# PARENT-CHILD RELATIONS
## An Introduction to Parenting

SEVENTH EDITION

# PARENT-CHILD RELATIONS
## An Introduction to Parenting

**JERRY J. BIGNER**
Colorado State University

PEARSON

Merrill
Prentice Hall

Upper Saddle River, New Jersey
Columbus, Ohio

**Library of Congress Cataloging-in-Publication Data**
Bigner, Jerry J.
  Parent-child relations : an introduction to parenting / Jerry J. Bigner.-- 7th ed.
    p. cm.
  Includes bibliographical references and index.
  ISBN 0-13-118429-6
  1. Parenting. 2. Parent and child. 3. Child development. 4. Family. I. Title.
  HQ755.8.B53 2006
  306.874--dc22                                      2005004052

**Vice President and Executive Publisher:** Jeffery W. Johnston
**Publisher:** Kevin M. Davis
**Acquisitions Editor:** Julie Peters
**Editorial Assistant:** Michelle Girgis
**Production Editor:** Linda Hillis Bayma
**Production Coordination:** Lea Baranowski, Carlisle Publishers Services
**Design Coordinator:** Diane C. Lorenzo
**Photo Coordinator:** Sandy Schaefer
**Cover Designer:** Terry Rohchach
**Cover Image:** Getty Images
**Production Manager:** Laura Messerly
**Director of Marketing:** Ann Castel Davis
**Marketing Manager:** Amy Judd
**Marketing Coordinator:** Brian Mounts

This book was set in New Caledonia by Carlisle Communications, Ltd. It was printed and bound by Hamilton Printing Company. The cover was printed by The Lehigh Press, Inc.

**Photo Credits:** Shirley Zeiberg/PH College, pp. 5, 67, 96, 100, 101, 197; Anne Vega/Merrill, pp. 7, 15, 32, 57, 58, 97, 142, 147, 154, 167, 175, 179, 180; National Gallery of Art, Washington, DC, pp. 9, 10; The Art Institute of Chicago, p. 11; Myrleen Ferguson/PhotoEdit, p. 21; Deborah Davis/PhotoEdit, p. 30; Todd Yarrington/Merrill, pp. 35 (left), 60, 65; Jerry Bigner, pp. 35 (right), 133 (bottom), 218, 260; Scott Cunningham/Merrill, pp. 56, 158, 181, 200, 239, 250; PH School, pp. 59, 195; D. Young-Wolff/PhotoEdit, p. 68; Michal Heron/PH College, pp. 77, 82; Marc Anderson/PH College, p. 92; Ken Karp/PH College, p. 104; Will & Deni McIntyre/Photo Researchers, Inc., p. 107; Peter Chen/The Image Works, p. 111; Bruce Johnson/Merrill, p. 116; Julie & Todd Bigner, p. 124; Barbara Schwartz/Merrill, p. 128; Wendy Douglass, pp. 133 (top), 137; Lloyd Lemmerman/Merrill, p. 144; Gail Meese/Merrill, p. 157; Ben Chandler/Merrill, p. 232; Zigy Kaluzny/Getty Images Inc.–Stone Allstock, p. 242; Charles Gatewood/PH College, p. 279; RealCare Baby II, courtesy of Realityworks Inc., 2709 Mondovi Rd., Eau Claire, WI 54701, (715) 830-1416, http://www.realityworks.com, p. 283.

**Pearson Prentice Hall**™ is a trademark of Pearson Education, Inc.
**Pearson**® is a registered trademark of Pearson plc
**Prentice Hall**® is a registered trademark of Pearson Education, Inc.
**Merrill**® is a registered trademark of Pearson Education, Inc.

Pearson Education Ltd.                              Pearson Education Australia Pty. Limited
Pearson Education Singapore Pte. Ltd.        Pearson Education North Asia Ltd.
Pearson Education Canada, Ltd.               Pearson Educación de Mexico, S.A. de C.V.
Pearson Education—Japan                    Pearson Education Malaysia Pte. Ltd.

10 9 8 7 6 5 4 3 2 1
ISBN: 0–13–118429–6

SEVENTH EDITION

# PARENT-CHILD RELATIONS

## An Introduction to Parenting

**JERRY J. BIGNER**
**Colorado State University**

PEARSON

Merrill
Prentice Hall

Upper Saddle River, New Jersey
Columbus, Ohio

**Library of Congress Cataloging-in-Publication Data**

Bigner, Jerry J.
  Parent-child relations : an introduction to parenting / Jerry J. Bigner.-- 7th ed.
    p. cm.
  Includes bibliographical references and index.
  ISBN 0-13-118429-6
  1. Parenting. 2. Parent and child. 3. Child development. 4. Family. I. Title.
  HQ755.8.B53 2006
  306.874--dc22                                  2005004052

**Vice President and Executive Publisher:** Jeffery W. Johnston
**Publisher:** Kevin M. Davis
**Acquisitions Editor:** Julie Peters
**Editorial Assistant:** Michelle Girgis
**Production Editor:** Linda Hillis Bayma
**Production Coordination:** Lea Baranowski, Carlisle Publishers Services
**Design Coordinator:** Diane C. Lorenzo
**Photo Coordinator:** Sandy Schaefer
**Cover Designer:** Terry Rohchach
**Cover Image:** Getty Images
**Production Manager:** Laura Messerly
**Director of Marketing:** Ann Castel Davis
**Marketing Manager:** Amy Judd
**Marketing Coordinator:** Brian Mounts

This book was set in New Caledonia by Carlisle Communications, Ltd. It was printed and bound by Hamilton Printing Company. The cover was printed by The Lehigh Press, Inc.

**Photo Credits:** Shirley Zeiberg/PH College, pp. 5, 67, 96, 100, 101, 197; Anne Vega/Merrill, pp. 7, 15, 32, 57, 58, 97, 142, 147, 154, 167, 175, 179, 180; National Gallery of Art, Washington, DC, pp. 9, 10; The Art Institute of Chicago, p. 11; Myrleen Ferguson/PhotoEdit, p. 21; Deborah Davis/PhotoEdit, p. 30; Todd Yarrington/Merrill, pp. 35 (left), 60, 65; Jerry Bigner, pp. 35 (right), 133 (bottom), 218, 260; Scott Cunningham/Merrill, pp. 56, 158, 181, 200, 239, 250; PH School, pp. 59, 195; D. Young-Wolff/PhotoEdit, p. 68; Michal Heron/PH College, pp. 77, 82; Marc Anderson/PH College, p. 92; Ken Karp/PH College, p. 104; Will & Deni McIntyre/Photo Researchers, Inc., p. 107; Peter Chen/The Image Works, p. 111; Bruce Johnson/Merrill, p. 116; Julie & Todd Bigner, p. 124; Barbara Schwartz/Merrill, p. 128; Wendy Douglass, pp. 133 (top), 137; Lloyd Lemmerman/Merrill, p. 144; Gail Meese/Merrill, p. 157; Ben Chandler/Merrill, p. 232; Zigy Kaluzny/Getty Images Inc.–Stone Allstock, p. 242; Charles Gatewood/PH College, p. 279; RealCare Baby II, courtesy of Realityworks Inc., 2709 Mondovi Rd., Eau Claire, WI 54701, (715) 830-1416, http://www.realityworks.com, p. 283.

Pearson Education Ltd.
Pearson Education Singapore Pte. Ltd.
Pearson Education Canada, Ltd.
Pearson Education—Japan

Pearson Education Australia Pty. Limited
Pearson Education North Asia Ltd.
Pearson Educacíon de Mexico, S.A. de C.V.
Pearson Education Malaysia Pte. Ltd.

10 9 8 7 6 5 4 3 2 1
ISBN: 0–13–118429–6

For my family of choice

(You know who you are!)

But very especially for

Duane, the wind beneath my wings . . .

# Preface

This seventh edition of *Parent-Child Relations* differs considerably from the first edition published 28 years ago when only a limited amount of research was available, most of it based on studying mothers and their parenting styles. Research on fathers was almost nonexistent. Theory about parenting was limited to adapting Erikson's psychosocial model and inferring from Piaget's cognitive theory. Changes in families over time were explained using the only developmental model available called the *family life cycle*, which was severely limited by placing its focus on white, middle-class families with children.

The essence of the text's approach remains the same, but we now have greater detail for explanations, more comprehensive and elaborate theory, and considerably more complex research addressing issues that have evolved over these past 28 years. We still lack a definitive answer about how to raise children to become effectively functioning adults.

More important, however, the world has changed, which has changed the context of parenting. We have greater diversity in families today, and those families must contend with different political and social issues and perhaps greater uncertainties. For most Americans, the world changed forever on September 11, 2001. Some issues parents and children confront today are similar to those we observed 28 years ago, but many are totally different.

The socialization of children has always been a primary caregiving function of parents, and this continues to be the case for parents today. However, a greater concern among parents today is how to teach children those skills and abilities that will enable them to cope with the rapidly changing society of their future.

Many years ago, Arlene and Jerome Skolnick (1971) proposed that the central challenge facing contemporary parents would be to keep the burden of obsolete knowledge of the past from interfering with the necessary changes taking place in society now and in the future. They suggested that to make this possible, parents need to teach children how to be open to new knowledge and experiences throughout their lives. To accomplish this, they proposed that the idea of the adult as an ideal human model should be considered as obsolete as many other ideas from the past. The traditional notion of an adult implied stagnation of learning and unresponsiveness to change since an adult was considered to be the finished product of his or her experiences while growing up. The Skolnicks believed that the ideal model for humans was not an adult but rather a child—someone who is curious about the world, gathers information, is open to options, and is willing to adapt and change in the light of new information.

I encourage you to keep this in mind as you read and study the material presented in this seventh edition: Look at the issues of parent-child relations through the eyes of a child who is open to examining the complexities of this important family relationship. Examine as well your own opinions, beliefs, and attitudes about parent-child relations. Then decide what you want to keep and what you want to adapt and change in light of what is likely to be new information on this topic. In this context, perhaps you will begin to understand the statement attributed to Heraclitus, a Greek philosopher (540–480 BC): "There is nothing permanent but change."

## FEATURES OF THE TEXT

The organization of this edition has been revamped. Based on the recommendations of reviewers and students, I believe this reorganization of topics makes for a smoother flow as I move from general to specific information over the course of the text.

Features retained from previous editions include:

1. an emphasis on family systems theory as a means for understanding and explaining parent-child relations over the years as children are reared toward adulthood;

2. continued application of the concepts of nurturance and structure as a means for understanding how parents shape their behavior and practice in raising children;

3. continued application of the *Frequently Asked Questions* feature that allows students to see parenting concerns and issues through the eyes of a parent but also of a therapist who consults with the parent; and

4. continued use of the *Focus On* feature to highlight information discussed in the text.

## NEW TO THIS EDITION

Several features are new to this edition:

1. The text maintains a sharper focus on parenting per se as students using this text are assumed to have basic child development information.

2. Updated research information is presented on *all* topics discussed in the text.

3. A new pedagogical feature, "Parenting Reflections," provides opportunities for readers to check their understanding of the content they've just read about parent-child relations. In addition, these reflections allow students to examine personal values and beliefs and develop empathy with what parents face in certain situations.

4. The family life cycle model has been replaced with the systemic family development model to explain family functioning at different developmental times. This model is illustrated by using the case study method, with a hypothetical family system featured at the different stages of child rearing. See the "Systemic Family Development Snapshot" feature in chapters 7–12. The model is also used to show how to study different family structures as the family structures experience different stressors.

5. New content is featured in many chapters, including discussions on immigrant parents and children, grandparenting, caring for older parents, and foster care issues.

## SUPPLEMENTS FOR INSTRUCTORS AND STUDENTS

### For Instructors

An *Instructor's Manual and Test Bank* is available for downloading from a Prentice Hall website. Ask your Prentice Hall sales representative for details. The manual includes lecture notes, supplementary media resources, test items, and learning projects.

An online Syllabus Manager™ is also available at www.prenhall.com/bigner. See details on page xi.

New PowerPoint® slides have been created to assist discussions and lectures.

### For Students

A Companion Website, consisting of self-assessment items, focus questions, and Web links, is provided at www. prenhall.com/bigner. For more details, see page xi.

## ACKNOWLEDGMENTS

Although my name appears as the author of this text, it would not be possible to provide this information without the efforts of many others. I am especially indebted to my colleagues who conducted the research I discuss here. Students and colleagues have provided feedback that is helpful in making improvements and changes. I am especially grateful to Jerold P. Bauch, Vanderbilt

University; Barbara Keating, Minnesota State University-Mankato; Gail Lee, University of Wyoming; Robert Moreno, Syracuse University; and Gisele Ragusa, University of Southern California. They provided comments specifically for this edition.

I am also grateful to Julie Peters at Merrill/Prentice Hall who has guided my work on this edition with sensitivity, astuteness, and candor.

My work on this project was made possible as well through the support and understanding of my family of choice and especially my partner. I am indeed fortunate to be connected with these individuals as part of my life.

*Jerry J. Bigner, PhD*
Professor Emeritus

*E-mail: bigner@lamar.colostate.edu*
*Website:* http://lamar.colostate.edu/~bigner

*Companion Website to this text:*
www.prenhall.com/bigner

# Discover the Companion Website Accompanying This Book

## THE PRENTICE HALL COMPANION WEBSITE: A VIRTUAL LEARNING ENVIRONMENT

Technology is a constantly growing and changing aspect of our field that is creating a need for content and resources. To address this emerging need, Prentice Hall has developed an online learning environment for students and professors alike—Companion Website—to support our textbooks.

In creating a Companion Website, our goal is to build on and enhance what the textbook already offers. For this reason, the content for each user-friendly website is organized by topic and provides the professor and student with a variety of meaningful resources. The site accompanying this text is **www.prenhall.com/bigner**.

### For the Professor

Every Companion Website integrates **Syllabus Manager™**, an online syllabus creation and management utility.

- **Syllabus Manager™** provides you, the instructor, with an easy, step-by-step process to create and revise syllabi, with direct links into Companion Website and other online content without having to learn HTML.
- Students may logon to your syllabus during any study session. All they need to know is the web address for the Companion Website and the password you've assigned to your syllabus.

- After you have created a syllabus using **Syllabus Manager™**, students may enter the syllabus for their course section from any point in the Companion Website.
- Clicking on a date, the student is shown the list of activities for the assignment. The activities for each assignment are linked directly to actual content, saving time for students.
- Adding assignments consists of clicking on the desired due date, then filling in the details of the assignment—name of the assignment, instructions, and whether it is a one-time or repeating assignment.
- In addition, links to other activities can be created easily. If the activity is online, a URL can be entered in the space provided, and it will be linked automatically in the final syllabus.
- Your completed syllabus is hosted on our servers, allowing convenient updates from any computer on the Internet. Changes you make to your syllabus are immediately available to your students at their next logon.

### For the Student

- **Focus Questions**—Specific questions about the key issues and concepts in the chapter to help students review and facilitate retention of what they have read.
- **Parenting on the Internet**—A variety of websites related to topics covered in the chapter.
- **True or False Items**
- **Multiple-Choice Items**

# Educator Learning Center: An Invaluable Online Resource

Merrill Education and the Association for Supervision and Curriculum Development (ASCD) invite you to take advantage of a new online resource, one that provides access to the top research and proven strategies associated with ASCD and Merrill—the Educator Learning Center. At **www.educatorlearningcenter.com,** you will find resources that will enhance your students' understanding of course topics and of current educational issues, in addition to being invaluable for further research.

## HOW THE EDUCATOR LEARNING CENTER WILL HELP YOUR STUDENTS BECOME BETTER TEACHERS

With the combined resources of Merrill Education and ASCD, you and your students will find a wealth of tools and materials to better prepare them for the classroom.

### Research

- More than 600 articles from the ASCD journal *Educational Leadership* discuss everyday issues faced by practicing teachers.
- A direct link on the site to Research Navigator™ gives students access to many of the leading education journals, as well as extensive content detailing the research process.
- Excerpts from Merrill Education texts give your students insights on important topics of instructional method diverse populations, assessment, classroom management, technology, and refining classroom practice.

### Classroom Practice

- Hundreds of lesson plans and teaching strategies are categorized by content area and age range.
- Case studies and classroom video footage provide virtual field experience for student reflection.
- Computer simulations and other electronic tools keep your students abreast of today's classrooms and current technologies.

## LOOK INTO THE VALUE OF EDUCATOR LEARNING CENTER YOURSELF

A four-month subscription to Educator Learning Center is $25 but is **FREE** when packaged with any Merrill Education text. In order for your students to have access to this site, you must use this special value-pack ISBN number **WHEN** placing your textbook order with the bookstore: 0-13-197194-8. Your students will then receive a copy of the text packaged with a free ASCD pincode. To preview the value of this website to you and your students, please go to **www.educatorlearningcenter.com** and click on "Demo."

# Brief Contents

# Contents

## CHAPTER 4
## Parenting Strategies   64

## PART II
## The Work of Parenting   89

## CHAPTER 5
## The Transition to Parenthood   91

## CHAPTER 6
## Pregnancy and Childbirth   115

Note: Every effort has been made to provide accurate and current Internet information in the book. However, the Internet and information posted on it are constantly changing, so it is inevitable that some of the Internet addresses listed in this textbook will change.

# PARENT-CHILD RELATIONS
## An Introduction to Parenting

# PART I

# Parenthood in Social Context

The role of a parent is a complex combination of many different but related behaviors. Parents today consciously define what their role is, which behaviors are acceptable and appropriate in their role, and how their particular role functions in their family system. However, in developing and conducting their parenting role, people generally have little guidance other than the model they observed from their own parents.

The caretaking relationship an adult creates with children in families has only recently come under the scrutiny of behavioral scientists. Until modern times, our culture viewed parenting and parent-child relationships as something of a sacred cow. The belief was that this family relationship was beyond reproach and too basic to the survival of society to warrant scientific study. Until recently, it was thought that people did not need training in parenting skills nor in preparation to become a parent. The idea was that parenting skills were acquired naturally from living in a family and that these skills were handed down successfully from one generation to the next.

These ideas are changing in relation to other social changes taking place in our society today. Many people question the ability of parents to give children the attention and guidance they need to become effectively functioning adults. The prevalence of violence in homes, delinquency and crime, drug use, pregnancy, and poorly developed academic, interpersonal relationship, and life skills among children and youth today are often cited as results of the inability of parents and schools to perform adequately as teachers. Regardless of the source of such problems, it becomes increasingly obvious that people who are parents today or who desire to become parents need assistance, education, and information in learning how to conduct this family role and how to interact effectively with children.

Contemporary families differ in their structure and functioning from those of the past. Because of significant changes in family life, what we learned as children in our families about how to be a parent may not be applicable when forming our own families today. The diversity observed among family forms today also creates challenges for effective parenting that differ considerably from what families of the past encountered in the process of raising children to adulthood.

1

This part of the text focuses on this family role and the rich social contexts in which parenting takes place. To understand parenting and parent-child relations, we must establish the significance of this role within a family system. We must understand how the contexts in which a family functions shape parenting roles and interactions with children. Exploring the origins of and influences on parental behavior establish the foundation, even in these uncertain times, for studying parent-child relations.

# CHAPTER 1

# Dimensions of Parenthood

### Focus Questions
■ ■ ■ ■ ■ ■ ■ ■ ■ ■

1. Why is it important to learn about parenting?
2. What attributes describe the nature of parenthood?
3. Why has the relationship between parents and children traditionally been viewed as unidirectional? How is this relationship seen differently today?
4. How have our ideas about parenthood and childhood changed as a result of social evolution over the years?
5. What are six stages of parenthood?
6. What factors significantly influence the contexts of parenting behavior and parent-child relations?

■ ■ ■ ■ ■ ■ ■ ■ ■ ■

## THE NEED FOR PARENTING EDUCATION

One of the most significant and intimate relationships among humans is that between parent and child. The parent-child bond is unique both in its biological foundations and in its psychological meanings. For a child, this essential relationship ensures survival and helps to shape his or her destiny. For an adult, it can be one of the most fulfilling of human experiences and a challenging opportunity for personal growth and development.

Contemporary ideas about the nature of parent-child relations are the result of years of social evolution and artifacts of many historical changes. Our concepts of the relationship between a parent and child carry numerous complex meanings and implications. These perceptions influence an adult's decision to become a parent and shape his or her parenting behavior. Our understanding of this significant family relationship has improved over the years with increased knowledge in the behavioral sciences. However, experts continue to study parent-child interactions in the hope of gaining a clearer understanding of how this relationship changes over time. Researchers seek to determine how interactions influence relations among all participants, what can be learned about competent parenting behaviors, and how children's actions influence their parents' behavior.

Serious events occurring in families and in our society today point to the need for preparing people to perform competently as parents. It is becoming more clear how the nature of this relationship can harm or benefit a child's development. The widespread prevalence of various addictions to substances, behaviors, and relationships among adults today are traced to early family of origin experiences in which poor and ineffective parenting is thought to play a major role (Di-Clemente, 2003; Jones, 2004; Wajda-Johnston, 2003). Similarly, awareness and concern are increasing about the effects of sexual, emotional, and physical abuse perpetrated upon children by parents. Many family experts and practitioners believe these situations result partially from poor preparation for parenthood and lack of adequate skills for coping with the stresses of parenting (Adams & Fey, 2003; Donnelly, 2000; Reeves, 2003).

For many years, few people saw the need for formal training or education to be parents. However, many people who work closely with parents today concur that such training is sorely needed. Our society goes to great lengths to train people for most vocational roles. A license indicating training and preparation is required to drive a car, possess a firearm, pilot a plane, and sell insurance or real estate, for example. However, no state or federal statute requires people to have training or preparation to become a parent.

The media sometimes depicts parenthood in unrealistic ways. People may be influenced by such depictions and hold idealistic expectations about parenting and parent-child relations. For example, one may gain an impression that parents and children have smooth interactions generally; that children improve their parents' marriage; that children will turn out well if they have good parents; that children generally are compliant with parents' requests or demands; or that parents are solely responsible for their child's character, personality, and achievements. Learning what parenting is all about in classes, observing parents and children interact in natural settings, and hearing parents share their experiences may help to deconstruct these stereotypes and myths.

Although most parents would agree they could profit from learning new ways to be effective in their role, we lack clear guidelines about what qualities or behaviors make someone a competent parent. Perhaps we will never achieve complete agreement in our society about this issue. However, researchers continue to make much progress in helping parents to find more effective ways to perform their tasks in raising children to become competent adults.

The relationship between parents and children is complex and is characterized in a variety of ways that are explored in this chapter and throughout this text. Contemporary and historical perspectives of this interactional relationship are discussed. Parenthood is described as a developmental role that changes over time, usually in response to changing developmental needs of children. Factors that significantly influence an adult's behavior as a parent are identified and described.

Clearly, people can learn how to be effective in raising children to adulthood and may be able to improve their behavior as parents. By studying the research, theories, issues, and approaches that have been developed and examined by practitioners and investigators, it is possible to develop a better understanding of parent-child relations.

## Parenting Reflection 1–1

Suppose you are in charge of developing a parenting course for first-time, new parents. What are some topics you would include in the course (even before you have studied parent-child relations)?

*Focus Point.* It is important for parents to learn how to raise children, to understand their developmental needs, and to become more effective in their role.

## CONCEPTS OF PARENTHOOD

The parenting role is associated with several different concepts or ideas in our society. Originally, the idea of parenthood referred singularly to the reproduction aspect that is so prominent in this role. Our society, like all others, values the function of reproduction within a family setting because this is the only way that the population has been sustained until recently. Although advances have been made in medical technology that allow for reproduction to take place in the laboratory and embryo transfers to be successfully performed, the usual mode of reproduction is generally preferred.

**FIGURE 1–1.** Our society conceptualizes parenthood in a variety of ways. The ideas of nurturing, teaching, and caring for children are prominent.

Other ideas are also embedded in our society's concepts of parenthood. These include the notion that parents are responsible for nurturing, teaching, and acting as guardians for their children until the age of legal maturity (see Figure 1–1). This long period of providing care for children is unique among most species found on earth. Human infants and children have a long period of dependency on adults due in part to the immaturity of their brains and the length of time it takes for maturity in all aspects to be attained (Marieb, 2003). The brain of a human infant, unlike the brain of offspring of most other species of mammals, is not completely functional at birth and for many years following. Infant humans' survival is dependent on being protected by adults. In contrast, infants of many other species walk within hours of birth and are capable of running to escape danger. Human infants do not master these same motor functions until many months following birth. Differences in brain size and function account for such disparities between humans and other species.

Parents were also originally considered to be a child's principal teachers. This instruction function related to the responsibility given to parents by society to prepare children for adulthood by teaching them how to behave ap-

propriately, what rules they must follow, what values to hold, and how to make decisions, for example. This process is referred to as **socialization,** or learning how to conform to the conventional ways of behavior in society.

In the past, parents also served as educators for their children, teaching them the essential skills needed to survive in society, such as reading, writing, and calculation. They helped children learn the job skills necessary to provide a living upon attaining adulthood. These functions today are accomplished by schools and other agents in society, but parents are expected to help children learn the basic rules of social functioning and to impart values that are held in esteem by their family to guide their behavior and decisions.

### Parenting Reflection 1–2

Try to imagine yourself as the best parent you could possibly be. What characteristics would you have? What are some things you would always try to do and always try to avoid doing?

••••••••••••••••••••••••••••••••••••••••••••••••••

***Focus Point.***   A number of concepts are embedded in the role of a parent. These concepts act to define the different meanings associated with the role.

••••••••••••••••••••••••••••••••••••••••••••••••••

# CHARACTERISTICS OF PARENTHOOD AND PARENT-CHILD RELATIONS

The relationship between parents and children can be characterized in several ways. This relationship has been taken for granted and assumed to be the most natural and ubiquitous of all human associations, largely because of the biological basis upon which it is founded. It is considered to be a bastion of our culture, for society could not continue if new members were not produced and socialized.

Our ideas and philosophies about the nature of parent-child relations are derived from diverse cultural and historical influences. Until recently, the relationship between parent and child was described as based upon a **unidirectional model of socialization.** In this model, the relationship traditionally patterns the role of the adult as a teacher responsible for inculcating appropriate behavior patterns, values, and attitudes that prepare children for effective participation in society upon reaching maturity. The child's role is that of being an active learner. According to this model, the flow of information is solely from parent to child. Clearly, this model features the adult as having a significant effect and influence on the child; however, the child is not seen as having influence on the adult, due to his or her subordinate role and lack of social power. Until recently, this basic notion about parents and children received strong support culturally and within the scientific literature on parenting (Ambert, 1994).

Today, our ideas about the nature of parent-child relations are shaped by the new information gained from research that reframes this bond as being **bidirectional** in nature (Ambert, 1994). By this, we mean that both adults and children influence one another as their relationship experiences developmental changes over time. Characteristic traits and qualities about this relationship are summarized briefly here and discussed in more detail in later chapters.

1.   *The relationship between parents and children is a subsystem of the larger social system we call a fam-*

*ily.*   One of the most salient models for understanding how family groups function is family systems theory (Bongar & Beutler, 1995; Mikesell, Lusterman, & Mc-Daniel, 1995). We discuss this model in detail in Chapter 3. **Family systems theory** describes how a family functions in ways that resemble other systems found in nature, such as the solar system and ecological systems. The model explains how everyday functioning takes place in a family, how rules evolve to govern the behavior of members, how roles are assigned to regulate behavior, and how these relate to goals the family group seeks to accomplish. It also explains how a family group strives to maintain its stability over time and to adapt or make changes in rules, behaviors, roles, and goals. The model recognizes that family members experience developmental changes, resolve interpersonal conflicts, or confront crises that challenge effective, continued functioning.

Several subsystems exist simultaneously within a larger family system, such as the committed relationship or marriage between adults and the relationships between siblings. A subsystem is a microcosm of the larger family system that mirrors the functioning of this group. The same principles and concepts that explain the functioning of the larger family system relate to how subsystems, including the parent-child subsystem, function (Figure 1–2).

The main priority of the relationship between parents and children is to nurture children so that they may learn to become effectively functioning adults upon reaching maturity. However, the family systems model describes the parent-child relationship as being bidirectional in nature. The flow of influence goes both ways. Children's behavior and development are strong factors that contribute to the quality and scope of interactions with parents. As children experience developmental changes, parents change their behavior and adapt by changing rules, the ways they interact with children, and their goals of child rearing. In this manner, interactions between parents and children evolve in tandem with children's developmental changes. Similarly, children respond to changes in parenting behavior in ways that help them to achieve specific developmental tasks appropriate for the particular stage they are experiencing in their life span.

2.   *Parenthood is a developmental role.*   Unlike most adult social roles, parenting behavior and interactions must adapt to developmental changes in children

**FIGURE 1–2.** Parenthood is a distinctive role that differs from others adults hold.

as they grow. Similarly, changes arising from a parent's own personal development affect his or her caregiving behavior. The age and developmental status of both parent and child affect the nature and context of this relationship.

The parental role is sensitive and responsive to changes within the family system. For example, when one adult is removed from the family through divorce or death, the remaining adult's quality and style of parenting change. The parenthood role is also heavily influenced by factors arising from what is known as the *family ecology,* the influences of the larger environments within which a family system exists.

3. *Parenthood is a social construct.* The parental role is a social institution based on a complex of values, beliefs, norms, and behaviors that focus on procreation and the need to care for young (LaRossa, 1986). As un-

likely as it may seem, people who are not parents can experience this role vicariously as parents experience it directly. The role is universally understood throughout cultures. Despite the ubiquitous understanding of parenthood, its meanings largely require explanation in a particular historical time. A visit to a nearby bookstore to examine the numerous titles on parenting illustrates this point. Every society defines what is appropriate behavior in this role. In addition, people who assume this role may be considered by a particular society to be of higher moral stature than those who do not. In other words, people who are not parents may be devalued by societies in which parenthood is valued.

••••••••••••••••••••••••••••••••••••••••••••••••••••••••

***Focus Point.*** Parent-child relations were traditionally described as unidirectional; that is, the adult had complete jurisdiction, power, and control of the relationship. Today, however, we describe this relationship as bidirectional, meaning that a child is acknowledged as an active participant and contributor to the relationship. Each person influences the behavior of the other. The parent-child relationship is unique to family systems and can be described in various ways.

••••••••••••••••••••••••••••••••••••••••••••••••••••••••

## HISTORICAL CHANGES IN PARENT-CHILD RELATIONS

Contemporary ideas about the nature of parent-child relations are very different from those of the past. Current ideas have evolved from earlier beliefs and concepts. The nature and quality of parent-child interactions are influenced significantly by cultural values and by the historical time in which individuals actively conduct themselves in this role (Coontz, 1998).

Most people believe that our culture values the well-being of children and supports this notion by providing numerous social institutions—the family, schools, social service agencies, and so on—to meet children's needs. We tend to think of our society as child-centered. We see childhood as a special time in one's life span, a time of preparation and education for functioning in the later years of life and a time for happiness and freedom from anxiety. We believe children have special needs that are met first by those in their family system and later by institutions, groups, and agencies outside their family system.

Our current concerns and ideas about the unique nature of childhood developed only as a result of many years of social change and transformation in Western culture (Coontz, 1998). Contrary to what we may assume, the ideas of childhood, parenthood, and the family are viewed differently now than during the Middle Ages, or even during the Colonial period of the United States. Our current ideas about what children need and how adults can conduct their parenting effectively are characteristic of contemporary times. These notions are thought to be particularly related to the manner in which family systems function and how this has changed over the years.

Most social historians agree that the basic contextual nature of parenting children probably has not changed over time. However, changes are noted in the ways adults define and conduct appropriate parenting behavior. In other words, although parenting always has had a strong nurturing context, the specific ways adults define and express nurturing have changed in the culturally approved ways at particular points in history. Child-rearing practices have changed throughout history in accordance with changing ideas about what children need from adults to prepare them for their future as adults. Studying the evolution of these ideas will help us understand why we have particular beliefs and attitudes today about the nature of parent-child relations, parenthood and childhood roles, and the proper way to conduct this relationship. A brief review of this evolution follows, beginning with the ancient cultures that influenced contemporary Western societies.

## Ancient Greece and Rome

The ancient cultures of Greece and Rome recognized that the experiences of childhood gave rise to character in adulthood. There was concern, however, about the quality of these early experiences and how best to provide these to children. The philosopher Plato believed that children could best be prepared for their future by separating them from parents and having the state assume the responsibility of child rearing (French, 1995). Later, Aristotle was the first to recommend that parents adapt the strategies they employed in raising children to meet children's individual natures. Both of these philosophers recognized that parental behavior heavily influenced child outcomes. The darker side of this early

culture, however, witnessed the widespread practices of child sacrifices, infanticide, and slavery.

Child rearing in ancient Roman culture differed only slightly from that of ancient Greece. Advantaged families faired considerably better than others in that children were provided with educational experiences in learning to read and write. Conditions changed during the Middle Ages.

## The Middle Ages to Renaissance

The Middle Ages were a time in which Western societies functioned in a rural, primitive manner. Formal education was minimal and generally restricted to the clergy of the Roman Catholic Church. Families were generally structured according to a form known as the extended family, involving several generations living together. In these premodern times, children were raised in a manner that we would interpret today as being indifferent to their special needs. There was no idea that infants needed to learn to trust their caregivers. Assimilation into the adult world came early, usually between the age of 5 and 7 years. According to Aries (1992), childhood apparently was not recognized as a distinct stage of the human life span prior to the 17th century. A child's education—probably his or her only schooling—came from observing and imitating adult models. A parent in the Middle Ages probably had the notion that children needed adult supervision and care, but apparently this did not include close emotional ties with adults (see Figure 1–3). Parents did not appear to provide warm nurturance to children, since many died in infancy and childhood from diseases that are preventable today. During this period, parenting was only one of many functions individuals performed in families, and it did not seem to have a high priority. What most concerned family members were the production of food, clothing, and shelter to ensure daily survival.

From about the 14th to the 17th centuries, there were conflicting views about the nature of children. On the one hand, they were thought to be symbols of purity as represented by the early depictions of cherubs in artistic works of the times. On the other hand, children were perceived to embody evil and innate wickedness, which called for strict parental control, punishment, and continual supervision to rid them of what was believed to be original sin.

**FIGURE 1–3.**   These paintings from the early to late medieval period illustrate a significant shift in the poses of mothers and infants toward depicting a more loving, nurturing relationship. This may be due to a decline in infant mortality rates and changes in the attitudes about the nature of children.

*Source:* (left) Margaritone d'Arezzo (c. 1270). *Madonna and Child Enthroned.* Samuel H. Kress Collection. Image © Board of Trustees, National Gallery of Art, Washington, DC. (right) Raphael (c. 1508). The Niccolini-Cowper Madonna. Samuel H. Kress Collection. Image © Board of Trustees, the National Gallery of Art, Washington, DC.

## Europe and Colonial America

Attitudes were being refined along these same lines during the 17th and 18th centuries in both Europe and colonial America. Two separate camps of thought emerged about the nature of children and how parents could best raise them into adulthood. On the one hand, the view promoted by Jean Jacques Rousseau (1712–1778), a French social philosopher, held that children were inherently good but could be corrupted by their caregivers.

He strongly advocated that children could be best raised outside of the influence of parents and teachers by allowing them to follow a natural tendency to learn at their own pace (later referred to as **maturationism**). He believed, however, that the most important relationship was that between mothers and their children, especially during the first years of a child's life.

The other major philosophy regarding children and child rearing was advocated by John Locke (1632–1704),

**FIGURE 1–4.** This painting of the Sargent family in the late 1700s reflects early Americans' attitudes about parents and children. Children's dress styles particularly illustrate that they are viewed as miniature copies of adults. Note, however, that the tone of the painting is one of emotional warmth, although it appears to be strained, especially in regard to the youngest child and the infant.

*Source: The Sargent Family* (c. 1800). Gift of Edgar William and Bernice Chrusler Garbisch. Image © Board of Trustees, the National Gallery of Art, Washington, DC.

an English philosopher and physician, which took a strong **environmentalist** position. Locke promoted the notion of *tabula rasa,* suggesting that children's minds were like blank slates at birth. Their character or personality upon attaining adulthood was thought to be the result of child rearing or learning experiences and interactions with the social and physical environments. From this viewpoint, children were neither inherently good nor evil but became one way or the other because of their experiences. As a product of these two differing views, childhood came to be seen as a distinct and unique period of the human life span. In colonial America, however, the view of the inherent evil nature of children remained prominent primarily because of the religious tone of the culture at the time.

## Industrial Revolution Era

The Industrial Revolution that occurred in the late 19th century changed American family life in dramatic ways. Prior to this time, a father's central role in a family system consisted of providing economic support, moral and religious education of children, and discipline. Following the Industrial Revolution, fathers began to be employed increasingly in nonfarm jobs that placed them away from their families for greater lengths of time. To compensate, mothers assumed increasing responsibilities for the character development and socialization of children (see Figure 1–5). Mothers soon became responsible for managing their entire households. During this time, health and survival rates improved considerably for infants and children. When coupled with a new interest in psychological research, attitudes about children and child rearing shifted focus to become increasingly child-centered. The responsible parent of this era attempted to meet a child's physical as well as emotional, social, and psychological needs. With the shift away from a rural society to an urban and industrial orientation, the economics of child rearing factored significantly into family life by reducing the numbers of children produced. Children increasingly became economic liabilities rather than assets to families.

## Twentieth Century Era

The 20th century has witnessed a vast array of attitudes about children and child rearing that range from the promotion of permissiveness, encouraged by the writings of Sigmund Freud (1856–1939) and Benjamin Spock (1903–1998), to the restrictive, authoritarian,

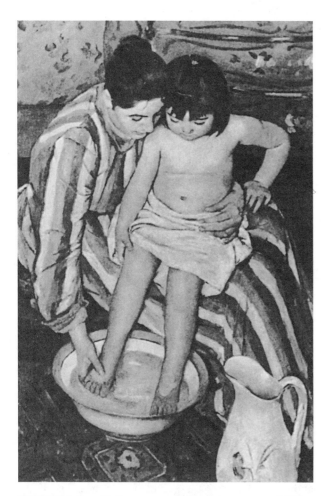

**FIGURE 1–5.** Mothers assumed greater responsibilities and duties in child rearing as a result of fathers becoming employed in jobs that removed them from family life for increasing amounts of time. Our modern-day attitudes about mothering can be found in artwork that depicts the predominance of women in child rearing, such as in this painting by Mary Cassatt, completed in 1892.

*Source:* Mary Cassatt, American, 1844–1926, *The Bath*, oil on canvas, 1891/92, 39 1/2 × 26 in., Robert A. Waller Fund, 1910.2. Photograph © 1996. The Art Institute of Chicago. All Rights Reserved.

and stern approaches advocated by John Watson (1928) and others (Bigner & Yang, 1996). As scientific information increased in respectability, numerous child-rearing experts offered copious, often conflicting advice to parents on how child rearing should best be conducted. With the advent of the child-rearing expert, the emphasis in disciplinary practices shifted to those that were more psychological in nature. Behavior modification based on parental use of positive reinforcement or reward gained over reliance on physical punishment as the recommended method of socializing children.

Changes in laws and attitudes led to less stigmatization and greater acceptance of divorce. This, in turn, led to the emergence of the single-parent family as the predominant family type. Changes in American society following World War II also contributed to the demise of the traditional nuclear family. Increases in divorce were accompanied by a rise in the numbers of remarriages and stepfamilies in the United States. By the end of the 20th century, diversity in family forms and structures became the norm rather than the exception.

Today, a variety of family forms are considered functional, healthy, and effective in meeting the needs of their members. The insidiousness of poverty was never eliminated during this century and continues to affect families, children, parent-child relations, child rearing, and society at large.

● ● ● ● ● ● ● ● ● ● ● ● ● ● ● ● ● ● ● ● ● ● ● ● ● ● ● ● ● ● ●

### Parenting Reflection 1–3

Why don't all parents raise their children using the same methods, styles, and approaches? How would such standard uniformity in child rearing result in what people are like as adults?

● ● ● ● ● ● ● ● ● ● ● ● ● ● ● ● ● ● ● ● ● ● ● ● ● ● ● ● ●

● ● ● ● ● ● ● ● ● ● ● ● ● ● ● ● ● ● ● ● ● ● ● ● ● ● ● ● ● ●

***Focus Point.***   The concepts of parenthood and childhood have experienced many changes in the last 2,000 years. Contemporary ideas of these roles and of this relationship are derived from these past notions. In many ways, contemporary ideas reflect the changes in cultural values about these roles.

● ● ● ● ● ● ● ● ● ● ● ● ● ● ● ● ● ● ● ● ● ● ● ● ● ● ● ● ● ●

## PARENTHOOD AS A DEVELOPMENTAL ROLE

So far in this chapter, we have described the nature of the parenthood role in various ways. Now it is important to reemphasize the notion that individuals experience changes in how they conduct themselves in their role as a parent. These developmental changes occur in association with the passage of time.

Like other patterns observed in family systems, this role must adapt and evolve in relation to the needs of children and of the individual acting as a parent. Most people assume parenthood with many misconceptions about what it is like to be a parent, how they should act, and what they might expect from children in return. Few people fully understand the reality that they must also evolve in their parenting skills and abilities, often in response to the developmental changes that children experience. This notion was first expressed in the first edition of this text, published in 1979. Several other writers, such as Ellen Galinsky (1987), have expanded the topic in greater detail.

From a traditional point of reference, parenthood is considered to be a normal developmental task of adulthood. From conventional viewpoints, this is not necessarily seen as an essential component of adult development, but many people choose to pursue parenthood as part of the psychosocial development that occurs in adulthood (Erikson, 1950, 1964). Galinsky (1987) describes six stages in the evolution of the parenthood role that may be observed among many individuals as they grow and change in response to the developmental changes being experienced by their children. In this text, we refer to this process as **reciprocal interaction** (from family systems theory)—the motivating factor that produces such mutual developmental changes in children and parents.

Drawing on the theoretical work of Levinson et al. (1978) and Erikson (1950, 1964) on adult development, Galinsky outlines the following six stages of parenthood, which are briefly discussed here.

1. *Image-Making Stage.* During this period, a potential parent uses imagery to rehearse what it must be like to be a parent. In many respects, this is a time for individuals to develop their vision of what kind of parent they wish to be. Their preparation for parenthood is particularly stimulated by the initiation of a pregnancy. Pregnancy brings many changes, especially for a woman. Her body changes, her image of her body changes, and she experiences the unique feeling of a new life that exists within her body. During this stage individuals examine their relationship with their own parents, which often serves as a guide for how they may act as parents

themselves. It is a time for evaluating how changes might occur in the relationship between parenting partners. Both partners prepare for the child's birth and confront fears, especially fears of the unknown if this is the first pregnancy.

2. *The Nurturing Stage.* The major focus of this stage of parenthood is establishing an attachment with the new infant. For new parents, especially, this also involves reconciling the reality of what having a child actually is like with how they may have imagined it. This stage necessitates redefining a couple's relationship and their relationships with their parents, in-laws, friends, and work associates. Paradoxically, by getting to know the baby, each parent has the opportunity to get to know themselves even better than before. The experiences of nurturing a baby reflect back to the parent an idea of what kind of person she or he is.

3. *The Authority Stage.* This period is characterized by the realization that parenthood involves a strong element of adult authority. This is partially stimulated by the changes taking place in children that allow them to master an increasingly wider context of skills that challenge parental interactions. The changing nature of children at this time calls for greater reliance on the parent as a person of authority who decides much of what is right or wrong and appropriate or inappropriate regarding children's behavior. Essentially, adults must accept their responsibility for guiding the life, behavior, and development of their child. The authority stage involves the emergence of rules as a means for governance and the clear establishment of personal boundaries between parents and children.

4. *The Interpretative Stage.* At this time in parenting, adults assume the responsibility of acting as interpreters of the world as they see it for their children. This means they now begin to impart their interpretation of their own worldview and family values to their children. Parents answer children's innumerable questions, help them to acquire skills for making personal decisions about their behavior, and pass on the value system deemed important by their particular family system. This stage ends with the child's entrance into adolescence.

5. *The Interdependent Stage.* This period of parenting adolescent children demands that adults reexamine the issue of parental authority and how this is

to be played out at this time. The new child who emerges during adolescence increasingly demands to be independent of parental control and authority. The reality of development for both adults and children is that although parents must recognize this desire for independence, it is not reasonable to permit adolescent children to have complete control over their decisions and behavior. The challenge of this stage of parenthood is for parents and adolescents to adapt and redefine their relationship to one that includes negotiation and discussion about rules, appropriate behavior, and limits.

6. *The Departure Stage.*   At this time, parents must reexamine their whole experience in raising children. Parents must begin to truly let go of their children and relinquish authority over them. They must recognize that their parenting career is indeed at last coming to an end and that the tasks of parenthood are almost completed. To be truly mastered, the relationship between adult children and parents must be redefined to encompass the new adult status of the children. Essentially, this means that the relationship takes on more of an adult-to-adult quality rather than one in which the authority of the parent is paramount over the child.

• • • • • • • • • • • • • • • • • • • • • • • • • • • • • • • •

## Parenting Reflection 1–4

Is it possible for parents not to adapt and change their approach to parenting children? Why? Why not?

• • • • • • • • • • • • • • • • • • • • • • • • • • • • • • • •

• • • • • • • • • • • • • • • • • • • • • • • • • • • • • • • •

*Focus Point.*   Galinsky describes six stages of parenthood that explain how parent-child relations and the role of a parent are modified as children grow and develop into adulthood.

• • • • • • • • • • • • • • • • • • • • • • • • • • • • • • • •

## CONFIGURING THE PARENTHOOD ROLE

We now have the opportunity to integrate what has been presented and discussed thus far in this chapter and extend the discussion about the nature of the parenthood role. Let's examine the significant factors that contribute to the arrangement or configuration of people's master blueprint for their parenthood role and their resulting behaviors.

As children, many of us had occasion to wonder why one or both of our parents behaved as they did. Sometimes the parents' behavior made no sense at all. At other times, our parents' actions were clearly in line with what we expected, but we did not fully understand their intent or reasons. A variety of factors contribute to the nature and context of someone's notions of how to act as a parent (see Figure 1–6). Several variables are known to contribute to the way adults configure their parenting role. By configuring one's parenting role, an individual combines a variety of factors or parameters into a workable blueprint that guides behavior. A good metaphor for this process is what happens when someone takes pieces of a puzzle, manages to perceive how they all fit together, and acomplishes a complete solution to the task of puzzle making.

Some factors that contribute to an adult's configuration of parenting behavior come from past experiences, and new ones are added as the person gains experience in parenting children. Certainly the contribution of a child to the configuration of parenting roles is apparent. Family ecological factors, attitudes about discipline, and an individual's past experiences all influence parenting style.

These predisposing factors that combine to influence parenting style and form a parenting blueprint include the following:

■ **Cultural influences** such as social class or peer value systems
■ The **developmental time** in which adults and children are actively engaged in the child-rearing process.
■ **Primary parenting functions** that fall into two basic categories of actions that serve as the basis for parenting behaviors: providing structure and nurturance to children
■ **Family of origin influences** such as the role model one observed as a child from one's own parents
■ **Child influences** or the myriad ways in which children can impact parental behavior
■ **Disciplinary approach** or the program of discipline adopted in tandem with a child's developmental level
■ **Family ecological factors** such as the particular structure of a family system and the trends that have affected family form
■ **Attitudes about parenting** such as beliefs about how one should behave as a parent

**FIGURE 1–6.** Parental role behaviors are configured according to the interaction of a variety of factors.

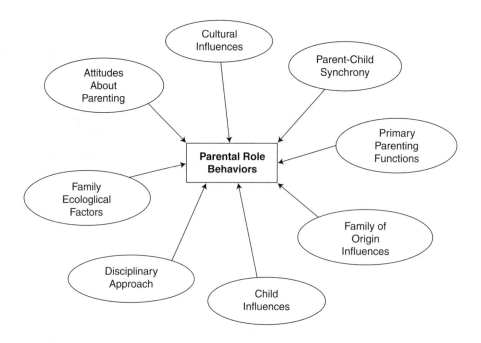

## Cultural Influences

Much research conducted over the past 60 years related to the assumption that cultural variations in child-rearing patterns result in personality and behavioral differences in children. In theory, differences in social class value systems cause corresponding differences in the ways children are reared. The patterns in child rearing found in the social class groupings are thought to be perpetuated from one generation to the next, although individual parents interpret them in different ways.

Numerous studies report considerable differences among socioeconomic groups in the ways that children are reared and in the values that are promoted (Coontz, 1998). For example, middle-class families were believed to use more psychologically harsh methods in attempting to control children's behavior than lower-class families. Middle-class families were thought to teach children to delay the immediate gratification of their needs, while lower-class families tend to promote gratifying needs as conveniently as possible. Lower-class families also appeared to place greater emphasis on children's conformance to parents' values than do middle-class families.

Generally, however, differences between families of different socioeconomic class backgrounds have diminished over the years. There are perhaps more similari-

ties than differences in the child rearing patterns in the family systems of society today. This has been attributed in part to the ubiquitous presence of television in most homes, which offers many programs portraying middle-class values, and to the fact that more families can achieve a middle-class lifestyle due to the increased availability of education and better-paying jobs.

Although the general differences in child rearing among social groups have diminished, differences in certain values and patterns in children's behavior persist. For example, the learning styles and ability to process information of children from disadvantaged families differ drastically from those of children from middle-class families (Coontz, 1998). This suggests that the potential for children's mental growth may be strongly influenced by the differences in language and the teaching styles of mothers from these two social groups. The value placed on education and academic achievement among middle-class family systems may result in patterns of interaction that promote children's problem-solving skills.

A parent's behavioral style is guided in part by the value system of the social class with which he or she identifies. Each group maintains essentially the same common objective in child rearing—that is, to support children's growth and development. However, the style of each group in interactions with children differs considerably. For example, as compared to lower-class parents, middle-class parents tend to value social achievement of children, to encourage children to acquire knowledge, and to expect independence early in their children's lives. These differences in values translate to differences in parents' child-rearing styles and what they teach their children (Coontz, 1998).

## Synchrony of Parental Style and Child Development

Parenting style will be congruent, or synchronized, with children's developmental level. For example, parenting style at the infancy stage focuses on nurturing and providing the tremendous amounts of physical caregiving infants need. When families have a broad age range of children, parenting styles must be mixed, in general, while continuing to focus on being congruent with a particular child's developmental level.

Further complicating this situation are the developmental experiences that parents are involved with at the time they are raising their children. Parents must attend to the developmental needs of their children while attempting to meet their own developmental demands. For example, interactions with children may be tempered by the pressures on working parents who must juggle family and work roles.

## Primary Parenting Functions

Parents' behavior and ways of interacting with children are usually purposeful attempts to meet what they perceive children's needs to be (Clarke & Dawson, 1998), which in turn relate strongly to the goals adults wish to accomplish in their socialization of children for adulthood. Two broad categories describe parenting behavior aimed at meeting children's needs in preparing them for their future: *structure* and *nurturance* (Clarke & Dawson, 1998). These constitute two principal functions parents perform in socializing children.

**Structure** describes those aspects of parenting behavior aimed toward providing children with the means to regulate their lives and to lay the foundation upon which a child's personality is formed and expressed. Structure involves teaching children about personal boundaries, teaching them the limits to which they may go in their behavior so that they do not infringe on others' needs and rights, providing the experiences that

**FIGURE 1–7.**   Most parents are aware that their children have particular needs. Parents attempt to meet these needs in the ways in which they provide structure and nurturance.

promote their acquiring a healthy sense of self-worth, and providing a sense of safety and security so that they will learn to be appropriately trusting of others. Structure also involves helping children to develop healthy habits in thought and behavior; learn values and ethics; acquire healthy character traits such as honesty, integrity, and personal honor; and develop personal responsibility for their actions. Structure helps to provide a child with a healthy, strong sense of self-esteem that permits growth toward meeting personal potential and becoming a well-differentiated individual who is valued for distinct qualities and traits (see Figure 1–7).

**Nurturance** is the second function involved in parenting children. It relates to those parenting behaviors intended to meet children's needs for unconditional love. This is necessary for children's healthy growth and well-being. By learning that he or she is lovable, a child learns that others can be loved as well. The assertive care and support that are given in unconditional ways to children form the basis of nurture. **Assertive care** involves noticing, understanding, and responding to the behavioral cues and verbal requests that children pose to parents. It is expressed to children when adults determine children's needs and respond to those needs in loving, predictable, and trustworthy ways. **Supportive care** is expressed at those times when adults offer care to children, but allow them the freedom to accept or reject the offer since parents give it in terms of unconditional love. Adults provide structure to children by teaching them rules and skills, which in turn allow children to accept nurturing more willingly. These two aspects of parenting are explored more fully in the later chapters that describe child rearing at each stage of children's development.

## Family of Origin Influences

Because we become parents without the assistance of instinct to guide our behavior, we rely on other means to help us learn how to care for a dependent child. One of the major influences comes from the observation of our own parents. Essentially, we appear to use our parents as models of how to act as a parent (Marsiglio, Hutchinson, & Cohan, 2000). This statement may be an over-simplification, however. The reactions, perceptions, and feelings we have about how we were raised also influence how we approach our own children when we become parents. Generally, people who are satisfied about how they were raised and how they feel about themselves as adults will probably duplicate the methods and attitudes of their parents upon assuming a parenting role (Clarke & Dawson, 1998). Conversely, people who are dissatisfied with their parents' methods may try to be just the opposite when acting as parents. Another type of response is the feeling that one's parents did not provide enough love or physical affection, in which case the reaction may be to overcompensate with one's own children.

The experiences we have as children provide a blueprint for a number of interactional patterns manifested when we grow up and become parents ourselves (Marsiglio, Hutchinson, & Cohan, 2000). There are several sources of this blueprint: (1) the goals our parents had for our growth and development, (2) the model of parenthood we observed from our parents' behavior, and (3) the influence of parenting models that have been handed down from one generation to another. For these reasons, the blueprint we assimilate for how to act as a parent may not be especially helpful when the time comes to assume the role ourselves. It may be outmoded, inappropriate,

and unrealistic based on the particular circumstances in which we conduct ourselves as parents.

Additionally, not every family system is healthy or functions in healthy ways. For example, one or both adults can be affected by addictions to substances, mental or emotional disturbances can thwart effective and healthy functioning, and living conditions can hamper one's ability to parent. Most such families attempt to hide the emotional pain that results from their inability to function healthily. When this occurs, the adults often adopt certain parenting behaviors (possibly learned from the models of their parents) and assign children certain roles that mirror their own family's dysfunction. This illustrates the concepts of wholeness and interrelatedness in family systems theory: What affects one person in a family system affects everyone to some degree. Patterns for coping with the stress of an unhealthy family of origin tend to carry over into future generations.

Based on observations of numerous adults acting as parents, several models of parenting behavior have been developed that illustrate how an unhealthy family of origin influences a person's own patterns or styles of parenting (Framo, Weber, & Levine, 2003). There is never a pure assimilation of one particular model into a person's potential parenting behavior; rather, a mixture or composite of behaviors usually resembles several aspects of the various models.

## Influence of Children on Parents

Our culture traditionally ascribes to children the role of learner. Children and adolescents are thought to need numerous learning experiences to prepare them for adulthood. They are the objects of adults' intensive socialization efforts. The relationship between parents and children focuses in many respects on the configuration of the adult as teacher and the child as learner. From this viewpoint, there is support for maintaining the unidirectional model of socialization.

Our culture also constructs the concept of children as people who are in need of adults' protection. Children obviously need assistance in learning the many skills considered necessary to their effective functioning as adults. Today, children are dependent on parents for a longer time than they were earlier in history. The relationship between parent and child has become one of the last human interactional relationships in which the use of social power by an adult is largely unquestioned. Because of the inherent teacher-student quality of this relationship, the power of adults is accentuated in interactions with children. In addition, the greater physical size and strength of adults also contribute to the greater use of their power over children. According to many psychologists and sociologists, this has caused the child to become something of a victim.

Power may not be the culprit, but rather the way in which it is used. Some adults use power to control and manipulate, rather than to facilitate, children's growth and development. This causes difficulty in the relationship, especially as children grow older (Ambert, 1992).

With the advent of family systems theory, which describes interactions within family relationships as having a reciprocal effect upon participants (discussed in Chapter 3), researchers have begun to acknowledge that children have an impact upon their parents' behavior (Ambert, 1992). Initial work points strongly to the effects that children can have upon adults' lives in at least 11 areas: (1) parental health; (2) adults' activities; (3) parental employment status; (4) use and availability of family financial resources; (5) parents' intimate relationship; (6) parents' interactions; (7) parent's community interactions; (8) parental personality development; (9) parents' values, attitudes, and belief systems; (10) parents' life plans; and (11) adults' feelings of having control over one's life.

These effects are perhaps even more broad than are outlined here. We may wonder why it has taken so long for behavioral and social science to acknowledge the impact of these kinds of influence by children on adults' lives. Perhaps this is because it has not been socially proper for adults to admit that children can influence them (Ambert, 1992).

## Disciplinary Approach

The approach parents take in teaching their children the values and beliefs their family hold will shape parenting style in a variety of ways. Goals that parents hold for their children's growth and development usually arise out of altruism. What adults desire for children and how most people shape their parenting activities and behavior relate to what they believe children need to become effective adults. Ordinarily, most parents want their children: (1) to have a happy and fulfilling life, (2) to become a person who functions independently and gets along well in

work and in relationships with others, and (3) to acquire the skills and competencies that permit effective functioning as an adult in society (Elkin & Handel, 1989).

Parents think about those behaviors and social competencies they feel are important for children to acquire to become effectively functioning adults. These constitute another aspect of what adults believe children need, and parenting behaviors may be directed toward shaping these as part of children's behavior repertoire. **Social competence** usually refers to a group of attributes that are believed to be essential in assisting a person to make full use of his or her personal resources to cope productively with the circumstances of life. The ways that parents provide structure for children in their child rearing or disciplinary program are usually shaped to help children acquire these essential social skills.

The goals that parents establish for their child rearing or disciplinary approach are influenced by both personal and societal sources. Adults' perceptions of what children need are based on complex personal opinions but also reflect the realities of what life presents as part of a family experience. Parents' general opinions about what children need are based on their past experiences, the values the parents were taught by their own families of origin, the philosophies of parenting they have developed since becoming adults, and so on. However, these perceptions can be tempered by specific situations, such as when one has a child with some type of physical or mental disability or when divorce changes one's status to that of a single parent.

Adults also come to understand that what children need changes with age and developmental stage, and they adapt their parenting behavior accordingly. As they establish goals, most parents come to understand they must change how they relate and interact with children if children are to attain the new goals. It is not unusual for parents to seek out sources of information and assistance in learning how to adapt and change their behavior in response to developmental changes taking place in children as they grow (Bigner & Yang, 1996). This constitutes one of the major challenges to effective parenting behavior.

## Family Ecological Factors

The influence of various environmental systems on the functioning of the parent-child microenvironment can be observed in a variety of ways, but they are often difficult to anticipate completely or measure accurately. Each of us is influenced in our behavior by a number of environmental factors. Our past experience with children is one factor. Our behavior can be influenced by internal factors, such as blood sugar levels, hormone balances, and emotional states. Sociocultural factors that affect our behavior include value systems and beliefs about appropriate role behavior. Other factors are more physical; for example, where we live (in an apartment or in a single-family residence, in the city or in a rural area) may affect parent-child interactions. Even the time of day that interactions occur can be an important consideration. All of these factors from the past and present tend to influence and cause variability in parents' behavior and affect the way interactions take place between parents and children.

Family ecological factors such as the level of family income (poverty-level vs. middle-class income), ethnic identity, or type of family structure can influence parenting styles in a variety of ways. These factors affect a family's ability to provide equipment and services such as medical or dental care, clothing, and food that can influence the quality and nature of interactions between parents and children. Parents' goals in their child-rearing efforts may also be tempered by these family ecological factors.

## Attitudes About Parenting Behavior

Closely associated with other factors are the attitudes adults hold about children and child rearing in general. These attitudes and beliefs are the result of a person's socialization and past experiences. In many respects, they form the implicit rules, or "shoulds," that guide a person's behavior as a parent and have a significant influence on the behavioral choices a person makes in interacting with his or her child. The attitudes about how one should act as a parent may also be seen more clearly in the parenting style that expresses a program of discipline.

The range of attitudes about how to parent children appropriately and effectively may be viewed as a continuum (see Figure 1–8) ranging from strict (authoritarian) to lenient (permissive). Typically, attitudes serve to guide actual parenting behavior and can be expected to shift along the continuum in tandem with the changing developmental stages of children. Some parents may adopt a particular parenting attitude and style once a child is a

| Authoritarian | Authoritative | Permissive |
| --- | --- | --- |

**FIGURE 1–8.** Attitudes about parenting influence parental behaviors and can be represented as lying on a continuum.

family member and never stray from this as the child grows older. Others may adopt a particular attitude and parenting style that can shift and change in relation to children's changing developmental stages and abilities. These attitudes begin to have significant influence on parenting style when children reach preschool age (see Chapter 8).

• • • • • • • • • • • • • • • • • • • • • • • • • • • • • • • • •

## Parenting Reflection 1–5

Suppose you are a parent of a 4-year-old; you and your child are grocery shopping. Which of the factors just described will influence how you behave in public as a parent when your child misbehaves?

• • • • • • • • • • • • • • • • • • • • • • • • • • • • • • • • •

• • • • • • • • • • • • • • • • • • • • • • • • • • • • • • • • •

*Focus Point.* Eight major categories of factors contribute to the nature and context of an adult's potential behavior as a parent and act to influence the configuration of the parenting style that someone adopts: (1) cultural influences, such as one's social class background and associated values and beliefs systems; (2) synchrony of parental style and a child's developmental stage; (3) primary parenting objectives that guide parental behavior in achieving child rearing goals, such as the manner in which nurturance and structure are provided to children; (4) family of origin influences, such as the model of parental behavior observed in one's own parents; (5) children's myriad ways of influencing parental behaviors; (6) the disciplinary approach adopted by parents in emphasizing the goals they wish to accomplish in their child-rearing efforts; (7) family ecological factors such as ethnic identity, level of family income, or type of family structure; and (8) attitudes about parenting behavior, such as authoritarian, permissive, and authoritative beliefs.

• • • • • • • • • • • • • • • • • • • • • • • • • • • • • • • • •

## POINTS TO CONSIDER

■ Individuals in our society need training and education to be effective parents, just as they do to perform other roles in adulthood. Until recently, little preparation has been given to those who plan to become parents.

■ The parenthood role is associated with a variety of different concepts and ideas in our society.

■ Four basic traits characterize the parenthood role in contemporary society.

■ Our current ideas about the nature of parent-child relations have evolved over time. What were considered appropriate traits for this role in the past are different from what are held today about this family role.

■ Parenthood may be viewed as a developmental role where one's behaviors change in response to the changing developmental needs of children.

■ Eight factors significantly contribute to the manner by which one's behavior is patterned in the parenthood role.

# CHAPTER 2

# Diversity of Contemporary American Families

## Focus Questions

1. How is a family defined today, and what are the functions of families in contemporary society?
2. What features characterize contemporary American families?
3. What are the principal types of forms and structures found in contemporary American families?
4. What is the nature of parent-child relations in ethnic minority families in the United States?
5. How is parenting influenced in interracial-interethnic families?
6. How do immigrant families conduct parent-child relations?

To understand how parenthood roles function within family systems, it is essential to describe the various factors that may be collectively grouped as family ecological influences. These factors serve as part of the social context in which parent-child relations take place. While the topic of family ecology is discussed in greater detail in Chapter 3, we may tentatively describe this now as the various social, psychological, and physical environmental systems in which parenting operates. For example, the level of a family's income (poverty vs. middle-class income) as well as the ethnic identity of a family system can influence parenting style or behavior.

This chapter discusses a variety of issues that expand on the topics introduced in Chapter 1. More specifically, this chapter first presents information about how a range of family systems are defined, structured, and characterized in contemporary American society. Then we explore the ecological factors of ethnicity and cultural background as they influence parent-child relations.

## CONCEPTIONS OF FAMILIES

### Family Characteristics and Concepts

The family is a ubiquitous social institution. This group has the responsibility for producing and socializing children to become effectively functioning members of society. Although families have always been the basic component of the society in which we live, they have changed significantly over the years in composition, size, and functioning, as well as in the characteristics that give them meaning.

In earlier times, when hunting provided the primary form of sustenance for humans, the predominant family form was the **nuclear family,** a group composed of a man, a woman, and their children (Figure 2–1). This family form enabled the fast, efficient movement of the family group as they followed the migration of animal herds over large geographic areas. As evolution occurred,

**FIGURE 2–1.**   A nuclear family is one of the basic family structures found in American society.

the use of plants and domesticated animals as food sources gave rise to agriculture and animal husbandry. Families, in turn, became less mobile and remained in specific geographic areas for longer periods of time. This encouraged the development of large **extended family** groupings that often included several generations living together in close physical proximity.

Agriculture and a rural lifestyle are no longer the predominant ways of life for most people in our society. Rather, we tend to live in urban areas, and many adults support families by holding highly complex occupations in technological fields. The predominant family form today has shifted back to the nuclear form with its many variations. Apparently, the return to the nuclear family unit is traced in part to economic factors, particularly the need for people to relocate to areas where jobs are plentiful (Coontz, 1998).

The traditional foundation of a family begins with the committed relationship of two adults. Since our society does not currently recognize such relationships between homosexuals, a legal marriage (with exceptions in two states) is necessarily one between an adult male and an adult female. Traditionally, *family* implies an adult opposite-sex couple and their children sharing a physical residence and mutually agreed-upon goals for their relationship.

Recent societal changes have instigated a reexamination of this traditional conception of family. It is becoming more accepted that today's family must be defined by different standards (Lamanna & Reidman, 2003). For example, childless couples are now considered to be a family. Likewise, we recognize a single parent and his or her children as a family. Two adults of the same sex who have a committed relationship can be called a family. Even a single individual who belongs to a **family of choice,** a network of significant others and friends who provide emotional and social support, can be considered part of a family.

Today, people often determine their own definition of family. Some consider themselves to be members of several different families. The current definition of family is more global than in the past. However it may be defined, the family remains the basic element of society. It performs specific functions for individuals and for the larger society. These are discussed in the next section.

*Focus Point.* The definition of family has changed in modern times. Families formerly were conceived as being composed of two opposite-sex adults and their children. This kind of family is known today as a *nuclear family*. In contrast, the extended family is usually composed of several generations. Diversity is the rule today; there are many different ways to define a family.

## Family Functions

Many years ago, anthropologist George Peter Murdock (1949) described the nuclear family as a universal feature of human societies. He contended that four functions were found in all families in all cultures: (1) reproduction of new members of society, (2) legitimizing sexual relations between adults, (3) maintaining reciprocal economic relations between the family group and the larger society, and (4) socializing children for their future adult functioning in society. Evidence can be offered to refute the universality of these four functions. Still, Murdock's functions can be observed in a variety of American families today, regardless of the form they take.

Some observers believe that the loss of family functions to other institutions has led to the disintegration of the family. Indeed, the family may appear to be much less functional today than in the past. Many writers suggest that the socialization of children is the only principal function it retains and that it is performing this function poorly.

This gloomy appraisal is probably exaggerated (Stacey, 1996). Rather than completely lost, traditional family functions have become underemphasized. As other groups have assumed many of these instrumental functions, the contemporary family has been freed to specialize in meeting emotional needs and in socializing children to become adults in society. The survival of family groups may now depend on how well they meet members' emotional needs. The smaller size of today's families means that members' interactions are intense and frequent. The family is still the primary arena for teaching effective interpersonal skills to children. As other family functions have become underemphasized, parenting is the major focus of a family group today. In many families with divorced adults, single parents, and stepchildren, for example, people may be challenged to accomplish this task successfully.

## Parenting Reflection 2–1

Try to predict how parenthood and parent-child relations will be conceptualized in the year 2100 or even 2200. How would you rate contemporary families in their abilities to socialize children effectively for their future?

*Focus Point.* Families comprise the basic element of society. The family group has changed considerably over the years in structure, size, and diversity of form. Socialization of children may be the principal function of the family group in society.

## WHAT ARE CONTEMPORARY FAMILIES LIKE?

### Features of Contemporary Families

Societal changes are reflected in families. For example, an economic recession greatly affects families. Family members may lose their jobs, and the family system may find its buying power drastically decreased. Society and the families within it have a reciprocal relationship. What affects society affects families, and vice versa.

Sociological data are useful in understanding what contemporary American families are like and the conditions under which they operate. This information, much of it collected by the U.S. Bureau of the Census, is helpful in evaluating changes in family and population characteristics and for making predictions about American family forms. Contemporary American families exhibit trends and features that help to provide another dimension that shapes parenthood and other family functions and relationships.

**Marriage.** Americans continue to value marriage as a social institution (Thornton & Young-DeMarco, 2001), but important changes in marriage behavior affect family formation and the assumption of parenting roles. For example, there are fewer married couples today than 30 years ago. This implies that there may be more people who choose to cohabitate prior to or in place of marriage, an increasing number of nonfamily households (consist-

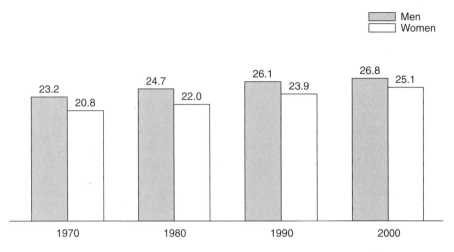

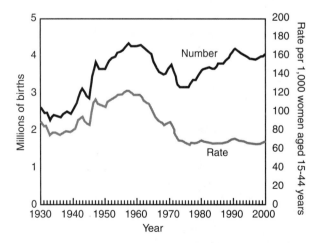

**FIGURE 2–2.** Median age at first marriage for men and women between 1970 and 2000.

*Source:* Fields, J., & Lynne, M. C. (2001). *America's Families and Living Arrangements: March 2000.* Current Population Reports, P20-537. Washington, DC: U.S. Census Bureau.

ing of people who are not related), and increases in the numbers of single-parent families and unmarried women who are parents.

The age at first marriage has been gradually increasing since the mid-1960s after experiencing a long-standing trend of occurring at younger ages (U.S. Bureau of the Census, 2003). For example, in 1970, the median age at first marriage was 23.2 years for men and 20.8 years for women. By 2000, the median age at first marriage climbed to 26.8 years for men and to 25.1 years for women (see Figure 2–2).

The higher median ages at first marriage appear to be related to economic and social issues. It takes longer for young people today to complete their education and training and to establish themselves in an occupational path. It is also associated with the desire of more women to complete their college education or establish their career path than in years past. The higher median age of women relates as well to women's participation in the labor force for longer periods before marriage. Later marriage has contributed to delayed childbearing, smaller families, and greater marital stability (Fields & Lynn, 2001; Hobbs & Stoops, 2002).

Another indication of the delay in first marriage is the increasingly larger numbers of young unmarried adults. From 1970 to 2000, the number of people who remain unmarried between 25 to 34 years of age more than tripled (U.S. Bureau of the Census, 2002). Apparently, increasingly larger numbers of both men and women are choosing to remain unmarried or to cohabitate rather than marry. Combining this data with statistics about births indicates that a sizable number of

Americans are deciding whether to become parents independently from their choices about marriage.

**Births.**   The number of children born in the United States has been relatively stable since about 1975, following a significant decline in births from 1958 (see Figure 2–3). The number of births declined slightly between 1990 and 1997 but has increased slightly since then. The number of births increased dramatically among unmarried women within recent years while those among adolescents has declined significantly. Asian and Hispanic

**FIGURE 2–3.**   Birth rate and number of live births to women in the United States between 1930 and 2000.

*Source:* Martin J. A., Hamilton, B. E., Ventura, S. J., Menacker, F., & Park, M. M. (2002). Births: Final data for 2000. *National Vital Statistics Reports, 50*(5). Hyattsville, Maryland: National Center of Health Statistics.

women tend to have higher fertility rates (the number of births a typical woman will have over her lifetime) in recent years than women in other ethnic groups.

The average number of births per family in 2000 was about 2.1 children, which accounts for today's smaller families. The number of children who die either before birth or during infancy has declined over the last 100 years, resulting in a smaller number of conceptions and births today. Small family size produces other ripple effects observed in society, such as the overall age structure of the population, school enrollments, and social programming needs.

**Divorce.**   Divorce data is reported in many forms by different government agencies. This presents complicated and often contradictory information. In addition, the federal agency that is charged with collecting vital statistics on U.S. citizens discontinued collecting data on divorce in 1996. Hence, much of the detailed information about divorce is based on aged data.

The rate of divorce appears to have stabilized within the last 20 years, although at a level that is the highest in our history (Figure 2–4). Predictions are that if the current rate of divorce continues, one out of every two first marriages contracted in the early 1970s will be dissolved through divorce. The high incidence of divorce has given rise to the prevalently observed family form called the **single-parent family.**

As divorce has become more common, it has lost much of its social stigma. It is difficult in these more liberal times for many couples to maintain long-term commitments to marriage for several reasons (VanLaningham, Johnson, Amato, 2001): (1) changes in the status and roles of women in society, (2) changes in laws that make obtaining divorce less complicated and less stigmatizing, and (3) the strong desire to achieve personal happiness.

● ● ● ● ● ● ● ● ● ● ● ● ● ● ● ● ● ● ● ● ● ● ● ● ● ● ● ● ● ● ● ●

### Parenting Reflection 2–2

You are the mother of a young woman who is contemplating marriage. She has only one concern that she wishes to discuss with you: Why do people continue to get married given the current likelihood of a divorce happening? What would you say to her in defense of marriage?

● ● ● ● ● ● ● ● ● ● ● ● ● ● ● ● ● ● ● ● ● ● ● ● ● ● ● ● ● ● ● ●

**Remarriage.**   Remarriage is more likely to occur among those who leave a first marriage via divorce (U.S. Bureau of the Census, 2002), although there has been a general decline in the rate at which remarriages occur since the mid-1960s. The median length of first marriage in the United States has remained at about 7 years since 1980. The median interval between divorce and remarriage is about 3 years. Men tend to remarry more quickly after their first divorce than women do. Racial group identity also influences remarriage rates; whites are more likely to remarry than are blacks. These rela-

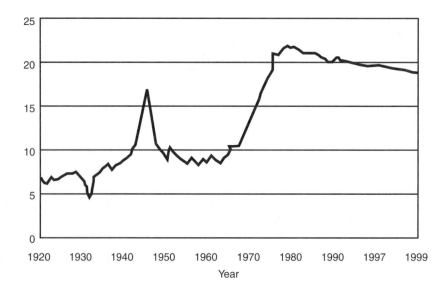

**FIGURE 2–4.**   The refined divorce rate (number of divorces per 1,000 women) of women aged 15 years and older in the United States between 1920 and 1999.

*Sources:* U.S. Bureau of the Census. (1997). *Population profile of the United States: 1997.* Current Population Reports (Ser. P23, No. 194). Washington, DC: U.S. Government Printing Office; U.S. Bureau of the Census. (1999). *Statistical abstract of the United States.* Washington, DC: U.S. Government Printing Office.

tionships are considered to be at high risk of divorce, often within six years.

Remarriage tends to create stepfamilies for many individuals. The result is that many remarried adults can expect to parent children of other people as well as their own. About 9 percent of children lived with a stepparent and a biological parent in 1996, the most recent data available (Fields, 2001). Researchers who study stepfamilies disagree about the effects of this family form on children's welfare and that of adult family members (Ganong & Coleman, 2000; Visher & Visher, 1996). Issues relating to parenting in stepfamilies are discussed in greater detail in Chapter 12.

**Family Income and Working Mothers.**   Employment of both adults in contemporary families has become the norm in recent years. Family income may have a more influential effect on the quality of family life and on parent-child relations than other factors that have been previously discussed. When both adults are employed, challenges in family life take several forms: who does what household work, how child care is arranged and financed, how much time can be devoted to child rearing and parent-child interactions, what kinds of extracurricular activities children may participate in, how children can be assisted in schoolwork, how personal and leisure time are spent, what quality of medical and dental care may be provided, and what amount of attention can be devoted to marital relationships.

The median income of families in the United States provides an idea of how finances influence quality of life. The median income of all family types in the United States has risen considerably since the mid-1940s (DeNavas-Walt, Cleveland, & Webster, 2003; U.S. Bureau of the Census, 2002). The main reason is due to the employment of both adults in intact family homes. In 2002, this figure, representing total income prior to withholding taxes, was $42,409 (see Figure 2–5). The lowest median income ($28,126) was among single-parent families headed by a mother. This compares to a median income of $59,343 for married couple families. These sharp differences in family income have a significant influence on quality of life experienced in these families. Quality of life issues play a central role in parenting and parent-child relations.

The increase in the numbers of married women in the labor force has resulted in a concomitant increase in dual-earner families. The largest segment of these are married mothers of children between the ages of 6 and 17 (U.S. Bureau of the Census, 2002). In 2001, about 62 percent of all married women in the United States were employed outside their home. Employment of both adults in an intact family produces ripple effects in other areas of family life and parenting. For example, supplementary child care must be financed and arranged, and household tasks must be shared.

**Poverty and Homelessness.**   Family well-being is threatened when homelessness occurs and a family exists at poverty level or below. Poverty varies considerably in the United States relative to family structure, racial group, and ethnicity. For example, poverty is

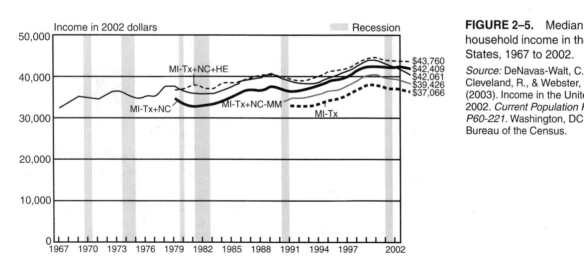

**FIGURE 2–5.**   Median household income in the United States, 1967 to 2002.

*Source:* DeNavas-Walt, C., Cleveland, R., & Webster, B. H., Jr. (2003). Income in the United States: 2002. *Current Population Reports, P60-221.* Washington, DC: U.S. Bureau of the Census.

more common among single-parent families headed by women than among married couple families (see Figure 2–6).

The number of individuals and families living in poverty, along with the rate of poverty, increased in 2002 from previous years (Proctor & Dalaker, 2003). Black and Hispanic families with children were the most likely and white families the least likely to be poor. The higher incidence of single-parent families headed by women among minorities is a major factor in the differences in family income among racial groups. Two trends in those affected by poverty continued to be observed in recent years: (1) the feminization of poverty, as noted by the increasing numbers of women and children who are poor, and (2) an increasing number of the working poor or those who may work one or more jobs earning low wages with few or no benefits.

Economic conditions are a leading factor in producing poverty-level incomes and the likelihood of homelessness for many families. Other factors such as unemployment, disabilities, or unstable family life may also contribute to homelessness. Although it may appear reasonable to assume that anyone who wishes to work can make an adequate income, this is not so. In 2002, about half of the low-income adults in the United States were employed full-time (Proctor & Dalaker, 2003).

•••••••••••••••••••••••••••••••••••••••••••••••••

***Focus Point.*** The ways that parenthood is defined, child rearing is conducted, and parent-child relations are valued vary based on how each family system experiences different ecological factors. Contemporary family life in America has certain features: (1) Both men and women are marrying for the first time at later ages. (2) One marriage in two will terminate in divorce, usually after 7 years. (3) There is a high probability of remarriage following divorce, leading to a sizable number of children who grow up in stepfamilies. (4) The birth rate has declined over the past 30 years, resulting in smaller families. (5) Family incomes have increased significantly in the years since World War II. Today, about two-thirds of all married women over 18 years of age work outside the home. (6) Poverty and homelessness affect an increasing percentage of families in the United States each year. This situation affects minority families to a greater extent than others.

•••••••••••••••••••••••••••••••••••••••••••••••••

**FIGURE 2–6.** Poverty rates in the United States in 2002 by family type.

*Source:* Proctor, B. D., & Dalaker, J. (2003). Poverty in the United States: 2002. *Current Population Reports, P60-222.* Washington, DC: U.S. Bureau of the Census.

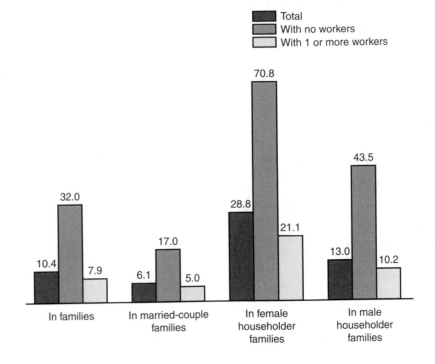

## DIVERSITY IN CONTEMPORARY FAMILY FORMS AND STRUCTURES

The family has become more important as a source of stability in our rapidly changing and increasingly complex society. It can be a refuge when individuals feel buffeted by impersonal forces. The United States was founded on the idea that people have the right to pursue personal happiness. Since the 1960s especially, the pursuit of individual happiness has been heavily emphasized. At the same time, Americans have become more sensitive to other human rights. We are today more conscious of discrimination based on age, gender, race, sexual orientation, and ethnic group identity.

These social changes are reflected in family life. Some observers think that the traditional nuclear family with husband-breadwinner, stay-at-home wife, and two-plus children is virtually a relic. This is especially the case for those groups in which the male serves as the principal economic provider and the female acts as the principal homemaker. This type of family today is in a distinct minority of all U.S. families, accounting for only 7 percent of these in 2002 (Population Reference Bureau,

2003b). A trend reported recently by the U.S. Census Bureau is an increase in the number of nonfamily households accompanied by a decrease in the number of family households (Fields & Casper, 2001). For example, 81 percent of all American households in 1980 were family households (at least two people related by blood, marriage, or adoption) while these kinds of households accounted for 69 percent of all households in 2000 (see Figure 2–7).

Social conditions such as the high probability of divorce for married couples have changed the face of the American family. Families have changed in size, structure, form, and function. Today, diversity in family form and structure is the norm. The predominant types that include children are outlined briefly here. These will be discussed in greater detail in other chapters.

### Single-Parent and Binuclear Families

One of the more common types of families in the United States today is composed of one adult parent and one or more children under 18 years of age. Whether headed by a man or a woman (most often a woman), this is called

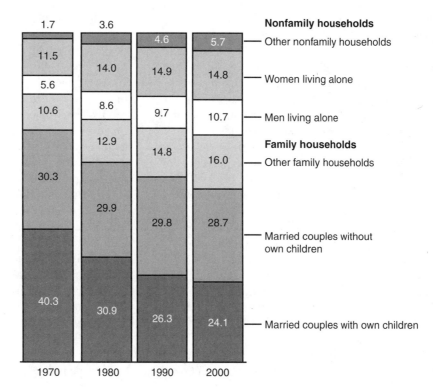

**FIGURE 2–7.** Percentage of different types of households in the United States between 1970 and 2000.

*Source:* Fields, J., & Casper, L. M. (2001). America's families and living arrangements: March 2000. *Current Population Reports, P20-537.* Washington, DC: U.S. Bureau of the Census.

**FIGURE 2–8.** Percentage of children with single parents or cohabitating single parents, 2002.

*Source:* Fields, J. (2003). Children's living arrangements and characteristics: March 2003. *Current Population Reports, P20-547.* Washington, DC: U.S. Bureau of the Census.

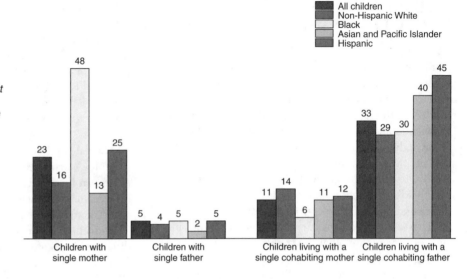

a **single-parent** or **binuclear family.** The latter term refers to the presence of two families shared by children. The single-parent family is increasing faster in number than any other family form today (Federal Interagency Forum on Child and Family Statistics, 2003; Fields, 2003). In 1970, approximately 3.8 million families were headed by a single parent. In 2000, this number increased to almost 16 million families (Fields & Casper, 2001). Single-parent families accounted for about 28 percent of all families with children in 1998. Recent data from the U.S. Census Bureau estimates that in a significant number of households children live with their single father (33 percent of these) or mother (11 percent of these) and their unmarried partner (Fields & Casper, 2001). Single-parent families are more prevalent among blacks as a group (South, 1999). About 48 percent of all children living with a single mother are black, 16 percent are white, 13 percent are Asian, and 25 percent are Hispanic (see Figure 2–8).

A single-parent family is created through one of three means: (1) divorce, desertion, or separation of the adults; (2) death of one adult; or (3) having a child out of wedlock. The most common means is through divorce, and generally the mother is given custody of the children. The vast majority of single-parent families are headed by women because courts typically award full or physical custody to women in the United States.

Quality of life is a major issue for single-parent families (Hildebrand et al., 2000). Any type of disruption in

family life can produce a crisis, and divorce is one of the most stressful experiences that one can have in adulthood (Lamanna & Reidman, 2003). It can also be traumatic for children. Although divorce has become commonplace, it is a crisis event that forces many short- and long-range adjustments on a family.

The experience of being a single parent is different for women and men. Women generally can expect to have financial difficulties, and there are significantly more children who live in poverty because they live in a female-headed, single-parent family (Federal Interagency Forum on Child and Family Statistics, 2003). The implications for children growing up in single-parent families, especially those headed by mothers, can be serious. While most studies report that children generally fare well when living in a single-parent family, those who live in poverty are at greater risk than those from more affluent families to experience school problems, to become teen parents, and as adults to earn less and be unemployed more frequently.

Life is not easy for most single-parent families. Yet many people choose to divorce rather than remain in an unhappy relationship, even though they know they will have to make a multitude of difficult adjustments. For many people, this type of family arrangement is more efficient and harmonious than a household marked by tensions and strife between the adults. This family type is discussed in greater detail in Chapter 11.

## Parenting Reflection 2–3

You have been elected as mayor of a large city running your compaign on social reform. What are some things you can do as a political figure to improve the quality of life of single-parent families headed by women in your community?

## Stepfamilies

Stepfamilies are also known as *blended families*. Stepfamilies include an adult couple and children of one or both of them from a previous marriage or relationship. This family type is based on the remarriage of at least one of the adult partners (Hildebrand et al., 2000). Since the vast majority of single-parent families are headed by women, the person usually filling the vacant adult family role is a man in the new stepfamily. He may or may not have been divorced and have children of his own.

Remarriage is popular today. The median length of first marriages in the United States is about 7 years (U.S. Bureau of the Census, 2002). Most people who divorce remarry within five years following divorce (Bramlett & Mosher, 2002). The median interval between divorce after the first marriage and remarriage is about 3 years. Stepfamilies by definition involve children of one or both remarried partners. About 9 percent of all children in the United States in 1996 (the most recently analyzed data) lived in a stepfamily (Fields, 2001).

Popular perception holds that stepfamily life is highly problematic for all involved. Researchers have found that this family form may be no better or worse than other family forms, however, although the challenges are distinct (Hildebrand et al., 2000). These include the need to deal with a complicated extended family network, difficulty in establishing parenting roles, an uncertain developmental life career, and unique developmental tasks. This family form is discussed in greater detail in Chapter 12.

## Families with Renested Adult Children

Families with renested adult children are a modern phenomenon. This **renested family** type emerges when children who have been launched into adult lives of their own return to the home base of their family of origin (Steinmetz, Clavan, & Stein, 1990). The young adult children

are also referred to as *boomerang kids* (Mitchell & Gee, 1996). Most children who return to their parental home are males under 20 years of age. Some estimates suggest that more than 60 percent of all young adults between 18 and 30 years of age will at some time return to their family of origin to live temporarily (Piper & Balswick, 1997).

The phenomenon of renested families occurs primarily when young adult children experience some type of economic or personal crisis, such as job loss or divorce, and turn to their family for support. Some renested families are also formed when young adults return to their elderly parents' home to care for them.

Very little is known about the interaction patterns or lifestyle of renested families (Mitchell, 1998; Mitchell & Gee, 1996; Veevers & Mitchell, 1998). This type of family system probably needs to be adaptable to respond effectively to the developmental level of a young adult. Family rules may need to be changed and new boundaries established as parents and young adult children work through interaction issues. The kind of arrangement arrived at will involve new definitions of parent-child relations that depend less on the social power of the parents. Parents were more likely to provide greater support when their boomerang kids reciprocated with their own support for parents and were more autonomous, for example.

## Gay and Lesbian Families

A common misconception about gays and lesbians is that they are antifamily and prefer to maintain a single lifestyle. People are often surprised to learn that many homosexual men and women form families that may include children (see Figure 2–9). **Gay and lesbian families** are difficult to distinguish from other family types today. Many more gay men, especially, have long-term, committed relationships than in the past (Bigner, 2000).

Children are a part of many gay and lesbian families. Their presence is more likely in lesbian than in gay families, probably because women generally receive custody of children after a divorce. Researchers have found few differences between homosexual parents and heterosexual parents (Bigner, 2000; Patterson, Fulcher, & Wainright, 2002; Tasker, 2002). Many people are surprised to learn that homosexuals are involved in something that is so heterosexual in nature as having children and parenting them. Most homosexuals became parents when they were young adults and often were denying their homosexual orientation by attempting to lead a

**FIGURE 2–9.** Gay men and lesbian women form families that resemble other family forms but differ in many respects.

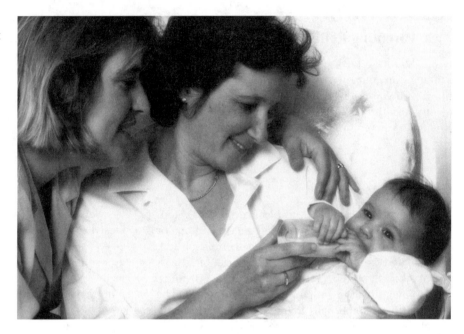

heterosexual lifestyle. Some lesbian couples, though, choose to become parents. To accomplish this, one partner usually is artificially inseminated.

There is no valid research data that demonstrates unquestionably that having a homosexual parent has any significant negative effects on children (Allen & Burrell, 2002; Buxton, 1999; Golombok & MacCallum, 2003; Patterson et al., 2002; Tasker, 2002). In fact, a gay or lesbian parent is as effective as nongay parents in raising children and may in some respects be even more efficient. Because our society continues to support heterosexist attitudes that favor heterosexuality over homosexuality, these facts are not widely known or accepted by the public at large.

Of course, gay and lesbian families have a different family life and different problems than other families. In many respects, however, homosexual families are like heterosexual blended families (Bigner, 2000; Laird, 2003). This is particularly true among lesbian mothers, who frequently have custody of their children from past heterosexual marriages. The distinctive problems of gay and lesbian families do not make them pathological. Rather, they reflect the difficulties of conducting a family system in a society that looks askance on such arrangements. This family form is discussed in greater detail in Chapter 11.

## Parenting Reflection 2–4

Suppose you are a family therapist advising a lesbian couple who are contemplating becoming parents. What would you help them to consider in this decision-making process?

## Coresident Grandparents and Grandchildren

The newest variation in family structure was first noticed in the early 1990s by researchers, public policy makers, and the media (Bryson & Casper, 1999). This new family structure involves grandchildren who live in grandparent-maintained households. In 1970, there were about 2.2 million of these households involving children 18 years of age and younger living with at least one grandparent. By 1997, this number increased to about 3.9 million children and constituted about 5.5 percent of all American children under 18 (Bryson & Casper, 1999). By 2001, this number reached about 8 percent of all children in the United States living with a grandparent (Fields, 2003). The parents of the grandchildren may or may not be present in these households.

The grandmother maintains the household in the large majority of coresident grandparent/grandchildren families (Fields, 2003). Coresident grandparent/grandchild families typically are created when parents experience some type of personal problem that prevents them from performing effectively in their caregiving role. Examples of such debilitating personal problems include drug abuse, addictions, child abuse, AIDS, chronic physical or emotional illness, or even death. Grandparents often step in to assume custody of grandchildren under such circumstances rather than having the children placed into foster care. The motivation to assume primary caregiving responsibilities is to provide their grandchildren with a stable environment.

The children in these families (1) are likely to be age 6 and under, (2) are mostly white, (3) live in poverty, (4) lack health insurance coverage, and (5) are likely to receive some form of public assistance (Fields, 2003).

Coresident families have difficult challenges not usually faced by other family structures (Caputo, 2001; Hayslip & Goldberg-Glen, 2000). Many grandparents, while acting compassionately in the best interests of their grandchildren, find that their plans for a serene retirement must be postponed or abandoned to provide for their grandchildren. Others find it necessary to apply for public assistance upon assuming custody of grandchildren due to the increased expenses involved that tax an already-limited fixed income. The grandchildren may also arrive with multiple problems that can be traced to parental divorce, parental addictions and dependencies, and inconsistent parental caregiving. Additionally, grandparents in coresident households are more likely to be poor and to experience all the negative aspects associated with poverty. They are less likely to be insured and especially lack health insurance coverage for grandchildren. Furthermore, grandparents may not be able to cope with providing the educational needs of grandchildren. Many have not completed high school and may not be completely aware of how to guide children's educational experiences.

***Focus Point.*** Diversity, in structure and form, is the principal characteristic of contemporary American families. Significant variations in the ways that families are defined and how they are composed reflect changes occurring in the larger society. The most commonly observed family types are (1) two opposite-sex adults with an intact marriage and their children, (2) single-parent adults and their children, (3) stepfamilies composed of two opposite-sex adults who have remarried and the children of one or both, (4) renested families composed of adult parents and their adult children who have returned to the home base, (5) gay and lesbian families composed of two same-sex adults and sometimes the children of one or both, and (6) coresident grandparent-grandchild families. These emergent family forms do not represent a pathological or dysfunctional orientation to family life in the United States.

## ETHNIC DIVERSITY AND CONTEMPORARY FAMILIES

Cultural diversity has always been a hallmark of American society, the product of the immigration of various ethnic groups to the United States since pre-Colonial times. In recent years, ethnic identity has been reemphasized as Americans have become more curious about their family roots. Americans have always considered themselves to have a culturally diverse society. This diversity is reflected in the numerous ethnic and racial groups that have emigrated from other countries to make new homes in the United States.

Ethnic identity is a central family ecological factor that influences how most of these family systems are organized and how they function. It continues to play a role in each subsequent generation. Many ethnic minority families have created new lives and discovered new opportunities, but they have also struggled with the prejudice and discrimination that limits educational experiences, job opportunities, and the ability to function fully in communities. Because of such problems, family systems with ethnic and racial backgrounds experience problems not usually shared by those with an Anglo, or white, middle-class background.

Researchers examining family structure and functioning have tended to classify minority families according to stereotypes promulgated within the larger society. Early researchers examining Hispanic families, for example, identified the concept of **machismo** as the prime factor shaping the dynamics of this ethnic group's family life (Staples & Mirande, 1980). More recent research refutes this and other findings as not relevant to the contemporary Hispanic family (Skinner, 2001).

Today, we are concerned about building bridges between all families that make up American society. Diversity and its essential importance in our society is not just a politically correct term but a critical element that has made American society what it has become today and predicts how the future can become. Ethnic diversity is a part of the sociocultural ecological system in which we live. It encompasses the values in which people believe, how their families operate as a social system, how they teach their children to function effectively, and how resources are used to promote daily functioning.

This section examines issues that challenge parents and children within those cultural and racial groups representing large numbers of minority families in the United States. Specifically, this section focuses on the parenting and child rearing practices of African American, Hispanic, Asian American, and Native American Indian families.

## African American Parents and Children

The child rearing practices of African American family systems are found to be similar to other groups in several aspects (Figure 2–10) (Julian, McHenry, & McKelvey, 1994). When compared with Latino families, blacks tend to encourage early autonomy of children, are intolerant of wasted time, appear to practice authoritative methods of discipline based on reasoning with children, and encourage egalitarian family roles (Bluestone & Tamis-LeMonda, 1999; Wiley, Warren, & Montenelli, 2002). This approach may vary, however, depending on the socioeconomic status of the parents and other factors.

One of the greatest obstacles to effective parenting among African American families relates to economic pressures (Jones et al., 2002; Weis, 2002). In spite of dire financial circumstances that can exacerbate stressfulness in family life, effective African American parents use encouragement and sharing activities with children that tend to counteract the negative influences of harsh economic family conditions.

Ethnicity is a major family ecological factor in child rearing practices. It contributes to how children are socialized in developing a personal identity considered appropriate to their ethnic background as African Americans. As are children in other minority groups in the United States, black children are generally raised by parents who emphasize the importance of educational success as a means of bettering one's quality of life (Balkcom, 2002; Thompson, 2003; Trosper, 2002). When black parents consistently use authoritative methods in child rearing, their children generally perform successfully in school.

African American parents, like other minority parents, are challenged in teaching their children to have a positive ethnic group identity while learning to cope

**FIGURE 2–10.** Despite misconceptions and stereotypes, African American families possess many strengths that assist in their healthy functioning.

with the problems associated with societal prejudice and discrimination (Hughes, 2003). Even being a middle class black family does not completely protect parents and children from acts of prejudice and discrimination. Most black parents make efforts to ensure that children are prepared with the means to place such attitudes and treatment into proper perspective. The challenge is to teach children what it means to be an African American in a society that has strong racist overtones (Staples, 1999). But even the simple task of choosing toys can be problematic in this regard. For example, should children be encouraged only to choose black dolls, or is it appropriate to allow a white doll?

Other aspects of parenting are unique to African Americans. For example, it is estimated that more African American parents spank their children in comparison with parents of other ethnic groups (McLoyd et al., 2000; Straus & Stewart, 1999). Spanking is not likely to be seen as negative, inappropriate parenting behavior among African American parents. Rather, using corporal punishment is more likely to be viewed as an appropriate positive parental behavior by both parents and children.

In addition, parenting frequently occurs within the context of single-parent family structure headed by women who may or may not have been married (Federal Interagency Forum on Child and Family Statistics, 2003). Given that these family systems are characterized by low-income or poverty-level status as well as living in an inner-city environment, children are often at risk of experiencing difficulties in school, participating in high-risk behaviors such as drug use and gang involvement, pregnancies, health problems, and other difficulties. Many African American parents, however, are successful in buffering their children from these problems by monitoring their leisure time and social contacts. They may also require younger children to tag along with older siblings who are responsible for their care (Jarrett, 1995).

*Focus Point.* African American families currently constitute the largest number of minorities in the United States. Although many stereotypes and myths characterize these families and their members, research indicates that they are far from pathological in their nature. Most problems associated with these family systems can be traced to the insidious effects of poverty;

about half are single-parent families headed by a woman. African American parents prepare their children to handle racist attitudes and their future adult roles in society by promoting education. African American parents possess many strengths that enable them to cope with adversity.

## Hispanic Parents and Children

Hispanic families constitute a diverse group (see Figure 2–11). What all may hold in common is the use of Spanish in addition to English as a second language (Hildebrand et al., 2000). Hispanics may have the distinction of becoming the largest minority group in the United States by 2010 (U.S. Bureau of the Census, 2002). The increases in this segment of the population are due largely to immigration from Mexico and other Latin American countries.

The role of family ecological factors has a significant influence on the nature of parent-child relations in Hispanic families. While the increasing size of this group is a significant characteristic, Hispanic families may be characterized in other ways (Hildebrand et al., 2000; McLoyd et al., 2000; Therrien & Ramirez, 2000):

■ Hispanic families are more likely to live in large families (four or more people) as compared with non-Hispanic white families (three people or less).

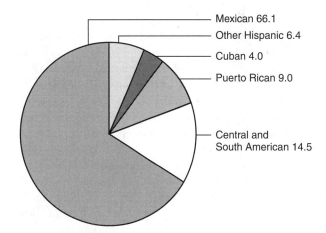

**FIGURE 2–11.**  Hispanic population in the United States by origin, 2000.
*Source:* Therrien, M., & Ramirez, R. R. (2000). The Hispanic population in the United States: March 2000. *Current Population Reports, P20-535.* Washington, DC: U.S. Census Bureau.

- There is a greater tendency for these parents and children to experience substandard levels of education. Over half of this population group has not graduated from high school and one-quarter has less than a ninth-grade education.
- About 23 percent of Hispanic parents and their children live in poverty, compared to 8 percent of non-Latino whites.
- Religion plays a significant role in daily family life.
- Hispanics may be more family-oriented than whites and use a more extensive kinship-based support network than whites.

In matters of child rearing, Hispanic parents are challenged by the traditional scripts they learned as children themselves that may have a poor fit with the realities of raising children in a different cultural environment. For example, a generation gap problem between parents and children in differences of English and Spanish language fluency can color parent-child interactions with frustration and even resentment (Becerra, 1998). In a similar vein, the conditions produced by having low income due to lack of educational attainment tend to promote a more authoritarian-like approach to child rearing known as **hierarchical parenting.** This parenting style combines emotionally warm support for children within the context of demanding exceptional respect for parents and others such as extended family members. This approach is noted for promoting a collective value system among children as opposed to the individualism promoted among whites in their child rearing approaches (McLoyd et al., 2000).

Within the context of hierarchical parenting, children learn the importance of the "three Rs" of Hispanic family values: personal relationships, respect, and responsibility (Hildebrand et al., 2000). Children also learn the role of cooperation (as opposed to competition) and other-centeredness (as opposed to self-centeredness) in their family relationships. Children are taught to make decisions based on the impact on others in their families. In this manner, they learn about family loyalty and the strength of family bonds in providing support, which in turn spills over into relationships outside their families. The emphasis on learning these values promotes the notion of **la familia** and the high importance placed on the family group and its ability to meet the needs of all members.

•••••••••••••••••••••••••••••••••••••••••••••••

***Focus Point.*** Their family structure, values, and parenting styles give Hispanics a unique position among ethnic minority families in the United States.

•••••••••••••••••••••••••••••••••••••••••••••••

## Asian American Parents and Children

Less information is available about Asian American and Pacific Islander families in comparison with other ethnic groups in the United States. This is perhaps because these families make up a smaller percentage of the population and are located in fewer geographic areas (Figure 2–12). In addition, these families are not likely to be viewed as abnormal nor as a problem in society (Hildebrand et al., 2000). The majority live in the western states and in Hawaii, with substantial populations in the largest northern cities such as Chicago and New York City (U.S. Bureau of the Census, 2002). These families constitute less than 3 percent of the total U.S. population and less than 10 percent of the groups labeled as minorities (Grieco & Cassidy, 2001).

Educational achievement is highly valued among Asian American parents for their children (McLoyd et al., 2000). For example, more than 42 percent of Asian Americans have completed four years of college or more (U.S. Bureau of the Census, 2002). Some researchers attribute this high level of achievement educationally to the Asian American parenting style, which is commonly compared with authoritarianism (Greenfield & Suzuki, 2001). Other Asian American researchers have explained this as the **Confucian training doctrine,** which is similar to the hierarchical parenting concept discussed in the section on Hispanic parents and children. The Confucian training doctrine emphasizes the blending of nurturance, parental involvement, and physical closeness with strict and firm control over children (McBride-Chang & Chang, 1998).

•••••••••••••••••••••••••••••••••••••••••••••••

***Focus Point.*** Asian American families may be stereotyped as the "model minority" since parents heavily invest in their children and in their educational achievements. These families value strong parent-child relationships and encourage children while providing a stable family life that emphasizes closeness within a strict adherence to family rules.

•••••••••••••••••••••••••••••••••••••••••••••••

**FIGURE 2–12.** The diversity in family forms found among Asian Americans can be traced to different national cultures of origin.

**FIGURE 2–13.** Contemporary Native American Indians have a rich cultural heritage that continues to be passed on to children.

## Native American Indian Parents and Children

There may be similarities between Native American Indian family systems and those of other minority groups (John, 1998; Yellowbird & Snipp, 1998), (Figure 2–13), especially African Americans. These groups have long histories of being viewed as pathological and largely have been studied from a cultural deviance model. Characteristics typically describing Native American Indian family systems include high fertility rates, large numbers of illegitimate births, prevalence of female-headed households, and high rates of unemployment and substance abuse, especially alcoholism (John, 1998).

Problems indigenous to life on the reservation include high rates of adult alcoholism, homicide rates higher than the rest of the U.S. population, accidents, and suicides. These problems put some Indian children at a higher-than-usual risk of experiencing the loss of parents, siblings, relatives, and friends. In many tribes, the paternal uncle and male cousins, in addition to the child's father and brothers, play an important role in a child's life. Because children continually lose family members due to situations particular to reservation life, they are challenged to acquire coping strategies not usu-

ally found in children of other ethnic groups. Their response patterns frequently include disruptive, aggressive behaviors at school and home; emotional depression; feelings of low self-worth and self-esteem; substance abuse; developmental delays; flattened emotional affect; interpersonal distancing; self-destructive behaviors, including suicidal gestures; sexual acting out; and running away from home (Hildebrand et al., 2000).

Native American families may view children differently from other groups in the United States (Hildebrand et al., 2000). Children typically are seen as treasured gifts. Parents and other extended family members are charged with discovering the unique characteristics of a child at birth to determine her or his place within the tribe. Infants are carefully observed for several months to learn about their nature. The child's name as well as his or her sexual orientation and gender role is determined relative to the characteristics family members observe. Only then is the naming ceremony conducted, sometimes many months after birth.

Because most Native American Indian tribes value personal autonomy and independence of members, individual differences in children appear to be tolerated and accepted as part of their nature. Children are generally reared through grooming these traits as they are encouraged to learn to make personal choices and learn by the consequences of their actions. This parenting style may appear to be permissive to outsiders since parents often ignore children's behavior that is considered inappropriate.

Native American Indian parents might be thought to use more permissive styles of raising their children in comparison with other ethnic groups (John, 1998). However, some tribes may use methods that are more punitive and controlling. Like Asian American parents, Native American Indian parents tend to combine nurturance with control in guiding children's development, especially when the children are young. Traditional styles of child rearing emphasize teaching children to maintain a sense of unity and cohesiveness with their tribal and immediate family groups and to suppress the tendency to experience conflict with others. While these practices may be useful in facilitating daily life among the people living on reservations, they may not be effective in teaching Indian children to function well in urban settings when they live in families away from the reservation.

Contemporary Native American Indian parents usually teach their children traditional values based on practical application of personal belief systems. For example, children are taught to perceive things and people according to intrinsic rather than extrinsic traits and characteristics. Children are taught to be in touch with the rhythms of nature and to be sensitive to the needs of others. Sharing personal resources, thoughts, and knowledge is considered appropriate in smoothing interpersonal interactions.

........................................................

***Focus Point.*** Native American Indian parents and children are challenged by sociocultural factors not experienced by other ethnic minorities. These relate to reconciling traditional ways and values with the necessity of adapting and acculturating to modern contemporary society. Native American Indian parents and children may have competing allegiances to both sociocultural worlds. The family structure and functioning of tribes may be difficult for outsiders to understand and appreciate. Native American Indians appear to have a unique approach to child rearing and family life.

........................................................

## Interracial-Interethnic Parents and Children

The number of interracial and interethnic married couples has doubled since 1980, although only constituting about three percent of all marriages in the United States (Fields & Casper, 2001). Not long ago these relationships were against the law in the United States. As early as 1761, colonial laws prohibited marriage or sexual relations between people of different races. These laws remained in effect until 1967 when the U.S. Supreme Court ruled that these laws were unconstitutional.

The reasons why these marriages have increased in the years since 1967 are varied. First, the general desegregation of American society presents greater opportunities for people of different racial groups to mingle socially and work together. Increased socioeconomic opportunities available today encourage the upward social mobility of ethnic minorities that increases contact between people of all racial and ethnic groups in housing, employment, school, work, and leisure activities (McLoyd et al., 2000). In some cases, upward social mobility may be a factor, especially for white women who marry black men of higher status. The increases may also reflect changes in attitudes about interracial marriages, despite the continuing threat of discrimination and even verbal abuse aimed at such couples (Kalish, 1995).

The challenges their children would face as biracial, biethnic individuals is a serious concern for many interracial, interethnic couples considering marriage (Funderberg, 1994). They fear their children will experience rejection and isolation from peers and others because of their heritage. This concern also exists for parents who adopt children of a different race. In the end, however, it appears that most biracial individuals have learned to look at their challenges due to their status with humor and a determination not to let other people's prejudices discourage them.

Research is limited on how biracial children manage and learn to cope with their situation. Many do not experience significant adjustments, but most must resolve issues relating to ambiguous ethnicity and their need to define their identities in a society where racial issues are prominent (Gibbs, 2003). One explanation for these children's healthy outcomes is in the efforts of parents to provide support, encourage activities that build ethnic identity, instruct children how to respond when their identity is questioned, and expose their children to effective adult role models in both racial and family groups.

## Parenting Reflection 2–5

How would you explain to a child why interracial-interethnic families continue to experience discrimination in their communities and neighborhoods? What would you suggest to the child about how to react when hearing offensive remarks of this nature?

*Focus Point.*   Interracial-interethnic parents and children have particular challenges related primarily to identity issues and preparing children to cope with discrimination.

## Immigrant Parents and Children

The United States was formed by the immigration of many different nationalities and ethnic groups over the centuries. Large numbers of people arrived in this new country to pursue their dreams of freedom, wealth, and personal happiness. Many individuals and families arrived legally and eventually assumed respected positions in their adopted communities. The amalgam of so many different ways of life, languages, family lives, parenting styles, and perspectives has given strength to the diversity of American culture.

Revisions in federal legislation in 1965 changed the criteria for lawful entry into the United States. Priority was given to those who possessed valued work skills, refugees from foreign aggressions, and those who already had relatives living in the United States. In fact, the final criteria has accounted for about two-thirds of all legal entrants into the United States (Fix, Zimmerman, & Passel, 2001; Martin & Midgely, 1999).

The number of immigrations into the United States has increased steadily since 1960 (Fix et al., 2001). Today, immigrants constitute about 11 percent of the total U.S. population. Most come from Latin American and Asian countries, now causing the greater metropolitan cities on the west coast to become the new "Ellis Islands" that receive large numbers of these individuals and families.

Many native individuals and families in the United States have become more aware of immigration issues, both legal and illegal in nature since the terrorist attacks of Sept. 11, 2001. Restrictions are more stringent because of security issues, and immigrant families may be scrutinized more than in the past. Many families report tension associated with this heightened attitude about their presence in communities.

Economic difficulties are often associated with many immigrant parents and children because of language barriers and general acculturation problems. These challenges affect everyone in a family and hinder parent-child relations. For example, economic well-being of immigrant families only improved slightly between 1998 and 2001 (Capps, Fix, & Reardon-Anderson, 2003), and there was significant concern about food availability and cost. Many parents and children are reported to be living in crowded housing units, and an estimated half of a typical family's income goes toward rent or mortgage payments. Many immigrant parents and children do not have health insurance coverage, although substantial increases have occurred in Medicaid and SCHIP (State Children's Health Insurance Program) coverage for many individuals and families (Morse, 2003).

Immigrant parents encourage their children to achieve high levels of education and become good citizens of their new country (Detzner & Xiong, 1999). However, parent-child relations in immigrant families may be strained by negative family ecological factors and by discrepancies observed in parents who may have problems with acculturation (e.g., difficulties in learning a new language) and in those observed in parents of native children. Immigrant children may also experience problems with reconciling the traditional standards and expectations of their parents with the consumer-oriented culture of contemporary American society. When immigrant families come from war-torn pasts in other countries, the entire family system is likely to be challenged even more by the post-traumatic stress resulting from these past experiences.

## Parenting Reflection 2–6

What is your opinion about states or cities that enact legislation requiring English as the official language? What might be the impact of such legislation on immigrant parents and children?

*Focus Point.* Issues confronting newly arrived immigrants involve the marginal nature of these families. Economic difficulties, problems in acquiring and using a new language, and general acculturation issues present a special challenge for immigrant parents and children.

## POINTS TO CONSIDER

■ People may define their "family" in a variety of ways.

■ Functions of families have changed over the centuries. Perhaps the major function of families today is to socialize children for adulthood.

■ Families in contemporary American society are diverse in form and structure. Single-parent families are the fastest growing family form today.

■ Stepfamilies usually are formed when a biological mother remarries. These families usually include children from the previous marriage, and remarried couples frequently have children of their own. Stepfamily maintenance requires that members rework their former family system into one that is pertinent to new participants. These families have many strengths to offer members.

■ A renested family is formed when children who have been launched into adult lives of their own return to their home base to live temporarily. Very little is known about how these families function.

■ Gay men and lesbians form families that resemble those of heterosexuals. These families may include children of one or both partners from a former heterosexual marriage or children who are adopted or conceived by artificial insemination. Contrary to popular belief, homosexuals do not differ from heterosexuals in their ability to parent children effectively or in their commitment to long-term relationships.

■ Coresident grandparent/grandchildren families are formed when an adult child cannot function in their parenting role. Coresident grandparents often need help and financial assistance in providing adequate care for their grandchildren.

■ Families of diverse racial/ethnic origins must deal with racist attitudes and bigotry and, for many, the insidious effects of poverty.

■ Many African American parents raise their children based on an authoritative style. Many parents must contend with severe economic conditions but use approaches that temper this severity on family life. Ed-

ucational advancement is encouraged, and children are equipped with ways for coping with societal prejudice and bigotry.

■ Hispanic parents and children come from diverse groups themselves. This ethnic group is likely to grow the largest of all ethnic groups in the United States in the future. Children are taught family values such as developing a strong sense of belongingness and loyalty, respecting other family members, and cooperation with other family members. Child rearing is characterized as hierarchical parenting, a style based on authoritarianism that combines emotional warmth with strictness. Children learn about the high value placed on family membership.

■ Asian American parents and children constitute the smallest ethnic group in the United States. Asian American parents typically use a parenting style known as Confucian training doctrine.

■ Native American Indian parents and children come from even more diverse groups. The notion of what constitutes a family usually is relative to a particular tribe. A variety of child rearing approaches may be employed in different Native American Indian tribes, but children generally are taught to respect authority and their elders. Because there is a division in those who live on and those who live off of reservations, Native American Indian families are challenged by different acculturation issues than other ethnic families. Many families must cope with the insidious effects of poverty and associated problems.

■ The number of interracial, interethnic marriages in the United States are increasing, with an accompanying larger number of biracial, biethnic children. Many parents involved in these marriages are concerned about their children's welfare, especially when they are rejected by other children. These children generally fare well in spite of their particular challenges.

■ Immigrant parents and children face challenges unique to their situation. Many problems arise from severe economic conditions as well as difficulties in dealing with language barriers and other acculturation issues. Quality of life is at risk as well as quality of parent-child relations. Parents desire that their children become good citizens and responsible individuals. Children may experience conflict between parents pressing for adoption of traditional values in a contemporary society that does not support these values from the countries of origin.

# CHAPTER 3

# Theoretical Perspectives on Parent-Child Relations

**Focus Questions**
■ ■ ■ ■ ■ ■ ■ ■ ■ ■

1. How can a family be described as a social system?
2. What major concepts describe how families function as a social system?
3. How can we best describe developmental changes that occur over time within family systems?
4. How can ecological theory assist the understanding of individuals within the context of their family system?
5. How does psychosocial theory address issues in parent-child relations?
6. How do other psychological theories address issues in parent-child relations?

■ ■ ■ ■ ■ ■ ■ ■ ■ ■

One of the ideas discussed in Chapter 1 is that a parent is an agent of socialization and a child is the object of the adult's socialization efforts. This notion has been labeled the *unidirectional model of socialization*. Stated simply, this model focuses on the adult's behavior as a stimulus that causes or produces some particular response or outcome within a child. Interpreted more broadly, this model of parent-child relations implies that if an adult behaves well as a parent, the child will grow to become a good person. That is, adults can achieve their parenting goals if they act properly as parents by doing and saying the appropriate things at the appropriate time and in the appropriate manner, thereby providing appropriate caregiving. Following this logic, there is a formula for effective parenting based on consistently good parental performance over the years of child rearing. By accepting this model as an accurate depiction of what occurs in the relationship between parents and children, society has been able to make judgments about success in child rearing in our culture and the process by which this is accomplished.

This traditional notion about parenting makes several assumptions about the process and the factors that influence someone's parenting style and behavior. Upon more careful study and observation, behavioral and social scientists have discovered that this traditional idea about parenting and what occurs as a result in children is too simplistic and imprecise for several reasons (Ambert, 1992). First, it does not realistically address the changes that take place as both child and parent experience growth and development over time. Second, it does not recognize the complexity of interactions over a long period of time between these individuals as they experience dynamic interchanges. Third, it disregards a child's contribution to and impact on the exchange of information or the behavior and conduct of an adult as a parent. Fourth, it assumes that adults are solely responsible for the outcome of their parenting experiences as manifested in children's character, behavior, and competency upon attaining maturity. In reality, although parents have a strong and vital influence on children's development, other factors also play a part, and effective parenting cannot be judged strictly in this manner. The *bidirectional model* is suggested in Chapter 1 as a more accurate depiction of parent-child relations. This model portrays the give-and-take flow of information and influence between parents and children; each person has an influence and impact on the behavior of the other.

This chapter introduces several theoretical explanations that describe the bidirectional nature of the process involved in parenting children. These explanations describe the parenting process more realistically and provide a basis for understanding how the relationship between parents and children takes place, which factors influence how it functions, how it changes over time, and how child rearing is a unique statement of personal and family philosophy. These explanations help to describe how adults shape the nature of their parenting behavior in relation to a variety of factors. The parent-child relationship is seen as a means of providing a primary opportunity for the psychosocial development of both children and adults, especially the adults. Parents are assisted in their growth and development as adults by parenting children while children are socialized into adulthood by parents. Although the theories presented in this chapter do not directly address issues in parent-child relations, it is possible to describe how the theories and their concepts may be applied to understanding this relationship.

This chapter also describes the family as a social system and the relationship between parents and children as a subsystem within this system. From this view, the parent-child relationship mirrors the larger family process. More specifically, using this perspective on family systems, it is possible to describe how the developmental changes being experienced by all members of a family system, typically two generations or more, affect the specific individuals involved as well as all other members of the system.

## FAMILY SYSTEMS THEORY

The discussion in Chapter 2 of the diversity found among contemporary American families stressed the notion that a family is a social system characterized by certain features and traits. Despite the myriad nature of forms to be found among contemporary American families, each family operates according to certain principles that govern how it performs and functions in meeting goals, making decisions, and resolving conflicts between its members.

Behavioral scientists who study families have devised various methods to describe these groups and the ways they function. For example, one of the first theoretical approaches explaining family functioning was derived from sociological thought known as *structural functionalism*. This explanation of family functioning focused on the social roles of family members and addressed the manner in which the family (as seen via the roles of its members) became integrated with other social institutions such as schools, churches, and business and service organizations (Lamanna & Reidman, 2003).

The approach that will be used extensively in this text to explain family functioning, and especially that between parents and children, employs the concepts of **general systems theory.** This theoretical approach has been applied largely in the physical sciences to explain the complex workings of naturally occurring systems such as biological ecological systems and the solar system (von Bertalanffy, 1974). As applied to humans, families are described as operating in ways that are similar to those of other systems observed in nature. This way of looking at family functioning describes the operation of a family as a social system (Becvar & Becvar, 1998; Broderick, 1993). Systems theory is useful in explaining the complex interactions of a family and the factors that influence the processes by which a family makes decisions, sets and achieves particular goals, and establishes rules that regulate behavior, for example. The model provided by systems theory describes how these processes govern daily interactions and work to maintain stability of the family group over time. The theory also explains how a family responds to change, both developmental changes in family members and external changes that challenge its ability to function effectively as a group.

Several subsystems exist as part of a family group. For example, the relationships between parents and children, between two adult marriage partners, and between brothers and sisters are recognized as subsystems that reflect the patterns observed in the larger family system. The concepts and processes that describe the functioning of a family system also describe how these smaller subsystems function.

To understand how families operate according to **family systems theory,** let's consider some basic concepts in the following sections.

## Wholeness

A family is not simply a group of individuals who operate or behave independently of one another. Rather, a family operates on the principle of **wholeness.** The family group must be considered in its entirety to understand how it works. It is not possible to do so by studying only one person from the group. In other words, a family is seen as being greater than the sum of its parts.

## Interdependence

**Interdependence,** which is related to the principle of wholeness, means that anything that affects one person in a family also affects every other person in the family to some degree. A mobile is a good way to illustrate this concept of family systems theory (see Figure 3–1). All parts of a mobile are connected, so when one part is moved abruptly, other parts are affected and respond accordingly, although to a lesser degree (Satir, 1972a, 1972b). The parts of the mobile represent different family members and the wires connecting each piece of the mobile represent the different relationships found in a family system. Thus, the mobile illustrates the interdependence of family members.

When one person in a family system experiences some type of change, such as becoming seriously ill, leaving the family, or receiving a job promotion, everyone in the system is affected to some degree by the change. Whether the change is good or bad, beneficial or detrimental, all members of a family system react and attempt to compensate for the imbalance caused by a change that directly affects just one member. The ob-

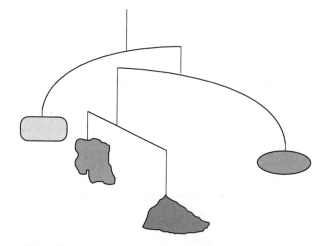

**FIGURE 3–1.**  A mobile graphically illustrates the concepts of wholeness and interdependence in family systems theory. If one part of the mobile is moved, all other parts react by also moving, although to a lesser degree.

jective is to return to the state of balance that existed prior to the change that caused the imbalance.

## Patterns

Within a family system, **patterns** evolve that serve to regulate the behavior of members and allow members to anticipate one another's behavior. These patterns are unique to each family system, although some patterns follow general guidelines that are common to all family systems. The patterns that usually can be found in most family systems include rules, roles, and communication styles.

**Rules.**  A family system usually develops **rules** to govern members' behavior. Rules provide common ground for understanding which behaviors are acceptable and appropriate within each family system. In turn, the consistent application of rules helps to maintain the stability of a family system over time in general and especially in times of uncertainty or crisis. Rules govern the behavior of both adults and children in families. To be effective, rules also outline the consequences that occur when they are obeyed and disobeyed.

Each family system evolves its own rules, usually through negotiations of the adults. In many instances, the rules that become established in a family system have their roots in the adults' families of origin. Rules can be explicit and implicit. **Explicit rules** are known, stated, and outlined clearly so that all people in the family know and understand them. Because these rules are clear to all, family members can discuss them and change them if they prove ineffective. **Implicit rules** are unspoken, and are often inferred from nonverbal behavior. Explicit rules are often stated verbally, especially when transgressions occur ("You know the rule is that you must be home by 10"). Implicit rules are not usually discussed openly or otherwise acknowledged by family members, yet everyone is expected to know and obey them. For example, some family systems do not allow the expression of anger. In such families, everyone is expected to be pleasant and not to engage in open conflict with one another. When conflict is imminent, one person leaves or is told, "Don't be so silly. You're acting childish." It is difficult to discuss such rules and to change them when necessary, since they are not readily acknowledged by family members despite their strong influence on behavior. Generally, healthy family systems operate with an abundance of explicit rules and few implicit rules, whereas those that are unhealthy have a greater number of implicit rules (Clarke & Dawson, 1998; Richardson, 1999).

**Roles.** Roles are also used in family systems to outline acceptable behavior and to regulate the system's functioning. Roles generally have associated rules that establish appropriate behavior of the person who occupies that particular role. For example, a family system may be expected to evolve rules that describe and outline the role of the mother. The mother's behavior is regulated by rules that reflect family members' beliefs about how a mother should act. For example, to be a good mother, she should attend all school-related functions of her children, maintain a clean and orderly home, be employed outside the home, and so on. Rules that describe the child's role might be that the person should be a willing learner, should be able to perform some family tasks, but not as efficiently as an adult, and so on. The rules, or shoulds, provide the script enacted by the person filling a particular role in a family system.

Unhealthy families often evolve implicit roles that are largely governed by implicit rules. Because such families often cannot or do not know how to cope with stresses effectively or in healthy ways, one family member may assume—either willingly or unknowingly—a special role in which he or she acts out the stress on be-

half of the family member under stress or for a particularly dysfunctional member (Becvar & Becvar, 1998). For example, a child may act as the family scapegoat by becoming depressed emotionally or acting out delinquently as a means of expressing stress in the parents' unhealthy marriage. In this instance, the child's role reflects an unhealthy implicit rule prohibiting or regulating the expression of conflict between the married spouses. In a different family system, a child's implicit role may be the "best little boy." In this system, the role carries a heavy expectation of perfectionism in the child's behavior. This child acts out the script of an implicit rule that states, "We are better than other families. We are special and are expected to achieve things that others only dream of."

**Communication Styles.** Communication styles relate strongly to the nature of relationships within a family system. Three basic styles are found in most families: verbal, nonverbal, and contextual (Becvar & Becvar, 1998). **Verbal communications** relate to the words used to convey information between people in the family system. Taken at face value, verbal communication is essentially meaningless. For example, the message, "It's cold outside today," simply provides descriptive information to the listener by the sender.

**Nonverbal communications** that accompany a verbal message include tone of voice, facial expressions, body posture, and hand gestures. The purpose of the nonverbal message is to inform the receiver about what to do with the verbal message. It hints at the intent of the message and often contains an implicit command or request. For example, the message "It's cold outside today," from a mother to her daughter, may contain nonverbal elements that communicate an implicit message such as, "Wear a sweater today." Hence, nonverbal communications relate to the way a relationship is outlined or defined.

**Contextual communication** is allied closely with nonverbal communication, and usually the two are considered together. The context often refers to where and under what circumstances the verbal and nonverbal communications occur. If a mother says "It's cold outside today" before the daughter dresses for school, the message has an entirely different meaning than if it occurred as the two were leaving the house.

Communication styles are unique to each family system, especially the contextual and nonverbal aspects of information exchange between members. These

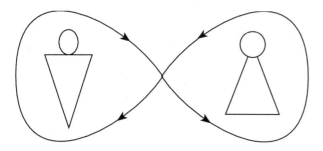

**FIGURE 3–2.**   Interactions between people in subsystems in families involve reciprocity and feedback. People react to one another's actions and communications; behavior serves as both stimulus and feedback in interactions.

styles emerge as each family system evolves and develops its own meanings to communications. The more frequently members interact and exchange information with each other and the outside world, the more flexible and receptive to change the system becomes. This flexibility occurs in ways that act to stabilize rather than disrupt healthy, effective functioning.

## Reciprocal Interaction and Feedback

Systems theory does not support a cause-and-effect process of interaction between members of families or between family systems. Rather, causality is seen as a **reciprocal interaction** between people and systems (Becvar & Becvar, 1998). For example, a cause-and-effect pattern is implied in a child asserting, "I behave as a child because you treat me as a child," and the parent responding, "I treat you as a child because you behave as a child." Taken from a family systems perspective, this assertion would be reframed as, "This has become a never-ending cycle: I act as a child because you treat me as a child, which makes me act in even more childish ways, which makes you continue to treat me as a child." Essentially, systems theory stresses that people in relationships or subsystems and in a family system as a whole influence one another's actions and behavior (see Figure 3–2). Behavioral interactions become intertwined as one person reacts to another, setting up a chain of interactional sequences. One person's action serves as a stimulus that elicits a reaction or response from another; this reaction, in turn, acts as a stimulus that elicits a different reaction or response from the other; and the cycle continues. Behavior serves as both

*stimulus* and *feedback* to maintain reciprocal interaction between people in a relationship or subsystem.

## Boundaries

**Boundaries** serve to establish limits that distinguish a family system from all others and differentiate between the people who are members of a particular family system (Knowles, 1997; Minuchin, 1974; Wood & Talmon, 1983). These abstract, psychological dividers are based on implicit as well as explicit rules that also outline who participates in a particular subsystem and the role that they have in that subsystem.

Boundaries assist in keeping subsystems distinct from one another as well, since a family member can be a participant in several of these within a family system (Orthner, Bowen, & Beare, 1990). In this regard, boundaries help prevent overlap between subsystems. For example, when conflicts occur within one subsystem, boundaries help prevent the conflict from overlapping into other subsystems in which family members participate. When the adults experience disagreements related to their committed relationship, boundaries help them keep the dispute from affecting the relationship with their children.

Boundaries act to regulate the degree of closeness or intimacy permissible according to a particular family system with other families and between the members of that system (Goodrich, 1990). In this respect, the boundaries maintained between people and family systems assist in regulating information exchange, communication, identities, and behavior. Although boundaries can be changed and may vary by situation, families typically either have flexible boundaries, resulting in an open family system, or rigid boundaries, resulting in a closed system (see Figure 3–3). Likewise, the boundaries that delineate the different subsystems within a family system usually are closed as well. For example, healthy family systems maintain closed boundaries for the married adult couple relationship that do not allow for the participation of children in this relationship.

Family systems theory describes an *open* family as one with flexible boundaries that permit the easy flow and exchange of information and interaction between other families and individuals. When this is the case, the family system is *open* to input or new data from outside the system and is receptive to change. Essentially, healthy families operate as an open system. Some families, however, operate as a *closed* system; the boundaries

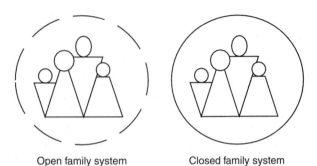

Open family system          Closed family system

**FIGURE 3–3.** Families may be either open or closed systems based on the type of boundaries used to regulate interaction and information exchanges within the system and with others in the environment. Those that are open have flexible boundaries while those that are closed have rigid boundaries. Boundaries also define roles and relationships within a family system.

serve to maintain the status quo of the group rather than allow external input to bring about positive changes within the system. Change is resisted rather than accepted as healthy (von Bertalanffy, 1974). When this is the case, family systems theory predicts that personal boundaries between family members in a closed system will become fused or *enmeshed* (Minuchin, 1974). For example, children are not encouraged to differentiate themselves as individuals as part of their normal developmental process in growing toward maturity. Rather, implicit rules promote prolonged emotional attachment between family members and blurring of personal boundaries to maintain dependency between family members (Bowen, 1978).

In healthy family systems, boundaries are valued for helping to differentiate one person from the other, even though a high level of intimacy is permitted. In such families, boundaries highlight individual differences without eliciting high degrees of anxiety among other members. Personal differences are viewed positively as another means by which the family system is enriched by behavioral, philosophical, and emotional variety among its members. In these families, the implicit rules that serve as the foundation for personal boundaries promote the balance between individuation and intimacy among family members. Some unhealthy family systems, however, view differences in members as threatening the welfare and effective functioning of the family system. Such families demand lesser degrees of individuation and maintain less rigid personal boundaries that differentiate each member

(Richardson, 1999). These families foster an expectation of similarity among members rather than distinct differences. They support the strong belief that everyone must hold the same beliefs, philosophies, opinions, and attitudes. Rules in these families are exceptionally strict and serve to promote the idea of sameness and maintain weak or diffuse personal boundaries between members.

## Entropy

Although a family system maintains separateness from other family systems, the degree of closure is never thought to be complete (von Bertalanffy, 1968). There will always be some exchange of information between systems. **Entropy** is disorder or chaos in system functioning that results from lack of input or information from outside the system as a means of resolving a crisis or problem. A family may react to the presence of entropy in two basic ways. Positive actions involve movement of a system away from disorder and chaos by accepting and using information and energy from outside itself, such as from other family systems. Negative actions occur when movements of the system enhance the level of entropy to even greater chaos or disruption. Such actions by the system may entail dedicated efforts to maintain the status quo, refusing to allow the exchange of information between the family and other environmental systems, or using denial to resist acknowledging that some problem or crisis exists.

In family systems with more open and flexible boundaries, energy and information input is accepted and used to maximize group functioning. For example, some energy in such a family system is directed toward organization and some is directed toward performing family tasks. By accepting and using information about how other family systems solve certain problems, open systems work effectively to achieve healthy solutions to their problems. In family systems that are rigidly closed, little new energy or information is allowed. This tends to promote greater family disorganization and greater expenditure of energy in random and inefficient ways. The continued maintenance of rigid boundaries enhances higher levels of entropy in such families (Becvar & Becvar, 1998).

## Equifinality

All subsystems have goals that substantiate the reason for their existence. Likewise, all family systems develop goals that influence functioning and behavior. The concept of

**equifinality** holds that families share common goals but reach these goals in different ways. For example, the ultimate goal of the parent-child subsystem may be to raise children to become effectively functioning adults. All parent-child relationships may have this goal as the primary endeavor. However, different family systems in society accomplish this goal in diverse ways. The concept of equifinality significantly differentiates family systems theory from a unidirectional model of cause and effect.

## Adaptation

A family system is challenged by both internal and external events and processes to restructure patterns to accommodate these changes. Change is a constant threat to effective functioning of a family system, because nothing is ever completely stable for families over the long term. All persons within the family system experience constant developmental changes over time. If the system is to continue to function effectively, patterns must be readjusted periodically upon discovering that they are not working properly. For example, rules developed at the beginning of a couple's parenting career may reflect a lack of experience with children more than knowledge of an infant's developmental abilities. After gaining experience, the parents' rules are **adapted** or changed to permit a more realistic experience in nurturing an infant. By rigidly maintaining rules that clearly don't work to everyone's benefit, a family system risks becoming unhealthy by virtue of its inability to function adequately.

## Homeostasis

The ultimate goal of family system functioning is to maintain stability or **homeostasis** over time. This is also known as *dynamic equilibrium*. There may seem to be a fundamental contradiction between a family system's needs for adaptation and stability. To address this seeming contradiction, two other terms are often used to illustrate the more fundamental need for stability over time. *Morphogenesis* describes the tendency of a family system to respond to variables that cause change by experiencing growth, change, innovation, and creativity and adapting its structure and patterns accordingly (Hoffman, 1973). *Morphostasis* describes the desire of a family system to remain stable over time by attempting to retain its organization, structure, and patterns. To understand these concepts, it may be helpful to visualize them as residing at opposite ends of a continuum

and to view homeostasis as an attempt to achieve dynamic equilibrium between them. Healthy family systems seek continually to maintain homeostasis between the dynamic factors of change and stability. The rules of such systems allow changes in patterns, rules, and boundaries to accommodate changing situations and conditions.

During times of stress, morphogenesis is thought to be more desirable than morphostasis in allowing a system to work out means that will ensure its continued existence and functioning. However, too much and too frequent experiences in morphogenesis call for greater and more extended efforts to maintain morphostasis.

● ● ● ● ● ● ● ● ● ● ● ● ● ● ● ● ● ● ● ● ● ● ● ● ● ● ● ● ● ●

### Parenting Reflection 3–1

What are some advantages and disadvantages of using family systems theory to explain family functioning? Could this theory have application in family therapy? How?

● ● ● ● ● ● ● ● ● ● ● ● ● ● ● ● ● ● ● ● ● ● ● ● ● ● ● ● ● ●

● ● ● ● ● ● ● ● ● ● ● ● ● ● ● ● ● ● ● ● ● ● ● ● ● ● ● ● ● ●

*Focus Point.* Family systems theory explains the complex interactions of a family group. It addresses the factors that influence the manner in which the group makes decisions, sets and achieves goals, and establishes patterns that govern members' behavior. It explains how these processes work to maintain the group's stability over time. Concepts central to this theory include wholeness, interdependence, patterns (rules, roles, and communication styles), reciprocal interaction and feedback, boundaries, entropy, equifinality, adaptation, and homeostasis (morphogenesis and morphostasis). The relationship between parents and children is one of several subsystems that make up a family system.

● ● ● ● ● ● ● ● ● ● ● ● ● ● ● ● ● ● ● ● ● ● ● ● ● ● ● ● ● ●

## SYSTEMIC FAMILY DEVELOPMENT THEORY

Many years ago, pioneer sociologist Ernest Burgess (1926) described the family as a "unity of interacting personalities." Unity in this context alludes to the concepts of wholeness and interdependence used today in family systems theory. The reference to interacting personalities denotes Burgess's observation that interaction among family members serves a vital purpose in the functioning of a family system by promoting the psychological welfare of each family member.

A family system provides an expressive function for members. This means that each member has the opportunity for being nurtured and assisted as a developing individual by others, and thus is provided with the means for realizing his or her emotional needs. The idea of unity among interacting personalities implies that a family is a dynamic system that responds to changes taking place in members and to those that come from external sources and impinge on its functioning. The inescapable reality implied in this description is echoed in the concepts of homeostasis and adaptation from family systems theory. These concepts hold that family members are dynamic, developmentally changing individuals, and hence a family system must change over time in response.

Just as individuals follow predictable stages in their personal development, families likewise experience stages that follow a predictable course (O'Rand & Krecker, 1990). The progression of stages a family follows from its establishment to its demise (Aldous, 1978; Duvall, 1988; Duvall & Miller, 1985; Mattessich & Hill, 1987) has been labeled the **family life cycle,** although this is a misleading notion in some respects. The term *cycle* connotes an alternating repetition of some factor or pattern. Because no readily identifiable repetitive patterns are commonly observed in all families, family studies experts disagree as to whether the changes that take place in a family system over time can be appropriately considered cyclical (Aldous, 1978; Mattessich & Hill, 1987).

The family life cycle model presents several other problems: (1) it was based on the notion that all families experience developmental changes in the same way and in predictable stages; (2) it excludes the diversity of family structures found in contemporary American society (e.g., gay and lesbian families, stepfamilies); (3) it assumes that ethnic minority families experience developmental changes in the same way that white families do; (4) it was first developed in the 1950s based on a white, middle-class family representation; (5) it excludes families that are affected by poverty and homelessness; (6) it focuses on the notion of a progression of stages where there may be only one generation in a family at times when in reality more than one generation is involved in family life; and (7) developmental progress is dependent on the increasing age of the first-born child through many of the stages, thus excluding those families that lack children with the reality that many families do not include children at all.

A more realistic model that describes how families change in association with the passage of time is the **systemic family development theory** model (Laszloffy, 2002). This process-oriented model addresses the problems inherent in traditional family development theory. It uses concepts derived from family systems theory to challenge the principal assumptions of the older model: (1) all families develop in the same way; (2) there is a single generation focus at certain stages such as before children are produced and following their launching into adulthood; and (3) all families include children. Instead, the systemic model promotes the notions that families are both similar and diverse and that the concepts of wholeness and interrelatedness are strong characteristics of the complexity found in their intergenerational composition.

## Common Developmental Process in Families

All families share a common process of developmental change over time, but how this occurs in a particular family varies widely. The common developmental process shared by all families according to the systemic development model is the experience of **stressors** at various times in their existence (Laszloffy, 2002). Stressors are those phenomena that force a family system to adapt, resulting in what is referred to as a **transition** (see Focus On 3–1). The transition typically produces changes in family roles and relationships.

Most transitions relieve the pressure that comes from the stressor. However, sometimes a family finds this to be a difficult task and cannot make a successful adaptation or transition. When this occurs, the group finds itself experiencing a **snag point** or general inflexibility in the face of the pressure to make changes (Pittman, 1987). This is likely to prevent a family from using resources to cope with the stressor and the associated stress increases accordingly. The end result of the snag point is a **family crisis,** which keeps the group from progressing and making necessary adaptations to dismantle their dilemma (Joselevich, 1988).

The experience of a single stressor event usually can be dealt with by making appropriate changes or using helpful resources to reduce the stress associated with the event. For example, the birth of a child is stressful in the sense that the routine in the home is altered (e.g.,

---

**Focus On
3–1**

## Examples of Stressors Common to Families

- Marriage
- Work
- Birth of children
- Developmental stages of children
- Chronic illness of family members
- Retirement
- Divorce
- Death of family members
- Dating
- Simultaneous stressors happening in all generations
- New family roles (e.g., in-law, grandparent)
- Financial problems

---

adult sleep patterns are disturbed by the need to feed and care for the baby) and financial resources are strained. People make changes in their roles and routines to adapt to the needs of the new baby. Stressors do not become problematic unless several occur simultaneously or within a short time. When this happens, the snag point emerges because of the accumulation of higher levels of stress from each of the events.

As stress continues to pile up in the family, a crisis emerges that prevents the family from adapting and making appropriate changes. For example, suppose a family has experienced a new birth, the oldest child has begun school for the first time, and the father loses his job, all within a two-week period. This is enough to produce a family crisis since the group is incapacitated by the cumulative stress occurring from these events within a short time and is unable to cope successfully. Taken individually and spread out over a longer period of time, the stressor events might be managed more successfully. What may help a family to avoid chaos is to use effective stress management skills or to locate and use resources that will allow the group to cope effectively with the stressors. In this way, the family may prevent the crisis or at least head off devastating effects (Boss, 1988).

## Family Systems Are Complex and Multigenerational

The systemic family developmental model also emphasizes the notion that families must be taken as a whole at any point in developmental time to understand how they function, change, and adapt. This notion comes from the

concepts of wholeness and interrelatedness found in family systems theory. Unlike the stages proposed in the family life cycle model, the systemic model assumes that it is not possible to reduce a family system to only one generation at any point in developmental time. This notion also acknowledges the diversity of family structures, thereby avoiding a principal criticism of the family life cycle model.

## A Metaphor

Laszloffy (2002) suggests the use of a metaphor to illustrate how the concepts of the systemic model are applied to understanding family development. She has chosen the depiction of a round layer cake as a representation of the life span of a family system (see Figure 3–4). The

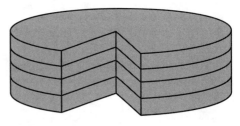

**FIGURE 3–4.**  A round layer cake serves as the metaphor for a family system in the systemic family development model.

*Source*: Laszloffy, T. A. (2002). Rethinking family development theory: Teaching with the systemic family development (SFD) model. *Family Relations, 51*, 206–214. Copyright 2002 by the National Council on Family Relations, 3989 Central Ave. NE, Suite 550, Minneapolis, MN 55421. Reprinted by permission.

cake represents the family boundaries or definition as well as the concept of wholeness. We view the cake in its totality just as we must view a family in its totality to understand it. The metaphor continues with comparing the individual ingredients of a cake recipe to individual family members. When mixed together and baked, the particular ingredients result in a particular type of cake; individuals form a family when brought together through the processes of marriage, birth, adoption, or choice. The different cake layers represent the different generations found in a family. The roundness of the cake represents the passage of developmental time during a family's life span. As the family metaphor revolves in a circular manner, old layers of the cake (older generations) are eliminated through death while new layers (younger generations) are being added. These changes represent a certain type of stressors commonly experienced by all families. By losing layers (generations) and adding new ones, the cake is required to make adjustments. If the cake cannot accommodate these changes, pressures increase that distort the cake. If the cake continues to be unable to adapt, the pressures increase to the point of a crisis that might cause the cake to collapse. And so it is with families.

To perceive what may be occurring developmentally in a family, we would observe the entire group for a short time. In the metaphor, we would be cutting a slice from the cake. What would be revealed in observing a "slice" of family life are the particular stressors being experienced by each generation (see Figure 3–5). By examining and studying the slice of the family's place in devel-

opmental time, we could determine how the family needs to adjust to the pressures produced by the stressors each generation is experiencing. Those adjustments allow the family to cope with a crisis. Family members could realign their roles, patterns, and boundaries accordingly to reestablish the degree of homeostasis that existed before the crisis or to achieve a higher degree of cohesion and balance.

● ● ● ● ● ● ● ● ● ● ● ● ● ● ● ● ● ● ● ● ● ● ● ● ● ● ● ● ● ● ● ● ● ● ● ●

### Parenting Reflection 3–2

How can families locate resources to help them learn to cope with stressors before they occur? Does advance knowledge about something truly help to prepare people to react appropriately? Or does this information make people fret more?

● ● ● ● ● ● ● ● ● ● ● ● ● ● ● ● ● ● ● ● ● ● ● ● ● ● ● ● ● ● ● ● ● ● ● ●

● ● ● ● ● ● ● ● ● ● ● ● ● ● ● ● ● ● ● ● ● ● ● ● ● ● ● ● ● ● ● ● ● ● ● ●

***Focus Point.*** Systemic family development theory makes allowances in understanding how families are highly complex and diverse. By examining a family at a particular point in developmental time, it is possible to see that families share common stressors that challenge each generation involved. This model has significant practical application in working with all families.

● ● ● ● ● ● ● ● ● ● ● ● ● ● ● ● ● ● ● ● ● ● ● ● ● ● ● ● ● ● ● ● ● ● ● ●

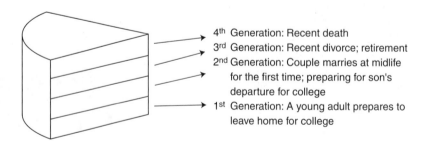

4th Generation: Recent death
3rd Generation: Recent divorce; retirement
2nd Generation: Couple marries at midlife for the first time; preparing for son's departure for college
1st Generation: A young adult prepares to leave home for college

**FIGURE 3–5.** A slice taken from the metaphorical layer cake represents a snapshot in developmental time of a family system. Stressors affecting each generation of a family (represented by each layer of the cake) and the effects of these on members of each generation may then be examined.

*Source:* Laszloffy, T. A. (2002). Rethinking family development theory: Teaching with the systemic family development (SFD) model. *Family Relations, 51,* 206–214. Copyright 2002 by the National Council on Family Relations, 3989 Central Ave. NE, Suite 550, Minneapolis, MN 55421. Reprinted by permission.

**Focus On
3–2**

## Case Study

The systemic family development model can be illustrated by studying a hypothetical family periodically over three periods of developmental time (after Laszloffy, 2002). In this case, we will examine what is occurring in the family's developmental progress at an arbitrarily chosen time and then, at intervals of two and four years later. We will note the stressors each generation is experiencing that call for transitions at each point in time.

Because this model recognizes diversity in family structures, this example is useful largely in illustrating how the various stressors affect individuals within each generation and across all generations. Thus, each slice of time serves as a **snapshot** of the family's functioning and options for reacting to the stressors.

### Background

The Smith family is composed of six family members from three generations: Generation 1 is comprised of the grandparents, Hank and Joan; Generation 2 is composed of their only child, Mark, Sr., and his wife, Karen; and Generation 3 is comprised of the young couple's children, Mark, Jr., and Jessica. The Smiths have lived in a Midwestern state for the past 150 years, owning the same property, which has been handed down from generation to generation. Additional homes were built on the property as needed.

### Slice 1

This slice is taken at a point in developmental time when a stressor is being experienced directly by two generations. Having a child marry and leave the family of origin to begin his own family is being experienced by both adults in Generation 2 and by the children in Generation 3. Mark, Jr., (age 18) is to be married. His leaving the family of origin eases the tension between himself and his little sister, Jessica (age 15). However, this is affecting his parents (Mark, Sr., age 43, and Karen, age 40) as they are becoming less involved in his life. They must now renegotiate their relationship with their son and his wife-to-be and take on roles they have never had before: being in-laws. Mark, Jr., now will assume a new family role of spouse. With the new marriage comes new responsibilities and adjustments. He and Lisa, his new wife, must negotiate how to define their spousal roles, how work will be accomplished in the new home, and how to define the boundaries for their new family. The parents in Generation 2 face another stressor: They must find a way to revitalize their marriage relationship since they focused intensely on their parenting responsibilities. Now that these responsibilities will be diminished, they will not have to direct as much energy and attention away from their marital relationship. Generation 1 is not exempt from this impending change in the family system. The grandparents (Hank, age 60, and Joan, age 58) must redefine their family roles as grandparents as they accept a new family member. All family members must devise shifts in their roles, patterns, and boundaries to adapt to the stressor of a child's and grandchild's impending marriage.

### Slice 2 (two years later)

Mark, Jr., is now 20 and has just become a father. He and his wife now have their own quarters on the family property in the form of a manufactured home they have recently acquired. They have more financial responsibilities than ever before, and the routine that was established in the marriage and in the home requires adjustments to accommodate the presence of a new baby. The birth of a child acts as the stressor in this case. And we now have a fourth generation in the Smith family. Mark's sister, Jessica, is now 17 and facing the decision about whether to attend college or become a part of the family business. The adults in Generation 2 are now older. Mark, Sr., is 45 and Karen is 42. The baby's birth affects them as they must now assume new family roles as grandparents.

Mark, Sr., has additional pressures because he is in the depths of his midlife transition experience. He questions many things in this life such as decisions made earlier, whether he is happy in his marriage,

*(continued)*

**Focus On 3–2**

*(continued)*

and whether he is happy with his work. This disturbing self-examination is acting as a trigger for Karen's own midlife transition experience. She also has been thinking deeply about her own life and how it has unfolded. She questions the same issues as her husband. This introspection occasionally surfaces in heated discussions between the two as they try to reach answers and solutions to serious questions. Divorce is always a possibility as are life-changing choices to move to a different place of residence, a different job, a different lifestyle. Generation 1 participants now must also make adjustments to add the new role of great-grandparent and determine how they will fit in with the new great-grandchild and his family. The Smiths may be brought to a crisis if they are unable to adapt successfully to these tremendous stressors. The family's resources for coping with the severity of the stressors are their willingness to help one another, to discuss issues head-on and rationally, and to seek outside assistance if necessary (through therapy, for example).

**Slice 3 (two years later)**

Mark, Jr., age 22, has again become a father with the birth of his second child. His wife, Lisa, is mindful of their need for additional income and is thinking about entering the workforce in their community as soon as possible. This child was born with a birth defect that requires additional family resources in time and money. The child's grandparents from Generation 2 (Mark, Sr., now age 47, and Karen, age 44) have weathered the more severe aspects of their midlife transition experiences and have become more attached and bonded as a couple because of a rededication to their marriage relationship. What spoils the totally positive outlook at this point is a strong economic downturn in the community, which has brought a financial stressor in the form of a potential bankruptcy to the couple. This has caused much concern for Jessica, now age 19, who is in her second year at the local community college. She is fearful that the financial conditions facing her parents will jeopardize the opportunity to continue her education at the state university. The participants of Generation 1—Hank, now age 64, and Joan, age 62—face their own particular stressor of Hank's retirement. This will necessitate making adjustments in roles, finances, and quality of life for these two family members. The multiple stressors taking place in this family at this point in developmental time are critical. The manner by which each stressor affects individuals within and across generations is noticeable. How each stressor is dealt with by each and all generations will determine the stability and cohesion of the family as a whole.

## FAMILY ECOLOGY THEORY AND PARENTING

The **ecological theory** proposed by Bronfenbrenner (1979, 1986, 1993) extends our attention to the role of different environments and how these affect individual and family functioning as well as parent-child relations. Bronfenbrenner focuses on the role of five distinct but related environmental settings to explain how an individual and his or her family system are influenced in his or her development, how relationships function, and how interactions take place. A person is at the center of a set of environments (see Figure 3–6). From this standpoint, an individual is not a passive recipient of interactions with other people and other environments but is actively involved in direct interactions. The first environmental setting with which he or she interacts is that comprising the environments provided by family, peers, school, or neighborhood. This is known as the **microsystem.** The next environment is known as the **mesosystem,** which encompasses the microsystem. This system involves relations between the first and all other systems that affect the person. For example, the family has relationships and interactions with the school the child attends. The child's relationships at school, then, are influenced by what takes place in the family setting and vice versa. If one or both parents have some type of addiction or substance abuse problem, this will affect a child's interactions and relationships within the family setting and influence interactions and relationships within the child's school setting. Academic performance as well as social relationships and interactions

**FIGURE 3–6.** Bronfenbrenner's ecological theory can be visualized as a composite of five distinct but related environmental settings that influence an individual directly and indirectly.

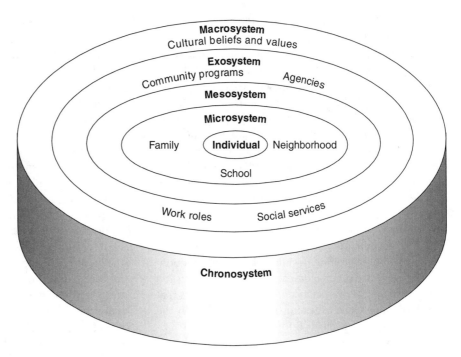

with peers and teachers are influenced by what happens in the child's family life and vice versa.

An **exosystem** also influences the individual. This setting may be visualized as encompassing the mesosystem (see Figure 3–6). The individual does not have an active role in this context but is influenced by it nevertheless. An exosystem may be government agencies, community programs, employment settings of parents, and so on. For example, the work responsibilities or assignments of one parent may change, requiring different and extraordinary work hours. When the parent begins to work longer hours or during the night rather than day shift, the parenting experiences of the child are affected accordingly. Another example would be how the quality of the child's life is affected by funding cutbacks to community recreation programs sponsored by local governmental agencies.

A **macrosystem** is an even larger context that affects an individual (see Figure 3–6). This environment involves the larger culture in which the individual lives and encompasses the exosystem and all others affecting the person. In this context, the person is affected by the broad, generalized beliefs, behavior patterns, and value systems deemed appropriate to be adopted by all members of a particular society. These influence how a person interacts with all other environmental settings.

The last environment is the **chronosystem,** which encompasses the entire network of other systems (see Figure 3–6). This context involves the organization of events and changes of an individual over his or her life span at a particular historical time. For example, we know that adults are influenced in their current behaviors and interactions by events and interactions that took place at earlier stages in their lives. In this regard, it is generally understood that if a person was abused as a child, the effects can last a lifetime. With therapeutic assistance, these effects can be minimized but perhaps not completely ameliorated and can continue to influence the person in various ways for years. Likewise, changes in cultural attitudes are reflected within the chronosystem to affect individuals at different historical times. Attitudes about gender roles in society are different today in many respects than what were held 100 years ago. Androgyny is more acceptable today in this context, for example, than a century ago.

Bronfenbrenner's ecological approach resembles some of the features found in family systems theory, especially with regard to the concepts of interdependence, reciprocal interaction and feedback, equifinality, and adaptation. His explanation adds another valuable dimension to understanding how individuals and families are affected by one another and the larger contexts in which they exist.

It is possible to view society as an immense collective of families. As such, what goes on in families is reflected in society and vice versa. A family system cannot function independently of the physical, social, economical, and psychological environments of which it is a part. The family ecology perspective outlined by Bronfenbrenner emphasizes the dual influence between families and societies locally and throughout the world. Essentially, what happens in one environmental aspect influences what occurs in others as well as in families that make up a society. Likewise, what occurs in families affects the various environments in which they live. The family ecology view leads to an examination of the ways that various sociocultural environments influence family form and functioning. The presence of a reciprocal feedback loop between families that make up society and the environments that impact them produce a dynamic model described by the family ecology perspective (Bubolz & Sontag, 1993).

There is increasing alarm about the health of contemporary American families. Observers note the high incidence of family violence, child abuse, substance abuse, divorce, and other problems that disrupt family life. Some believe that the family is declining as an effectively functioning social institution. There is much discussion about basic issues relating to family life and values, including the conscious choice to become a parent, a couple's determination of when and how many children to produce, the possibility of changing careers several times in adulthood, and early retirement, for example. Family life may be different today because these kinds of choices were much less commonly observed in the past.

Some people attribute many of the social problems in contemporary America to recent changes in family structure and functioning. However, some family sociologists who have studied the issue speculate that these same changes indicate the family's ability to adapt to societal changes. They therefore regard these changes in family structure and functioning as healthy.

The success of family life is closely related to conditions found in the larger society. Families have changed today in size, structure, composition, and function as a response to changes taking place in the larger society. A significant portion of family life in the past was devoted to fulfilling cultural and socioeconomic functions, especially the reproduction of new members for society and the production of necessary goods and services. Family functions today center on the expression and fulfillment of the needs of family members, especially their emotional and social needs, and on training children to become effective members of society upon reaching adulthood. In today's smaller families, members find that their interactions within the family group are intense and frequent. The survival and continuation of families may depend on how well each member's personal needs are met by the group.

Survival of the family as a social institution may also depend on how successful families are in responding to changes taking place in society. Parents today must deal with many new and difficult situations that are different from those encountered by families in the past. These include rapidly changing societal economic conditions, severe social pressures on children, restricted family size, the hazards of living in urban environments, and the need for both parents to work outside the home in occupations that are often highly stressful. Many families do not know how to react or adapt in healthy ways to these kinds of changes. Family life today is described as *asynchronous*; that is, family leaders (the adults) depend on personal past experiences to guide their current behavior and to prepare children for future functioning as adults. The problem is that there is little guarantee that the future will be anything like the past, especially if societal changes continue to occur as rapidly as they have over the last 50 years.

The ways that parenthood is defined, that child rearing is conducted, and that parent-child relations are valued will vary based on how family ecological factors are experienced differently by each family system. While almost every family system adheres to the central role expectations of parenthood, including an emphasis on nurturing, teaching, and caring for children, variations occur because of differences in the environments in which each family lives. Because of such variations, it is impossible to speak of families using only one definition, one form, one structure, or one method of defining parenthood and child-rearing methods.

••••••••••••••••••••••••••••••••••••••••••••••••••••

***Focus Point.*** Bronfenbrenner's ecological theory supplements some of the family systems theory concepts and explains how individuals and families are affected by a variety of interacting environments and vice versa. An individual's family, by being part of the total environment, also is influenced by these other systems.

••••••••••••••••••••••••••••••••••••••••••••••••••••

## PSYCHOSOCIAL DEVELOPMENT THEORY AND PARENTING

Most modern developmental theories focus on the development of an individual child during the years between birth and the end of adolescence. Extensive abstract explanations have been formulated about how the interaction between heredity and environment influences individual development. To date, the years of childhood and adolescence have received the greatest attention. Few developmental theorists have attempted to explain or interpret what takes place in the years of adulthood and old age. The psychosocial theory of Erik Erikson (1950, 1964, 1982; Erikson, Erikson, & Kivnick, 1986) is a notable exception. Erikson's theory features developmental change as a process that continues throughout the life span between birth and death, not just during the growth years of infancy, childhood, and adolescence.

Erikson's explanation of the continuing psychosocial development of an individual is a modern reinterpretation of Freudian psychology. It differs from earlier theories in that it describes the developmental and social tasks that a person is expected to accomplish at each stage of development as a series of childhoods that occur throughout the individual's life. Developmental change is viewed as an evolutional process based on a universally experienced sequence of biological, social, and psychological events that take place between birth and death. According to Erikson's theory, an individual enters each stage of psychosocial development with the goal of developing the specific skills and competencies appropriate to that particular stage. Hence, the individual never has a static personality, but always is in the process of reshaping and revising his or her personality.

Each stage of the life span has its own developmental theme, which Erikson terms a **psychosocial crisis,** or a challenge to attain a healthy rather than unhealthy attitude or generalized feeling. Developmental change is enhanced or retarded by a person's experiences in confronting and handling each psychosocial crisis that occurs within each stage of the life span. The person must confront a central problem—a specific psychosocial crisis—at each life stage and is given the opportunity to develop strengths and skills leading toward a particular attitude that is healthy or unhealthy. Provided with a social and psychological environment that is conducive to developmental change, an individual faces each problem at that stage with the potential for healthy, normal

accomplishment. If the person experiences overwhelming difficulty in accomplishing what is expected at one stage of the life span, the result will be difficulty in dealing with the psychosocial crises at future stages.

Developmental change, however, does not occur within a vacuum free of other influences and factors. The process is not structured so that a person is forced to face the challenges and trials of life alone. Developmental change usually occurs first within the context of a supportive family atmosphere, then within an increasingly wider social radius of friends, then within the school environment, and so on as life progresses. **Significant others**—those who are singularly important to a person—assist or inhibit his or her developmental progress at each life stage. An individual proceeds to the next stage after meeting the particular requirements of biological, social, and psychological **readiness.** This readiness to progress further along one's developmental path is influenced significantly by others in one's social environment, especially by the parents in the case of a developing child.

The psychosocial crises at each stage of the life span present the individual with the challenge of acquiring what Erikson calls **psychosocial senses.** Psychosocial senses are attitudes or general feelings that result from how adequately a person can meet and master the crisis at a particular stage of psychosocial development.

Erikson describes eight stages of psychosocial change over the life span and labels each in terms of healthy or unhealthy psychosocial development. It is important to note that a person's mastery of a psychosocial attitude or sense is not an all-or-nothing matter, but is continually being weighed on a balance. It is possible to gain some measure of unhealthy, as well as healthy, feelings related to the psychosocial attitude associated with a particular life stage. In the balance of experiences, attitudes and feelings that promote healthy psychological development derive from attaining healthy experiences that outweigh those that are unhealthy (see Figure 3–7). In early childhood, for example, children are thought to experience a psychosocial stage during which they have opportunities to acquire the ability to function independently, or what Erikson calls a sense of autonomy. Positive experiences that lead children to conclude that they can function autonomously result in a healthy sense of autonomy. Negative experiences, if constituting the majority of a child's experiences or occurring with sufficient consistency and strength, lead the child to feel shame and doubt about his or her ability to function autonomously. The result is an

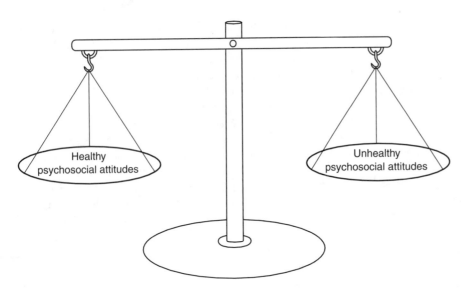

**FIGURE 3–7.** Psychosocial development at any particular stage can be viewed as having a majority of experiences that promote one attitude (sense) or the other. Some unhealthy feelings inevitably occur at any particular stage. Healthy development results when healthy experiences outweigh those that are unhealthy.

unhealthy sense of shame and doubt. In Erikson's theory, at each of the eight stages, progress in development occurs when the healthy attitude in that stage is acquired, whereas future difficulty in psychosocial development will occur when the unhealthy attitude results from that stage.

The establishment of each of the eight healthy senses at the corresponding stages of the life span implies that an individual acquires the competencies required for healthy psychological and social functioning in society. For example, in infancy each individual is faced with the challenge of developing what Erikson terms a sense of basic trust. Through their parents, infants are provided with numerous experiences to interact with their physical and social environment. Gentle handling, attentiveness, and consistency in the care provided by parents help infants learn to trust others. Conversely, rough handling, neglect, and chaotic caregiving can cause infants to learn to mistrust others. The establishment of either a sense of trust or mistrust will affect how each child experiences subsequent stages of psychosocial development. A healthy psychosocial sense facilitates healthy development at subsequent stages, while an unhealthy attitude hampers the person's future psychosocial development.

Erikson's theory is optimistic, however, in holding that the possibility of redemption exists at each stage of psychosocial development. Although success in meeting the developmental tasks at any stage implies the readiness to advance to the next, failure or difficulty in estab-

lishing what is required at one stage does not condemn the individual to complete failure at attaining healthy development in the next stage. Erikson believes that the door to a developmental stage does not slam shut when one reaches the chronological age at which the stage ends, but that problems experienced at any stage can be addressed later in the life span.

Erikson uses a timetable to illustrate his eight stages of psychosocial development (see Table 3–1). Although the ages listed are flexible guidelines for the times at which people experience the stages, the first five occur during the growth years of infancy, childhood, and adolescence, and the remaining three occur during adulthood. We will discuss only the first seven stages of Erikson's theory as they relate directly to parent-child relations.

## Stage 1: Basic Trust Versus Mistrust

The primary developmental task of early infancy (birth to 18 months of age) is that of developing a sense of basic trust in one's environment and in those who populate it. Erikson recognizes the traditional orientation within our culture whereby the mother is charged with providing the primary care of an infant and assisting the infant to develop a trusting attitude. The caregiving procedures and the type of handling a baby receives during this period are thought to determine whether it develops a sense of trust or a sense of mistrust. Erikson believes that the

**TABLE 3–1.** Erikson's Timetable of Developmental Stages

| Stage | Psychosocial Crisis | Radius of Significant Others | Theme | Ages |
|---|---|---|---|---|
| I. | Trust vs. Mistrust | Maternal person | To get; to give in return | Birth to 18 months |
| II. | Autonomy vs. Shame/Doubt | Paternal person | To hold on; to let go | 18 months to 3 years |
| III. | Initiative vs. Guilt | Family | To make; to make like | 3 to 6 years |
| IV. | Industry vs. Inferiority | School; Neighborhood | To make things; to make together | 6 to 12 years |
| V. | Identity vs. Role Confusion | Peer groups | To be oneself; to share being oneself | 12 to 18 years |
| VI. | Intimacy vs. Isolation | Partners in friendship, sex, competition | To lose and find oneself in another | 18 to 24 years |
| VII. | Generativity vs. Self-absorption | Partner | To make be; to take care of | 24 to 54 years |
| VIII. | Integrity vs. Despair | Mankind | To be through having been; to face not being | 54 years to death |

*Source:* Adapted from E. H. Erikson. (1959). Identity and the life cycle: Selected papers. *Psychological Issues 1*(1).

process by which the baby achieves basic trust is by "getting and by giving in return" (see Table 3–1). An infant gets the attention and stimulation it needs from its parents and gives social stimulation to its parents in return.

One of the most significant factors that helps an infant to establish the sense of basic trust is the consistency of care the parent provides. The quality of the interaction process between the mother and baby is seen by Erikson to be of special importance. From his point of view, anyone can simply feed a baby. The establishment of a consistent pattern of holding, cuddling, speaking to, smiling at, and expressing love to a baby is best performed, in Erikson's opinion, by a nurturant mother figure (see Figure 3–8).

Learning to trust the environment occurs when a baby experiences consistency in his or her interactions with the physical world. The baby learns that the day proceeds according to a routine: The baby experiences rhythms of wakefulness and rest, and he or she demands and receives food at certain intervals. Consistency in the environment is also learned when objects are released and the baby notices that they always fall. The factor of predictability cannot be underestimated, for a sense of mistrust derives from unpredictability and inconsistency in caregiving as well as in interactions with the environment.

## Stage 2: Autonomy Versus Shame and Doubt

By the infant's second birthday, many different events have occurred in his or her developmental progress. The infant is beginning to talk and to communicate with others, to walk, and to eagerly explore the environment. Many of the events experienced during the period from 18 months to 3 years of age lead the toddler toward greater independence and autonomy (Table 3–1). For the most part, the child is trying to communicate to the world the attitude, "I am BIG! I am as strong as you are! I can do *anything* BY MYSELF!"

This can be a bewildering experience for both a child and adults. The toddler discovers that she or he has a strong drive to try to stand alone and assertively take positions of autonomy. Most parents discover that the terrible 2-year-old maintains this strong-willed attitude through the third year. It is a period of tension and conflict, not only between parents and child but also within the child. Having learned to be dependent on others, the child discovers that this is no longer a satisfying experience. Negativism becomes a way of life, expressed by the proverbial "No!" in response to almost every adult request for cooperation.

**FIGURE 3–8.** A sense of basic trust is facilitated by consistent nurturant parental behavior toward an infant that fulfills its basic needs.

**FIGURE 3–9.** One aspect of a sense of initiative is established as preschoolers discover their world through play activities.

Erikson believes that children become concerned at this stage with "holding on and letting go." They experience a basic conflict between their need for assistance from others and their desire to function independently. During this period, children learn tasks that ensure autonomy, such as toilet training, self-dressing, and self-feeding. The father takes on additional importance in helping the child to relax the close emotional ties that were established between them in the earlier months of infancy. From a family systems theory view, the toddler (through the assistance of parents) begins to establish personal boundaries that define a rudimentary personal identity distinct from parents and others. This healthy self-differentiation lays the foundation for feelings of self-worth and autonomy and prevents unhealthy dependency on others at later stages of developmental progress.

## Stage 3: Initiative Versus Guilt

Ages 3 through 6 are a time for aggressive exploration of the child's social and physical worlds. At this time, a child devotes much attention to discovering what he or she can accomplish. Erikson calls this stage the time for acquiring a sense of initiative, an attitude of "I can" (see Table 3–1 and Figure 3–9). Behavior during this stage is characterized by the theme of "making and making like." Children attempt many acts and are concerned with developing an awareness of the variety of social roles present in their environment. The basic social framework during this period is the child's family, and the value of siblings, grandparents, cousins, and other relatives as significant others in the child's life increases.

The sense of guilt may be established if children of this age are penalized too severely or too frequently for their attempts to express initiative. Rather than learning that it is a positive matter to try new and different things, they may learn that it is far safer not to try too much. A pattern of passivity may be set for future behavior. Adults are challenged to reinforce acceptable behaviors as the child explores and discovers his or her environment and capabilities. The basic problem for the child at this stage is to learn to be responsible for his or her own behavior. Patterns evolve in family systems at this time to help children begin to learn appropriate behaviors. These are usually communicated through rules that a family system evolves to define appropriate limits. For most children, learning experiences that teach structure and socialization are now begun in earnest by parents.

**FIGURE 3–10.** A sense of industry is acquired when school-age children master basic skills such as reading, writing, and calculation as well as a work ethic.

## Stage 4: Industry Versus Inferiority

The middle childhood years between 6 and 12 are designated by Erikson as the period when children are challenged to develop a sense of industry (see Table 3–1 and Figure 3–10). The major theme of this period of psychosocial development is the child's determination to master what our culture considers age-appropriate developmental tasks. Great efforts are made by family systems to teach children a work ethic and sense of responsibility and duty in contributing to the welfare and functioning of their family system. Children now are expected to complete tasks they have been assigned and to learn work habits in performing small jobs that help the family to function, such as taking out the trash and setting the table.

The conflict many children experience during this stage is a fear of not being able to do enough, to be enough, or to be as good as others their age. School-age children become more involved in learning to relate to and communicate with the individuals who are most significant to them at this time of their life: their peers. They strive to accomplish, to do something well, and to be the first or the best in some endeavor. Play activities and personal feelings reflect competition rather than autonomy or cooperation with others. Self-imposed segregation of the sexes during play is common among children of this age and may promote sex-role identification.

A child's fear of inferiority is founded on the knowledge that she or he is still a child, an incomplete person who lacks the skills and abilities to cope successfully in the adult-oriented world. As a consequence of these feelings, the child is ambivalent about growing up. The child aspires to have the responsibilities and privileges of the adult world, yet wishes to retain the prerogatives of childhood.

A sense of inferiority develops in school-age children when they come to believe that they cannot succeed or accomplish as much as they expect of themselves or as much as is expected of them by the school, their family, or their peers. A child's basic identity as a member of a peer group and status within that group become endangered when he or she perceives his or her abilities or tools—academic skills, athletic skills, and so on—to be inferior to those of others the same age.

## Stage 5: Identity Versus Role Confusion

The fifth stage of psychosocial development begins with puberty at about age 13 and lasts through age 18 (see Table 3–1). The challenge presented by this stage involves one of the major questions an individual confronts during life: "Who am I?" By experiencing a wide variety of roles and relationships during the years of childhood and adolescence, a person comes to form idealistic impressions and concepts about how things should be

**FIGURE 3–11.** Adolescents establish a sense of identity through interactions and activities with peer groups. Identity is expressed in other ways as well such as dress style.

within himself or herself, within the family system, and within social relationships. The resolution of the primary task of this stage represents an integrative process of assimilating and resolving the issues that emerged in all of the previous stages of psychosocial development. A clear identity of who one is, what one values, what types of attitudes are important, and how to become involved in an occupational role becomes more focused during this stage. Parents have almost completely been replaced by the peer group as the essential element of social support (see Figure 3–11). The adolescent continues to use the family system to assess her or his place in society and the values the family has supported during the growing years of childhood.

The sense of role confusion results from failing to reach a certain degree of clarity about the primary role the teenager will assume in adulthood. This attitude reflects uncertainty about one's ability to contribute in some way to society, how to go about choosing a vocation, and which values are important to one's role as an adult. The support of parents during these years is important to help the adolescent in questioning life's purpose and determining how he or she fits into society.

## Stage 6: Intimacy Versus Isolation

Having established an idea of who one is and where one is going in life, the individual is prepared for the next stage

of development between 18 and 24 years, which, according to Erikson, involves "losing and finding himself or herself in another" (see Table 3–1). During this stage, a person is presented with the challenge of learning the skills necessary for conducting an intimate relationship with another. A series of experiences with people is necessary for learning when to lower personal boundaries, how to be vulnerable with another, and how to relate to someone in an intimate manner. The sense of trust that was learned in infancy and reinforced over the years of childhood and adolescence will assist the person in sharing his or her identity as a unique, worthwhile human being with another without fear of losing that identity in the process.

If a sense of intimacy is not learned at this optimal stage in the life span, a sense of isolation may be established. This attitude is reflected in a growing degree of self-devaluation. Experiences that reinforce a sense of isolation are those in which the individual learns that others cannot be trusted in a close, intimate manner. It becomes too painful psychologically to be vulnerable; it is much safer for the individual's ego to face life alone.

## Stage 7: Generativity Versus Self-Absorption

The productive years of adulthood constitute the longest stage of psychosocial development between 24 and 54 years (see Table 3–1). During this period, productivity

**FIGURE 3–12.** Parents play an important role in facilitating children's psychosocial development and vice versa.

may be seen in the establishment of a family system and in achievements in one's occupation or creative endeavors. Erikson (1950) describes the attitude of generativity as the "interest in establishing and guiding the next generation or . . . the absorbing object of parental kind of responsibility" (p. 114). The person who fails to establish this sense of caring for others or to become involved with creative production becomes preoccupied with his or her own personal needs and interests and ignores those of others. He or she becomes what Erikson calls "his own infant and pet" (p. 115) and develops a sense of self-absorption.

## Application to Parent-Child Relations

Erikson does not specifically indicate in his theory how it might be applied to parent-child relations but we may infer from his writings how this may be accomplished. His theory provides a basic framework for understanding the psychosocial changes experienced by an individual. A family system, however, is composed of several individuals of differing ages and developmental levels, each of whom is involved in resolving the challenges of his or her own particular psychosocial stage. The parents are at the stage of psychosocial development termed generativity versus self-absorption. If several children have been produced by a couple, they are likely to be at

different developmental stages (see Figure 3–12). For example, the oldest child may be involved in accomplishing the tasks leading toward a sense of industry versus inferiority, the middle child may be addressing the tasks involving a sense of initiative versus guilt, and the youngest may be learning to accomplish the tasks of basic trust versus mistrust.

This intertwining or congruence of developmental stages being experienced by parents and children is referred to as **reciprocal interaction** in family systems theory. In the everyday interactions taking place between parents and children, each participant in this subsystem promotes the acquisition of the healthy psychosocial sense being experienced by the other. Providing appropriate parental caregiving assists the children in achieving the particular psychosocial attitude they are attempting to master at that particular developmental point in time. In turn, by providing a source for parents to provide caregiving, children assist their parents in mastering their sense of generativity.

It is also in this manner that parenting behavior becomes adapted or modified as children grow older. By passing through the various stages of psychosocial development, children's needs change and parenting styles must be adapted to meet these new needs. Using the concepts of reciprocal interaction and adaptation, homeostasis is achieved in parent-child relations when parenting behavior becomes congruent with meeting the needs of children at their different stages of growth and development. For example, a child who is striving for autonomy during the latter part of infancy prompts entirely different patterns of caregiving from parents than were called for when the child was focused on developing a sense of trust. The course of parent-child relations proceeds according to these interactional sequences: The child assists or inhibits the parents in their development of a sense of generativity, as the parents assist or inhibit the child in meeting the challenges of each developmental stage. Like the larger family system of which it is a part, the parent-child subsystem must adapt to changes in the individual participants to maintain stability and effective functioning.

●●●●●●●●●●●●●●●●●●●●●●●●●●●●●●●●●●●●●

### Parenting Reflection 3–3

What are some ways at each stage of Erikson's theory that inappropriate and ineffective caregiving by parents could impede a child's psychosocial development and encourage their acquiring the unhealthy attitude?

●●●●●●●●●●●●●●●●●●●●●●●●●●●●●●●●●●●●

●●●●●●●●●●●●●●●●●●●●●●●●●●●●●●●●●●●●

***Focus Point.*** Erik Erikson's framework for explaining the process of psychosocial development over the life span provides another means for interpreting the relationship between parents and children. The framework focuses on developmental changes in individuals that occur in association with the passage of time. These changes are couched within the context of the social environments individuals experience throughout their life span. Parent-child relations change in response to the concept of reciprocal interaction.

●●●●●●●●●●●●●●●●●●●●●●●●●●●●●●●●●●●●●

## OTHER RELATED THEORIES AND PARENTING

### Vygotsky's Views of Children as Apprentices

Lev Vygotsky (1962) proposes that children accomplish many developmental tasks within the context of what he terms the **zone of proximal development (ZPD)**.

Many tasks that are too difficult for children to master alone can be accomplished successfully with the guidance and assistance of adults who are more skilled than children. The lower limit of the ZPD is what a child can accomplish in learning a task independently of adult assistance. The upper limit of this zone is what can be accomplished when assisted by an adult. The ZPD represents an idea of a child's learning potential. It emphasizes the interpersonal context in which learning such tasks occurs for children by implying that learning is a shared experience.

Young children are assisted by parents and other caregivers by motivating their interest in accomplishing a task that appears difficult for them to achieve successfully. By providing children with verbal instruction and by helping them to learn by doing things themselves with guidance, parents and others assist children to organize the information they already possess in existing mental structures and transform these to allow them to accomplish increasingly more difficult tasks.

Some researchers use the term **scaffolding** to refer to any parental behavior that supports children's efforts at more advanced skill development until the children become competent at that behavior. In the context of this text, we refer to such assistance as *assertive* and *supportive care*, which comprise the concept of nurturance and refer to the ways parents provide this to children in appropriate, healthy ways. When parents provide this kind of instruction for their preschool-age child, it often happens in this sequence: (1) recruiting the child's interest in performing a task or activity; (2) simplifying the task to a number of steps that lead to a correct solution; (3) maintaining the child's interest in the task; (4) pointing out errors as they occur and providing guidance toward correction; (5) controlling the child's frustration by discounting the distress caused by making mistakes; and (6) demonstrating or modeling correct solutions (Astington, 1993; Rogoff, 1990). When viewed in this manner, children learn best when parents model problem-solving skills or mentor the child in ways for learning how to reach solutions to problems. In this manner, Vygotsky's views approximate that of social learning theory.

Parents and other adults working with young children may observe them talking out loud, frequently to themselves, as they play and go about other activities. Vygotsky (1987) describes this as **private speech,** noting that young children probably use this for self-guidance and direction as they attempt to accomplish difficult tasks or to work through their confusion about how to go about solving a problem. It appears that humans retain this practice throughout life, but the speech becomes internalized and silent or restricted to lip movements or whispers (Berk & Landau, 1993).

## Cognitive Theory

Several theoretical approaches explain how people acquire their thought processes and problem-solving abilities as well as organize and use information. One of the more useful in application to parent-child relations is that proposed by Jean Piaget. His writings (Piaget, 1967; Piaget & Inhelder, 1969) on this topic were based initially on observations of his own children.

This theory is a comprehensive guide to understanding mental processes and how these are acquired and change as a person grows and develops from birth through the years of childhood and adolescence. Central to Piaget's explanation is the role of personal experience with one's environment, both physical and social, in influencing how we come to think and reason. Parents are an essential component of a child's experiences in the ways that they interact with a child and provide a variety of experiences both physical and social in nature. For example, parents provide physical experiences for infants through the toys given for play, the food for meals, and the destinations they take children in the community. These shape children's understanding of their physical environment and how they can operate in this setting. Parents also provide a social environment to their infants by talking with them, playing with them, and teaching them certain rudimentary social skills in late infancy. These actions by parents continue throughout the years of childhood and adolescence. For example, when parents read to their children and encourage them to look at picture books, the children learn that information can be acquired from printed materials. What parents provide as experiences for children influences the quality of their cognitive development. The manner in which this occurs in parent-child relations is discussed in greater detail in later chapters.

### Parenting Reflection 3–4

Has information from behavioral science improved or only served to complicate matters even more for adults who are trying to parent children effectively?

*Focus Point.* Other theoretical approaches may be useful in understanding the social context of parent-child relations. Learning theory components (behavior modification and social learning) explain how parents teach children by using rewards to reinforce the behaviors they desire of children and by serving as models of behavior. Vygotsky's views expand on social learning to explain how parents teach skills to their children. Cognitive theory stresses the importance of the experiences parents provide for children that are both physical and social in nature as a means for shaping their mental life and understanding of the world in which they live.

## POINTS TO CONSIDER

- Several different but related theories can be applied to understanding and studying parent-child relations. Each provides insight into a particular aspect of this relationship. Some describe how the relationship is subject to being changed over time; others describe how the relationship functions in more general terms.
- Systems theory has been applied to the study of families. Family systems theory is useful in explaining the processes by which a family group makes decisions, sets and achieves particular goals, and establishes methods for governing the behavior of its members. The theory is helpful in describing how these processes work to maintain the stability of a family group over time and how the family reacts to changes affecting individual members and the group. According to the theory, several subsystems often can be found within the larger family system. These are usually based on relationships between two or more members, such as the adult spouses, parents and children, or brothers and sisters. Each subsystem has its own patterns that mirror those of the larger family system.

- Family systems theory uses several concepts to explain family functioning: wholeness, interdependence, patterns (rules, roles, communication styles), reciprocal interaction and feedback, boundaries, entropy, equifinality, adaptation, and homeostasis.

- Systemic family development theory is an extension of family systems theory that is useful in understanding how a family group changes in response to stressors that occur as part of normal developmental processes of individuals. This realistic model of family life recognizes that families are complex and composed of several interrelated generations. By taking a snapshot or slice of developmental time being experienced by a family, it is possible to examine the stressors affecting each generation in a family and study how a family copes with these stressors in response. By making adaptations in patterns, families are able to make necessary changes in order to re-establish their stability in functioning.

- Ecological theory proposed by Bronfenbrenner offers an additional way to understand family functioning. Bronfenbrenner suggests that five distinct environmental settings explain how an individual is influenced in his or her developmental progress and how relationships function in interaction with various environments and people in those environments.

- Erikson proposes a theory of eight stages that describe the psychosocial development of individuals over the life span. This theory stresses: (1) the continuity of developmental changes over a person's entire life span; (2) the resolution of a central crisis or challenge at each stage; (3) the mastery or acquisition of a healthy or unhealthy psychosocial attitude at the completion of each stage; and (4) the assistance and support from significant others who assist or impede an individual's development progress. The theory may be applied to parent-child relations by examining the congruence between the psychosocial stages of parents and children. By applying the concepts of reciprocal interaction and adaptation, parenting behavior changes in response to the changing developmental needs of children. In turn, children help parents to achieve their particular psychosocial attitude by virtue of being the recipient of their care giving behavior.

- Other theories can also be applied to understanding parent-child relations. Vygotsky's observations emphasize how parents structure learning experiences in teaching children to master skills. Cognitive theory described by Piaget focuses on the role of physical and social experiences provided by parents in shaping how children come to understand their world.

# CHAPTER 4

# Parenting Strategies

## Focus Questions
■ ■ ■ ■ ■ ■ ■ ■ ■ ■

1. What qualities characterize a competent parent?
2. How is discipline defined? What are some guidelines that help parents to be effective disciplinarians?
3. How are structure and nurturance provided to children through discipline?
4. What basic methods of discipline can be used by parents? What elements do they have in common? How are they applied to a program of discipline?
5. Why are behavior problems considered a normal aspect of children's development?

■ ■ ■ ■ ■ ■ ■ ■ ■ ■

Our culture provides little preparation or assistance in training people to act as competent parents. Parental behavior may be guided by trial-and-error learning, self-education, intimate self-knowledge, the model provided by one's own parents, and a clear idea of what is to be expected of children at each stage of their developmental progress (Simons et al., 1991). It is also influenced by those factors and variables discussed in previous chapters, such as family ecological factors.

For many years, a prevalent belief has been that people in our society do not need formal training or education to be parents. However, professionals and others who work closely with parents today believe there is considerable need for such training (Smith, Perou, & Lesesne, 2002). For example, family sociologist E. E. LeMasters (1977) states:

> It is usually assumed in our society that people have to be trained for difficult roles; most business firms would not consider turning a sales clerk loose on the customers without some formal training; the armed forces would scarcely send a raw recruit into combat without extensive training; most states now require a course in driver's education before high school students can acquire a driver's license. Even dog owners go to school to learn how to treat their pets properly. This is not true of American parents. (p. 18)

Although most people involved in parenting would agree that they could profit from learning new ways to be effective in their role, no clear guidelines identify the qualities or behaviors that make someone a competent parent. It is possible that our culture will never reach a consensus on this issue. However, researchers continue to make much progress in helping parents find more effective ways to perform their tasks in working with children and attaining goals established for their child-rearing efforts.

Many people discover their lack of knowledge about parenting skills after serious problems have developed in their family systems. Those problems may relate to ineffective guidance and communication within the group, for example. Professionals who promote education for parenting believe that people can be offered opportunities to learn a variety of means and methods to improve their parenting abilities (First & Way, 1995). Education is seen as a means for preventing or minimizing problems in child rearing. This is preferable to some interventionist approaches designed to deal with the aftermath of problems (Figure 4–1).

Clearly, people can learn how to be more effective parents. By studying the research, theory, issues, and approaches developed and examined by parent education practitioners and investigators, it is possible to develop a better understanding of the challenges and adventures of parenting children.

This chapter presents information about specific methods and techniques of child rearing that are recommended today by child development and family experts. These methods have emerged from changes in social attitudes about how to raise children properly and from information derived from behavioral science research on such issues as what children need and the long-term effects of child-rearing methods on personality development and self-esteem. Thus, unlike the advice on child rearing passed down from grandmothers and great-aunts, these methods have added credibility in being derived from research and clinical study.

## DEALING WITH DISCIPLINE

Teaching and guiding children are perhaps the greatest concerns parents have in performing adequately as caregivers to growing children. As discussed in Chapter 1, cultural ideas have evolved about what children need and how best to teach them the behaviors, values, and beliefs adults consider important for their effective future functioning. Advice on how to raise children has proliferated in modern times. Information on a variety of topics pertaining to parenting, child development, and guidance techniques is available in magazines, books, and pamphlets. Such materials tend to be used more frequently by today's parents than they were in

**FIGURE 4–1.**   Parents are expected to teach discipline to their children. This does not refer to punishment for transgressions but teaching appropriate behaviors, including self-control.

previous generations (Bigner & Yang, 1996; Francis-Connolly, 2003).

Uppermost in many parents' thinking is the issue of how to provide adequate and appropriate discipline in guiding children's growth and development (Chamberlain & Patterson, 1995). A survey of child-rearing advice in popular literature between 1950 and 1970 found discipline to be a common topic (Bigner, 1972). Articles during this period also emphasized: (1) helping children gain self-control through psychological means rather than through physical punishment, (2) using positive reinforcement to achieve desired results in children's behavior, and (3) using a variety of strategies and methods for child training. Another survey of popular literature articles appearing between 1972 and 1990 also found that the topic of discipline and socialization of children received a sizable degree of writers' attention (Bigner & Yang, 1996). Articles published during this period reflected the same general themes found in the earlier period surveyed, but also emphasized the emergence of many new ways of working with children that are described in this chapter. Many of the themes discussed during the past 40 years in popular magazine articles appear to be perennial issues with parents, such as how to communicate with children so that they learn how to listen and comply with parental concerns about their behavior.

## Some Generalizations About Discipline

The concept of discipline is largely misunderstood. The term is derived from an old English word meaning instruction. A derivative of the term is *disciple*, which means pupil or student. Contrary to its definition, most people equate discipline to the use of punishment or penalties in response to children's misbehavior. For discipline to be effective, however, parents need to view it in light of the term's original meaning.

First, discipline is teaching children to behave in ways considered appropriate by their parents, teachers, and other caregivers. Discipline is the means by which children are taught to internalize the rules, values, and beliefs that will help them to become effective individuals as adults.

Second, discipline involves measures that help children learn to control their impulses so that they can learn to reason and make appropriate choices for their behavior before acting. These measures also help children learn social skills in considering others' needs as well as their own, which will facilitate their future participation in work and family life and in other interactions with people.

Third, to be effective, disciplinary actions of a parent must be positive, reasonable, and temperate.

Fourth, methods and strategies of discipline should be geared to a child's age and developmental level.

Fifth, to discipline a child effectively, an adult must understand the child and his or her particular needs and problems.

Finally, discipline provides structure in children's lives by means of the rules developed within their family system. Rules are found in both healthy and unhealthy family systems. These act as the means for helping everyone know the guidelines of what serves as acceptable and unacceptable behavior and the consequences of both actions. In healthy family systems, negotiable rules abound. Children in healthy families learn that the rules are for their protection and freedom. They know they can talk with their parents about making occasional exceptions to the rules. The topic of rules as

applied to the practice of discipline is discussed in greater detail later in this chapter.

Children's misbehavior is often a primary focus of parental attention. This preoccupation, which may be more of a problem to the adult than to the child, can be traced to the following questions: (1) Are adult expectations too high for the child's age and abilities? (2) Are instructions to children given in a negative framework involving an excessive number of "don'ts" rather than "do's"? (3) Is the adult consistent in enforcing some rules and policies that are not negotiable and at the same time flexible to debate negotiable rules to teach the child conflict resolution and discussion skills? (4) Is the emphasis on teaching children how to arrive at win-win solutions to problems with parental or family rules instead of on the deliberate, conscientious expression of parental power over children when problems arise in their behavior? Environmental factors discussed in Chapter 1 that influence both parents' and children's behavior and interaction also influence disciplinary actions.

Children may misbehave because of varied and complex reasons, including the following: (1) they may be ill or becoming ill; (2) they may lack knowledge and experience in knowing how to behave appropriately and as expected; (3) they may feel unloved, discouraged, or rejected, and hence are attempting to gain their parents' attention; (4) they may feel inadequate or incapable of living up to parental standards; or (5) they may have forgotten about a rule or not had sufficient learning experiences to internalize it.

Parents can learn certain skills and gain understanding and knowledge that will guide them in teaching children acceptable and responsible behavior. However, no child development or family expert can offer programs of discipline and guidance that will work effectively for all families or for all children.

Each family system must develop its own rules, policies, and values of child rearing and socialization. How these evolve in a particular family system depends on a host of factors, such as personalities, family of origin backgrounds, values, financial and social status, and the number and birth order of children. Experimentation with what works, what feels comfortable, and what is reasonable contributes to the program of discipline parents use. The ability of a family system to adapt or change rules that either don't work or are no longer functional because children have grown older is also an essential feature of a healthy program of discipline.

The concepts and possible approaches outlined in the paragraphs that follow may prove helpful to parents attempting to develop a program of discipline for their family system:

1. *Understand how the concept of equifinality applies to a program of discipline.* The equifinality concept from family systems theory implies that families attain similar goals in different and varied ways. Hence, different methods of socializing children may result in adult individuals who hold similar values, attitudes, and behaviors. A variety of techniques, methods, and practices can help accomplish similar goals of socialization. No single, correct program of discipline will accomplish these goals (Figure 4–2).

2. *Do not use abusive corporal punishment.* Contrary to popular opinion, spanking and other abusive corporal punishment are not effective means to achieve desired behavior from children (Kazdin & Benjet, 2003; Straus, 1994). Instead, such forms of physical violence model this behavior as appropriate ways to resolve conflicts and lead to habitual use of violent behavior by children (Kyriacou, 2002; Straus & Yodanis, 1996). Recent work also strongly substantiates the connection between harsh physical, abusive punishment in childhood and violence in adult romantic involvements (Swinford et al., 2000). Many adults were spanked by their parents in at-

tempts to control their misbehavior as children. However, researchers increasingly note that it is the consistency with which this and other punishment measures are used rather than the act itself that helps children learn to control their actions (Kazdin & Benjet, 2003). Spanking and other forms of physical punishment usually occur within the context of expressions of parental anger, which can result in overly aggressive actions that harm the child (Figure 4–3).

Considering this danger along with the negative effect on a child's self-esteem, alternatives such as positive reinforcement, time-out, and other less damaging methods are viewed as more appropriate disciplinary measures (Whipple & Ritchey, 1997) (see Focus On 4–1).

One study, however, reports that parental reliance on reasoning alone to shape and guide a disciplinary program for toddlers is ineffective (Larzelere et al., 1989). When the reasoning approach is combined with noncorporal, nonabusive punishment (e.g., time-out, withdrawal of privileges), then disciplinary programs become more effective and toddlers learn to comply with parental wishes. And as all parents of toddlers learn, there are times when even this kind of procedure may not work well. In these instances, the authors recommend that parents use a nonabusive corporal punishment as a back-up for the reasoning and use of noncorporal

**FIGURE 4–2.** Competent parenting today differs from what occurred in the past. Today, competent parenting requires more than providing love and nurturance.

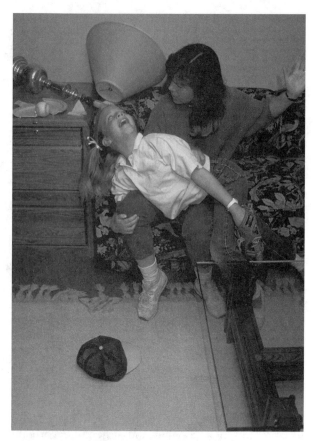

**FIGURE 4–3.** Many parents believe that physical punishments, like spanking, are an appropriate way to teach children to obey family rules. What do you think about this practice?

punishment. A two-swat hand-slap, for example, is advocated in these circumstances. Not every parent, however, may wish to go even to this as a last resort in working with a noncompliant toddler. The authors of this study note that how parents use disciplinary tactics may be more critical than which ones they choose to use.

● ● ● ● ● ● ● ● ● ● ● ● ● ● ● ● ● ● ● ● ● ● ● ● ● ● ● ● ●

### Parenting Reflection 4–1

Does anyone have the right to intervene when parents use physical punishment as a disciplinary technique with their child, especially in public? What would you say to a parent who is a stranger about what he or she is doing?

● ● ● ● ● ● ● ● ● ● ● ● ● ● ● ● ● ● ● ● ● ● ● ● ● ● ● ● ●

3. *Try to understand children's feelings and motivations.* Many parents consider the misbehavior of a child to be a personal attack motivated by the child's malicious intent. This is rarely the case. The child's misbehavior may be a learned response or action that is logical enough to him or her at that particular time. Parents who attempts in a loving, noncritical way to develop an understanding of their children will feel less hostile when they misbehave. As a result, the parents will be more rational in developing corrective action that teaches children to think before they act. Such an approach will also facilitate the parent's position as the child's ally in solving a particular problem. On the other hand, the parent who sees misbehavior as a personal attack with malicious intent will likely respond with anger and frustration, which will only serve to intensify the problem.

A parent has various means to gain understanding of a child's feelings and motivations for behaving in unacceptable ways. The parent can listen carefully to a child's verbal and nonverbal communications and reflect the feelings being expressed back to the child. This exercise will help the child express himself or herself and help the parent to understand the emotional aspects that underlie the child's actions. To employ this technique effectively, the adult must respect the child as a fallible human being who is by nature prone to making mistakes and errors. This attitude is based in compassion and empathy. Parents who are angry and critical of a child because of misbehavior often dictate their own solution to a problem, which tends to thwart thinking and reasoning on the child's part. Such behavior serves to discount the child rather than foster an understanding of why the child acts as he or she does.

A parent might also attempt to help the child identify and rectify the cause of the misbehavior. This approach is similar to that used by a mechanic fixing a malfunctioning engine. Ordinarily, mechanics do not scream in anger, condemn, or strike an engine because it has malfunctioned. They simply discover the cause of the malfunction and make repairs. A parent can approach a malfunctioning child in similar ways, first by attempting to identify what caused the problem behavior and then by helping the child make the necessary adjustments to his or her behavior.

4. *Facilitate children's opportunities to learn to think and reason and make choices for their actions.* A child who is granted the right to make personal decisions and to experience the consequences, both positive and negative, of those decisions will learn to be responsible

**Focus On 4–1**

**Is It OK to Spank?**

Consider these issues and findings from research studies on the effects of spanking children. Draw your own conclusions as to the advisability of using spanking as a means of discipline.

- There is a very strong association between experiencing harsh, abusive, physical punishment in childhood and being a perpetrator of violence in intimate relationships in adulthood (Swinford et al., 2000).
- Spanking as a means of discipline appears to be strongly ingrained in certain ethnic and cultural groups.
- Nevertheless, it appears to be a prevalent means of child maltreatment, frequently used as a last resort in gaining children's compliance to adult wishes (Buriel et al., 1991).
- Most spankings occur when adults are angry with children (Graziano & Namaste, 1990).
- Parents who are considered abusive to children by mental health professionals and by the court system consider spanking to be an acceptable means of discipline (Kelley, Grace, & Elliott, 1990).
- Spanking is used frequently as a replacement for positive communications with children about their behavior and parent's ideas about appropriate behavior (Larzelere et al., 1989).
- More boys than girls are spanked by parents (Day, Peterson, & McCracken, 1998; Lytton & Romney, 1991; Simons et al., 1991).
- Younger children (infants through preschool-age) are spanked by parents more than older children (school-age through adolescent) (Day, Peterson, & McCracken, 1998; Power & Chapieski, 1986; Walsh, 2002).
- Mothers are more likely to spank children than fathers, especially if they are young (Day, Peterson, & McCracken, 1998).
- Children who are spanked exhibit more aggressive behaviors than children who are not spanked (Aggarwal & Verma, 1987).
- Spanking is associated with children's negative feelings of self-esteem and personal worth (Larzelere et al., 1989; Straus, 1994).
- Males are more likely than females to approve of spanking children (Kelder et al., 1991).
- Spanking may produce a child's conformity to parental wishes in an immediate situation, but its long-term effects may include increased probability of deviance, including delinquency in adolescence and violent crime in adulthood (Straus, 1991a, 1991b).
- Children who are emotionally disturbed (and have been physically or sexually abused) are more likely to endorse (approve of) physical punishment than nonemotionally disturbed children (Strassberg et al., 1994).
- Parents who are members of fundamentalist Protestant religious groups prefer the use of spanking (corporal punishment) over alternate methods of discipline (Wiehe, 1990).
- Adults who spank children are likely to have been spanked by their parents as a primary means of controlling their misbehavior (Simons et al., 1991).
- Males who exhibit Type A personalities and behavioral tendencies—perfectionism, stressful feelings about time pressures, extraordinarily high achievement expectations for self and others, and high risk of coronary heart disease—experienced more frequent physical punishment by parents as children (McCranie & Simpson, 1986).
- Few children recommend that adults use physical punishment as a means of discipline (Carlson, 1986).
- Individuals who are considered to be bullies have been subjected to physical punishment/abuse as children and have learned that the use of physical force is an acceptable means of resolving conflicts with others (Floyd, 1985).

for his or her actions. Here the parent's role is to help in generating alternatives without supplying all the answers, options, or solutions all the time. The adult must determine which decisions a child can make and at what age. The parent who continually makes all the child's decisions and accepts responsibility for all the child's actions fosters dependency rather than autonomy in the child. By making their own decisions and living with the results, children learn to differentiate themselves from others and to establish personal boundaries.

5. *Learn to value the individual differences of children as interesting and positive tools for personal growth rather than require that everyone in the family system be the same.* Some family systems value sameness or rigid conformity in all members rather than seeing the benefits of individual differences in values, opinions, ideas, or means of self-expression (Richardson, 1999). Parenting and disciplining children in such family systems is approached with a "cookie cutter" mentality: Children are required to think and act like their parents and hold identical values and beliefs. The demand for sameness can kill a child's spirit and self-perception as an autonomous, unique human being who has the ability to reason and think and the right to be who he or she is.

Faced with the demand for sameness among family members, a child may react in one of several ways:

■ The child may comply with the rule of sameness by denial of his or her true self. The child will avoid conflict and seek peace at any price.

■ The child may rebel and seek self-definition by not acting as the parents wish, often in ways that are contrary to his or her own wishes.

■ The child may project blame on others rather than admit his or her own part in conflicts. A power struggle with parents is a typical result.

■ When the demand for sameness becomes overwhelming, the child may disengage emotionally from parents.

6. *Maintain a clear understanding that discipline should be based on helping children develop internal structure that is based on healthy self-esteem rather than fear, guilt, or shame.* Structure refers to the internalized controls that people acquire through socialization experiences that guide their behavior (Clarke & Dawson, 1998). Parents provide socialization experiences to their children through care, instruction, and rules that

result in children's self-disciplined actions (see Focus On 4–2). This differs drastically from the experiences of children who are raised by parents who use criticism, sarcasm, nagging, discounting, shame, and guilt to provide children with internal controls for their behavior. When parents attempt to shape and motivate children's development by instilling fear and shame about misbehavior, the children suffer a loss of self-esteem. Such children internalize what psychologists refer to as a critical parent aspect of their personality to motivate and regulate their behavior. As adults, such individuals respond to committing an error or transgression with guilt and shame. These emotions tend to block effective problem solving because the person's thinking skills become frozen and ineffective at reaching rational solutions to the problem at hand (Burns, 1999).

Rules provide an important aspect for helping children learn structure. When applied appropriately, rules provide children with a sense of protection and foster a sense of trust and security. Parents must teach children rules that are rational and serve to outline the limits to which children can go in their behavior by maintaining personal boundaries. If rules derive from parents' critical, judgmental, unloving positions promoted by authoritarian attitudes, the resulting discipline and structure provided for children will tend to be rigid and inflexible. Such rules and the ways parents enforce them become similar to the poisonous pedagogy of authoritarianism that causes children to acquire negative rather than positive structure.

Some parents provide implicit rules and inconsistent experiences, resulting in what is called *marshmallowing*, or abandonment of children's needs for adequate structure. Some rules will be negotiable while others, by necessity, will not. Negotiable rules will lead to healthy feelings of self-esteem in children. On the other hand, rigidity, inflexibility, having the majority of rules be nonnegotiable, and abandoning children's needs will damage children's self-esteem. An example of how these different parenting styles are applied to a hypothetical teenager's infraction of a family rule is given in Focus On 4–2. In four of these styles the structure provided for children is negative in nature and results for children. In two of these, which feature degrees of flexibility in applying rules, the structure parents provide is positive in nature and results for children.

When enforcing rules, it is wise for parents to decide how and when to use their authority, when to be lenient,

**Focus On 4–2**

## Identifying Positive and Negative Structure by Parenting Style

There are six possible ways that parents provide or fail to provide structure for their children. These are arranged below from left to right in order of degree of strictness. For example, the parenting style *Rigidity* is characterized by having the highest degree of strictness, whereas the parenting style *Abandonment* has no rules. Although these two styles lie at opposite ends of the continuum, they are similar in their effects upon children. The two parenting styles *Nonnegotiable Rules* and *Negotiable Rules* are the patterns that support and facilitate children's development of healthy structure and are the most helpful to both children and parents. The other four parenting styles, *Rigidity*, *Criticism*, *Marshmallow*, and *Abandonment*, do not provide children with healthy structure and are considered negative in their effects.

### Hypothetical Situation: Fifteen-year-old drank alcoholic beverages.

| *Rigidity* | *Criticism* | *Nonnegotiable Rules* |
|---|---|---|
| *Characteristics:* | | |
| Rigidity, supposedly for the child's welfare, springs from fear. It consists of old rules "written in concrete" sometime in the past and usually for someone else. These rules often ignore the developmental tasks of the child. It threatens abuse and/or withdrawing love to enforce compliance; doesn't believe children should have a say in working things out. | Criticism labels the person with bad names rather than setting standards for acceptable behavior. Criticism often includes global words such as "never" and "always." It negates children and suggests ways to fail. Ridicule, which issues a bitter and mocking invitation for contemptuous laughter, is a devastating form of criticism. | Reasonable, nonnegotiable rules build self-esteem in children. Nonnegotiable rules must be followed. Children come to know they can count on these rules and that there are rewards when they are followed and negative consequences when they are broken. However, even though nonnegotiable rules are firmly set and firmly enforced, they are not "rigid" and can be rewritten for the welfare of the family and its members. |
| *Example:* | | |
| "If you ever touch alcohol again, don't bother coming home." | "You're always doing something stupid. Now you are drinking, just like your dad." | "You may not drink alcohol until you've reached legal age. There are penalties. They are . . . " |
| *Underlying Messages Children Hear:* | | |
| You are not important. Don't think. Don't be. You will be abandoned if you make a mistake. Don't trust your own competence. | Don't be who you are. Don't be successful. Don't be capable. You are not lovable. | Your welfare and safety are important. Your parents are willing and able to be responsible and enforce the rules. |

| *Negotiable Rules* | *Marshmallow* | *Abandonment* |
|---|---|---|
| *Characteristics:* | | |
| Negotiable rules teach children how to think clearly and to problem solve, helping them raise their self-esteem. These rules are negotiated and then firmly enforced. When they are designed to support a nonnegotiable | Marshmallow parenting grants freedom without demanding responsibility in return. It sounds supportive, but it implies the child does not have to or is not capable of following rules. It discounts the child's ability and | Abandonment consists of a lack of rules, protection, and contact. It tells the child the adult is not available for him. If teasing is offered when a child needs structure or approval, that teasing, constitutes abandonment. |

*(continued)*

**Focus On 4–2**    *(continued)*

rule, they can be adjusted to match maturing skills and needs. The process of negotiating provides children an opportunity to argue with parents, learn about the relevancy of rules, and learn to be responsible for themselves in new ways.

gives the child permission to be irresponsible and to fail, to be helpless and hopeless. At the same time, it lets the parent look good, play the martyr, or feel in control.

*Example:*

"You may find yourself around kids whose number-one priority is drinking. Find other things to do so you don't spend all your free time with those kids."

"If all the kids drink, I suppose you can," or "You're too young to drink and drive, so you can have a kegger here," or "Boys will be boys!"

"I don't want to talk about it," or makes fun of pain or humiliates the child. Parent is not available (either physically or emotionally), is drunk, irrational, or ignores or teases instead of responding to the child.

*Underlying Messages Children Hear:*

You can think, negotiate, and initiate. Your needs are important and others' needs are important. You must deal with how things really are. You are expected to be powerful in positive ways for yourself and others.

Don't be competent or responsible. Don't be who you are. Don't grow up. You can have your way and be obnoxious and get by with it. I need to continue taking care of you. My needs are more important than your needs.

I am not willing to care for you; I don't want you. Your needs are not important; mine are. No one is here for you. You don't exist.

### *Rigidity*

### *Criticism*

### *Nonnegotiable Rules*

*Common Responses of Children:*

Feels oppressed, distanced, angry, scared, hopeless, imperfect, discounted, mistrusted, abandoned, no good.

Feels powerless and diminished, rejected, hurt, humiliated, squashed, angry, unimportant, inadequate, scared, discounted.

Feels safe, cared for, powerful, helped, responsible, accounted for, and may feel frustrated, irritated, and resistant at times. Learns to follow rules and be responsible.

*Decisions Children Make:*

I am not wanted. Parents don't care about me. Rules are more important than my needs. I will let others think. I will comply, rebel, or withdraw. I will blame myself.

I have to know what I don't know. I will try harder, be strong, be perfect. If I don't do things right, I am a bad person. I can't be good enough. I am hopeless. Why bother?

There are some rules I have to follow. I can learn from my mistakes. I am a good person. I'm lovable and capable. They care about me and take care of me.

**Focus On 4–2**    *(continued)*

| **Negotiable Rules** | **Marshmallow** | **Abandonment** |
|---|---|---|
| *Common Responses of Children:* | | |
| Feels respected, cared for, listened to, powerful, important, loved, intelligent, safe, and sometimes frustrated. Learns to evaluate rules and participate in the making of rules as well as to follow rules and be responsible. | Feels patronized and kept little, remains incompetent in order to please parent. Feels undermined, crazy, manipulated, discounted, unloved, unsatisfied, and angry. | Feels scared, terrified, hurt, angry, rejected, discounted, baffled, unimportant, upset, like a nonbeing. Perhaps suicidal. |
| *Decisions Children Make:* | | |
| It's OK for me to grow up and still be dependent at times. I can think things through and get help doing that. I continually expand my ability to be responsible and competent. | I must take care of other people's feelings and needs, or I don't need to care about anyone but me. I am not capable of learning how to value and take care of myself. If help is offered, mistrust it or at least expect to pay a price for it, but don't expect helpful structure from others. | Don't ask for or expect help. No one cares. If I am to survive, I will have to do it by myself. If help is offered, mistrust it. Help and trust are a joke. |

*Source:* Adapted from Clark, J. L., & Dawson, C. (1998). *Growing up again: Parenting ourselves, parenting our children* (2nd ed.). Minneapolis, MN: Hazelden.

and when to penalize children for misbehavior. Rules constitute a significant aspect of the patterns that govern the functioning of the family system and the parent-child microenvironment. Without some form of rules, the family system cannot function effectively for the benefit of its members. It is essential that rules for children's welfare and development be formed rationally rather than emotionally.

7. *Discipline is most effective when provided to children within an atmosphere of nurturance.* By nurturing their children, parents show them that they are loved and are lovable unconditionally (Clarke & Dawson, 1998).

Nurturance relates to all the ways in which we demonstrate love, not only for others but also for ourselves. Nurturing another involves touching, noticing, and caring for that person in ways that are healthy. Nurturance is expressed to children in two basic forms and in many variations of these forms. **Assertive care** is expressed when a parent knows and determines what a child's needs are and responds to those needs in loving ways that generate a sense of trust within the child. Assertive care involves noticing and listening to the child and understanding the cues and requests the child offers. **Supportive care** is provided as children grow older and can make decisions for themselves about what kinds of attention and care they need from their parents. In providing supportive care, parents offer care at appropriate times, and children are free to accept or decline the care (see Focus On 4–3).

**Focus On
4–3**

## Identifying Positive and Negative Nurturance

Unconditional love for a child is generated through parental actions that represent the two facets of nurturance known as assertive care and supportive care. These lead children to experience joy, hope, self-confidence, and self-esteem. When children are loved conditionally, parental actions demonstrate that there are limits and controls to when and how a child is loved and under what conditions or circumstances. Such conditional parental actions are observed when parents abuse children physically, mentally, and/or emotionally; provide conditional care; act indulgently; and neglect children physically, mentally, and/or emotionally. Such treatment leads children to experience despair, joylessness, depression, and loneliness, all of which are damaging to self-esteem and feelings of self-worth.

### Situation: School-age child has a badly scraped arm.

| *Abuse* | *Conditional Love* | *Assertive Care* |
|---|---|---|
| *Characteristics:* | | |
| Abuse is relating to a child by assault, by physical or psychological invasion, or by direct or indirect "don't be" messages. Abuse negates the child's needs. | Parents who use conditional care connect with the child by the use of threats and conditions. The care the parent gives the child is based on the parent's needs and expectations, not on the child's needs. | Assertive care is comforting and loving. It is freely given; it is helpful to the child, responsive to the child's needs, and appropriate to the circumstance. |
| *Example:* | | |
| Parent does not care for wounds. Says, "Stop sniffling or I'll give you something to cry about." Parent yells at or shakes child. | Parent says: "Stop crying or I won't bandage your arm." | Parent gives loving care and a hug, cleans and dresses the wound, and says, "Your arm is scraped! I'm sorry." |
| *Underlying Messages Children Hear:* | | |
| You don't count. Your needs don't count. You are not lovable. You don't deserve to exist. To get what you need, you must expect pain. | I matter and you don't. Your needs and feelings don't count. You can have care as long as you earn it. Don't believe you are lovable; you have to earn love. | I love you and you are lovable. You are important. Your needs are important. I care for you willingly. |
| *Common Responses of Children:* | | |
| Pain in the heart, as well as pain in the scraped arm. Fear, terror, rage, withdrawal, loneliness, despair, shame. | Pain in the heart, as well as pain in the scraped arm. Fear, terror, anger, mistrust of own perceptions, shame, feelings of inadequacy. | Pain in the arm and warmth in the heart. Feels comforted, accepted, important, satisfied, relieved, secure, safe, loved. |

**Focus On 4–3**   *(continued)*

| Supportive Care | Indulgence | Neglect |
|---|---|---|

*Characteristics:*

Nurturing support offers help, comfort, and love. It encourages the child to think and do what he or she is capable of doing for himself or herself.

Indulgence is a sticky, patronizing kind of love. It promotes continuing dependence on the parents and teaches the child not to think for himself or herself and not to be responsible for self or to others.

Neglect is passive abuse. It is lack of attention, emotionally or physically, by parents who are unavailable or who ignore the needs of the child. These parents may be "there, but not there."

*Example:*

Parent, who has already taught child how to clean a scrape, says in a concerned and loving tone, "I see you've scraped your arm. Does it hurt? Do you want to take care of it yourself or would you like some help from me?" Offers a hug.

Parent rushes to child. Says, "Oh, look at your arm, you poor thing. That really stings! I'll bandage it. Go and lie down in front of the television and I'll do your chores for you."

Parent ignores the scrape. Says, "Don't bother me."

*Common Responses of Children:*

Pain in the arm and a heart filled with confidence. Child feels cared for, comforted, challenged, secure, and trust-worthy.

Pain in the arm and uncertainty in the heart. Self-centered satisfaction, temporary comfort. Later on: helplessness, confusion, obligation, resentment, defensiveness, and shame.

Pain in the heart, as well as pain in the scraped arm. Feelings of abandonment, fear, shame, rage, hopelessness, helplessness, abject disappointment.

| Abuse | Conditional Love | Assertive Care |
|---|---|---|

*Decisions Often Made by Children:*

I am not powerful. I deserve to die, or the reverse, I will live in spite of them. It's my fault, or the reverse, I'll blame everything on others. I'll be good, or the reverse, I'll be bad. Big people get to abuse, or I can abuse those smaller than me, or I will never abuse. I won't feel or have needs. Love does not exist. I am alone; I keep emotional distance from, and don't trust, others. I blame or strike or leave first.

I am what I do. I must strive to please. Big people get what they want. I can never do enough. I must be perfect. I don't deserve love. There is a scarcity of love. I must be strong. Love obligates me and is costly. I don't trust. I do keep emotional distance, run away, or blame others.

I am important. I deserve care. It's OK to ask for what I need. I belong here. I am loved. Others can be trusted and relied upon. I can know what I need. It's OK to be dependent at times.

*(continued)*

**Focus On
4–3**

*(continued)*

| *Supportive Care* | *Indulgence* | *Neglect* |
|---|---|---|

*Decisions Often Made by Children:*

| | | |
|---|---|---|
| I am loved. I can know what I need. I am capable. I can be powerful. I am not alone. It's OK to ask for help. I am both separate and connected. I can decide when to be dependent and when to be independent. | I am not capable. I don't have to be competent. I don't have to know what I need, think, or feel. Other people are obligated to take care of me. I don't have to grow up. I must be loyal to my indulging parent. To get my needs met, I manipulate or play a victim role. It's OK to be self-centered. Later on: be wary and don't trust. | I don't really know who I am or what's right. I am not important or powerful. I am not lovable. I die or survive alone. It isn't possible or safe to get close, to trust, or to ask for help. I do not deserve help. What I do doesn't count if someone has to help me. Life is hard. |

*Source:* Adapted from Clarke, J. L., & Dawson, D. (1998). *Growing up again: Parenting ourselves, parenting our children* (2nd ed.). Minneapolis, MN: Hazelden.

Both forms of care derive from love that is unconditional. This means that love is given freely, without expectations, without limits, and without measure. The parent's message to the child is, "I love you because you are who you are."

In reality, both assertive and supportive care can be given by parents in ways that are both positive and negative. When assertive and supportive care are offered positively and consistently, children's growth and development as individuals are facilitated in healthy ways. When care is offered negatively or inconsistently, love is conditional rather than unconditional and manifests as conditional care, indulgence, or abuse and neglect (Clarke & Dawson, 1998). These represent harshness in relating to children, resulting in negative and harmful effects that are seen in children's unhealthy self-esteem. Parents' treatment of children when applying discipline teaches children about themselves and leads them to make conclusions about their self-worth.

• • • • • • • • • • • • • • • • • • • • • • • • • • • •

### Parenting Reflection 4–2

What is the difference between child abuse and disciplining children?

• • • • • • • • • • • • • • • • • • • • • • • • • • • •

• • • • • • • • • • • • • • • • • • • • • • • • • • • •

*Focus Point.*    Many people believe that discipline is synonymous with punishment. However, discipline refers to teaching children appropriate behaviors through positive means. Parents need to discuss those ways of discipline that are acceptable to them by developing rules and boundaries that provide children with structure and teach them to internalize self-discipline.

• • • • • • • • • • • • • • • • • • • • • • • • • • • •

## METHODS AND APPROACHES

In Chapter 1, we noted that changes have taken place in parenting as various strategies of child-rearing rose and fell in popularity. What was appropriate for one generation became inappropriate for the next. Knowledge gained from studies of human development and behavior contributed to much of this vacillation. In the process of applying the various strategies to interactions with children, parents have come to realize that there is no single, adequate method for being an effective, competent parent. However, many publications on this topic continue to appear each year, and they sell very well.

A plethora of child-rearing experts has emerged within the past 50 years, each advocating a particular approach to discipline. Three strategies that have survived the tests of time and practice are discussed in this section: behavior modification and social learning, the democratic approach to child training, and Parent Effectiveness Training. The popularity of these strategies derives from their effective, but not absolute, methods that parents can learn and apply in daily interactions with children to achieve long-range goals. Each of these strategies is representative of modern applied behavioral science. None guarantees consistent results in children's behavior or in parents' interactions with children.

## Behavior Modification and Social Learning

**Behavior Modification.**  Using behavior modification techniques (Bloch, 2003), parents teach children acceptable behavior by weakening undesirable behavior and reinforcing desirable behavior. All behavior is a learned response, according to this view. Just as a child is taught to read, so he or she is taught to behave in a given manner in a variety of situations. A parent intentionally or unintentionally encourages and shapes certain behaviors in a child by responding to how the child acts. A child learns to adopt a given behavior pattern if it accomplishes a desired goal. Several publications describe how behavior modification procedures shape desired responses and acts of children by parents (Van Houten & Hall, 2001).

***Basic Concepts.***  The basic concepts and approaches used in behavior modification are: (1) all behavior is learned; (2) behavior is a function of its consequences; (3) a given behavior is encouraged and taught when it is immediately rewarded or reinforced; (4) reinforcement may be either positive or negative in nature; (5) learning may generalize from one situation or setting to another.

All approaches based on behavior modification emphasize that an awareness of environmental events as well as the context in which behavior occurs are necessary to fully comprehend the nature of stimuli that control behavior. Not only do such approaches stress that all behavior is learned, but that whatever is learned can be unlearned, changed, or modified.

The basic premise of behavior modification theory is that individuals adjust their behavior according to its consequences. Essentially, people behave in ways that result in positive consequences and avoid behaving in ways that result in negative consequences (Figure 4–4). Stated thus, this view may seem overly simplistic. However, several factors influence the development and occurrence of behavior and the ways in which behavior can be changed or modified.

***Reinforcement.***  The concept of reinforcement maintains that a *reinforcement* (reward) that immediately follows a particular behavior increases the likelihood that the behavior will occur again in the future. All

**FIGURE 4–4.**  Parental responses to child behavior that are positive in nature, like hugs and smiles, can shape future child behavior.

reinforcers are considered to be stimuli and are either positive or negative. A *positive reward* (positive reinforcer) increases the likelihood that a particular behavior will occur again. An example of positive reinforcement might be praising a child for using good table manners. It is important that the positive reinforcement (praise, in this instance) *immediately follows* the occurrence of the desired behavior. Performance of the act thus becomes associated with its reinforcement. *Negative reinforcement* occurs when an unpleasant stimulus is removed, thus increasing the likelihood that a particular behavior will occur again. An unpleasant stimulus associated with a certain type of behavior becomes reinforcing when its withdrawal is a positive or pleasurable experience. For example, the discomfort of having something stuck painfully between one's teeth is removed by flossing. In this example, flossing is a negative reinforcer because it removes an unpleasant stimulus rather than adds one to a behavioral act.

### Parenting Reflection 4–3

If positive reinforcement is so effective in producing desirable behavior from children, why do so many parents continue to use physical punishment as a means to gain the same effect with children?

**Extinction.** Behavior modification includes the concept of extinction of behaviors that are undesired or unpleasant. This concept is illustrated by a student teacher who ignores the whining behaviors of children. The undesirable behavior is not reinforced when the teacher's attention is not given. Likewise, undesired behaviors of children that are not reinforced by attention from parents will eventually cease. This is a difficult process for many parents, however. The number of times a behavior must be ignored is often excessive, and it may take a long time for the child to eliminate it from his or her repertoire of behaviors.

**Reinforcement Schedule.** Another factor that is important to the success of behavior modification approaches is the frequency with which reinforcers are used. Researchers have discovered that continuous reinforcement of behaviors is not desirable. Rather, reinforcement that is intermittent may achieve most effective results. Two dimensions distinguish this approach to reinforcement. First, the desired behavior may be reinforced according to the number of occurrences. For example, a child may receive reinforcement only after he or she correctly pronounces five words consecutively. Second, the amount of time between behaviors may determine when reinforcement is given. For example, the child may receive reinforcement every other minute while he or she is talking, or there may be a variable amount of time between reinforcements, such as once after 1 minute, again after 3 minutes, and again after 10 minutes.

These methods involving reinforcement to teach children desirable behaviors are among the most powerful tools of discipline available to adults. However, the reinforcement process can be applied by children to adult behavior as well. Through reciprocal feedback, children also teach behavior patterns to their parents by applying their own brand of reinforcers. When an adult nags loudly, for example, a child usually tunes out the adult's unpleasant behavior by not listening, thus reinforcing the nagging behavior. Similarly, a child who wishes the attention of parents learns to act in a manner that reinforces parental attention.

**Social Learning.** Social learning theory explains how learning may occur when there is no visible reinforcer or reward. This theory is especially useful in explaining how socialization occurs or how someone learns appropriate behaviors based on family beliefs and values. According to this theory, an individual responds to a number of complex stimuli in forming associations between appropriate and inappropriate behavior. Conscious thought, rather than automatic response to a stimulus, assists in shaping behavior and actions.

This approach focuses on the importance of the role of a **model** or the effect of observation learning also known as *imitation*. Many kinds of behaviors are believed to be acquired by watching the behavior of another person and then replicating the observed behavior in one's own actions.

Research into this type of learning shows how children learn to express such social behaviors as sharing and cooperation as well as aggression and violence by watching such behaviors demonstrated by a model. Models include both real people and characters seen in media presentations. Research reveals that when children see a model being rewarded for acting aggressively, for instance, they are more likely to demonstrate that same kind of behavior in their own play.

Social learning theory also explains how people acquire social values and attitudes. Social roles are learned in this manner. Children imitate behaviors they observe in adults and in other children they perceive as models. For example, social learning accounts for how sex-role behaviors or scripts are acquired in childhood.

••••••••••••••••••••••••••••••••••••••••••••••••••

***Focus Point.***    Behavior modification is a highly reliable method for eliciting desired behaviors from children through the effective, conscientious application of positive reinforcement. Behaviors can be shaped by using reinforcement and paying close attention to the time when reinforcement is given. Social learning theory emphasizes the influence of modeling and observation as a means for learning a variety of social behaviors and roles.

••••••••••••••••••••••••••••••••••••••••••••••••••

## Democratic Child Training

The democratic approach to child training is based on principles from Adlerian psychology, an approach used in family therapy. Rudolf Driekurs (1950) and his colleagues present a strategy for parenting and discipline that emphasizes democratic means of family operation such as encouragement, setting appropriate limits, practicing mutual respect for members, and collective decision making. A parent education curriculum that teaches this strategy is called Systematic Training for Effective Parenting (STEP). Compared to other strategies, the democratic approach appears to show more consistently significant outcomes as a means of attaining parenting goals, according to some researchers (Dembo, Switzer, & Lauritzen, 1985; Krebs, 1986; Ring, 2001).

The democratic approach is based on the following assumptions (Dinkmeyer, 1979; Dinkmeyer & Driekurs, 2000; Dinkmeyer & McKay, 1981; Driekurs, 1950): (1) behavior is purposeful and caused; it does not happen by chance; (2) it is necessary to understand behavior within its social context; (3) goals of misbehavior explain unacceptable actions of children; (4) to understand a child's behavior, one needs to understand the child's interpretation of the events he or she experiences; (5) belonging to social groups is a basic need of people, regardless of age; (6) people, including children, develop a life plan (script) that guides their behavioral decisions, even though these decisions may be based on faulty assumptions and logic.

These assumptions form the basis for parents' interactions with a child (Magen, Levin, & Yeshurun, 1991). The starting point for developing an effective, loving relationship with a child is for the adult to learn the impact of the family system in shaping the child's emerging patterns of behavior. The family system is seen as the child's model for all social interactions with others (Driekurs, 1950).

The *life plan* or *script* is the consistent pattern of decision making by which people make choices for their behavior. It is encouraged and developed first within the family system. The life plan is based on decisions about how to act, which relate to the goals one works for in his or her actions. A child discovers this plan for behavior to be effective in solving certain interaction problems within the family system and especially within the sibling and parent-child subsystems. As children grow older, they develop a personal logic to justify actions that make up the life plan. Different life plans emerge under each of the different parenting conditions outlined in Focus On 4–3: abuse, neglect, conditional love, indulgence, assertive care, and supportive care. If a parent consistently responds to children's behaviors in an indulgent manner, the child may adopt a life plan that involves being manipulative, self-indulgent, and self-centered (see section labeled "Decisions Often Made by Children" in Focus On 4–3). When children are taught in ways that cause them to reach faulty conclusions about themselves or they draw these conclusions on their own, they develop life scripts containing behavioral choices that support these faulty conclusions.

Four basic goals of misbehavior occur from flaws in the logic of the life plan (see Table 4–1).

1. *Attention getting.* The child exhibits positive or negative behaviors that make others notice him or her, such as showing off or crying.
2. *Social power.* The child controls others by only doing what he or she wants and refusing to cooperate.
3. *Revenge.* The child retaliates for being hurt and feeling unloved by misbehaving.
4. *Displaying inadequacy.* Failure in all endeavors becomes expected and is used by the child to escape participation in interactions with others.

**TABLE 4-1.** The Goals of Misbehavior

| Child's Faulty Belief | Child's Goal | Parent's Feeling and Reaction | Child's Response to Parent's Attempts at Correction | Alternatives for Parents |
|---|---|---|---|---|
| I belong *only* when I am being noticed. | Attention | *Feeling:* Annoyed. *Reaction:* Tendency to remind and coax. | Temporarily stops misbehavior. Later resumes same behavior or disturbs in another way. | Ignore misbehavior when possible. Give attention for positive behavior when child is not making a bid for it. |
| I belong *only* if I am in control or am the boss, or when I am proving no one can boss me! | Power | *Feeling:* Angry, provoked, as if one's authority is threatened. *Reaction:* Tendency to fight or to give in. | Active- or passive-aggressive misbehavior is intensified, or child submits with "defiant compliance." | Withdraw from conflict. Help child to see how to use power constructively by appealing for child's help and enlisting cooperation. Realize that fighting or giving in only increases the child's desire for power. |
| I belong *only* by hurting others as I feel hurt. I cannot be loved. | Revenge | *Feeling:* Deeply hurt. *Reaction:* Tendency to retaliate or get even. | Seeks further revenge by intensifying misbehavior or choosing another weapon. | Avoid feeling hurt. Avoid punishment and retaliation. Build trusting relationship; convince child that she or he is loved. |
| I belong *only* by convincing others not to expect anything from me. I am unable; I am helpless. | Display inadequacy | *Feeling:* Despair; hopelessness. "I give up." *Reaction:* Tendency to agree with child that nothing can be done. | Passively responds or fails to respond to whatever is done. Shows no improvement. | Stop all criticism. Encourage any positive attempt, no matter how small; focus on assets. Above all, don't be hooked into pity, and don't give up. |

*Source:* Reprinted by permission of American Guidance Service, Publishers' Building, Circle Pines, MN. *Parents' handbook: Systematic training for effective parenting* by Don Dinkmeyer, Sr., and Gary D. McKay. Copyright © 1981. All rights reserved.

Democratic child training recognizes the impact of a child's sibling subsystem in influencing behavior. Driekurs believes that a child's birth order and position among siblings in the family system act to shape the life plan the child adopts. Competition for parents' attention, alliances that emerge between siblings, and different parental expectations for behavior of siblings account for differences in life plans and personalities of children from the same family system. For example, a first-born child may learn to adopt behavior patterns that work toward achieving the goal of power, or of power with revenge, first in interactions with siblings and parents and later with persons outside the family system. Being the oldest child generally brings heavy responsibilities and high expectations from parents. Competition for parental attention and affection may be intense, with the next child in the sibling constellation seen as an adversary who usurped the position of the first born in receiving the majority of attention from parents.

According to Driekurs, the second child is made to feel inferior to the older child through their interactions. The older child makes the younger child feel that he or she has to catch up with or be better than the older sibling. This child may learn patterns of behavior designed to meet goals of displaying inadequacy or power with revenge in interactions with others.

The middle child may learn power-oriented or attention-getting types of behavior to make himself or herself noticed among siblings. The youngest child—the baby of the family—may learn patterns that achieve goals of getting others' attention or displaying inadequacy.

**Logical Versus Natural Consequences.**   A key element of this strategy featured strongly in the STEP program is teaching children the logical consequences of their behavior as opposed to using rewards or punishment. In this guidance technique, authoritarianism is replaced with allowing the child to assume personal responsibility for his or her own actions (Ring, 2001).

A natural consequence results obviously and immediately from a given action: If you touch a hot stove, you get burned. Natural consequences are sometimes either too dangerous to be allowed or too remote in time to be effective in teaching children the results of their actions. In such cases, the parent must substitute a logical consequence, a consequence that is a rational result of a given action. For example, if a child arrives home after the evening meal has been served, the logical consequence to the child's tardiness (which should have been established and agreed to by all family members in advance) is that the child must prepare his or her own meal or else eat cold food. When this logical consequence to tardiness is administered consistently, the child eventually concludes that to avoid the unpleasant consequence of not being on time for meals, he or she must watch the time more carefully. This technique places the

---

**Parenting FAQs 4–1**

**My mother is critical of me for always praising my child. She says that too much praise is bad for her because she'll learn to depend on praise from everyone when she does something well. Is my mother right about this?**

**A:**   Not exactly. Praise in and of itself isn't harmful for children. It sounds like your mother is speaking of the old-fashioned notion that too much parental attention spoils children. It is true that you can give so much praise and recognition that these become ineffective. Children either learn to tune you out or they might even become dependent on approval. This might be the reaction your mother fears. However, dependency on parental approval usually develops when children grow up with parents who are severely critical of just about everything they do and consequently fail to get enough praise and recognition. A parent who praises is preferable to one who is constantly critical of children. However, you will be doing your child a great injustice if you do not teach her how to learn to praise and reward herself when she does something well or appropriate. People who develop healthy self-respect know that self-praise and recognition help to maintain those personal good feelings about oneself. It also helps in learning to be less dependent on others for their approval.

responsibility for both the choice of behavior and its consequences on the child, not the parent. Thus, a child learns to think, make plans, weigh consequences of decisions, and accept responsibility for those decisions.

A consequence must be experienced fully and consistently by a child before it can be an effective learning tool. Parents must resist the temptation to intervene and prevent the child from experiencing the consequence. When parents take pity on children and intervene, children learn that someone else will take responsibility for their actions. They also learn to pity themselves when they must endure the consequences of their actions.

**Encouragement Instead of Reward or Punishment.** A major tenet of this strategy is that stimulation from within is more effective in producing desirable behavior than is pressure from without (Edgar, 1985). In this strategy, encouragement replaces reward and logical consequences replace punishment. Encouragement and reward are different in both timing and effect. Encouragement is given before an act takes place; a reward is given afterward. Encouragement is given not only upon success, but upon experiencing difficulty or failure; a reward is given only when one succeeds.

**The Family Council.** The democratic basis of this strategy is reflected in the use of the family council or meeting as a means of reaching agreements, communicating effectively, and helping children develop a sense of participation in the family (Figure 4–5). It is suggested that these meetings occur on a regular basis, and that children be allowed an equal voice and vote in reaching family decisions. Such decisions may relate to establishing logical consequences to family rules, determining use of family resources, and resolving disputes among members.

••••••••••••••••••••••••••••••••••••••••••••••••••••

***Focus Point.*** The democratic approach to discipline strives to help children learn to become self-disciplined by experiencing the logical consequences of their behavior. Children's misbehaviors are seen to relate to the particular goal they wish to achieve through their behavior, which in turn is related to their particular life script. Encouragement is an important tool that is preferred over rewards or punishment. Family councils are recommended as a means to enable children to participate in family decision making.

••••••••••••••••••••••••••••••••••••••••••••••••••••

## Parent Effectiveness Training

Thomas Gordon's text *Parent Effectiveness Training* (1975/2000) represents a humanistic strategy for promoting a healthy relationship between parents and children. It is an outgrowth of a course Gordon developed to teach parents how to be more effective in their caregiving and disciplinary activities. The strategy focuses primarily on communication skills developed by the par-

**FIGURE 4–5.** Families can gather to discuss issues, reach agreements, and develop a sense of togetherness. Meal times may be the most convenient time for such meetings in contemporary families.

ent and a method of resolving conflicts that occur between the parent and child. As with other humanistic methods, such as those promoted by Ginott (1965), this strategy teaches the parent when to act as a counselor to children regarding their behavior. The strategy is grounded firmly in proven counseling methods developed by other professionals and applied to parenting skills by Gordon. The Parent Effectiveness Training (PET) program provides a useful battery of techniques for parents to use in their program of discipline (Wood & Davidson, 2003). Although there is a good possibility that these work well when performed appropriately by parents, their overuse may lead a child to tune out the parents, rendering their efforts ineffectual. Children of parents who have received this training exhibit greater self-reliance on problem solving and a higher degree of self-esteem. Like other strategies, PET is designed to achieve a more effective manner of communicating and interacting with children.

1.  *The parent acts as a counselor when a child has a particular problem.*    In this role, the parent engages in active listening, a common therapeutic technique used in many counseling methods. Instead of rescuing the child by offering solutions and suggestions for solving the problem for the child, the parent listens to the child and sifts through the child's statements to determine the feelings being covertly communicated. The parent then responds with what he or she perceives the problem to be as stated by the child. The goal is for the parent to empathize with the child, thus providing a nurturing response, objectively reflect back to the child the parent's perception of the problem, and allow the child to search for his or her own solution. In the following example, notice how the father uses active listening to help the child solve his problem.

DAD: Why aren't you playing with the other kids?

BOY: Nobody wants to play with me.

DAD: You feel that you don't have any friends and that makes you feel bad, huh? (*paraphrasing what is not being said but is assumed to be embedded in the message; reflecting the emotions in the message*)

BOY: Yeah. I hate Tommy and all the others.

DAD: You just hate them all. (*reflecting the emotion in the last message*)

BOY: Yeah. Especially Tommy.

DAD: He's the worst, huh? Why is that? (*reflecting the meaning and the emotion of the last message; taking an investigative stance*)

BOY: He makes fun of me because I don't always throw the ball right.

DAD: It really makes you feel bad when he teases you. (*reflecting the meaning and the emotion of the last message*)

BOY: You bet. He shouldn't do that to me. It hurts people's feelings when they get teased.

DAD: You think it's OK to make mistakes and Tommy needs to feel that way, too. (*reflecting the meaning and the emotion of the last message*)

BOY: Yeah. He calls me names. I don't like that. I don't do that to him when he goofs up.

DAD: You would get along better with Tommy if he didn't call you names when you goof up, and you wish he'd treat you like you try to treat him. (*reflecting the meaning and the emotion of the last message*)

BOY: You bet. I'm his friend, but I don't like it when he calls me names.

DAD: You think you're Tommy's friend, and friends should try to treat each other fairly and decently. Seems like you've got a problem about this. What do you think you can do to straighten things out? (*reflecting the meaning and emotion of the last message; bringing closure to the discussion by indicating that the solutions generated are the child's responsibility*)

BOY: Well, I think I need to tell Tommy how I don't want him to call me names when I goof up. Maybe I can ask him to show me how to throw the ball better. Then he won't call me names!

This hypothetical interchange allowed the father to help his son express feelings about the real issue that bothered him: being treated unfairly by his friend. The child's initial statement had many underlying feelings, implications, messages, and meanings that the father helped the child identify. The father did not offer his own solution to the child's problem ("You're bigger than Tommy. Get out there and knock his block off!"), nor did he admonish the child ("You're acting like a baby. Get used to being teased; there'll be a lot of it in your lifetime."). The father did not moralize ("You're a bigger person than Tommy. Now get out there and show him what you're made of!") or discount his son for those feelings ("You shouldn't feel like that. If I were you, I'd start

**Parenting FAQs 4–2**

**What do you think about using threats to gain children's cooperation with parents' wishes? Do these work?**

**A:**   Not really, especially in the long term. Threats usually are used when parents are feeling exasperated, tired, powerless, or otherwise at their wits' end. Sometimes *they* are used because a parent doesn't know of any other way to gain children's cooperation. Threats often act to stimulate children's noncompliance with parental wishes, promoting an "I-dare-you" stance between parents and children. These can develop into power plays between parents and children that are not healthy for the relationship. Instead of helping children learn about how to achieve win-win solutions to problems, threats force a no-win attitude upon children. Using forceful threats can also promote a fear of adults in children and damage their self-respect by the discounting nature of some threats.

A major problem with using threats is that they often involve hollow consequences or ones that are difficult to enforce. Imagine the reaction of a 5-year-old to hearing a mother's threat, "If you don't stop doing that, I'll slap you so hard you'll be looking backwards the rest of your life!" Such threats do not make sense to children and may instill fear and mistrust about parents to children.

Using positive alternatives such as choices rather than threats may help to gain children's cooperation with rules that have clearly identifiable consequences. For example:

> **Threat:** This is the last time I'm telling you to stop what you're doing and come to dinner or else you'll go hungry tonight.
>
> **Alternative:** It's time to stop playing and put your things away where they belong. You can have either 5 or 10 minutes to do this now.
>
> **Threat:** If you don't stay with me while we're in the store, you'll have to sit in the car by yourself until I'm finished shopping.
>
> **Alternative:** The rule is that you must stay with me while I'm shopping. If you can't do that, I'll have to take you back home and call the sitter to stay with you while I do my shopping.
>
> **Threat:** I'm going to turn this car around and head back home if I hear one more scream from anybody in the back seat.
>
> **Alternative:** I can't drive the car safely when there's all this screaming and loud noises coming from children. I'll have to pull over if it doesn't stop now. We'll be late and may not be able to see the movie because you kids won't calm down.

*Source:* Adapted in part from A. Faber. (1995). *How to talk so kids can learn—at home and in school.* New York: Rawson Associates.

practicing right now on my ball throwing so nobody could have the chance to tease me."). These responses fall into the categories of conditional love and criticism and would not promote healthy structure and nurturance. The father provided assertive and supportive care by recognizing the child's feelings of hurt and rejection and helping him reach his own solution to the problem.

2.   *Parents can express their feelings to children about troublesome behavior in nondamaging ways.*   On those occasions when a child's behavior is a problem to a parent, the child may not know that he or she is causing a problem, or the child may be testing a parent's limits. At times, children just can't seem to resist the temptation to misbehave, even though they know they will get into trouble for doing so. In such situations, where the parent "owns" the problem (that is, the child's behavior is a problem because it is troublesome to the parent), Gordon suggests that the adult use a strongly phrased "I" message to communicate the problem to the child.

Without having learned to do otherwise, most adults phrase an initial sentence about someone's offensive behavior with a sentence beginning with *you:* "You're acting stupid," "You are doing that all wrong," or "You are driving me crazy with all that noise." Such "you" messages occur especially in cases where the adult is angry about the other person's behavior. Gordon suggests that a different sentence format be used when adults want children to pay attention and listen to what they are saying. First, Gordon proposes that rather than begin a message with "you," start with the word "I." Next, he suggests adding how the parent feels ("I get angry . . . "), and then labeling the problem ("I get angry when I see you hit your sister," "I'm upset because I can't talk on the phone when you have the TV so loud," or "I feel bad when you don't listen when I'm talking to you").

According to Gordon, "I" messages differ from "you" messages in that they enable parents to effectively communicate a message to a child without damaging the child's self-esteem. Recall from the example of active listening given earlier that the father started many sentences with "you." In that context the father was acting as a counselor, so using sentences beginning with "you" was appropriate because they showed that he was listening to the child.

The "you" messages the father used did not contain content that would hurt the child's character or self-esteem, as do the "you" messages in the preceding paragraph: "You are acting stupid" or "You are doing that all wrong."

"I" messages are used to get a child to listen to what an adult has to say, to communicate facts to the child, and to help the child modify the unacceptable behavior. When parents learn to use this communication format, children also acquire the skill and begin to express their feelings to parents in nondamaging ways. "I" messages place the responsibility for changing the child's behavior on the child rather than on the parent, and they are less likely to promote resistance and rebellion in children. Additionally, these methods may be more effective with preschool- and school-age children than with adolescents.

3. *When conflicts occur that cannot be avoided, Gordon suggests that parents use the no-lose method of conflict resolution.* All too often, individuals in families believe that in resolving conflicts there must be someone who wins and someone who loses. This belief tends to promote adversarial situations in which parent and child are pitted against one another in a power struggle, each attempting to win by gaining his or her own way. In employing the no-lose strategy, parent and child strive to reach a win-win solution based on a compromise that is satisfactory to both. Neither parent nor child wins or loses in resolving the conflict; they come to an understanding that mutual needs must be satisfied to some degree in order for both people to be happy with the solution.

Gordon lists six steps for implementing this method. The steps are listed here, along with an example of a parent-child interaction.

1. Identify and define the conflict.

   PARENT: I've been very upset lately because you've been coming home late from school. I worry so much about you that I can't concentrate on my work until I know that you're home OK.

2. Generate possible solutions.

   PARENT: What can we do to solve this problem? Perhaps you should ride the bus home instead of staying after school to play.

   CHILD: I suppose I could keep better track of the time. If you would buy me a watch, I could set an alarm to let me know when to stop playing and leave for home.

3. Evaluate the solutions.

   PARENT: How much would a watch cost?

   CHILD: There are some kinds that aren't very expensive. I'd rather have a watch to remind me when to start home than not be able to stay after school and play with the kids.

4. Decide on the best solution for both parties.

   PARENT: OK, if we can find the right watch at the right price, I think that's a good idea.

5. Work out ways to implement the solution.

   PARENT: We can go to the department store after dinner tonight and shop for a watch. If you'd like, I'll help you learn how to set the alarm.

6. Evaluate how well the solution worked.

   PARENT: You've been doing a great job at being home on time now that you've got a watch. I'm proud that you learned how to do this yourself.

**Parenting FAQs 4–3**

My partner and I often disagree about how to discipline our children. We usually get into arguments about who's right and which rules our children have to follow—hers or mine. Sometimes the kids will play one of us against the other to get what they want. How can we resolve this?

**A:** There are always going to be differences between parenting partners. These usually happen because we were raised by different families having different rules and different values. Many people believe that both parenting partners *must* agree on everything—every rule and every consequence to rules for children. However, it may be essential to reach an agreement about how to prioritize those rules that are more important than others and those rules that fall into the categories of negotiable and nonnegotiable upon which both parenting partners can agree. Rather than reaching this consensus by trial and error, it is best to do so by explicit discussion and agreement. This will help everyone to know that there are some things that both parenting partners do not budge on, whereas there are other rules that are one parent's while not being an issue with the other. Such arrangements usually are not harmful to children.

There are several advantages to this method: (1) part of the responsibility for conflict resolution is placed with the child; (2) the child's cognitive skills in generating solutions are developed; (3) increased communication between parent and child results; (4) communications have no destructive emotional effects for parent or child; (5) the parent does not exert power over the child; and (6) autonomous behavior from the child is encouraged.

Gordon's strategy is significant in recognizing the influence of children's behavior on parents and in showing how to teach children to recognize the rights and needs of parents. Perhaps even more important, the strategy provides ways for parents to interact on a more equal basis with children instead of relying on power-assertive methods that damage children's self-esteem.

Gordon recognizes that there are times when active listening, "I" messages, and the no-lose method are inappropriate, as when children's safety is endangered or there are time pressures. These methods, however, generally are useful for anyone who works with children or with people in general.

Different effects are reported by researchers who have compared the behaviors of parents who attended training sessions in behavior modification and PET with those of parents who had no training in either strategy (Wood & Davidson, 2003). PET-trained parents felt that they had tools for working with children that enabled them to have a healthy relationship.

*Focus Point.* Parent Effectiveness Training stresses communication between parents and children and gives specific formats for such communication. It recognizes that there are times when adults can be helpful to children by simply listening to their problems, and it recommends the technique of active listening. When a child's behavior is offensive or problematic, parents need to communicate this to the child in nondamaging ways by using "I" messages. With the no-lose strategy for conflict resolution, parents and children learn to develop satisfactory compromises. The methods promoted in PET help parents provide structure and nurturance to children in healthy ways.

## Ineffective Disciplinary Methods

A review of the research literature on parental disciplinary practices suggests that there are at least four methods that do not work well or effectively in providing structure for children and gaining their compliance (Chamberlain & Patterson, 1995). These include: (1) discipline or parental behavior that is inconsistent, (2) irritable explosive practices, (3) inflexible rigid discipline, and (4) low parental supervision and involvement.

*Inconsistency* in parental behavior and especially that which constitutes a program of discipline serves primarily to confuse children about how they are expected to behave. For example, children receive mixed signals when a parent enforces a rule with its attendant consequences but at another time relents and does not enforce the rule or its consequences. When parents fail to agree on certain policies or rules about child behavior, children may also interpret this response as parental inconsistency.

Some parents appear to have only one type of reaction to all manner and types of children's transgressions such as loud emotional outbursts like yelling, screaming, or using violent physical acts of aggression. The intensity of the parental reaction and the degree of punitiveness usually escalates in relation to the frequency that the child misbehaves.

When parents employ inflexible, rigid discipline, they appear to rely on one type of punitive strategy regardless of the nature of a child's transgression. No matter what a child does that is unacceptable, the parent reacts the same way. What is lacking is a hierarchy in an organization of parental reactions that links the seriousness of the offense to the nature of the parental reaction. Typically, when parents rely on this inflexible approach, they do not employ verbal reasoning with a child when transgressions occur. Rather, the parent reacts in the same manner with little assistance given to the child on how to learn from the mistake.

When parents provide poor supervision or involvement, children become abandoned and neglected emotionally. Left to their own devices under such circumstances, children become at risk for experiencing a wide range of behavior problems and poor school performance and for failing to develop effective interpersonal skills.

## NORMAL BEHAVIOR PROBLEMS OF CHILDREN

One of the major preoccupations of many parents focuses on problems in children's behavior and development. Frequently, conflicts occur between parents and children over socialization tasks, relationship concerns, and gaining compliance from children. Many situations that are termed "normal" behavior problems are actually a problem for the adult and not the child. Similarly, many problems are simply a normal part of development as children strive to accomplish specific tasks but experience difficulties in mastering them. These may relate to the child's age: What is normal be-

havior at one stage may be problematic at another and may indicate some type of developmental or emotional disturbance.

Parents need to be aware of the difference between normal behavior problems and problems that are indicative of a serious disorder that calls for professional attention. Each of the chapters that follow includes a section about the normal behavior problems that parents can anticipate as a part of the development of children. These range from sleep problems in young children to eating disorders in adolescents. For many individuals, the major sources of information on these common problems are parenting books, articles in popular magazines, and discussions with friends.

••••••••••••••••••••••••••••••••••••••••••••

*Focus Point.*   Some misbehaviors of children constitute problems that are a normal aspect of their development. A competent parent today gains knowledge about child growth and development to learn what to expect at each stage of development. The competent, effective parent learns a variety of methods for handling problems that present difficulties in interactions with children.
••••••••••••••••••••••••••••••••••••••••••••

## POINTS TO CONSIDER

- Today, a competent parent actively acquires knowledge about child growth and development and gains experience in using a variety of methods and strategies that facilitate healthy parent-child interactions.
- One of the greatest concerns of most parents is how to provide adequate and proper discipline for children. Discipline refers to those methods used to help children learn to behave in appropriate ways, according to the patterns supported by their family system. To be effective, discipline should be positive, moderate, aimed at a child's particular age and developmental level, and based on an understanding of a particular child's needs.
- Discipline often is considered to refer to those behaviors and methods that involve punishment used to control children's misbehaviors. In truth, spanking and other forms of physical punishment are not recommended as part of any discipline program. Effective discipline aims to provide children with structure (self-discipline) and nurturance.

- It is also important for a caregiver to remember that there are a variety of reasons for children's misbehavior.
- Discipline is facilitated when caregivers: (1) attempt to identify and understand a child's feelings and motivations; (2) discuss and adopt a consistent plan of discipline methods; (3) attempt to accomplish effective communication with children by listening to their opinions and feelings; (4) allow children to learn to make decisions as well as mistakes and to take responsibility for their actions; and (5) base discipline on the use of rules, some negotiable and others nonnegotiable, as well as assertive and supportive care.
- A variety of methods or strategies is available to contemporary parents for use in establishing disciplinary programs for children.
- The disciplinary strategies discussed in this chapter are derived from modern behavioral science and range from reward and reinforcement to ways that facilitate effective communications between parents and children. Those strategies include behavior modification, the democratic approach, and Parent Effectiveness Training.
- Four characteristics describe these discipline strategies: (1) each seeks to reduce parental power over child behavior and fosters reacting in positive ways that do not damage children's self-esteem; (2) children are taught to learn self-discipline in controlling their actions; (3) caregivers are provided with proven, effective means of communication that help reduce conflict and facilitate healthy interpersonal interactions; and (4) each seeks to help parents gain a better understanding of child growth and development.
- Behavior modification involves the use of positive rewards and reinforcement of desired child behaviors by parents. Caregivers use these methods to teach children how to behave in an appropriate manner. Reinforcers must immediately follow a desired act to be effective. Caregivers may teach a complex task to children in sequential stages using reinforcement as children master progressively difficult behaviors. In addition, caregivers must be aware of the ability of children to reinforce certain parent behaviors.

- A central tenet of the democratic approach to parenting is based on several assumptions: (1) there are reasons for children's actions; (2) parents must attempt to understand children's behavior by determining and analyzing the child's reasoning for his or her behavior; (3) everyone has a basic need to belong to a social group; and (4) people develop a life plan that guides decisions to behave in certain ways, and that life plan may be based on faulty assumptions. A child's birth order in a family has a strong influence on the kind of life plan the child develops. Goals of misbehavior may explain reasons underlying most behaviors of children. Parents are encouraged to teach children that there are logical consequences, either positive or negative, to behavior. These consequences teach children to behave in accordance with family rules and policies. Encouragement is suggested as being more appropriate in shaping children's behavior than rewards. Family councils or regular meetings of the family group are recommended to establish policies and rules, consequences to the rules, and to resolve conflicts. Children should have an equal voice with that of parents at such councils.
- Parent Effectiveness Training focuses on enhancing communication skills between parents and children and on ways to resolve conflicts. Effective communication is thought to occur when: (1) the parent acts as a counselor when a child has a problem; (2) a child's behavior is causing a problem for the adult and others; and (3) conflicts between parents and children are resolved through compromise.
- There are several ways that parental discipline can be ineffective with children and can be damaging rather than helpful to children.
- Most children will experience problems in their behavior that is an anticipated aspect of normal developmental progress. Parents need to learn to distinguish between such normal behavior problems and those that are serious in requiring professional assistance.

# PART II

# The Work of Parenting

The work of parents in actively producing and socializing children into adulthood usually lasts for about 25 years. As we have seen in the first part of this text, on-the-job learning, especially regarding how to rear the first-born child, is required.

One of the distinctive characteristics of parenting children is the changing nature of the style or actual behavior that occurs in tandem with children's changing developmental needs. The shifts, refinements, and adaptations made in parenting style that occur in the interactions between parents and children are examined in the chapters of this part. For example, as a child matures and grows, parents must change from being physical helpers to psychological helpers and assist the child in coping with cultural as well as family expectations of how to behave appropriately.

Other expressions of caregiving also change as parents adapt their ways of providing structure and nurturance to accommodate the needs of growing children. When children are young, physical expressions of nurturance dominate parenting styles with increasing emphasis on experiences that teach structure. As children grow older, these are replaced by verbal methods such as encouragement, reassurance, and listening to their problems. Parents change their methods of controlling a child's behavior as part of the adaptation of providing structure. Physical means of control that are used frequently with young children are replaced with psychological and verbal guidance methods when children enter their school-age and adolescent years.

This part of the text first examines the issues that adults consider in deciding to become a parent or not. We discuss pregnancy and childbirth as important aspects of parenting children and providing for a healthy start in life. Next, we focus on parenting infants and toddlers and then young children. The focus shifts to a discussion of parenting strategies, which become a major issue as children grow into their preschool years and into middle childhood and adolescence. The remaining chapters discuss parenting issues involved in rearing school-age children, adolescents, and young adults. Portions of some chapters examine slices of family developmental time (using the Systemic Family Development model) as a means for understanding what is taking place in an entire family system when children are of particular ages.

# CHAPTER 5

# The Transition to Parenthood

## Focus Questions

■ ■ ■ ■ ■ ■ ■ ■ ■ ■

1. What major factors influence a person's decision to become a parent?
2. What adjustments and reactions do people have to pregnancy and childbirth?
3. Is first-time parenthood a "crisis" experience for many adults?
4. How does first-time parenthood affect a couple's committed relationship? What other factors may influence someone's adjustment to becoming a parent?
5. What new medical technologies assist people with reproductive difficulties in becoming parents?
6. What major factors and issues relate to adopting children?
7. What are the different types of adoption?
8. Should adopted children be informed of their birth circumstances?
9. What kinds of support are available for new parents?

■ ■ ■ ■ ■ ■ ■ ■ ■ ■

## DO I WANT TO BE A PARENT?

Before the advent of modern contraceptives, it was taken for granted that married couples would have children if they were biologically able. Circumstances are different today. People have greater freedom of choice to decide whether and when they will have children and how many children they will have. In many cases, couples plan to have children in advance of their conception and birth (Figure 5–1). Couples often discuss how many children they want and prepare for the entry of children into their family system. In this section we explore some of the factors that influence how people reach the decision to become a parent in contemporary times.

**FIGURE 5–1.** Many contemporary couples discuss and make plans before beginning a pregnancy.

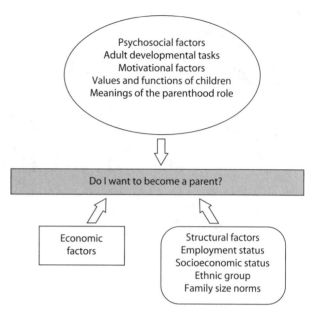

**FIGURE 5–2.** The decision about whether to become a parent is influenced by a complex of interrelated factors.

The decision to become parents is a serious one that usually involves discussions between a couple. Complex issues are considered in this decision (see Figure 5–2). Today, economic considerations play a central role (Lino, 2003). Children are no longer considered an economic asset as they were in the past. To a contemporary American family, children can be an economic liability, and for this reason many people delay childbearing until they have established a sound financial base to support the many expenses involved. Others delay having children until decisions have been made about their desired lifestyle and whether children will play a part. In addition, a variety of social pressures influence one's decision to become a parent. For these reasons, the desire to become a parent has a strong psychological and emotional basis. Potential parents must examine the notion that children can fulfill different needs, values, and functions within a particular family system. These and other related factors are discussed in more detail in the following sections.

## Parenting Reflection 5–1

How does our society view someone who does not want to be a parent? What factors may motivate someone to remain childless? Can someone who does not want children be considered to be emotionally and/or socially healthy?

## Economic Factors

People apparently consider the economic costs of having children today more carefully than they did in the past. Economic factors also relate to a couple's desired lifestyle. These issues contribute to the delayed ages at which many couples have their first child (see Figure 5–3). Although accurate costs of childbearing and child rearing are difficult to obtain, it has been estimated that about one-fourth of the total lifetime income of a typical middle-class family in the United States is devoted to meeting the costs of having and raising a child from birth through age 18 (Lino, 2003). Another way to look at the financial outlay is the estimated total costs required for child rearing. For a child born in 2000, this may require

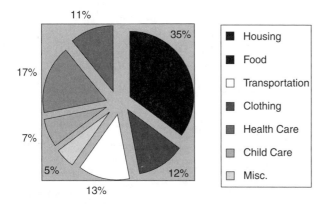

**FIGURE 5–3.**   Percentages of income spent by a typical middle-income family during the first two years of a child's life.

*Source:* Lino, M. (2003). *Expenditures on children by families, 2002.* U.S. Department of Agriculture, Center for Nutrition Policy and Promotion. Miscellaneous Publication No. 1528-2002. Washington, DC: U.S. Government Printing Office.

$165,630 to age 18. This immense figure relates to family expenses for a single family home, health care, and child care, for example (Lino, 2003).

Family expenditures to provide housing, child care, transportation, and food consume the majority of a family's income. These costs account for about half of the total outlay necessary in raising children to maturity (Lino, 2003) (see Figure 5–3). Another cost of child rearing not often considered by those contemplating parenthood is the potential loss of family income due to the mother not being employed. Many women choose not to enter the workforce or leave upon having a child and do not return to work until the child enters kindergarten. The loss of income due to the desire that children receive full-time parental supervision is an important issue to potential parents.

## Structural Factors

Several structural factors that relate to and influence economic considerations enter into the decision to become a parent. First, the employment status of the mother is frequently an important consideration (Federal Interagency Forum on Child and Family Statistics, 2003). A related factor is the necessity of planning for child care should the mother return to the labor force. Finding a source of reliable, economical child care, especially for

an infant, calls for careful consideration. Many families in the United States rely on relatives or in-home (family) day care of children when mothers are employed outside the home. Others rely on agencies, nonprofit organizations, or proprietary services for substitute child care. Use of these services is often seen as less desirable than parental care, although research strongly suggests that children are not harmed by nonparental care during the early years of their lives (NICHD Early Child Care Research Network, 1999, 2000a, 2000b). The relative advantages and disadvantages of nonparental child care are discussed in later chapters.

The socioeconomic status and ethnic group membership of a family also influence the decision to pursue parenthood. These factors are associated with the values and functions adults apply to having children and the number of children a couple desire.

A group's *fertility rate*—the actual number of children to whom a woman gives birth—reflects these factors as well (see Figure 5–4). Hispanics are currently the fastest growing minority group in the United States due in part to a fertility rate that is considerably higher than other ethnic groups (Population Reference Bureau, 2003a). In addition, middle-class women tend to have fewer children than those of blue collar status (U.S. Bureau of the Census, 2003). This may be due in part to the higher level of education generally received by middle-class women, which is related to more prevalent use of birth control methods, differences in rate and type of employment, and a tendency to limit family size to maintain a certain lifestyle.

Due to our culture's strong **pronatalist** bias, adults who are married experience great social pressures to become parents (May, 1997). Perhaps the greatest pressure comes from a couple's parents in their desire to become grandparents. At the same time, there is considerable pressure on couples to limit the number of children they produce, which arises from societal concerns about overpopulation and from economic pressures.

## Psychosocial Factors

A complex of psychosocial factors contributes significantly to people's decision to become parents. The reasons for having children have shifted from a strong economic base in the past to one that is psychological and social in nature today. An equally strong emotional component is tied in with parenthood and parenting.

**FIGURE 5–4.** Total fertility rate by race/ethnicity, 1990–2001.

*Source:* Population Reference Bureau (2003). "U. S. fertility rates higher among minorities 2001." From http://www.prb.org/ Ameristat Template; Martin, J. A., et al. (2001). Births: Final Data for 2001, *National Vital Statistics Report, 51*(2); and Ventura, S. J., et al. (1999). Births: Final Data for 1997, *National Vital Statistics Report, 47*(18).

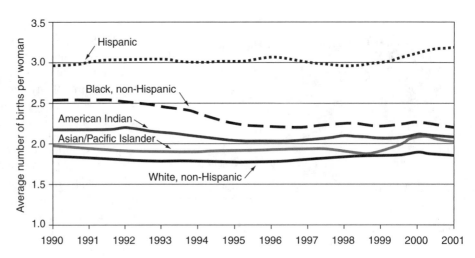

This psychosocial complex is well illustrated in a series of questions that may be considered prior to beginning a pregnancy.

● ● ● ● ● ● ● ● ● ● ● ● ● ● ● ● ● ● ● ● ● ● ● ● ● ● ● ● ● ● ●

## Parenting Reflection 5–2

What happens when one person in a committed relationship wants to have children but the other does not? How might this conflict be solved so that both persons can be satisfied to some degree?

● ● ● ● ● ● ● ● ● ● ● ● ● ● ● ● ● ● ● ● ● ● ● ● ● ● ● ● ● ● ●

**Parenthood as a Normal Developmental Task of Adulthood.** A traditional concept depicts parenthood as an important developmental task of adulthood (Erikson, 1950, 1964, 1982; Erikson, Erikson, & Kivnick, 1986). This expectation that normal, healthy development in adulthood includes procreation may reflect the pronatalist bias of our culture. From our culture's point of view, the years of adulthood represent the culmination of an individual's maturation, a time when one is expected to assume mature responsibilities such as earning a living, entering into parenthood, supporting a family, pursuing occupational and personal goals, and making some type of contribution to society. In Erikson's theory of psychosocial development, the adult years constitute a period in which society encourages an individual to meet these responsibilities and, in doing so, to prepare himself or herself for the next and final stage of the life span.

Traditional cultural ideas carry the expectation that once an individual reaches adulthood, that person will establish a family-oriented lifestyle. In other words, heterosexual adults are expected to marry and to have children, and every adult is assumed to be heterosexual unless proven otherwise. Population statistics confirm this belief in showing that about 90 percent of persons 18 years of age and older marry at some time and that about 50 percent have at least one child (U.S. Bureau of the Census, 2003).

These figures have implications for decisions about parenthood. For example, do people become parents because they feel it is expected of them as adults and because they do not wish to be different from the majority of their peers? What mechanisms promote the desire to procreate as part of an individual's adult development?

One explanation of why people become parents is provided in Erikson's psychosocial theory. He believes that when we reach the adult years, several physical, social, and psychological stimuli trigger a sense of generativity. A central component of this attitude is the desire to care for others. For the majority of people, parenthood is perhaps the most obvious and convenient opportunity to fulfill this desire. Erikson believes that another distinguishing feature of adulthood is the emergence of an inborn desire to teach. We become aware of this desire when the event of being physically capable to reproduce is joined with the events of participating in a committed relationship, the establishment of an adult pattern of living, and the assumption of job responsibilities. According to Erikson, by becoming parents we learn that we have

**Parenting FAQs 5–1**

**I've been married for more than five years now and have a wonderful relationship. There are no children and probably won't be any in the future. However, there are times when I'm uncertain that this is what I want. Can you offer some guidance on what to consider about making this decision about having kids?**

**A:**   It's good that you are making a conscious effort to make the decision about parenthood. Many people don't do this or don't have the opportunity for a number of reasons. Here are some points that you might include on your list of issues to examine:

■ What do you want out of life for yourself? What do you think is important?
■ How would a child interfere with your growth and development as an individual? How would a child enhance this process?
■ Do you like doing things with children? Do you enjoy activities that children can do?
■ Do you want a boy or a girl child? What if you don't get the one you want?
■ Would you try to pass on to your child your ideas and values?
■ What if your child's ideas and values turn out to be very different from yours?
■ Does your partner want to have a child? Have the two of you discussed your reasons for wanting a child? Suppose one of you wants a child and the other doesn't? Who decides?
■ Are you financially prepared for caring for a child?

*Source:* Adapted from Baker, C. (1977). *Am I parent material?* Washington, DC: National Alliance for Optional Parenthood.

the need to be needed by others who depend on our knowledge, protection, and guidance. We become entrusted to teach culturally appropriate behaviors, values, attitudes, skills, and information about the world. By assuming the responsibilities of being primary caregivers to children through their long years of physical and social growth, we concretely express what Erikson believes to be an inborn desire to teach. Through the production and care of children, we contribute to the continuation of our culture. By doing so, we begin to develop a sense of generativity as adults.

● ● ● ● ● ● ● ● ● ● ● ● ● ● ● ● ● ● ● ● ● ● ● ● ● ● ● ● ● ●

### Parenting Reflection 5–3

What are some advantages and disadvantages of having children in contemporary society? What are some ways that society's expectations of parents can be made more realistic in today's world?

● ● ● ● ● ● ● ● ● ● ● ● ● ● ● ● ● ● ● ● ● ● ● ● ● ● ● ● ● ●

**Motivations (Reasons) for Becoming a Parent.**   Many different personal reasons enter into a person's debate about assuming parenthood, and most people appear genuinely to want children (Figure 5–5). These reasons may have their basis in the beliefs of one's family of origin, social class, or ethnic group. Motivations for becoming a parent may be present long before an individual has children and are seen as antecedents of the varying attitudes people have toward this role in adulthood. When and if children are produced, adults' underlying reasons for becoming parents may be played out in a child rearing script they follow without questioning. In many ways, the reasons for wanting to be a parent may be associated closely with the experience a person expects to have interacting with a child. Although these reasons are highly personal and unique to each individual, a strong psychosocial theme reflects pleasure in child rearing, feelings of love and affection, and attitudes of generativity.

There is a fatalistic component to some individuals' desire to be a parent. Some people may be strongly motivated to become a parent because they believe that procreation is the primary reason for their existence. People with such beliefs believe that contraception is immoral because it interferes with God's will. These beliefs are grounded strongly in many individuals' religious orientations.

A different aspect of a fatalistic reason to have children is to ensure continuation of one's family name. In

**FIGURE 5–5.** There are a variety of reasons for wanting to become a parent. Children represent many things to parents, and the parenthood role holds different meanings for adults.

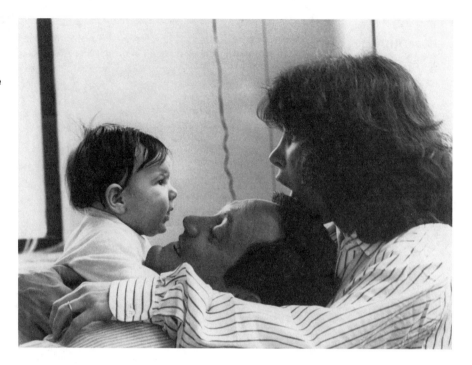

some ethnic subcultures and family systems, males continue to be highly valued because family names are perpetuated through them.

The primary motivations for having children and becoming a parent can be altruistic in nature. These reasons include an unselfish desire to express affection and concern for children. The ability to express one's sense of generativity may be provided through parenting experiences.

Parenthood provides an outlet for having one's psychological need to be needed fulfilled, according to Erikson's concept of generativity. This aspect can also be considered a narcissistic motivation to become a parent. Narcissism in this context refers to the expectation that having children will reflect on the goodness of a person and serve as a concrete, visible statement of maturity and adequacy as a sexually mature and active adult. It is also related to the need to achieve similarity with peers.

Another narcissistic aspect is the notion that children will provide their parents with emotional security and love. There is no guarantee, unfortunately, that children will reciprocate a parent's love.

Other reasons for assuming parenthood are instrumental in nature. For example, many parents may wish children to achieve specific goals for them. Their expectation is that children will reach levels of achievement that they have not been able to achieve, such as getting a college education, learning a particular skill, or being successful in a certain career. In essence, such individuals view the parenting experience as a second chance at life. Some parents may unconsciously believe that they can relive their own childhood through their children. Similarly, many are motivated by the hope and determination that their children will not repeat their mistakes. Interestingly, some men may desire to become fathers because they missed having a close relationship with their own fathers and hope to relive this in a potential parenting relationship (Gerson, 1993).

Another instrumental reason for assuming parenthood is to secure a relationship. Some people mistakenly believe that having children will rescue a troubled marriage, when the presence of children does not appear to help or hinder marriage satisfaction. Unfortunately, the increased strain on adults caused by managing multiple roles is likely to contribute to difficulties in a marriage. Studies that compare marriages with and without children consistently find that marital satisfaction is greatest among couples who do not have children (Houseknect, 1987; Somers, 1993).

Yet another instrumental reason for assuming parenthood is having a child to please one's own parents.

It is not unusual for older parents to place pressure— subtly and not so subtly—on their adult children to become parents. The desire to be a grandparent may be the paramount explanation. Middle-aged parents may wish to conform with their peers who are grandparents. Adult children may give in to these pressures to reduce the guilt that arises from being childless.

•••••••••••••••••••••••••••••••••••••••

### Parenting Reflection 5–4

Is it possible for some people not to adapt successfully to becoming a parent? What happens when someone has a surprise pregnancy that was not planned, does not want to have an abortion, and does not believe that it is appropriate or moral to give a child up for adoption?

•••••••••••••••••••••••••••••••••••••••

**The Values and Functions of Children for Adults.** The decision to become a parent is based in part on adult needs and values that children fulfill. Ultimately, the question focuses on the reasons why people choose to have children. These reasons relate, in turn, to the number of children a couple will produce during their childbearing years.

Researchers have examined the values and functions of children as a part of adult development (Arnold et al., 1975; Hoffman & Manis, 1979). Most of these studies analyzed questionnaire responses of adults in several cultures around the world, including the United States, Asia, and the South Pacific islands. The values, functions, and advantages of having children (becoming a parent) derived from responses given by these groups include: (1) conferral of adult status and identity, (2) continuation of the family name, (3) confirmation of personal morality, (4) a sense of family, (5) fun and pleasure (Figure 5–6), (6) a sense of accomplishment, (7) a position of influence over someone's life, (8) proof of personal fecundity, and (9) economic benefits (in some cultures). These values are believed to influence the fertility rates of couples in that they define the circumstances under which pregnancies are initiated and influence the number of children produced.

The values adults hold for children in their lives are influenced by structural variables such as age, place of residence, sex, and ethnic background of adults, as well as the age of children. Studies of young adults' perceptions of the values and functions of children for adults report that individuals of this age group may have less positive attitudes about having children than do older individuals (Bigner, Jacobsen, & Phelan, 1981; Gerson et al., 1991; Gormly, Gormly, & Weiss, 1987). Young adults

**FIGURE 5–6.** Children represent a number of values to adults. For example, children may provide their parents with many pleasurable experiences.

apparently picture themselves as being highly involved in careers and occupations that make such great demands on their time, energy, and finances that parenthood is placed at a lower priority. It would appear that having children takes less precedence in young adults' personal goals today than in previous years, when single provider incomes and early marriages were in vogue.

Where one lives may play an important role in how children are valued. For example, as compared to urban mothers, rural mothers generally express more traditional values in that they view children as a means of perpetuating the family name and as giving loyalty and support to parents throughout life (Bigner et al., 1982; Bormann & Stockdale, 1979). African Americans are reported to express stronger beliefs than whites that having children promotes personal happiness and success in marriage, increases personal security, and gains approval from others. Males are reported to feel that having children is a greater personal and social asset than do females. This may explain why males in some ethnic groups tend to place stronger pressures on females to have children (Jacobsen, Bigner, & Hood, 1991; Roxburgh et al., 2001).

**Meanings of the Parenthood Role.** The last of the psychosocial factors we examine are the cultural meanings associated with the parental role. In most cultures, individuals have ideas about the characteristics and functions that are ideal in the social roles they have found to be necessary in that culture. These ideas are often exaggerated notions that shape an individual's thoughts, reactions, and behaviors. Many times, individuals accept these ideal notions as valid and do not question them.

The social meanings of parenthood and nonparenthood existing in our culture are described by psychologist J. E. Veevers (1973). These interpretations of parenthood come from behavioral and social science research. It is important to understand the influence of these social meanings on individuals' behavior. Belief in the social meanings of parenthood may place social pressure on people and motivate them to become parents rather than remain childless.

Veevers uses six main themes to classify the social meanings of parenthood: morality, responsibility, naturalness, sex, marriage, and normality and mental health.

1. *Parenthood Is a Moral Obligation.* Many individuals may interpret parenthood as a moral obligation associated with adulthood. According to Veevers, the Judeo-Christian traditions that influence our culture arise from the Old Testament directive to be fruitful and multiply. These traditions support the pronatalist position of our culture that adults are obligated to reproduce and replenish society with new members. Procreation becomes a moral obligation for those who devoutly practice the teachings of religious groups that favor this position.

2. *Parenthood Is a Civic Responsibility.* Parenthood may be interpreted as a civic obligation in that the continuation of a culture depends on the reproduction of children. Veevers identifies a cultural belief that the alarmingly high costs of child rearing are not disadvantages or acceptable excuses for not having children. Individuals who have the financial and social resources to be competent parents and yet choose to remain childless are traditionally considered by society to be selfish and irresponsible. It is partially for this reason that homosexuality traditionally is not valued by society, because most individuals of this orientation do not reproduce and have children.

3. *Parenthood Is Natural for Adults.* Traditional belief holds that parenting is an expected and natural behavior of adulthood. According to Veevers, this attitude refers to the belief that conception is a natural consequence of sexual intercourse between opposite-sex adults. This idea of parenthood is carried over from the period before the introduction and acceptance of reliable contraceptives. People have assumed that a childless individual had some type of physical problem that prevented procreation and, therefore, that the individual was an unnatural or abnormal person who had little value to society. Veevers states that this assumption is erroneous. According to her logic, if humans had an instinctual drive to reproduce and provide for children's care, then the method of socializing children and performing caregiving would be common to every culture of the world. In fact, anthropologists have shown that there is much cultural variation in parenting styles, and hence human behavior is not governed by instinct.

4. *Parenthood Is a Statement of Human Sexuality.* Parenthood has sexual meanings and implies that an individual adult is capable of reproduction. Since parenthood validates, communicates, and confirms heterosexuality, it may be considered an

aspect of a person's sexual identity. This view calls into question the psychological and physical condition of childless adults.

5. *Parenthood Is a Confirmation of Marriage.* Closely associated with the sexual meanings implied in parenthood is the notion that parenthood gives true meaning to a committed relationship between adults. Traditionally, children are believed to round out a marriage, improve the relationship between a couple, help a troubled or stagnant relationship, and prevent divorce.

6. *Parenthood Is Normal Adult Behavior.* The final idea discussed by Veevers is the normality of individuals who have children. Traditionally, childbearing is thought to fulfill a personal destiny for women more than for men. From this view, a woman who is childless is seen as unnatural, abnormal, and lacking in normal mental health. Implicit is the assumption that parents are socially mature people. Having a child is considered to be a means of achieving adult social status and being recognized for it. Parenthood implies caring for dependent children and being concerned for their welfare; conversely, nonparenthood implies caring more for one's own well-being than for that of others.

It is difficult to determine exactly the extent to which these beliefs continue to be held in the general population. As Veevers notes, several organizations have been formed in reaction to these pronatalist attitudes, such as the National Alliance for Optional Parenthood. Certainly, the impact of the women's movement also has contributed to reducing the prevalence of these beliefs. A growing segment of the adult population of the United States appears to be choosing not to become parents. About 18 percent of adults over age 18 who are married apparently are voluntarily childless (U.S. Bureau of the Census, 2003). Furthermore, traditional attitudes about the social meanings of parenthood seem to be more prevalent among older people than among younger individuals (Bigner et al., 1981; Callan & Gallois, 1983). Young adult women, for example, tend to describe a childless adult as happy, normal, natural, sensitive, and emotionally stable, whereas middle-aged adult women describe this individual as maladjusted, inappropriate, unloving, and sexually inadequate. Young women today apparently hold more positive attitudes about nonparenthood due to exposure to alternatives to parenthood as acceptable options of adult life (Coll, 1991).

Another way to study the meaning of parenthood is to examine the concept of *responsible fathering* (Doherty, Kouneski, & Erickson, 1998; Levine & Pitt, 1998). This concept implies a set of social and ethical notions that constitute what this role means within families and within society. It also reflects a desire to include nurturance within a traditional male sex- and gender-role ideology that is in balance with the instrumental functions of enforcing limits on children's behavior. Furthermore, it emphasizes the moral duties of men to children once they have taken the reproductive responsibility of helping to create a human life. A responsible father, then, is one who (Levine & Pitt, 1998):

■ waits to make a baby until he is prepared emotionally and financially to support his child.
■ establishes his legal paternity if and when he does make a baby.
■ actively shares with the child's mother in the continuing emotional and physical care of their child, from pregnancy onward.
■ shares with the child's mother in the continuing financial support of their child, from pregnancy onward.

These ideas about how to configure someone's role as a father can serve as a template for future behavior and a means for evaluating one's behavior and conduct in this role.

*Focus Point.* Several factors operate to influence the decision of many adults to become parents or to remain childless. These include: (1) economic considerations that relate to the costs of childbearing and child rearing and affect other factors such as employment of both adults in a family, the kind of lifestyle desired, and number of children produced; (2) structural variables such as the employment status of the adults, socioeconomic and ethnic group backgrounds of the family members, and desired family size; and (3) psychosocial factors such as parenting as an expected developmental task of adulthood, personal reasons or motivations to become a parent, the values and functions that children may serve for adults, and meanings ascribed to the role of parent. Making a decision about prospective parenthood is a critical issue for many couples in their marriage relationship.

**FIGURE 5–7.** The initiation of a pregnancy signals many changes for a couple in their family and work roles, daily routines, resources of time and money, self-image, and committed relationship.

## ADJUSTING TO PARENTHOOD

The birth of a first child transforms individuals into parents. Assuming this new family role in addition to others already held is both challenging and rewarding. People evolve gradually into parenthood roles as they assume increasing responsibilities in raising and caring for a child. The transition is usually initiated when a couple learns that a pregnancy is in progress (Figure 5–7).

### Expectant Parents' Reactions to Pregnancy

When a couple learns of a pregnancy, especially their first, they can expect several reactions. Many of the direct experiences of pregnancy apply mainly to a mother, of course. However, a pregnancy also affects the mother and her partner in several ways, although the experience is unique to each.

Pregnancy has been found to be the 12th most stressful life event that adults experience (Holmes & Rahe, 1967). An expectant mother undergoes a variety of changes that can cause her stress. These include adjusting to a changing body image as the pregnancy pro-gresses, challenges to physical and psychological well-being, feelings about what it is like to be pregnant (especially for the first time), dealing with fears of the unknown, and shifting mood states that may be related to fluctuations in hormone levels (Schneider et al., 1999). Emotional reactions in pregnancy are important as well because high levels of anxiety in mothers have been associated with increased fetal activity, which may contribute partially to lower birth weights in these infants. High activity levels continue to be observed in these babies following birth (Monk et al., 2000).

For the most part, most women and their partners react favorably and with great anticipation to the news that a pregnancy has begun. This appears to be especially the case when the pregnancy is the first one and when the pregnancy is desired.

Like parenthood, pregnancy has different connotations and meanings for different individuals. For some, pregnancy validates one's sexuality and verifies one's femininity or masculinity in serving as proof that one is capable of conceiving or impregnating. For many individuals, the initiation of a pregnancy revives memories of childhood and brings anticipation of the parenthood role.

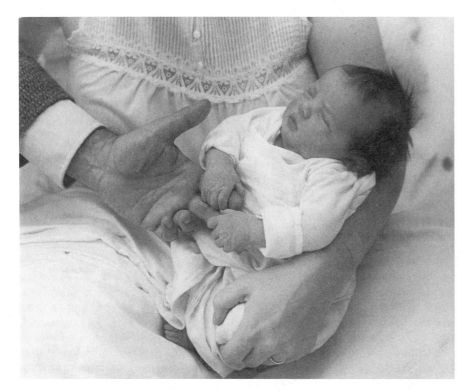

**FIGURE 5–8.** First-time parenthood requires many personal adjustments for a family system. Adults typically experience a variety of reactions not only to a pregnancy but also to the birth of a child.

Not everyone who learns of the beginning of a pregnancy reacts with joy, pleasure, or anticipation, however. Emotional reactions that are less than positive are attributed to: (1) feelings of ambivalence about the possibility of becoming a parent, (2) marital difficulties, (3) lack of a suitable social network to provide emotional support during the pregnancy, or (4) lack of desire for the pregnancy (Fleming et al., 1988). These negative attitudes also have a bearing on the manner in which labor and delivery are experienced.

When a pregnancy is confirmed, a couple must often focus on new issues they have not yet considered in their relationship (Figure 5–8). For example, many begin to ponder what it will be like to have a child and to be a parent, what kind of parent they will be, in what kinds of activities they will participate, and what kind of person the child will be and become. Perhaps one of the benefits of the 9 months of pregnancy is that it allows such mental preparations to take place before one actually has to perform as a parent. Expectant parents have time to begin thinking of themselves as a family in the traditional sense rather than as a couple. By attending childbirth education classes, reading books and articles about child rearing and child development, and arranging and participating in prenatal medical care, couples begin preparations for this change in their family system. They equip a nursery, receive baby showers, and shop for the things they will need in caring for an infant. This change is to be a significant one, and it will prompt related changes in the family system as the couple moves from being newlyweds to being a couple in the process of producing children. These changes are discussed in more detail in the next chapter.

••••••••••••••••••••••••••••••••••••••••••••••••••

***Focus Point.***   The potential of new parenthood causes changes for both the woman who is pregnant and her partner. Women who anticipate motherhood positively adjust better to being pregnant and to experiencing labor and delivery. Pregnancy signals impending changes in personal and marital identities for a couple. It prepares them to make adjustments in moving to the next stage of their family life career.

••••••••••••••••••••••••••••••••••••••••••••••••••

## EFFECTS OF THE BIRTH EXPERIENCE FOR ADULTS

A variety of outcomes can be anticipated in association with the type of delivery a couple experiences. Today, childbirth is recognized as being a psychological as well as a physical event that has implications beyond the immediate (Hoffnung, 1992). Reactions to childbirth can be experienced as feelings of ecstasy and intense spirituality or as one of the more singularly negative experiences of one's lifetime (Kendall-Tackett, 2001). One of the most significant aspects of this event is the importance and role of the birth experience in promoting bonding between parents and the child (Garbarino, 1980). Some research suggests that the first few minutes following birth are crucial in this respect and constitute a critical period for the parent-child relationship (Waldenstroem, 1999a). Skin-to-skin contact between each parent and the newborn, as well as expressing physical affection and maintaining eye contact, are believed to facilitate emotional bonding. Family-centered childbirth methods may also enhance the process. It has been speculated that a birth experience that promotes bonding between parent and infant prevents later parenting difficulties that have been associated with prolonged separation of the adult and child at birth.

The active involvement of the father or partner in childbirth may serve to make this experience more positive and thus more meaningful (Waldenstroem, 1999b). Research generally indicates that preparation during pregnancy by both partners, but especially by the adult male, assists the woman in coping more positively with the experiences of pregnancy and delivery and leads to greater satisfaction. In addition, the father's participation in childbirth appears to stimulate his interest in the child, in child rearing experiences, and in his role as a parent.

Immediate access to the newborn by the mother and father that is accomplished by rooming-in experiences, for example, may act to increase the confidence of the parents in performing competent child care under supervised conditions. This may also lead to fewer incidences of future parenting inadequacy. However, there do not appear to be any long-term deficits in the mother-child relationship when these early contacts do not occur (Eyer, 1992).

Adults experience stress reactions to delivery in different ways (Haig, 1995). The level of stress experienced may be higher among those who are first-time parents.

This relates more directly to the transition first-time parents are experiencing into their new role and the varied related changes occurring in conjunction with this transition. These are discussed in more detail later in this chapter. For parents who are having their second or third child, there continues to be some stress associated with childbirth. This may relate, in part, to memories of past experiences of being a new parent of a newborn. These stimulate a more realistic appraisal of the impact that a newborn child has on changing family life, routines, and resources. In addition, a mother's satisfaction with the birth experience is related in part to the frequency of obstetrical interventions (surgical procedures, fetal monitors, episiotomies, enemas, etc.). More extensive use of these procedures is associated with lower levels of satisfaction (Kyman, 1991).

### Parenting Reflection 5–5

What parting advice would you offer to new parents who are taking their new baby home about what to expect in the months to come in their marriage, home routines, and social life?

*Focus Point.*  Adults can expect to experience several different types of outcomes in association with childbirth. The type of delivery may influence the adults' reaction, especially affecting the quality of emotional bonding that occurs between parents and the newborn. The active involvement of the newborn's father in the birth experience may facilitate his involvement in child rearing experiences. Contemporary trends in childbirth such as rooming-in may facilitate emotional bonding of parents and child as well as bolster the confidence of parents in their ability to provide competent care for their infant.

## EFFECTS OF NEW PARENTHOOD ON MOTHERS AND FATHERS

When adults become parents for the first time, profound changes may be expected to take place in every aspect of their family life and relationship (Cox et al.,

1999). The absence of children typically during the first few years following marriage or commitment allows a couple to focus on each other's needs and on their own. They evolve routines, rules, policies, and roles that establish boundaries and expectations for behavior as a married couple. These serve as the foundation for the myriad adjustments and transitions they will experience over the career of their family system.

Most people do not make rapid adaptations and changes in response to the beginning of a new stage of development. Rather, a series of events and happenings signal that changes must be made in order for the family system to maintain its balance and ability to function effectively. The events surrounding the pregnancy and delivery of the first child signal that a couple must now begin to shift their thinking and identities to accomodate their new role as parents. As individuals move into this new developmental stage of family life, they are also moving into a new stage of their own psychosocial development, which Erikson calls the sense of generativity.

The presence of the new baby produces many profound changes in both the individuals and the family. The relationship of the parents as marriage partners becomes transformed into a more complicated interactional network (see Figure 5–9). In accordance with the principles of wholeness and interrelatedness in family systems theory, the new baby's presence affects the entire family system in some manner and causes realignments to occur in response to this new situation. The adjustments required of a couple in order to incorporate a new baby into the family system appear to be facilitated when they have established a highly competent marriage relationship and functional patterns to regulate behavior prior to the child's birth (Rholes et al., 2001).

Many adults may find this period of new parenthood to be especially disconcerting. Some new parents feel that they have had inadequate or insufficient preparation for the adjustments they must make in their marriage and their personal lives, and they are unsure of their ability to nurture a small infant. Alice Rossi (1968) and others (Belsky & Rovine, 1990; Cowan & Cowan, 1992; Levy-Shiff, 1994) describe several factors that contribute to difficulty in adjusting to first-time parenthood:

■ Specific educational experiences that prepare people for parenthood are not readily available in our society.
■ The experience of pregnancy involves only a limited degree of preparation for parenthood.

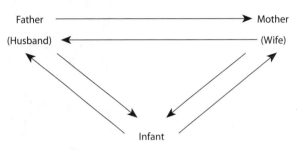

**FIGURE 5–9.** The addition of a baby into a family system changes the interaction patterns already established between the mother and father. The interactional bonds increase from two to six, creating a more complex social environment and affecting the family ecology.

■ Our society provides little guidance on how to ensure successful parenting behavior and experiences.
■ The transition into the new role of parenthood is abrupt and disruptive.

## "Parenthood as Crisis" Studies

A number of early research studies on new parenthood are considered to be the classic forerunners to the contemporary view of first-time parenthood. These early studies laid the foundation for contemporary studies that focus on the problems, challenges, and adjustments individuals face as they make the transition into parenting roles for the first time. When this topic was first being investigated, the early research viewed new parenthood as a crisis event in a couple's marriage career. Through greater understanding of the issues involved in new parenthood, it is now seen as a transition experience rather than as a negative, crisis-producing event in the career of a family system (Figure 5–10).

The abruptness of change into new parenting roles served as the basis for family sociologist E. E. LeMasters' (1957) proposal that the birth of the first child is a crisis event in a couple's marriage relationship. LeMasters proposed that our society supports a romantic complex about parenthood.

**FIGURE 5–10.** First-time parenthood is no longer considered to be a crisis event but rather a transition in one's personal development in adulthood and in a couple's committed relationship.

Extensive folklore about the joys of parenthood creates unrealistic impressions and expectations about what is involved in child rearing and what it is like to be a parent. LeMasters reported data suggesting that people become disenchanted with their marriage after having their first child. He interviewed 46 middle-class couples who had had their first child 5 years prior to the interview, and 83 percent reported an extensive or severe crisis in adjusting to the baby's presence and subsequent influence on their relationship. Mothers reported experiences or feelings such as losing sleep, worrying about their appearance and housekeeping standards, being chronically tired, and giving up social contacts and the income from employment outside the home. Fathers reported similar reactions and also mentioned dissatisfaction with a decline in the sexual responsiveness of their wives.

Although the LeMasters study brought attention to the effects of the first child on the parents' marriage relationship, other researchers questioned the validity of these findings. Everett Dyer (1963) performed a subsequent investigation in an attempt to replicate the results of the LeMasters study. Dyer's results confirmed the prediction that the severity of the crisis was dependent on: (1) the degree of cohesiveness of the marital and family organization at the time of the baby's birth; (2) the couple's degree of preparation for parenthood and marriage; (3) the degree of adjustment required in the marital relationship after the birth; and (4) other variables

such as the number of years the couple had been married before the child's birth. Most couples in Dyer's study who reported a severe crisis in reaction to the first birth were able to recover and reorganize their relationship within several months following the birth.

Family sociologist Dan Hobbs (1965) performed additional research that focused on the reports of a more representative group of new parents than those interviewed by LeMasters and Dyer. In his study, Hobbs found that 86 percent of the couples reported having only slight crisis reactions, a finding that was diametrically opposed to that of LeMasters and Dyer.

Later studies have confirmed Hobbs's initial findings (Hobbs & Wimbish, 1977; Russell, 1974). This research prompted a reevaluation of the challenges of a first birth and brought about a revised viewpoint labeling the change in a family system a **transition** rather than a crisis. More recent research has addressed other factors that influence adjustment to the new parenthood role for first-time parents. These are discussed in the following paragraphs.

## Timing of First Birth

Researchers generally report that the timing of the transition to new parenthood in a person's life and marriage career is determined by rather complex social factors (Chakraborty, 2002). There is a trend in the United

States to delay first marriage and childbearing to later ages in adulthood than was customary in the past (U.S. Bureau of the Census, 2003). Children are typically produced by most couples within 2 years following their first marriage. However, many couples delay having their first child for a variety of reasons. The postponement of parenthood to later ages is attributed to unfavorable economic conditions and the pressures of career and educational goals. Many of these structural factors influence a married couple's decision to enter into parenthood. Later ages at which marriages occur today are also associated with fewer numbers of children being produced. However, the reduction in numbers of births is not due solely to age at first marriage, but to complex social structural variables such as those just described (Morgan et al., 1999).

The age of parents at the birth of their first child is associated with other effects observed in various areas of their lives. A particular dilemma is when a person's becoming a parent is off time developmentally according to what is normative for peers and age-mates, such as the case of teenage pregnancies. When people have their first child at a young age, their ability to pursue educational goals is hampered. Similarly, the more education people have, the older they tend to be when having their first child (Hofferth, Reid, & Mott, 2001).

## How Does Parenthood Affect a Couple's Committed Relationship?

The committed relationship of a couple acts as a foundation for their family system. Forming such a relationship requires time, effort, and commitment to resolving conflicts, developing patterns, and achieving a level of healthy functioning. The focus of the first years following marriage and commitment are devoted to achieving these ends.

Our culture supports romantic notions about parenthood and child rearing that may deceive adults about what these roles involve and require. Folklore implies that parenthood improves a couple's marriage relationship and that a truly successful marriage is one in which happiness predominates.

However, these notions are usually cast aside in light of the reality of everyday life as a couple. Becoming a parent causes a restructuring and reorganization of a couple's committed relationship. A new baby, especially the first produced by a couple, produces obvious effects that are both positive and challenging. Researchers who study the effects of parenthood on marital satisfaction have consistently reported that, rather than improving a couple's relationship, the presence of children is associated with decreasing martial satisfaction (Bradbury, Fincham, & Beach, 2000) (see Figure 5–11). The quality

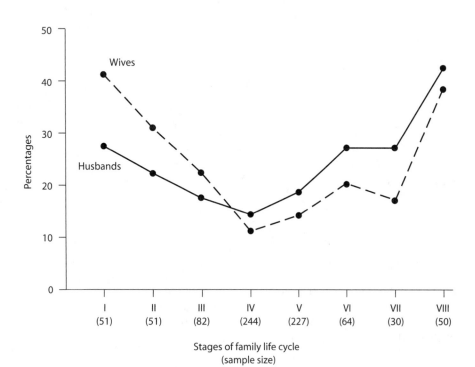

**FIGURE 5–11.** The percentage of individuals at different stages of family development who reported that their marriage was going well "all the time."

*Source:* Rollins, B., & Feldman, H. (1970). Marital satisfaction over the family life cycle. *Journal of Marriage and the Family, 32*, 25. Copyrighted 1970 by the National Council on Family Relations, 3989 Central Avenue, NE, Suite 550, Minneapolis, MN. Reprinted by permission.

of marital satisfaction declines in association with increasing age of children, culminating at its lowest point when children reach middle childhood and then increasing as children grow through adolescence and into early adulthood. This phenomenon is more marked among wives than among husbands (Glenn, 1990).

At first examination of this information, it may appear that children are detrimental to a couple's marital happiness. However, researchers who study the topic believe that the increasing amount of **role strain** during the initial years of child rearing causes the decline in marriage satisfaction rather than the mere presence of children. Role strain occurs when adults attempt to fulfill several competing social roles simultaneously and to a high degree of performance and efficiency. In most family systems today, this means that both adults attempt to cope with the multiple roles of worker, parent, and marriage partner. When individuals try to perform all of these roles at a very high level of proficiency, the effect is that performance in all roles suffers to some degree. Since most individuals understand that children's needs often must take priority over personal needs, their roles as marriage partners are allowed to take less precedence and priority in terms of expending energy and resources.

This information strongly suggests that it is important for couples to develop a strong marriage relationship prior to the production of children, since the relationship usually does not receive considerable attention while they are actively involved in child rearing. Most couples have some idea that their lives will change when they become parents. However, most are unaware that their marriage relationship will be challenged to some degree. Many more are equally surprised to discover that the introduction of children tends to reorganize the marriage into a traditional sex-role orientation. In many cases, women assume traditional mothering and housekeeping roles while men gravitate more toward their careers and their role as provider. This tends to occur even among couples who have agreed to promote an egalitarian philosophy about roles within the home and family (Bird, 1997; Coltrane, 1990). Several explanations have been suggested for this phenomenon:

■ Women, because of their biology (e.g., the ability to breast-feed), may have a different reaction to childbearing than men, one that causes a greater motivation and interest in parenting (Rossi, 1977).

■ Social scripting acquired in early childhood about parenthood becomes activated when individuals assume this role in adulthood (Cox, 2001).
■ Economic considerations may dictate who performs what jobs and responsibilities in the family. For example, because men are typically paid more for their work than women, many women assume parenting and home responsibilities while men assume the role of family provider (Cox, 2001).

The arrival of a child is not likely to destroy a couple's relationship, but it is not likely to salvage one that is troubled. Although both partners may expect to observe decreases in opportunities for shared leisure activities, there are more opportunities to enjoy activities involving both adults.

• • • • • • • • • • • • • • • • • • • • • • • • • • •

## Parenting Reflection 5–6

How can couples prepare and cope successfully with the projected declines in their marital satisfaction if they know in advance of having children that this is likely to occur?

• • • • • • • • • • • • • • • • • • • • • • • • • • •

• • • • • • • • • • • • • • • • • • • • • • • • • • •

*Focus Point.* New parents experience a period of adjustment to their new roles following the birth of their first child. Although early researchers viewed this as a crisis event in the family career, a more contemporary view is one of transition. The transition to new parenthood is influenced by several factors, such as the timing of the first child's birth in the adults' lives and the sex of the adult. One of the major adjustments that occurs is the shift in the priorities of the marriage relationship toward the individuals' new roles as parents. Researchers report that satisfaction with marriage often declines because of the stress adults experience in managing their new roles.

• • • • • • • • • • • • • • • • • • • • • • • • • • •

## NEW AVENUES TO PARENTHOOD: ASSISTED REPRODUCTIVE TECHNOLOGIES (ART)

Many people wish to become parents but are unable to do so in the usual fashion. The reasons preventing their ability to reproduce are often medically related, such as

**FIGURE 5–12.** Couples experiencing difficulties in conceiving or who have a history of genetic disease have a number of medically assisted options available to help in becoming parents.

when a man has an abnormally low sperm count. In other instances, the reasons are more social in nature, as when a woman decides that she wants to become a mother but is not cohabitating or is not married.

Medical technology has advanced to levels that were unimaginable in the past that allow people to have children under some of the most incapacitating reproductive situations (Figure 5–12). Although the success rates of these methods are fairly low (12 to 20 percent) and they may cost thousands of dollars that may or may not be covered by insurance plans, many people are willing to endure such hardships to achieve biological parenthood. Other individuals who have fertility problems adopt children as a means for achieving parenthood.

## Artificial Insemination

One of the oldest assisted technologies available involves injecting sperm into a woman's cervix. Several routes may be taken with this method. For example, when a man has a low sperm count, the sperm from several of his ejaculations are combined into one injection. If the man is infertile or a woman has no male partner available, it is likely that artificial insemination by donor (AID) will be used. In these situations, the donor is matched according to characteristics desired such as physical appearance. When AID is used, the donor's identity is often anonymous.

## In Vitro Fertilization (IVF)

This method is being used by an increasing number of couples who have difficulty conceiving a child. It is the most promising avenue for parenthood among those women whose infertility results from blockage of the fallopian tubes. In the course of this treatment, fertility drugs are administered to the woman to facilitate overproduction of ova. At the time of ovulation, a mature egg is removed surgically, fertilized by sperm from her partner or from a donor in a laboratory dish, and then implanted into the mother's uterus. It is customary for several ova to be fertilized in this manner since the rate is fairly low for the successful implantation and survival of the zygote. As a result, this method frequently results in multiple births.

Two newer methods have higher success rates. These include: (1) gamete intrafallopian transfer (GIFT) and (2) zygote intrafallopian transfer (ZIFT). Both of these techniques involve implanting an egg or sperm or a fertilized egg (zygote) into a woman's fallopian tube.

## Ovum Transfer

This procedure is used when a woman produces poor quality ova or has had her ovaries removed. This method is the female counterpart of AID where an egg is provided by a donor female (usually anonymous) that becomes fertilized in the laboratory using the sperm of the woman's partner or by an anonymous male donor. Sometimes, the donor egg is fertilized inside the donor by artificial insemination. The donor's uterus is flushed out several days following the insemination, and the zygote is retrieved and implanted in the woman's uterus. One of the advantages of this procedure is that it can be used with post-menopausal women.

## Surrogate Motherhood

Sometimes a couple who experiences fertility difficulties will contract with a fertile woman to conceive a child by artificial insemination, often by the sperm from the man. The surrogate mother is paid a fee for performing this service in addition to expenses covering prenatal care and delivery. According to the usual contractual terms, the surrogate mother agrees to relinquish all parental rights to the father and his partner when the baby is born.

This method of assisted conception is fraught with legal problems and, according to some, ethical issues. The legal problems are traced to the groundbreaking case of Baby M in 1988. A surrogate mother changed her mind about relinquishing custody of the child at birth. The court decided that she was not allowed to have custody but did grant her visitation rights. Some states have laws prohibiting surrogate parenthood or have limited the terms of the contracts that are written for this purpose. While many states prohibit payment for adoption, surrogate parenthood is not adoption since the legal parent is the father. Some ethicists worry that to allow surrogate parenthood would encourage the practice among poor or disadvantaged women as a means for livelihood in providing a questionable service for more advantaged individuals and families. Other questions that this practice raise include the right of access by others such as singles or cohabiting couples and how to resolve the problems that would arise if a contracting couple divorced or separated prior to the birth of a child carried by a surrogate mother. Other issues that are likely to arise following the child's birth include the child's right to information about the surrogate mother's medical history.

Some concerns also exist about the quality of parenting among those who have used medically assisted conception procedures. Basically, these relate to the role of biological parenthood in influencing the strength of psychological attachment between children and parents that is assumed to be lacking in these cases. One study suggests that this factor is not as important as it might

appear since the quality of parenting was judged to be better among those using these techniques for conception when compared with parents who conceived children naturally (Golombok et al., 1995, 2003). In fact, adoptive and medically assisted parents scored similarly in this regard. Apparently, the great desire and the lengths to which couples with fertility difficulties go to attain parenthood act as significant motivations to perform well in parenting roles. Children conceived via various assisted reproductive technologies are reported to be no different from children conceived naturally (Blasco & Verney, 2003; Tully, Moffitt, & Caspi, 2003).

### Parenting Reflection 5–7

Is it likely that one day in the future all pregnancies will be managed by in vitro methods? What would be the circumstances involved that lead to and result in this situation?

*Focus Point.*   Assisted reproductive technology is now available for helping many individuals experiencing fertility difficulties to become parents. While these methods are costly and not widely available, they include a variety of approaches that attempt to circumvent various problems of reproduction that a man or a woman or both have in causing a conception to take place.

## ADOPTION ISSUES

Adoption is the oldest solution to adult infertility and a way of caring for children whose biological parents are unable to do so (Ostrea, 2003). It involves the legal, social, and psychological processes of including a younger person into a family system and coming to accept this person as one's relative (Schwartz, 2000). Because our culture's legal and social heritage comes from England, American attitudes and laws tend to stigmatize adoption (Pavao, 2004). When adoption laws were originally written in the United States, custom placed a significant emphasis on the importance of blood ties among family members. This was particularly important because of the way family property was inherited. In more recent times, however, laws in this country have been revised to make adoption easier and more accessible to more diverse individuals and couples. Before the 1970s, agencies largely restricted adoption to middle-class, white, affluent families. Today, it is possible for single people (both heterosexual and homosexual), older people, dual-career families, and others to adopt children of different racial and ethnic backgrounds (DeBlander & DeBlander, 2004; Mallon, 2004; Pavao, 2004; Varon, 2003).

The status of adoptive parents continues to be marginalized by society (Schwartz, 2000), and a variety of cultural beliefs surround adoptive families and their children. Adoptive parents tend to believe that, regardless of their degree of emotional stability or maturity, regardless of how much they try, it is impossible in the long run for them to replace or compensate for a child's loss of biological parents (Adesman & Adesmec, 2004). It is likely that this perception is also present in society as a whole. Involuntarily childless women tend to believe that society promotes the notion that the biological tie between natural parents and children is important for psychological bonding and love (Eshleman, 2004). When it occurs between adoptive parents and children, the love and bonding in this relationship is perceived as second rate at best. Society may consider adoptive children to be second rate because of their unknown genetic past and may not consider adoptive parents to be bona fide parents. Some people also believe that the attachment between adoptive children and their parents is problematic, especially when children are adopted at older ages when the critical period for establishing emotional attachment or bonding in infancy has passed.

These perceptions of societal beliefs may influence the success or failure of the adoption process for the families involved (Wegar, 2000). In effect, the degree to which individuals accept and internalize such beliefs may influence their ability to learn to be parents. Adoption agencies may need to consider ways to assist new adoptive parents in learning parenting skills that will counteract negative views of adoption, adoptive parents, and the reasons for adoption (Caldwell, 2004; Pavao, 2004).

There is a heavily heterosexist, pronatal cultural belief in the United States about marriage and family life. According to this belief, reproduction and childbearing are glorified and romanticized, and childlessness is devalued as a viable option for married individuals. As more people begin to devalue the presence of children in their lives and make the conscious decision not to reproduce, there may be a greater acceptance of this status among adults. In addition, as foster parenting, stepparenting, and other types of family forms become more common, society may begin to accept the greater diversity of family forms (see Chapter 2). Furthermore, advances in reproductive technology that were unheard of 15 years ago have allowed more infertile couples to become biological parents. These methods tend to devalue the importance of biological ties and encourage the consideration of alternative family forms as viable means of creating family systems.

Several additional factors are associated with the decision to adopt a child (Bitler & Zavodny, 2002; Keck & Kupecky, 2004; Ostrea, 2003; Pavao, 2004):

- The reduced population of adoptees and the downward trend in adoption continues to occur but seems to have slowed in recent years and may be due to the increased number of illegitimate births and the decreased number of unmarried mothers who retain custody of their children.
- Adopting a child is primarily a function of childlessness, infertility, and age.
- Adopted children are as economically advantaged as children raised by never-married, single-parent mothers.
- More white women with out-of-wedlock children seek to place children for adoption than do black women of similar status.
- Children of either sex are acceptable to those adopting, while minority children and those with disabilities are preferred less. There is a greater preference for children under 13 years of age and the preference increases as the age of children decreases.
- Between 1989 and 1995 (the most current complete data available), about 1 percent of children born to never-married women were relinquished for adoption, as compared with 9 percent who were relinquished before 1979. The tendency for unmarried mothers to keep their infants has made adoption increasingly more difficult in recent years.

## Types of Adoptions

Today a variety of adoption options are available to potential parents and to those placing children for adoption (Caldwell, 2004). No local, state, or federal registries maintain a central database for matching potential parents with adoptive children. This is partially due to differences in laws governing adoption from state to state and from nation to nation. However, the presence of laws that govern adoption, the age and developmental status of an available child, and the potential compatibility between the parents and an available child also may play a role in the type of adoption a couple might pursue.

**Public Adoption.**  Public adoption typically takes place through an agency licensed for placing children for adoption (Neil, 2002). These agencies may be nonprofit and sponsored by charities or religious organizations. Potential parents often locate the agencies through word-of-mouth, ads in local newspapers or Yellow Pages, Web searches, or referral from lawyers, social workers, or medical sources. The agencies typically offer counseling and education for potential parents regarding the adoption process and what to expect following adoption. Often there is a waiting period for five years or longer as the potential parents experience screening procedures and the search is made for an appropriate child for placement. Potential parents can expect to pay an application fee (often quite high), the legal fees involved in formalizing the adoption, and even the medical costs incurred by the birth mother.

**Private Adoption.**   Private adoptions do not involve an agency but occur by the involvement of a third party, often an attorney, who arranges the adoption between the potential parents and the birth mother (Varon, 2003). These adoptions offer greater control to the potential parents but may be significantly more expensive than public adoption. However, it is not unusual for this to be a more risky adoption in that the birth mother has greater latitude in changing her mind, even after the potential parents have paid her medical expenses.

**Closed, Open, or Semi-Open Adoption.**   Whether public or private, an adoption may be closed, open, or semi-open. Until recently, all adoptions were **closed** in that the identities of both the adoptive and biological parents were unknown to each party and no communication took place between these families. It was thought that this was the best way to handle identity and attachment issues in the adoptive family for both parents and children. An increasing number of adoptions in the last few years are **open,** meaning that it is possible to determine identities of biological parents. Adoptees and their adoptive parents have access to information records. A **semi-open adoption** permits access to information for all parties but no contact.

However, open adoption arrangements are controversial (Sobol, Daly, & Kelloway, 2000). Adoptive parents may find open records relating to their adopted child's biological parents and birth circumstances to be ominous (Grace, 2003; Rushton, 2003; Townsend, 2003). Biological parents may wish for their anonymity to be intact regardless of the desires of a biological child to know their identity. On the other hand, adoptees often cite the need to know the medical history of biological parents and family for a variety of reasons. Because many states have laws allowing an adoptee access to records of their adoption, **reunions** with birth parents, most frequently the mother, are occurring more frequently (Pavao, 2004). These have unpredictable outcomes that may be very positive, very negative, or a mix.

**Transracial Adoption.**   The problems encountered among adoptive families sometimes are heightened when the race of the child is different from that of the parents and other family members. Several issues have been identified as critical adjustment challenges for multiracial adoptive families (Kennedy, 2004). (1) When adoptive parents see themselves as "rescuing" a child from a potentially disadvantaged life, they tend to cast the child into a victim role and expect the child to be grateful for their generosity. (2) Some extended family members are not likely to accept a child who is of a different racial group; this child will feel discrimination. (3) The insidious influence of racial stereotyping may affect adopted families; for example, an Asian child may be expected to excel in academics or an African American child in athletics (4) A racially different adopted child may experience prejudicial treatment by peers at school because of his or her adoptive status in a racially mixed family. Despite these challenges, research has demonstrated repeatedly that transracially adopted children are not harmed by their experiences, although there are reports of identity issues (Figure 5–13). In fact, children may benefit from such placement (Swize, 2002).

The issues involved in transracial adoption are especially accentuated for African American and Native American children. These groups of children are overrepresented in the foster care population when compared to the representation of children in the general population (Perez, O'Neil, & Gesiriech, 2004). Interracial adoptions are viewed skeptically today because of objections raised by professional groups based on questions about children's identity issues and assertions of cultural genocide (Swize, 2002). As a consequence, interracial adoptions declined to about 8 percent of all adoptions in the late 1980s. The position disfavoring interracial adoption is accentuated by the passage of the Indian Child Welfare Act of 1978 that requires placement of adoptive children into the child's extended family, other members of their tribe, or other Indian families. Congress has acted to support this type of adoption, perhaps in contradiction of earlier legislation. The Multi-Ethnic Placement Act of 1994 and the Adoption and Safe Families Act of 1997 prohibit the delay or denial of placement of children based on race, color, or national origin of the parents. The difficulty in enforcement of these laws may explain why transracial adoptions continue to occur (Barth, Webster, & Lee, 2002).

## Parenting Reflection 5–8

You are the parent of a transracial adopted child. You've been asked to address a group of potential adoptive parents who are likely to pursue this option for creating an adoptive family. What advice would you provide for these adults about what to expect, what to avoid, and ways to react to others who would make negative judgments about this decision?

**International Adoption.** Some potential parents tire of the bureaucratic procedures and lengthy wait period often involved in domestic adoption and turn to agencies that assist in placing children for adoption from foreign countries. The numbers of these adoptions have increased in recent years. Americans adopted orphans from China (4,600), Russia (4,200), South Korea (1,700), Guatemala (1,600), the Ukraine (1,200), Romania, Vietnam, and Kazakhstan (700 each country), and other foreign countries in 2001 (Delahunt, 2002). The majority of these children were infants at the time of adoption, lessening the problems encountered with older adopted children involving cultural issues. One benefit that has aided adopting families was enactment of the Child Citizenship Act of 2001, which confers U. S. citizenship to foreign-born children when adoption is finalized.

**FIGURE 5–13.** Families formed by transracial adoption have unique needs and challenges; however, research shows that children are not harmed by such experiences.

International adoptions, however, are noted for their high risk of many kinds of difficulties (Bowie, 2004; Layne, 2004; Murphy & Knoll, 2003). Prospective parents must arrange for large payments such as all agency and in-country expenses, medical checkups, documents, visa and travel expenses, meals, and lodging. They may not be able to choose a desired child. In addition, they may experience obstacles in gathering a health history about the child and frustrations with agencies and government restrictions. On the other hand, international adoption is more likely to occur successfully for single, gay or lesbian, or older adults seeking to become parents. Regardless, as a result of this option in adoption, more American families are multicultural as part of their nature. Multicultural adoptive families also have more resources to call upon today than in the past. Numerous Web sites, for example, offer information, links for support, and opportunities and guidance in the adoption process involving nonnative-born children (e.g., Adoption Associates, Inc., http://www.adoptassoc.com/; International Adoption Clinic at the University of Minnesota, http://www.peds.umn.edu/iac/). In the end, however, the success of an international adoption may depend on the ability of children to function at high levels of overall competence (McGuinness & Pallansch, 2000).

## Parenting in Adoptive Family Systems

What is the nature of parent-child relations in family systems that only have adopted children as compared with those who have children born as well as adopted into the family? Relatively little is known about parenting and the result of parenting experiences among adoptive families (Borders, Black, & Pasley, 1998; Brodzinsky & Pinderhughes, 2002; Chiang & Finley, 2001; Lal, 2002; Noy-Sharav, 2002; Pavao, 2004; Schwartz, 2000). However, when compared to families with only natural children or both natural and adopted children, those children in all-adoptive families generally tend to score lower on social and personal adjustment measures than children in natural families. Children in mixed families are similar to those in natural families on such measures. The natural children in these mixed families do not differ from those in all-natural families. This seems to indicate that the placement of adopted children into a mixed family situation does not adversely affect the natural children's adjustment and may have a positive influence on adoptive children.

Adoptive parents are challenged in their ability to adjust to their new status (Brodzinsky & Pinderhughes, 2002). The transition to parenthood is abrupt for adoptive parents as compared with the opportunity natural parents are afforded by a 9-month pregnancy and the physical experiences that accompany a pregnancy. In addition, adoptive parents often do not receive the social support that natural parents are afforded by being given baby showers, for example. This adjustment challenge is especially heightened when an older child is adopted as compared to an infant.

### Parenting Reflection 5–9

You are the Adoptive Parent Trainer for an adoption placement service. What would you include as important topics to cover in preparing new adoptive parents of infants for what to expect from this "instant family" experience that lacks the benefit of preparation provided by a pregnancy?

**Disclosing Adoption.**   In the distant past, adoptive parents were advised to keep the true status of their adoptive child a secret. More recently, however, adoptive parents are urged to tell children about their adoptive status, but to provide few details about their known origins. This is a topic of considerable controversy (Perry, 2004). The general consensus is that a dialogue must be established about a child's adoptive status. The age at which it should occur is highly debatable. Parenting FAQs 5–2 illustrates the major issues relating to disclosure for adoptive parents.

*Focus Point.*   Some adults who wish to be parents adopt children. Potential parents may choose to pursue one of several types of adoption. Multiracial adoptive families and those involving international adoption have unique challenges. Many factors influence the decision to adopt a child. The process of adoption often follows a predictable path that may be long and costly. A key issue among adoptive parents is telling children that they are adopted. Later, many adult adoptees often seek to reunite with birth parents for a variety of reasons.

**Parenting FAQs 5–2**

**We are the adoptive parents of a beautiful baby boy. He's a preschooler now, and I think it's time to begin telling him about his adoption. My wife disagrees with me. She says we should wait until he's older, like in elementary school or junior high school. What would you advise us to do about this disagreement?**

**A:** I think it's important that adoptive children know of their situation. Experts advise parents to begin a dialogue during an adoptive child's preschool years regarding his or her adoptive status. This dialogue is a continual one, stretching throughout the child's growing years in the family and even extending into adulthood. Parents should consider the following guidelines when they inform children of their adoption:

■ Tailor the details of the child's adoption to his or her age and/or developmental abilities.

■ Do not necessarily wait for the child to bring up the issue. Adoptees may be reluctant to bring up the topic because they do not want to seem disloyal. However, too much discussion about the topic can indicate that parents have not resolved the issue of their infertility or are not yet comfortable with the topic.

■ Start the story of the adoption at the child's beginning. For example, talk about where the child lived before the adoption.

■ Refer to the biological parents as real people who exist somewhere.

■ When discussing the biological parents' decision to place the child for adoption, try to show empathy for the difficulty of their position. This is best accomplished by telling the child that the biological parents made a difficult decision that was in the best interests of the baby. Do not say, however, that the biological parents gave the child for adoption because he or she was loved so very much. This serves to confuse rather than elucidate the child's questions.

■ Inform the child that there are many other children like him or her. Explain that adoption is no cause for shame.

■ Help the child understand that even though he or she has two sets of parents, the adoptive arrangement is permanent and the adoptive parents are responsible for his or her well-being and rearing.

*Source:* Adapted from Melina, L. R. (1986). *Raising adopted children: A manual for adoptive parents.* New York: Harper & Row.

## FACILITATING THE TRANSITION TO PARENTHOOD

The discussion thus far has identified adjustments and some difficulties in becoming a parent, especially for the first time. There is considerable agreement about what produces these problems for individuals and couples. How can those considering parenthood or those who are expectant or new parents prepare for what awaits them? What kinds of support can assist these individuals and couples in their transition to parenthood?

First, support groups may offer a means for people to gain information and education about parenthood (Cowan & Cowan, 1992). These groups assist individuals and couples in several ways. (1) Men are included and welcomed, giving the message that they are essential participants in the parenting process. (2) People gain reassurance that others share similar fears, misgivings, and stressfulness about becoming parents or on becoming parents. (3) Expectations about parenthood and child rearing can be examined in a safe environment. (4) Such experiences help couples to network with one another and to form social supports that often take the place of family support that may not be available.

Second, parenting classes may be particularly helpful to new parents, especially in the first few weeks and months following a child's birth. These classes may be structured according to topics (e.g., infant nutrition, physical care) and meet for several weeks. The classes may be informal and combine educational as well as supportive experiences. For example, an emerging parenting education experience in many large cities is known by various names, such as Boot Camp for Dads (Murphy, 2003). The daylong session is offered on a weekend, and new fathers are asked to bring their child to the session with them. They are assigned to an experienced father who has previously graduated from the Boot Camp experience and whose children are older. This exposes new fathers to a mentor to whom they can relate more effectively. The fathers gain insights about what it means to be a new father, what infants are like and what kind of care they need, what to expect from themselves and their partners, and so on. Such educational experiences help new parents to learn about resources, equipment, and methods of child care.

Families continue to provide support for new parents but usually for a limited period following the child's birth. Grandparents are often called upon to provide assistance with older children, help with household chores, provide information about child care, and generally be supportive.

## POINTS TO CONSIDER

■ The decision to become a parent is often based on a conscious decision-making process by many adult individuals. The decision to become a parent can be influenced by complex issues, such as: (1) economic considerations relating to the costs of childbearing and child rearing; (2) structural factors such as employment status of the adults, values and beliefs, and the desired family size; and (3) psychosocial factors such as parenthood as an expected developmental task of adulthood, personal reasons or motivations, the values and functions that children may serve for adults, and meanings ascribed to parenting roles.

■ A topology describing the kinds of couples who have decided to remain child free or to become parents, whether by a conscious decision or by accepting a surprise pregnancy, is offered by Cowan and Cowan (1992).

■ The birth of a couple's first child prompts a transition of a family system into the childbearing family stage of the family life career. The adjustments that adults make initially focus on realignment of patterns set up early in a marriage.

■ The difficulties some couples experience at the birth of their first child relate to inadequate preparation for parenthood and the abruptness with which these changes take place. Several factors mediate these adjustments: (1) the timing of the birth in the adult's personal developmental path, (2) the level of personal self-esteem, (3) the employment status of the mother, (4) the quality of patterns established in the family system prior to the first child's birth, (5) the degree of commitment to being a parent, (6) the good health of the mother and child, and (7) the expectations (either positive or negative) of what it will be like to be a parent.

■ The economic, social, and psychological costs of childbearing are considered when individuals decide whether to become parents. Parenthood affects a couple's committed relationship in that satisfaction usually declines during those years that a family is involved in child rearing. This is believed to be due to role strain of the adults rather than to the presence of children within the family system.

■ New medical technologies are available for assisting individuals and/or couples who have fertility difficulties to conceive and become parents. These technologies are expensive and not widely available. They include: (1) artificial insemination, (2) in vitro fertilization, (3) ovum transfer, and (4) surrogate motherhood. Some of these involve ethical and legal issues.

■ New parents may need assistance as they become adjusted to their new family role. Sources of assistance include support groups for new mothers, new fathers, or both; parenting classes; and assistance from family members.

■ Adoption involves challenges for both adults and children. Adopted children usually have greater chances of an improved life situation, although society tends to stigmatize adoptive families.

■ There are a number of reasons why people choose to become adoptive parents.

■ Prospective parents may choose to pursue different options for adoption, each with its own advantages and disadvantages.

■ Parenting in adoptive families offers unique challenges not found in other family systems.

■ Adults are encouraged to discuss the circumstances surrounding a child's adoption openly.

## CHAPTER 6

# Pregnancy and Childbirth

**Focus Questions**
■ ■ ■ ■ ■ ■ ■ ■ ■ ■

1. What critical factors influence the course of pregnancy?
2. What are current trends in providing prenatal care?
3. What are current trends in childbirth management?

■ ■ ■ ■ ■ ■ ■ ■ ■ ■

The birth of a baby is a significant event in the lives of parents and for the family system into which it arrives. The baby's arrival is anticipated with an array of feelings ranging from great excitement to high anxiety. This may be particularly so when a couple is having their first child, whose conception was desired and planned (see Chapter 5).

This chapter discusses the experiences that arise from a pregnancy and the options associated with childbirth. Many Americans today carefully plan and time the conception of their children. The high cost of bearing and rearing children is one important reason this occurs. Pregnancy provides the first opportunity for parents-to-be to offer nurturing caregiving to their unborn child. It is a highly critical period in the life of the unborn child. The environment the mother provides for the child she carries can have long-term consequences for the baby, its parents, and the entire family system. Pregnancy and childbirth are important aspects of parenting (Figure 6–1).

## PREGNANCY CONSIDERATIONS

The period in the uterus before birth is one of the most crucial stages in an individual's life span. During the average 280-day period, biological foundations are established that will influence much of the person's developmental potential over his or her lifetime.

In earlier times, development before birth was surrounded by mystery. Because much of what occurs during this period is hidden from direct observation, the beginnings of life were largely misunderstood and explained through superstition and speculation. Folklore about pregnancy encouraged the notion that almost everything a pregnant woman experienced would ultimately affect the developing child. Physical defects in a baby were believed to be caused by maternal experiences. For example, birthmarks were thought to result from the mother's having spilled wine or eaten too many strawberries

**FIGURE 6–1.** The birth of a baby is a significant event and initiates numerous changes for a family system.

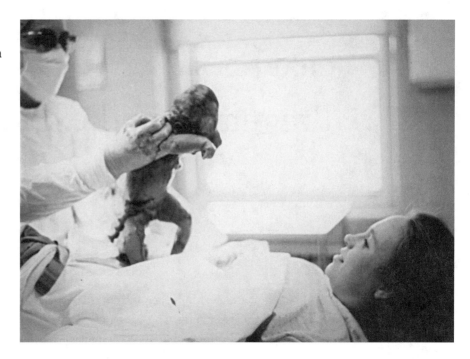

during pregnancy, and a harelip was thought to result from the mother's having seen a rabbit. Similarly, it was believed that if a pregnant woman listened to classical music or read classical literature, the child would have strong musical or literary tendencies.

Such folklore has been discarded as scientists have gained information on how life begins, how the genetic code is transmitted, and how the internal and external maternal environments actually influence fetal development. Dramatic advances have been made in knowledge about caring for babies prior to their birth, especially for premature neonates and those of low birth weight. Genetic science has progressed to where it is now possible to clone or make an identical genetic copy of many species, including human beings. Cloning human embryos, however, has been banned in the United States (Itzkoff, 2003).

## Characteristics of Prenatal Development

The time before the birth of an individual is significant and unique in many ways. Many experts consider this time in the life span to be the most important because of its crucial effects on later stages. It can be characterized briefly in the following three ways.

1. *It is the shortest stage of the life span.* The average length of pregnancy is 280 days, although the period does vary somewhat for every pregnancy. Remarkably, during this relatively short time the individual develops from a one-celled organism at conception to having more than 200 billion cells at birth.

2. *It is the period of most rapid growth and development in the human life span.* The first trimester (90 days) of pregnancy is the *embryonic stage*, or the formative phase of an individual's growth and development. During this stage the fertilized egg differentiates into specialized cells that make up the body and organ systems. By the end of this embryonic stage, the body has a distinctly recognizable human form and contains all the organs essential for functioning after birth. The second and third trimesters are the *fetal period* of the pregnancy. During this time, the body experiences refinements and the most rapid increase in weight and length. At the beginning of this period, the fetus weighs approximately 1 ounce and is about 1½ inches long. At birth, the infant weights about 7½ pounds and is about 21 inches long.

3. *It is a highly critical period in human development.* The embryo is vulnerable to many factors that

can enhance or hinder its development. Environmental and genetic factors can have permanent effects, adversely or positively, on the embryo. These factors can result in congenital birth defects, miscarriage, prematurity, low birth weight, and tendencies toward certain behavioral traits.

••••••••••••••••••••••••••••••••••••••••••••••

***Focus Point.***  The period of prenatal development is one of the most crucial stages in the life cycle. During this short period of rapid growth, myriad factors can affect the individual's future development.

••••••••••••••••••••••••••••••••••••••••••••••

## CRITICAL FACTORS OF PREGNANCY

During pregnancy the developing baby is exposed to a number of environmental influences that can have both short- and long-term effects on the baby's development (Eisenberg, 2002). Environmental influences that can be harmful to an unborn child, such as smoking or drinking alcohol (Eisenberg, 2002), should be avoided during pregnancy. Appropriate parenting before a child's birth involves being mindful of these factors and how they can impact a child's development over their life span.

### Age of the Mother

The age of the mother is one factor that contributes to the probability of having a baby with low birth weight

(Newburn-Cook et al., 2002). Babies who weigh 5½ pounds or less at birth are considered to be of low birth weight (Federal Interagency Forum on Child and Family Statistics, 2003). Low birth weight is often associated with death, brain and central nervous system damage, and mental retardation (Newburn-Cook et al., 2002). For these reasons, low birth weight is considered to be a congenital birth defect that has implications for the health and well-being of the infant, not only at birth but later in life. For example, learning difficulties and cognitive problems among school-age children are highly associated with low birth weight (Lawrence & Blair, 2003).

Women under 20 and over 40 years of age have a higher probability of delivering babies of low birth weight, especially if they are African American (Federal Interagency Forum on Child and Family Statistics, 2003) (see Figure 6–2). These women generally experience what is termed a high-risk pregnancy, due both to their age and to related social factors. For example, there is a greater frequency of high-risk pregnancies in certain ethnic groups, although this factor alone does not fully account for the phenomenon. In addition to low birth weight, other complications arising from high-risk pregnancies include circulatory and respiratory difficulties, brain damage, and physical and mental handicaps.

Older women experience higher rates of miscarriage and giving birth to children who have some type of genetic disorder. For example, the incidence of Down syndrome, a type of genetic disorder that causes mental

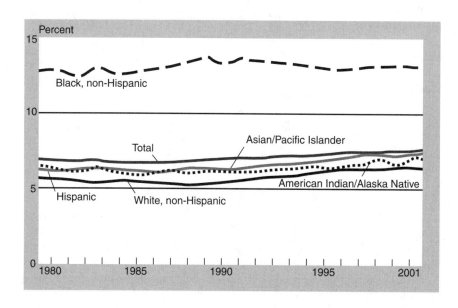

**FIGURE 6–2.**  Percentage of infants of low birth weight by mothers' race and Hispanic origin.

*Source:* Federal Interagency Forum on Child and Family Statistics (2003). *America's children: Key national indicators of well-being: 2003.* Washington, DC: U.S. Government Printing Office.

retardation and certain physical abnormalities, increases significantly among women who bear children after 40 years of age (Vontver, 2003). This is thought to result from chromosomal disturbances in the ova older women produce and hormonal changes that take place with aging. On the other hand, adolescent girls who become pregnant deliver babies with problems that are more likely due to attitudinal and behavioral causes rather than physical problems. For example, improper nutrition and lack of adequate prenatal care and supervision contribute to the high incidence of birth complications among teenage mothers. A more detailed discussion of adolescent childbearing is found in Chapter 12.

Other factors contributing to rates of low birth weight in the United States include: (1) the increasing numbers of large multiple births resulting from fertility treatments and (2) the general trend in delaying childbirth to later years in adulthood.

What are the ideal ages for women to bear healthy children? Apparently, because of both physical and social factors, many women experience healthy pregnancies with positive outcomes between the ages of 24 and 35 years of age (Vontver, 2003).

## Nutrition During Pregnancy

The nutrition and health of a pregnant woman are important related factors that influence the quality of development of the growing child (Anderson, 2003). These factors have a strong impact on the well-being of both the fetus and the mother, and they can influence the course of subsequent pregnancies. One of the most significant aspects of nutrition during pregnancy is the association between adequate weight gain by the mother and an increase in the infant's birth weight.

The United States has one of the highest rates of newborn death among the developed nations of the world (Federal Interagency Forum on Child and Family Statistics, 2003). This has been attributed to restrictions on weight gain in pregnant women on the advice of health care workers. Weight gain is a normal result of pregnancy and is important in its influence on neonatal birth weight and on the mother's ability to produce breast milk following the baby's birth. Until recently, weight gain was restricted to about 21 pounds, on the assumption that a relatively low-weight infant would be quicker and easier for the mother to deliver. Today, the recommended weight gain is between 26 and 35 pounds for most pregnant women (Allgeier & Allgeier, 2000). It

is anticipated that this change will result in a lowered infant mortality rate, decreases in numbers of infants of low birth weight, and better health overall for babies.

Maternal nutrition during pregnancy is critically important because the quality of the mother's diet will be reflected in the health and well-being of her baby. A woman generally does not need to increase her caloric intake considerably during pregnancy to have a nutritionally balanced diet. It is more important that she eat a well-rounded diet consisting of a variety of foods (Eisenberg, 2002), including dairy products, fruits and vegetables, and grains. Following prescribed guidelines, dietary intake during pregnancy should be increased by about 300 to 500 calories and include an extra serving of protein. Sodium intake may need to be monitored and the diet adapted if indicated as a means of managing certain metabolic conditions that can develop in pregnancy, such as toxemia. If weight gain occurs according to these guidelines and nutrition is adequate, the possibility of miscarriage or of having a stillborn or infant with low birth weight is significantly reduced (Federal Interagency Forum on Child and Family Statistics, 2003).

Some nutrients may play a critical role in influencing the quality and nature of a baby's development before birth. For example, a lack of adequate amounts of folic acid (a type of B vitamin) in a pregnant woman's diet is associated with high risk of spinal cord defects in a developing baby. In the United States, grain products are supplemented with this nutrient (Honein et al., 2001). It is also available in prenatal vitamin/mineral supplements and is available naturally in fresh fruits and vegetables.

An expectant mother's nutritional and health status can be adversely affected by her emotional state (Nelson et al., 2003). High levels of anxiety and depression during pregnancy can interfere with the mother's appetite and interest in eating a nutritionally sound diet and therefore adversely affect the health and well-being of the baby (Dipietro et al., 2003).

## Exercise

Expectant mothers need to prepare their bodies for pregnancy and child birth by participating in moderate levels of physical exercise. Examples of these activities include jogging, swimming, walking, cycling, and tennis. Women generally are the best judge of this level of exertion, but they should avoid pushing themselves above their reasonable limits of physical endurance in these kinds of activities (Committee on Obstetric Practice, 2002). Regular exercise provides many health benefits to an expectant mother such as maintaining regularity and improving respiration, circulation, and muscle tone. Regular exercise also is associated with an elevated mood.

## Prenatal Medical Supervision

Part of good prenatal parenting is providing the mother with medical supervision. Mothers who have at least five or more prenatal visits with a health care professional that begin during the first trimester increase the chances of having a healthy, full-term baby (Gabbe, Niebyl, & Simpson, 2003). Medical supervision for expectant mothers includes obtaining a health history, appropriate medical examinations and tests, and counseling about a variety of concerns and issues, such as method of child birth, appropriate nutrition, supervision of any drugs and prescriptions, and preparation for child birth. Most importantly, these visits with health care professionals can help expectant mothers manage weight gains appropriately and provide screening for a number of conditions affecting the health of both the mother and her unborn child.

## Drugs and Chemical Agents

Physicians generally urge their pregnant patients not to take *any* type of drug—prescription, nonprescription, or recreational—without medical advice (American Academy of Pediatrics Committee on Drugs, 1994). Although a developing baby is well protected within the uterus, certain drug and chemical agents can cause malformations and other problems. The developing embryo is most sensitive to interference from these agents, because it is during the embryonic period (first 90 days of gestation) when organ systems are being formed (see Figure 6–3). Effects of drug use during pregnancy can be manifested following a child's birth as well. For example, some of the daughters of women who took a synthetic hormone during their pregnancy developed a rare form of reproductive system cancer, had abnormalities in their genitals, and had higher risks of miscarriage (Treffers et al., 2001).

A number of drugs and other kinds of chemical agents are known to have *teratogenic* effects—that is, they cause the abnormal development of an embryo. Among the most widely publicized is thalidomide, a

drug used in the early 1960s to control the nausea or morning sickness that pregnant women sometimes experience. Thalidomide was later found to cause birth defects, such as absent or deformed limbs and organ translocations and malfunctions. Other drugs that may be prescribed in clinical level dosages that are teratogenic include the antibiotic tetracycline, certain psychotropic medications, and certain anticancer drugs.

Other drugs can cause developmental problems. Thyroid drugs taken by the mother can produce congenital goiter in the developing baby. Conflicting views exist about whether ingesting LSD and marijuana in pregnancy correlates with birth defects in babies. Even aspirin has deleterious effects if taken frequently in late pregnancy, in that it can cause problems in blood clotting for the baby and delay the normal beginning of labor. Exposure of the baby to female sex hormones through the mother's ingestion of contraception pills during the very early stages of pregnancy can cause defects in the baby's heart, reproductive system, anus, and central nervous system.

Other drug substances must be carefully avoided during pregnancy. These include:

**Alcohol.**   Attention has been directed recently to alcohol consumption during pregnancy and its association with birth defects in babies (Miller, Astley, & Clarren, 1999). Moderate consumption of two or more ounces of alcohol daily by a pregnant woman increases the risk of having a child with **fetal alcohol syndrome.** It is estimated that more than 12,000 infants are born each year in the United States with defects related to this syndrome (CDC-NCBDDD, 2002). These can range from a combination of several conditions, such as slowed growth both pre- and post-natally, brain and central nervous system disturbances, mild mental retardation, organ malformations, and malformed facial features. Many of the immediate and short-term disturbances affecting children with this syndrome eventually disappear a short time after birth. However, several serious, long-term effects can cause problems for many years, such as learning disabilities and hyperactivity that affect school performance (Sokol, Delaney-Black, & Nordstrom, 2003).

Even moderate drinking, one or two drinks daily, appears to cause harm to a developing baby (Sood et al., 2001). Because the risks for damage to the baby are so high, physicians urge women to avoid alcohol completely from the time they begin thinking about becoming

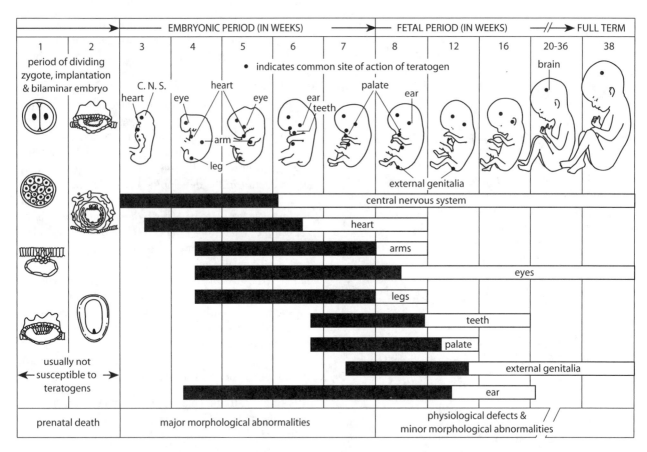

**FIGURE 6–3.** Critical periods occur in embryonic and fetal development in which the developing baby is sensitive and vulnerable to the influence of teratogens (substances known to cause developmental malformations) it experiences as part of the maternal environment. Major organ system deformities, as indicated by the black lines, occur when growth is occurring most rapidly. Minor physiological and structure damage is indicated by the white lines.
*Source:* Moore, K. L. (1974). *Before we are born.* Philadelphia, PA: Saunders.

pregnant to the time when they wean their child from breast-feeding (American Academy of Pediatrics Committee on Substance Abuse, 1993, 2001.)

• • • • • • • • • • • • • • • • • • • • • • • • • • • • • • • •

## Parenting Reflection 6–1

Should a mother who has a substance addiction be allowed to have custody of a new baby? Would the decision to allow custody have conditions such as the mother participating in a treatment program? Do medical personnel have an obligation to report such mothers to child protection agencies?

• • • • • • • • • • • • • • • • • • • • • • • • • • • • • • • •

**Cigarettes (Nicotine).** When an expectant mother smokes, nicotine and other chemical agents found in cigarettes can have an adverse effect on the developing child (Bourgeois, 2004). One of these includes an increased risk of miscarriage. The general finding is that mothers who are chronic heavy smokers (more than one pack a day) are more likely to have babies of low birth weight and to be at greater risk of miscarriage and stillbirth, as well as other complications (Martin et al., 2002). Pregnant women who smoke are also more likely to experience bleeding. Substances in cigarette smoke may elevate the heart rate and blood pressure of a fetus, causing it to increase its movements within the uterus and depriving it of adequate nutrients by reducing the mother's appetite. This reduction of essential nutrients contributes to low birth weight for these babies. Long-range effects in children of mothers who smoke during their prenatal development include poorer school performance, hyperactivity, perceptual-motor difficulties, and learning disabilities (Gabbe, Niebyl, & Simpson, 2003). In this regard, the effects of nicotine resemble the effects of alcohol on prenatal development.

**Caffeine.**   It appears that caffeine found in coffee, tea, chocolate, or soft drinks does not harm a developing baby prior to birth (Leviton & Cowan, 2002). This is relative to the expectant mother drinking small to moderate amounts of any of these substances. However, drinking large amounts (four or more cups of coffee daily) appears to be associated with a significantly higher risk of sudden infant death syndrome occurring following birth (Studd, 2004).

**Recreational Drugs (Cocaine, Heroin, Marijuana).** The high use of recreational drugs, such as marijuana, heroin, ecstasy, and cocaine, in the United States is of great concern due to the effects observed in infants whose mothers used these substances during pregnancy. However, some research is unclear about the effects of certain substances (Schutter & Brinker, 1992).

Cocaine (including crack cocaine, which is smoked rather than inhaled as a powder) is a particularly addictive substance. Infants born to women who are addicted to cocaine are also addicted and must receive special medical care following birth. The short- and long-term effects of this substance in infants are especially troublesome (Macmillan et al., 2001). Typically, these infants are of low birth weight and often are not carried to term before birth. They tend to be undersized in general and have smaller heads than average. Babies exposed to cocaine before birth often have urinary tract defects, and are apathetic, fretful, and less alert (Scher, Richardson, & Day, 2000).

Some states have enacted legislation or social policy regarding the welfare of so-called "crack babies" born to addicted mothers. While the U.S. Supreme Court overturned these laws in 2001, many people hold the perception that these infants have been abused by their mothers' addictive behavior. To the contrary, research has confirmed that the infants of addicted mothers studied were no worse off in a variety of developmental domains than children of mothers who smoked tobacco or marijuana, consumed alcohol, or provided a poor home

environment (Beeghly et al., 2003; Frank et al., 2001; Rose-Jacobs et al., 2002).

Although evidence is not conclusive, findings from research suggest that heavy marijuana use by pregnant women is associated with developmental problems in their offspring. These include information-processing problems, low birth weight, attachment problems, and higher risk of using drugs later in life (Anand, 2003; Mereu et al., 2003; Reichman & Teitler, 2003). These findings and others indicate that it is not wise for a woman to risk such conditions in her children by heavy use of marijuana during pregnancy.

## Infectious Diseases

Several types of infectious diseases can be transmitted from mother to child, both before birth through the placental membrane and during birth from contact with the mother's vaginal tract. The severity of these infections depends on when the disease is contracted by the mother during the course of her pregnancy.

German measles (rubella) is one of the best known examples of disease agents that can harm a developing embryo. Infection of the developing baby with this viral agent can result in deafness, blindness, heart defects, central nervous system damage, mild mental retardation, or a combination of these conditions, depending on when the pregnant woman contracted the disease. The greatest potential for harm to the developing baby exists during the embryonic stage of development. Unfortunately, because the symptoms of this disease in the mother closely resemble those of the common cold or an upper respiratory infection, detection of the disease is difficult. Fortunately, most women in the United States have been vaccinated against this disease (Plotkin, 2001).

Other diseases are known to damage the baby's central nervous system during the fetal stage of development. For example, conditions caused by the *cytomegalovirus* and the disease *toxoplasmosis* can contribute to brain damage, learning disabilities, sensory problems, and even death (March of Dimes Foundation, 2002).

The cytomegalovirus appears to be associated with improper or poor hygiene. It enters the nasal and throat passages of a fetus during birth and quickly makes its way into the central nervous system. It can be easily contracted among older children in day-care centers if proper personal hygiene is not practiced with great care.

Toxoplasmosis is an infection caused by a parasitic agent that normally is found in farm animals, pets, and poultry. Because it completes its life cycle only in cats, infection can occur from inhaling the dust created when cleaning a litter box. It can infect humans, especially when immune responses are not fully functional, as is normally the situation with young infants and newborns or in individuals who are infected with the HIV virus that causes AIDS. Toxoplasmosis results in various disorders in infants, such as encephalitis, which causes brain damage, central nervous system dysfunctions, and digestive disorders (Kravetz & Federman, 2002). If a pregnant woman transmits the disease to her fetus, the newborn may suffer blindness or mental retardation. Pregnant cat owners are well advised to relegate litter box cleaning to someone else.

Sexually transmitted diseases such as syphilis, gonorrhea, and HIV (human immunodeficiency virus), which causes AIDS (Acquired Immune Deficiency Syndrome), can also be transmitted by a pregnant woman to her developing baby (Williams, Norris, & Bedor, 2003). AIDS is an especially dangerous disease for all concerned. The HIV agent disables the fetal immune system, often resulting in the child's death within a short period of time following birth. Mothers who are infected with this virus become exposed in several ways, such as having sexual intercourse or sharing contaminated needles with an individual who is infected or from contact with infected blood. They may not develop AIDS symptoms themselves until a later time. Congenital HIV infection is believed to take place in late pregnancy and is affecting an increasing number of babies born to infected mothers worldwide (Kourtis et al., 2001). The AIDS virus can also be transmitted via a mother's breast milk to her infant. In the United States, the incidence of AIDS among women is increasing dramatically, and 75 percent of women with AIDS are of childbearing age (Bulterys, 2001). Currently, it is estimated that more than 80 percent of children with AIDS in the United States contracted this disease from their mothers during pregnancy. Pregnant women who are infected with HIV can be treated with AZT, a drug commonly prescribed for those with AIDS or HIV infection. This treatment can substantially reduce the likelihood that an infant will be born with this virus, especially if mothers avoid breast-feeding following birth.

Venereal diseases contracted by a woman in pregnancy also have a negative influence on developing babies. Syphilis germs transmitted from mother to baby across the placenta affect the child's bones and body organs. Women with gonorrhea pass the disease agents to their child during birth, often leading to blindness in the neonate if not treated properly. Genital herpes is caused by a virus that also may be passed to an infant during birth (Sullivan-Bolyai et al., 1983) and is believed to be responsible for about one-third of all deaths in newborns. If the mother is known to be infected, the risk of transmission can be minimized by a cesarean (surgical) rather than vaginal delivery.

## Metabolic Disorders

Women who are diabetic and become pregnant have a significantly high incidence of miscarriages, stillbirths, and infants born with multiple defects. Diabetes is not ordinarily transmitted to the child but does have an important influence on the child's development. This disorder is an inability of the mother's pancreas to produce a proper amount of insulin, the hormone that metabolizes sugar. As a result, an excessive amount of sugar exists in the mother's blood and urine. To compensate, the pancreas of her fetus enlarges and produces greater than usual amounts of insulin. Babies who manage to survive in this environment are usually overweight and have a bloated appearance at birth. In addition, their adjustment following birth is more difficult (Studd, 2004).

Another metabolic disorder is *phenylketonuria* (PKU), which is an inability to metabolize protein. Mothers with PKU and certain thyroid disorders face a greater risk of having a child who is mentally retarded (van Spronsen et al., 2003).

## Blood Type Incompatibility

Everyone's blood has a chemical factor identified as either Rh+ or Rh− (from *Rhesus*, the type of monkey used in the research on this blood factor). The **Rh factor** is an inherited characteristic and a dominant genetic trait. About 85 percent of whites are Rh+ compared with 93 percent of blacks and 99 percent of people of Asian descent (Bourgeois, 2004). The Rh blood type becomes a problem only when an Rh− woman conceives a child by an Rh+ man and the child inherits the father's dominant Rh+ factor. The Rh+ fetus produces substances called *antigens*, which pass across the placenta into the mother's bloodstream and cause her body to produce antibodies to the blood of the baby. This can also occur when small capillaries in the placenta rupture or during birth when the placenta passes from the mother's uterus and the baby's blood mixes with that of the mother through contact with small lacerations in the vaginal tract. Because of the antibodies, subsequent pregnancies may produce infants who exhibit a condition known as **erythroblastosis fetalis,** which is characterized by severe anemia, low birth weight, jaundice, severe brain damage, or mental retardation. The condition can be prevented by injecting the mother with a substance called *Rhogam* (Rh immune globulin), which prevents her body from producing antibodies to Rh+ blood factor of other developing babies when she is pregnant. This must be performed within a short period following her first delivery. The potential condition can be detected long before a pregnancy begins through blood tests performed as part of a standard marriage license procedure required in many states.

## Paternal Risk Factors in Prenatal Development

Mothers are not solely responsible for situations that place a developing baby at risk for harm. While the evidence points largely to what the maternal environment presents for better or for worse to a developing baby, certain situations from fathers can cause problems for the baby as well. For example, abnormal sperm development can be attributed to a man's exposure to lead, recreational drugs like marijuana and cocaine, cigarettes, alcohol, radiation, and environmental chemicals such as pesticides (Westheimer & Lopater, 2004). As with women, the reproductive cells (sperm) of men are likely to experience genetic mutations as age increases. These changes occur more frequently in the sperm cells of aging men than in the ova of women as age increases and may be a significant cause of birth defects in the children fathered by older men.

### Parenting Reflection 6–2

What can government agencies do to help disadvantaged mothers-to-be to have healthier pregnancies?

*Focus Point.* The quality of an individual's development before birth may be influenced positively or adversely by a number of factors, including age of the mother; the quality of her diet; the quality of medical care during pregnancy; her exposure to certain drugs, chemicals, or disease agents; the presence of certain metabolic conditions, such as diabetes; and blood incompatibility problems. Certain risk factors are also related to fathers.

## CURRENT TRENDS IN PRENATAL CARE

Every individual's right to be normal is encouraged and assisted by adequate care prior to birth. The field of **perinatology** is one area of medical science that has emerged in recent years to address this important need. Perinatology is concerned with the detection and treatment of illness in developing individuals during the prenatal stage. This new field of medical care has brought about advancements in knowledge and techniques for diagnosing the health status of individuals while they are still in the uterine environment (Sinclair, 2003).

Adequate prenatal supervision may be an important factor in reducing the incidence of low birth weight and prematurity in infants (Lawrence & Blair, 2003), a condition that has long-range implications for parents as well as children. However, the quality of prenatal care women receive varies according to their social, ethnic, and demographic backgrounds. Black mothers are generally reported to receive little care or to start their care late in the course of their pregnancy (Federal Interagency Forum on Child and Family Statistics, 2003). Adolescents and women over age 45 are likely to receive the least amount of prenatal care of the age groups usually surveyed. Amount of education is an important factor affecting whether women seek prenatal care. Mothers who do not complete high school are more likely to begin care late in pregnancy or receive no care.

**Medical genetic counseling** is an example of new advances in prenatal medical care. Until recently, physicians could only provide a minimal amount of information to parents who already had a child with birth defects about why the defects occurred and how to prevent them in future pregnancies. Expectant parents could be given only general advice about the probability that their child would be defective in some way at birth. Intensive research efforts to learn more about hereditary influences on birth defects have led to the development of remarkable new diagnostic tools and methods. Parents and potential parents can be given accurate information to assist them in making decisions about beginning a pregnancy or about the progress of a particular pregnancy. A genetic counselor investigates parents' medical backgrounds by obtaining their family history. Blood and other tissue samples are obtained to perform a chromosome analysis in order to identify genetic abnormalities. If a pregnancy is already in progress, various types of prenatal diagnostic tools are available to determine the status of the baby's health.

● ● ● ● ● ● ● ● ● ● ● ● ● ● ● ● ● ● ● ● ● ● ● ● ● ● ● ●

### Parenting Reflection 6–3

Is it a good idea to require couples, as part of the process of obtaining a marriage license, to submit blood samples for screening for potential problems with pregnancies?

● ● ● ● ● ● ● ● ● ● ● ● ● ● ● ● ● ● ● ● ● ● ● ● ● ● ● ●

## Prenatal Diagnostic Methods and Equipment

**Ultrasound** allows the creation of a **sonogram** (see Figure 6–4). This is much like an X-ray picture without the hazards of radiation. This method may be used to measure the growth of a fetus, to assess gestational age and structural abnormalities in the fetal body, to allow early detection of multiple pregnancies, and as a guide in other procedures such as amniocentesis.

**Sonoembriology** is a more recently developed advancement in ultrasound technology. High frequency transvaginal probes are analyzed with digital image processing that make early detection of abnormalities in the embryonic part of prenatal development (Kurjak et al., 1999).

**Amniocentesis** is one of the better known and widely used prenatal diagnostic tools (see Figure 6–5). This procedure, usually performed at about the 16th week of gestation, allows a physician to determine early in pregnancy whether a child has a hereditary disorder. Amniocentesis involves withdrawing a sample of the amniotic fluid that surrounds the fetus and examining a va-

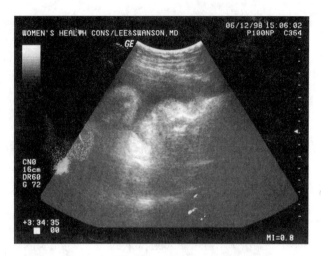

**FIGURE 6–4.**　A sonogram of a fetus can assist in determining important information such as fetal age, sex, and the presence of certain abnormalities.

riety of cells shed from its skin. First, fetal position in the uterus is located by means of ultrasound scanning. Next, the physician inserts a long needle into the mother's abdomen and through the uterine wall, avoiding both the placenta and the fetus, and withdraws a small amount of amniotic fluid for testing.

The fluid sample is placed into a centrifuge and spun rapidly to separate the cells from the fluid. The liquid portion then can be analyzed for a variety of biochemical abnormalities caused by genetic disturbances, such as Tay-Sachs disease, a crippling central nervous system disorder that leads to early death. The remaining cells from the fluid are cultured for a short period and examined under the microscope for any abnormal genetic patterns. This examination assists in diagnosing abnormalities caused by missing, broken, or additional chromosomal matter. The sex of the developing fetus can also be determined by this method, which allows for diagnosis of sex-linked genetic diseases such as hemophilia. Many genetic diseases can be detected early through amniocentesis. A new type of ultrasound test measures the nose bone of a fetus, allowing for early detection of Down syndrome (a type of mental retardation) (Cicero et al., 2001). This test is used in place of amniocentesis, especially when miscarriage is a risk for the expectant mother.

**Alpha-fetoprotein (AFP) screening** (Hui et al., 2003) may be performed as early as 16 weeks following conception. This test, or series of blood tests, may be used to detect the presence of spinal cord defects such as spina bifida (a condition where the spinal cord is exposed, leading to paralysis and other central nervous system disorders) and anencephaly (the absence of normal brain formation). Because this test can produce false positive results, other diagnostic methods, such as amniocentesis or sonography, are used to confirm the results.

Another newly developed procedure available to health care professionals is **chorionic villi sampling** or biopsy (Studd, 2004) (see Figure 6–6). Chorionic villi are small hairlike structures that precede the developmental structure of the placenta. These are derived from tissue of the early embryo following implantation into the uterine wall. Ultrasound is used to locate the embryonic tissue mass in a woman's uterus, and a small catheter is inserted through the vaginal opening into the cervix. A very small section of the villi tissue is then removed from the uterine wall. An analysis similar to that performed with amniotic fluid can then be carried out

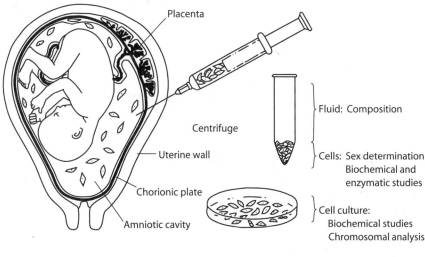

**FIGURE 6–5.** The procedure for performing amniocentesis and analysis of amniotic fluid.

*Source:* Friedman, T. (1971). Prenatal diagnosis of genetic disease. © Scientific American, Inc. All rights reserved.

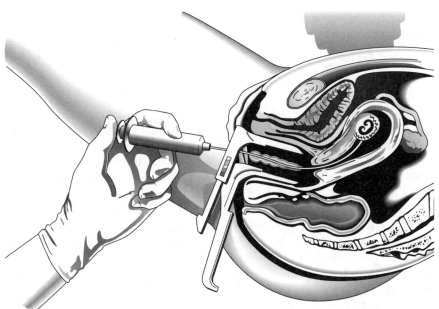

**FIGURE 6–6.** In chorionic villi sampling, a biopsy is made of the tissue forming the early placenta structure by entering the uterus via the vagina and cervix. The tissue can be examined microscopically for disorders, and chromosome analysis can be performed to detect genetic disorders.

*Source:* Turner, J. S., & Rubinson, L. (1993). *Contemporary human sexuality.* Upper Saddle River, NJ: Prentice Hall.

on the villi tissue. This procedure, performed between the 8th and 11th week of pregnancy, allows for an even earlier diagnosis of genetic disorders than is provided through amniocentesis. This information is especially important for women who conceive when they are over age 40, because the probability of genetic abnormalities in infants increases significantly as women approach this age. A major disadvantage of this procedure is the risk of spontaneous abortion (Bourgeois, 2004).

A procedure known as **umbilical cord sampling** allows tests to be performed for infections, anemia, certain kinds of metabolic disorders, and other medical conditions (Chinnaiya et al., 1998). Using ultrasound for guidance, a sample of the developing baby's blood can be withdrawn from its umbilical cord for these tests. While these tests provide essential information for medical intervention, the procedure carries risks, such as miscarriage and hemorrhage.

When medically assisted technology, such as in vitro fertilization, is being used for conception, **preimplantation genetic diagnosis** can be made for identifying genetic defects before a zygote is implanted into a woman's uterus (Damewood, 2001). While this procedure can prevent the progression of a pregnancy producing a baby with genetic disease, other ethical issues can be raised if the procedure is not used judiciously.

**Embryoscopy** is a technique in which a small viewing instrument is inserted into an expectant woman's abdomen to allow visual examination of an embryo as early as 6 weeks after conception. This permits early diagnosis and possible treatment of structural abnormalities (Studd, 2004).

Physicians may also use an instrument called an **endoscope** for direct examination of a developing fetus (Studd, 2004). The endoscope is especially useful for investigating defects not detectable through amniocentesis. The procedure is similar to amniocentesis in that a hollow needle is inserted into the uterus. The endoscope needle, however, contains a fiber optic device that allows the physician to visually inspect the fetus to detect structural defects. An additional needle also may be used to withdraw a small blood sample from the fetus; the blood can be analyzed to diagnose a number of genetic problems, such as sickle-cell anemia.

An electronic **fetal monitor** is also a useful instrument in providing prenatal care (Bourgeois, 2004). This instrument amplifies the heartbeat of a fetus and can be used as early as five months after conception. The device permits health care professionals to study the fetal heart rate for significant variances from normal patterns. The instrument is also useful in following the progress of labor and its effect on the fetus. Any significant change in heart rate is a signal of distress in the baby during labor and signals the need for immediate care.

**Fetoscopy** allows a fetus to be examined while inside the uterus via fiber optics (Cox et al., 2001). In addition to allowing direct observation, a sample of the fetal blood can be removed for testing, especially for genetic disease. This permits early treatment via surgery, or with drugs, prior to birth for a variety of conditions.

••••••••••••••••••••••••••••••••••••••••••••••••

*Focus Point.* The medical field of perinatology is a new source of prenatal care and supervision. Other advancements include medical genetic counseling, new methods of diagnosing fetal health conditions, and equipment for monitoring prenatal development.

••••••••••••••••••••••••••••••••••••••••••••••••

## THE BIRTH EXPERIENCE

The birth of a baby is a momentous event for a family system. It is a particularly memorable occasion for couples who are experiencing it for the first time. Until recently, Western culture has approached birth as a medical event rather than as a family affair (Molter, 2003). However, today adults can choose from a variety of options for childbirth. Perhaps one of the advantages of these options is the return of childbirth to a family-centered experience and the recognition by medical personnel that the birth of a child is more than a matter of medical concern.

### Types of Delivery

In the past, the majority of women in the United States delivered their babies by one standard, traditional method, which involved the use of medications that rendered the woman unconscious during the birth of the child. Physicians and women came to disapprove of this method for several reasons. Birth had become a highly managed medical affair rather than a family-centered experience. In addition, the anesthetics used for delivery eliminated the woman's participation in the event and had undesirable effects on the baby during labor. The period of recovery from the birth experience lengthened for both mother and child.

Medications used in delivery have been regarded negatively in recent years. Nevertheless, their use is warranted in certain instances. Physicians and certified midwives today know how to administer and monitor the effects of such drugs more carefully. At the same time, alternatives to medications have been developed that tend to enhance the birth experience and offer many benefits both to parents and the infant.

The various options to traditional childbirth are discussed in the following paragraphs.

**Medicated Deliveries.** Numerous drug agents are used in labor and delivery to minimize discomfort to the mother. Such drugs include **analgesics,** which primarily relieve pain and produce a semiconscious state; **amnestics,** which are used in combination with analgesics to produce "twilight sleep" and depress memory formation; **sedatives,** which produce a calming effect; and **tranquilizers,** which have a stronger, more soothing effect than sedatives (Studd, 2004).

All medications used in labor and delivery affect the fetus as well as the mother. Although these drugs enhance some body mechanisms, they usually work to depress most bodily functions, such as respiration, heart rate, blood pressure, and kidney function.

Use of regional anesthetics is also appropriate in some situations (Bourgeois, 2004). These agents, such as novocaine, block sensations in the mother's uterus, pelvic area, and vaginal region, preventing her from feeling pain during delivery. Such drugs allow a woman to be conscious during the birth process but limit her participation. In some instances, the drug can pass across the placental barrier and affect the fetus to some degree as well. The methods using local anesthetics include the **spinal** or **saddle block,** in which analgesic drugs deaden the nerves leading from one specific area of the spinal cord, such as that affecting the uterus and pelvic areas; the **pudendal nerve block,** which deadens the nerves functioning in the vaginal area; and the **paracervical nerve block,** which deadens the nerves supplying the uterus, cervix, vagina, bladder, and rectum.

All medications used during labor and delivery today are administered with great care, with special attention given to their effects on the well-being of the fetus. Some evidence suggests medications used during delivery have long-range effects on the child (Studd, 2004), such as delays in developmental progress (e.g., sitting, walking, talking). Hence, decisions about whether to use these drugs in delivery and to what degree warrant serious consideration.

**Cesarean Deliveries.** In some situations it is not possible or desirable for a woman to experience a vaginal delivery. In such cases, a **cesarean section delivery** is performed to protect the health and well-being of both fetus and mother. Conditions indicating cesarean delivery include diabetes in the mother; an extremely large fetus; genital herpes in the mother, which can be transmitted to the infant during a vaginal delivery; an insufficiently dilated cervix; the possibility of severe hemorrhaging by the mother; multiple births; or breech presentation of the fetus (Cox et al., 2001).

The cesarean section is a surgical procedure named after Julius Caesar, the ancient Roman emperor who, according to legend, was born in this manner. The procedure is performed by making an incision through the woman's abdominal wall and into the uterus. The fetus and placenta are removed through this small opening. To prevent discomfort to the mother, a local anesthetic is usually administered in the form of a saddle or spinal block. It is not unusual today for some women to undergo more than one cesarean section.

There are different reactions to having a cesarean rather than a vaginal delivery for the mother and infant (Cox et al., 2001). There appears to be a greater risk for the infant's survival following birth by this procedure in comparison to a vaginal delivery. However, few long-range effects have been conclusively identified. Mothers who have experienced abdominal delivery appear to be at higher risk of mild depressive reactions following delivery as compared to other procedures. This especially may be the case when a vaginal delivery has been anticipated but prevented by circumstances warranting the abdominal procedure. Some women report having great feelings of loss of control due to their inability to participate in their delivery when this procedure is used. Another compounding factor is the lengthy convalescent period and use of highly technical equipment in the delivery and aftercare, which tend to create a more impersonal birth experience for both mother and newborn.

Parents appear to react differently to children born through the abdominal procedure. They are reported to be more involved with children's activities, to see their children in more positive tones, and to value their children more when compared to parents who have experienced the vaginal delivery of children. This may be attributed to the greater risks taken in giving birth through this procedure as compared with other approaches (Fenwick, Gamble, & Mawson, 2003).

**Hypnosis.**   Hypnosis is sometimes used as an additional means of reducing the use of drugs and anesthesia during delivery. The method has a limited use, however, because not everyone can be trained to enter a hypnotic state, and because special training is required for the physician or health care professional and the patient.

**Prepared Childbirth.**   Various methods used today emphasize the parents' preparation for childbirth, such as training for the delivery through educational experiences and learning specific techniques of pain control, encouraging the conscious participation of the mother by minimizing the use of drugs during labor and delivery, and encouraging the participation of the mother's partner in labor and delivery. Such approaches stress that, even though women have been socialized to expect discomfort and pain during labor and delivery, prepared childbirth techniques can help them relax and redirect their conscious attention away from those discomforts.

### Parenting Reflection 6–4

What are some advantages and disadvantages of allowing older children, relatives, and friends to observe and participate in a couple's birth experience?

One of the more popular approaches to prepared childbirth is known as the **psychoprophylactic method** or **natural childbirth** (Cox et al., 2001). This technique was originally developed in the former Soviet Union based on Pavlovian concepts of classical conditioning. Its aim is to substitute a neutral response for the conditioned response of fear and tension. The neutral response is an acquired breathing pattern that is learned and performed in association with a uterine contraction. Fernand Lamaze (1958), a French physician, studied this method while visiting the Soviet Union and introduced it to the Western world. He refined the technique, emphasizing the increased participation of the mother during delivery (Figure 6–7).

These methods have great appeal to both physicians and couples for many reasons. The minimized use of drugs in labor and delivery enhances the well-being of both mother and child. Babies born through such deliv-

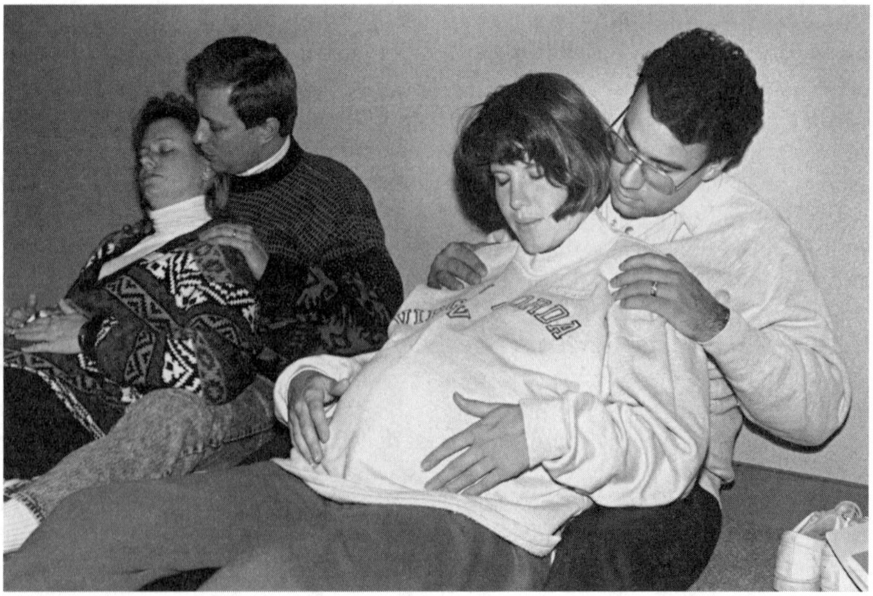

**FIGURE 6–7.**   In many communities, prospective parents may take classes that prepare them for childbirth. Many are based on the Lamaze method and include a coach (usually the mother's partner) who assists during labor and delivery.

eries typically have significantly higher-rated health status. The mother's recovery is speedier, and there are usually fewer complications from the delivery. Furthermore, delivery of the baby becomes a family matter in that it involves the active participation of both the mother and her partner. The mother's partner often acts as a coach in assisting her to perform the breathing patterns properly and offers encouragement and support. Their relationship may become more enriched as a result of the months of training and preparation for the birth (Vontver, 2003). The information gained from these experiences also helps to reduce fear and anxiety surrounding labor and delivery.

## Contemporary Childbirth Trends

Many hospitals and birthing facilities offer a homelike atmosphere for the labor and delivery experience (Cox et al., 2001). More couples are coming to view the birth of a child as a family experience and not as an illness requiring strict hospital care routines.

**Birthing rooms** are more comfortable and relaxed than traditional labor rooms, which are usually sparse

and functional in design. Birthing rooms are furnished much like a bedroom in a home, with a large bed, decorated walls, plants, and draped windows. Children, other relatives, and friends are welcome in this room. Should complications occur, medical equipment is nearby. The birth of a baby in this environment occurs much like the home deliveries that were common earlier in the last century.

Another innovation in the birth experience is called **rooming-in,** in which the baby is placed in a bassinet near the mother's bed and the mother takes the major responsibility for caring for the baby after delivery. This is thought to enhance opportunities for families to share in the birth experience and to develop stronger and more meaningful emotional bonds earlier in the baby's life (Cox et al., 2001).

Birthing centers and home deliveries are an option for low-risk deliveries (Cox et al., 2001). Birthing centers provide facilities similar to those found in hospital settings that are hotel-like while providing easy access to medical equipment and staff. Home birth entails giving birth in one's home environment with the attendance of a nurse-midwife or physician. This setting is not often

**Parenting FAQs 6–1**

My wife wants me to help her when it's time for her to give birth to our child. This is our first. I want to be supportive of her, but I'm just not sure if this is such a great idea. It seems to me I'd be out of place at the time. I always thought the father wasn't welcome during childbirth. None of my friends have done this so I don't know who to ask about it. What are the benefits and disadvantages of having me there during childbirth?

**A:**   It's good that you want to be supportive of your wife because being a part of the childbirth experience can be a good way to show your support at a time when she really needs you. Things have changed considerably about childbirth since your father and mother gave birth to you. Today, most young couples like yourself make childbirth a team effort by using prepared childbirthing methods that weren't so popular when you were born. The idea many women have today about the issue is that if their partner was interested in being present at conception, he can certainly be there at the time of birth as well. The benefits of your presence and involvement are many and some may be long term in nature. For example, being involved in childbirth helps you to see how you played a role in the conception of your child. It helps you to bond with your child and to take ownership in the child's presence in your life and that of your wife. Your presence makes childbirth a family experience rather than one that is strictly a medical situation. Sorry, but I can't think of any significant disadvantages of you being involved. Some men fear, for example, that they will lose interest sexually in their wives by witnessing them giving birth. On the contrary, many men find that their participation has stimulated their interest in their wives and helped to develop a greater respect for them.

used due to difficulties in having access to emergency medical equipment and the high cost of malpractice insurance for health care professionals.

Although most deliveries in the world are by midwives (Daly, 2003), in the United States the use of midwives had become rare until recent years. Today, many women are choosing to use the services of a midwife rather than a physician to provide prenatal care and delivery of their baby. There are two classes of midwives in the United States: the **direct-entry midwife,** who is not a certified health care professional but has learned midwifery skills and is allowed to deliver babies in some states, and the **nurse-midwife,** who is a certified health care professional with advanced training in obstetrics, maternal nutrition, family planning, and related topics. The involvement of midwives in prenatal care and obstetrics is a controversial issue, especially within the medical community.

A **doula** is someone who cares for a new mother, particularly after she has begun to breast-feed her new baby. Doulas are like midwives in having been present in numerous cultures worldwide for centuries. These individuals provide important and useful social, emotional, and physical support for new mothers and have a positive impact on the mother's experiences in the days following birth. Women who have the support of a doula are reported to have shorter labor, cope more effectively with the responsibilities of being a new mother, and have fewer labor and delivery problems (Gordon, 2000).

Many women today wish to use alternative birthing centers rather than the impersonal labor and delivery suites found in a typical hospital environment. Some even go so far as to ensure the type of delivery they desire by arranging for home births to be supervised by a midwife. Where the delivery takes place is often influenced by factors considered important by the parents. For example, those who choose home delivery typically do so to avoid separation from the newly born infant, whereas those choosing hospital delivery do so to ensure safety for the mother and infant.

Health care professionals working with pregnancy and delivery are becoming more concerned about the birth experience of the fetus as well as of the mother. The impression thus far about the birth experience is that it is a stressful event for all, but perhaps more for the fetus be-

cause of its less advanced state of development than the adults involved in the process. In response to this impression, an alternative approach to traditional delivery methods has been proposed by Frederick Leboyer (1976), another French physician. Lehoyer's method seeks to minimize the adverse effects of the birth experience for the fetus. Birth occurs in a quiet, softly lighted room, and immediately after birth the baby is placed on the mother's abdomen to be stroked and handled nurturantly. After the umbilical cord is cut and tied, the baby is bathed in warm water. This is believed to soothe the baby while the vernix is being cleaned from the skin. This approach is in stark contrast to the usual, traditional environment and approach used in most delivery suites. These rooms typically are brilliantly lit, and the baby is handled vigorously following birth to help it begin breathing. Leboyer views his method as a gentler and more humane way to introduce a baby to life outside the mother's uterus. Leboyer's approach is controversial, however.

In addition to these differences in procedure promoted by LeBoyer, delivery tables are giving way to the use of *birthing chairs*. Delivery tables, which place the mother-to-be on her back with her legs raised and feet anchored in stirrups, were originally designed for the convenience of physicians delivering the baby. The birthing chair is believed to be more helpful to the mother and does not hamper the ability of the person assisting in the delivery (Barber et al., 2000). It typically resembles a captain's chair design but may have a portion of the seat cut away in a semicircle to allow access to the woman's vaginal area. By placing the delivering mother in a comfortable semi-squatting position, she is able to make use of gravity and her anatomy to push when necessary during the delivery.

● ● ● ● ● ● ● ● ● ● ● ● ● ● ● ● ● ● ● ● ● ● ● ● ● ● ● ● ● ●

### Parenting Reflection 6–5

If you had a choice between using a medical doctor or a midwife for your delivery, which would you choose and why? Should states allow greater use of midwives as a means for helping more women have greater access to health care prior to and during childbirth?

● ● ● ● ● ● ● ● ● ● ● ● ● ● ● ● ● ● ● ● ● ● ● ● ● ● ● ● ● ●

*Focus Point.* Childbirth has become, once again, a family event rather than one closely managed in hospitals under strict medical supervision. New methods of childbirth promote the involvement of both partners in this event, and some institutions provide facilities that allow participation of others in the experience, such as relatives, older children, and friends. This greater involvement of the family in childbirth is thought to promote emotional bonding of these individuals with the baby following birth, thereby producing beneficial effects for all. Some families choose to use the services of a midwife to conduct prenatal and childbirth care. Leboyer suggests alternative ways for conducting childbirth that are believed to minimize the stress of birth for the baby.

## POINTS TO CONSIDER

■ Development before birth has unique characteristics in that it is: (1) the shortest stage of the human life span; (2) the stage during which growth occurs most rapidly; and (3) a highly critical period of human development due to the extreme vulnerability of the embryo to a variety of factors.

■ Factors that can positively or adversely influence the developmental progress of a fetus include: (1) age of the mother; (2) maternal nutrition; (3) exposure to drug and chemical agents in the mother's bloodstream; (4) exposure to infectious disease agents contracted by the mother; (5) the mother's metabolic disorders; and (6) blood type incompatibility between the mother and the fetus.

■ A variety of childbirth approaches are available to families today. The contemporary trend is toward the increased use of family-centered methods that feature: (1) a more relaxed, homelike atmosphere; (2) more active involvement of the mother's partner; (3) less frequent use of drugs during labor and delivery unless warranted; (4) more active involvement and participation of both the mother and her partner in preparing for childbirth; and (5) active caretaking of the newborn by the parents before discharge from the health care facility.

■ A variety of procedures are also available that provide diagnostic information about the health and well-being of an embryo or fetus prior to birth such as sonography, amniocentesis, chorionic villi sampling, umbilical cord sampling, endoscopic examination, and use of a fetal monitor.

# CHAPTER 7

# Parenting Infants and Toddlers

## Focus Questions
■ ■ ■ ■ ■ ■ ■ ■ ■ ■

1. How do two principal schools of thought describe the nature of an infant?
2. What are the principal developmental landmarks of infancy that parents should know?
3. What is the nature of parent-infant relations?
4. What kinds of community supports do families with infants need?
5. What stressors and coping mechanisms are revealed by a systemic family development snapshot of families with infants and toddlers?

■ ■ ■ ■ ■ ■ ■ ■ ■ ■

**Infancy** is the period of the life span that extends between birth and 3 years following birth. Most individuals perceive a baby as being passive and dependent on others. However, findings from new studies about the nature of infant development depict an infant as showing highly competent behaviors and being actively involved in learning to master his or her interactions with the environment (Miller & Albrecht, 2004).

Most people are aware that infants require much attention, supervision, and care to grow and develop properly. Theorists and researchers also acknowledge infancy as a landmark stage in the human life span (see Figure 7–1).

## CONCEPTS OF INFANCY

There are two principal views of the nature of an infant. One is the **psychoanalytical** concept of infancy, which is based on Freudian psychology and places importance on the early experiences of an infant in determining characteristics later in the life span. The other is the **developmental view,** which depicts an infant as an adaptable individual who can initiate behaviors and make responses in interacting with the environment. Early experiences are important in this framework as well, but they are considered to be less final in their impact on a child's future developmental progress.

**FIGURE 7–1.** Infancy is a time of life when children experience many new things for the first time as they discover their world.

## The Psychoanalytical View

The psychoanalytical view of infancy derives from the writings of Sigmund Freud. Stated in general terms, this view holds that the early experiences of children, especially during their infancy, have a profound effect on determining their adult personality structure and traits. These early experiences are primarily provided through the caregiving of parents, especially by the mother, during an infant's first months and years.

Proponents of this view place an immense amount of psychological pressure on parents to perform the right actions in their caregiving in order for children to grow into healthy adults. From this view, how well the parents conduct their child-rearing activities determines whether a child develops a healthy personality or is handicapped with personality and behavior problems. The belief is that the human personality is permanently formed in infancy and early childhood, and that it cannot be changed later in life except through a long and involved examination of the personality through psychoanalysis. Thus, under the psychoanalytical view, parenting and the experiences of growing up are an all-or-nothing matter. Although there is little empirical evidence to support this view, it has become part of the folklore of parenting.

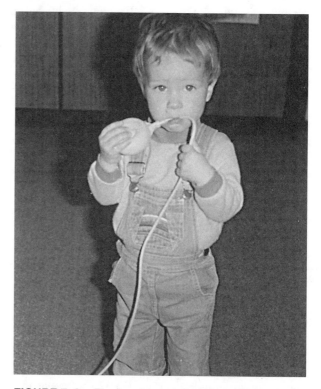

**FIGURE 7–2.** The psychoanalytical view of infancy emphasizes that the expression of certain drives and the frustration of these drives influences personality development. In infancy, an individual experiences the oral stage, where stimulation is gained from placing things in the mouth as a source of pleasure.

## The Developmental View

The developmental view holds that an infant is an actor, as well as a reactor to, his or her physical and social environment. Developmentalists believe that a baby can initiate and react to a large number of stimuli. Unlike the psychoanalytical view, a single event or circumstance is not thought to be a turning point in either a positive or negative manner in affecting future developmental progress. Difficulty occurs when a traumatic event is repeated or continually reinforced during the course of a child's developing years. An example would be a baby who was once frightened by a large dog and subsequently is reminded of the traumatic event by his parents each time a dog approaches. The child is never allowed to touch or to play with dogs and is not permitted to have a dog as a pet.

From the developmental point of view, the infant is not simply a human sponge who absorbs and responds to stimulation, but an integrated psychological system capable of selectively choosing those stimuli from the environment to which to respond. An infant is believed to be an interactor with the environment and those who populate it, but on a selective basis. Developmental researchers have confirmed the notion that infants discriminate between stimuli and in many instances selectively choose those to which they respond (Chugani et al., 2001). Numerous empirically based research studies support this view and are discussed throughout this text.

### Parenting Reflection 7–1

What are some sources of contemporary ideas about the nature of infants? Are these depictions realistic?

*Focus Point.* Two major conceptual views describe the nature of an individual in infancy. The psychoanalytical view stresses that early experiences, especially those that occur in infancy, have a profound influence on a child's later development and personality formation. In this view, parents are seen as solely responsible for the quality of their child's developmental outcome.

The developmental view emphasizes that individuals are adaptable and plastic in nature, that infants are actors upon, as well as reactors to, their environment, and that a variety of factors influence the course of developmental progress, including the ability of infants to influence the behavior of adults who provide for their care.

## DEVELOPMENTAL LANDMARKS OF INFANCY

As with other stages of the life span, infancy has its own unique developmental tasks and landmarks that lay the foundation for current and future developmental progress. Many complex developmental changes and events are singular to this time of life. Many developmental events that occur in infancy are the product of maturational changes, such as changes in size, weight, and body proportions; changes in physiological structures and functions; and the development of particular physical skills, including walking and speaking. Other significant developmental events that occur in infancy are more psychological in nature and are more sensitive to environmental influences. These are important as well in influencing how the relationship between parents and children takes shape and becomes configured in particular ways unique to the individuals and their family system.

Healthy adjustment in infancy focuses on accomplishing the challenges of the developmental tasks and landmarks appropriate to this time of life. These are outlined in Focus On 7–1. Traditionally, these lead from complete dependence and helplessness at birth to the ability to function independently of adults to a certain degree. For this development to take place, infants necessarily need to acquire a trusting attitude about their caregivers and their environment and establish initial personal boundaries that permit self-individuation.

Knowledge of developmental events that occur at each stage of a child's life span is important to parents and other caregivers. All humans are born with a capacity for experiencing certain events that have been programmed to occur and for experiencing other events subject to modification by the environment in their impact. Infants are active participants in influencing their social environment and the responses of those who provide their care. As a result, parents and caregivers need to be aware of certain cues that a baby

<br>

**Focus On 7–1**  **Major Developmental Landmarks in Infancy**

### The Newborn (birth to 2 weeks)
- Establishing respiration within normal limits
- Establishing circulation to the lungs and away from the umbilical cord
- Establishing body temperature regulation
- Establishing digestion and elimination processes
- Exercising neonatal reflexes
- Adjusting to light and sound
- Establishing sleep pattern

### The Infant (3 weeks to 18 months)
- Acquiring self-regulated skills of locomotion (walking), manipulation (hand skills), and self-feeding with solid food
- Maintaining a sleep-wake cycle
- Exploring sound production in preparation for speech
- Establishing initial sensorimotor schemes and mastering object permanence
- Establishing an emotional attachment to parents or primary caregivers
- Experiencing basic emotional states germane to infancy (e.g., social smiling and crying) as a means for communication
- Establishing an attitude of basic trust versus mistrust

### The Toddler (18 months to 3 years)
- Refining self-regulated skills
- Establishing early speech patterns
- Refining and modifying basic sensorimotor schemes and establishing elementary logic and reasoning
- Learning to control the elimination of body wastes
- Establishing an attitude of autonomy versus shame and doubt
- Establishing self-differentiation and exploring personal boundaries
- Initial conscience development

will provide to assist caregivers in their behavior. These cues are often a part of the developmental process, and to recognize them, caregivers need to observe a baby's behavior and know what occurs appropriately at different times.

Although chronological age is a convenient indicator of events that may be expected as part of the normal developmental process, it should be considered primarily as a guide to landmarks that punctuate the different developmental stages of the life span. No particular child will fit the textbook definitions of age-appropriate characteristics perfectly. Nevertheless, the value of such norms lies in showing the organization and trends in development that are typical of human beings.

## PARENTING INFANTS AND TODDLERS

### Meeting the Needs of Infants and Toddlers

Most adults are cognizant of the extreme degree of dependency of an infant on its parents or caregivers. The need for dependence on adults is necessary for survival and for enhancing a child's developmental progress. The nature and degree of dependency in infancy and childhood among humans differs from that observed among the young of other species. Anthropologists have attributed this to the larger brain of humans that allows for higher order mental processes not found in other species (Morris, 1986, 1996). It takes much more developmental time for a human's brain to be "built" in laying down the myriad neural circuits to reach maturity. For example, the brain at birth weighs only 25 percent of its total adult weight but by age 3, the brain has attained about 90 percent of its adult weight. However, there is more to attaining maturity than achieving an adult brain weight. Socialization and education continue for many years beyond age 3.

For most of the developmental periods between infancy and early childhood, parents provide caregiving that is largely physical and emotionally nurturing in nature. As children grow older past these years, physical caregiving diminishes relatively while psychological caregiving increases.

**Feeding.** The sucking reflex is one of the earliest reflexes to appear during prenatal development and is exceptionally well developed at birth in full-term newborns. This necessary reflex, which is easily elicited by almost any stimulation to the lips, cheeks, or mouth area, ensures that an infant can obtain nourishment before teeth emerge for chewing.

One of the initial decisions in providing care at this time is whether to breast- or bottle-feed an infant. This is a choice that affects all family members and should be fully discussed before implementing a final decision,

ideally before a baby is born. Focus On 7–2 presents a summary of the advantages and disadvantages of both feeding methods that may be considered in making this decision.

There are important reasons why a couple should discuss this decision prior to a child's birth. Several research articles have addressed the problems some men experience when their wives breast-feed a newborn baby (Spock, 2004). While most men are supportive and encourage their wives' breast-feeding, some men experience stress and generally troublesome negative reactions to this feeding practice. The most common negative reaction is jealousy or feelings of being displaced by the infant as the primary focus of the wife's affection. Suggested ways to prevent or alleviate such negative reactions include: (1) improving the birth experience for the husband by involving him in the process, (2) promoting early physical and social contact between the father and the infant, (3) improving communications between the husband and wife during the postpartum period, and (4) encouraging the father to become more actively involved in routine caregiving activities of an infant following birth.

Most normal infants require a feeding once every 3 or 4 hours during the first few months after birth. After adding solid foods to a baby's diet, usually during the 4th to 6th months, the number of feedings is reduced

---

### Focus On 7–2    Advantages and Disadvantages of Breast- and Bottle-Feeding

**Advantages**

| *Breast* | *Bottle* |
|---|---|
| Economical | Frees the mother |
| Readily available at correct temperature | May involve the father |
| Assists uterus in returning to pre-pregnant size | Doesn't distend breasts |
| Contains natural antibodies | May have psychological effects not found |
| Does not cause constipation | with breast-feeding |
| May have psychological effects not found with bottle-feeding | |

**Disadvantages**

| *Breast* | *Bottle* |
|---|---|
| Sometimes difficult to establish | Requires heating and sterile equipment |
| Does not involve the father | Contains no antibodies |
| Amount produced varies | Conducive to constipation in infant |
| Can be painful for mother | May cause allergic reactions in infant |

throughout the day and continues to decline as the baby grows older. Babies can generally feed themselves after they have developed the motor skills and coordination necessary to hold a cup and drink from it and to bring food to their mouths and chew it properly. These events are a result of maturational processes and cultural expectations or experiences. Developmental norms have been established that show the times at which these events can be expected to occur.

••••••••••••••••••••••••••••••••••••••

### ■ Parenting Reflection 7–2

Why should a father be involved in the decision to breast-feed a new baby?

••••••••••••••••••••••••••••••••••••••

**Weaning and Introducing Solid Foods.**   The shift from liquid to solid foods involves the process of **weaning.** Although extended breast-feeding may continue through the second and third year following birth, most infants are weaned when they indicate a readiness to begin taking solid foods. Such indications include drinking from a cup, grasping a spoon easily, drinking more than a quart of formula daily, and enjoying playing with food (Figure 7–3).

A major concern in the weaning process is providing an adequate amount of protein and iron to meet the infants' growth requirements. Lack of adequate sources of these nutrients can lead to malnutrition and eventually to permanent damage, especially to the brain and central nervous system (Spock, 2004).

There is much disagreement about when to introduce solid foods into an infant's diet. Some infant specialists recommend that solid foods can be safely started between 3 and 4 months after birth, while others suggest waiting until 6 to 8 months after birth (American Academy of Pediatrics, 1999).

**Health and Medical Care.**   If a woman experienced relatively good health during her pregnancy, then it is likely that the baby will also enter the world in a healthy state. However, certain physical conditions that appear to be of concern are relatively normal for infants. These are briefly outlined here:

- Spitting up or vomiting is common; caregivers learn to be prepared for the inevitable in this regard.
- Wheezing, sneezing, and hiccuping are to be expected, especially in the first few months following birth.
- Constipation is more common among babies who are bottle- rather than breast-fed. Diarrhea also can be expected frequently because of an immature digestive system.

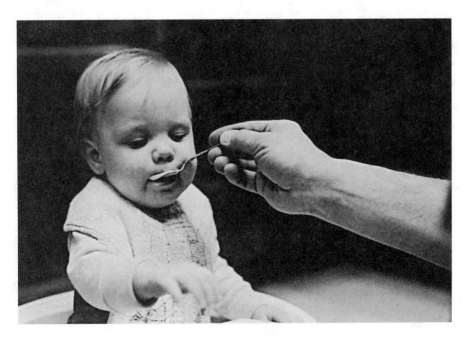

**FIGURE 7–3.**   Solid foods are introduced sparingly to infants. There is much disagreement about when to begin this process.

- Rashes occur commonly, especially in the diaper area, because of sensitive skin and exposure to acidic urine. Other kinds of rashes are attributed to yeast and bacterial infection.
- Other skin conditions may be observed such as cradle cap (seborrhea) caused by an overly oily scalp; prickly heat rash that occurs in hot weather; and impetigo, a highly contagious skin infection.
- Thrush is a yeast infection in the mouth due to an immature immune system.
- Obstructed tear ducts sometimes develop due to an infection and are not considered serious but something that needs medical attention.

It is important to provide well-baby medical care that will allow health care professionals to examine the baby regularly. Many physical disorders can be detected early if babies are receiving this care. Immunizations also must be received in infancy to provide protection from communicable diseases such as measles, diphtheria, mumps, and polio. While most families can provide this care and have medical insurance coverage, families living in poverty or who have employment difficulties often forego this treatment due to financial constraints. Fortunately, most states provide treatment for those who are medically indigent.

**Sleep-Wake Cycle.** A popular belief about infants is that they sleep a great deal of the time. This may be the situation in the early months of this life stage, but individual sleeping patterns are subject to wide variations (Spock, 2004). Some infants require long periods of sleep, while others sleep for only short, restless periods. Sleep during the first several months after birth is interrupted only long enough for the baby to feed. This round-the-clock pattern of alternating periods of sleep with feeding extends to longer intervals of wakefulness after the third month. During the remainder of the time until the baby approaches age 2, sleep needs decrease to 10 to 14 hours daily. Most toddlers need a morning and afternoon nap through the preschool years, which is definitely welcomed by most parents as a means of obtaining uninterrupted work time.

As most infants approach their second birthday, a pattern of **negativism** often appears in their willingness either to take a nap or go to bed at night. A child's resistance to bedtime may be a means of expressing a growing sense of autonomy or may arise from a fear of the dark or of being left alone. Children may express their difficulty in developing self-regulated sleeping patterns by resisting the establishment of bedtime routines. Parents may respond to these behavioral cues by staying with the child to provide reassurance and by not asking

---

**Parenting FAQs 7–1**

**We have a toddler who just doesn't want to stay in her bed once she's put down at night. She'll get up five or six times before going to sleep. It's exhausting for us to go through this every night. What can we do?**

**A:** Children this age often experience separation anxiety in relation to bedtime. Some children, however, perform this kind of routine as a matter of gaining parental attention. Try to analyze why this may be going on with your child. If your child is being cared for by someone else during the day, it might be helpful to sit with her with the understanding that it will only be for a short period during which she is to go to sleep. This can get out of control, however, because she can routinely expect one of you to stay with her.

Remember that you are helping your child to develop a bedtime routine at this time in her life. To develop one that is healthy for all concerned, consistently but firmly lead her back to bed over and over again each time she reappears after being put down for sleep. Don't be tempted to lock the child's bedroom door. This can generate fears that are difficult for her to control and create another problem. You might install a radio or tape player to provide soothing music at bedtime as well. Developing a bedtime routine of reading calm, peaceful stories also helps children to settle down; a pleasant bath time is also helpful for many children. It is important, however, to continue to enforce the ultimate rule of bedtime: Once you are put to bed, it's time to go to sleep.

the child if she or he is ready to go to bed, since the response will most likely be negative. American society is perhaps the only major Western culture that expects its children to develop this self-regulated pattern early in life, with little guidance from adults. American parents simply place an infant into a crib and close the bedroom door, while parents in many other cultures typically sing a short, soft lullaby or rock an infant to sleep.

**Providing Structure and Nurturance for Infants.** The psychosocial focus of an infant is on learning to trust the integrity of caregivers and the environment in providing and meeting the infant's needs. At some level of consciousness, infants are likely to make decisions about themselves, others, and things in their world that relate to trust (Clarke & Dawson, 1998). Interactions with people, with the environment, and with things in the environment lead the infant to conclusions and expectations about how his or her needs will be met.

Interactions between parent and infant experiences are congruent at this time. Adults are experiencing interactions with infants that assist in establishing their sense of generativity. While adults are learning "to make be and to take care of," the infant is learning "to get and to give in return." The reciprocal nature of this interaction helps to ensure that each participant experiences opportunities to fulfill his or her particular psychosocial need.

Listed in Table 7–1 are the behaviors of parents that meet their infant's needs for structure and nurturance. Behaviors that can be detrimental to infants by not meeting their needs appropriately are also listed. Understandably, most of the parenting behaviors that are observed in providing care for infants between birth and 6 months of age are nurturant in nature, whereas those that are observed in providing care between 18 months and 3 years include increasing elements of structure. All of these, however, communicate messages that promote healthy self-esteem for infants and toddlers, promote the establishment of personal boundaries, and affirm their basic sense of self-worth.

**TABLE 7–1.**   Parenting Behaviors for Infants

| Age | Behaviors Providing Structure/Nurturance | Behaviors Not Providing Structure/Nurturance |
|---|---|---|
| Birth to 6 Months | • Affirming infant's attempts to meet developmental tasks. | • Not responding to infant's behavioral cues. |
| | • Giving loving, consistent care. | • Failing to hold and touch infant sufficiently. |
| | • Responding appropriately to infant's behavioral cues. | • Responding rigidly, angrily, and agitatedly to infant. |
| | • Thinking on behalf of infant; anticipating needs. | • Providing food before infant has given cues of hunger |
| | • Holding infant lovingly and maintaining eye contact during feeding. | • Punishing infant for his or her behavior. |
| | • Providing nurturance by touching, looking, talking, and singing to infant. | • Failing to provide a healthy physical environment. |
| | • Seeking help and information when uncertain about what to do. | • Failing to protect infant from harm and danger. |
| | • Acting in reliable and trustworthy ways toward infant. | • Criticizing infant for anything he or she does. |
| | | • Acting in ways that discount an infant's existence, i.e., acting irresponsibly in ways that fail to meet the needs of an infant. |

*(continued)*

**TABLE 7–1.** Parenting Behaviors for Infants *(continued)*

| Age | Behaviors Providing Structure/Nurturance | Behaviors Not Providing Structure/Nurturance |
|---|---|---|
| 6 to 18 Months | • Continuing to affirm infant's attempts to meet developmental tasks.<br><br>• Continuing to offer love, safety, and protection.<br><br>• Providing a safe, child-proofed environment.<br><br>• Protecting infant from harm and danger.<br><br>• Continuing to provide food, nurturing touch, and encouragement.<br><br>• Saying "yes" twice as often as "no" to infant.<br><br>• Providing a variety of experiences for infant.<br><br>• Providing feedback about infant's behavior to him or her.<br><br>• Refraining from interrupting infant's speech or behavior.<br><br>• Responding to infant's invitations to play. | • Continuing to fail to protect infant from harm and danger.<br><br>• Restricting infant's freedom of movement.<br><br>• Criticizing, punishing, or shaming infant for attempts to establish personal autonomy or to explore the environment.<br><br>• Expecting infant not to want to touch things.<br><br>• Expecting infant to become instantly toilet-trained.<br><br>• Acting in ways that discount infant, i.e., acting in ways that prevent the infant from accomplishing basic developmental tasks and needs. |
| 18 Months to 3 Years | • Affirming toddler's attempts to meet developmental tasks.<br><br>• Continuing to offer love, cuddling, safety, and protection.<br><br>• Encouraging toddlers' ability to think.<br><br>• Encouraging child to reach conclusions based on information.<br><br>• Explaining rules, reasons, how to's, do not's, and other information to toddler.<br><br>• Accepting toddlers' expressions of positive and negative emotions.<br><br>• Teaching toddler about options for expressing negative feelings.<br><br>• Setting and enforcing reasonable limits that have been discussed with partner in advance, if possible.<br><br>• Remaining calm in times of toddler's emotional outbursts, neither giving in nor overpowering the child.<br><br>• Giving simple and clear directions to toddler; encouraging and praising accomplishments.<br><br>• Expecting toddler to begin thinking about own feelings and those of others.<br><br>• Reframing attitude about toddler as a "terrific two." | • Communicating too many "don'ts" about toddler's behavior.<br><br>• Getting involved in power struggles with toddler.<br><br>• Trying to create a compliant child in order to maintain image of self as a "good" parent.<br><br>• Referring to toddler as a "terrible two" both to the child and to others.<br><br>• Refusing to set limits consistently or provide expectations for toddler's behavior.<br><br>• Setting expectations for toddler's behavior that are appropriate for an older child.<br><br>• Expecting toddler to play well with other children.<br><br>• Failing to teach toddler about how to make simple choices in behaviors.<br><br>• Shaming toddler for anything.<br><br>• Acting in ways that discount toddler. |

*Source:* Adapted from Clarke, J. I., & Dawson, C. (1989). *Growing up again: Parenting ourselves, parenting our children.* Minneapolis, MN: Hazelden.

Parents of toddlers are especially concerned about beginning efforts to control their child's behavior and to elicit the child's compliance with their requests and demands. One study provides insightful information on how parenting style influences how parental demands are shaped and their influence on children's compliance (Kuczynski & Kochanska, 1995). The researchers observed a group of 70 mothers and their toddlers in a naturalistic setting. Three types of maternal demands were observed: (1) *caretaking demands* that were related to providing physical care and supervision (e.g., "Wash your hands," "Watch out for the stairs"), (2) *demands for appropriate behavior* that involved teaching and reinforcing rules for acceptable behavior (e.g., "Don't do that"), and (3) *demands for competent action* that would help the child or others (e.g., "Please share your toy"). Younger toddlers received more of the first type from mothers while older toddlers received more of the third type.

The parenting style was found to be associated in this study with the type of demand that a mother used with her toddler. Those who were using an authoritarian style peppered their demands with prohibitions for the toddler's behavior while those using an authoritative style couched their demands in terms that promoted the child's competencies within a rationale of guidance. Interestingly, the researchers found that those mothers using an authoritative style were more likely to gain compliance from their toddler than mothers using an authoritarian style. When the children and their mothers were again observed by the researchers after the children had reached 5 years of age, fewer behavior problems were observed among the children of the authoritative-style mothers.

**Communication.** Infants do not acquire the ability to communicate adequately using speech until after their second birthday. However, other means are used to communicate with caregivers. Crying is the first method in letting others know of needs. Parents must learn what a particular cry means from each infant. Crying can have a number of different meanings such as expressing hunger, needing a diaper changed, being hot or cold, teething discomfort, needing to sleep, or becoming ill, for example. At other times, the reason for an infant's crying may be an expression of fatigue. And sometimes, crying occurs as an expression of fretting and does not have any apparent meaning for caregivers. Crying also occurs in association with physical conditions known as

*colic.* This occurs when babies develop an extended abdomen and are gassy. Some infants are excessively fretful and can cry for lengthy periods. Colic is difficult for caregivers since a highly fretful or hypertonic infant can be inconsolable.

The parents' job is to discover the meanings of the different types of crying by which a baby communicates needs. Sometimes it takes several attempts to discover just exactly why a baby is crying. Most parents quickly learn what their baby needs after spending time with the child. Many infants simply want attention or to be held and can be comforted in this way. Others respond to being rocked or walked by their caregiver. Some more fretful infants seem to respond best when held on a caregiver's lap and rocked on their abdomen. Still others quiet down if taken for a ride in a car.

The question of spoiling an infant often arises, especially if the baby is highly fretful and cries much of the time in its first few months after birth. *Spoiling* refers to the fear that infants will demand a great deal of parental attention if they receive it in excessive amounts. While it is not unusual for some parents to feel that they are being controlled in this manner by a needy infant, most experts in infant care report that spoiling is not likely to happen even in such circumstances (Spock, 2004). It is more important for parents to understand the need for providing such attention, at least before 9 months of age, to facilitate an infant's development of a sense of basic trust.

**Facilitating Attachment.**    **Attachment** is an attraction to someone that is based on psychological bonding. Attachment is also described as a strong affectional tie between an infant and his or her primary caregivers (Ainsworth, 1973) (Figure 7–4). It is one of the few developmental phenomena that appears to be found universally in all humans and in all cultural settings. It is essential for an infant's survival and well-being. When an infant fails to attach properly to caregivers, the consequences are damaging to his or her emotional, physical, social, and psychological well-being.

Attachment is constructed through interactions of an infant with primary caregivers. An infant who is experiencing normal developmental progress behaves in ways that signal a desire to be near caregivers, and the behaviors usually serve to attract caregivers' attention. Infant behaviors that stimulate attachment to caregivers include crying, smiling, clutching, and touching. Such infant behaviors elicit responses from caregivers that

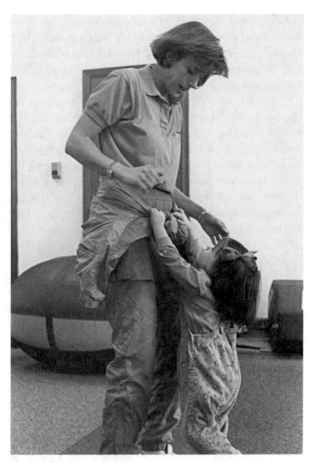

**FIGURE 7–4.** Attachment of an infant to an adult caregiver is a significant developmental task that facilitates the development of basic trust.

facilitate the attachment process—smiling at, gently handling, stroking, feeding, and talking to the infant, for example.

Attachment is important in establishing an infant's sense of basic trust in people and the environment and in helping the infant feel secure in exploring the environment (Ainsworth, 1977). Children who successfully attach to caregivers learn to express curiosity in their world, which helps promote mental and social growth throughout their life span. Children who have successfully attached in infancy appear to have a greater capacity to deal with novel situations, to cope with failure, to exert greater perseverance in problem solving, to participate in loving relationships with others, and to maintain healthy self-esteem.

**Social referencing** appears to be related to attachment. This behavior is observed when infants look to their parents' faces as a means of obtaining informational cues (Baldwin & Moses, 1996). Facial cues guide infants' decisions about how to act and how to react to situations. Apparently, cues and emotional information from parents program many reactions that become automatic and habitual responses to similar situations that arise later in life.

A controversial issue about contemporary family life relates to attachment during infancy. In about 97 percent of all married-couple families in the United States, both adults are employed outside the home (U.S. Bureau of the Census, 2003). Most single parents are employed as well. The daily separations that result raise concerns about the ability of infants to form attachments with caregivers and the quality of those attachments. The issue of whether such repeated separations are harmful cannot be settled as yet. Some studies find significant differences in the attachments between infants of employed mothers versus infants of unemployed mothers, while others do not. A mother's attitude about her employment may play a role in the nature and quality of her infant's attachment. For example, infants of employed mothers who were highly anxious about not being able to care for them around the clock tended to develop avoidant attachments rather than secure attachments (Stifter, Coulehan, & Fish, 1993).

**Facilitating a Sense of Basic Trust.**    According to Erikson (1950, 1964), the development of a sense of **basic trust** is one of the primary tasks of psychosocial development in infancy. Impressions gained from both informal observation and empirical research suggest that an infant's sense of basic trust emerges through interactions with the mother or the person who consistently acts in this capacity. The feeding situation provides ample opportunities for an infant to explore the mother through both vision and touch. Feeding is considered to be a significant opportunity for an infant to identify the caregiver as the primary source of physical and psychological nurturance. For example, a caregiver who holds an infant in a consistent manner and has a consistent pattern of feeding behavior enables the infant to trust the caregiver's integrity. Through consistent caregiving, an infant learns that there is predictability in how life occurs, which in turn helps the infant to predict that certain behaviors on his or her part will cause particular events or sensations to occur. For example, a baby learns that a lusty cry will cause caregivers to attend to his or her needs.

**Facilitating a Sense of Autonomy.**   Erikson (1950, 1964) proposes that infants begin to establish a sense of autonomy versus shame and doubt between 18 months and 3 years of age. Parents may view this time as a series of troublesome encounters with their child because so much of the child's behavior is directed toward developing an initial identity as a person independent of his or her parents.

From a family systems theory perspective, the experiences of an infant at this period in life are those that teach about personal boundaries. The attachment process in the early period of infancy apparently leads an infant to believe that there is a symbiotic relationship between him or her and the parents. This may especially be the case with the mother, as she is very often the principal caregiver. In terms of family systems theory, the relationship is described as emotionally enmeshed. Because of the intense closeness and intimacy of their relationship, both infant and mother may have difficulties in perceiving the personal boundaries that distinguish them as distinct individuals. The infant may have difficulty in perceiving that he or she is not an extension of the parent, and vice versa. Lack of such distinctions between the self and others cannot continue indefinitely,

however, as that would be psychologically unhealthy. Self-differentiation from others begins when an infant learns to erect personal boundaries by behaving in ways that establish personal autonomy.

Some parents are unaware that these difficult interactions are a necessary part of the child's healthy psychosocial development. As a result, they are inclined to use power to gain control over their child's unacceptable actions. Adults whose own parents used strict, rule-oriented methods are likely to repeat this approach in raising their own children. This is done without thinking, because our society does so little to train people to be parents. Such parents consider imposing rules and rigid standards of acceptable behavior on children as appropriate child-rearing practice at this time. Since so much of a toddler's behavior appears directed against parental authority, attempts to control the child's rebelliousness are seen as necessary and appropriate. However, many parents apparently can be too successful and relentless in trying to achieve this end. The result is that many children emerge from this period of their lives with a negative self-concept and doubts about their worth as human beings. They come to believe that they are bad, flawed, unacceptable, undesirable, and unlovable. This unhealthy mental outlook is what Erikson calls an attitude of shame and doubt, and it stems in part from parents' overreaction to the negativistic behavior that is normal at this time in a child's life.

**Parenting FAQs 7–2**

**Do you have any suggestions for how to handle a toddler's temper tantrums? These seem to happen everywhere, at home and in public.**

**A:**   Reacting to temper tantrums is an exercise in parental control. However, it is helpful to understand that these are not a personal attack on you but what happens when toddlers' or preschoolers' emotions become uncontrollable. Even adults can have temper tantrums, better known as *outbursts*. Children can learn to control these with a fair degree of success if taught by patient parents.

With toddlers, you can begin the learning process by remembering to stay calm yourself. Try to analyze why the tantrum is happening: Is it because the child is tired and needs to nap or be fed, for example? If this is the case, just holding the child firmly and rocking gently will often help to calm things down. Going to a quiet place, if in public, may also contribute to calming the child. Some children kick and/or bite when upset emotionally in this manner, so restrain the child carefully to avoid injury to yourself. If you can reframe the temper tantrum experience your child is having as being similar to an electrical power outage, it can help you to stay calm. We don't plan an outage; it just happens, and often we just need to be patient and stay calm until the power returns.

Erikson's framework of psychosocial development includes the father as a new significant other for the toddler at the autonomy stage. Although research shows that a father may begin to influence his child's development in infancy, according to Erikson, the father's function at this stage is to assist the child's development by helping to lessen the intensity of the bond between child and mother. As a toddler shows an increasing ability to be less dependent on adults, the father may take a greater interest in interacting with his child. Fathers may become more willing to take their toddler on short errands with them, or on special outings, such as to the zoo or the supermarket. These experiences are stimulating psychologically and socially for both the father and child. The toddler learns that Dad can be trusted as much as Mom. The more frequently father and child experience enjoyable and successful interactions, the easier separations from the mother may become. The mother can influence the success of the father's initiations of the child's separations from the mother by encouraging them and by reassuring toddler and father that these interactions and events are appropriate. The assumption here is that the toddler who learns to trust the father and has successful experiences in separating from the mother will come to generalize this trust to additional significant others in the family system. The path to effective social interactions with others is smoothed by such experiences.

***Toilet Training.*** Training for society's standards for handling bodily eliminations usually begins when infants are between 24 and 30 months of age and typically is completed by 36 months. The process of learning to control the release of urine from the bladder and feces from the bowels is usually accomplished easily by most individuals. In some situations, however, difficulties occur. Many adults are unfamiliar with ways and methods for toilet training that are successful and unstressful for both the infant and themselves. Opinions and directions can be found in most child care books, from pediatricians and family physicians, or from relatives and friends who have accomplished this with other children.

Some parents believe that shaming an infant for accidents or mistakes in toilet training will motivate him or her to achieve this developmental task successfully and speedily. Instead, toilet training is likely to become a power struggle between parent and child. The unhealthy attitude of shame and doubt that results can cause the child to question his or her ability to be autonomous.

Fortunately, most children who experience problems with toilet training eventually are able to accomplish the task (Figure 7–5). For example, being exposed to children in day-care programs who are toilet trained can help them to adopt the appropriate behavior cue to a desire to conform to other children.

● ● ● ● ● ● ● ● ● ● ● ● ● ● ● ● ● ● ● ● ● ● ● ● ● ● ● ● ● ●

## Parenting Reflection 7–3

What would be the long-term effects of the development of basic trust and of the development of mistrust during infancy?

● ● ● ● ● ● ● ● ● ● ● ● ● ● ● ● ● ● ● ● ● ● ● ● ● ● ● ● ● ●

**FIGURE 7–5.** A sense of autonomy is established when toddlers accomplish self-differentiation in new ways, such as setting personal boundaries via temper tantrums or mastering toilet training, for example.

| Focus On 7–3 | Age-Appropriate Play Equipment for Infants | | |
|---|---|---|---|
| | *Birth to One Year* | *One to Two Years* | *Two to Three Years* |
| | Rattles | Bath toys | Tricycle |
| | Crib mobiles | Simple puzzles | Outdoor swings |
| | Teething rings | Musical instruments | Picture books |
| | Texture balls/boxes | Toy phone | Scene toys |
| | Crib gyms | Simple picture books | Crayons |
| | Stuffed toys | Interlocking blocks | Puzzles |
| | Push-pull toys | Ride toys | Wooden blocks |
| | Shape sorters | | Wheel toys |
| | Squeak toys | | Musical toys |
| | Nesting/stacking toys | | Wagon |
| | Cloth/hard cardboard books | | |

**Providing Appropriate Toys and Play Equipment.**
Infants need appropriate play equipment and materials to stimulate cognitive development and social interaction skills. Simple toys are often all that is necessary in this regard. This is especially reassuring for parents who lack financial resources to provide what they see in stores and being used by other families. Infants can develop adequate cognitive skills by parents providing toys and play equipment that encourage visual and tactile exploration. Materials that encourage these behaviors also promote the development of curiosity in the world, which will have long-range effects.

One of the most important factors parents should consider in choosing infant toys is safety. While most large manufacturers are mindful of this in developing and making infant toys, parents need to keep these points in mind when selecting toys for infants and older children: (1) no sharp edges, (2) no small parts that can be swallowed or inhaled, (3) no cords or strings, and (4) no loud noises (Consumer Product Safety Commission, 2004).

Parents can choose appropriate toys and play equipment by considering the chronological age of their baby. Focus On 7–3 shows a listing of examples of age-appropriate play equipment.

••••••••••••••••••••••••••••••••••••••••••••••••••

*Focus Point.*   Development in infancy is characterized by developmental tasks that are unique to this time of the life span. The infant achieves a variety of physical, social, and psychological abilities, such as walking, learn- ing elementary communication and self-help skills, and acquiring healthy attitudes of basic trust and personal autonomy.

••••••••••••••••••••••••••••••••••••••••••••••••••

# EVOLVING PERSONAL CONCEPTS OF PARENTHOOD

As discussed in Chapter 5, becoming a parent for the first time is a critical adjustment for the adults in a family. The first child has a major role in shaping the emergence of parenting skills for the new mother and father. While an infant is experiencing the psychosocial stages of establishing the senses of basic trust and autonomy, parents are usually experiencing a new challenge in their own personal development in acquiring a sense of generativity. For many adults, the parenthood role adds a new, different, and perhaps more meaningful experience in acquiring their attitude of generativity. When children are being produced, the adults now turn their psychosocial focus more directly on the dimension of parenthood. They develop initial ideas about what it means to be a parent, what they understand to be the needs of children, what goals they have in child rearing, and what kind of parenting style they find appropriate and comfortable.

People may not think much about parenting or how to behave in this role until the need arises. However, when children are being produced, adults discover ample opportunities to examine their existing beliefs, attitudes, and behavior as parents. This seems to be the time when adults consider and develop the self-regulating patterns for parenting behavior and parent-child interactions. These self-regulating patterns form the basis for guiding how each adult should act as a parent, what rules the adults wish to have in regulating and evaluating children's behavior as well as their own, and what goals or outcomes they wish to accomplish with their children. (Review the discussion in Chapter 5 pertaining to the transition to parenthood and that in Chapter 3 relating to patterns that guide the operation of a family system.)

It is crucial to discuss and agree on these issues. Even more pressing are the day-to-day concerns about how to act as a parent in providing care and nurturance for an infant whose daily needs are rapidly changing. Initially, the tasks that parents perform involve providing safety and care for the infant. Later, as the infant grows and changes, parents need to provide psychological and social stimulation. Later still, especially following the second birthday, parents must use different parenting skills to support the child's socialization tasks related to gaining personal autonomy. For example, parents must deal with the expressions of anger and negativism a child exhibits at this stage of development. New parents need to examine just how they wish to respond to these outbursts of emotion from their child. Parents must find ways to allow independence to be expressed without damaging the child's belief about his or her inner nature or self. During this stage of the family life career, parents learn an important lesson about working with children: One's behavior as a parent must change in tandem with the changing behavior and needs of children. Children have an important influence on one's conduct as a parent.

## Learning About Parenting

Although people want to be competent as parents, they do not always know what infants and toddlers need or how to meet those needs effectively. Parents usually don't have access to the information about what contemporary researchers have learned about infants. This lack of knowledge may cause them to under- or overestimate what infants are capable of in their behavior. For example, a classic study of adolescent parents noted that there was gross underestimation of the times when significant developmental events occur in infancy

(deLissovoy, 1973a, 1973b). The implications of such lack of knowledge are significant. Of particular concern is the potential for parental abuse stemming from incorrect expectations about children's normal development. Parents who become impatient and push a child to achieve a developmental task long before the child is ready are likely to cause harm to the child's self-esteem, and perhaps even to the child's physical well-being.

A variety of programs for educating and training adults in parenting skills are usually successful in helping adults accomplish parental goals (Johnson et al., 2003; Paris, 2000). Many studies find that adults who participate in such programs are more satisfied with being a parent, are more knowledgeable about children's behavior and needs, and feel more competent as parents. In addition, infants of parents with this type of training are found to be more responsive to their child. Some programs use parent educators to train the adults in a classroom setting, and others rely on in-home instruction. Unfortunately, such training opportunities are limited and are unavailable to many adults who could benefit from them.

### Parenting Reflection 7–4

Should new parents be given a parenting kit to take home following delivery? What are some things that such a kit might contain that would be helpful, especially to first-time parents of an infant?

## Are There Differences Between Mothers and Fathers of Infants and Toddlers?

There is considerable variation in the infant care practices found among other cultures. For example, in certain societies of Africa, infants typically are left unattended for long periods of time (Hewlett et al., 1998). From this standpoint in relation of one culture to another, we can conclude that parental roles and caregiving styles are socially constructed (see Chapter 1) (Doherty, Kouneski, & Erickson, 1998). In other words, parenting roles are not necessarily influenced by biology. In American culture, fathers typically employ a style of interaction and play with infants that is highly physical in nature (Figure 7–6). This is not the case in other cultures (Roopnarine et al., 1993).

**FIGURE 7–6.** Men can be expected to be competent caregivers for infants, although there may be subtle differences from women in the way they provide care.

Women are traditionally the parents who assume the primary caregiving role in child rearing. The involvement of fathers in child rearing has increased steadily as a function of the increasingly larger numbers of women employed outside the home. The benefit to children of both parents' involvement can be observed in enhanced levels of development in all domains (Coontz, 1998).

As fathers have become more involved with child rearing, behavioral scientists have labeled this as **responsible fathering** (Coley, 2001; Doherty et al., 1998, 2000; Silverstein & Auerbach, 2002; Walker & McGraw, 2000). This parenting style is characterized by a heightened motivation and commitment to parenthood and child rearing, beliefs about parenting, involvement in providing for a family, the relationship with his child's mother, the degree of encouragement the mother gives him, and his self-confidence as a parent.

Overall, there are likely few differences between mothers and fathers in terms of interaction styles with infants. Differences that do exist might be attributed more to the manner in which men act out their psychological script of a father (which is likely to be rather traditional in nature) and to the time men are able and willing to devote to caregiving responsibilities. Generally, fathers who are likely to be actively involved with child care are younger, happily married men who were present at their child's birth and are willing to modify their work schedules to share parenting responsibilities with their partner. Fathers do make important contributions to a child's developmental progress in infancy. Their involvement as parents by providing emotional support to mothers also tends to improve both adults' parental performance.

## Androgynous Parenting Roles

Many men and women who become parents today are likely to hold attitudes different from those of their parents about how parental responsibilities are to be conducted. Many adults today may espouse egalitarian concepts about parenthood roles. Researchers label these as *androgynous* in that parenting roles may be shared rather than being distinct or based on gender. Although both partners tend to say they want to share parenting responsibilities equally, women continue to perform more of these tasks than men (Bianchi et al., 2000). Today, many men fully expect that they will be actively involved in providing care and support for their infants (Fox, Bruce, & Combs-Orme, 2000). Although the involvement may be configured to the role of "father as a helper to mother" in providing child care, the expectation is for full fatherly involvement nevertheless. Adults can experience some difficulties in sharing child-care responsibilities. The most difficult area reported is employers' rigidity about the time frame for performing work responsibilities.

••••••••••••••••••••••••••••••••••••••••••••••••••

***Focus Point.***    Few significant differences are found in the overall performance of men and women in providing care for infants. Some differences are noted in interaction styles that relate more to the enactment of psychological scripts of appropriate parenting. Many middle-class men and women attempt to develop androgynous parenting roles rather than those based on traditional sex-role stereotypes of fathers and mothers. Such parents share in performing parenting roles.

••••••••••••••••••••••••••••••••••••••••••••••••••

## SUPPORTS FOR PARENTS OF INFANTS AND TODDLERS

The issue of child care has received a great deal of attention in recent years. Consider the following statistics relating to the use of nonparental child care by families of infants and young children in the United States (Federal Interagency Forum on Child and Family Statistics, 2003; U. S. Bureau of the Census, 2003):

■ The changing structure of American families has resulted in dramatic increases in the number of single-parent families in which the mother is the primary economic provider and in the numbers of dual-earner families in which both adults are gainfully employed.
■ About 62 percent of all married women over 18 years of age were employed outside the home in 2001.
■ About 73 percent of all women with children under 6 years of age were in the labor force in 2001.
■ About 75 percent of all children in the United States 5 years of age and under have been in some type of child-care arrangement since they were born. Sixty percent of these children are under 2 years of age.
■ Even if a mother is unemployed, many families use day care and nonparental child care as enrichment experiences for children and to provide time for mothers' personal enrichment.

Given this information, questions may arise about who is raising America's children and the quality of care being given. Use of nonparental child care has not had a good reputation in the past in the United States, especially when infants are involved. Traditionally, the preferred mode of child care in our culture has been for

parents, typically the mother, to provide care. Many families today obviously are finding this type of child-care arrangement impossible, and perhaps in some respects even undesirable. One study reports that many dual-earner families are turning increasingly to the use of the father rather than other relatives or paid caregivers to provide care for infants following birth (Federal Interagency Forum on Child and Family Statistics, 2003). Apparently, major cost savings result when this arrangement is used. Fathers may not necessarily provide a great deal of the infant care nor help to make child-care arrangements easier or more satisfactory, but the incentive provided by using them results in halving child-care costs. This may be a primary motivation for many young families.

Concerns about the effects of day care or large group care on children, and especially on infants, have been expressed for many years (Azar, 1997). Debate has continued about providing care for infants by someone other than the mother in someplace other than the home. Maternal deprivation was found to have serious deleterious effects on infant growth and development and was interpreted as strong evidence that infants should be cared for by their own mothers.

Opinion continued in this vein until the 1960s, when increasing numbers of women began to return to the workforce. Use of nonparental child care increased accordingly. Researchers reversed the attitude that such care produced harmful effects on infants and children when it became apparent that attachment to parents was not adversely affected. However, a national study rated only 10 percent of infant child-care sites as high quality (NICHD Early Child Care Research Network, 1999). This study and others suggest the following interpretations:

■ Nonparental care of infants can offer an enriching experience that enhances and stimulates their developmental progress.
■ Quality care for infants had the greatest impact on infants from disadvantaged families.
■ Some less desirable behavioral traits, such as boisterousness, heightened physical and verbal aggressiveness, and lack of cooperation with adults, could be observed at later ages in children who had been in infant group-care settings.

Controversy has surfaced among developmental researchers who have studied the effects of group care on infant and child development and reported disturbing results (Belsky, 1990; Belsky & Rovine, 1988). Belsky, for example, reversed his earlier beliefs and concluded in a 1988 study that infants spending more than 20 hours a week in nonparental care are at risk of developing an insecure attachment. Other researchers question this contention (NICHD Early Child Care Research Network, 2000a, 2000b). At issue are differences of opinion and interpretations of research findings by the investigators. Most of the studies have found beneficial effects of nonparental infant care.

The main source of nonparental care of infants today is by a nonrelative in a private home, or by what is known as *family day care* (Federal Interagency Forum on Child and Family Statistics, 2003). The employment status of mothers contributes significantly to choosing a day-care provider who is a relative. Fifty-three percent of employed mothers tend to have a relative rather than a nonrelative provide care for their babies. In fact, the majority of mothers in one study preferred the father to provide this care (Riley & Glass, 2002).

The stability or consistent use of a nonparental care provider of infants is a major concern for both parents and researchers. Changes in the nonparental care provider occur less frequently for infants than for older children. In all, only about one-fourth of the families change nonparental care providers within a year. Changes occur more commonly when the provider is not a relative.

It may not be possible to conclude at the present time what long-term effects may occur as a result of non-parental group care for infants. What may be interpreted from research findings is that infant care apparently is not harmful (NICHD Early Child Care Research Network, 2000a, 2000b). However, the problem of how to provide care adequately for individuals at this vulnerable time in their lives has not been completely resolved.

***Focus Point.***   Due to the large number of women who are employed outside the home, an increasing number of families use nonparental care of infants. Concerns have been expressed about whether such experiences harm the adequate attachment of infants to parents. This is a controversial issue to which there are no clearly definite answers today. Some researchers report that nonparental care causes no harm to infants while others suggest it does. The stability of care and quality of experiences may be crucial factors in determining the effects of nonparental care on infant and child development.

### Parenting Reflection 7–5

What are some pros and cons of using nonparental child care for an infant when both parents must work outside the home?

# SYSTEMIC FAMILY DEVELOPMENT SNAPSHOT

*(Before reading this section, it may be helpful to review the systemic family development model and the metaphor used to illustrate its concepts from Chapter 3.)*

We will use the metaphor of a round layer cake and a slice taken from the cake to discuss a point in developmental time in a hypothetical family system in the chapters dealing with parenting infants and toddlers through parenting adolescents and young adults. The slice will reveal the stressors being experienced by each generation so that we may gain a better understanding of what is affecting the entire family system at this point. We will also identify and discuss the means for coping with the stressors and observe hypothetically how various family roles, patterns, and boundaries might be reestablished to regain a degree of homeostasis previously experienced by the family. To illustrate the discussion, we will use a hypothetical family system, three generations of the Curtis family.

## Examples of Stressors Affecting Each Curtis Family Generation

### First Generation (Grandparents)

■ Adjusting to the aging process experienced in middle age
■ Adjusting to the midlife transition experiences

- Assisting adult children in completing their individuation process
- Adjusting to the death of parents, relatives, and colleagues
- Beginning preparations for retirement
- Establishing grandparent and in-law roles

### Second Generation (Young Adult Parents)

- Establishing work roles and objectives
- Balancing work and family roles
- Maintaining a household that meets the needs of infants and toddlers; providing finances for this household
- Deciding on family size
- Adjusting to pregnancy, childbirth, and infants
- Adjusting to changes in their committed relationship related to additional family roles (e.g., parenthood, in-laws)
- Learning to parent infants and toddlers

### Third Generation (Infants and Toddlers)

- Establishing an attachment with parents
- Establishing the attitudes of trust and autonomy
- Mastering cognitive tasks of infancy
- Mastering toilet training

Typically, families that are in the process of producing children remain focused on this family task for 3 to 5 years. This phase in family life is preceded by the adjustment period following a formal marriage or upon an agreement to become committed as a couple. The median age at first marriage in the United States was about 28 years for men and about 25 years for women in 2000. We would estimate the ages of both sets of the hypothetical couple's parents at the time of their marriage as: (1) groom's father to be 52; (2) groom's mother to be 50; (3) bride's father to be 49; and (4) bride's mother to be 47.

The young couple in the hypothetical family, Butch and Lisa Curtis, have produced two children; their first, Mary, was born 2 years after they married, and Joey was born 2 years later. The stressors and means for coping that affect each generation will be discussed separately.

At the time we are taking a slice of developmental time, Mary is 2½ and her brother, Joey, is 6 months old. This places the ages of the various adults as fol-

lows: (1) groom's father, George Curtis, is 56; (2) the groom's mother, Joan Curtis, is 54; (3) the bride's father, Harry Scott, is 53; (4) the bride's mother, Susan Scott, is 51; (5) Butch Curtis is 32; and (6) Lisa Curtis is 29. These ages are important in that they provide clues as to where all family members are in developmental time.

## First Generation (Grandparents)

We will address the older generation first in examining our slice of developmental time. All of the older adults compose the first generation in this particular family system. All have entered middle age in their adult development and are experiencing a typical progression through this developmental stage. The oldest of the four generation members, George Curtis is beginning to look forward to retirement. He has worked as a post office employee for almost 30 years. His father recently died from Alzheimer's disease, and George is having a difficult time acknowledging his father's death. His mother passed away several years ago, and George doesn't understand why he seems to be paying little attention to this recent significant family event. Joan Curtis is also stymied by his reaction but is attempting to persuade George to enter into therapy as a way of discovering his feelings about his father's death. For now, George is resisting this suggestion. Joan has had her own challenges recently with a new supervisor who is much younger than she and, in her opinion, much less experienced. Her work is enjoyable, but she is starting to question whether to seek other employment or stay put because of seniority status.

The Scotts are dealing with a particularly difficult situation in that Susan was diagnosed with breast cancer 6 months ago and has been undergoing chemotherapy treatments. It has been especially challenging for Harry because he feels there is little he can do to protect his wife from the dreadful side effects of the treatments and even less from the distinct possibility she may die soon. Luckily, their medical insurance provides for most of the cost, and they can attend support group meetings as well as couple therapy to deal with stresses from this situation. However, Harry has turned to alcohol as a way of handling his uncertainties, which Susan finds to be another source of stress. She has found solace in her spiritual life, and for now this is what sustains her.

All this has also affected their daughter and son-in-law. Lisa Curtis is fearful both for her mother and for herself as she can envision developing this same condition at some point in her future. To make matters even more confusing for this family, no one talks about the situation, the feelings associated with their fears, or what the future could hold.

## Second Generation (Adult Parents)

Butch Curtis has recently changed jobs after experiencing a long period of unemployment that was difficult on everyone in his immediate family. Financially, things look better than they have in a long time. Lisa carried a heavy burden in being the sole provider for her family while Butch was unemployed, a position she was thankful for but also found to be uncomfortable in some respects. Now that Butch is working again, they are faced with finding child care for both their children. Lisa is not especially satisfied with group care and wants to find someone to care for the children in their home. Calling on her parents or in-laws is not feasible because of their own situations. Butch has also brought up another issue that they had talked about off and on for several months now. This is whether to have another child. Lisa is unclear on her feelings about this and has discussed the issue with several friends to learn about the pros and cons of having three versus two children.

Both Butch and Lisa have managed to adjust to being parents for the first time and find that taking care of a new baby is more manageable than what they experienced after bringing Mary home. However, both have expressed discontent about not having much of a social life or getting private time. They feel fortunate to have Butch's parents nearby, and George and Joan have been generous in offering to take the children overnight occasionally.

## Third Generation (Children)

The children of this family are highly dependent on the adults for their care. Luckily, they have had good health and are growing as expected. The only major difficulty at this time is with Mary's toilet training. She appeared to have accomplished this about the time her brother was born. The change in things at home with the new baby resulted in her loss of control, and she is having accidents more than usual. Lisa anticipates that this will not improve with Butch going back to work and other changes in the home routine. At times, Lisa feels that she is neglecting the children because she can't be a full-time mom. However, she is working through these feelings when she sees how well the children's needs are being met and with the equipment, food, medical care, and clothes they can provide for the children.

Joey is having some problems with separating from his mom and dad when taken to the sitter's home, and Lisa experiences the most difficulties when this happens. Perhaps more than her husband, Lisa feels torn between the difficulties her parents are having, her own situation, and the developmental changes her children are undergoing. This is a stressful time for the first and second generations of this family system.

### Parenting Reflection 7–6

Can you identify the ways that this Snapshot reveals how the concept of interrelatedness (from family systems theory) can be observed in this family system at this particular point in developmental time? What were some ways that the family system used to adapt or cope with the effects of the various stressors being experienced?

## POINTS TO CONSIDER

■ Two principal concepts describe the nature of infants: (1) *the psychoanalytical view*, which stresses the primacy of early experiences in determining an infant's later development, and (2) *the developmental view*, which emphasizes the adaptable nature of an infant in manipulating and responding to the environment.

■ Basic developmental tasks of infancy focus on achievement of significant physical milestones, mastery of basic motor competencies, and emerging social competencies.

- Parenting infants and toddlers focuses on meeting a variety of needs of children at these ages: (1) providing structure and nurturance; (2) providing food and helping establish self-feeding; (3) attending to health and medical needs; (4) recognizing how an infant communicates and encouraging speech development; (5) observing an infant's sleep-wake cycle and encouraging good sleeping habits; (6) facilitating the attachment between parents and an infant; (7) facilitating the child's development of a sense of basic trust versus mistrust and a sense of autonomy versus shame and doubt; (8) providing toilet training at a developmentally appropriate time; (9) providing appropriate toys and equipment.

- Becoming a parent, especially for the first time, is a significant event that requires a critical adjustment for the adults of a family system. New parents evolve concepts of parenting from many sources, including social scripts developed from their families of origin, exposure to society's expectations of appropriate parenting behavior, and personal interpretations of what constitutes appropriate parenting behavior. New parents evolve ideas that serve as self-regulating patterns for how they fulfill this role within their family system. It is helpful if new parents develop a vision of how their parenting experiences should take place.

- First-time parents may take advantage of educational programs to help learn how to parent infants effectively. Participation in these programs may increase satisfaction with parenting and boost confidence.

- Researchers have found few significant differences in comparing mothers with fathers of infants. Men appear to be effective as parents to infants. Some family systems attempt to conduct parenting as an androgynous role. To do so may require some adjustments on the part of the adults, especially in relation to their work roles.

- Many families with infants use the services of nonparental child care, especially when both parents work outside the home. In many situations, nonparental care by a relative is the major source of supplemental child care. Controversy exists as to the effects of nonparental child care on infants.

- A systemic family development snapshot reveals the stressors that may affect different generations of a family system and the ways members cope with these stressors in healthy and unhealthy ways.

# CHAPTER 8

# Parenting Preschoolers

### Focus Questions

......

1. What are the principal developmental landmarks of early childhood that parents should know?
2. What is the nature of parent-preschooler relations?
3. What are some common behavior problems observed among young children?
4. What kinds of community supports do families with preschoolers need?
5. What stressors and coping mechanisms are revealed by a systemic family development snapshot of families with preschool-age children?

......

**Early childhood** is the period in a person's life between the ages of 3 and 6. Children of these ages are also known as *preschoolers*. The interactions within a family system change to reflect an increasing involvement of young children as participating members of the family. A major challenge to parents at this time is to adjust to a developing child whose behavior and personality traits are emerging rapidly. Preschoolers are adventuresome creatures who are curious about their world and quickly learn many things. Parents and others typically find much pleasure and enjoyment from their preschool-age child but also begin to experience conflicts as the child tests limits and boundaries adults have set for them. The rate of developmental change is slower during these years relative to what was observed in infancy and prenatal development.

## DEVELOPMENTAL LANDMARKS OF EARLY CHILDHOOD

There is much to be learned and accomplished during the years before a child enters formal schooling. The basic skills of locomotion, communication, and interaction are acquired by most individuals in infancy. In early childhood, expansion in the size of a child's vocabulary and in other elements of language development allows him or her to perform unlimited tasks. It is a time to begin learning in earnest the basic social skills necessary for effective interactions with others. Language becomes the tool of socialization and personal expression. Young children learn through modeling and observation of others and

**FIGURE 8–1.** Early childhood is the life stage between age 3 and 6. This period is viewed as a special time during childhood.

come to comprehend their parents' expectations and instructions by these means. As young children acquire a number of physical and social skills, they become other-oriented rather than largely self-oriented. This important change in perspective enables a developing child to capitalize on a wide range of experiences as she or he learns to cope with and master the environment.

As with all other life stages, several unique developmental tasks and landmarks are associated with the early childhood stage. These are listed in Focus On 8–1.

• • • • • • • • • • • • • • • • • • • • • • • • • • • • • • • • • •

*Focus Point.* Early childhood is characterized by unique developmental tasks and specific landmarks. The period is notable as the time when young children actively acquire knowledge and basic skills that are both physical and social in nature.

• • • • • • • • • • • • • • • • • • • • • • • • • • • • • • • • • •

# PARENTING YOUNG CHILDREN

## Meeting the Needs of Preschoolers

Parenting behavior will undergo modification as children grow from infancy into the years of early childhood. These changes occur in response to the changing developmental needs and abilities of preschoolers. From the perspective of family systems theory, parenting changes in response to meeting new and different needs presented by preschoolers. The children present different challenges to parents in attempting to master the developmental tasks presented at this stage.

The behavior of preschoolers is enhanced by parents who are responsive to changes in their children's needs. At the same time, parents find that their need to be needed by their children changes accordingly. Children, in effect, shape and modify the parenting behavior of adults. Parents learn that their growing preschooler also recognizes the changes in his or her maturity and will resist being treated as a younger child might be. Older preschoolers are particularly sensitive to adults who attempt to interact with them in a patronizing manner that fails to recognize their perceived status as big kids. From ages 3 to 6, the child's increasing attempts to express initiative act as a psychological flag to parents that they can no longer take their child's behavior for granted. Throughout the years of early childhood, a child tries to prove to parents that "I can! Let me show you that I can!"

As children become more capable of verbal communications with others, parents react by shifting from physical methods of child rearing to those that are more verbal and psychological in nature. Parents who believe in permissive and authoritative methods of child rearing may begin to use an increasing amount of reasoning and verbal directions in interacting with preschoolers. These reactions to children's changing nature assist and guide the autonomous behavior that prepares children for their next stage of development.

**Meeting Nutritional Needs.** Preschool children typically have a small appetite, which results in consumption of small amounts of food. Young children now eat meals with their families and are taught to use utensils rather than hands. Table manners also may be taught at this time. Preschoolers are eating the same types of food as other family members and usually don't require special dietary foods. Because they require

---

**Focus On 8–1**   **Major Developmental Tasks and Landmarks in Early Childhood**

### Physical

- Slower rate of growth in weight and height
- Small appetite; may be a picky eater
- Uses a preferred hand
- All primary teeth erupt
- Major gross motor skills mastered (e.g., running, climbing); fine motor skills emerging (e.g., art work)
- Prevalent upper respiratory diseases
- High energy level

### Psychosocial

- Expanding awareness of self, others, and things
- Gaining independence and some self-control
- Mastering a sense of initiative versus guilt
- High curiosity level
- Beginning socialization experiences (e.g., appropriate social and sex-role behaviors)
- Learns by doing and from mistakes
- Play is more social and creative in nature

### Cognitive

- Thought is both preoperational and intuitive, related dynamically to perception, and largely prelogical in nature
- Building a database of information about the world
- Preoccupation with classification and grouping things
- Expanding vocabulary
- Memory improving
- Flaws in thinking include egocentrism, animism, jumping to conclusions, and centering

---

fewer calories, parents begin to learn that they will eat at meals but often in smaller portions than other family members. Most parents understand that children require good nutrition to grow properly and that they need adequate amounts of protein, calcium and other minerals, and vitamins from a variety of food sources and supplements. Most parents also are aware that preschoolers can develop preferences for foods that are not healthy, such as those containing large amounts of refined sugar or those considered to be empty calorie foods such as potato chips. Eating problems can develop in early childhood that can lead to obesity in later years. Parents may unwittingly contribute to these by requiring children to eat all food that they are served (Rolls, Engell, & Birch, 2000). These problems are discussed in greater detail in the Dealing with Behavior Problems section of this chapter.

**Focus Point.** Preschoolers can be expected to have small appetites. They need to be encouraged to try different foods and food preparations. Parents may unwittingly encourage the later development of eating problems by enforcing strict eating requirements.

**Health and Safety Issues.** Young children do not yet have a fully mature immune system nor have developed antibodies to combat many illnesses. The wide availability of immunizations against a large number of formerly debilitating and fatal diseases has helped to extend life expectancies of people in many countries around the world. Most deaths today among young children are caused by injury in or near the home rather than illness (Federal Interagency Forum on Child and Family Statistics, 2003).

Accidental injury is the leading cause of death in childhood and adolescence in the United States (U.S. Bureau of the Census, 2003). In early childhood, this often occurs in relation to car accidents as a pedestrian, a passenger, or on tricycles. Use of appropriately designed children's car seats are required now in all states for both infants and young children.

Many accidental deaths and injuries to young children occur in or near their home. Many of these involve a child's ingestion of poisonous or toxic substances, such as fertilizer, gasoline, or cleaning products. While parents are urged to store these safely, it is also wise to have the telephone number of a local poison control center, emergency facility, or physician handy in case it is needed quickly. In addition, it is important for parents to insist on childproof caps for medication bottles. Other safety measures include the use of helmets for skiing and tricycle riding. Parents need to teach their children rules of safety when walking or playing outside the home. Some children are more impulsive than others and can experience greater numbers of injuries and close calls (Schwebel & Plumert, 1999). These children require an extra-strict parental eye and perhaps more intensive safety instruction than other children. Perhaps just as important is making sure that play equipment both indoors and outdoors is safe and can be used safely by young children.

***Focus Point.*** Preschoolers generally have good health but may experience a number of illnesses. Accidental injury is the leading cause of death of preschoolers, with the majority of these occurring within or near the home.

**Providing Structure and Nurturance for Young Children.** During the early childhood period, child rearing increasingly includes greater attention to teaching children about structure as it is interpreted by the particular family system. Structure comes in several forms, such as the rules promoted by the family, the roles taught to children by precept and by example, and the ways family members communicate with one another. In family systems theory, these are referred to as *family patterns.*

Nurturance is provided when parents consistently attempt to meet the particular needs of young children and act in ways that are supportive of their psychosocial growth (see Table 8–1). There is a greater emphasis on providing assertive care rather then supportive care because preschoolers are not yet able to take greater control over their actions.

**TABLE 8–1.** Behaviors of Parents of Preschool-Age Children

| Behaviors Providing Structure and Nurturance | Behaviors Not Providing Structure and Nurturance |
|---|---|
| • Affirming child's accomplishment of developmental tasks | • Teasing child |
| • Continuing to provide for safety, protection, and love needs | • Behaving inconsistently |
| • Supporting exploration of the environments of people and things | • Not allowing child to learn to think and make independent choices |
| • Encouraging acceptance of gender identity; teaching acceptance of both sexes | • Not providing information or direct answers to questions |
| • Encouraging expression of feelings and associating feelings with actions | • Responding with sarcasm and ridicule |
| • Providing information that is as accurate as possible; correcting misinformation | • Using messages with mixed meanings |
| • Providing appropriate positive and negative consequences to behavior | • Discounting child |
| • Giving clear, concise directions | |
| • Encouraging the separation of fantasy from reality | |

*Source:* Adapted from Clarke, J. I., & Dawson, C. (1989). *Growing up again: Parenting ourselves, parenting our children.* Minneapolis: Hazelden.

At this time in a child's life, several types of parental behaviors can promote feelings of guilt that may inhibit developmental progress and lead to unhealthy self-esteem. Most of these behaviors are considered to be variations of acts that serve to discount or belittle a child (Clarke & Dawson, 1998).

**Using Rules in Teaching Structure.** The discussion in Chapter 3 indicated that rules are used in family systems as a primary means for maintaining the group's efficient functioning. Rules are one means by which parents teach structure to children and help children to internalize controls that guide their behavior (Clarke & Dawson, 1998). When a family system evolves and formulates rules that promote healthy parent and child behavior, some are negotiable and others are nonnegotiable. **Nonnegotiable rules** cannot be debated or changed, while **negotiable rules** are subject to discussion and alteration. In healthy families, a mixture of such rules guides the behavior of family members. In these families, nonnegotiable rules generally relate to safeguarding children's well-being in reasonable ways. These are not arbitrarily derived by the parents, nor are they abusive or rigid in nature. Instead, the purpose of such rules is to teach responsible behavior, good citizenship, and effective interpersonal skills. Nonnegotiable rules may define limits as well as appropriate behaviors with which children are expected to comply for their own well-being. For example, the rule "play in the back yard, not in the street" informs a preschooler that a parent cares about the child's well-being and is willing to define the places where the child can play safely. Other nonnegotiable rules might include: "You must go to bed at eight o'clock" or "You must eat breakfast every day."

Negotiable rules can be questioned by children and discussed with parents. Young children quickly learn which rules are negotiable and which are not. For example, the implicit rule in some families is that children are to eat whatever is served to them for meals, but children may learn that they can question what they are expected to eat. Perhaps children may resist eating spinach because of its odious taste, smell, or appearance. They may bargain with their parent for what they will eat at the meal and what they will not until some agreement is reached between them. In essence, negotiable rules help to teach children how to think and use discussion as a means of conflict resolution (see Figure 8–2).

**FIGURE 8–2.** Family systems evolve rules as a means of providing structure to children. Some rules are negotiable and others are not. Rules are used as a means of socializing children into appropriate behavior patterns. Consequences help to enforce rules. Children learn that some behaviors are acceptable but others, such as expressions of physical aggression, are not.

● ● ● ● ● ● ● ● ● ● ● ● ● ● ● ● ● ● ● ● ● ● ● ● ● ● ● ● ● ●

## Parenting Reflection 8–1

Can a family system have too few or too many rules that govern the behavior of family members? What effect would each of these situations have on young children, and what would be the implications of each on children's future development?

● ● ● ● ● ● ● ● ● ● ● ● ● ● ● ● ● ● ● ● ● ● ● ● ● ● ● ● ● ●

Enforcing rules and consequences of rules can be a problem for parents, especially those who are first-time parents of young children. It is often just as difficult for parents to remember to use positive reinforcement to help teach structure as it is to enforce the consequences of transgressions to rules. Such structure is most effective when administered with nurturance and love by parents.

*Focus Point.*   Young children need to learn about structure from their parents. This is typically taught via rules that are both negotiable and nonnegotiable in nature. Consequences of rules help preschoolers begin to learn self-control of their actions.

**Facilitating a Sense of Initiative.**   Young children experience the challenges of developing a **sense of initiative** between their third and sixth birthdays. This attitude represents further adaptation to the environment, reflects the full confidence of young children in their desire to achieve mastery of relationships, objects, and activities, and is boosted by the accomplishments that occurred in the last psychosocial stage (Figure 8–3). The sense of autonomy prepares a young child to develop feelings of accomplishment, the pervasive psychological attitude that "I can!"

## Parenting Reflection 8–2

Is it possible for a young child to have an over-developed sense of initiative? How would this take be expressed?

The significant others in a young child's life now include the family system as a whole. These individuals, taken singly and as a group, assist and support a child's efforts to express initiative and adjust to others. Parents are an important influence in helping preschoolers discover the variety of personal abilities they possess as individuals such as asking questions to gain information, exploring their world through their senses, trying new things, and experimenting with play equipment and toys. When parents establish an accepting attitude that these are appropriate behaviors within limits, then preschoolers gain confidence in themselves and learn that it is OK to be curious and to learn.

The alternative to acquiring a sense of initiative is acquiring a **sense of guilt,** which is the psychosocial hazard faced both by young children and those who assist them in their developmental progress. Young children show an almost unlimited interest and curiosity about life and their environment, and their exuberant behavior can fre-

**FIGURE 8–3.**  A sense of initiative is established when children are encouraged to learn, ask questions, and discover their world. This attitude is one of self-confidence in learning to master the environment.

quently lead them into conflict with those who provide their care and guidance. When caregivers' responses cause the young child's psychosocial focus to become centered on guilt rather than initiative, action is inhibited.

••••••••••••••••••••••••••••••••

### Parenting Reflection 8–3

How would you, as a parent of a preschooler, use rules to manage their behavior to encourage a sense of initiative rather than a sense of guilt?

••••••••••••••••••••••••••••••••

Guilt differs from shame, the unhealthy attitude that may have been acquired in late infancy. Shame is the feeling that one's inner self is flawed in some manner, whereas guilt focuses on the negative aspects of one's behavior. Essentially, one feels guilt about behavior that is somehow perceived as wrong or bad, and this bad behavior can serve as proof and reinforcement of the belief the one's inner self is indeed shameful (Burns, 1999).

••••••••••••••••••••••••••••••••

***Focus Point.***  Parents as well as the family system help preschoolers to acquire a healthy sense of initiative. This positive attitude toward themselves and their abilities helps young children to be inquisitive about their world and to learn how they fit into their particular family system.

••••••••••••••••••••••••••••••••

**Beginning Socialization. Socialization** refers to the processes by which children are taught to conform to social rules, to acquire personal values, and to develop attitudes and behaviors typical or representative of their cultural environment. The socialization process begins in earnest during early childhood, when parents and other caregivers begin to take an active role in teaching a young child these lessons. The lessons are not always given by formal instruction. Some are learned by observing the behavior of others.

Young children are expected to learn the patterns by which their family system functions and operates and to adopt the rules, behavioral expectations, and limits or boundaries their family system establishes for them. Some psychologists call this helping a child to inter-

nalize behavioral standards promoted by parents and other caregivers. This is what is referred to in this text as providing experiences that teach *structure* to children. A child who has learned structure has the information about which to judge any action as appropriate and acceptable or inappropriate and unacceptable. At the level of preschool children, such lessons are introductions to family functioning. Implicit is the understanding that transgressions and mistakes are to be expected from young children as they learn.

Depending on the nature of a particular family system, certain standards may be promoted more than others. Despite the diversity of families today, almost all teach certain kinds of behaviors and values to children. For example, nearly all families attempt to teach children to acquire prosocial behaviors such as learning to be empathic, controlling impulsiveness, gaining self-control, and limiting aggression. These are briefly discussed in the following paragraphs.

***Prosocial Behaviors.***  Most young children are taught to show some degree of social interest in others. **Prosocial behaviors** promote helpfulness and concern for others. These altruistic behaviors show an awareness of other people's feelings and appropriate ways of reacting to those feelings. This calls for knowledge in using a social skill known as **empathy,** which is the ability to accurately comprehend the thoughts, feelings, and actions of others. Empathy differs from sympathy, which is the ability to feel the same way that others do. Learning to be sympathetic, however, is the first step toward becoming empathetic.

The origins of sympathetic behaviors can be found in infancy when children are observed to comfort another child's distress (Radke-Yarrow, Zahn-Waxler, & Chapmen, 1983). In early childhood, empathic responsiveness is observed when children share belongings and comfort or help others who are distressed. However, these behaviors are not performed as spontaneously or as frequently as parents and others would prefer.

It is unclear at this time how an adult model facilitates empathic behaviors in young children. It appears that when children have opportunities to observe such behaviors, they tend to behave more frequently in empathic ways toward others (Rock, 2002). Researchers note, however, that these behaviors are observed throughout infancy and childhood regardless of the degree of parental influence or instruction.

*Aggression.* Psychologists define **aggression** as any hostile action that causes fear and leads to forceful contact with another (Parens, 1995). Aggressive actions directed at people or things can be verbal, physical, or both, and they can be either positive or negative.

Our culture values nonviolent social aggressiveness. An example is a steady, determined, and controlled effort in reaching solutions to problems and exploring learning experiences. In effect, this cultural concept of aggressiveness is synonymous with, and a logical extension of, the idea of initiative. Concern arises, however, when aggression is expressed as hostile or violent behavior that harms others or excludes children from social interactions with others.

Some researchers believe that aggressive expressions in childhood follow a normal developmental progression. Aggressive expressions steadily increase from late infancy into the years of early childhood (Parens, 1995), then peak in early childhood and decline thereafter. Thus, aggression in preschoolers is part of their normal growth and development. It may serve healthy functions such as helping them discover personal boundaries and communicate or enforce these with others.

Some researchers suggest a genetic tendency toward aggressive behavior (Parens, 1995). Other researchers believe that the family environment promotes such behavior. The premise for this observation is that children who are treated in harsh, aggressive ways by parents also act aggressively toward others (Delfos, 2003). Another possibility is that children adopt the model of aggressive behaviors they observe on television and in the movies. Despite the variety of explanations, young children clearly act aggressively at times for various reasons, and parents and other caregivers frequently are challenged to teach young children how to control aggressive impulses. Children are given a confusing message when they are spanked by adults for hitting others. Research points to the role of reinforcement as a powerful means for helping children learn to act in nonaggressive ways. When adults positively reinforce prosocial behaviors that are incompatible with aggressiveness, children learn that there are more beneficial ways to express themselves. One popular method is to isolate children from others briefly. Social learning theory suggests other alternatives, such as modeling for children appropriate ways of handling the feelings that motivate aggression.

*Delaying Gratification.* Adults often ask preschoolers to delay getting what they immediately want to have. This is a difficult task for a young child to master. The expectation for this behavior from young children is especially characteristic among middle-class families. Children are expected to defer having a smaller need satisfied immediately in exchange for receiving a greater benefit later. This is an important lesson in self-control. It helps to bring impulsiveness under willful restraint.

Individuals will cope with difficult situations in later life more successfully if lessons about delaying immediate gratification are introduced in early childhood (Schwarzchild, 2000). Teaching young children to think "It is good if I wait" can also help them in controlling impulsiveness.

**Encouraging Positive Sex-Role Development.** An important aspect of an individual's self-concept is **gender identity,** the knowledge that humans are either male or female. An individual's biological sex immediately predicts a variety of reactions from others at birth. Children first learn gender or sex roles according to parents' interpretations of masculinity or femininity. In early childhood, parents and other caregivers use reinforcement to shape gender identity. These become modified and refined in middle childhood and adolescence. The result of such socialization experiences is that individuals make personal interpretations of masculinity and femininity at later ages. Sex-role development, then, has both cognitive and behavioral aspects. It is not clear whether gender-related differences in behavior are due to cultural factors or to biological factors (Bornstein & Masling, 2002). However, gender roles appear to vary from one culture to another in some respects. For example, the practice in some cultures that women and girls are allowed to eat only after the males in the family have eaten is obviously a cultural factor. On the other hand, the fact that males tend to exhibit more aggressive behaviors than females regardless of culture would appear to point to a biological factor.

Young children appear to acquire rigid stereotypes of what it means to be male or female (Dresner, 2000). This rigidity is largely due to the inflexible thought processes typical of young children. It is only to be expected that young children understand whatever they see as something that is factual. For example, preschoolers typically use visible physical cues, such as clothing and hair style, to recognize someone as either male or female (Bem, 1989). It is not unusual for many young children to believe that long hair always indicates that a person is female, even when other features indicate the person is a male. The notion that gender conforms to external genitalia is not mastered until age 6.

A child's sex-role development begins at birth, when parents are told, "It's a boy!" or "It's a girl!" This immediate classification is made more permanent and public by naming the child, usually with a name that conforms to the child's sex (although androgynous names are becoming more common). From this point forward, children are channeled into one sex role or another by being dressed and given hairstyles that identify them as a male or female and cause others to treat them accordingly (Lester, 2003).

A preschool-age child's knowledge of sex-appropriate role behaviors comes from several sources. These behaviors are reinforced and modeled to children by adults and others in the family system (Maccoby & Jacklin, 1974). In addition, reinforcement from other same-sex children helps to promote sex-appropriate behaviors, especially among boys.

Teaching young children about androgynous sex roles is difficult but not impossible. The challenge lies in encouraging preschoolers to avoid stereotypes about sex roles. One method is to promote their involvement in activities and with toys traditionally associated with both genders. For example, boys can be encouraged to take on feminine play roles such as playing house, and girls can be encouraged to play with building blocks and trucks. In addition, observing adult behavior in nontraditional roles can affect children's ideas about sex roles. Children form a more balanced impression, for example, when they see Dad doing the laundry and Mom mowing the lawn.

It may be helpful to recognize that preschoolers' rigid interpretations of sex-role orientations and behaviors help them to understand these social roles and organize their behavior accordingly. However, encouraging children to maintain inflexible beliefs indefinitely may limit their full potential as human beings. Traditional sex-role orientations are problematic in that they tend to be rigid and restrictive. Higher levels of self-esteem and social competence are found among adults who adopt more androgynous sex-role orientations (Woodhill & Samuels, 2003).

**Teaching Young Children About Sexuality.** It is commonly believed that children are not interested in or

aware of their sexuality until puberty. This is a misconception, as many parents soon discover when their children reach preschool age. Rather than relating just to physiological functioning and behavior, *sexuality* refers to the broad aspects of sexual interests, attitudes, and activities that are an expression of a person's total being. Sexuality plays a significant psychological role throughout an individual's life span, not just following puberty. Although it is difficult for behavioral scientists to study the sexual interests and activities of children, childhood sexuality has been investigated for many years. It has had an important impact on the psychoanalytical theory of personality development proposed by Sigmund Freud.

Young children commonly ask many questions as a means of gaining information about their world, and questions relating to sexual issues and bodily functions are an expression of this interest. A typical question that can be expected from most 4-year-olds is "Where do babies come from?" It is also common for sexual themes to emerge in dramatic play activities such as when young children play house or the proverbial scenario of doctor.

Parents are the primary source of sexual socialization and information for young children (Westheimer & Lopater, 2004). Most parents are aware of their responsibilities in this regard, although some are anxious about answering a child's sexually oriented questions or feel incapable of providing accurate information due to their own ignorance about such matters. Although the accuracy of information parents provide in addressing young children's sexuality and sexual interests is important, perhaps of greater importance are the emotional tones and affect that parents communicate. For example, although young children are unable to comprehend the mechanics involved in human reproduction due to their level of cognitive development, they easily absorb any feelings of embarrassment that accompany a parent's answers to sexual questions.

Parents may read an abundance of excellent printed material about what kinds of sexually related questions to expect from young children. It may be helpful for parents to rehearse the answers they might provide to their preschoolers. Parents should understand that the messages they convey about sexuality, both verbal and nonverbal, will affect children's attitudes and values when they have reached maturity.

**Teaching Young Children About Dying and Death.** Until recently, sexuality was a stringently taboo topic in parent-child relations. Today, parents are encouraged to take an active role in shaping children's values and attitudes about their sexuality. However, teaching children about the realities of dying and death remains a topic of socialization that many parents find especially difficult (Cook & Oltjenbruns, 1998).

As unpleasant and difficult as discussion of this topic may be, parents should attempt to teach young children about the reality of mortality (Cook & Oltjenbruns, 1998). Parents need to remember that very young children cannot understand the finality of death. For example, when preschoolers play cops and robbers, they are able to resume normal functioning after playing dead. When they watch cartoon characters experience serious injury, they see them spontaneously recover. Another difficulty in this regard is the inability of preschool-age children to comprehend the full meaning of "forever" as relating to the finality of death. Many young children also reach the conclusion that death happens only to those who are old, sick, or fatally injured. This belief leads to questions when a parent or sibling becomes ill, for example, that relate to whether the person will die. As with socialization experiences that teach young children about sexuality, there is no specific design for how parents can teach young children about dying and death.

*Focus Point.* Parents of preschoolers begin instructing their preschooler about appropriate behaviors that are expected of them by their family and by society. Instruction also is directed at helping children understand gender or sex roles, sexuality, dying, and death.

**Facilitating Cognitive Development.** Children shift to a new type of thought process typically around age 3. Piaget (1967) calls this a change to the **preoperational** mode of thinking. Parents and other caregivers readily recognize that a preschooler, unlike an infant, thinks. Thinking becomes more noticeable as young children solve problems in their play and daily activities. They now have an active memory and information-processing skills. They also show indications of the ability to use elementary logic (Flavell, Miller, & Miller, 2001).

Parents may need to be informed that preschool-age children do not understand the world as an adult or even an older child does. Piaget described the nature of preschool-age thought as intuitive in nature, meaning that these children often jump to conclusions, make de-

cisions, and interpret the world based on insufficient facts. Since children this age do not rely on reasoning, they will have many erroneous thoughts. Parents who may not be aware of the significantly different way that preschoolers think may assume they know more than they do. For example, Piaget noted that preschool-age children's thought processes are slanted in terms of what he called **egocentrism.** This is the child's belief that he or she is the center of the universe, that things happen simply because he or she exists, and that everything revolves around the child. This may be why preschoolers often believe that things happen magically, and it may explain the wonderment of magic acts for children this age.

Piaget also noted that a wide variety of experiences allows children to be exposed to the infinite elements of their world and stimulates cognitive development during these years. Parents play an important role in supervising preschoolers' experiences and providing a number of these for their children. Shopping at the supermarket, taking a walk, going on a trike-hike, or just reading to children are examples of ways parents can take advantage of stimulating their child's mind. Parents also become recognized by their preschooler as a resource of information about the world. This is particularly appealing to a 4-year-old who poses an endless stream of questions to parents. While this constant bombardment of questions may become irritating at times, parents need to understand that they play a significant role in their child's life by acting as an interpreter and helping to give meaning to children's understandings of their world. It is also in this manner of interacting with preschoolers that parents may begin to share their family values, beliefs, and worldviews to children.

*Focus Point.* Cognitive development in early childhood focuses on children acquiring a database of information about their world. Language skills facilitate this process. In addition, parents facilitate appropriate cognitive development by providing a variety of experiences and equipment for preschoolers.

**Providing Appropriate Toys and Play Equipment.** Toys and play equipment help preschool-age children to develop a number of different skills and abilities. Play is how young children begin to gain an understanding of the world in which they live socially, physically, and mentally.

Preschool-age children progress through various types of play as they gain in social and mental skills. Three-year-olds may prefer and enjoy solitary play activities where they have no competition in exploring objects and things. Children this age do not share possessions easily with others and will often do well simply by playing alone or with the same kinds of play equipment being used by another child. Four-year-olds are becoming more creative in using their imaginations and are learning how to share and play with other children. A number of different kinds of toys and play equipment appeal to children this age as they master gross motor skills and begin to explore fine motor skills. Five-year-olds can play fairly well in a small group of other children and participate in more complex types of play and equipment such as building blocks, pretend play, art activities, and science activities (see Focus On 8–2). Many young children today are fairly computer literate in that they have been exposed to games using their family's home computer equipment. Many of these are educational as well as recreational.

---

**Focus On 8–2**

## Examples of Preschool Toys and Play Equipment

### Physical activity/Gross motor skills equipment

- Wagons
- Tricycles
- Scooters

### Outdoor equipment

- Swing/gym sets
- Playhouses
- Wading pools

### Manipulative play equipment (hand-eye coordination skills)

- Blocks
- Connecting pieces
- Simple puzzles
- Bead Stringing
- Sorting boxes
- Lotto matching toys
- Sandbox equipment
- Bath toys

### Educational toys

- Picture and storybooks
- Computer games
- Simple board games
- Sorting/nesting toys

### Creativity equipment

- Art and craft equipment (e.g., crayons, paint, playdough, clay, markers, round-ended scissors, paper)
- Rhythm instruments
- Chalk

### Dramatic play equipment

- Dress-up clothes and accessories
- Dolls
- Play kitchen equipment
- Role-play equipment
- Action figures
- Theme equipment
- Trucks and cars

Parents should always keep safety factors in mind when choosing toys and play equipment for preschoolers. In addition, affordability may be an issue when selecting toys. Some community agencies have toy-lending libraries that are especially helpful to budget-minded families or those wishing children to be exposed to a wide variety of toys without making a large financial layout.

••••••••••••••••••••••••••••••••••••••••••••••••

*Focus Point.*   Preschoolers need appropriate toys and play equipment that encourage the appropriate physical, psychosocial, and mental skills germane to this stage of development.

••••••••••••••••••••••••••••••••••••••••••••••••

## DEALING WITH BEHAVIOR PROBLEMS OF YOUNG CHILDREN

Many young children will experience to varying degrees any one of a score of possible problems as a normal part of their developmental progress. Although these problems are not necessarily detrimental to their progress, they are troublesome, especially from the parents' point of view.

Most of the behavior problems young children experience are temporary in nature. As such, these behaviors present challenges for young children in their interactions with others, especially within their family system. Most problems are stage-specific. In other words, certain problems observed among preschoolers are unique to their stage of the life span, whereas others occur more commonly among older children.

Parents are often disturbed by the appearance and continued presence of certain kinds of behavior problems among preschoolers. An immediate response is to attempt every possible means to eliminate the troublesome behavior from the child's repertoire on the notion that once ingrained, such behaviors become permanent and habitual. Some parents turn to professionals, such as pediatricians, family physicians, child psychologists, and early childhood education specialists, for guidance in dealing with these problems. Others seek information from articles and books that address specific problems of young children such as toilet training, bed-wetting, or eating difficulties. The more problematic cases may require professional consultation and custom-designed treatment approaches. Those that occur more commonly among preschoolers are briefly discussed in the following paragraphs.

## Bedtime and Sleeping Problems

The most common bedtime problems among young children include crying, resisting going to bed, repeatedly getting out of bed, and getting into bed with parents (Spock, 2004).

Resistance to going to sleep is especially troublesome, since a young child who gets too little sleep is irritable the next day (Tobin, 2002). Several issues may account for resistance to sleeping. First, parents may have trained their child improperly from the time of early infancy. Infants normally whimper when they are going to sleep. Parents who interpret this as cries of distress and rush in to pick up the infant train him or her to expect such attention at bedtime. Eventually, a young child may not be able to go to sleep without being held and rocked by a parent or other caregiver. Second, a young child may not be allowed time to relax and wind down prior to bedtime. In some homes, parents are not aware that it is important to promote what experts call *sleep hygiene routines* beginning in early childhood. In some homes, the period shortly before bedtime is used as playtime, especially with a father who may encourage active, rough-and-tumble play that can excite rather than relax the child.

Parents can help preschoolers develop good sleep hygiene habits that promote relaxation and preparation for sleep. Restful activities such as baths, reading stories, or quiet play serve as signals to preschoolers that bedtime is approaching. One of the more successful approaches is to use "planned" ignorance (Spock, 2004), whereby parents provide their full attention to a preschooler during the quieting-down period prior to bedtime but do not reenter the child's bedroom after the child is in bed. This policy of "Once in bed, you stay in bed" is established with the child's full knowledge and expected compliance. Usually, preschoolers will go to sleep within about 20 minutes after being put to bed.

**Bad Dreams and Nightmares.**   Fears are common among young children and can take on additional dimensions in the fantasy world of dreams and nightmares. Although a nightmare may last only a few minutes, a young child can recall it in intricate detail. Bad dreams or night terrors can last much longer, and a child is usually unable to recall specific details that were frightening. These are commonly observed among children who are experiencing extreme stress in their lives, as when parents are divorcing, for example (Spock, 2004).

Talking with young children about their fears is often an appropriate approach for helping them to understand how fears can be manifested in frightening dreams. It may be helpful to hold the preschooler nurturantly and rock him or her for a short time. Comments that inform the child that such frightening experiences are not real but are created by the imagination help in reassuring a preschooler. Parents also might examine the preschooler's bedtime and sleep hygiene routines and eliminate activities such as watching television shows that stimulate harmful fantasizing.

## Problems of Elimination

Preschoolers can experience problems with bodily elimination functions occasionally. Typically, these include regression. Loss of elimination control (e.g., bedwetting) is not considered problemmatic until a child reaches the school-age years.

Regression in toilet training might happen: (1) as a reaction to the birth of a new baby into the family system; (2) as a reaction to extreme fatigue, excitement, or illness; (3) as an expression of anxiety; or (4) as a result of forgetfulness during periods of intense concentration during play activities or television viewing.

Commonsense measures help young children overcome these periods of regression in their elimination training. Reminding a child to use the bathroom may be all that is required to resolve the problem. In addition, protecting a child from situations that are overstimulating or frightening may be an easy solution.

### Parenting Reflection 8–4

How would you advise a parent of a young child that a behavior problem might be serious enough to warrant professional consultation but is not indicative of abnormal developmental progress?

## Eating Problems

Young children are included in eating meals with other family members and sharing the family diet. Most parents understand that young children may eat the same

foods as other family members, but in smaller portions. They are aware that the particular nutritional needs of young children include adequate amounts of protein, calcium, and vitamins from a variety of food sources. Many parents also know the unhealthy aspects of allowing young children to eat a lot of "empty calorie" foods in their diet, such as snacks with high amounts of sugar and/or fat.

Young children may gravitate toward acquiring problems with eating such as (1) resistance to eating, (2) dawdling over food served at meals, and (3) developing peculiar desires for nonfood items (Tobin, 2002).

Because some parents are knowledgeable about what constitutes an adequate diet, they become conscientious about what foods are served to young children. However, overzealousness can cause young children to become resistant to eating. When children feel pressured to conform to parental desires and eating policies, they tend to resist eating certain foods. For example, if parents firmly believe that vegetables must be consumed when served at meals, some young children resent the pressure to comply with parents' expectations and stop eating vegetables altogether. Parents may react by becoming greatly concerned about the child's nutrition and fret about the short- and long-term effects on the child's health and well-being. At times, some parents pressure children to eat "something" at meals, which may exacerbate the problem even more.

*Focus Point.* Many parents observe certain kinds of behavior problems among preschool-age children as a normal part of development. Many of these are related to conflicts between parents and children and with other family members. A variety of sources can help parents work with children in such situations.

## SUPPORTS FOR PARENTS OF PRESCHOOLERS

Community services that provide alternative forms of nonparental caregiving are more numerous and accessible to families with preschool-age children than to families with infants. About two-thirds of 5-year-olds in the United States have parents who are employed and need assistance in providing child care (U.S. Bureau of the Census, 2003). The type of supplemental care provided for children varies according to their age and the type of child care parents desire (Federal Interagency Forum on Child and Family Statistics, 2003). While infants are more typically placed in home-based care by either a relative or nonrelative, preschoolers who are not yet enrolled in a kindergarten program are more likely to be placed in a group center-based program.

The most common type of supplemental care for those who are not enrolled in kindergarten is a nursery school program. This is unlike day-care situations for infants, who most frequently are cared for by a nonrelative. Families today use such services for a number of reasons. Many mothers of young children are employed outside the home, for example, and this type of care is necessary to help the family provide for children's needs. Other families wish young children to have enriching experiences that are not usually available in the home. Others wish their child to experience educational opportunities in preparation for public school. Most programs today provide educational stimulation for young children in addition to custodial care.

Relatives provide about half of the child care for families of preschool-age children (Federal Interagency Forum on Child and Family Statistics, 2003) (see Figure 8–4). Of those who are relatives providing care, fathers and grandparents provide the greatest amount of child care for preschool-age children when mothers are employed outside the home. Among providers of child care who are not relatives, slightly over half of preschool-age children are cared for by day-care centers and by non-relatives in their homes.

There continues to be much discussion about the advantages and disadvantages of nonparental child care for preschoolers. A variety of concerns have been raised about the short- and long-term effects of such care on children's developmental progress. Researchers have examined issues such as attachment, the quality of parent-child interaction, the degree of children's compliance, and other behavioral effects in children who have experienced nonparental care. In reviewing the research on such issues, Belsky (1990) cites several important factors. When nonparental care is sensitive and responsive to children's needs, for example, young children are observed to be compliant, cooperative, and achievement-oriented. In many respects, nonparental child care is like that which is provided by parents: The relationship that nonparental adults promote with children has a greater impact than the methods used in working with children. This parallel implies consequences based on the quality of nonparental care. Negative emotional attitudes of nonparental caregivers and their failure to respond to children's needs are thought to result in problem behavior. Generally speaking, the intellectual gains offered by preschool programs are greatest for low-income children rather than middle-class children, due to the differences in home environments (Erel, Oberman, & Yimiya, 2000).

The features of each type of supplemental child-care program are discussed here briefly.

**FIGURE 8–4.** Percentage of children from birth to age 6, not yet attending kindergarten, by type of child care arrangement in 2001.

*Source:* Federal Interagency Forum on Child and Family Statistics (2003). *America's Children: Key national indicators of well-being: 2003.* Washington, DC: U.S. Government Printing Office.

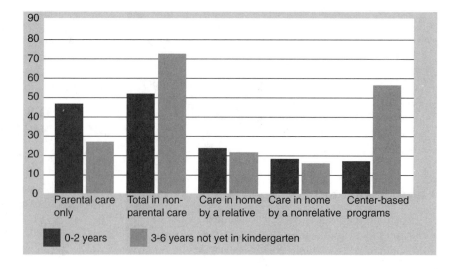

## Child-Care Centers

These programs are used more commonly when young children are not enrolled in kindergarten (Figure 8–5). Child-care or day-care centers typically offer care of children for varying lengths of time. The kinds of programs used most commonly by families with preschoolers involve groups of children. Some programs are nonprofit and are sponsored by companies, community agencies, or educational institutions. Others operate as a business venture for profit.

Day care in the United States has not had a respectable reputation until recently. In the past, most day-care programs provided nothing more than custodial care. Today, this is changing as more staff members are trained in early childhood education. In many respects, there are few differences between preschool and day-care programs today.

• • • • • • • • • • • • • • • • • • • • • • • • • • • • • • • • •

### Parenting Reflection 8–5

Should early childhood educational experiences be required prior to a child's enrollment in first grade? Why or why not?

• • • • • • • • • • • • • • • • • • • • • • • • • • • • • • • • •

**Is Day Care Harmful to Young Children?**   Researchers continue to investigate this question and have learned that it involves complex issues (Belsky, 1990; National Institute for Child Health and Human Development, 1999, 2003). The context in which young children receive care may be associated with different child outcomes. It is important to take both the quality of child care and the characteristics of a family into consideration when examining long-term influences on children's development. For example, young children show the least competence in peer relation skills when they acquire insecure attachments to both parents and nonparental caregivers. This does not occur when they have a secure attachment to their day-care provider but not to their mother. Apparently, incompetent peer relationship skills are counterbalanced by the context of the nonparental caregiver-child relationship as compared with the parent-child relationship.

For the present, it may be safe to say that there appears to be little difference in the effects of parental and nonparental care on young children. There is one caveat to this statement: The quality of nonparental care must be high (National Institute for Child Health and Human Development, 1999, 2003). Child development experts describe factors indicative of a high-quality nonparental care program as: (1) clean, (2) safe, (3) adequately

**FIGURE 8–5.** Many families with preschool-age children rely on nonparental child care. A variety of programs and services are available to assist families with child care.

**Parenting FAQs 8–1**

**My husband and I are in the process of choosing where we'll place our 4-year-old for child care because I'm returning to work. We're not sure what to look for when we evaluate the different alternatives and options. What's important for us to consider in choosing what's best for us as parents and for our child?**

**A:** You will want to consider the advantages and disadvantages of family day care (where individuals provide child care in their home for a small group of children), center day care (where larger groups of children are supervised in a private or agency program), and relative day care (where someone who is a family relative usually comes into your home to provide supervision). If you are fortunate, child care may be available at your place of employment as part of your work benefits.

When investigating the various options, visit each center and look for these factors and ask for answers to these questions:

**Providers**

- What is the ratio of adults to children? (It should he rather small for good supervision.)
- Is there a high turnover in providers?
- Are the program and its employees licensed?
- What educational training do providers have?
- Can you discuss matters with the provider? How does the provider respond to a variety of questions, such as, "What if a child is injured?" "What do you do when children misbehave or hit one another?" "What happens if a child becomes ill while in your care?"
- What is the tone of interactions occurring between providers and children?
- Can you receive references from other parents about the providers and the program?

**Programming and Environment**

- Is the area clean and well managed?
- What kinds of activities are the children doing while you are observing?
- Are there a variety of materials, toys, and equipment?
- Is the outside play area fenced and in safe condition?
- What kind of food is served? Is there a sample menu you can examine?
- Is the program focused just on supervision of children playing or does it emphasize education as well?
- Are adults interacting with children or merely supervising from a distance?
- Does the local or state Department of Social Services have inspection reports that you may review about the programs you are considering?
- What are the policies of the program regarding discipline, parent-teacher contacts, costs and billing, fees for bringing children early or picking them up late, and providing care for children who become ill during the day?
- Is this a place where you would enjoy being yourself?

*Source:* Adapted from National Association for the Education of Young Children. (1991). *Accreditation criteria and procedures of the National Academy of Early Childhood Programs* (rev. ed.). Washington, DC: Author.

staffed, (4) providing opportunities for comfortable play with other children, and (5) showing respect for children's individual needs. Not all day-care programs are rated high in these factors. Until researchers examine the complete array of circumstances that affect children's development, this question will remain unanswered.

## Parenting Reflection 8–6

Would you be more likely to work for an employer who provided day care for children of employees as an employment benefit over an employer who did not? Why or why not?

## Preschool Programs

Preschool programs are more educational than custodial in nature. Many young children have some type of preschool experience rather than day care. Most communities have several types of programs available for families with young children. Preschool programs are typically short-term in duration, with sessions for 2 to 3 hours in the morning or afternoon. Children can attend for varying numbers of days throughout a week. The more common types of programs are outlined briefly in the following paragraphs.

**Specialized Curriculum Programs.** Some preschool programs offer a particular curricular focus, such as one based on Piagetian cognitive theory, the Montessori method, or an open classroom model. The theoretical philosophy of a particular program is emphasized over other factors. The materials used in a Montessori program foster sequential thinking skills. Young children are taught to proceed sequentially to reach goals or solutions to problems. A cognitive-based curriculum may provide opportunities for young children to classify objects as one of many activities.

**Special-Needs Programs.** Some families have a child with atypical needs. These children can benefit from preschool programs designed to meet their needs. Such programs typically involve children with special physical or mental handicaps. There is a trend, however, to incorporate children with special needs into other preschool programs, due to a belief that all children will benefit by gaining greater empathy for one another.

**Compensatory Programs.** Compensatory preschool programs are specially designed to provide a variety of experiences for children from disadvantaged families. Head Start is an example of such a program. Activities promote a preschooler's acquisition of language, social, and cognitive skills to enhance the child's self-concept and a sense of initiative. Nutritional and health needs are addressed as well. Unique to these programs is parental and family involvement, which serves to strengthen family functioning.

Excellent long-range benefits result from participation in these programs (National Institute for Child Health and Human Development, 1999, 2003). Children who have attended Head Start programs score higher on achievement tests and have higher grades in elementary school. These children are also less likely to be placed into special education classes or to repeat a grade. Their preschool experience in compensatory programs makes them similar to other children in this regard.

*Focus Point.*   Many parents seek assistance in providing child care by using services from sources outside their family systems. These are frequently provided by agencies and institutions that provide child care or by services offered by individuals in their homes. Generally, these are stimulating experiences for preschoolers if an educational component exists in the services provided. Parents are concerned about the quality of these services and the effects on children's developmental progress. A variety of types of programs serve different needs and purposes in supplementing parental care for preschoolers.

# SYSTEMIC FAMILY DEVELOPMENT SNAPSHOT

Our slice of developmental time is taken at the midpoint of the early childhood stage of the oldest child in the Curtis family. Mary Curtis is now 4 years old. This slice is taken about a year and a half after the first we made in the previous chapter when Mary was a toddler. We begin examining the snapshot with a brief review of the stressors that can be affecting a family system at this time. The second generation in this family is experiencing an increasing level of stress due to **role strain** affecting the young adult parents. Role strain refers to the pressures experienced when several competing roles must be managed simultaneously. When this occurs, role performance typically declines in at least one or two of the roles while another is given priority attention. The role given priority shifts and changes even during the course of a day. In the case of the second generation Curtis family, the roles that must be juggled by both young adults are work, parenting, and marital relationships. Typically, this challenge is first encountered by families that have at least one preschool-age child. The relationship most often selected to receive the least amount of attention and maintenance is the marriage relationship. Because of this, people notice they are experiencing a decline in marriage satisfaction, which can be confusing and upsetting (Talmadge & Talmadge, 2003). Women typically experience this role strain to a greater degree than men, perhaps because they often bear the greater involvement and responsibilities in parenting and household maintenance (Bianchi et al., 2000). Couples cope with this initial awareness of dissatisfaction in a variety of ways that can be healthy or unhealthy in nature.

## Examples of Stressors Affecting Each Curtis Family Generation: 1½ Years Later

### First Generation (Grandparents)
■ Continuing adjustments to the aging process experienced in middle age
■ Continuing assistance to adult children in completing their individuation process.
■ Continuing adjustment to the death of parents, relatives, and colleagues
■ Continuing preparations for retirement

### Second Generation (Young Adult Parents)
■ More challenges in balancing work and family roles
■ Maintaining a household that meets the needs of preschoolers and toddlers; providing finances for this household
■ Refining parenting behaviors and styles
■ Meeting personal adult needs while performing family and work responsibilities
■ Maintaining a healthy committed relationship while coping with marital dissatisfaction
■ Cultivating relationships with other friends and families

### Third Generation (Preschooler and Toddler)
■ Completing developmental tasks and milestones of infancy and early childhood

At the time of this slice of developmental time, here are the ages of all members of this family system: (1) groom's father (George Curtis) is now almost 58; (2) the groom's mother (Joan Curtis) is now 56; (3) the bride's father (Harry Scott) is now 55; (4) the bride's mother (Susan Scott) is now 53; (5) Butch Curtis is now almost 34, and (6) Lisa Curtis is now 31. The first child, Mary, is 4, and her brother, Joey, is 2 years old.

## The Third Generation (Children)

The children have changed the most rapidly of all family members in the short period of time since the last snapshot. Mary Curtis is very much an inquisitive preschooler who attends a full-time day-care program provided at her mom's place of employment. Mary had some problems initially being away from her mom and dad for the entire day but has since learned to look forward to her "school." Sometimes she gets to spend the day with one set of grandparents or the other. This usually happens if she is sick and can't go to the day-care center. Her parents have some concerns about some problem behaviors she now manifests when she is angry or upset. Apparently, she has learned these from other children or from not being watched closely enough by the center staff. She now bites and pulls others' hair when she wants her own way. Her mom has arranged a meeting with her child's teacher to discuss this undesirable new behavior. Lisa also wants to discuss what she perceives as Mary's poor eating habits and interests with the teacher. This concerns her considerably.

Mary's younger sibling Joey is attempting to master toilet training, which is a strain on his parents. They feel they aren't able to give him the attention he needs to master this task and may have to delay this for awhile. Joey also attends a half-day care program and is picked up for the rest of the day by one of his grandparents. Lisa and Butch feel fortunate to have parents who are willing to help out with this child-care arrangement.

For the most part, the children seem to have normal developmental progress relative to that of their friends' children these ages. Mary and Joey seem to have frequent upper respiratory illnesses, and Joey picked up a case of impetigo not long ago. Apparently, being in day care with many other children exposes them to a greater-than-average number of microbes. When Lisa asked the children's doctor about this, she was told that this is normal and helps children to develop a strong immune system.

## The Second Generation (Adult Parents)

This generation is experiencing the greatest amount of stress. Lisa and Butch now must juggle work and family responsibilities that are even greater than the last time we saw the family development snapshot. Butch now is working longer hours and has taken on more work responsibilities to help meet their financial needs. This means he is often and unpredictably late for evening meals. Lisa, who also works, is taking on more overtime work to help with expenses. They have recently experienced increases in several critical areas of their budget, including mortgage, medical insurance, and food costs. They want to replace some furniture from days before they were married and would like to have a short vacation away from the children in the summer. Both have recently remarked that they miss seeing each other and the increasingly less time they have for social and romantic time together.

Butch and Lisa are finding that they appear to have splintered aspects of their life as a family and as adults. On the one hand, they acknowledge the necessity of working and working hard to get ahead. They also understand that to get the material possessions and to maintain a household requires that both of them work. However, trying to do this while meeting the needs of their preschooler and toddler is becoming a real challenge. This is especially the case when one of the children becomes ill while at day care and needs medical attention. Day-to-day parenting obligations require both

of them to switch quickly between attending to the entirely different needs of a preschooler and a toddler. By the end of the day, they are exhausted and have little energy to give to one another. They occasionally leave the children with a sitter or with a set of grandparents so that they can have some quality alone-time together. But those times are becoming less frequent as the children grow older. Lisa is more unhappy with what seems to be a more stressful marriage arrangement than she ever expected. Sometimes they argue more than usual, and the arguments sometimes don't get resolved, possibly because they are tired. They have discussed the possibility of seeing a marriage therapist and may do so at some point in the future to work on improving their relationship.

The relationship between both parents and Mary is good. They enjoy playing with her and watching her grow and develop. They are discovering the need, however, to begin discussing what rules they will have for regulating Mary's misbehavior and the consequences of these rules. Fortunately, Lisa and Butch come from similar family backgrounds where both sets of parents raised them in similar ways with similar rules. They have managed to agree on most of the rules they have formulated for Mary and how they will enforce them. Lisa has taken a child development course and a parenting course at a local college, so she knows some of the basic ways of working with children these ages. Butch is allowing Lisa to take the lead as he learns how to talk with Mary instead of talking "down" to her as a parent. They both enforce time-outs as a way for helping Mary become composed after an emotional outburst. They both learned a great deal about parenting from their earlier experiences with Mary and find that this helps tremendously in working with Joey. Apparently, Lisa and Butch are evolving an authoritative parenting style that they will use with both children for a number of years to come.

## The First Generation (Grandparents)

The grandparents continue to deal with stressors that were observed in the previous developmental snapshot. All are becoming more involved as grandparents as they actively assist with child care. Lisa's parents appear to be more comfortable with this greater involvement than Butch's parents. These roles seem to be evolving as each set of grandparents works to define what they want their role to mean and become.

Susan Scott (Lisa's mother) has had a good response in treatment of her cancer, and the disease is now in remission. The experience has made her take stock of what is truly important in life; one of her conclusions is that the people in her life are treasures, and she takes nothing for granted about time and how she uses it. The cancer episode took a toll as well on Harry, her husband. He is deeply thankful that they have a new lease on life with time that he also sees as a precious commodity. They have truly fallen in love all over again as they experience a depth in their relationship that was not there before the disease struck. This illness has affected other family members as well. Lisa has seen what her mother has had to endure and wonders if she also will develop this disease later on in her life. It is frightening for her to think about, and she has come to value her mother's presence more deeply. Butch's parents also have reacted in similar ways as they have observed what the Scotts have experienced. Joan Curtis sees Susan Scott as a role model of courage and bravery as she has dealt with the serious aspects of the disease. Now that Joan has had the opportunity to see how someone else copes with the challenges posed by cancer, she feels as if she, too, will know how to face similar challenges in her future.

George Curtis now sees retirement on the horizon. While viewing this as a great escape from the stressfulness of his work, he also now is beginning to have some twinges of uncertainty about his future. He's never felt like this before about anything and is attributing his mixed feelings to simply growing older. Joan, his wife, occasionally becomes frustrated with George as he ruminates about what retirement may hold for him. And she also wonders how he will fare in a new life where his identity will not be rooted in being an employee.

### Parenting Reflection 8–7

If changes occuring in one generation affect the other generations to some degree, how are stressors occurring in the third generation affecting the first generation? Is Butch and Lisa's marriage at risk for divorce because of the increasing levels of role strain being experienced? How does this role strain of the parents affect the children?

## POINTS TO CONSIDER

■ The time of a child's life between age 3 and 6 years constitutes the stage of early childhood. During this time, a child's developmental tasks and milestones focus on continued physical changes, new psychosocial skills and abilities, and changes in mental development that allow for greater use of language skills and information processing. Preschoolers are characterized as (1) being highly curious in learning about their environments, (2) discovering emerging personal competencies and gaining in self-awareness, (3) beginning to learn family and cultural expectations for appropriate behavior, and (4) discovering social roles and family interaction patterns.

■ Parenting behavior changes in response to the particular needs of preschoolers. Parents continue to provide nurturance in the form of greater degrees of assertive rather than supportive care. Structure is introduced for the first time, often through the use and enforcement of rules to control children's behavior and to help them begin to learn self-control. Parents begin to expose their preschooler to socialization practices for the first time. Young children begin to learn family as well as cultural expectations of appropriate behavior. Typically, these may involve certain behaviors that a family values as well as behaviors that are necessary for functioning in social interactions (e.g., prosocial behaviors). Parents also teach preschoolers about their gender- or sex-role as a part of the socialization process. Socialization of children this age also typically includes some instruction about sexuality and about dying and death.

■ Parents assist young children in acquiring a sense of initiative, which involves a positive outlook on themselves and their abilities to function in their environments. A healthy sense of initiative helps a preschooler to learn and develop a wide database of information about the world. Young children become aware of their membership in a particular family and gain a certain sense of self from family interactions. They also begin to learn about their role as a sibling in many families. Parents assist their young child in developing appropriate cognitive skills by providing a variety of different kinds of experiences through play and equipment and in other activities.

■ The general decline in the rate of physical growth during these years prompts parents to hold different expectations regarding how to provide appropriate nutrition for young children.

■ While the health of preschoolers is good generally, parents provide assertive care in protecting them from accidents and injuries, which largely occur within or near the home.

■ Behavior problems considered to be normal can be expected among many young children. These are due largely to problems children experience in learning appropriate behaviors, problems parents experience in teaching children what is expected of them, or daily adjustment difficulties.

■ Supports for caregiving in early childhood include the use of alternative types of nonparental child care that includes child-care centers, home-based care by relatives and others, and other substitute caregivers. Child-care programs vary according to philosophy and objectives in assisting families with young children. A variety of outcomes, mostly positive and beneficial, can be anticipated from a child's participation in such programs.

■ A systemic family development snapshot reveals examples of the stressors that may affect the different generations of a family system in healthy as well as unhealthy ways.

**CHAPTER 9**

# Parenting School-Age Children

### Focus Questions
▪ ▪ ▪ ▪ ▪ ▪ ▪ ▪ ▪ ▪

1. What are the principal developmental landmarks of middle childhood that parents should know?

2. What is the nature of parent/school-age child relations?

3. What are some common behavior problems observed among school-age children? How do these differ from what was observed among young children?

4. What challenges affect the ability of parents of children with special needs to raise their children effectively? What kinds of assistance are available for these families?

5. What kinds of community supports do families with school-age children need?

6. What stressors and coping mechanisms are revealed by a systemic family development snapshot of families with school-age children?

▪ ▪ ▪ ▪ ▪ ▪ ▪ ▪ ▪ ▪

The period of the life span termed **middle childhood** begins when a child enters school at about 6 years of age and extends to puberty, which can be expected to begin near the end of the 12th year. The developmental events and changes that occur during this time lead to increased maturity and responsibilities.

Parents and others now hold greater expectations of school-age children than they did with preschoolers. They take a more serious approach to supervising and providing care for children of these ages. Parents and children now must work with the school system to ensure a successful academic experience and mastery of basic academic skills. Children now begin to detach from their dependency needs for parents as they separate from their families for longer periods during the day. There is an increasing orientation to peer rather than to parents and family members. School-age children are also faced with the central psychosocial task of developing a healthy sense of industry as opposed to a sense of inferiority. Although this focus constitutes the major concern of children at this time, many supplementary developmental tasks arise during this period as well. These tasks complement a child's emerging sense of self, and achieving these skills assists a child in developing healthy self-esteem that extends to many different, but related, aspects of his or her life.

Parents continue to experience the challenges of interacting with a child whose emerging self-concept is sensitive to psychological bruises inflicted by increasingly complex interactions with others outside the family system. Parenting style and behaviors in caring for growing children become modified during this period. The changing nature of school-age children requires major modifications in the style and nature of parental interactions. The methods and techniques of parenting or guiding children that were successful during a child's earlier years no longer are as efficient or effective. Essentially, parents, must become psychological rather than physical helpers of a school-age child. The change in the nature of caregiving often comes about rather subtly as a child progresses through the years of elementary school.

## DEVELOPMENTAL LANDMARKS OF MIDDLE CHILDHOOD

During the years of middle childhood, children are challenged by developmental events and changes that lead to increased maturity and responsibilities. They are faced with the central task of acquiring a sense of industry as opposed to a sense of inferiority, according to Erikson (1950, 1964). Although this challenge becomes the primary psychosocial focus of children in middle childhood, they also expected to achieve many additional developmental tasks during this period. These tasks complement a child's emerging sense of self, and achievement of these skills helps children acquire healthy self-esteem during their school-age years (Figure 9–1).

The events of early childhood lay the foundation for the developmental tasks and milestones addressed during middle childhood. The higher expectations held for children during these years are reflected in a significant change. Both parents and school systems expect children to acquire an attitude or feeling of duty and accomplishment (industry) as a result of the successful experiences they have in middle childhood. This attitude may be described in several ways: (1) a positive attitude toward work assignments and routine jobs leading to the development of a positive work ethic; (2) "tools," or mental and social skills our culture expects children this age to master over time (i.e., academic skills such as reading, writing, and calculation and learning group politics through group and individual activities with peers); and (3) an emerging ability to take responsibility for personal actions and behavior.

The development of a healthy attitude toward work and duty in performing one's responsibilities means that school-age children are expected now to begin an assignment or task and to complete it satisfactorily without having to be continually reminded to do so. The nature of the task may not be as important as the process of beginning the job and performing it to acceptable standards outlined by those in authority. The overall feeling or reaction that should emerge during this life stage is pride in accomplishing a variety of skills and in demonstrating one's dependability in performing assigned tasks. Learning a basic American work ethic is accomplished in this manner as children learn that they are rewarded accordingly if assignments and tasks are performed satisfactorily in the eyes of parents, teachers, and other authority figures.

**FIGURE 9–1.** School-age children are expected to begin mastering basic skills required for effective functioning in society, such as reading, writing, and calculation.

Entrance into the school environment signals changes and adjustments for the child, the parents, and the family system. An additional social group now takes on increasing importance in children's lives. This group is composed of other children, approximately the same age and with similar abilities, who become a child's peers. As a child progresses through this stage and through adolescence, the peer group assumes an increasingly significant role in facilitating a child's socialization process.

Throughout these years, the cultural expectations of parents and other adults in authority concerning how children should behave and what they should be learning combine with the maturation process to include new developmental objectives for school-age children. These objectives, which are largely social and mental, are communicated to children through their parents, the school environment, peer groups, and social programs in which they participate.

## PARENTING SCHOOL-AGE CHILDREN

### How Does Parenting Change?

The nature and style of parenting change when children reach the school-age years. The major source that motivates these changes is the different nature of a school-age child. The developmental tasks and milestones school-age children experience are entirely different from those experienced by preschoolers. They are more complex than those of infancy and early childhood and are more social and psychological than physical in nature. However, physical skills acquired in this period play a significant role in shaping children's self-concepts.

Parenting children in middle childhood, as in earlier stages, focuses on helping them accomplish their essential developmental tasks and milestones. Parents learn that they must respond to, or interact with, a school-age child differently than they did when the child was younger. Methods and parenting styles that were effective with preschoolers lose a high degree of effectiveness with school-age children. Children have new accomplishments and emerging abilities during middle childhood, and they may not permit parents to continue a response style or interaction pattern that was appropriate when they were younger. Parents essentially learn that they must now become psychological rather than physical helpers for their school-age children.

Parents begin training children for increased self-control in early childhood. This previous training results in a greater sharing of social power between parents and children during their school-age years. This sharing results in **coregulation** as a predominant parenting style. Parents of school-age children exercise general supervision while children gain in moment-to-moment self-regulation (Maccoby, 1984), and parents tend to exercise their power more typically when children misbehave in their presence.

Parents increasingly use psychological methods as a means for helping children achieve a higher level of self-control. These methods often consist of reassuring children, helping them to recover from social blunders, and giving positive reinforcement for efforts to learn new skills. School-age children continue to need their parents but in ways that are very different from preschoolers.

The expectations parents hold for school-age children change, which also reflects the shift to coregulation. For example, parents of school-age children expect that they will: (1) gain more refined social skills that reflect an increasing ability to cooperate with adults and other children; (2) show more sophisticated information processing skills that are reflected in school work; and (3) be able to begin assignments and tasks without being directed by an adult and complete them to a level of competence and satisfaction determined by an adult.

••••••••••••••••••••••••••••••••••••••••••••••••••••

*Focus Point.* The nature of interaction changes between parents and children during this stage of the family life career. Essentially, parents adopt different and more specific interaction styles based on the authoritarian, permissive, and authoritative models. Parents also change from being primarily physical to being psychological helpers of school-age children. These changes are initiated in response to the developmental needs and nature of school-age children, which differ from those of preschool-age children.

••••••••••••••••••••••••••••••••••••••••••••••••••••

### Meeting the Needs of School-Age Children

**Promoting Healthy Nutrition.** We are more aware today than in the past that the typical American diet is based on large amounts of saturated animal fat, high calories, and use of refined ingredients such as sugar and flour. This dietary lifestyle is associated with the high levels of coronary heart disease, hypertension and strokes, diabetes, and some cancers found in adulthood. Some evidence points to the beginnings of these conditions in middle childhood when children eat this type of diet (Center for Disease Control and Prevention, 2002). Of major concern is the increasingly high incidence of Type II diabetes among school-age children, obesity, and even under-nutrition. Several factors complicate this situation: (1) many school-age children do not have adequate physical activity and exercise daily; (2) many eat unhealthy lunches; (3) many eat snacks that consist of "empty" calories; and (4) many arrive at school without having eaten breakfast.

Helping school-age children develop healthy eating habits and food preferences can be challenging for parents and other adults. Perhaps the best approach is to have healthy foods in the family's diet and adults modeling good eating habits for children. School-age children may not be immediately attracted to or satisfied by eating the proper kinds of vegetables and fruits without adult supervision and encouragement. By simply preparing meals at home that include these kinds of foods, parents help children learn these habits without being admonished that healthy foods are "good for you." Adults often mistakenly indicate that such foods aren't tasty, but "you have to eat them anyway." Or they attempt to develop good eating habits by bribing children (e.g., "eat your spinach so you can have dessert"). When parents stock up on and serve healthy foods, they help children avoid empty calories. Many parents resist pressure from children to purchase soda pop, potato chips, and sugary breakfast cereals.

**Providing Structure and Nurturance.**    Parents and other adults who work with school-age children recognize the value of children's experiences in earlier stages, which assist them in learning about structure. During middle childhood, adult caregivers are interested in helping children acquire even more refined abilities, as children are expected to become more skilled at internalizing their own structure. An appreciation for rules is a basic part of experiences that help school-age children internalize or become more self-directed.

A focus on **nurturance** helps parents guard against the negative aspects of an exclusive emphasis on rules in experiences that teach structure. The nurturance of school-age children requires that parents and other caregivers be sensitive to children's developmental needs and emerging abilities at this time (Clarke & Dawson, 1998). Adapting parenting styles is a major challenge for many parents; they must shift to more responsive methods than those established in a child's preschool years. This shift moves away from focusing attention, energy, and resources on providing physical care to providing psychological care that is supportive of school-age children. Table 9–1 outlines a guide to parental caregiving behaviors that may either facilitate or hinder effective experiences in providing structure and nurturance to school-age children.

Parenting school-age children focuses on reinforcing their efforts to attain appropriate developmental tasks. Parents often accomplish that goal when they shift their styles and interactions to psychological assistance and guidance of children. For example, psychological controls such as reasoning are more effective with 9-year-olds than with 3-year-olds. Taking privileges away is another method that some parents find useful, as compared with a less-useful method, such as spanking.

Psychological guidance primarily consists of reassuring children, helping them to bounce back from social blunders with friends, and providing positive reinforcement for their efforts in acquiring new skills. The competitive nature of school-age children and the high degree to which they expect immediate results and success in almost every endeavor compels their need for secure and stable adults. These adults appear, from the child's perspective, to weather every imaginable adversity or difficulty.

## Parenting Reflection 9–1

What are some examples of family rules that promote structure for school-age children? What are both positive and negative consequences of such rules?

Responding to a child's changing developmental demands in middle childhood means learning to lessen the more stringent controls imposed during early childhood. It means allowing the child to gain freedom to practice making decisions within safe limitations. In other words, parents learn that children desire and require increasing degrees of freedom during this time in their lives. The

**TABLE 9–1.** Behaviors of Parents of School-Age Children

| Behaviors Providing Structure and Nurturance | Behaviors Not Providing Structure and Nurturance |
|---|---|
| • Showing approval for child's efforts to achieve developmental tasks | • Enforcing rules inconsistently |
| • Showing approval for child's establishment of personal learning style | • Insisting on perfection from child in every respect |
| • Providing generous amounts of positive reinforcement for acquiring learning skills | • Expecting child to learn everything without proper instruction or assistance |
| • Acting as a reliable resource for child's questions about others, the world, and sexual matters | • Failing to provide child with adequate amounts of unstructured time to explore personal interests and learn the relevance of rules |
| • Helping child consider choices and options in his or her behavior; promoting cause-and-effect reasoning | • Failing to allow child to experience periods of moodiness |
| • Establishing and enforcing negotiable as well as nonnegotiable rules | • Maintaining rules that are rigid and inflexible or failing to provide and enforce rules that govern behavior |
| • Reminding child that he or she is loved and cared for even when child disagrees with parent | • Maintaining many nonnegotiable rules; failing to examine personal values; expecting child to provide for his or her own supervision |
| • Taking responsibility for personal actions and encouraging child to do the same | • Discounting child |
| • Encouraging child to develop personal interests by providing instructional experiences from trained individuals who act as models and examples | |

*Source:* Adapted from Clarke, J. I., & Dawson, C. (1989). *Growing up again: Parenting ourselves, parenting our children.* Minneapolis: Hazelden.

psychosocial focus of school-age children is facilitated when parents and other adults reinforce the greater desire for independence and provide opportunities for learning a sense of industry.

The increased involvement of children with peers, school activities, and activities outside the family system means more frequent periods of absence from the home. Parents may find it difficult to keep a stable and predictable schedule of routines in the home. Keeping children's schedules from becoming chaotic and allowing periods of unstructured personal time can be challenging for many parents.

Letting go of school-age children also means that parents need to accept the reality that they increasingly value peers and best friends as significant others in their lives. Letting go of children involves allowing them to take overnight trips to a friend's home and, in the later years of middle childhood, to go to overnight slumber parties or on camping trips with youth groups. Many children experience their first extended absence from

their family system during summer camp sessions and visits with relatives.

**Facilitating a Sense of Industry.** A sense of **industry** can be described in several ways. Taken literally, it is the development of a positive attitude toward work and a mastery of the *tools*, or academic and social skills that are appropriately learned at this time of the life span. The development of a healthy attitude toward work means that a school-age child is expected to apply himself or herself to an assigned task under the direction of someone in authority and to complete it satisfactorily. The task may vary, but regardless of its nature, the feeling that should emerge is one of pride in being able to accomplish one's duties. School-age children should also acquire the perspective that all people are expected to contribute to their communities by performing certain jobs adequately. This stage of psychosocial development differs from establishing a sense of initiative because new expectations are determined for a child's develop-

**FIGURE 9–2.** Adults expect school-age children to begin acquiring more responsible behaviors and to contribute to family functioning. Household chores often are a means of teaching a work ethic to children.

mental progress. Related to these expectations is the knowledge that children must expect their behavior and performance to be evaluated more objectively by those in authority. Essentially, school-age children are expected to acquire the basic notions of a work ethic that will guide their behavior as adult workers in jobs and occupations. In the initiative stage, curiosity about the world and what children can discover about themselves are the primary objectives of psychosocial development. In middle childhood, this curiosity is transformed into mastering the environment by achieving goals that "everyone" knows how to achieve (see Figure 9–2).

### Parenting Reflection 9–2

When parents want to promote a sense of industry for school-age children, is it more helpful to purchase kits that children can use for some specific arts-and-crafts activity or to supply children with a variety of materials and let them decide what they might wish to do with them?

*Focus Point.* A healthy sense of industry involves a positive attitude about work, duty, and responsibility. It also involves mastery of basic social and mental skills considered essential for effective functioning in society. School-age children are influenced by family and school systems but more by peer groups in acquiring this attitude.

**Promoting Peer Relations.** Our culture is a composite of different subcultures, such as familiar racial, ethnic, and age groupings. Individuals have experiences with a number of subcultures throughout their life span. During the middle years of childhood children experience one of the first and most important subcultures: the childhood **peer group** (see Figure 9–3).

Parents and teachers are aware that some children will not fit easily or readily into peer groups and can sometimes be rejected by other children. When this occurs, adults often seek an explanation about why other children view the rejected child in negative terms (Rys & Bear, 1997). For example, children who are seen as unpopular may be viewed as hostile and overly aggressive, immature, impulsive, different in appearances, or insensitive to others (Smith et al., 2002). Adults should be concerned when children have experiences with rejection since these may contribute significantly to a negative self-image, conflicts with other children, and impaired social development at later stages in the life span. Adults can arrange occasions for supervised play with other children so that children can learn social skills that lead to more positive peer experiences.

**FIGURE 9–3.** Peer groups become an important social force that serves a number of functions among school-age children.

● ● ● ● ● ● ● ● ● ● ● ● ● ● ● ● ● ● ● ● ● ● ● ● ●

### Parenting Reflection 9–3

What are some things you could do as a parent or teacher to "bully-proof" a child who is being picked on constantly by another child? What would you do to help the child who is the bully?

● ● ● ● ● ● ● ● ● ● ● ● ● ● ● ● ● ● ● ● ● ● ● ● ●

**Promoting Cognitive Skills.** School-age children increasingly use mental skills as part of their daily life, much of which involves school activities. Parents and other adults play an important role in facilitating a school-age child's cognitive development in several ways. For example, children at this time are making use of a large database of information they acquired earlier in the preschool years. They are attempting to make greater sense of their world. Adults hold more challenging expectations of them than of preschoolers. As a result, it is often easy to expect things of school-age children that are beyond their capabilities at this time. By understanding that school-age children still are not able to think logi-

cally all the time and are learning the basics of such thinking, parents can customize the ways they provide structure and nurturance at an appropriate developmental level. By understanding that school-age children see the world differently than adults, parents will not expect understanding beyond their child's ability.

**Helping Children Adjust to School.** Entrance into the school system is a significant event that influences a number of social and cognitive changes in middle childhood. For example, in this setting a school-age child is introduced to peers, often for the first time. The child is also exposed to other adults in authority, such as teachers and youth group leaders, who assist in the child's growth process. New expectations for behavior change yearly as children progress through the school system (Figure 9–4).

Although the education of children was once the responsibility of a family system, it is now institutionalized in other agencies in the United States. The school system has gained in significance as our culture has become more technologically oriented. Children in middle childhood are expected to become proficient in basic skills, such as reading, writing, and calculation. They are also expected to learn a lot of facts and information about the world. Parents expect that children will succeed in their learning experiences if they are assigned to properly trained teachers. Teachers are also expected to conduct effective educational programs that equip children with basic skills.

Some parents assume that once children become a part of their school environment, they need to relinquish more responsibility to teachers to help children achieve academic success. However, many teachers feel that they cannot be expected to assume the degree of responsibility that supports children's academic success. Perhaps the best arrangement in this regard is teaming the efforts of both parents and teachers to help children to be academically successful (Bickart & Jablon, 2004). When researchers study how to motivate parental involvement in children's homework, they have found that parents are more involved when they are prompted both by children and the school to provide assistance with assignments. However, parental involvement had little effect in improving children's academic performance. The researchers point out, though, that other positive outcomes could result from greater parental involvement in children's homework, such as being more aware of what was going on with their children at school.

**FIGURE 9–4.** The school environment acts as an important source of socialization for school-age children.

● ● ● ● ● ● ● ● ● ● ● ● ● ● ● ● ● ● ● ● ● ● ● ● ● ● ● ● ● ●

### Parenting Reflection 9–4

Beyond the basics, what are some topics that elementary schools should and should not teach children?

● ● ● ● ● ● ● ● ● ● ● ● ● ● ● ● ● ● ● ● ● ● ● ● ● ● ● ●

● ● ● ● ● ● ● ● ● ● ● ● ● ● ● ● ● ● ● ● ● ● ● ● ● ● ● ● ●

*Focus Point.*   School-age children are challenged by a variety of developmental tasks that focus on complex social, mental, and physical skills that lead to increased maturity. Social development in middle childhood relates to adjusting to the school environment, establishing relations with peers, and experiencing refinements in self-concept. New mental skills reflect refinements in cognition, allowing a child to learn reading, writing, and calculation. Parents and teachers are also more concerned today about school-age children's exposure to violence and how this can be prevented and controlled.

● ● ● ● ● ● ● ● ● ● ● ● ● ● ● ● ● ● ● ● ● ● ● ● ● ● ● ● ● ●

**Teaching About Sexuality.**   Children's education about sexuality continues to take place during middle childhood. Schools now play an important role in working with parents to help children grow up with healthy attitudes about sex and sexual matters. Many school systems in the United States provide units on sex education, beginning in kindergarten and continuing throughout the elementary grades. Often these units are

presented in conjunction with input provided by parents who serve on school district advisory committees. Most parents apparently wish to have some assistance in helping children learn about sexuality and welcome the professional abilities of trained teachers to introduce the topic to school-age children.

School-age children continue to ask occasional questions about their bodies and sexual matters that deserve honest answers from parents. In this situation, parents may act as interpreters and narrators of family values for their children. Some parents fear that school systems replace them in this role by providing children with formal educational experiences about sexuality. However, most teachers prefer that parents take an even more active role in teaching children about such matters (McElderry & Omar, 2003).

Parents have an important responsibility in preparing older school-age children for the approaching physical and psychological changes related to puberty. Beginning when children are about age 9, most parents can initiate discussions about this approaching developmental event. Opportunities for discussion are important because preteens are more likely to listen to parents' views on topics relating to sexuality than are children who have already entered adolescence. For example, it is important that girls be prepared for menstruation and that boys understand about nocturnal emissions. Both boys and girls are also interested in their anatomy and desire more detailed information about the functioning of the reproductive system than do preschool-age children. Many excellent resources are available to assist parents in becoming more knowledgeable about sexual issues and preparing children for puberty.

**Computers and the Internet.** It's an inescapable reality that children today need to become computer literate to prepare for their future. The Information Age that was predicted in the 1970s has definitely arrived. The use of computers has become commonplace in homes, schools, and workplaces and the vastness of the Internet has grown beyond all expectations. It is likely that computers will have an even larger place in our society in the future.

The use of the Internet and home computers can augment what children are learning in school and how the school is using these as instructional tools. School-age children should be able to use computer software for writing reports, researching topics, and playing educational games. Some children may even desire to learn how to write software and develop the skills necessary for developing Web sites.

Most adults are aware now that children need supervision when using computers to cruise the Internet. Parents need to learn about software filters that protect children from sites containing pornography and chat rooms that can draw people who want to exploit children. Forbidding access to computers and the Internet because of inherent risks is not in the best interests of children. Rather, parents need to understand that children should learn to negotiate this arena safely. To be computer illiterate can place children at a distinct disadvantage in their present and future.

Parents should develop rules and regulations that outline how much time a child is allowed to use the computer and the Internet and that specify behavior while using the Internet. For example, children should be taught never to give out personal information to anyone or any Web site. They should know how to deal with accidental viewing of unacceptable material and how to observe rules of "Netiquette" and controlled supervised use of instant messaging services. If rules are not observed, parents may need to investigate installing hardware and software that limit time use by children. A contract is available for parents to use with children in regulating Internet and computer use. Some children can be determined to work around rules, regulations, and limitations that parents have placed to prevent them

from being exposed to the Internet's more unsavory elements. In this event, parents might wish to consult Web sites for helpful assistance in fine-tuning methods to protect children (e.g., see http://www.komando.com)

## NORMAL BEHAVIOR PROBLEMS OF MIDDLE CHILDHOOD

The types of behavior problems observed in school-age children reflect the difficulties they experience in adjusting to the challenges of developmental tasks; therefore, these problems are considered to be age specific. Some, but not all, involve conflicts between parents and children regarding expectations the adults hold about appropriate standards of behavior. Others may be negative, attention-getting behaviors. Some problems, such as learning disorders, are diverse in their origins and can involve inherent developmental difficulties. Several types of commonly observed behavior problems are discussed here briefly. They include noncompliance, antisocial behaviors, and learning disorders.

### Noncompliance

One of the most common complaints of parents is that school-age children fail to comply and cooperate with parent requests and disobey rules established by the family system. This issue, which begins to appear when children are preschool age, can escalate during middle childhood into a full-blown power struggle between adults and children.

Children at this age tend to test the limits of adults' patience, particularly if they are asked to do something they do not want to do. Standard replies to parental requests include, "In a minute, Mom," or "Just let me finish what I'm doing, OK, Dad?" Parents are adapting their expectations for children; instead of asking a child simply to get involved in an activity or chore, they insist that tasks be completed satisfactorily. Some adults may believe that a child needs only one prompting to perform the task before the consequences of the family task completion rule are enforced. But initially, most parents are patient, understanding that children must adjust as they learn the mechanics and limits of family expectations.

There comes a time, however, when parents know that their school-age child should be complying with rules and policies without great resistance or hesitation. Some of the most frequently prescribed methods of prompting children's compliance involve the use of behavior modification techniques. One technique teaches parents how to phrase their requests in ways that communicate exactly what is expected of children in keeping with family rules and policies. Essentially, parents are taught how to give clear, concise directions so that school-age children can understand parental expectations. Parents are told to give a child at least five seconds to comply and to provide positive consequences or rewards for their appropriate, cooperative behavior.

Another method stresses the use of positive social reinforcement by using what is called *time-out,* or separating a child from an activity to be alone for a specified period of time. Although rewards, such as hugging, tend to promote the appearance of compliant behavior, the use of time-out becomes associated in the child's mind with being noncompliant.

## Antisocial Behaviors

Antisocial behaviors promote ill will between others, interfere with effective communications and interactions, constitute negative ways of getting attention, and serve as a means of expressing anger and hostility or of coping with frustration and anxiety (Paul, 2000). Although some of these behaviors begin appearing in the latter part of early childhood, a number are observed more typically during middle childhood. They reflect problems in adjusting to the demands of developmental tasks during these years and can act as a challenge to effective, healthy functioning. Several are observed more commonly than others during middle childhood, and they cause particular concern among adult caregivers. These behaviors include lying and stealing.

**Lying.**  Lying refers to the deliberate falsification of information with the specific intent to deceive the listener (American Psychiatric Association, 2000). Although young children are often unable to separate fantasy from reality, the ability to understand what is true and what is not follows a child's level of moral and cognitive development. Typically, most children come to understand the importance of truthfulness in their interactions with others at about age 6 or 7.

Parents can assist children with problem lying in several ways. First, it is helpful for a parent to evaluate his or her own behavior and actions so that children do not learn from the model the parent presents. For example, parental honesty helps children learn how to be trusting and how to generate others' trust in their own integrity. Second, when parents observe children lying, they should tell the children that lying is unacceptable behavior and will jeopardize their effective interactions with others. School-age children can be helped to understand how the consequences of such behavior relate to the nature and degree of their personal integrity. In such instances, reading the Aesop's children fable "The Boy Who Cried Wolf" may be an effective instructional method for helping them understand the importance of truthfulness. Third, quizzing children about their misbehavior often promotes defensive lying. Parents can avoid this approach by informing a child that they are aware of his or her misbehavior. Discussions can proceed from this point in a straightforward manner to resolve the problem behavior. Fourth, parents should try to determine the causes that underlie a child's lying behavior (Spock, 2004).

**Stealing.**  Stealing occurs more commonly among school-age children than most people imagine. Although many parents feel that stealing is an innocuous behavior in early childhood, it becomes a matter of concern among parents of school-age children and adolescents.

Children steal for a variety of reasons: (1) they may lack training in a sense of personal property rights; (2) they may be trying to bribe friends, perhaps to avoid being teased or to gain their approval; (3) stealing may occur as a means of coping with feelings of inferiority or of being different from others in some manner; (4) they may steal simply because they cannot resist the temptation to have something they want very much; and (5) they may steal to express revenge against parents or as a means of gaining their attention.

The problem of stealing is handled first by informing children of the unacceptability of this behavior. Parents and other adults should deal fairly and honestly with instances of stealing. They may review their own behavior and reveal instances in which they have modeled dishonesty to children. Then parents can consciously work to avoid having their own actions contribute to the problem behavior of their child. Scrupulous attention to the details of property rights is important as well; parents should explain the difference between a child's property and that of others. It may be helpful to give children allowances if they are not receiving them. Allowances can help them learn the work ethic of their family system, which may be associated with financial rewards. Removing temptation from children or reducing it by keeping money put away or protected may also be helpful.

## Learning Disorders

Learning disorders that affect poor school achievement are frequently observed in association with other types of behavior problems in middle childhood (American Psychiatric Association, 2000). Children with behavior problems also tend to demonstrate other types of maladaptive patterns during this period.

Five basic conditions are classified as learning disorders (American Psychiatric Association, 2000); several are discussed here. They interfere with an ability to process information correctly to facilitate learning and formal instruction. Researchers generally understand that learning disorders involve a complex variety of different but related conditions and factors that hamper the ability of a child to learn and progress in school. The complexity of the situation becomes compounded by the effects observed in other types of troublesome behaviors that relate to a child's inability to learn and perform adequately in the school environment. (1) *Ability deficits* may account for many of the problems school-age children experience with school performance. (2) Many professionals attribute learning problems to children's *emotional disorders* such as anxiety, depression, and unhealthy self-esteem. (3) *Biological factors* can account for learning problems that stem from prenatal or postnatal exposure to harmful substances, such as maternal intake of alcohol or cocaine, deprivation of oxygen, accidents involving the central nervous system, infections, and inadequate protein intake. (4) *Ecological factors* contribute to learning disorders when, for example, labeling a child as troublesome or as a slow learner can negatively influence his or her behavior and learning skills. (5) Children may lack *adequate knowledge* of how to learn, which may also contribute to such problems.

**Attention Deficit Disorder (ADD).  Attention Deficit Disorder (ADD)** has recently received a significant amount of study by behavioral and medical researchers. This condition is the most commonly diagnosed behavior disorder in childhood and is believed to have strong neurobiological and genetic bases (Satyen, 2003). Some studies identify biological factors that influence its oc-

currence, such as the use of alcohol during pregnancy, while others identify tendencies that are due in part to genetic disturbances transmitted in some families.

Children who are diagnosed with this learning disorder have been found to be at high risk of failure in their educational experiences (American Psychiatric Association, 2000). They are unable to concentrate for long periods of time, are often hyperactive, and have difficulty processing information. The disruptive effects of these children within classrooms also interfere with the ability of other children to participate in learning experiences. Children with this disorder are found to have average or higher-than-average intelligence.

Families, especially the parents of children with ADD, are challenged with dealing with the extreme exasperation and frustrations of the condition and how it affects everyone. Children with ADD can be in constant motion from the time they awake in the morning until the time they finally go to sleep at night. They have difficulty following directions, appear to constantly forget rules and parental admonitions, and generally are a handful for parents and teachers. It is not unusual for many parents to blame themselves for how their children with ADD behave, because the children essentially appear to be out of control. The fact is that children with ADD cannot control their actions, but parents are not responsible for their children's behavior. Most adults respond to the diagnosis of ADD with relief that the problem finally has a label and that they are not at fault.

Although the ramifications of this disorder are discouraging for children and parents, the condition is responsive to a variety of treatments (Paul, 2000). For example, drugs such as Ritalin may produce a calming effect on a child's behavior. Behavior modification techniques may be used in training children to increase their attention when performing tasks. Family therapy may be helpful in assisting a family system to deal with the crises associated with a child whose behavior has an extremely disruptive effect on family functioning. When parents and children consult with therapists who are trained in working with children with this disorder and their families, significant progress can often be expected in helping everyone involved cope with the great stress associated with ADD (Sayten, 2003). Parents can also obtain information and support from the National Resource Center on ADHD (http://www.chadd.org/). Many other Web sites also provide information.

**Specific Reading Disability.** Reading difficulties can be associated with a number of causes, but **dyslexia** is a primary culprit in causing many reading problems. This condition ranges from mild to severe in its effects on reading and information processing. It is most frequently associated with perceptual problems in dealing with word comprehension and in processing information into forms the brain recognizes. Specifically, dyslexia is associated with the following difficulties or combinations of these problems: (1) an inability to perceive the significance of the relation of one written symbol to another, (2) failure to correlate written and spoken words and to synthesize them into meaningful words, and (3) difficulties in perceiving the meaning of words or groups of words.

Some children tend to reverse the order of letters in certain words; they perceive *was* as *saw* and *dog* as *god*. Other children confuse a letter with its mirror image: *p* as *d* or *b* as *d*. Typically, children who have reading problems are thought to have average or higher-than-average intelligence before entering school. They fail to learn to read during their first 2 years of school, and the problem may become compounded but undetected for the next several years of elementary school. This is because children learn to memorize and develop other schemes that mask their inability to read adequately. Children who experience dyslexia or another reading disability recognize that their inability to read adequately places them at a disadvantage in comparison with peers who do not have this problem (Kim, 2004). As a result, they experience feelings of deep shame and guilt about something over which they have little control. Their self-concept and self-esteem are harmed by such feelings. Parents and teachers may not recognize the problem until a child is well into the intermediate levels of elementary education.

In the primary grades of elementary school, children with reading problems usually make their best grades in mathematics. In the intermediate elementary and later grades of junior high school, however, they begin having trouble calculating figures (Kim, 2004).

Intervention strategies are frequently tailored to the specific needs of a child with a learning disorder. Once a trained specialist has diagnosed the problem, treatment can begin in the form of specialized educational experiences or placement into a special educational environment. Current awareness of learning problems is particularly acute among most well-trained educators. Children who have such problems are usually identified and assisted early so that more serious problems may be prevented from interfering with later experiences in school (Hallahan & Kauffman, 2004).

Parents may find a number of resources useful in learning about these disorders and appropriate treatment. Local libraries and bookstores usually hold a variety of text titles on this topic. In addition, Web sites are also useful in beginning the search for information (e.g., KidSource Online http://www.kidsource.com/kidsource/pages/dis.web.html). Ultimately, however, children will need professional screening to determine the type, nature, and extent of a learning problem before any particular method of treatment can be considered. Medical and educational specialists can provide referrals to appropriate professionals for treatment.

*Focus Point.* Many problems of school-age children's behavior relate to difficulties in achieving the developmental tasks of this period. Others relate more specifically to interaction difficulties with parents and peers. Some are more specific to learning disorders that are discovered through experiences in the classroom. A variety of methods may be helpful in dealing with these problems.

## PARENTING CHILDREN WITH SPECIAL NEEDS

Our society has only recently begun to understand and recognize that some children, often because of circumstances beyond their control, have unique needs. These needs relate to a group of disabilities that involve problems in seeing, hearing, walking, talking, climbing, or lifting or in providing self-care tasks known as **activities of daily living (ADLs)** (Hildebrand et al., 2000). These needs create unusual demands on family systems and parents. In some situations, children have unique developmental difficulties and problems that label them as **exceptional.** In this regard, the term refers to individuals who are different in some manner from the large majority of others their age. Other children have special needs because of chronic, life-threatening illnesses, such as AIDS, diabetes, or cancer.

In the past, little support was available in most communities for assisting these individuals and their families in meeting their special needs. For some children, negative community attitudes and labels served as forms of discrimination that prevented access to the life experiences and community services available to those with normal developmental abilities. In many respects, early efforts to provide services for individuals and families with special needs could be called *segregated services*, since these were provided under separate support when children were isolated from others (Hildebrand et al., 2000). Negative social stigma is still evident in many cases, particularly for those individuals with chronic illnesses, such as AIDS.

Community-based programs for assisting these individuals and their families have been developed only recently. Generally, the field of special education, which serves those individuals who need such services in their hometowns, has emerged only within the last 30 years. Certainly, a variety of legislative acts at state and federal levels have assisted in bringing about the widespread availability of such services at the community level.

## Characteristics of Children with Special Needs

The definition of exceptional children, or those with special needs, was formerly restricted to those with emotional, developmental, or mental difficulties that placed them at a disadvantage in comparison with others or that incapacitated them in their ability to function within the larger society. More recently, however, the meaning of exceptionality has broadened to include those groups of individuals with learning disabilities and other handicaps, as well as those with chronic and terminal illness (Rigazio-DiGilio & Cramer-Benjamin, 2000). Children with special needs in the student population of the United States are generally about 13 percent. In general, males outnumber females who have special needs. For example, Attention Deficit Hyperactivity Disorder (ADHD), formerly included as a learning disability, stands on its own as a separate and distinct condition requiring special needs attention. The classification scheme is so broad that intellectually gifted children also have been termed exceptional because these individuals and their needs are often misunderstood by others in their community. The process of including a child in any of these categories often involves extensive, comprehensive evaluations by a variety of medical, psychological, and educational professionals.

## Family Reactions

Unless there has been some indication prior to birth that a child is likely to have a developmental disorder, parents and other family members usually have little preparation for accommodating a child with special needs. Parents experience a limitless variety of reactions to having a child who has special needs. These reactions may vary according to the nature of the exceptionality, the degree of impairment, the socioeconomic status of the family system, the availability of professional assistance, the financial resources available to supply the assistance, and the presence of unimpaired children in the family (Leyden, 2002). Parents can be expected to experience a grief and mourning process in reaction to the confirmation of a child's disability. The discovery that a child has special needs essentially represents a loss for most parents, in particular the loss of a future of normal developmental progress for the affected child (Osborn, 2004).

In many respects, the news serves as a crisis or as a stressor event for a family system, and additional reactions follow for most families. The family as a system must adjust to this newly recognized status of the affected child and begin to search for the numerous ways and means to meet the child's particular needs and those of family members. This process can take months, even years, as the family strives to accept and reconcile their unique situation in comparison with other families. Ways must be found to include the child into the family's routines and patterns. Parents, especially, must learn ways to strengthen their committed relationship and find ways to meet the needs of other children in the family. Those family systems that use the crisis and stresses of this situation to their advantage are likely to become stronger by developing healthy coping strategies that may also be applied in other future family crises. On the other hand, those families that acquire unhealthy coping strategies experience even higher levels of stressfulness and greater levels of family disorganization. Ultimately, some will dissolve as the result of the chronic strains experienced under such circumstances.

Generally, many parents experience a process in adjusting to having a child with special needs by which they attain acceptance of the situation although others may experience ambivalence and even rejection of the child. For many, it is difficult to overcome the tendency to personalize this unfortunate circumstance. In some respects, mothers may react differently from fathers when it becomes known that their child is exceptionally different from others.

Parental attitudes about an exceptional child and the circumstances involved in having this child as a family member influence the nature and quality of caregiving (Ripley, 2003). Mothers tend to become the family member assuming the greatest amount of caretaking and nurturing for a child with special needs. However, because fathers and other male family members are expected to be more actively involved in child care today, it is not unusual to see levels of family stress diminish and come more under control when this occurs.

The siblings of a child with special needs are also affected by the child's presence (Meyer, 2003). It is possible to observe the interrelatedness concept found in family systems theory. Having a sibling with special needs brings some benefits to other children such as learning empathic skills, gaining in tolerance and compassion for those who are seriously different from others, and developing a greater appreciation of personal health status. On the other hand, siblings often report negative effects such as feelings of jealousy because of lack of parental attention, resenting the affected sibling's presence in the family, or shamefulness and guilt about the affected sibling. Parents should be mindful of the possibilities of these negative reactions. In addition, girls often complain that brothers aren't expected to assume surrogate parent or caregiver roles to a similar extent. By equalizing these responsibilities between male and female siblings, the psychological risks—to girls, especially—may be minimized.

Cultural backgrounds of families also influence their reactions to an exceptional child. Cultural beliefs color differences in what it means to have a child with special needs as a family member. For example, in an Anglo-European family, a child's disabilities are described and understood in medical and scientific terms; in Native American Indian families, the child's disability is placed on spiritual intrusion or the breaking of cultural taboos. Other cultures may attribute the situation to bad luck, an evil influence on a family, or punishment for ancestral sins (Rigazio-DiGilio & Cramer-Benjamin, 2000).

Chronic stress is one of the most frequently observed family reactions to having a child with special needs (Krauss, 2000). Family members can learn healthy coping strategies such as attending support groups, journaling, participating in individual and family therapy, tapping into spiritual resources, and sharing caretaking responsi-

bilities, for example. Networking with other families experiencing similar circumstances is also a helpful source of coping with stress. Unhealthy coping also may manifest in some families when the child with exceptional needs is scapegoated, abused, and emotionally mistreated.

## Supports for Families with Exceptional Children

Families with a child with special needs tend to be smaller than average in size and to have lower incomes than the general population (U. S. Bureau of the Census, 2003). Because of their unique circumstances, these families typically make use of more community services and resources in gaining assistance for their child. Several sources provide infrastructural support for these families.

**Federal Legislation.**   Federal legislation has helped to address the needs of exceptional children and their families. Public Law 94–142, first enacted in 1975, is based on two assumptions: (1) that all children with special needs have a rightful and appropriate place in the public school system, and (2) that all parents have an important role in the education of their children with special needs. Essentially, the law gives parents the right to monitor and judge the appropriateness of the educational experiences their children with special needs receive. The law provides for appointing a surrogate parent for children who are without parents and for funding for special education programs. The law requires that each child with special needs enrolled in public school systems be provided with an individualized educational program (IEP) developed by an education specialist working in conjunction with the child's parent(s). An IEP must be written, tailored to meet the child's specific needs, and signed by the child's parent(s). It must include a statement of present level of educational performance at the time of initial implementation, a list of goals and objectives, and specific educational services and support to be provided. It must also include plans for the child's participation in the classroom, length of institutionalization (if applicable), and the way goals and objectives will be evaluated at the completion of the plan. Although IEPs are controversial, their value may be shown by the attention now given to meeting the needs of children and their parents along with the more intense involvement of parents in children's educational experiences.

Public Law 99–457, enacted in 1986, has also influenced the assistance provided to families with exceptional children. It requires states to establish comprehensive multidisciplinary approaches to provide early intervention to infants and toddlers with special needs. It extends the ages of children being served from birth through age 25, emphasizing a focus for services during the prekindergarten years. This law requires that individualized family service plans (IFSP) be provided to children with special needs. An IFSP is written for each child between birth and age 3 by a multidisciplinary group of professionals and the parents. It includes the following: (1) an assessment of the child's present level of functioning and developmental status; (2) a statement of the family's strengths and needs in facilitating the child's developmental progress; (3) a list of goals and objectives for the child's progress; (4) the means by which the child is expected to achieve these goals and objectives or the experiences that will promote their accomplishment; (5) the means by which the child will be transitioned from early intervention experiences into a preschool program; (6) the time frame during which these will be provided; and (7) the name of the child's case manager.

In 1991, another federal law, Public Law 102–52, provided states with an additional 2 years to develop systems to serve eligible children with special needs. Public Law 102–119, also enacted in 1991, reaffirmed the early intervention approach to the 1975 Education of the Handicapped Act and strengthened the involvement of families in the educational process of children with special needs.

Taken together, all of these laws comprise the Individuals with Disabilities Education Act (IDEA) (Turnbull & Cilley, 1999). In complying with this legislation, states have established an Interagency Coordinating Council that oversees the delivery of early intervention services to families and children with special needs. Families are protected from having to advocate individually for their children with special needs, as each state is required to provide a state education representative. This person has sufficient authority to actively provide policy planning and implementation for children with special needs and their families.

The IDEA has not sailed through Congress without hitches. There have been disagreements about providing for the costs of these services to individuals and families and resistance to policies relating to disciplining children with special needs at school. President Clinton was finally able to sign the legislation authorizing the IDEA in 1997. In its finalized form, this legislation: (1) reduces incentives to segregate students with special needs, (2) increases federal funding for services, (3) increases the involvement of teachers and parents in developing IEPs for children, (4) generally increases the flexibility of states to provide services, (5) affirms the importance of classroom discipline for all students, and (6) enhances the provision of services to infants and toddlers.

The Elementary and Secondary Education Act of 2001 (also known as the No Child Left Behind law) contains provisions that address the needs of exceptional children in supplementing other legislation. This legislation, considered controversial by some observers (see http://www.nea.org/esea/), allows school districts to provide programming that may increase parental involvement, reallocate financial resources to provide research-based curricula, and heighten accountability of instruction. This law also permits children with disabilities to become classified as having cognitive disabilities, which qualifies special education classrooms and programs for financial assistance.

**Community Services.** The kinds of services needed to assist exceptional children and their families often depend on the age and specific problems of the child. Some problems become evident long before a child enters the public school system. In some instances, these problems are noticed at birth or when expected developmental progress fails to occur within the months or years after birth. It is also not unusual for problems to be discovered through special screening activities that regularly occur in many communities. When infants and young children are seen on a regular basis by a physician or health care professional, the doctor or nurse may discover and evaluate the child's current or future developmental problems. Early detection is crucial because treatment and therapy can often alleviate many potential difficulties if begun soon in a child's development. Available community services for parents of infants and young children with special needs include day-care centers, hospital programs, public school programs, Head Start programs, and programs offered through colleges and universities.

Respite care is a community service for families and disabled individuals. This service provides temporary relief for developmentally disabled individuals who live at home and also acts as an important element in preventing their institutionalization. This supervisory service assists families in coping with emergency situations that require the absence of primary caregivers and also provides relief from the daily stresses involved in caring for a disabled family member.

**Educational Programs.**   School-age exceptional children are included to the maximum extent possible in existing public school programs, a practice known as **mainstreaming,** or more recently **inclusion** (Leyden, 2002). These programs are supplemented by special education classes. Because all children do not profit from this educational arrangement, some may be placed exclusively in special education classes. School districts offer a variety of programs and services for exceptional children, which often change as the needs of the children change (Ripley, 2003). These services may include the following:

■ *Regular classroom experiences,* in which the child receives special attention and an individualized program
■ *Resource room experiences,* in which the child is enrolled in a regular classroom but goes to a specially equipped room to receive part of the daily instruction
■ *Consulting teacher experiences,* in which the child's instruction by a regular teacher is supplemented by a special education teacher
■ *Day school,* in which special educational programs are conducted in a separate room or building (for cases in which the child's needs cannot be met by including him or her in a regular classroom program)
■ *Residential schools,* which provide education and other treatment experiences that cannot be provided through any other means (usually reserved for those children who are visually or hearing impaired, severely mentally retarded, emotionally disturbed, or severely physically handicapped)
■ *Hospital or home-bound programs,* which serve the needs of a child who must be confined to bed or experience a lengthy convalescent period as the result of some type of disability.

Parents and family systems are especially concerned that children with special needs be provided with appropriate environments (Rigazio-DiGilio & Cramer-Benjamin, 2000). However, they typically experience mixed feelings about this issue. For example, children with special needs are protected and supported when they are placed in special education environments but miss out on important stimulation and interaction experiences because they are segregated from other students. When inclusion all but eliminates the unique attention these children require, they tend to suffer from not receiving such specialized services. The decisions about where and how to provide services for children involve complex issues. Complicating these decisions is the lack of training and experience that creates antipathy among mainstreaming teachers toward students with special needs (Ripley, 2003).

**Other Services.**   In addition to involving parents in the educational experiences of exceptional children, some kinds of support help the adults and other children in the family system. These families often need professional counseling, and several helpful strategies have been developed for these family members. Three methods are usually applied in these situations (Rigazio-DiGilio & Cramer-Benjamin, 2000):

1. *Informational counseling* occurs when children are first diagnosed and parents are informed of test results, prognosis, and treatment approaches.
2. *Psychotherapeutic methods,* most prominently behavior modification and reflective counseling, are taught to parents and siblings who use the methods in working with the exceptional child or sibling. Pediatric psychotherapy is offered to the affected child in dealing with emotional and behavioral problems.
3. *Group therapy approaches* place a number of parents or siblings into a support network in which individuals share feelings, reactions, and experiences to help each other cope with the stresses in their family systems.

*Focus Point.*   Parents of children with special needs deal with issues in child rearing not usually confronted by other parents. Child rearing in these circumstances can be difficult but can have particular rewards as well. Members of such family systems experience numerous reactions and effects, which invariably influence the quality and nature of parent-child relations. These families need and receive a variety of community resources that assist them in dealing with their particular challenges. Federal legislation efforts continue to provide needed support.

# SYSTEMIC FAMILY DEVELOPMENT SNAPSHOT

Our slice of developmental time is taken at the midpoint of the middle childhood stage of the oldest child in the Curtis family. Mary Curtis is now 9 years old. This slice is taken about 5 years after the snapshot we examined in the previous chapter when Mary was a preschooler. We begin examining the snapshot with a brief review of the stressors that affect a family system at this time. The second generation in this family continues to experience even greater levels of stress due to role strain affecting the young adult parents. However, the first generation now faces a critical adjustment following the death of Lisa's mother, Susan Scott, from complications relating to breast cancer. The third generation of the children also has had to deal with adjustments of their own, although children are often more resilient than adults in accepting the necessity of making changes.

## Examples of Stressors Affecting Each Curtis Family Generation: 5 Years Later

### First Generation (Grandparents)
■ Adjusting to the aging process that continues in the latter part of middle age
■ Adjusting to increasing frequency of deaths among spouses, colleagues, coworkers, and friends
■ Making final preparations for retirement

### Second Generation (Young Adult Parents)
■ Continuing adjustments in balancing work and family roles
■ Adding new roles to existing array
■ Adjusting household and work routines to meet the needs of school-age children
■ Adapting parenting behaviors and styles to meet the needs of school-age children
■ Avoiding divorce and coping in healthy ways with the lowest level of marital satisfaction that will be experienced
■ Attempting to meet personal adult needs

### Third Generation (School-Age Children)
■ Mastering developmental tasks and milestones of middle childhood

At the time of this slice of developmental time, here are the ages of all members of this family system: (1) the paternal grandfather (George Curtis) is now 63; (2) the paternal grandmother (Joan Curtis) is 61; (3) the maternal grandfather (Harry Scott) is 60; (4) the maternal grandmother (Susan Scott) is deceased; (5) Butch Curtis is 39; and (6) Lisa Curtis is 36. The first child, Mary, is 9 years old and the second child, Joey, is 7 years old.

## The Third Generation (Children)

The children are in elementary school now; Mary is in fourth grade and her brother, Joey, is in second grade. Mary's parents perhaps had the greater adjustment to make when Mary first entered first grade since she was their first child to embark on this major change. Joey's entrance into first grade in the last year was not quite so earth-shaking for the parents. Mary has become a typical trail-blazing, first-born child who coaches her little brother about the ins and outs of what he will encounter in each new school grade. She has enjoyed this advantage and likes helping her little brother with learning to read, write, and make calculations. Now that she is 9 years old, she is allowed to participate in the local Girl Scout program and is excelling with these activities. This coming summer, she will get to go to camp for one week as a reward for her sales in the annual cookie drive. Joey also belongs to a youth program called the Tiger Cubs, a program especially geared to boys in the first and second elementary grades. Both children are involved in other activities that take place throughout the week. Both children are on separate soccer teams, and Mary has gymnastics class twice weekly and dance classes on Saturdays.

Both children are doing relatively well with their schoolwork. Mary loves to read and has a current interest in biographies of famous people from the past such as Eleanor Roosevelt. She is particularly fond of the computer games available at school and at home. Right now, she is learning how to use the instant messaging feature so that she can visit with friends at night; sometimes they participate in online games together. Mary's mom has placed some restrictions on just what she can and cannot do on the Internet, and Mary is closely supervised with time limits as well. Joey seems to enjoy math more than reading and plays with educational games when he has his share of computer time at home.

Mary feels the importance of the trust her parents have placed in supervising herself and her little brother when they can't be home some days after school is out. She has learned to act responsibly in these situations and observes the rules her parents have established about what can and cannot be done when they aren't around. She knows, for example, how to answer the phone if someone calls for one of her parents, how to prepare snacks without using the stove, and what to play with Joey when both have finished homework assignments.

Both children experienced stress during this past year when their maternal grandmother died from cancer. This is their first encounter with this life event, and they don't completely understand why their grandmother died. All both children know and remember most vividly was that everyone in their family was very upset and cried a great deal. They were allowed to attend the funeral but didn't understand very much about what was going on. They miss their grandmother and wish that their grandfather would not be so unhappy. They have been with their parents to visit the cemetery on Memorial Day when they were given flowers to place on the grave site. Joey brought along one of the toys that his grandmother had given him for his last birthday and left that as well. Lisa and Butch have been very open with the children in answering their questions about dying and death. Although this has been difficult at times to discuss, they know it is important for their children to learn about this part of life and not to be confused about the issues.

## The Second Generation (Adult Parents)

Lisa and Butch have experienced some difficulties over the past several years. Butch was promoted in his work position and now works longer hours that also take him away from the family for short periods of time as he travels. This situation is very different from the family's experience when Butch was unemployed about 7 years ago. Lisa finds this change more challenging than she anticipated since she has the primary responsibilities of managing her own work role in relation to what the children require from her. Because of the children's different, hectic, and often conflicting schedules, she has found it necessary to call on her father and her in-laws to lend their time and help when Butch is unavailable. At times Lisa feels like she's living in a three-ring circus instead of a normal family because of all the running around that

must be done. Her day often begins at 5 A.M. to get her part of the housework done and get everyone in the family off to begin their day. Sometimes, she feels exhausted by 9 A.M. The day often is not over until 11 P.M. By then the children have taken care of their homework and gone to bed while Lisa has finished other housework chores and has finally had time to watch a bit of TV. There seems to be little time for family fun and interaction.

Butch and Lisa have noticed that they have more conflicts with each other now than ever before. The arguments lately have centered on Butch's lack of involvement with the family and with his household responsibilities. Lisa is beginning to feel that she can't take on anything more than what she is doing right now. She feels an increasing resentment about Butch giving greater priority to his work over his family and household responsibilities. He maintains that if they are to have a future with some financial safety, then they must accept this current situation. Their personal time together has dwindled almost to nothing, and Lisa sometimes thinks that when they do have time together, it becomes focused on settling arguments rather than expressing affection. She fears that her marriage may be threatened by the possibility of a divorce if things don't improve soon. Both of these young adults are tired, more emotionally distanced than ever before, and uncertain of how things are headed in their future.

Both Lisa and Butch are aware that their conflicts are affecting their children, and they are working to reduce and restrict their heated discussions to protect the children's anxieties. Not long ago, Lisa heard Mary weeping while in her room. When she came to Mary's bedroom, she quickly asked her to explain what was bothering her. At first, Mary didn't want to discuss anything with her mom but with Lisa's gentle encouragement, she found the words to tell her mother she was afraid she was going to become like many others in her class. She told her mother that about half of her classmates had parents who were either divorced or divorcing. When Lisa asked Mary why she thought this was happening to her parents, Mary responded that she had heard many arguments late at night between her mom and dad. Rather than discounting or diminishing Mary's fears, Lisa was truthful in admitting that she and Butch "had issues right now," but she went on to assure Mary that she and Butch were committed to each other, to their relationship, and to their children and family members. In doing so, she was trying to show Mary that while children can't be involved in adult matters, she and her brother had parents who were working on their problems together and expected to ride out the difficult times by learning now to work together more closely.

Complicating an already stressful situation was the death of Lisa's mother about 6 months ago. They had anticipated that this would happen one day but remained hopeful and optimistic as Susan Scott managed her illness and treatments with a good attitude. However, Susan experienced a turn for the worse as the cancer was detected in her pancreas and lungs. In less than 6 weeks, she died. Lisa and Butch were with the other family members (except the children) when she died. She and her mother had the opportunity to bring some closure before she died and Lisa was thankful for this. They were able to make peace with one another and settle some old issues that had not been completely addressed. Butch was supportive to Lisa during this time, and she sees this commitment as evidence that he still loves her very much. Perhaps this event was what both needed to help bring them closer after feeling some estrangement. They have recently discussed entering therapy to work on their current problems. In talking with friends who have weathered similar problems, Lisa has gained some pointers and has discussed with Butch some ways that they might improve their marriage and home life. Butch has agreed, for example, to take complete charge of the children on the weekends so Lisa can have some personal time to use as she wishes.

## The First Generation (Grandparents)

The first generation has been affected more so by Susan Scott's death than they expected. Losing parents was difficult, but Harry Scott never thought he would survive his wife. Now, being alone after so many years of marriage, he feels lost and uncomfortable. It is hard at times to fight the feelings of depression and loss. He has not slept well in the months following Susan's death and has avoided dealing with some issues he knows he will have to attend to eventually. Lisa is attentive to her father as he struggles with a new identity of being a widower. She also is attentive because she has heard from friends that when older men reach this new status, they often become emotionally depressed to the point of committing suicide. She is in daily contact with her father to monitor

him as closely as she can. Harry has recently joined a support group for cancer survivors and their partners. He finds it difficult to talk about his feelings but has learned a great deal just from listening to others. The group is helping him to learn about these feelings and how to deal with a new lifestyle. Harry also finds that helping to care for his grandchildren is a much needed and welcomed distraction from his own problems. He enjoys spending time in play with both grandchildren. He also understands how helpful this is for his daughter and son-in-law and that he is playing a useful role in his family.

Butch's parents, Joan and George Curtis, also have been affected by Susan's death. They have become closer as a result and value their time together more deeply now than ever before. As such, their marriage has been strengthened. As they observed Harry and Susan deal with their own issues, they have learned how to lean more upon each other for support and nurturance. George now is looking forward to his retirement because this will allow him to have more time with Joan and do some things they have had to put off until now, such as travel. Both have taken a greater interest in their health since this may be an important key to having time together following retirement.

The three surviving older adults have noticed how their adult children are struggling with issues in their work and family life. They know they can't intrude by offering unsolicited opinions and suggestions about what they think Butch and Lisa need to do, but they have indicated they are willing to listen and discuss anything if their children so desire. In some ways, they don't understand the issues because these are different from what they encountered at a similar point in their own development as a family.

### Parenting Reflection 9–5

Can you determine how each generation in the snapshot uses boundaries? Is this family system one that is open or closed? Does morphogenesis or morphostasis appear to be functioning in this family system when this snapshot took place?

## POINTS TO CONSIDER

■ The time between 6 and 12 years is called *middle childhood*. During this period, children master several developmental tasks and milestones, including: (1) achieving a sense of industry vs. inferiority; (2) developing a new individuality; (3) establishing relationships with peers; and (4) refining existing skills and acquiring new physical, social, and mental skills.

■ Parenting increasingly shifts to psychological assistance and guidance when children are of school age. Parenting styles change and become adapted in relation to the new developmental needs of children. Coregulation becomes a predominant approach by most parents of school-age children. Children take on greater responsibility to police their own actions. Children are also allowed greater latitude in their activities and behavior because of their more advanced abilities. Parents increasingly provide more advanced levels of structure, best conveyed in nurturant terms. Many parents also incorporate new models of parenting styles in providing structure and nurturance to children at this age.

■ Socialization experiences continue to occupy the efforts and energy of most parents of school-age children, especially focusing now on facilitating children's moral development. Parents serve an important function in providing interpretations and acting as narrators. This role assists children in learning how to reason morally, consider options and choices for their behavior, and gain knowledge about family values and a sesnse of what is right and wrong. The school may assist parents in helping school-age children learn in greater detail about their sexuality. It is important for parents to prepare preteen-age children for their approaching puberty.

■ Certain behavior problems can be expected in some school-age children that are specific to diffculties in adjusting to the developmental tasks of this life stage. They may involve: (1) problems in cooperating with adults' expectations of appropriate behavior, (2) difficulties in attending school and in mastering the skills essential to successful functioning in an academic environment, and (3) problems in adjusting to interpersonal skills and achieving appropriate standards of behavior expected by those in authority.

■ Families of children with special needs have particular problems not usually shared by other families. Parents and family members experience a variety of reactions to having a child with special needs present; this child has a number of influences on the family system as a whole. The ability of families to cope with the stresses and demands of having a child with special needs often depends on the availability and nature of a variety of sources of assistance. Community programs and federal legislation work to address the needs of exceptional children and their parents.

■ A systemic family development snapshot reveals examples of the stressors that may affect the different generations of a family system as well as the ways that members cope with these in healthy as well as unhealthy ways.

**CHAPTER 10**

# Parenting Adolescents and Young Adults

### Focus Questions

■ ■ ■ ■ ■ ■ ■ ■ ■ ■

*Parenting Adolescents*

1. What are the principal developmental milestones of adolescence that parents should know?

2. How is parenting conducted with teenagers and young adults? How is this different from when children were younger?

3. What are some common behavior problems observed among adolescents? How do these differ from those observed among younger children?

4. What stressors and coping mechanisms are revealed by a systemic family development snapshot of families with adolescent children?

*Parenting Young Adults*

1. What are the unique challenges of parenting young adults?

2. What is the nature of grandparenting in contemporary families? What styles may be observed? What are some unique challenges in grandparenting roles today?

■ ■ ■ ■ ■ ■ ■ ■ ■ ■

**Adolescence** is the stage of the life span that represents a transition period between childhood and adulthood. Chronologically, it begins at age 13 and extends through age 18. The developmental event of puberty, which usually occurs at the beginning of adolescence, signals the end of childhood; at this time individuals become sexually mature and capable of reproduction. The stage of adolescence is technically divided into two periods: (1) *early adolescence,* which begins at puberty (about age 13), ends at age 16, and involves a variety of physical changes associated with the achievement of sexual maturation; and (2) *late adolescence,* which begins at age 16, continues until age 18, and involves many psychosocial changes (Steinberg, 2004).

Parents may anticipate the adolescent stage of their children's life span with mixed feelings. Traditionally, the period is described as one of storm and stress, not only for the teens who experience it but also for their parents and family systems. Parents may fear that their worst nightmares will come true about their children. A more contemporary view of adolescence describes this stage as one of increasing autonomy as children gain increasing degrees of personal responsibility and a time of significant transitions (Steinberg, 2004). Parents may view these gains in more realistic terms colored by trepidation and apprehension about the many hazards that can threaten the health and well-being of adolescent children. As with other stages of the life span, adolescence presents both children and their parents with unique challenges for growth and adaptation. Those challenges are briefly outlined as characteristics of this life stage.

## DEVELOPMENTAL LANDMARKS OF ADOLESCENCE

Two changes distinguish a child's development during adolescence from previous stages. The first is characterized by *rapid physical and psychological change.* Adolescence is a period of metamorphosis in an individual's life involving dramatic changes in body proportions, physical size, sexual maturation, and personality shifts. The second change involves *individual emancipation.* Western culture emphasizes the teenage years as the appropriate time for establishing one's independence as a mature person and assuming full responsibility for oneself (Figure 10–1). The specific developmental tasks and milestones that individuals

encounter in adolescence focus on acquiring and refining more advanced skills, abilities, and attitudes that lead toward preparation for adulthood. These are outlined in Focus On 10–1.

## PARENTING ADOLESCENTS

Many parents anticipate that when a child reaches adolescence, it is like going to war since this stage of the life span is associated with rebellion, tension, conflict, and emotional turmoil. In reality, this depiction is not far from the truth since adolescence is a difficult time both for children and parents. While some teenagers reach the outer limits in their behavior and attitude, however, most adolescents do not act out and the stereotypes described here do not normally apply.

Parenting styles and behaviors must adapt once again to meet the needs of a different child. And once again, the adaptation often is not initiated by the parents but rather by the adolescent who may demand to be treated differently now that he or she is older. Meeting the developmental needs of a child who is attempting to become autonomous and eventually to individuate from the family system presents challenges not found in previous periods of parenting children. Most parents understand that adolescents continue to need guidance, rules, and support in this process of growing toward maturity.

**FIGURE 10–1.** Adolescence is a time of rapid changes as individuals seek to establish a personal identity and embark on individuating from their family of origin.

**Focus On 10–1**

**Developmental Landmarks of Adolescence**

- Establishing a sense of personal identity as opposed to role confusion
- Establishing new and more mature relationships with peers of both sexes
- Accepting the physical changes that accompany puberty
- Determining one's sexual orientation and accepting one's sexuality
- Initiating emotional independence from parents and other family members
- Initiating the process of individuation
- Initiating financial independence
- Selecting and initiating preparations for an occupation or higher education
- Initiating the learning of skills involved in participating in healthy intimate relationships
- Manifesting socially responsible behaviors
- Determining a set of values and an ethical system that will guide behavior

Family professionals stress that one of the more difficult challenges of parenting adolescents is the fine line parents walk between being supportive of a teen's efforts to individuate and maintaining certain limits and boundaries for appropriate behavior (Gnaulati & Heine, 2001). Adolescents need experience in making personal decisions, but sometimes these decisions can have traumatic consequences. Family systems become unhealthy when there is a demand for complete uniformity and conformity among all members, when everyone is expected to adhere to the same beliefs, values, and behaviors. Although parents and adolescents must agree on rules and other family patterns, this agreement occurs ideally through negotiation and input from all concerned. When no latitude is permitted for individual expression and differences are not tolerated, a family system becomes endangered in its ability to function in a healthy way. This approach may have been appropriate at earlier stages of the family life career as a reflection of the developmental limits and inabilities of children to participate fully in family life and decisions; however, it becomes less appropriate as children reach the adolescent years.

## Revised Parenting Styles

A common misconception of many parents is that a particular style of child rearing does not change once it is established; they assume they will use the same style throughout the years of child rearing. In reality, children's changing developmental progress affects changes in parenting styles throughout childhood and adoles-

cence. Most parents make adaptations in child-rearing strategies, methods, and interaction styles to meet the particular needs of adolescents. Because of the different developmental status of adolescents, parents must shift to accommodate these needs by altering their parenting style to become more authoritative, less authoritarian, and eventually more permissive in nature.

Parenting during this stage is particularly challenging for a variety of reasons (Santrock, 2004). Adults must discover ways to help teens learn to make decisions that minimize potential harm to themselves and others. Communication between parents and teens requires patience and effort to achieve effective functioning of this family system microenvironment. A unique challenge is adjusting the relationship to allow an adolescent to individuate from the family system. By doing so, adults must gradually relinquish control and place increasing amounts of personal responsibility on teens to become self-regulated.

Research consistently shows that adolescent-parent relations are best when decisions are perceived by both as being consistent and collaborative, the needs of all family members are respected, and decisions are seen as fair and reasonable as opposed to arbitrary (Steinberg & Silk, 2002). As in previous stages of parenting children, the authoritative parenting style continues to be associated with positive adolescent outcomes.

••••••••••••••••••••••••••••••••••••••••••••••

***Focus Point.*** One of the challenges to the relationship between parents and teens relates to how parents must adapt in providing structure and nurturance. A significant task involves the ability of parents and teens to communicate effectively. Adults who use democratic styles in parenting adolescents usually have improved interactions. Those using stricter styles have more conflicts, which are frequently related to adolescent attempts at individuation.

••••••••••••••••••••••••••••••••••••••••••••••••

## Meeting the Needs of Adolescents

**Health and Safety Issues.** Adolescence and young adulthood are perhaps the time in one's life span when health and well-being are at their peak. However, health and safety issues occurring during these times often have a significant impact in the present as well as in the future.

Adolescents should begin having an annual visit with a health care professional for screening for a variety of health issues. These visits also allow for confidential discussions of issues of a personal nature that a health care professional can address. Health care professionals can also bring other issues up for discussion with the teenager relating to health, exercise, and sexual matters. Other situations involving the health and well-being of teens call for monitoring by parents and other family members.

**Substance Abuse.** Parents and other members of society are extremely concerned about adolescent use of drugs and chemical substances. Estimates vary considerably about the extensiveness of drug use among teenagers. Indications are that adolescent drug abuse remains stable in comparison with past years in which information has been gathered (Federal Interagency Forum on Child and Family Statistics, 2003). Despite this decline, one high school student out of four uses marijuana, and two out of three use alcohol regularly.

Despite the influences of the media and peers, adolescents who have been reared by parents who rely on an authoritative style appear to have stronger internalized standards that help to insulate them from pressures to abuse substances (Collins et al., 2000). Teens who apparently care what parents think about such matters (e.g., parents who disapprove of smoking and/or drinking) are less likely to drink alcohol, smoke cigarettes, or use other drugs (Figure 10–2).

**Suicide.** Suicide is the second leading cause of death, following fatal accidental injuries and death from firearms, among individuals between 15 and 21 years old (U.S. Bureau of the Census, 2003). Contemporary teenagers increasingly complete suicide successfully; the

**FIGURE 10–2.** Substance abuse is a serious problem of adolescence that can continue into later years of life.

rate has more than tripled within the last 30 years (Federal Interagency Forum on Child and Family Statistics, 2003). While suicide occurs more commonly among white youth, no ethnic group is spared this phenomenon among adolescents. Most adolescents attempting suicide are female, although males are more likely to succeed in completing the act (U.S. Bureau of the Census, 2003).

It is not completely clear why some adolescents want to commit suicide, particularly at a time when, for many people, their lives are just beginning. Suicide may be related to a variety of issues (Groleger, Tomori, & Kocmur, 2003). Many teenagers who contemplate suicide and attempt to end their lives are emotionally depressed. Depression distorts a person's ability to reason logically and clearly to reach solutions to personal problems. Living situations frequently seem hopeless to people who are emotionally depressed, and suicide appears to be the only solution to their life situations. Suicide among adolescents is also related to substance abuse, which is frequently accompanied by depression (Tubman, Wagner, & Langer, 2003).

Many teenagers who attempt and succeed in committing suicide may also be emotionally depressed about their sexual orientation (Savin-Williams & Ream, 2003). Gay and lesbian youths are about six times more likely than nongay youths to attempt suicide; they account for about 30 percent of those who complete suicide successfully. These individuals apparently experience much anguish and inner turmoil because of the social stigmas associated with homosexuality. They choose to commit suicide rather than suffer rejection, disapproval, and shame, reactions they anticipate from family and friends.

**Teen Pregnancy and STDs.** There has been a decline in the number of teen pregnancies in recent years (Martin et al., 2003), but the decline has not eliminated this problem. Teen pregnancy continues to be a matter of concern for society, schools, and the adolescents and families who are affected. Teen parents, their child, and their families face many serious short- and long-term consequences. This problem is discussed in greater detail in Chapter 14.

Sexually transmitted diseases (STDs) are a new health concern occurring for the first time in adolescence. These may be transmitted via heterosexual or homosexual acts. The most common types in our society are syphilis, gonorrhea, chlamydia, herpes simplex, venereal warts, and HIV infection and Acquired Immune Deficiency Syndrome (AIDS). The high fre-

quency of unprotected sexual behavior and multiple sex partners results in about 3 million new cases of STDs yearly among adolescents (Centers for Disease Control and Prevention, 2003).

••••••••••••••••••••••••••••••••••••••••••••••••••••

**Focus Point.** A variety of issues involve the health and safety of adolescents. These ordinarily do not affect all teenagers, but a significant number are sidetracked into avenues that have short- and long-term adverse effects on their development.

••••••••••••••••••••••••••••••••••••••••••••••••••••

**Providing Structure and Nurturance for Adolescents.** A recurrent theme stressed in this text is that the nature of the relationship between parents and children is renegotiated and redefined as parents respond to the changing developmental needs and demands of developing children.

Much parental reluctance to accept any changes in their children is related to the functioning of the family system. The cohesion of a family system is threatened when any change takes place that affects the system's functioning. Systems have a strong tendency to seek to maintain the status quo because change in any aspect threatens the system's integrity. Family systems, in particular, face challenges that call for changes. When a child becomes an adolescent, his or her desire for individuation poses a serious threat to the family's functioning and its ability to maintain cohesion as a system. The family reacts in ways typical to other stressful situations it confronts.

Parents may seem particularly reluctant to release a teen from the controls, limits, and boundaries that were established in earlier developmental stages. Although many parents realize that this change must take place eventually, the equalization and transfer of power toward greater self-regulation occurs more slowly than most teens prefer.

Nevertheless, researchers have consistently validated the benefits of authoritative parenting styles in mediating positive developmental outcomes for children (Gray & Steinberg, 1999). The benefits for adolescents from this parenting style continue to remain in effect while parents make alterations in response to the individuation process of their teenagers. For example, behavior problems of adolescents appear to be diminished while academic competence can be enhanced when parents maintain what can be termed *detached in-*

*volvement* or supervision. This variation on the authoritative parenting scheme relates to the perception adolescents hold of their parents as being involved in their lives while allowing them enough slack from parental supervision to feel autonomous. Parents, in this vein, are still providing structure for adolescents, but the structure is perceived as being fairly administered, yet firm and warm in its tone.

## Parenting Reflection 10–1

Is there such a thing as a **generation gap** or is this a media fabrication? How would this influence interactions, communications, and mutual understanding between generation members in families with adolescents?

Table 10–1 outlines some ways in which parents of teens can be responsive and supportive or unhelpful in providing structure and nurturance.

## Parenting Reflection 10–2

Is it a good idea for parents to forbid their teenagers from activities and people of which they disapprove? If not, what can parents do when their teen makes what seems to be unwise decisions?

*Focus Point.* One of the challenges to the relationship between parents and teens relates to how parents must adapt in providing structure and nurturance.

**Promoting the Individuation Process.** The experiences of adolescence are a struggle toward the eventual emancipation of a teenager from the family system in which he or she has been raised. The process leading to emancipation, or **individuation,** is part of the identity formation that is central to adolescent development. Although this process begins in adolescence, it may not be

**TABLE 10–1.**  Behaviors of Parents of Adolescents

| Behaviors Providing Structure and Nurturance | Behaviors Not Providing Structure and Nurturance |
|---|---|
| • Showing approval for teen's efforts to achieve developmental tasks | • Responding to teen in uncaring ways |
| • Continuing to offer love, safety, and protection | • Withholding love, especially nurturing touch |
| • Accepting teen's feelings and sharing own past feelings about puberty to build empathy with teen | • Responding inappropriately to teen's developing sexuality |
| • Not discounting teen's behavior, feelings, and attitudes | • Using rigid rules, having no rules, or enforcing rules inconsistently; refusing to negotiate rules |
| • Understanding teen's need for individuation and supporting efforts to establish it | • Failing to expect teen to think and reason about solutions to problems |
| • Celebrating the teen's growing independence and gains toward attaining adult status | • Engaging in negative teasing about teen's emerging sexuality, interests, dress styles, friends, or idealisms |
| • Encouraging, supporting, and accepting teen's emerging personal identity; accepting that it may be different from what you desired or hoped for the teen | • Failing to confront teen's self-destructive behaviors, such as substance abuse |
| | • Thwarting and sabotaging teen's efforts to individuate from the family |
| | • Refusing to accept teen's wide range of emotional expressions and feelings |
| | • Discounting teen's behavior, feelings, and attitudes |

*Source:* Adapted from Clarke, J. I., & Dawson, C. (1989). *Growing up again: Parenting ourselves, parenting our children.* Minneapolis: Hazelden.

**FIGURE 10–3.** Employment helps adolescents learn work skills that can be applied to future occupations and helps them individuate from their families of origin.

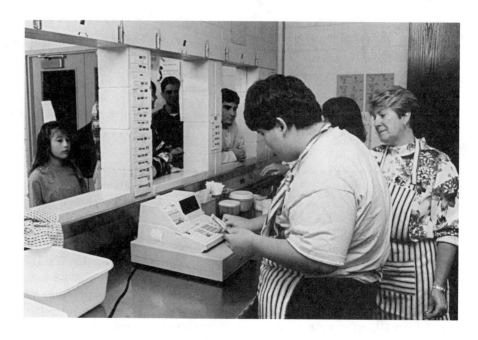

completed until years later in adulthood. Some individuals, however, never completely achieve the degree of emancipation or individuation they truly desire or that is expected by society as an appropriate developmental task. It involves becoming a true individual in that one develops a personal belief system to guide decisions and behaviors, acquires financial independence, and assumes emotional self-care. The process requires questioning and challenging and may account for some of the tension experienced between parents and adolescents.

Often a teen's advancement toward emancipation includes working at full- or part-time jobs (Figure 10–3). Making social decisions (such as choosing friends, dating, or becoming sexually active) also helps a teenager take greater developmental steps toward maturity and personal autonomy.

**Helping Teens Handle Puberty.** Puberty is perhaps the central developmental milestone of adolescence. It involves both physical and psychological aspects as part of the identity formation process. In this developmental event a child becomes a sexually mature individual. However, because adolescents are not yet mature emotionally, the feelings that accompany the physical changes of puberty can be confusing, conflicting, and difficult to understand. Many parents are also unsure about how to help their adolescent child handle the various aspects related to puberty. Perhaps the greatest part

that a parent can have is maintaining open lines of communication with their maturing child so that issues can be discussed openly and honestly.

***Sexual Orientation Issues.*** During adolescence, many individuals discover their sexual orientation, which serves as the foundation of sexual identity. **Sexual orientation** is the self-awareness and knowledge that one is sexually attracted to and directs emotional affection toward people of the same or opposite sex. Those who orient to others of the same sex are known as *homosexuals*. Those who orient to others of the opposite sex are known as *heterosexuals*.

There is no clear, definitive explanation of how a person's sexual orientation is determined (Strong, 2004). Apparently, the foundations for someone's sexual orientation are influenced by genetic and biological factors interacting with environmental factors that occur beginning prior to birth. The large majority of adolescents are heterosexual. Estimates vary about those having a homosexual orientation. Adolescents who are gay or lesbian commonly experience great difficulty in accepting their homosexuality. Adolescents are sensitive to any behavior or social position in which they might be seen as different from others. Young adolescents are especially fearful of rejection by peers because they interpret such reactions from others as an invalidation of self. Given the deeply ingrained negative societal opinion about homosexuals, most teenagers who discover their homosexual orientation are reluctant to acknowledge it publicly, afraid of risking even further rejection. This reluctance is especially common among boys who are gay.

Many gay and lesbian adolescents react by hiding their homosexuality, which leads to unhealthy and negative outcomes (Hatheway, 2003). Role confusion, rather than a fully integrated personal identity, may begin for these individuals if they fail to incorporate this aspect into their personal identity. Those having difficulty accepting their homosexual orientation typically make strong efforts at denial, trying to pass as heterosexual to avoid social stigmatization and isolation. Unhealthy self-esteem, alienation from others, fear of intimacy, social isolation, and stifled emotional expression are frequently observed during this denial. Gay and lesbian teens usually are not afforded the equivalent types of dating experiences available to nongay teens, which may contribute to those feelings.

### Dating and Sexual Activity.
Dating is the first interpersonal social experience that many teens have with heterosexuality. The way in which teens date has changed over the last 30 years. In the past, a boy traditionally approached a girl with a proposal for socializing at his expense. Their behavior was ritualized because both knew what was and was not expected to occur during the date.

Today, heterosexual teens are much more informal in the way they socialize together. Much of this socialization is part of peer group activities rather than between individuals. Interaction is more casual and informal than in the past. For example, teens enjoy hanging out at shopping malls or having small parties where everyone comes together to enjoy the company, meet new people, and have fun. The age at which adolescents begin to date is a significant predictor of the age at which sexual activity also begins (Steinberg, 2004). Both activities are initiated earlier today than they were in the past. The age at which sexual activity begins also varies according to a teen's ethnic background. For example, black teens tend to experience intercourse for the first time at earlier ages than white teens do (about age 15 to 16 for blacks versus age 18 to 19 for whites). Other predictors of early sexual involvement include opportunity (being in a steady relationship), sexually permissive attitudes, association with delinquent peers, and alcohol use.

While it is unlikely that completely accurate statistics can ever be obtained about the ages at which adolescents first become sexually active, it does appear that this occurs earlier among more adolescents than previously (Bernstein, 2004). However, use of condoms and other birth control methods is more prevalent than in the past, resulting in fewer teen pregnancies.

Sexual activity places teens at risk for pregnancy as well as exposure to sexually transmitted diseases. Use of contraceptives, especially condoms, is known to reduce this risk considerably. The increased used of condoms may reflect the influence of more effective sex education, especially regarding the transmission of AIDS.

### Supporting Sex Education for Teens.
Exploration and experimentation are necessary behavioral components that motivate the identity formation process in adolescence. Many adults are uncomfortable acknowledging that adolescents are curious about their sexuality, particularly because puberty has made them capable of reproduction; it is no longer an abstraction (Steinberg, 2004). Some adults object to school courses that provide teenagers with explicit sexual information. They may object for several reasons: (1) fear that sexual information will stimulate experimentation with sexual activities, (2) concern about moral issues, (3) fear that teens will be taught values that differ from those of their family system, (4) lack of parental control over what is taught, or (5) fear that schools will undermine parental authority. Most adults favor sex education in schools, however, and only a few appear to prohibit their teenage children from participation (Bellows, 2004).

Compounding the issue of the need for sex education is the fact that teens do not think logically about hypothetical issues in general (Flavell, Miller, & Miller, 2001). Sexual decision making involves some of the many different kinds of skills that teens must acquire in their identity formation process. They may obtain much information in sex education courses; however, it is unclear how teens use this information in making sexual decisions that affect their behavior. Some adults fear that if teens are given information about sexual behavior or methods of birth control, they will become more curious, which may lead to sexual activity. But this response does not appear to be the case. Exposure to sexual information may have the effect of delaying the age at which adolescents begin to experiment sexually rather than stimulating it (McKay et al., 2001).

One of the most important contributions parents can make to their teen's exposure to sexual information is providing them with the skills to make healthy sexual decisions. For some parents, this means helping their teen to understand the desire for sexual abstinence. For others, it means being sure that their adolescent understands the principles but most especially the importance of safer sex practices. Each family system will need to determine how it will approach and deal with this aspect of an adolescent child's identity development and act accordingly. Many will want to take advantage of the opportunities provided by most school systems today for professionally guided educational experiences for their teens, while others will seek strict control over the information that is presented and in a particular context.

Equally important is the balancing of information that is strictly factual with that which addresses the emotional aspects of sexuality. Teens need support as they explore their first romantic encounters and preparation for all that this entails as best as is possible. For many par-

ents, this experience is a reminder of what they encountered as adolescents. However, when most contemporary parents were teenagers, sexually transmitted diseases were not fatal and teen pregnancy was less acceptable than today. In this regard, many parents of contemporary adolescents need updating on sexual information to discuss these issues with their adolescent children.

## Parenting Reflection 10–3

The AIDS epidemic has changed a long-running debate on what public schools should and should not teach in sex education courses. What should adolescents learn in these courses and when should this be taught? Some high schools have clinics where teens may obtain condoms and other methods of birth control. Do you think this practice encourages sexual activity or serves as a means of realistically assisting adolescents in making healthy sexual decisions?

# SYSTEMIC FAMILY DEVELOPMENT SNAPSHOT

Our slice of developmental time is taken at the midpoint of the adolescence stage of the oldest child in the Curtis family. Mary Curtis is now 15 years old. This slice is taken about 6 years after the snapshot we examined in the previous chapter when Mary was a school-age child. We begin examining the snapshot with a brief review of the stressors that can affect a family system at this time. Perhaps the greatest levels of stress are being experienced now by both the third generation (the adolescent children) and their parents. However, the first generation is experiencing major life changes. Altogether, this is a time of challenges for the entire family system as homeostasis has been disrupted at all levels.

At the time of this slice of developmental time, here are the ages of all members of the family system: (1) the paternal grandfather (George Curtis) is now 69; (2) the paternal grandmother (Joan Curtis) is 67; (3) the maternal grandfather (Harry Scott) is now 66; (4) there is now a maternal stepgrandmother (Kim Scott) due to Harry's remarriage—she is 63; (5) Butch Curtis is now 45; and

(6) Lisa Curtis is now 42. The first child, Mary, is 15 and the second child, Joey, is 13 years old.

## Examples of Stressors Affecting Each Curtis Family Generation: 6 Years Later

### First Generation (Grandparents)

- Adjusting to the aging process that continues in the latter part of middle age and in the first years of late adulthood
- Adjusting to increasing frequency of deaths among spouses, colleagues, coworkers, and friends
- Adjusting to declines in personal health and that of one's partner
- Making final preparations for retirement and adjusting to the life changes precipitated by retirement
- Beginning life reviews
- Adjusting to widowhood and to remarriage in late life
- Preparing for one's death and of one's partner

## Second Generation (Adult Parents of Adolescents)

- Providing for widely different needs of all family members
- Experiencing recovery in marital satisfaction
- Bridging communication issues between adults and adolescent children
- Supporting the individuation process of adolescent children
- Reworking and adapting family roles and rules
- Adapting parenting styles to meet the needs of adolescents
- Managing provider and family roles effectively

### Third Generation (Adolescent Children)

- Mastering developmental tasks and milestones of adolescence (see Focus On 10–1)

## The Third Generation (Adolescents)

We begin our examination of the Curtis family snapshot with the third generation, the adolescent children. Mary Curtis is now a freshman in high school at age 15. She is both excited and nervous about beginning high school. Junior high was lots of fun, and she excelled in her schoolwork. Now, she knows things will change in many respects on entering high school. Academics are more difficult, but the payoff is new friends, old friends, and, of course, boys! She has her parents' permission to begin dating if she desires and if the boy meets a few standards set by her parents. There are many new freedoms now, but these are controlled by the rules her parents set with Mary's agreement. She has already been on several double-dates with friends and has gone to a few parties. Her first big school dance is coming up in a few weeks, and Mary has been asked out by three boys for the occasion. Luckily, Mike, the boy she likes the most, asked her first. She definitely has feelings about him as they have spent more time together. These feelings are confusing in some ways because she doesn't always understand what they mean. The feelings seem to peak when they are alone and making out. Some of her girlfriends have already "gone all the way" with their boyfriends and talk about their experiences quite a bit. Mary isn't sure what to do about all this but thinks she should try to talk things over with her mom before proceeding as her friends have done. She feels she could trust her mother's

thoughts and believes she is lucky to have a mom who is open-minded. Most of her friends keep secrets like this from their parents.

While Mary likes school, she is almost bored with some of her subjects and finds that her mind turns to daydreaming when she is uninterested in something during class. The daydreams focus on a variety of themes and ideas, such as what kind of work she will do when she grows up, if she will ever be married and have children, and if she will have a handsome husband someday with an important job and live in a trendy home. But reality soon returns as she knows she must do well in school now to be accepted to a good university.

She often thinks about new clothes and makeup, but her parents keep her on a small allowance in return for housework she does while her mother and father work. This isn't enough to cover the costs of what she really wants, so she had been investigating the possibility of a job at one of the local fast-food restaurants. She has even filled out an application but has not yet handed it in because she needs to discuss this with her parents. She has been exploring some what-if scenarios with her mother about working part-time, and her mom seems to think she could try this out as an experiment to see what would happen with her schoolwork. She needs the permission of both parents to get a job permit, however, so her mother has agreed to discuss this first with her dad to work out any objections he might have. Mary also is looking forward to getting her driver's license in a few months. Her parents have agreed she could do this if she has proven that she can be trustworthy and responsible this year. She has agreed to show this by observing curfew rules, keeping at least a B average in all her subjects, and being responsible about her household chores. Her parents recently added one other stipulation to this list—not getting into any trouble that involves her friends.

One of the biggest problems Mary faces now is what to do about hanging out with friends. Some are drinking alcohol and trying drugs like Ecstasy, especially the boys. Some have been smoking cigarettes now for over a year and some have tried pot. Some of them have pressured Mary to try these things, but she has managed so far to only try pot once. She didn't like the way it made her feel, and she got ill from the experience. This was yet another thing to talk over with her mom since she wasn't exactly sure what to do to keep her friends while saying no to drugs and other wild behaviors.

Mary's brother, Joey, is now 13 and in seventh grade. Mary is surprised at how much he has changed in the last year. He is taller but very skinny. His braces are the most prominent part of his facial expressions. And he is always doing dorky things either by himself or with his friends. Mary thinks they all need to be hung out to dry for another year. Not that high school boys are totally cool, but these kids are in a totally different class!

Joey seems always to be hungry. No matter how much he eats at a meal, he has hunger pangs 30 minutes later. His allowance goes quickly for junk food from vending machines near home and school. And he is always outgrowing his clothes, it seems, within weeks after his mom has replaced them. He sleeps a lot more than he used to, and it's not unusual for him to crawl out of bed by noon on weekends. His body confuses him in some ways; at times he seems uncoordinated and unsure of where his arms or legs are in space. He can just as easily fall or trip going upstairs as he can do fancy tricks on his skateboard. And he doesn't understand the changes he sees in his genitals. He listens with keen interest when his friends talk about such matters and it makes him feel better to know he isn't some kind of a freak. The exercise sport classes he takes now require that all the boys take showers, and this is a convenient place to make comparisons between himself and the other guys.

Joey looks at girls differently now; in fact, it seems that he has just discovered that girls share the planet. However, he feels shy and awkward when one looks at him and smiles, and he hasn't had the courage yet to even hang out with a girl. He has gone to only one dance at school so far, but only a few couples actually danced together; everyone else got into bunches with their friends and just jumped around.

His passion is playing video games with his buddies and going to the skateboard park after school and on weekends. These are places and times when they can get away from disapproving adults and older sisters and do their thing without interference. Joey has gotten into lots of arguments with his parents lately; it seems that is all they do at meals and other times. He thinks his father is especially bossy and has been driving hard rules that are difficult and unreasonable, like having to tell them everywhere he goes, who he is going with, and being back home at a set time. Joey's parents insist on meeting his friends before they allow him to go to their house for a weekend overnight; that is truly unreasonable, he thinks. And they always give him a once-over

after he comes back the next day. They seem suspicious of things like smoking, drinking, and who knows what else. He tried to dress like some of his buddies in that way-cool Goth style, but his parents put that off-limits the minute they saw him come home wearing black fingernail polish.

## The Second Generation (Adult Parents)

Lisa and Butch feel that they have learned many lessons about parenting adolescents from working with Mary, but lately parenting Joey has called their skills and patience into doubt. Boys must be more of a challenge and a handful as teenagers than girls, but then again girls present their own unique challenges for parents. All the questioning of just about everything, the defiance, the testing of rules and boundaries, the conflicts, and the rebellious experimentation that they had seen in varying degrees with both of their teens has had a definite impact on them as individuals, as parents, and as a couple.

Many conflicts have arisen between themselves and Mary about certain issues, such as her need to demonstrate responsible behaviors for them to trust her when she is away from home with friends. Now innumerable tugs-of-war occur with Joey about most everything. His negative attitude permeates their home life and shows up in a poor attitude about schoolwork, disagreements about dress style and hygiene, intolerance and insensitivity about his family members, his apparent lack of respect for people in authority, constant nagging to get him to perform tasks around the house, forgetting to keep commitments until the last minute, and the constant fear that he is getting in with the wrong crowd of kids. They had seen Mary grow away from these kinds of problems and knew that they have to hang in with Joey in trusting that this too would pass away some time in the future. They love their son very much and hate to see how difficult it is for him to be dealing with all these boundary issues.

Butch and Lisa have talked with friends who weathered the adolescence of their children about the situation with Joey and have gathered many opinions and ideas. Lisa even attended a parenting class offered through Joey's school by the PTA about "Surviving the Storm and Stress of Adolescence." What seems to work the best for now when they need to be strict about something is denying privileges and working out bargains with Joey. For example, they have learned that he responds well to arrangements where he is offered a reward such as staying out an hour later than normally past curfew in return for keeping to school assignment deadlines and doing his work as directed.

Lisa and Butch are not aware that they are going through what is known as the *midlife transition experience*. Perhaps there is some connection between the turmoil that their teenagers are experiencing in confronting their new selves and the many issues and decisions that must be made. Butch began to express this uneasiness before Lisa had as he tried to talk about his confusion about some things and the feelings of uncertainty that have come into his consciousness. He wonders about what it will take to make him feel really happy. He hasn't found it in his work, volunteer activities, or some aspects of his family life, especially in dealing with a young adolescent boy. And he has not yet mentioned unhappiness with their marriage. In fact, things between Butch and Lisa have improved considerably just within the last year or so. They have found more time to spend together just talking when the kids are out for the evening. They are doing more things together again, like shopping and working in the yard. They have even had some rare private time for several weekends when the kids were out of the home for visits with friends. They had almost forgotten what it was like to be able to go to a movie as a couple or just rent a video and have pizza and wine like they did before their kids arrived. Both of these adults have discovered that what makes the difference in their lives are the relationships with family and friends.

## The First Generation (Grandparents)

The first generation of this family system is confronting the full reality of what it means to grow old and become senior citizens. All four of these individuals have reached retirement status and have learned how to adjust to living on a fixed income while having the opportunity to enjoy the luxury of leisure time. There had been many adjustments to a new lifestyle produced by this new social status. At first, George Curtis felt wonderful about being released from the daily grind of having to go to work. However, the availability of too much time caused confusion, restlessness, and a sense of loss. Joan, his wife of almost 45 years, also struggled with the changes in the household routine in having her husband home all the time.

As he struggled to find a new direction in his life, George sometimes seemed like a child who was underfoot and in the way. Joan had heard from other wives in similar situations that this was a good time to offer options and choices for how George could find new meaning in his life. Some men developed hobbies (that could be expensive), others were content to plan and go on trips, and others resolved this issue in creative ways. As they explored what both of them could do with their newfound time and opportunities, George and Joan finally found an outlet that afforded good use of their time and was helpful to others. They now volunteer at a shelter for homeless people. Joan puts her wonderful interpersonal skills to good use in working with the literacy program that helps people of all ages learn or improve their reading skills. George found his place in working with the life skills program where he could share his vast experience in financial management by just helping people learn about budgets, credit management, and even balancing a checking account.

Harry Scott, Lisa's father, had taken longer to recover from the grief of his first wife's death than he had anticipated. It seemed that he had become stuck in his grieving process. Lisa became concerned that her father was emotionally depressed to the point of watching him closely for signs of suicidal ideations. Fortunately, after much discussion and persuasion, Harry agreed to enter therapy to work on the issues related to his grief. At the same time, he also sought help in dealing with his heavy involvement with drinking that had occurred in conjunction with Susan's death. After much hard work, he recovered from both problems and was able to pick up and go on with his life.

In an odd twist, Harry met the woman who became his second wife at a support group for widows. Kim Scott was widowed a short time before Harry's wife died. Coincidentally, both of the deceased spouses had died of cancer. As Harry and Kim participated in the group sessions, they listened to others' descriptions of problems similar to their own and the various ways that people managed their emotions and reactions. They became friends through informally continuing those discussions over coffee following the group sessions. The time spent talking for hours helped to lay the foundation for a strong intimate relationship based on sharing, authenticity, and mutual care and respect.

The remarriage came as a surprise to some members of the family but not to others. Lisa was overjoyed that her father had found love again and that the person was someone who truly cared for her father. She missed the close relationship with her mother but knew she could not impose the same expectations on this new relationship with her stepmother. On the good advice of a friend, she has learned to allow this to develop and grow in its own way.

The grandchildren have had different reactions to their grandfather's remarriage. Joey resents having to spend time with his maternal grandparents and flatly refuses to be seen in public with them. Mary, on the other hand, finds her new stepgrandmother to be a great ally, someone she can approach to talk about things she wants to run by her parents after rehearsing with Kim.

Death seems to be a more common denominator in the lives of all four members of the first generation. Not only had they experienced the deaths of spouses but now there are more and more memorial services to attend for friends, colleagues, and coworkers who are dying in greater numbers as they grow older. Each is also experiencing health problems that range from arthritis to hypertension to cataracts to dry eye syndrome. Conversations often focus on these health issues and related economic problems such as medical insurance coverage, social security payments, Medicare management, and the increasing cost of long-term care insurance. Prescription costs are becoming unbearable, and much discussion centers on how the government needs to do something about this problem. Such conversation topics are a sore point with Butch at times and with the teenagers most of the time because they find these topics boring and mundane.

Harry and George have found a common ground of interest: genealogy. Both are learning how to trace their family's backgrounds and have shared much information with each other as they learn to navigate the Internet as

a research tool. All this interest in the past has sparked an interest for Kim Scott to begin assembling the information she needs to write her memoirs. Joan is also caught up in the enthusiasm of the others by learning how to quilt so that she could pass heirloom quality hand-me-downs to her son's family.

This generation is relatively content in their old age, fortunately. And they are well insulated from the pressures their children and grandchildren are experiencing as they navigate the troubled waters of the "adolescent experience," as Joan calls it. They are there for support if their family needs them but are enjoying the fruits of their earlier labors in raising children into adulthood.

### Parenting Reflection 10–3

Is Mary experiencing situations that you would label as typical for most adolescent girls? Can you identify what she is employing to cope with her situations? Are these healthy or unhealthy in nature? Is Joey experiencing development as a normal adolescent could be expected? How would you describe his attitude in general? How do you think his parents generally perceive him at this time? Can you predict how what was described here as the midlife transition experiences of Butch and Lisa will affect the first and third generations of the family? What could be a less desirable outcome of the midlife transition experience for either Butch or Lisa or both? What are some factors, experiences, or situations experienced by each member of this family's first generation that have had an impact on other family members?

## PARENT–YOUNG ADULT CHILD RELATIONS

By the time someone's child has reached the years we designate as early adulthood (18 to 45 years), the general perception is that one's work and involvement as a parent ceases. The child is no longer considered to be an immature person but someone who is responsible for their own welfare, capable of making their own decisions, and owning the consequences of their behavior

and actions. The parenting relationship continues but in an altered form. The transformation of the relationship between parent and child has actually been taking place all along in keeping pace with the developmental changes occurring in the child over time. The child has long depended on the parent for protection, nurturance, and training.

Upon the child's attaining adulthood, the overall goal of parenting should have been accomplished: helping a child to become a fully functioning, effective person in adulthood. However, this transformation is not simply accomplished when the child becomes legally mature at age 18. Dependencies continue in some modified form between the adult child and the parent. But the dependencies are not like those observed among infants and older children. Rather, these share similarities to the dependencies found to some degree in all intimate relationships found in families among adults. The transformation is to a relationship originally based on power and responsibility of the older person in guiding and directing the development of the younger person to one in which the participants share a more balanced field of interaction. The relationship between parents and adult children ideally becomes one that is more distinctly adult in nature.

Parenthood does not come to a complete halt, then, when children reach their 18th birthday or even later; however, the relationship between parents and young adults is modified once again in response to the new developmental needs of adult children. Most young adult children experience these first years of adulthood as a transition period while they complete the final aspects of individuation from their family systems. For example, many are not yet completely financially independent while they complete their college educations or even for some time afterwards. Others, although involved in a marriage relationship, have not been employed long enough to equip their homes, build a sound financial base that provides for their own children's needs, or establish themselves in occupations to ensure a sound financial future. Parents continue to provide support, often in the form of financial assistance, to young adult children during this period. In addition, they may provide other aspects of support when young adult children temporarily return to live in the family home and the structure is shifted to a renested family system.

Relations between parents and children during this stage can be strained and confusing. Parents sometimes are unsure of how to relate and communicate with children who are quickly becoming independent adults but who are still dependent in many respects. They continue to feel responsible for giving advice to their children but may feel unprepared and ill-equipped to do so in ways that are truly helpful. Adult children probably feel as many conflicting emotions as their parents do in this regard. On the one hand, they may desire to confide in parents, but on the other, they may feel resentful of the intrusive and judgmental nature of parental advice.

## Prolonged Dependencies Between Parents and Young Adults

Prolonged dependency can take place in a relationship between parents and children that is unhealthy when children become young adults. Parents can maintain this state when adult children are supported financially and emotionally far beyond the time when such ties are normally severed and adult children fully individuate. Sometimes situations beyond the control of the family system maintain these ties. For example, higher education is extremely costly today, and young adults frequently seek assistance from parents to meet financial obligations. But other situations can also cause prolonged dependency, such as overparenting or prolonged investment in the aspects of parenting that promote children's dependencies.

Some parents foster extended dependency of adult children, for example, when they have intensely continued to be overinvolved in their children's lives. They may have given children too many material possessions and not enough limits. They may not have fostered analytical and decision-making skills or used a parenting style that encouraged and facilitated individuation during adolescence and early adulthood (Gordon, 2004). As a result, the adult child fails to individuate successfully from the family system, largely because dependency prolongs and even thwarts the normal individuation process. The usual, anticipated outcome of individuation is a redefined relationship between parents and adult children that is more adult in nature.

**How Do Parents Promote Prolonged Dependency of Adult Children?**   Most parents want their children to grow up and achieve an independent existence. Essentially, most healthy parents want their child rearing responsibilities to end at some point. Then why do some parents continue to create situations where they remain heavily and actively involved in a caregiving role? The answers are complex, just as the individuals involved are complex. However, several factors emerge as possible answers (Arnett, 2003; Ifejika, 2003).

Parents ideally shift away from authoritarian styles to those that are more democratic and equalitarian as children grow older. This shift occurs in response to the changing developmental nature of children as they grow and mature. Equalitarian parenting styles support a child's individuation process by shifting the source of social power to a more balanced position between parent and child. They recognize a child's more mature status and his or her ability to solve personal problems, learn from mistakes, and make his or her own way in the world. By reacting in ways that are authoritarian, overprotective, or disinterested, parents promote prolonged dependency in their adult children.

**How Do Adult Children Promote Their Prolonged Dependency on Parents?**    Prolonged dependency is not created and maintained by parents alone. A child also plays a part by maintaining a dependency role longer than is developmentally appropriate. Contributions stemming from the adult child that can promote abnormally prolonged dependence on parental involvement include factors such as: (1) an abnormal fear of assuming responsibility for one's own life and decisions, (2) addictions and substance abuse, (3) an abnormal fear of failure in the adult world, or (4) lack of motivation to leave the comforts of the parental home (Arnett, 2003; Ifejika, 2003; van Poppel, Oris, & Lee, 2004).

• • • • • • • • • • • • • • • • • • • • • • • • • • • • •

### Parenting Reflection 10–5

What happens when a family system does not accept or support the efforts of young adults to individuate completely from the system? What are short- and long-term effects of such prolonged dependence between family members?

• • • • • • • • • • • • • • • • • • • • • • • • • • • • •

**What Can Be Done to Normalize Parent-Adult Child Relations?**    Parents often realize that they are partially responsible for creating the dependency of adult children. Some understand what has happened when children do not progress in mastering appropriate developmental tasks for their age. Others become aware when adult children return home and do not move on with their lives after an extended period of time. Therapists suggest a number of ways that parents can help to remedy their role configuration in fostering this unhealthy situation so that all family members can move forward developmentally. For example, an obvious solution is to stop playing the role of a caretaker parent in enabling an adult child's lack of developmental progress. Parents can let go of the ways in which they have usually responded to children's dependency needs. For exam-

ple, boundaries are adapted within the relationship to reflect less involvement in the affairs of adult children. Another solution is to make a conscious and demonstrable change toward a more equalitarian stance in relating to adult children. When prolonged dependencies occur as part of improper or poor parenting skills, parents can change the relationship with their adult children by changing themselves (Adams, 2004).

However, parents sometimes wish to continue promoting their child's dependency, while an adult child wishes to individuate more fully. Often changes are initiated in the parent-child relationship when children become aware that they are, indeed, *adult children* of dysfunctional families (Ramey, 2004). This term comes from contemporary psychotherapy; it describes individuals who have experienced a stifling of their healthy emotional developmental progress at some point in their developmental past. This stifling occurs when children grow up in family systems where they are affected by physical, emotional, or sexual abuse; parental alcoholism or drug abuse; or ineffective and unhealthy parenting styles. Many people discover that they are adult children when they try to recover from various addictions manifested in early adulthood. These range from addictions to substances, such as food or drugs, to addictions to people or relationships.

When young adults struggle for individuation from dysfunctional parents and family systems, they can find assistance in psychotherapy, support groups, and 12-step programs. In this case, the adult child, not the parent, struggles to let go of dependencies and inappropriate patterns of interactions, but the struggle can be immensely difficult for everyone concerned.

Adult children make aggressive attempts to individuate from unhealthy parents as a means of resuming healthy developmental progress. The parents, however, often resist this significant change in their relationship. At this point, it is often best to have the assistance of a competent therapist. When one person in an unhealthy family system attempts to produce change, the system often reacts to the loss of equilibrium by experiencing even more chaos.

While the adult child who is attempting to change the nature of the relationship with their parent knows that freedom comes only from acting differently, the unhealthy family system abhors change. Parents who have a toxic relationship with their adult children can be expected to resist the children's attempts to individuate. However, many individuals recovering as adult children are parents themselves, and they do not wish to perpetuate unhealthy parenting patterns with their own children. By fully individuating from an unhealthy family system, these courageous individuals pursue a healthy developmental path toward their own full potential as human beings and the potential of their children (Clarke & Dawson, 1998).

## Functioning as a Renested Family System

Families in which children have become adults are characterized by the changes in status and roles of all family members. Those produced by the emancipation of the children can cause conflicts, adjustment problems, and even emotional crises for family systems. Launching their children into the adult world essentially may complete the parents' development of a sense of generativity. However, because of various social and economic circumstances today, some parents find that it takes many years to launch children successfully and completely into adult independence and autonomy.

Transitions of adult children into their own lifestyles do not happen as smoothly as research or textbooks describe (Secunda, 2004). Many young adult children, mostly males, return to their parents' homes to live temporarily. Usually this is a limited arrangement because the adult children become unemployed, seek retraining, change career objectives, or divorce.

The kind of family structure experienced during childhood and adolescence may have a bearing on when adolescents and young adults launch themselves away from their families of origin (Goldschneider & Goldschneider, 1998). The family structure factor can also influence their return into the family of origin at later times. Growing up in nontraditional family settings, such as stepfamilies, decreases the likelihood of an adolescent's enrollment into a program of higher education, for example, and increases the likelihood of leaving the family of origin early to become married or to attain full individuation. Under such circumstances, researchers find that there is also a lessened likelihood of returning to the family of origin after becoming individuated.

Undoubtedly, everyone involved in this type of family structure is likely to have mixed feelings about the situation (Secunda, 2004). On the one hand, parents understand the need to be supportive of their adult child and wish to be as helpful as possible. On the other hand, parents may be understandably resentful of the new demands on resources, time, and energy required in having an additional person or persons in their daily lives. The adult child may also harbor mixed feelings. He or she may appreciate what the parents are providing in a time of need and at the same time resent conflicts that can arise in the resumption of old interaction patterns between parent and child.

Both children and parents resent the dependency on parents and view this period as developmentally off-time. Many problems result from parents who continue to act intrusively in the lives of children who are used to independent functioning. For example, families describe conflicts about the hours adult children keep, the way they maintain their personal space, and lifestyle choices such as sexual behavior.

Researchers have not studied problems in these families adequately enough to know exactly how these conflicts are resolved. Most likely, they are not resolved unless the adult children can resist falling into old dependency patterns and parents can resist acting as caregivers. During renesting, both parents and adult children may need to renegotiate the rules and patterns that govern their relationship.

••••••••••••••••••••••••••••••••••••••••

### Parenting Reflection 10–6

Are teenagers and young adults different today than they were 20 or 30 years ago? What has changed and what has remained fairly constant about the nature of young people over the years?

••••••••••••••••••••••••••••••••••••••••

## GRANDPARENTING

At some point in time, it is likely that many parents will become grandparents when their children have become adults. The stereotypical image of grandparents is that of a kindly middle-aged or elderly person in a rocking chair dispensing advice and wisdom to one and all. Today, it is not unusual for someone in their late 30s or early 40s to be a grandparent. Rather than taking a sedentary approach to life, today's grandparent most likely is physically active, still employed, and at times providing full-time care for grandchildren (Kornhaber, 2002).

Today's grandparents and their activities as a grandparent are different from that of previous generations. First, more people are grandparents, and it is estimated that more than 90 percent of older people are great-grandparents (Kornhaber, 2002). When considering the greater length of life expectancy, it is more likely that children today will have the opportunity to know and have a relationship with both sets of grandparents. Since about 90 percent of Americans who are 65 years of age or older are great-grandparents, it is also more likely that today's children will have experiences involving this grandparent than previous generations.

Second, the high divorce rate in contemporary society has changed the nature of grandparents' relationships with grandchildren from what perhaps was observed in the past. The legal status of grandparents is a nebulous issue, and few states have enacted statutes that outline grandparental rights with regard to visitation with grandchildren (Taylor, 2001).

Third, many grandparents take an active role in raising and providing care for grandchildren (Fields, 2003). A substantial increase has occurred in the numbers of households headed by grandparents who provide the primary caregiving for grandchildren whether the children's parents are present or absent. This type of family was discussed in greater detail in Chapter 2.

Although some grandparents are not especially involved with grandchildren and their role is downplayed in family life, other grandparents make important contributions to family life and have significant influence on family systems. These include: (1) accepting behaviors and traits of grandchildren that adult parents are not able to tolerate; (2) providing nurturance for grandchildren that adult parents may not be able to provide; (3) providing instruction for grandchildren in values, ethics, and morals; (4) providing backup support for parents in raising grandchildren; (5) providing parents with options for solving interaction problems and conflicts with grandchildren; and (6) acting as an equalizer to provide balance within a family system (Kornhaber, 2003; Kropf & Burnette, 2003; Mueller & Elder, 2003).

## The Grandparent Role

While greater numbers of grandparents may be found in families today, the role continues to lack clear definitions and boundaries for outlining how someone is to act in this capacity. Grandparents do not readily know what is expected of them nor how they are to interact with grandchildren, and adult children and grandchildren are often equally unsure about these interactions.

It is more appropriate, perhaps, to view a person's grandparent role as having a variety of aspects, often based on the nature of the relationship with each particular grandchild (Mueller & Elder, 2003; Reynolds, Wright, & Beale, 2003). When viewed from this perspective, a grandparent role does not have a monolithic definition but one that is composed of different aspects. The relationships between grandparents and grandchildren vary in many respects. For example, one grandchild may be perceived as being special to the grandparent in certain ways while another may be viewed as an irritant and vexsome. Undoubtedly, the nature and quality of the relationship as well as how the grandparent conducts his or her interactions with a grandchild is mediated on such perceptions.

It is not clear how people make the transition into this role (Kornhaber, 2003). For many, the transition begins when they learn of the pregnancy of the adult child carrying the potential first grandchild. The older adult parents fantasize about what they will experience as grandparents. Because this is a first-time experience, the first grandchild often takes a special place in the lives of grandparents. The transition experience appears to vary from person to person, however. Some find this difficult, especially if becoming a grandparent is perceived as being developmentally off-time rather than on-time (Kopera-Frye, Wiscott, & Begovic, 2003).

Childhood experiences with grandparents appear to influence the current involvement of men and women with their own grandchildren (Hayslip, 2003). Apparently, people pattern their grandparenting role and behavior based on the models they observed as children.

Although there is general ambiguity about the grandparent role, it appears that several prominent aspects or components can be found in this role. (1) Grandparents may act as the family "watchdog" in providing support to adult children and grandchildren when needed and in ameliorating the negative impacts of serious family problems of adult children, such as drug abuse, divorce, or chronic emotional or physical illness. (2) Grandparents may provide nurturance to all family members, especially unconditional love that may not be available from other adults in a family. (3) Grandparents serve as the family historians in acting as the bridge between the past and the present that aids in developing a sense of family and family identity. (4) Grandparents may provide companionship for grandchildren in shared social activities that promote close emotional attachment.

---

**Focus On 10–2**

## Grandparenting Styles

| *Style* | *Traits* |
|---|---|
| Surrogate Parent | Primary caregiving; active involvement in child rearing |
| Remote | Infrequent contact with grandchildren; makes appearances on special holidays and events |
| Fun Seeker | Maintains recreational relationship focusing on leisure activities with grandchildren |
| Reservoir of Family Wisdom | Maintains strict boundaries based on patriarchal authority; passes on family legends, folklore, and information |
| Formal | Maintains stereotypical grandparent role; promotes distinct boundary between parental and grandparent role |

*Source:* Adapted from Cherlin, A. J., & Furstenberg, F. F. (1986). *The new American grandparent.* New York: Basic Books; McCready, W. (1985). Styles of grandparenting among white ethnics. In V. Bengston & J. Robertson (Eds), *Grandparenthood* (pp. 49–60). Beverly Hills, CA: Sage.

---

There appear to be at least four to five distinct grandparenting styles that typically change as grandchildren grow older. This evolution or modification of grandparenting styles that changes in tandem with grandchildren's development reflects similar changes in parenting styles that occur as children experience developmental changes. These styles are outlined in Focus On 10–2.

Grandparenting styles may be mediated by a variety of factors (Cherlin & Furstenberg, 1986; Kornhaber, 2002). First, gender may temper how someone approaches his or her grandparenting role. Women may be more actively involved with grandchildren than men because of their socialization and past experiences in parenting children. Grandfathers, for example, may emphasize interactions relating to tasks outside the family with grandchildren, while grandmothers may emphasize issues relating to interpersonal dynamics within the family.

Second, physical proximity is an important factor that mediates how the grandparent-grandchild relationship will be shaped and how it will unfold. The magnitude of physical distance between grandparents and grandchildren will frequently determine how involved the older adult is with grandchildren and how interactions will occur. Third, ethnic group influences grandparenting style. For example, a large majority of older Latinos report the desire to live in the same neighborhoods with adult children and grandchildren. In addi-

tion, grandparents who are heads of households where they raise grandchildren are likely to be members of ethnic minorities (Fields, 2003).

## Stepgrandparenting

Finally, divorce of adult children as well as that of grandparents themselves can temper how the grandparent-grandchild relationship will be conducted (Taylor, 2001). When the grandparents themselves divorce after years of marriage, some may diminish their involvement with grandchildren because of the circumstances surrounding their divorce. When adult children divorce, a different situation is created that leaves many grandparents uncertain as to their rights for access to grandchildren. Since mothers typically are awarded custody of children following divorce, the relationship between paternal grandparents and grandchildren is often weakened more in comparison with that between maternal grandparents and grandchildren.

Divorce of adult children can sometimes strengthen the relationship and involvement of grandparents and grandchildren. In this regard, grandparents assume the major caretaking responsibilities for raising grandchildren, often in the absence of the children's parents. These circumstances present unique challenges for both grandparents and grandchildren (Kopera-Frye, Wiscott, & Begovec, 2003; Reynolds, Wright, & Beale, 2003). For example, grandparents may not be aware of how to promote the educational progress of grandchildren in their school performance nor what is important for children to accomplish.

Grandchildren may be uncertain of the role of their parent in their lives when their grandparent has assumed the major responsibilities for providing nurturance and structure. These arrangements typically occur when some type of serious family problem affects the adult child. Quality of life issues become prominent due to the financial problems that typically affect older adults who may be on fixed incomes or dependent on public assistance for their support.

● ● ● ● ● ● ● ● ● ● ● ● ● ● ● ● ● ● ● ● ● ● ● ● ● ● ● ●

### Parenting Reflection 10–7

What kinds of support can be provided to assist coresident grandparents to provide appropriate and effective caregiving for their grandchildren?

● ● ● ● ● ● ● ● ● ● ● ● ● ● ● ● ● ● ● ● ● ● ● ● ● ● ● ●

Stepgrandparenting issues have received very little attention from researchers. If grandparent roles are nebulous in many respects, this is particularly the case for stepgrandparents. Because stepgrandchildren are usually older when remarriages of adult child parents occur, there may be little opportunity for the stepgrandparent-stepgrandchild relationship to develop. However, because both parties may have had experiences with this relationship prior to parental divorce, it is likely that both wish to take advantage of opportunities for the new relationship to develop.

## CARING FOR AGING PARENTS

It is highly likely that at some point in the lives of adult children that they will be called upon to provide care for an elderly parent. The American population is increasingly larger in the numbers of elderly individuals as well as in the longer life expectancies that most can experience (U.S. Bureau of the Census, 2003). Not all families desire nor can they afford to purchase caregiving services for elderly members as this is frequently seen as a responsibility of children to provide for aging parents (Connor, 2000).

Researchers who have studied parent-child relationships between adult children caregivers and elderly parents have found these observations:

■ Because more generations of families live longer than ever before, family relationships are more numerous and complex as younger members maintain ties with elderly parents, grandparents, great-grandparents, and even older relatives (Crimmins, 2001).
■ A serious consequence of increased life expectancy is that more people live longer with more serious health problems (Crimmins, 2001).
■ More adult children provide care for elderly parents from ethnic minority than white families (Smith, 2003).
■ The vast majority of adult children caregivers are women (Cancian & Oliker, 2000).
■ While many adult child caregivers are young, most are likely to be middle-aged, married, parents themselves, and work full-time (Himes, 2001).

Because there is the expectation that elderly parents will be cared for by children or even grandchildren, professionals refer to this provision of emotional support, services, and financial assistance as *eldercare* (Ingersoll-Dayton, Neal, & Hammer, 2001). There is a wide range of activities covered by this type of family work such as making phone calls, assisting with personal hygiene, chauffering for errands and appointments, housekeeping tasks, meal preparation and purchasing food, and paying bills. As such, adult child caregivers can expect to perform informal caregiving for an estimated 18 hours weekly or more depending on the needs of the elderly parent (Connor, 2000). When this type of caregiving is not feasible, adult children often resort to arranging for paid service providers to meet the needs of their parent.

Many adult child caregivers rely on siblings to help with the responsibilities they are faced with in caring for their aging parent. However, this is not always possible nor are some siblings reliable in providing assistance, making the care burden especially heavy for the principal adult child provider.

Elderly parent-adult child provider relations often follow a caregiving trajectory (Cancian & Oliker, 2000; Cicirelli, 2000). This begins with concern for the welfare of an elderly parent and expressing this to siblings and others. This progresses to giving advice to the elderly parent on conducting their affairs, for example, "Be sure to remember to take your medicine." Then, the adult child caregiver assumes greater responsibilities by providing services needed by the elderly parent while often consulting with family members and professionals in making decisions.

It is at this point, if not already occurred, that conflicts surface between the elderly parent and adult child provider. The elderly parent may become resentful of lost power and control over their life and activities and feel threatened by loss of independence. They may also resist deferring to the adult child provider's decisions causing increasing stress and tension within the relationship.

Fueling the problems within the already strained parent-child relationship is the significant role reversal that takes place as the adult child provider assumes greater responsibilities out of necessity in caring for an elderly parent who is likely to have one or more chronic illnesses or disabilities. When these points are reached, the adult child caregiver progresses more swiftly toward **burnout** resulting in poor quality of caregiving. This is especially the case when the adult child provider works full-time, tries to maintain a marriage relationship, seeks to conduct their own parent-child relationships and grandparent-grandchild relationships, and has little assistance from siblings or spouse. It is not unusual that caregiver stress of this magnitude can lead to elder abuse that is emotional, physical, and/or verbal in nature (Connor, 2000).

Several possibilities may help to alleviate situations that can prevent or minimize caregiver burnout. These might include: (1) encouraging men to become as responsible as women in providing eldercare, (2) involving wider community supports such as eldercare and respite programs, (3) more government funding support for programs that educate as well as provide services about eldercare, and (4) making this type of family work more financially rewarding through tax credits and other incentives (Cancian & Oliker, 2000).

*Focus Point.*   Family systems enter a new stage when the oldest child enters early adulthood. Parenting focuses on assisting adult children to individuate fully and to maintain a home base while this process is taking place. Parents in healthy family systems shift to a more equalitarian interaction style with adult children, which supports the efforts of adult children to emancipate completely into adult lifestyles.

Grandparenting roles are unclear for the most part although researchers have identified distinct aspects that make up the role. Grandparenting styles also have been identified and appear to be modified by several different factors, such as gender, ethnic identity, and geographic closeness. Divorce of grandparents or of adult children can also significantly alter the nature and conduct of this relationship.

Many adult children can expect to provide care for an aging parent, especially those having chronic illnesses or disabilities. A variety of characteristics define the nature of parent-child relations under these circumstances. The relationship can become strained and contribute to caregiver burnout.

## POINTS TO CONSIDER

### Parenting Adolescents

- Parenting adolescents presents new and different challenges that have not been encountered previously in child rearing. Stereotypes of teenagers are misleading in what most parents can expect during this period of a child's life. One of the more difficult challenges of parenting adolescents is the fine line parents walk between being supportive of a teen's efforts to individuate while maintaining certain limits and boundaries for appropriate behavior.
- Parenting styles and behaviors must adapt once again to meet the needs of a different child. And once again, the adaptation often is not initiated by the parents but rather by adolescent children who may demand to be treated differently now that they are older.
- The personal developmental tasks of adolescents initiate a rewriting of the rules and patterns that govern the conduct of parent-child relations. The relationship between parents and adolescents has two central objectives: to promote greater individuation and achievement of adolescent self-regulation and to develop an equalization of power within this subsystem in a family system. If successful, such redefinition can preserve the effective functioning of a family system. Essentially, the challenge facing most parents of adolescents is learning that they must relinquish control over their child for development to take place appropriately.
- Parents provide assistance in a child's development of a sense of personal identity as opposed to role confusion. This basic self-identity involves recognition that the self-concept is composed of many different but related aspects that make up the total personality.

- Teenagers are concerned about individuating, or establishing independence from the controls and influence of parents and other adults. Individuation is a healthy aspect of personal identity development at this time of the life span. Adolescents' emancipation is established in a variety of ways that can be both positive and negative. Positive demonstrations include working in part-time jobs, choosing their own friends, and showing responsibility in a number of ways. Less positive demonstrations include various acting-out behaviors such as substance abuse.
- Adjusting to the physical changes associated with puberty is a major developmental task of adolescence. Teens need assistance in understanding the physical, social, and psychological changes that take place. They may need particular assistance with sexual orientation issues. Parents also usually recognize the importance of education about sexual issues at this time of life. Teenagers especially need parental guidance in learning sexual decision-making skills considered appropriate by their family.
- A variety of issues relate to health and safety during adolescence. Some are associated with negative acting-out behaviors such as substance abuse, while others such as eating disorders often reflect significant problems taking place in the family system. Many teens are at risk of committing suicide, particularly if there are sexual orientation issues in question. Adolescents also are at greater risk to be the victims of serious violent crimes and of contracting sexually transmitted diseases.
- A systemic family development snapshot reveals examples of the stressors that may affect the different generations of a family system as well as the ways that members cope with these in healthy as well as unhealthy ways.

### Parent-Young Adult Relations

- The relationship between parents and adult children is different than those experienced previously. The relationship is more mature in nature, reflecting the new developmental status of the young adult. The individuation process usually is completed at some point in early adulthood, and parents support this process in a number of ways. Difficulties sometimes occur when either parents, adult children, or both experience problems in releasing their dependencies on one another.
- Changes also can take place in the family form as the renested family structure may emerge periodically to meet the needs of adult children. Renesting often takes place during times of personal crisis for the young adult child that relates to finances or changes in marital status.
- Many parents assume a grandparenting role during this time when their adult children become parents themselves. Grandparents typically evolve and custom-design the style they wish to conduct in this role.
- Adult children often provide care for elderly parents. These parent-child relationships have certain characteristics, such as more caregivers are from ethnic minority than white families and more are middle-aged women. The type of care provided is referred to as eldercare and is largely informal in nature but highly demanding of the caregiver's time and energies. While many providers rely on siblings and spouses for assistance, this may not always be available. The relationship between adult child providers and parents usually becomes strained over time. As stresses increase for the provider, the likelihood of burnout increases which can lead to elder abuse. Suggestions have been made for ways to help alleviate or prevent caregiver burnout.

# PART III

# Challenges for Contemporary Parents and Children

A commonly held belief is that the majority of families in the United States today meet the traditional notions of family form and composition. In this framework, the ideal family is depicted as having two opposite-sex adults, in which the man is the major provider and the woman is the housewife-mother, and their children. This belief in the prevalence of such a family form is misleading; in reality, less than 11 percent of all families in the United States today fit this form (U.S. Bureau of the Census, 2003). As noted in Chapter 2, diversity in form and structure is the norm among contemporary American families.

Today, the pluralistic context in which people define their families unseats the concept of a "typical" family. Over the past 50 years significant changes in many aspects of American society have influenced the kinds of families that have become more commonplace. These changes include the products of a high divorce rate resulting in increasing numbers of binuclear families. A related change has been the increasing numbers of remarriages, resulting in parallel increases in stepfamilies with their own unique challenges and issues. Adolescent pregnancies that are carried to term continue to take place in spite of declines in the numbers of teen pregnancies. Many adolescent girls and their families have chosen to retain custody of these children, creating unique parent-child relationship issues. Likewise, gay and lesbian couples and families are becoming more visible throughout American society. These families are currently in the spotlight politically and socially as our society debates the pros and cons of same-gender marriage.

Another common misconception about American families implies that people (and families) that differ from the perceived norm are unhealthy and dysfunctional. This myth holds that these differences are responsible for producing an environment in which children grow up to be unhealthy in their emotional, social, and psychological development. These notions are examined in the chapters of Part III as we discuss those family situations that appear to create differences among family systems in comparison with those that are more traditional in nature.

Many families in the United States, however, experience problems and situations that affect their ability to function in healthy ways. Effective parenting may be difficult to achieve due to a number of factors operating against this optimal goal. Some parents do not perform well in this capacity and may abuse their children. In extreme circumstances, parental rights may be temporarily or permanently suspended and children removed from their parental homes. When this occurs, the state assumes legal guardianship and children are placed into the foster care system where they may become adopted by another family. In the final chapter of the text, we examine those situations in which parents abuse their children physically, sexually, and/or emotionally. This serious parental behavior harms all family members and accounts for the placement of the majority of children into the U.S. foster care system.

# CHAPTER 11

# Parenting in Single-Parent Family Systems

## Focus Questions

■ ■ ■ ■ ■ ■ ■ ■ ■ ■

1. What major factors are responsible for creating single-parent family systems?
2. How does divorce affect parents as individuals and as caregivers?
3. How are children affected by parental divorce?
4. What important issues relate to child custody decisions?
5. What are the characteristics of a single-parent family headed by a woman and that headed by a man? How is parenting conducted in each of these family systems?
6. What major adjustment issues are encountered in single-parent families? What kinds of support are available to these families?
7. What stressors and coping mechanisms are revealed by a systemic family development snapshot of a single-parent family?

■ ■ ■ ■ ■ ■ ■ ■ ■ ■

Many people believe that the dominant family form in the United States today consists of an adult man who acts as the main provider, a woman who ideally is only a housewife and mother, and their several children. This kind of family is commonly depicted as the best and most acceptable type and is therefore frequently modeled on television programs and in other media. Over the years, people with traditional views of family life have promoted the belief that this ideal family is the only kind that is healthy and strong and least dysfunctional. It is touted as the best milieu in which to raise children.

Families that represent the traditional image have increasingly become a minority in the United States within the past 30 to 40 years (Figure 11–1). Today, these families constitute a distinct minority, accounting for only 11 percent of all families in the United States in 2002 (U.S. Bureau of the Census, 2003). Some observers of American family life attribute this decline to the demise of family values in society, values that are believed to promote the maintenance of the traditional type of family system. The increasing rate of divorce over the years parallels the increasing number of *binuclear* (a term seldom used by family sociologists) or single-parent families that are created when this alleged breakdown in values occurs (U.S. Bureau of the Census, 2003). However, divorce alone

**FIGURE 11–1.** Single-parent family systems have become a more common family form in the United States. Most of these are headed by women rather than men because women usually are awarded custody of children.

does not exclusively account for the diversity that is a global characteristic—the norm—of family systems in contemporary American society. Many adults who divorce also remarry, which creates in turn a new family system that resembles other families but is unique in its functioning and structure. These families are called *blended families* or stepfamilies. Other family systems are also formed in different ways and have different structures.

Being a single parent is not necessarily devastating for either adults or children. However, divorce is a stressful experience that can be uncomfortable for the family system because old familiar patterns are dismantled by the separation of the adults. Family systems theory describes divorce as an event that produces disruption in a family system. In place of the chaos that emerges when a marriage is dissolved, a new family form evolves known as a **single-parent family,** which is based on the former family system but has significant modifications. Essentially, the new family form reflects the children's membership in two separate and distinct households or families, one headed by the father and the other by the mother. Basically, these are separate one-parent households. Increasingly, both parents hold joint custody of the children. One usually is designated as the

physical custodian, meaning that the children reside the majority of time in this parent's household.

Researchers continue to explore issues that relate to the adjustment of individuals in the new single-parent family system following divorce (Knox & Liggett, 2000). New patterns, rules, roles, and modifications to the parent-child subsystem restore equilibrium and balance and allow the system to function. Researchers find that several factors influence healthy adjustment and that unhealthy dysfunction can also take place in certain circumstances.

This next section examines the myriad effects of family life on single-parent family systems, including a number of adjustments by both adults and children in adopting a new lifestyle and interaction patterns. For many individuals, these adjustments may be relatively temporary since the majority of divorced adults eventually remarry.

## DIVORCE, SINGLE-PARENT FAMILIES, AND PARENT-CHILD RELATIONS

Single-parent family systems are one of the more common types of families in the United States today. These are composed of an adult male or female parent and one

Percent

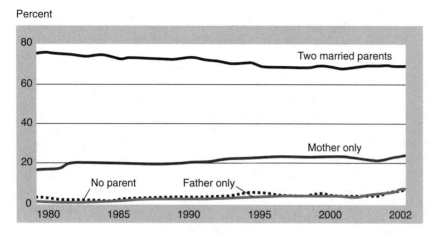

**FIGURE 11–2.** Percentage of children 18 years of age or younger by presence of married parents in household between 1980 and 2002.

*Source:* Federal Interagency Forum on Child and Family Statistics. (2003). *America's children: Key national indicators of well-being: 2003.* Washington, DC: U.S. Government Printing Office.

or more children under 18 years of age who reside in separate households following divorce. This family type is increasing at the fastest rate of all family forms (see Figure 11–2). In 1970, approximately 3.8 million families were headed by a single parent. By 2000, this number had increased to almost 16 million (Fields & Casper, 2001). One-parent families in the United States accounted for about 28 percent of all family types with children according to the latest data collected by the Census Bureau (U.S. Bureau of the Census, 2002). Although almost three-fourths of all single parents are white, this type of family occurs more prevalently among African Americans as a group (U.S. Bureau of the Census, 2003). One-parent families accounted for about 62 percent of all African American families as compared with 27 percent of all white families. Among Latinos, single-parent families accounted for about 36 percent of all family types.

A single-parent family system can be created in several ways: (1) divorce, desertion, or separation of the adults; (2) death of an adult; or (3) giving birth to a child out of wedlock. Of these reasons, divorce is the most common. The federal agency charged with collecting data on divorce ceased doing so in 1996, but it is still possible to gauge the prevalence of divorce by the living arrangements reported for children living in the United States. In 2002, for example, about 72 percent of all children in the United States lived with both biological parents as compared to 28 percent who lived with either a single-parent mother or father (Fields, 2003). The majority of single-parent families are those in which women have sole custody or are the physical custodian of chil-

dren, although there are significant increases in the numbers of such families where men are the head of households. Many of these families include an unmarried adult partner of the parent (Fields & Casper, 2001). An exception to this are those women who are financially independent who become single parents by choice (Mannis, 1999).

Because our society has promoted the belief that parenting is conducted best by families with two adults, much concern has been expressed about the effects of divorce and the experiences of growing up as a child in a single-parent family system. Family and child development researchers have been aware that differences may exist in families with one adult as compared to those with two adults. These differences are observed in a number of areas, such as interaction patterns, communication styles, parenting styles, and behavior problems among children (Knox & Liggett, 2000). As may be expected, the principal difficulties in single-parent family systems are traced in part to the lack of sufficient people to adequately perform the roles needed in an efficient family life.

This factor, however, does not disrupt family system functioning in dysfunctional ways. Furthermore, most research findings suggest that while similarities exist in single-parent families headed by women and those headed by men, the sex of the parent is an important factor in determining the type of family life experience in each family system.

Each family system that experiences the loss of one adult's presence through divorce adapts in distinct ways in responding to this stressful change. Divorce, in particular, forces such responses in the new single-parent

**Parenting FAQs 11–1**

I have some questions about divorce. What if my partner doesn't agree to this? How is child support determined? What happens if my partner doesn't obey the terms of our divorce agreement?

**A:**  These are good questions that most people don't know to think about before divorcing. First, in most states that have no-fault divorce laws, all it takes is for one person to declare legally that the marriage is irretrievably broken and the divorce proceedings may begin. You will need to consult a lawyer for legal advice on how to begin this process. Second, many states now have a formula by which child support is determined. Usually, a couple's gross annual income is the basis of the formula used to determine how much each adult will contribute to child support. In some states, this formula may include how health insurance, child-care, and/or educational expenses are shared by each adult, for example. Third, let's suppose your divorce agreement includes stipulations about child support and visitation. The agreement is that children are picked up at a designated time on Friday and returned by a designated time on Sunday. However, if your ex-partner habitually disregards those scheduled times or is not paying the amount of child support ordered by the court and is habitually late, you have recourse to these actions. You can return to court for legal redress of your complaints of the violations to the divorce agreement, and/or you can call upon the county sheriff's office for assistance in having the terms of your agreement enforced. Sometimes, mediation is helpful in such situations as well.

family system. Because this is the primary cause of its creation, the divorce process involves various aspects of adaptation (Kaslow, 2000). Divorce is one of the most difficult processes a family system can experience. It has short- and long-term effects on both the original first-marriage family system and on others that follow such as the single-parent family and the stepfamily created upon remarriage. In keeping with the prediction from family systems theory, everyone in a family system, adults and children, is affected to some degree and in various ways by the divorce.

In the case of the formation of two single-parent family systems following divorce, each family must reconstruct new boundaries and patterns (rules, communication styles, and roles) by adapting to the crisis of divorce. All in the family are affected to some degree but in different ways by the myriad changes resulting from parental divorce. But each family, to survive and adapt successfully to these changes, does so to maintain homeostasis and to avoid further confusion, disorganization, and chaos.

● ● ● ● ● ● ● ● ● ● ● ● ● ● ● ● ● ● ● ● ● ● ● ● ●

### Parenting Reflection 11–1

Are there any advantages or benefits in single parenthood as compared with married partnership?

● ● ● ● ● ● ● ● ● ● ● ● ● ● ● ● ● ● ● ● ● ● ● ● ●

## Effects of Divorce on Adults

Family systems theory predicts that all members of a family system are affected when some type of change takes place in just one person. Divorce dissolves the effective functioning of the committed relationship between the adult partners. In turn, it disrupts the functioning of the parent-child relationship as well as the functioning of the entire family system (Benedek & Brown, 2004). Divorce has a number of effects on both the adults and children in a family system. For example, one cultural belief holds that children are affected adversely because they are deprived of a "normal" two-parent family experience, because their quality of life declines due to difficult financial situations, and because they are more psychologically vulnerable to the disruptions produced by parental divorce. Researchers also acknowledge that the stressfulness of divorce affects adults as well. They consider divorce to be the second most stressful life event an adult can experience, exceeded only by death of a spouse in its negative effects on personal functioning (Kaslow, 2000). Adults experience a variety of reactions when divorce is pursued as a solution to marital difficulties (see Focus On 11–1) (Knox & Leggett, 2000). Other changes and adaptations may be implemented to restore homeostasis to a single-parent family system as an evolved family form (Kaslow, 2000).

---

**Focus On 11–1**

## Some Adult Reactions to Divorce

**Psychological**

- Sense of personal failure
- Depression and feelings of alienation
- Sense of relief
- Opportunities for personal growth

**Social**

- Changes in lifestyle
- New social networks
- Changes in parent-child relationship

**Financial**

- Different quality of life
- New place of residence
- New or altered employment

*Source:* Adapted from Benokraitis, N. V. (2002). *Marriage and families: Changes, choices, and constraints* (4th ed.). Upper Saddle River, NJ: Prentice Hall.

---

Because divorce affects all family members, it is important for adults to interpret what is happening to children so that they can understand the changes taking place in their family of origin, which include the following four areas:

1. *Family metacognition.* The system acknowledges that divorce is imminent and that adults no longer share similar feelings of love and attachment. It also acknowledges other feelings of adults and children, such as sadness and even hate.

2. *Physical separation.* Separation of the adults has highly disruptive effects on the family system by dismantling the boundaries, rules, behavior patterns, and roles that have made the system operate effectively. Removing the father's presence from the family system (which commonly occurs) can leave children with feelings of abandonment. In general, divorced fathers are more emotionally depressed than divorced mothers (Knox & Leggett, 2000).

3. *Family system reorganization.* Divorced adults forge a new relationship with different rules, roles, and interaction patterns. Their ability to resolve issues in healthy ways determines if the new single-parent family system will be reorganized in a func-

tional or dysfunctional manner. The new single-parent family system also adapts by evolving new rules, roles, and interaction patterns that respond to new living conditions.

4. *Family redefinitions.* As the new single-parent family system takes form and assumes higher degrees of effective functioning, the system is perceived differently by the members and by the noncustodial parent. The noncustodial parent also reorganizes interaction patterns, boundaries, and rules that govern how he or she relates to the single-parent family system and its members. Therefore, children often learn two sets of patterns because they are now members of two single-parent family systems composed of the custodial parent system and the noncustodial parent system.

## Parenting Reflection 11–2

Has the increased acceptability of divorce led to the breakdown of healthy family values in the United States, as certain organizations maintain?

A major challenge for many parents who divorce is their ability to acknowledge that they continue to share parenting responsibilities and relationships with their children, even though their marriage relationship has been dismantled (Knox & Leggett, 2000). Many people divorce with the expectation that their contact and involvement with the former spouse has been completely terminated. However, the relationship becomes transformed in several ways: '

■ Visitation rights of the noncustodial parent forces some type of contact with the former spouse.
■ Children may perpetuate the remnants of the relationship by sharing information about one parent with the other and discussing life and events in their new family systems.
■ If joint custody has been arranged, spouses are committed to making major decisions together that affect children's welfare.
■ While parents attend to their own particular reactions and adjustments to the divorce, they are often mindful of their children's reactions. That topic is explored in the next section.

••••••••••••••••••••••••••••••••••••••••••••••••••••

***Focus Point.*** Divorce has a variety of effects on adults. Most involve dealing with emotional adjustments as individuals make the transition from being a couple to being single people. Even though adults make different adjustments to the divorce, they continue to share a con-nection by being their children's parents. It seems that a person is never completely divorced when children are involved.

••••••••••••••••••••••••••••••••••••••••••••••••••••

## How Does Parental Divorce Affect Children?

About one-fifth (23 percent) of American children lived only with their mothers, 5 percent lived with only their fathers, and 4 percent lived with neither of their parents in 2002 (Federal Interagency Forum on Child and Family Statistics, 2003). The number of single-parent families has increased considerably in the United States since 1960. This type of family system now constitutes a sizable proportion of the population (U.S. Bureau of the Census, 2003). The marital status of parents influences where children will live and with whom, as well as the kind of quality of life they will experience. In line with the increase in single-parent families, there has been a concomitant decrease in the number of children living with two parents. In 2002, for example, about 69 percent of all children in the United States were living with two parents as compared with 77 percent in 1980 (Federal Interagency Forum on Child and Family Statistics, 2003) (see Figure 11–3).

Researchers have learned that children's reactions to parental divorce involve a process of adjusting to change rather than a single, simple reaction (Knox & Leggett, 2000). This process is tempered by other fac-

**FIGURE 11–3.** Female headed households with children, by race and ethnicity, 1970 to 2002.

*Source:* Federal Interagency Forum on Child and Family Statistics (2003). *America's children: Key national indicators of well-being: 2003.* Washington, DC: U.S. Government Printing Office.

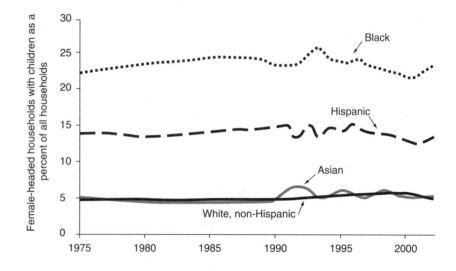

tors, such as the child's age, sex, and past experiences. For many children, the parental divorce involves significant losses, and children can experience a variety of grief reactions. Children appear to undergo this process in three distinct stages:

1. The **initial stage** occurs after parents inform children of their decision to separate. It is marked by high levels of stress during which aggressive conflicts markedly increase. A mood of unhappiness pervades.

2. The **transition stage** commences about 1 year after the parents' separation and lasts for up to 3 years. At this stage, high levels of emotionalism have diminished; it is characterized instead by the restructuring process of evolving new family system patterns, changing the quality of life, and establishing visitation routines with the noncustodial parent.

3. The **restabilization stage** occurs about 5 years after the separation when the new single-parent family system or stepfamily has been completely instituted.

Divorce may be one of the few major family crisis events in which adults become more focused on their needs than on those of their children (Benokraitis, 2004). In many respects, the functioning of the parent-child relationship is disrupted because of this change in focus. The effects of divorce on children may be due to this change rather than to the divorce *per se*. Researchers report different findings about the specific effects observed in children of divorcing parents (Kaslow, 2000; Knox & Leggett, 2000). Several factors have been identified in recent years that appear to influence the nature and course of children's adjustment to this family crisis:

■ Age and sex of children when parental divorce occurs
■ Adults' use of available social support networks to help children adjust to the process
■ Attitudes of the culture toward divorce and single-parent families

The effects of parental divorce on children may be either short- or long-term and positive or detrimental. Short-term effects, for example, include behavior difficulties at home and at school that occur in association with the initial reactions to parental separation.

Long-term effects may not appear until adolescence or adulthood when individuals become involved in intimate relationships and experience difficulties in establishing them (Price, 2004). Other long-term effects appear in the course of development as children experience the adjustments required at later phases in the process of reacting to parental divorce. For example, low quality of the parents' marriage is reflected in troubled parent-child relationships as long as 8 to 12 years prior to divorce. Sex of a child can also mediate such reactions. For example, boys have more adverse reactions to parental divorce than girls do, but girls react more adversely to parental remarriage.

The age of children at the time of parental divorce seems to be one of the driving factors in influencing how a child reacts and how he or she adjusts after the divorce. Researchers have identified certain kinds of reactions that vary according to the children's age when parental divorce occurs.

Regressive behaviors such as temporary loss of toilet training as well as increased aggressiveness, fretfulness, and negative attention-getting behaviors such as whining or destroying toys may be observed among preschoolers whose parents are divorcing or have divorced. School-age children may manifest feelings of being abandoned or rejected by their absent parent, a drop in school performance, adverse interactions with peers, or boundary shifts with their mother during or following parental divorce. Adolescents also may manifest similar feelings of abandonment or rejection, delinquency and negative acting-out behaviors, heightened conflicts with their parent, decline in school performance, and emotional depression (Price, 2004; Teybor, 2004; Weight, 2004).

The first year after parental divorce may be the most difficult and stressful for both children and parents (Pryor & Rodgers, 2001). However, the disruptive effects young children experience often continue beyond this first year. Boys generally continue to experience greater degrees of disruptiveness than girls do, especially it parents continue to experience high levels of discord and conflict. Figure 11–4 illustrates an 8-year-old's representation of her family following her parents' divorce.

Divorce is perhaps more problematic when children are adolescents. The context of the parent-child relationship is altered when adolescents experience the divorce of their parents (Price, 2004). Girls may experience more serious difficulties than boys do. Some research suggests that teenage girls may project anger about their noncustodial fathers onto their custodial

FIGURE 11–4. In this drawing an 8-year-old girl represents her family. Her mother and father have divorced, yet she is aware that she is a member of two distinct family systems. The line attempts to show how her father is a part of one family but not of the other. (Drawing by Brianne Pfaffly.)

mothers. These girls may also experience role reversal and blurring of boundaries between themselves and their mothers, a situation also occurring among school-age girls. Adolescent girls may resent this change in their relationship with their mothers. It is also not unusual for some adolescents to have divided allegiances to both parents. This division relates to high levels of conflict and hostility and a low degree of cooperation between parents. As a result, many teenagers feel caught between loyalties to individual parents, and researchers have noted that poor levels of adjustment are related to the disruptive changes associated with parental divorce.

The disruptive effects of parental divorce on children and adolescents may last a long time (Conway, Christensen, & Herlihy, 2003; Pryor & Rodgers, 2001; Wallerstein & Blakeslee, 2003; Wallerstein, Lewis, & Blakeslee, 2001). Many adolescents make adequate adjustments in the years following the divorce and arrive at adulthood as competent individuals. However, one-half of those studied in a comprehensive longitudinal investigation were found to enter adulthood as unhappy, angry,

underachieving, self-deprecating, and fretful individuals. Researchers believe that those unhealthy reactions were artifacts of the parental divorce that took place many years earlier. While some researchers believe divorce leaves children and adolescents emotionally scarred and handicapped in future intimate relationships, the issue remains essentially unresolved until more extensive research is conducted (Amato, 2003).

### Parenting Reflection 11–3

Can growing up or living in a single-parent family be a healthy experience for children? What benefits might they gain from this experience?

The numerous research findings about the effects of divorce on children present a highly negative, dour, and depressing picture. They may also be helpful. Parents who are considering divorce may be more aware of what can occur in single-parent family systems as a re-

**Parenting FAQs 11–2**

**My brother is getting divorced, and things seem to be pretty nasty. He just told me that the court has appointed another attorney to be a Guardian Ad Litem for the children. This seems unusual and something I've never heard of before with other couples I've known who have divorced. I don't understand this. Can you please explain?**

**A:**  It is not unusual for a court to appoint an attorney or another qualified professional to represent the interests of the children of divorcing parents. This person is called the Guardian Ad Litem (GAL), as you note, and serves as an agent of the court acting in the best interests of the children. This person acts as an advocate for the children in the divorce proceedings and will sometimes recommend actions that go against the parents' wishes. This is because of the unique representation of the GAL for the children instead of the parents. The appointment of a GAL usually happens when at least one parent requests it or because the court has reservations about the ability of either or both parents to act in the best interests of the children in the divorce proceedings.

sult. Thus, they can better prepare by making arrangements that assist children and themselves when they cope with this stressful event. Some generalizations about the research include the following:

- Children experience the effects of parental divorce in ways that are more disruptive and stressful than those experienced by parents.
- Divorce is a process rather than an event, and it is experienced by the whole family system rather than by adults alone.
- Divorce has both immediate and long-term effects on children, which vary with their age and sex at the time the divorce takes place.
- Children whose parents divorce during their developing years almost always see it as a milestone event in their lives that may shape many developmental aspects in their adulthood.

It is important to reiterate that the effects of divorce on children and adolescents are not clear-cut. Many conflicting, complicated, and complex findings are reported in the research literature. Some critics of these findings point to the samples of children studied, noting the small sample sizes and the fact that the children were often under the care of mental health professionals because of problems experienced in relation to parental divorce. It is safe to state that not all children whose parents divorce react in the exact manner described in these studies. However, it is equally safe to conclude that no child of divorced parents completely escapes the impact of disruption on a family system during divorce.

*Focus Point.*  Researchers have observed a number of effects on children when their parents divorce. They note that children's age at the time of divorce is an important factor in determining their reactions to this event. Many parents fear that their children will experience serious and harmful effects as a result of divorce. Researchers generally find that divorce produces disruptive effects but that most children successfully adapt and adjust within several years. However, observers note some residual effects that last for many years after the divorce.

## Custody Arrangements

Parents must confront a major decision when they divorce: Who will have custody of children, and how will the noncustodial parent and children have access to each other for visitation? The Family Law Section of the American Bar Association lists several standards that court officials may apply in determining the custody arrangements of children following the divorce of their parents (American Bar Association, 1996, 2001). The section includes the following five standards:

1. Custody should be awarded to either or both parents according to the best interests of the child.
2. Custody may be awarded to persons other than the father or mother whenever such award serves the best interests of the child.

3. If a child is old enough and able enough to reason and form an intelligent preference, his or her wishes about custody should be considered and given due weight by the court.

4. Any custody award should be subject to modification or change whenever the best interests of the child require or justify such modification or change.

5. Reasonable visitation rights should be awarded to parents and to any person interested in the welfare of the child, at the discretion of the court, unless such rights of visitation are detrimental to the best interests of the child.

Before the 1920s such decisions about child custody were not an issue in divorces because custody was automatically assigned to the father; women had no legal rights in this regard. They lacked the right to vote and to sign contracts. In subsequent years, however, women have gained legal status in the United States and the child-custody issue has changed. In almost 90 percent of cases, child custody is awarded to mothers rather than to fathers.

## Parenting Reflection 11–4

What can divorced parents do to prevent their child from feeling like a football that is continually being tossed from one parent to the other in order to meet the requirements of joint custody or noncustodial visitation?

Even though mothers stand a good chance of being awarded legal custody of children, divorcing couples still must negotiate to reach a decision about which parent should have full custody, or if both will share custody. They must reach visitation and support decisions and consider other important details relating to the best interests of children. These details might include, for example, how each parent will contribute to the children's medical and dental expenses, clothing costs, and college education, and in what percentage. It is not easy for many couples to reach these decisions in an objective, fair manner without involving some type of legal mediation or the intervention of a court's judicial decision.

When divorcing parents consider custody issues, five factors frequently favor one parent over the other (American Bar Association, 1996):

1. The wishes and preferences of children

2. Whether or not a parent wants custody

3. The perceived need to place a child with a same sex parent

4. The perceived need to keep a child with the mother because people believe she is the socially appropriate person for custody

5. A parent's ability to provide stable, continuing involvement in the same residence or geographical area

Courts apparently use certain specific variables relating to the quality of children's adjustment after parental divorce when they make decisions about custody, rather than rely on the general rule of assigning it to only one parent (American Bar Association, 2001). For example, according to such guidelines, a child is likely to be placed with a same-sex parent because he or she generally has better prospects of healthy social adjustment.

A single parent's sole custody of children can create problems that, at times, appear to outweigh the situation's advantages. The experiences of single-parent families, described later in this chapter, give the impression that they can be problem-ridden, stressful, and unpleasant for many individuals, especially women. Many of the problems associated with sole custody reflect the noncustodial father's resentment, anger, and frustration in dealing with what is perceived to be a no-win situation. Many men feel they are systematically disenfranchised from having input into important decisions about their children's lives and from having access to quality interaction time with their children. As a result, post-divorce conflict with the ex-spouse continues or escalates, which, in turn, affects the manner and context of children's interactions with their fathers. Noncustodial fathers typically disengage from the parenting relationship because their ability to function adequately in this role is greatly diminished by their withdrawal from the former family system (Kaslow, 2000).

Compounding the situation is the dismal record of consistent child-support payments by many noncustodial fathers (Grall, 2003). Many fathers feel they are cut out of their children's lives, and therefore, they should not have to maintain financial support. They often use

**Parenting FAQs 11–3**

**My husband's attorney has requested an evaluation for child custody since we can't agree on these arrangements. Just exactly what is involved in such an evaluation? Who should pay for it? How can I be assured that whoever does the evaluation isn't biased in favor of my husband? Why is this necessary anyway?**

**A:**    Having an evaluation performed by a qualified professional may be the best way to resolve the impasse between you and your husband regarding custody arrangements. Usually, attorneys representing you and your husband agree on a particular mental health professional who is highly regarded in your community for conducting fair, accurate, and appropriate evaluations of how custody arrangements best meet the interests of the children involved, not necessarily that of the parents. Sometimes the court will appoint the person to conduct the evaluation if the attorneys can't agree on someone. You will need to trust the recommendation of your attorney or the court that the evaluator has the reputation for being fair and unbiased.

Evaluations can be expensive, sometimes ranging between as much as 3,000 and $10,000 or more, depending on where you live. Costs typically are shared by both parents. An evaluation is conducted when both parents insist that they know what is best for their children even though the conditions of what each considers to be appropriate for the children differ. An evaluation helps the court to decide what is in the best interests of the children. It is not unusual, however, for the court to disregard what the evaluator recommends and determine its own orders concerning child custody. So, there is some risk that this expensive exercise will not result in what the evaluator recommends.

this claim when they live far away from their children, particularly when they live out of state.

Most divorcing couples must arrive at some decision regarding custody and visitation, which typically involves lengthy discussions and compromises. They may arrive at this decision with the help of lawyers, divorce-mediation professionals, or therapists. But even with this help, some divorcing couples have a hard time reaching decisions of any sort.

**Joint Custody.**    A recent trend in custody decisions involves **joint custody,** or awarding the responsibility for child care and supervision to both parents. In many cases, joint custody, rather than single-parent custody, may be a viable solution that is in the best interests of the children (Kaslow, 2000). This alternative has both advantages and disadvantages to those involved and in its implementation and execution. However, many feel that the advantages outweigh the problems if parents can work together in the mutual interest of their children.

Researchers find that joint custody has several positive effects (Everett & Everett, 2000; Kaslow, 2000; Lowenstein, 2002; Weinraub, Horvath, & Gringlass, 2002):

- More contact between ex-spouses
- Fewer problems in securing father's cooperation in consistently meeting financial-support agreements
- Fewer feelings of being overwhelmed by child-care responsibilities
- More access to beneficial interactions between children and fathers (typically not the case when mothers have sole custody)

### Parenting Reflection 11–5

Should joint custody become the norm among divorced parents with children? Why or why not?

Fathers who share joint custody with mothers are also more involved with parenting responsibilities, have more contact with their children, and use parenting resources more extensively than noncustodial fathers do (Knox & Leggett, 2000). They tend to be more satisfied with joint rather than sole custody arrangements, but mothers appear to prefer sole custody. When fathers hold joint custody with mothers for children, the mother is also more likely to receive support payments from the father, helping to prevent the children from experiencing a poverty-level existence (Grall, 2003).

● ● ● ● ● ● ● ● ● ● ● ● ● ● ● ● ● ● ● ● ● ● ● ● ● ● ● ● ● ● ● ●

### Parenting Reflection 11–6

Is it right to force men to pay child support when they fall behind or to garnish wages to do so? Should a noncustodial mother pay child support to a custodial father even though she earns less than he does? Would noncustodial fathers be more willing to pay for child support if the federal government made this a line-item credit on annual tax returns?

● ● ● ● ● ● ● ● ● ● ● ● ● ● ● ● ● ● ● ● ● ● ● ● ● ● ● ● ● ● ● ●

Although joint custody seems to sidestep problems associated with sole custody of children, it does create some problems (Everett & Everett, 2000; Kaslow, 2000):

- It is more expensive to maintain because each parent must supply housing, equipment, toys, food, and often clothing for children.
- It requires a degree of connection with ex-spouses that many people are not prepared for and may not desire.
- It will not work properly if the adults are not committed to maintaining civil discussions that remain on topic about child rearing issues.
- Constraints on relocation to another community or residence can impair decision making.
- Children may feel confused and overburdened because they have commitments to two family systems instead of one.
- Children may have problems adjusting to the transition from one family system to another.
- The possibility of disturbances in the relationship between siblings may occur due to split living arrangements with parents.

**Managing Coparenting Arrangements.** It is imperative that divorcing parents establish new rules and boundaries regarding their coparenting relationship with children that emerges when separation and divorce are taking place and following this event. The temptation for many is to involve children in the adult business of the divorce, and the children can become pawns in the matter. This is unhealthy for children and parents as well. Many children also feel forced or obligated to take sides with one parent or another to the detriment of all parties involved.

● ● ● ● ● ● ● ● ● ● ● ● ● ● ● ● ● ● ● ● ● ● ● ● ● ● ● ● ● ● ● ●

### Parenting Reflection 11–7

Are two parents really better for children than just one? Why or why not?

● ● ● ● ● ● ● ● ● ● ● ● ● ● ● ● ● ● ● ● ● ● ● ● ● ● ● ● ● ● ● ●

When parents are separating in preparation for divorce, it is important that they maintain lines of communication between each other to resolve their differences. Children are inevitably a part of the matters to be discussed. However, to avoid the feelings of anger, frustration, and guilt that can accompany the discussions involving children's affairs, divorcing parents might limit the topics to the health needs, educational concerns, and time sharing of children (Judges, 1985). When these new rules and boundaries involving discussions of children are followed, additional rules, patterns, and boundaries can be shaped to redefine the relationship between each individual parent and the children. This should allow for the development of the new family system that the children will experience, known as the single-parent family.

Sometimes divorcing parents are tempted to express their hurtful feelings about their divorce and the divorcing partner by playing "pain games" that can interfere with effective parenting (Judges, 1985). Basically, three types of games may serve as unhealthy ways to express unpleasant feelings associated with divorce:

1. *Cut Down.* This is any type of discounting of the other parent to a child, such as making negative comments or using derogatory labels. When children hear such statements, they may feel that these also apply to them because they are half of each parent.

2. *Messenger.* In this game, one parent solicits a child to be a messenger as a means of communicating with the other parent. Children can sometimes distort even innocent, simple messages they might be asked to give to the other parent. It is not healthy for children to play a middleman role in the altered relationship between divorcing parents.

3. *I Spy.* Divorcing parents may be tempted to use a child as a source of information about the other parent. This is a ploy to find out what the other par-

ent is doing, who he or she might be seeing socially, what purchases he or she might have made, and so on. Asking children to provide information about the other parent places them in a position where they can violate a sense of trust between themselves and the other parent, which is not healthy.

## Single-Parent Families Headed by Mothers

The majority of single-parent families in the United States are headed by women who have either never married or have divorced (U.S. Bureau of the Census, 2003). Among these families, quality of life is a major concern (Holyfield, 2003). Women appear to face more difficulties resulting from divorce than men. These difficulties are attributed to economic conditions related to employment and the support of children. Family income is lowest among single-parent families headed by women (U. S. Bureau of the Census, 2003). In 2001 the median income for families of married couples was $60,335. This figure contrasts sharply with the median income of $25,745 for single-parent families headed by women. The median income of single-parent families headed by men, by comparison, was $36,590. Because of the low level of income among these mothers, many of these family systems can expect to experience poverty-level existences that seriously affect the quality of life, especially for children (see Figure 11–5) (Population Reference Bureau, 2003a, 2003b). In addition, the overwhelming majority of these families are found in black and Hispanic communities in the United States.

**Financial Difficulties.**    Single-parent families headed by mothers can expect to experience financial difficulties. A father's child support and maintenance payments

are important sources of income for such families; they help provide an adequate quality of life. They do not, however, adequately reflect typical expenditures on children by mothers who are physical custodians (Peterson, Song, & Jones-DeWeever, 2003). Because of this dependence on typically inadequate support payments and other factors, such as less education or fewer years in the labor force, most single-parent families headed by women have lower annual incomes than those headed by men. To make matters worse, women do not always successfully obtain support payments from the absent father (Federal Interagency Forum on Child and Family Statistics, 2003). In 2001, about 63 percent of single-parent mothers were awarded some amount of child support (Grall, 2003). However, only about 45 percent of those received the full amount that had been awarded. This factor, in addition to differences in education, job experience, and training, creates the likelihood that more custodial mothers than fathers are poor.

State laws differ in the manner for determining how much someone must pay in providing child support. Most commonly, many have requirements that 17 percent of a nonresident, noncustodial parent's gross income should go toward child support. This figure increases as the number of children involved increases, and it can rise as high as 31 percent when four or more children must be supported. While these fathers most likely could afford to pay more in child support, many have established new families and must also contribute to the support of new biologically produced children as well as to those they have previously fathered. The conflict between honoring the responsibilities owed to children from former marriages and those produced in new relationships often creates a dilemma for all the affected individuals.

Child support is determined at the time a divorce becomes finalized by court decree. The divorcing

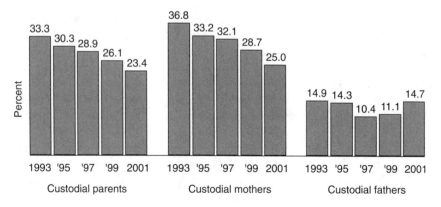

**FIGURE 11–5.**  Poverty status of custodial parents, 1993 to 2001.

Source: Grall, T. S. (2003). Custodial mothers and fathers and their child support: 2001. Current Population Reports, Series P60–225. Washington, DC: U.S. Bureau of the Census.

individuals often make arrangements finalized in a contractual agreement that the court legalizes. Both parties may make decisions that have adverse financial consequences due to the emotional coerciveness present in negotiations leading to such agreements (Schmitz & Teeb, 2003). It may be helpful, therefore, to include a therapist or a divorce mediation professional in the negotiations as a means of achieving objective decisions regarding child support. That person may assist both divorcing adults in securing arrangements that help to ensure children receive adequate financial support in accordance with other related variables affecting the agreement.

The most common reason for failure to pay support regularly and in its full amount is attributed to financial problems by the noncustodial parent (Weinraub, Horvath, & Gringlas, 2002). However, some parents fail to honor their child support agreement for other reasons, including: (1) withholding payment as a means for expressing anger toward the custodial ex-spouse; (2) feelings of discrimination about the amount awarded by a court; or (3) unemployment or underemployment. In other instances, many noncustodial parents provide support in forms other than money such as gifts, paying for medical and dental expenses, or clothing (Grall, 2003).

Becoming divorced means that most women with children will become employed to provide support for their families. Typically, they earn wages and salaries at levels lower than men, often because of different levels of education, training, and work experience. Economic conditions are a primary source of stress among single-parent families headed by women (Population Reference Bureau, 2003a, 2003b). One in three single-parent families headed by women exists below the poverty level, as compared with 1 in 10 two-parent families. This factor may significantly contribute to changing the quality of life, social functioning, context of the parent-child relationship, and various related effects in these family systems.

The implications of economic conditions in these families, then, have both short- and long-term consequences. Children who are not supported as they are entitled perhaps experience these consequences to a more serious extent than their mothers, although quality of life affects everyone in these families. Essentially, numerous ripple effects stem from such dire financial conditions in single-parent families headed by mothers.

**Role Strain.** Single-parent mothers experience additional role strain within their new binuclear family system.

Divorced women experience different degrees of role strain than divorced men. Because most women are granted full custody of children, they must now function as the sole full-time parent in their new family system. What was stressful in managing competing roles in a two-parent family system is even more stressful after divorce. The time demands in such systems are particularly stressful (Federal Interagency Forum on Child and Family Statistics, 2003). There is less time for most activities, and employment responsibilities receive the highest priority. Child care and personal needs receive the least time; however, quality of attention to children does not appear to decline.

As with role strain in intact families with children, role performance in all the competing roles falls as the number of roles and levels of stress increase concomitantly (Goode, 1993). Combined with other factors that produce stress such as financial problems, this factor may account for other changes taking place in this new single-parent family, one of which is discussed in the following section.

**Changes in the Parent-Child Relationship.** Many single-parent mothers experience changes in their relationship with their children. The parent-child subsystem changes as all participants redefine the parameters of the relationship in this new family form. In many respects, two distinct parent-child subsystems emerge. In general, there may be few differences in the relationship between mothers and daughters and mothers and sons in single-parent family systems when children are young. However, children in family systems headed by single-parent mothers continue to experience adjustment difficulties 4 to 6 years following parental divorce, as compared with children whose mothers have remarried (Nelsen & Delzer, 1999).

One effect of role strain on other factors operating in single-parent families headed by mothers is their increased reliance on more authoritarian patterns of interacting with children (Nelsen & Delzer, 1999). The functioning of the parent-child subsystem is generally disrupted following divorce, and this disruption is especially accentuated in the relationship of mothers and sons. It is less likely to affect mothers and their preadolescent daughters, who often forge a relationship that is more emotionally intimate and close. As the new family system evolves new patterns and establishes some degree of stability, many single-parent mothers generally shift to patterns of child rearing that are more authoritative. This tends to promote healthier, more positive adjustment among children.

After divorce, it is not unusual for single-parent mothers to institute changes in the boundaries, patterns, and rules that define the usual adult and child role behaviors (Everett & Everett, 2000). A mother may transform the definition of her role, particularly in relation to the oldest child, to that of a peer/partner. She may expect that child to be more mature than he or she is developmentally ready to be. As the mother transforms the nature of the relationship with this child, she significantly increases her shared personal feelings and opinions about a variety of topics. Accordingly, the child's role becomes transformed; he or she is now the mother's *confidante*. The mother increasingly relies on this child for emotional support and assigns him or her much of the missing adult partner's responsibilities. As a result, the child may be forced into interaction patterns calling for developmental maturity that he or she does not have or is not prepared to provide for the mother.

The pressures children experience in these situations come from not having their emotional needs met by their mothers, who are usually unaware of this problem. When a mother transforms the child's role to one similar to the absent adult partner's, a conflict can emerge that imitates the marital conflicts with the former spouse. The child discovers that he or she is in a no-win situation, pressured to assume the missing partner's role but punished for behaving like the former spouse. Some researchers also report a particular interaction between mothers and daughters. At times, they may experience competition, jealousy, and conflict that are not found between single-parent mothers and sons (Everett & Everett, 2000). When children find themselves in these situations, some may not feel comfortable expressing their feelings of frustration and confusion. More likely, they respond with psychosomatic reactions and acting-out behaviors that serve as symptoms of their concerns and fears. Not surprisingly, when mothers disclose intimate details about personal problems, such as financial matters or negative feelings about ex-husbands, daughters report strong feelings of emotional distress (Koerner, Jacobs, & Raymond, 2000).

Therapists and researchers working with single-parent families note that parents may encounter certain pitfalls that can develop into clinical issues, including responding to children as a reminder of the former spouse, developing overdependence on children, seeing children as a burden, and focusing on surviving rather than on parenting children and attempting to meet their developmental needs (Kaslow, 2000). One study, however, questions the pathological implications of most studies of single mothers for leaning on children for emotional support and advice (Arditti, 1999). This study reports that adult children instead viewed this as contributing to a sense of equality, closeness, and promotion of friendship with their mother. Rather than constituting boundary violations, these interactions may help, from this researcher's point of view, to build strength in single-parent families headed by women. However, more work will need to be done to fully substantiate this view.

••••••••••••••••••••••••••••••••••••••••••••••••••••••

***Focus Point.***    Most single-parent families are headed by mothers who have been divorced. These families can expect to experience financial problems due to several factors. Researchers commonly observe role strain among these parents, who must adjust to holding several competing roles simultaneously. The relationship between mothers and children also changes as the boundaries previously established between adult and child roles become blurred. Many women find their status as single mothers to be stressful but manage to adjust in a variety of ways.

••••••••••••••••••••••••••••••••••••••••••••••••••••••

## Single-Parent Families Headed by Fathers

Single-parent families headed by fathers constitute the minority of these family systems in the United States, although the percentage of families headed by men has increased steadily over the past 40 years (Figure 11–6). In comparison with single-parent mothers, fathers heading this type of family system earn considerably higher incomes, which promotes a different quality of family life.

Boys are more likely than girls to live with a custodial father. Some researchers attribute this tendency to the belief that boys in such situations benefit from being raised by fathers, while girls benefit from being raised by mothers (Jordan, 2003). This is often contrary to the bias of court officials, who may believe that it is in the best interests of all children to be raised by a single-parent mother than by a father as a single parent.

**FIGURE 11–6.** An increasing number of single-parent family systems in the United States are headed by men.

• • • • • • • • • • • • • • • • • • • • • • • • • •

## Parenting Reflection 11–8

Why is sole custody of children granted to fewer divorced fathers? Why are women reluctant to relinquish full custody to the father?

• • • • • • • • • • • • • • • • • • • • • • • • • •

Men assume the custodial parenting role following divorce for a variety of reasons. However, it continues to be customary in our culture for women to assume this role, although in the past a man commonly accepted single parenthood after the death of his spouse. The idea that men can conduct their parenting activities as capably as women and that children are not harmed by single-parent fathering experiences is a relatively new concept. Its increasing acceptance is reflected in the corresponding increase in the number of men who are awarded custody of children following divorce.

Unlike single-parent mothers, single-parent fathers gain custody of their children through two likely avenues:

1. Men may assert their right to gain custody of children because they feel capable and motivated to parent their children effectively, although the mother may contest their ability.

2. Men may consent to assume custody when mothers show no desire to continue their parental rights or are unable to do so because of emotional or physical problems.

Men make more positive adjustments to being a custodial single father when they have a strong desire to perform well in this capacity. Many men wish to continue positive parenting activities that may have been established when the children were born.

**Greater Financial Freedom.**   Single-parent fathers typically earn higher incomes than single-parent mothers. Fathers achieve greater economic security, due in part to a higher level of educational attainment and more years of employment. Those advantages enable them to hold jobs that earn higher levels of income and put them in a more favorable employment and financial situation after they become single parents (Kaslow, 2000).

Discrepancies in income between single mothers and fathers account for many of the differences in the quality of life in these family systems. As stated earlier, incomes of single-parent families headed by men are typically higher than of those headed by women. Single-parent families headed by men also tend to have fewer people who must be supported by the father's income, as opposed to those families headed by women. These differences contribute to the higher quality of life in single-parent families headed by men: Financial resources are more abundant.

**Role Strain.**   A single-parent father experiences role strain differently than a single-parent mother. Like the single-parent mother, he must adjust to the additional responsibilities of child rearing in addition to providing the family income. The challenges facing most fathers differ from those of mothers, however, in a variety of ways.

Many single-parent fathers were not involved in managing household tasks before the divorce, but they have little difficulty when they assume responsibility for home management (Everett & Everett, 2000). However, they report that meal preparation and food shopping can be major problem areas because many lack these skills. Single-parent fathers tend to share household management tasks with children rather than secure help from outside resources. Single-parent mothers, by comparison, tend to perform these tasks themselves rather than expect children to cooperate, which promotes greater levels of role strain. Single-parent fathers with daughters tend to expect them, more than their sons, to assist with household management tasks, possibly due to differences in the socialization of children. When the families of single-parent fathers are compared with two-parent families, however, children in the single-parent systems do not perform as many household management tasks. This difference may be due to several factors:

■ Single-parent fathers may intentionally not involve their children in tasks in an effort to prove their own competence as household managers.
■ These fathers may attempt to ease the transition and tensions that children experience when they shift to new family patterns after the divorce.
■ Children have difficulty becoming familiar with the routines and patterns of two different households.

Some single-parent fathers may have difficulty synchronizing child care, household duties, and wage-earning responsibilities into a workable and manageable routine. Arranging child care may be a major problem for many fathers, particularly those with young children. Rather than hiring housekeepers or sitters, single fathers generally rely on the same child-care resources as do other parents.

Structuring older children's activities is also a common problem among many single-parent fathers. Single fathers of older children typically rely on after-school activities, such as dance instruction or athletics, to help them adequately supervise children. Most fathers also adapt their work hours to increase their availability.

**Changes in the Parent-Child Relationship.**   Single-parent fathers can perform child-care responsibilities effectively (Kaslow, 2000). One concern of the authorities who make custody evaluations and recommendations often centers on a father's ability to perform effectively as a single parent. Today researchers generally recognize that most men can conduct caregiving responsibilities in a competent manner that is healthy and

beneficial to children (Cabrera, 2003). Fathers are particularly competent when they have been actively involved in providing care since a child's infancy and when they willingly accept child custody after divorce. Because individuals in our society have moved increasingly toward the creation and enactment of androgynous parenting roles, men have learned how to provide for children's needs and to express nurturance in caregiving.

Single-parent fathers tend to promote different expectations for their children than single-parent mothers (Knox & Leggett, 2000). For example, single fathers appear to demand more independence from children. As many gain experience in child rearing activities, they shift away from authoritarian methods to those that are authoritative in nature. They become less traditional, less discipline-oriented, more concerned about the quality of care they provide and the experiences children have with nonparental caregivers, more interested in children's educational experiences, and more protective about dangerous situations to which children might be exposed.

Many single-parent fathers also express concerns about raising a daughter in a family system that lacks the sex-role model provided by an adult woman. They wonder how they can provide socialization experiences for girls that will help them learn appropriate sex-role behaviors.

Single-parent fathers tend to seek support and assistance from others outside their family system when they need help as caregivers. These sources include relatives, such as their own parents, professionals, religious leaders, physicians, and teachers. Many discover that these sources are helpful in providing information and guidance about child care that improves the fathers' abilities to parent children effectively.

••••••••••••••••••••••••••••••••••••••••••••••••••••

***Focus Point.***   Single-parent fathers experience situations that are similar to those of single-parent mothers, but researchers also observe differences. Family systems headed by custodial fathers constitute a minority of single-parent families. Single-parent fathers are typically better educated than single-parent mothers and earn significantly higher incomes. They often have custody of sons rather than of daughters. Men may gain custody of children after a divorce because they actively seek it or because the mother has defaulted on her parenting rights. Like single-parent mothers, fathers experience role strain as they add increased involvement with child rearing to their other responsibilities. These men usually perform adequately as caregivers, but researchers notice certain differences in interaction patterns with children when these single families are compared with two-adult families.

•••••••••••••••••••••••••••••••••••••••••••••••

## The Dilemma of Nonresident, Noncustodial Fathers

Many individuals, both within and outside of family systems, may wonder if nonresident fathers are of any worth or value, other than paying child support, to their children. Even these fathers may ponder this issue. Researchers who have studied this issue have presented information and data that would tend to answer this negatively. The consensus of research, until recently, has given little strength to the notion that children's contact with their nonresident father has significant benefits for them (Wilcoxon, 2002). Evidence has been strong, on the other hand, in showing that nonresidential fathers' payment of child support is positively associated with measures of children's well-being.

Some aspects of the research regarding the relevance of nonresidential fathers in their children's lives may be problematic (Amato & Gilbreth, 1999). Two important dimensions influence the role of nonresidential fathers in their children's well-being. First is the degree to which children feel close to their nonresidential father and desire contact with him. The second hinges on whether the nonresidential father uses an authoritative parenting style when interacting with his children. Taking these dimensions together with regular payment of child support, a marked association appears with children's academic success and the tendency of children to deal with problems in healthy ways.

It is not uncommon for nonresidential fathers to want to make the little time they have with children during visitation to be the most positive experiences possible. Guilt over not being able to be a full-time parent may also contribute to the desire to minimize children's problematic behavior in this time with the father. Additionally, it is not uncommon for nonresidential fathers to approach parenting not from an authoritative but from an adult-companion position. When nonresidential fathers avoid this latter approach with children and act in authoritative ways, such as praising children,

disciplining their misbehavior, setting and enforcing limits, assisting with schoolwork, and talking about problems, positive effects are observed in children's well-being as measured by post-divorce adjustment and academic performance, for example (Amato & Gilbreth, 1999).

Results of an ongoing study of single-parent families (Ahrons & Tanner, 2003) report some long-term effects of relationship changes for adult children and their noncustodial fathers 20 years following the parental divorce. Most participants felt that the relationship had improved over time or remained stable. However, relationships worsened over time when conflicts between the biological parents increased, the father remarried early in the post-divorce years, and the father generally had low involvement with children in the early post-divorce years. Participants describing their father-child relationships as poor also reported having poor relationships with other family members involving biological relatives and steprelatives.

•••••••••••••••••••••••••••••••••••••••••••••••

***Focus Point.*** Child custody is a central issue for most divorcing parents. Legal decisions are made with the best interests of children in mind. Sole custody is customarily awarded to the mother rather than to the father. Decisions about sole custody are sometimes difficult to make and can involve lengthy, expensive legal assistance. Joint custody continues to gain favor as a means of overcoming the disadvantages of sole custody although it has unique problems.

•••••••••••••••••••••••••••••••••••••••••••••••

## Strengths of Single-Parent Families

The problems and challenges faced by single-parent families often overshadow their strengths. As noted earlier, the challenges experienced by these family systems tend to provide the opportunities for people to grow and develop in ways they might not imagine otherwise. Women, for example, generally say, in afterthought, that their single-parenting experience helped to build personal strengths and confidence. In addition, these family strengths also have been identified (Benedek & Brown, 2004; Jordan, 2003; Weight, 2004): (1) the ability to incorporate parenting skills traditionally found in two-parent families; (2) a positive attitude about the changes in family life; (3) effective communications between all family members; (4) family management skills; and (5) the ability to become financially independent.

It is also important to note that there are few differences between children raised by single-parent mothers and fathers (Everett & Everett, 2000; Kaslow, 2000). Children are often placed for custody with same-sex parents based on the notion that it is in their best interest for this type of arrangement. Conversely, it is believed that children raised by single-parent mothers or fathers are disadvantaged because they lack exposure to the opposite-sex parent. This finding of no significant differences in children regardless of this type of family structure may result from adults becoming more androgynous in their behavior. Modeling androgynous gender roles to children may offer many benefits that promote their well-being far beyond the years of childhood and adolescence into adulthood (Bem, 1975).

# SYSTEMIC FAMILY DEVELOPMENT SNAPSHOT

One of the strengths of the systemic family development model is its ability to be applied to all types of family forms and structures. For this reason, it is possible to examine what is taking place in single-parent family systems that are headed by mothers or by fathers. These families typically have experienced divorce, one of the most stressful life events producing numerous changes and challenges for individuals and their family systems. We will briefly examine an example of one single-parent family in which the divorced parents hold joint custody of children and in which the mother is the physical custodian. When the snapshot is taken, the two children in this family are 10 and 7; their father is 38 and their mother is 35; and the only grandparent living is their maternal grandmother who is 61. The parents were divorced about one year ago. The mother retained the family home, and the father moved into an apartment nearby. The children are members of a binuclear family system.

## Single-Parent Family Headed by a Mother

Ashley Miller was exhausted by the end of the day. She felt like this just about every day now. Ashley found it difficult to find happiness in anything any more.

Ashley had not worked full-time outside the home while she was married, but she was forced to take a job 12 months ago when her divorce from John Miller became final. She had reluctantly started work as a grocery store clerk because jobs were so scarce in their small community. Her job was demanding and her feet hurt from standing on a concrete floor every day. Sometimes customers were irritable and difficult; this was especially challenging on those days when she herself was not up to par emotionally. The hours were long and the pay was just enough to meet most of the expenses each month.

John had agreed to provide child support since he had a much larger salary than she did in his job at a local factory. Without his financial help, she knew that she would have to apply for food stamps. He had mostly been regular with the checks, but a few had come late and not in the complete amount. When she discussed this with him, he always explained that he had financial problems as well and would make up the missing amount in later checks. For the time being, she simply let this all go in hopes that she could trust his word as she could in the past. Still, when this happened, it forced her to cut corners, and she and the children often had to do without some things they would normally have.

The divorce had been a difficult experience. Things had progressively become more difficult and strained between Ashley and John over the years. They had married two years before their first child was born and appeared to be an ideal couple. But as the second child arrived, John increased his work hours and Ashley had taken a part-time job to help make ends meet. As the children grew older, John spent less time being a parent and more time working harder as a provider in order to gain a promotion that would bring in more money. And he helped less around the house as well. Many times, arguments focused on what Ashley regarded as his reneging on a commitment made earlier to share equally in parenting and housework responsibilities. He contended, in defense, that if she wanted the kind of home and furnishings she desired, then this was the price both of them had to pay. In the end, the price became their marriage. They had tried to work out things in therapy but this went nowhere because John maintained that he had become burned out on the marriage itself. He wasn't sure he wanted to be married anymore and only saw a great deal more unhappiness for everyone if they continued to be together.

One thing John and Ashley shared was a concern about how the split-up would affect their children. Now, in therapy, the direction turned to how to prepare the children for the imminent change in their family life. They were able to work out many details relating to their divorce with the therapist rather than with lawyers: how they would arrange joint custody, designating Ashley as the physical custodian; how often John would have visitation with the children; how medical and dental expenses would be handled under whose insurance; and what would happen to their house. The therapist helped them to understand how their children might react so they could be prepared as parents. They rehearsed telling the children about the divorce and why it was happening and other related issues.

The couple wanted to keep changes to a minimum. Toward this end, Ashley gained title to the house, keeping a change in residence at bay for a while and allowing the children to continue to go to their current school. Fortunately, their school counselor had recently organized a support group for children whose parents were divorcing and for those whose parents had divorced. The therapist strongly recommended this program to Ashley and John as a way of supporting their children in handling the stressfulness of their parents' divorce.

One other detail needed attention in this first year following divorce: how to arrange for her mother to have visitation with the children. John and his mother-in-law had not always gotten along, and following the divorce he had mixed feelings about his former mother-in-law having much involvement with her grandchildren. The children had complained several times about wanting to see their grandmother, but this had been delayed because of John's misgivings. When they had each worked with their own lawyers in finalizing the divorce agreement, John's had informed him that grandparents had no legal rights to visitation in their state. John informed Ashley about this information and had wanted to place a clause in the contract specifically stating that

Ashley had to gain his consent before letting the children have visitation with their grandmother. He feared that the hard feelings between them would be expressed by his ex-mother-in-law to the children. Ashley would not agree to this, and the point had delayed signing the contract for several months. They finally reached a verbal agreement by working with their therapist that they would discuss grandparent visitation before arranging it and that John would have veto power if he ever felt uncomfortable.

Lately, Ashley had discovered through the children that John had been entertaining lady "friends" during the time when the children were at his apartment. She was unsure how to handle this. She felt insecure and jealous, but was disturbed more about the appropriateness of this arrangement and how the children could be affected. She had made an appointment with the therapist to discuss this and learn of her options and how to handle her feelings about John's social life.

The school counselor had called her at work to discuss something that her daughter, Brittany, had shared with the support group. Brittany, age 10, had mentioned that her mother was sharing personal problems with her and that she felt helpless and unsure of what to say in response. The counselor had gently suggested that Ashley should rethink these interactions with Brittany. He told Ashley that sometimes this effort to involve a child in an adult's world was not in the child's best interest. He explained that this often forced children to attempt to become mature long before they were emotionally capable. Ashley, of course, was not aware these discussions could be harmful and quickly had discontinued them.

Being a divorced, single mother was not what Ashley had ever imagined would happen to her. She sometimes found herself daydreaming about what it would be like if she ever remarried. She had heard other coworkers who were in a similar position remark that they would live with someone instead of getting married again because of trust issues. She wondered if this would be a possible option for her if she ever fell in love again.

## Parenting Reflection 11–9

Does this binuclear family system have open or closed boundaries? How did boundaries change following the divorce of the parents between themselves and the children? How did this family system use resources to help cope with the crisis event of divorce?

## POINTS TO CONSIDER

- There are a variety of family forms in the United States. Differences in family composition and structure most likely result in differences in the ways in which adults conduct parenting functions.
- The single-parent family is one of the most visible types of family systems in the United States today. Most are headed by a woman who becomes the head of the household through divorce, separation, the death of her spouse, or birth out of wedlock.
- Divorce is the most common avenue through which single-parent family systems are created. There are four basic causes of divorce: (1) The society-level explanation stresses the kinds of social changes that have made divorce more acceptable today. (2) The legal explanation emphasizes the changes in laws that have made divorces easier to obtain. (3) The social-psychological explanation focuses on a variety of factors that contribute to the decision to divorce. (4) The personal explanation, or the reasons given by people who divorce, ranges from extramarital sexual affairs to a spouse's abusive behavior.
- While many mothers continue to be granted child custody, the trend is toward granting joint custody to both parents. This arrangement has many advantages if parents can work cooperatively and communicate with one another about parental role responsibilities. But joint custody also creates problems that must be addressed by everyone involved. When couples cannot reach agreements about custody, they may need to engage a mediator who can help bring closure to their divorce and custody proceedings.
- Women have different experiences as single parents than men do. Single-parent family systems headed by women are characterized by: (1) financial difficulties, (2) additional role strains for the mother, and (3) changes in the parent-child relationship.
- An increasing number of men are gaining custody of their children. Single-parent family systems headed by men are characterized by: (1) greater financial freedom in comparison with the families of single mothers, (2) additional role strain for the fathers, and (3) a less disrupted lifestyle than that experienced by single mothers.
- Divorce has several effects on adults: (1) rediscovering feelings of self-worth, (2) experiencing a sense of failure about the former marriage relationship, (3) developing a fear of intimate relationships, (4) experiencing depression and alienation, and (5) experiencing changes in lifestyle. The continuing relationship between adults, despite the divorce, presents challenges to adjustment.
- Parental divorce has several effects on children. The timing of divorce in a child's life results in different levels and types of adjustment. Generally, preschoolers exhibit regressive behaviors and a variety of other types of behavior problems, particularly during the first year after the divorce. School-age children react to their parents' divorce by feeling angry with their parents, experiencing pervasive fears, feeling helpless about the situation, and perhaps feeling rejected by the absent parent. These children become more involved in household responsibilities and experience changes in interactions with both parents. Adolescents often experience problems with personal identity; fears of being abandoned, rejected, and unloved; fears about the failure of their own marriages in the future; and delinquent behaviors. The effects of parental divorce on children are both short- and long-term. Researchers currently believe that some of these effects can be observed for many years after the parents' divorce.
- Single-parent families have strengths that derive from the experiences of these families in adapting to the crisis of divorce and the resulting challenges for all members of both binuclear systems. These strengths provide opportunities for personal growth that might not occur in other types of family systems.

# CHAPTER 12

# Parenting in Stepfamily Systems

## Focus Questions

∎ ∎ ∎ ∎ ∎ ∎ ∎ ∎ ∎ ∎

1. How are stepfamilies created, and what are their distinguishing characteristics?
2. What are similarities and differences in stepmother and stepfather roles?
3. Are developmental changes observed in stepfamily systems?
4. What are the strengths of stepfamilies? What are major adjustment issues and how are these resolved?
5. What stressors and coping mechanisms are revealed by a systemic family development snapshot of a stepfamily?

∎ ∎ ∎ ∎ ∎ ∎ ∎ ∎ ∎ ∎

One trend noted by demographers over the past 40 years in American family life is the increasing tendency of adults to divorce and remarry, often several times (Kaslow, 2000; U.S. Bureau of the Census, 2003). This pattern has been labeled serial monogamy, sequential polygamy, or conjugal succession (Pasley & Ihinger-Tallman, 1987).

A new type of family system is formed when a single parent remarries. Some researchers refer to it as a *reconstituted* or *blended family system*, but **stepfamily** is the more common label (Ihinger-Tallman & Pasley, 1997). Regardless of the name applied, remarriage of adults restores the adult family role that was vacant in a single-parent family system. Because the vast majority of single-parent families in the United States are headed by women, the person usually filling the vacant adult role is a man who may or may not have been previously married himself. Occasionally, two single parents and their families are merged by the remarriage of the adults (Figure 12–1).

The problems and challenges facing stepfamilies are different from those of other family systems, especially when children are involved. The adults face the usual tasks of establishing an intimate relationship as a newly married couple. However, when children of one or both adults are included, this process becomes more complicated because children are included as part of the remarriage and are not introduced gradually into the family structure. The ability of the new stepfamily system to survive and cope with these challenges occupies much of the time, attention, and resources of the system, especially in the early years following remarriage.

**FIGURE 12–1.** Stepfamilies are often formed by the remarriage of at least one adult. Researchers have observed wide age differences in children of these families.

# INCIDENCE AND CHARACTERISTICS OF STEPFAMILY SYSTEMS

Remarriages are not a new phenomenon of family life (Berger, 2000). In the past, many married adults became single and remarried after the death of a spouse. Divorce has only recently become the leading cause of single status after a first marriage.

Demographers have studied a number of factors and patterns in the occurrence of remarriage in the United States (Bramlett & Mosher, 2002; Kaslow, 2000). Remarriage is more likely to occur if an adult has been divorced rather than widowed (see Figure 12–2). The probability of remarriage is highest among white divorced women and least likely among black divorced women. Women who were under age 25 at divorce are more likely to remarry than women ages 25 and over at divorce. Remarriage is more likely if divorced women live in communities with lower rates of male unemployment, poverty, and receipt of welfare. And interestingly, women living in nonurban areas are more likely to remarry than those living in cities. These patterns may be explained in part by the age of individuals when they become single. People who are widowed are usually in their late adulthood years and are less likely to remarry because of their advanced age. Divorced individuals tend to be much younger by comparison.

Almost two-thirds of the people who divorce each year in the United States eventually remarry (Bramlett & Mosher, 2002). In the typical divorcing couple, the man is about 37 years old, the woman is about 33, and typically they are parents of at least one child (Federal Interagency Forum on Child and Family Statistics, 2003). This suggests that many men and women remarry when they are about 10 years older than they were at their first marriage. Generally, however, remarriage is more likely to occur among younger, rather than older, individuals (Bramlett & Mosher, 2002). The median interval between divorce and remarriage is about 3 years for women, with about half remarrying within 5 years of their divorce. Ethnic group identity also influences remarriage rates; for example, more whites tend to remarry than blacks or Hispanics.

Cohabitation occurs more commonly for many remarrying adults, which is another distinction from that of first marriages (Berger, 2000). This may reflect the desire to test a relationship before making the commitment involved in marriage. Cohabitation prior to remarriage appears to have little effect on a couple's relationship (Skinner et al., 2002). Another distinction of courtship prior to remarriage is the influence of the children's presence. Not only do single parents, especially those who hold custody of children, have a more

**FIGURE 12–2.** Probability of remarriage within 10 years of divorce by race/ethnicity and age at divorce: 1995.

*Source:* Bramlett, M. D., & Mosher, W. D. (2002). Cohabitation, marriage, divorce, and remarriage in the United States. *Vital Health Statistics, 23*(22). Hyattsville, MD: National Center for Health Statistics.

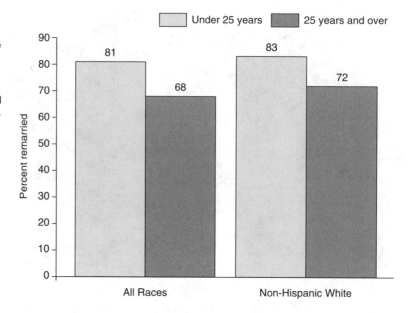

challenging time in locating prospective partners, they have other considerations as well. For example, single parents must figure out how to handle the presence of a potential partner spending the night when children are present or how to help children understand when a relationship with a potential partner has broken up. This may be especially challenging when children have developed an attachment to the potential partner.

Remarriages are also characterized by the difference in developmental levels of the adults at the time of remarriage as compared with those at first marriage. Because of what they have experienced in their first marriage and because of developmental changes, divorced people tend to have different expectations of a remarriage and of themselves (Gerlach, 2003). For example, many women with children who remarry have career goals and plans that may be stronger and more definite than those at first marriage. Many know that they can survive a divorce and are more committed to making another marriage work successfully, or their ideas of what a marriage requires are more clear as compared with the first marriage. Remarriages do not differ significantly from first marriages in terms of marital happiness or in the degree of partners' well-being (Ihinger-Tallman & Pasley, 1997). This lack of difference may be attributed to the issues just discussed.

## Parenting Reflection 12–1

Is it possible to distinguish a stepfamily from a first-marriage biological family?

Like other contemporary family structures, stepfamilies are characterized by their diverse nature (Berger, 2000). For example, some stepfamilies involve only one adult who has been married previously; in others, both adults may have been previously married only once; and both adults may have been previously married more than once. Some involve a remarriage when children were infants and thus perceive themselves as an ordinary family.

Because remarriage most frequently involves individuals who have been previously divorced, it is likely that children of one adult or both will be included as part of the new family system. Researchers describe seven characteristics of stepfamilies that distinguish them from first-marriage families (Berger, 2000).

1. *When children are involved, a new family system is created instantaneously without the benefit of gradually adding new members.* In the family life career of first marriages, adults can gradually develop new patterns (rules, boundaries, and roles) for their family

system that affect effective functioning. Stepfamilies are challenged by the immediacy of developing patterns without gradually adding children to the system. In many instances, the patterns formed for one adult's single-parent family system after divorce are the template for those initially used in the new stepfamily system.

2.   *The remarriage of adults may occur at a time when the necessities and tasks of the stepfamily life career are incompatible with the developmental needs and tasks of the adults.*   In some situations, there is a conflict between what is required for healthy, individual adult development and what is required to establish a new marriage relationship and new stepfamily system patterns.

3.   *Ex-spouses and ex-grandparents can continue to have input into and influence on the new stepfamily system.*   Unlike the family systems based on first marriages, stepfamily functioning is complicated and seriously challenged by the influence of past relationships from former family systems. For example, the adults may continue to be influenced by their former spouses because they are still the biological parents of children who are part of the new stepfamily system.

4.   *Wishes and expectations of adult marriage partners may not be fulfilled by the new marriage relationship in the stepfamily system.*   When adults remarry, they tend to anticipate that the new relationship will overcome or compensate for problems or deficiencies in the previous marriage. However, this expectation places an extra burden on the new marriage to fulfill needs that may be unrealistic.

5.   *Both children and adults may have mixed feelings of allegiance and guilt that interfere with effective stepfamily system formation.*   Children in stepfamilies can become confused about where their loyalties to others should lie because they are members now of two separate and distinct family systems. For example, it is not unusual for stepchildren to feel as if they are being pulled in several directions at once, which tests the strength of their personal boundaries. Adults also carry mixed feelings about their past and its influence on their present functioning into the new family system. It is not uncommon, for example, for remarried men to feel torn between the need to provide for their biological children from their previous marriage and to meet the needs of the family system to which they now be-

long. In addition, whereas many men are relieved that their former relationship has ended, some continue to resent the continuing degree of involvement with that severed relationship through children and financial responsibilities.

6.   *Children may not be willing participants in the new stepfamily system.*   Although adults may consult children about the new marriage relationship, they often do not seek child approval before deciding to remarry. Typically, children are not supportive or accepting of the new marriage, but they are often expected to cope with a situation they would rather avoid or ignore. Many children of divorced parents fantasize that their biological parents will somehow be reunited and that their family life will return to its former state. Many continue to hold resentments about the divorce, which tends to make life unpleasant and difficult in the new stepfamily system as children resist the efforts of the remarried adults to forge new family system patterns.

7.   *All stepfamily members experience role confusion.*   A major task of the system is to establish new patterns that regulate the functioning and behavior of all members. This task is common to all family systems, but it is especially difficult among stepfamilies because of the past histories of the adults and children involved. The role of stepmother or stepfather is not clear, and systems must develop patterns and concepts to define this role, often by trial and error. New rules must be established that all members can agree with for the system to function in a healthy way. Boundaries are a special challenge to effective stepfamily functioning. For example, they may relate to personal property, psychological intimacy, and family routines or traditions. Clear communication, commitment to the new family system, and willingness to discuss issues and reach agreeable solutions are necessary for these new patterns to become established and adapted.

••••••••••••••••••••••••••••••••••••••••••••••••••••••

***Focus Point.***   Stepfamilies are created by the remarriage of at least one adult. Many people who have been divorced remarry within a relatively short period of time. Children are frequently part of the new family system. Researchers note that these families can be distinguished from those based on first marriages in a variety of ways.

••••••••••••••••••••••••••••••••••••••••••••••••••••••

## STEPFAMILY FORMATION

The problems that challenge stepfamily systems are unique, and these systems may experience a greater level of stress than that usually encountered by family systems based on first marriages (Figure 12–3). Generally, problems may occur from the following sources (Pasley & Ihinger-Tallman, 1987):

■ Merging different family cultures and identities as the new system establishes roles and patterns

■ Developing new modes of distributing time, energy, material goods, finances, and affection

■ Establishing new bonds of loyalty to the stepfamily system while learning to manage loyalty bonds to former family systems

Stepfamily system formation involves different structures than does first-marriage system formation (Papernow, 1984, 1993). First-marriage families differ in having a history of time to allow the adults to develop an intimate relationship and areas of shared interests, values, and habitual patterns that guide interactions and conflict resolution. The gradual addition of children to a biological family allows the adults to develop and adapt parenting roles and patterns, learn to resolve their differences, and create a shared value system as needs arise.

When a first-marriage couple divorces, they create a single-parent family system that most prominently affects the children, who become members of two distinct binuclear systems. A major consequence of change in the parent-child relationships is the dismantling of the usual generational boundaries between adults and children. Adults look to children for the support and nurturance formerly provided by the spouse.

At the beginning of a stepfamily's life, the stepparent at first seems to be an outsider to the existing alliance between the biological parent and his or her children. This alliance is based on the patterns established in the former single-parent family system and has its own history, methods of problem solving, rules, boundaries, patterns, and operational styles firmly in place. The greatest challenge to the survival and effective, healthy functioning of a stepfamily system may be overcoming the obstacles and resistance encountered in adapting previously established patterns and styles to accommodate the needs of the new stepfamily system.

Patricia Papernow (1984, 1993) developed a model that describes stepfamily formation. She depicts three major stages that involve substages (see Focus On 12–1). It takes a relatively long period of time for a stepfamily to find itself and its identity. Many difficulties can challenge effective family formation and functioning. For example, one of the disadvantages that challenges effective stepfamily formation is that the children involved frequently are adolescents. Because of their developmental focus on individuation from their families, struggles can

**FIGURE 12–3.** Remarried couples face additional challenges in establishing new relationship bonds. The success of a new stepfamily often depends on the health of the new marriage relationship.

**Focus On 12–1**

## Stages in Stepfamily Formation

### Early Stages: Getting Started and Avoiding Pitfalls

#### Stage 1: Fantasy

Everyone involved commonly holds unrealistic expectations that they hope will be fulfilled in the new family system:

- Children will be rescued from problems associated with the divorce of their biological parents.
- Children will be able to get their biological parents reunited by sabotaging the biological parent's new relationship.
- The biological family will be healed by introducing a new adult into the vacated role.
- Stepparents will be adored by stepchildren and welcomed enthusiastically by the biological family.
- The biological parent will finally have unmet needs satisfied by the new partner.
- The biological parent will be able to share parenting responsibilities again with another adult.

#### Stage 2: Assimilating the New Adult

The biological parent attempts to merge the stepparent into the biological family but usually cannot accomplish this goal successfully at this time. The stepparent notices by now that he or she is an outsider and discovers feelings of jealousy, resentment, and inadequacy.

- Both stepparent and stepchildren experience problems in establishing and working on a relationship.
- Problems are perceived differently by everyone involved. The stepparent expresses frustration in dealing with what is seen as an impenetrable biological family solidarity. The biological parent doesn't understand the frustrations of the stepparent. The stepchildren may begin to experience loyalty conflicts toward their absent biological parent and the stepparent.
- The biological parent feels caught in the middle between wanting a good adult relationship and the problems experienced by children in dealing with a new adult in their family.

#### Stage 3: Awareness

Many stepfamilies stagnate in their development at this stage due to difficulties in communication between all parties. To avoid this, all family members need to:

- Apply labels to feelings being experienced
- Understand why the feelings are being experienced
- State personal needs more articulately
- Listen to what the stepparent describes as perceived rules and boundaries in the biological family that have failed to include the stepparent

### Middle Stages: Remodeling the Family

#### Stage 4: Mobilization

The stepparent's role to initiate changes intensifies at this point. A showdown becomes inevitable; if the changes and compromises cannot be made, there is considerable risk that the stepfamily will dissolve via divorce of the adults.

- Some changes and demands may appear to be trivial but these represent the need for further weakening of the biological family's alliances to accommodate the stepparent into a new family structure.
- The biological parent may feel pulled in two directions: meeting the perceived needs of children and giving more allegiance to the new relationship.

*(continued)*

**Focus On 12–1**  *(continued)*

■ If the changes and adaptations are successfully implemented (e.g., having more private time for the adult couple), the new stepfamily now can truly be formed.

### Stage 5: Action

This is when the changes and adaptations may be implemented on a larger scale to form the new stepfamily.

■ New family rituals and traditions are helpful to facilitate a sense of family.
■ Boundaries and rules are tested out to more clearly define the adults' committed relationship and the stepparent-stepchild relationship (e.g., restricting discipline of children solely to the biological parent and removing the stepparent from this responsibility).
■ The stepparent now plays an even larger role in the new family.
■ The adult couple work together more closely as a team in a variety of matters.

### Later Stages: Putting It All Together

### Stage 6: Contact

This stage serves to solidify the actions taken to forge a new stepfamily.

■ Children have been reassigned out of the primary relationship with the biological parent as it was modified in the single-parent family experience and maintained in earlier stages of stepfamily formation.
■ A workable relationship has been negotiated for the stepparent and stepchildren without involvement of the biological parent.
■ Each member's family role becomes validated and authentic.

### Stage 7: Resolution

The new stepfamily achieves a new identity.

■ The stepparent becomes accepted by the stepchildren as an "intimate outsider." A true friendship emerges between them.
■ The family gestalt differs completely from earlier; instead of uncertainty and stress, the feeling is one of confidence and comfort in relationships.
■ The family learns to let go of dependencies that helped in forming the new family structure.

*Source*: Adapted from Papernow, P. L. (1984). The stepfamily cycle: An experimental model of stepfamily development. *Family Relations, 33*, 355–363; Papernow, P. L. (1993). *Becoming a stepfamily*. San Francisco: Jossey-Bass.

be expected when the adults involved demand their teenager's participation in activities that are aimed to develop a family identity.

**Focus Point.** The structure of stepfamilies is different from that of biological families. Single-parent families are created when adults divorce from their first mar-

riage, which changes the relationship between the biological parents and children. When a biological parent's marriage to a new partner forms a stepfamily, other changes emerge in the parent-child subsystem such as the alliance between the biological parent and children adapting to include the stepparent. A stepfamily life career progresses through distinct stages that may occur over a long period of time.

## STEPFAMILY ROLES AND RELATIONSHIPS

A stepparent's role is distinct from that of a biological parent (Parenting FAQs 12–1). It differs in having a high degree of role ambiguity (Berger, 2000; Papernow, 1993). Our culture promotes many stereotypical images of stepparents that are largely negative in nature. These images can be found, for example, in stories and fairy tales told to children. Stepparents, particularly step-

mothers, are depicted as evil, uncaring, self-centered individuals who mistreat and abuse stepchildren. To a certain degree, popular television shows and movies reflect the lack of clarity in the stepparent role.

Belief in these negative stereotypes varies according to someone's current family situation. Perceptions of stepparents, and particularly those of stepmothers, are generally negative when compared with perceptions of biological parents. However, individuals currently living in single-parent family systems and stepfamilies tend to

---

**Parenting FAQs 12–1**

**I'm seriously considering marriage to a wonderful woman I've been dating for almost 2 years. There are school-age children involved. I've never been married before. I have no clue what it's like to be a father, much less what is involved in being a stepfather. Can you tell me what to expect if I become a stepfather?**

**A:** You are in a unique position that may be to your advantage. Since you don't bring any preconceptions about fathering to this situation, you may not already have certain ingrained ideas about what you should be doing as a parent. However, this is an instant family situation. You are the newcomer in an already established and long-term relationship between the children and their mother. It might help you to understand what you are confronting to consider these factors about the role of a stepfather:

- **Uncertainty about the degree of authority in the stepfather role.**  The challenge is accomplishing the transition from being a friend to stepchildren before remarriage to establishing a parenting relationship after remarriage.
- **Uncertainty about the amount of affection to show to stepchildren.**  Some stepfathers feel uncomfortable kissing and hugging stepchildren and do not always enjoy play activities with them.
- **Uncertainty about disciplining stepchildren and enforcing rules.**  A major source of conflict between stepfathers and biological parents involves agreeing on what needs enforcing and what is unimportant. It is difficult for many biological mothers, even if they have given prior approval, to deal with stepfathers' attempts to discipline their children.
- **Uncertainty about how to deal with financial conflicts.**  Many stepfathers feel sandwiched financially between two different families. Members of the new stepfamily often see the financial contributions of the stepfather as a measure of love and devotion to the new family system.
- **Uncertainty about dealing with guilt regarding perceived abandonment of one's own biological children.**  This feeling frequently interferes with establishing good relationships with stepchildren because a sense of allegiance remains strong toward the biological children.
- **Uncertainty in dealing with loyalty conflicts.**  Problems emerge regarding the time children spend with biological parents versus stepfathers.
- **Uncertainty in dealing with sexual conflicts.**  The incest taboo in families is weakened in stepfamily systems. Adults and children in these families can be sexually attracted to and involved with one another. This is unhealthy, illegal, and inappropriate abusive activity, especially for children.
- **Uncertainty in dealing with conflicts about surnames.**  Some stepfamilies have problems with the differences in last names of the adults and children.

*Sources:* Adapted from Robinson, B. F. (1984). The contemporary American stepfather. *Family Relations, 33,* 381–388; Coleman. M., & Ganong, L. H. (1991). Remarriage and stepfamily research in the 1980s: Increased interest in an old form. In A. Booth (Ed.), *Contemporary families: Looking forward, looking back.* Minneapolis, MN: National Council on Family Relations.

hold less negative opinions than those living in first-marriage families. Negative perceptions about stepparents seem to decrease as people become more sensitive, familiar, and appreciative of the problems and challenges that face stepfamilies (Bloomfield, 2004).

Expectations about how someone should perform a social role frequently influence actual behavior. Although research does not specifically detail exactly what may be expected of people in stepparent roles, it finds that stepparents are expected to share equally in the parental status of the new family system. However, the stepparent is expected to be involved to a lesser degree than the biological parent (Berger, 2000). Additionally, social disapproval is considerably less if a stepparent refuses to become involved with stepchildren than if a biological parent refuses to become involved with offspring.

Special parenting problems may arise for a person who occupies the vacant role in a former single-parent family system. Both men and women who become stepparents may approach their new role with some trepidation or fear of the unknown. These individuals come into a family situation in which they are often considered an outsider. The entire family interaction pattern must change to include the new person's cognitive style and personality pattern. For example, a single-parent mother who marries or remarries is confronted with relinquishing her sole authority in managing family affairs, and she must now share decision-making responsibilities with her new partner. Although many women welcome this change, others state that they must work hard to realign their role with that of the new partner (Pasley & Ihinger-Tallman, 1987).

Although some remarriages are generally reported to be happier and more successful than first marriages, most of the problems associated with stepfamily functioning are related to parenting children from the former marriages (Berger, 2000; Bloomfield, 2004). The difficulties of a stepparent may be enhanced when stepchildren live with the remarried couple rather than elsewhere, particularly if they live with a stepmother.

## Parenting Reflection 12–2

Why are clearly defined role functions and behaviors for stepparents lacking in our society?

## Stepmothers

The uncertainty associated with stepparent role expectations causes many problems for individuals who assume these roles (Berger, 2000). The stepmother role is made even more difficult by two basic myths: (1) a stepmother is bad, and (2) she requires instant love from the stepchildren. To counter these impressions, the stepmother who believes in these myths may overcompensate by contributing too much to the relationship between herself and her stepchildren. The situation becomes impossible, however, because the stepmother eventually realizes she cannot possibly please everyone involved, including herself. Her own children may complicate the situation by feeling that they are left out, ignored, or receiving less attention than their stepsiblings.

## Parenting Reflection 12–3

How do stereotypes about stepmothers depict these individuals? Are there similar ones about stepfathers? Do these truly influence the behavior of individuals in these roles? Could these become self-fulfilling prophecies about stepparents?

Families in which the mother role is filled by a stepmother are found to have more problems than those with a stepfather. This may be due to differences in the ways in which stepfamilies are formed. Fathers who gain custody of children after remarriage often do so because the mother has difficulty handling the child or because the child has experienced problems following the parental divorce. Another difficult situation among families with stepmothers involves a woman who has never had children of her own but who quickly assumes a parenting role after her first marriage or remarriage.

Relationships with stepchildren may vary depending on their sex. Stepmothers and stepdaughters are found to have the least favorable relationship of all steprelationships studied. The girls in these relationships who do not feel loved report more feelings of hostility and lowered self-esteem. A factor that may contribute to a poor stepmother-stepdaughter relationship is the child's regular contact with her biological mother.

This seems to create tensions within the stepfamily because children may find it more problematic to replace mothers than fathers in their lives.

Age of stepchildren is also a factor in influencing the nature of the relationship with their stepmother, especially among those who have live-in stepmothers. Preschool-age children have the least problems in interactions with stepmothers, whereas school-age and adolescent children have poorer relationships with their stepmothers by comparison. The stepmothers of these older children have more disagreements with their spouses, more conflicts over ways of disciplining children, and less satisfaction with their marriages than do stepmothers of younger children.

## Stepfathers

Stepfathers encounter similar kinds of problems in developing and performing their family role (Berger, 2000). Some research suggests that stepfathers are less likely to be authoritative in parenting style than are biological fathers.

The stepfather-stepchild relationship may be at risk for as long as 2 years following the remarriage. Unlike the stepmother, he is not handicapped with myths and stereotypes about his new role. The less-structured nature of his role has both advantages and disadvantages. On the positive side, he can forge a new identity and impression when establishing a relationship with his spouse's children. Problems abound, however, in several areas. For example, establishing disciplinary patterns and using controls related to stepchildren's behavior are often prime problem areas for stepfathers. Disagreements often result with the spouse over how the stepfather conducts his disciplinary actions with stepchildren.

Stepfathers also experience problems in relation to their financial affairs. Many must make some kind of child support payments to their biological children from a former marriage. This money may be very much needed by the new stepfamily, which can produce feelings of resentment about the former marriage experience. Guilt feelings may derive from the sense that biological children have been abandoned after the formation of the new stepfamily system. Some men feel, however, that when another man becomes involved as a stepfather to their biological children, then this man should help to bear the financial costs of raising and caring for these children. Researchers have suggested that biological fathers reduce their social and economic investments in children with whom they no longer live when they remarry and become involved in a stepfamily. One study reports that biological fathers in new stepfamilies are likely to adjust child support payments to nonresidential children to accommodate the financial needs for supporting the "new" biological children (Manning & Smock, 2000).

A man's satisfaction with being a stepfather is associated with several factors. First, being a biological father appears to work against a man's development of a positive relationship with stepchildren. Men who do not have children of their own and who become stepfathers appear to develop more positive relationships with stepchildren. Second, positive relationships between stepfathers and stepchildren are enhanced by the amount of communication that occurs between them. Third, when stepfathers feel that they have the biological mother's support to become involved in disciplining children, they report greater levels of satisfaction. This factor may also be due to the eagerness of younger children in accepting a new father into their lives. Older children and adolescents are less willing to make adjustments and to be tolerant and accepting of a new individual in their family life. Finally, a critical event takes place in stepfamily formation when the stepfather accepts the stepchildren as his own and makes the transition from being an outsider to being a paternal figure (Marsiglio, 2004). This is all dependent, of course, on the contingencies of stepchildren making a similar transition in accepting the stepfather into the family circle.

## Stepgrandparents

If we acknowledge that the family role of grandparent in contemporary times is ambiguous, consider the even more unique status of the stepgrandparent role. The legal status of stepgrandparents is even less clear. The little research available about this family role indicates that stepgrandparents are more likely to view stepgrandchildren like biological grandchildren if they are young when an adult child remarries. When stepgrandchildren live with the grandparent's adult children, the likelihood for a relationship developing between stepgrandparent and stepgrandchildren increases considerably. However, stepgrandparents appear to be generally overall less satisfied with relationships with stepgrand-children than biological grandparents (Christensen & Smith, 2002). One study (Haberstroh et al., 2001) reported on the perceptions of adult grandchildren of their stepgrandparents. The researchers suggested that stepgrandparents can improve the relationship with their grandchildren by behaving in a more actively parental manner, establishing a closer relationship with their adult child, and increasing their visits with the grandchild at family gatherings and holidays. The quality of the stepgrandchild-stepgrandparent relationship appears to be influenced to a greater extent by the adult children than by the factors exclusive to the stepgrandparent-stepgrandchild relationship. Stepgrandchildren perceived the quality of the relationship with their biological grandparent to be stronger than their stepgrandparent relationship.

## Stepchildren/Stepsiblings

Usually, the quality of life for stepchildren is thought to be enhanced when their biological mother remarries. As discussed earlier in this chapter, single-parent families headed by a woman typically experience either a poverty-level existence or a borderline standard of living. When children live in these conditions, they fare less well than children living in more affluent families in terms of quality of life, medical care, nutrition, education, and economic security (Federal Interagency Forum on Child and Family Statistics, 2003).

Researchers, however, report that children from stepfamilies fare no better nor no worse than children from single-parent families in terms of ratings of well-being (Berger, 2000). When compared with children from intact, first-marriage families, children from both stepfamilies and single-parent families are rated as less well-adjusted. It should be stressed, however, that most children in stepfamilies are not found to demonstrate serious problems.

The research literature is also ambiguous regarding whether children of different ages and gender adjust differently to the arrival of a new stepparent (Berger, 2000). Children are expected to make a series of adjustments when biological parents divorce and later remarry. These adjustments typically focus on making a transition in family structure and functioning. These adjustments are stressful and have manifestations in school performance, behavior, and other socioemotional factors. Obvi-

ously, children living in intact, first-marriage families do not experience anything comparable that can affect their development, providing one major explanation of why researchers report such disparate findings.

One finding remains consistent among the majority of studies about children growing up in stepfamilies (Berger, 2000): These children, especially girls, can be expected to leave their stepfamilies at an earlier age than those growing up in single-parent or two-parent households. Their reason for leaving is to establish their own homes and lifestyles prior to marriage or to become married. One explanation for these early departures is the tensions that exist between themselves and their parents and stepparents. Apparently, exiting the stepfamily is seen as a more viable way to resolve these tensions. Some researchers suggest that the friction that exists in stepfamilies involving female children is due to the disruption of the mother-daughter relationship by the mother's male sexual partner who has an ambiguous relationship with the daughter.

Sibling relationships become complex when stepfamilies are formed that involve children of both adult partners (Berger, 2000). Forging stepsibling relationships presents other challenges for stepfamilies to accomplish. The usual problems often observed in biological sibling relationships, such as rivalry and jealousy, can become even more intense when stepsiblings are involved. It is not unusual for coalitions to develop between siblings of each adult that create a "my children are being mistreated by your children" scenario. Furthermore, sexual tensions can exist when stepsiblings are pubertal or adolescent, although this topic has not been given credible attention by researchers. On a more positive note, stepsiblings can also develop strong relationships where mutual support can be found and friendships flourish (Anderson et al., 1999).

## Ex-Spouses and Ex-In-Laws

Relationships are not severed but become altered with ex-spouses and ex-in-laws for people in stepfamilies. It is typical for these individuals to feel displaced and alienated when divorce transforms their relationship (Berger, 2000). Although the rights and boundaries that define the altered relationship between ex-spouses begin with the divorce agreement, few legal rights or clear distinctions inform ex-in-laws about their altered relationship with one another.

It is not uncommon for ex-spouses to experience feelings of jealousy, anger, and competition with their former partners (Berger, 2000). Likewise, ex-in-laws may also harbor similar feelings of resentment about one another. However, in other situations, ex-spouses and ex-in-laws work to make the situations more tolerable and amicable.

••••••••••••••••••••••••••••••••••••••••••••••••••

*Focus Point.* Stepfamilies involve challenging and complex relationships. The stepparent role differs from that of a biological parent. It is characterized by certain definitions for both men and women, although many negative images and stereotypes are associated with the role. The expectations of a stepparent are ambiguous, and remarriages generally are happier than first ones. Most of the problems of stepfamilies relate to a stepparent's child-rearing function. The stepmother may encounter more difficulties than the stepfather does, and her relationships can be influenced by the age and sex of children. Stepfathers encounter many similar problems, but their role is less restricted by structure and expectations, which allows for greater freedom in creating a unique role identity. Several factors affect a man's satisfaction with being a stepfather. Stepchildren and stepsiblings also experience challenging situations as new relationships are defined and developed. Ex-spouses and ex-in-laws, as well as stepgrandparents, experience unique situations as their roles and relationships become defined in a new family structure.

••••••••••••••••••••••••••••••••••••••••••••••••••

## ISSUES AND STRATEGIES OF ADJUSTMENT IN STEPFAMILIES

The ability of stepfamilies to adjust to their new status, roles, and patterns depends on three central issues (Pasley & Ihinger-Tallman, 1987):

1. Giving up the dream, or discarding unrealistic fantasies and expectations of the new family system and its members
2. Clarifying the feelings and needs of each family member
3. Making a commitment to create and adapt new rules, roles, boundaries, and family routines suitable to the new family system

Stepfamily systems must successfully accomplish several tasks to make the transition from early disillu-

sionment to total commitment to the new family system (Bloomfield, 2004; Glenn, Erwin, & Nelen, 2000). A variety of strategies are useful in reaching this final point.

First, the biological parent and the stepparent need to determine long-range goals for the organization of the new family system. This vision is determined by thinking about the needs of all family members. One helpful way to initiate the process of planning is to have the remarried couple conduct a guided fantasy exercise. This allows them to visualize how they want things to be at some future time in their family life. Discussion about the stepparent's role function is especially important at this time. The couple can use input from the stepchildren, relatives, or a trained therapist in setting long-term goals.

Second, it is helpful if the remarried couple agrees that the biological parent is in charge of setting and enforcing limits for his or her biological children. It is recommended that when enforcing limits, the stepparent should learn to say, "Your parent says that you should." When the biological parent is away and has left the stepparent in charge, it is helpful to instruct children to obey the stepparent in much the same way that they are expected to obey a sitter. The biological parent gives instructions to children that they are expected to follow under the stepparent's supervision. When both adults have biological children, it is helpful for them to understand that it is OK to have different rules for the different children. There is a tendency for stepfamilies to try to follow the old first-marriage family system's model of developing and imposing the same rules for all children rather than understanding that the new family system is nothing at all like the previous one. Conflicts will probably occur between the biological parent and the stepparent, and couples may need assistance in learning how to negotiate compromises.

Third, stepparent-stepchild bonding often needs assistance. This occurs much in the same manner as it does between biological parents and their children during infancy. The process is characterized by nurturing without setting limits on children's behavior. When the stepparent insists that the biological parent should take over the limit-setting functions, bonding can occur between the stepparent and stepchildren. This process may take a year or longer, depending on the age, personality, sex, and other factors of the children. The stepparent must also learn about individual differences that characterize each stepchild.

Fourth, adjustment to becoming a new family system is facilitated when the stepfamily develops its own rules, boundaries, and traditions. This step may be as mundane, but important, as determining who performs what household chores. Negotiation is the usual method for developing rules and traditions, and it is helpful if the stepparent and stepchildren engage in their own discussions in this regard. However, if the biological parent and stepparent cannot reach agreement on a particular rule, it is important for the stepparent to concede to the biological parent because children usually will not obey any rule that their biological parent does not support. Children confirm their awareness of the biological parent's lack of agreement when they tell the stepparent, "You can't make me do that because you aren't my real parent."

Part of the negotiation strategy for the adults regards the biological parent's motivation to make compromises with the stepparent's point of view. This depends on the biological parent's perception of the stepparent's positive contributions to the children's lives. If the biological parent refuses to negotiate, the stepparent has the option of withdrawing this support to gain cooperation in discussion with the biological parent. Sometimes professional help is needed to assist the remarried couple in reaching a settlement on these issues (Figure 12–4).

Fifth, stepfamilies need to develop ways for interacting with the households of their ex-spouses. This is facilitated when the stepparent encourages the children's relationship with the same-sex parent in the other household and by avoiding competition with him or her. It is important for the stepfamily to differentiate itself from the other family by establishing recognizable boundaries. One way to accomplish this is to encourage the understanding that each family system has its own rules and that this difference is acceptable. Couples' groups also help in coping with conflicts between households. In these groups, the remarried couple learns new ways of dealing with these stresses and comes to understand that the situation is not unique.

● ● ● ● ● ● ● ● ● ● ● ● ● ● ● ● ● ● ● ● ● ● ● ● ● ● ● ● ● ● ● ● ● ●

### Parenting Reflection 12–4

What are some indicators that a stepfamily needs to seek assistance in resolving issues that fail to support family cohesion?

● ● ● ● ● ● ● ● ● ● ● ● ● ● ● ● ● ● ● ● ● ● ● ● ● ● ● ● ● ● ● ● ● ●

Other sources of support for stepfamilies come from self-help publications, educational experiences, and therapeutic intervention (Ziegahn, 2002). A variety of self-help books is available on the topic of stepfamilies. They primarily focus on the problems these family systems face and offer a number of strategies for dealing with these issues in healthy ways.

Educational strategies can include lectures, workshops, and seminars on the topics of stepfamilies and remarriage. These programs assist individuals in developing more realistic expectations of stepfamily life that facilitate the creation of long-term goals. Marriage and family enrichment programs are also offered by churches and other organizations, and they are intended to assist stepfamily development (Hawkins, 2003).

**FIGURE 12–4.** Family therapy can help stepfamilies learn new ways to resolve conflicts and problems.

Therapy is often the last resort when communication has failed and remarried couples seek assistance in resolving their conflicts (Berger, 2000). A variety of mental health professional assistance is available in communities to provide help to stepfamilies, including psychologists, marriage and family therapists, psychiatrists, counselors, social workers, and members of the clergy. Stepchildren may need to be included in the therapeutic program or may need other special attention. Therapeutic groups led by mental health professionals also offer educational and supportive means for promoting emotional closeness or family cohesion among stepfamily members. Children often call on teachers for help. When this occurs, teachers can play an important role in helping children understand that the problems unique to stepfamily life can be resolved. Teachers may work with parents or refer the family to professional assistance. It is important to stress here that because stepchildren may complain about problems in their new family, it may appear that the stepfamily home life is deleterious to their development. Adjustment problems are more prevalent among children in stepfamilies, and they can cause a higher level of stress than that experienced by children in first-marriage families. Even though this stress can affect school performance and other aspects of their lives,

the children are not necessarily harmed by having a stepfamily experience.

Support groups are another source of therapeutic assistance for stepfamilies. They allow a remarried couple to discuss and hear matters of mutual interest that relate to their problems. It is also helpful to hear how others in similar circumstances cope with problems and reach creative solutions (Smith, 2002).

## Parenting Reflection 12–5

Can stepfamilies have strengths not possessed by first-marriage families?

***Focus Point.***   The success of a stepfamily may depend on its ability to overcome obstacles that challenge the development of the new family system. The stepfamily may use several strategies to reach this objective as well as a variety of sources for support, such as therapy and support groups.

# SYSTEMIC FAMILY DEVELOPMENT SNAPSHOT

*(Before reading this section, it may be helpful to review the systemic family development model and the metaphor used to illustrate its concepts from Chapter 3.)*

We will examine the functioning of a stepfamily by taking a slice in developmental time from the new family formed by the remarriage of Ashley Miller, the mother of the single-parent family described in the Chapter 11 snapshot. This snapshot is taken six years after Ashley's divorce was final. She is now 41 years old; her daughter, Brittany, is now 16; her son, Michael, is now 13. The only living grandparent is Ashley's mother who is now 67. Ashley's new husband is Tim Matthews, age 47, a divorced father of three children living with their mother as physical custodian. Tim holds joint custody of his biological children with his ex-wife. Legally, he has no

parental rights with Ashley's children unless he decides to adopt them.

Tim moved into Ashley's home, to which she gained title following her divorce, following a brief courtship of slightly less than 6 months.

## A New Stepfamily

Ashley Matthews . . . she was just now getting used to having this new name. It still sounded somewhat unfamiliar to her, especially when someone called it out, but she knew that would pass. She had had the new name now for about three years. The first year after marrying Tim Matthews was like a long, extended honeymoon. Things had gone relatively smoothly when Tim moved into her home. They had dated for about 6 months prior to remarriage; she had had some reservations about getting remarried but felt that she knew Tim well enough to make a commitment. The children had seemed at the time to like Tim and thought he was relatively "cool" for someone his age. Now, almost three years into the new stepfamily, she was starting to have some doubts if this had been the good decision it seemed at first.

Ashley's misgivings related to feeling pulled in two directions in her new family. On the one hand, Tim had been complaining enough now that it required serious attention. His most common observation was that he felt like an outsider. This had come as a shock to Ashley because she had believed that Tim fitted in relatively well and easily into their routine. As it turns out, he had not felt a part of the group almost from the time he had moved in. On the other hand, her children also had their own complaints about Tim. They had loudly resisted any of his attempts to discipline them when he believed they were acting unruly. Their disputes were loud and sobering in how vociferously they had communicated that he was NOT their father and NEVER would be. In the end, these disputes had not been resolved to the satisfaction of anyone. Ashley often felt that if she didn't back up her children, she would lose their love and loyalty. Conversely, if she didn't back up her husband, she was afraid he would question her loyalty to him and to their relationship. It seemed to be a no-win situation, so she had kept her silence until now.

The tension in the home had become so heavy within the last several months that there were sometimes long periods when the children tried to avoid any communication, even during meals, or Tim would withdraw from interacting with any of them. Ashley had finally persuaded everyone that they needed to get professional help. In essence, she made an ultimatum for the entire family, including herself, that they must work out their differences. She would not allow anyone not to participate. She had practically begged, pleaded, and did whatever it had taken to get Brittany to agree. The children were told that if they had been determined to destroy their mother's remarriage, they had another thought coming because she and Tim had no intention of splitting up. This may have been what the children had needed to hear in order to understand why they needed to participate in the recovery process.

After several months in family therapy, Tim finally let out the long list of ways he felt he had been treated as an outsider. He was responding to the therapist's request for everyone to discuss at least two things they found uncomfortable in the new family. As it turned out, he had felt that Ashley was part of the problem, not just the children. Tim described many times over a meal when someone would mention what essentially was an "inside joke." Since he didn't understand it, he couldn't join in with the laughter that ensued. He hated the way certain meals were prepared but hadn't said anything because he felt this was imposing himself. In reality, he was also hurt that no one had asked what his favorite dishes were and how he liked certain dishes prepared. Everything had been business as usual just as they had established their routines as a family before he had arrived. He felt like a guest, even an unwelcome one at times.

The children then mentioned a laundry list of complaints. They felt that Tim was intrusive and had butted in to their family's way of doing things by wanting to impose his way of working with issues with no discussion. Other complaints were mostly the standard teenage fare of resenting the constant demands to do things together as a family and to have family vacations together.

Ashley was finally able in this session to voice her feelings of being pulled in two different directions by her loyalty and love. Tim was surprised to hear this, and the children reacted by being astounded that their mother would even consider putting Tim above their own interests. The therapist intervened at this point by stating that the children needed to understand the importance of the adults' marriage to the well-being of the new family. She explained that their mother needed to be supportive of her new husband and vice versa for the marriage to work. She also pointed out that preserving the integrity of the marriage was not any indication of lack of support, love, or loyalty to the children. These were two different relationships that worked independently as well as integratively within the entire family relationship.

At the end of the session, the therapist gave assignments to the different relationships in this stepfamily. The adults were to have discussions to work out discipline matters for the children. Ashley would be in charge of enforcing the rules, and Tim would back her up but not impose any rules of his own that had not been worked out with Ashley beforehand. In addition, they were to have "date nights" away from the home and from the children where they would have time to develop a closer, more intimate committed relationship. The therapist also assigned the children and Tim specific projects. She hoped that these exercises would allow Tim and the children to form a relationship that was not grounded in power assertion on anyone's part. By reconfiguring these relationships, they could form friendships. This might take a while to accomplish, but she had seen it happen with others when they shared a commitment to keep working on the matter.

Ashley and Tim knew their new family was at a crossroads, but by working with the therapist and allowing the teens in their family greater freedom to express feelings appropriately, taking these new roads would bring them into a different family configuration.

## POINTS TO CONSIDER

■ Remarriage in the United States involves several factors and patterns. It is more likely to occur among individuals who have divorced, and individuals who remarry generally are young adults. The median interval between divorce and remarriage is about 3 years. Ethnic background influences remarriage; for example, whites tend to remarry more frequently than blacks do.

■ Stepfamilies are distinguished from those formed by first marriages in a variety of ways. When children are involved, a family system is transformed and recreated instantly without the benefit of gradually adding new members. One remarried adult may be facing the developmental tasks of the stepfamily life career at a time when those tasks are incompatible with the other person. Ex-spouses and ex-grandparents can continue to make their influence known in the new stepfamily system. Spouses' wishes and expectations may not be fulfilled in the new marriage. Both children and adults may have mixed allegiances and feelings of guilt. Children may not want to be part of the new family system. All members of the new family system experience role confusion until patterns can be established through experience and negotiation.

■ Stepfamilies encounter a series of developmental tasks similar to those of single-parent family systems. They also experience a sequence of stages in their life career: (1) fantasy, which represents the time when all members hold unrealistic expectations for the new family system; (2) assimilation, in which attempts are made to include the new family member in the existing biological family network; (3) awareness, when members of the stepfamily can recognize and give labels to their confused feelings; (4) mobilization, or the time when the stepparent acts to initiate changes in the biological

family network to promote assimilation; (5) action, or the time when new boundaries are formed and erected, differences are negotiated, and new patterns of interaction are established; (6) contact, or the time that is characterized by developing and increasing the authenticity of interactions within the stepfamily system; and (7) resolution, or the period when strength is built into the relationships of the stepfamily system.

■ The stepparent role is distinct from that of a biological parent because it has a high degree of role ambiguity. This is especially the case for stepmothers. Typically, the role is characterized as one that includes many interaction problems with other family members, especially children.

■ Families in which the mother role is filled by a stepmother may have more problems than those with a stepfather. This difference may be due to the ways in which these new family systems begin their family life careers. The quality of relationships with children appears to depend on a child's sex and age.

■ Stepfathers have similar difficulties but are not hampered by stereotypes and myths about their role. They encounter problems in disciplining stepchildren and in dealing with complex financial arrangements involving two separate family systems. Sex and age of stepchildren are factors influencing the quality of the relationship with a stepfather.

■ Adjustment in stepfamilies hinges on resolving three basic issues: (1) giving up the dream, or discarding unrealistic fantasies and expectations of the new family system and its members; (2) clarifying the feelings and needs of each family member; and (3) making a commitment to creating new rules, roles, boundaries, and routines for the new family system.

■ A variety of strategies assist stepfamily members in adjusting to this new status. (1) Adults decide on long-term goals for organizing the new family system. (2) They agree that the biological parent is in charge of enforcing limits for his or her children. (3) They facilitate the bonding process between the stepparent and stepchildren. (4) They develop patterns involving rules, boundaries, and traditions for the new family system. (5) They develop ways of interacting with the households of ex-spouses. (6) They seek assistance from self-help literature, educational strategies, psychotherapy, and participation in support-group activities.

■ Stepfamilies have particular strengths that include: (1) opportunities for stepchildren to learn problem-solving, negotiation, and coping skills, as well as the ability to be more flexible and adaptable; (2) the presence of more adults for support; (3) exposure to a wide variety of people and experiences; (4) exposure to a good model of marital interaction; and (5) the possibility of a better experience than that offered by the single-parent family.

# CHAPTER 13

# Homosexuality and Parenting

## Focus Questions

■ ■ ■ ■ ■ ■ ■ ■ ■ ■

1. What challenges confront parents and family members who learn that a child is gay or lesbian?
2. Why are some gay men and lesbian women parents?
3. Does sexual orientation affect one's ability to parent children effectively?
4. Do children experience harm being raised by gay or lesbian parents?

■ ■ ■ ■ ■ ■ ■ ■ ■ ■

## HOMOSEXUALITY AND PARENTING

Homosexuality has always been recognized as an aspect of human nature and sexuality (Bozett & Sussman, 1989). However, in cultures with a strong Judeo-Christian heritage, homosexuality is labeled most negatively, and **homophobia,** the irrational fear, dislike, or disgust of homosexuality and homosexuals, and **heterosexism,** the belief that heterosexuality is superior and preferable to homosexuality, occur most strongly (Herek, 1984, 1993). Because of these beliefs, many people do not understand the nature of homosexuality and express hostility, fearfulness, intolerance, and unacceptance toward homosexuals.

A family is traditionally considered to be the one place where people are nurtured emotionally, loved unconditionally, and accepted for who and what they are. This may be an unrealistic expectation for many individuals, but for gays and lesbians it is especially so. Serious and painful problems are involved in being the only homosexual member of a family composed of heterosexuals in which heterosexuality is promoted as socially conventional and totally acceptable. It is especially difficult for many gays and lesbians to develop a healthy, positive self-esteem growing up in a heterosexual family because they fear rejection if they disclose their true sexual orientation (Connolly, 2005). Most homosexuals feel caught in a no-win situation. They risk rejection if they disclose their orientation; however, if they keep it secret, they deny their basic core identity, which also promotes poor self-esteem and other interpersonal disturbances as well.

Gays' and lesbians' fears of rejection are well founded on their personal perceptions as well as their observations of the actions and beliefs of others. There is little social affirmation for homosexuality in our society. Laws do not sanction homosexuals' committed relationships. Many states have enacted legislation limiting marriage only to opposite-sex individuals and/or banning recognition of domestic partner relationships. A movement is under way to amend the U. S. Constitution to ban same-gender marriage. Only in 2003 did the U.S. Supreme Court finally extend the right of privacy to homosexual activity in states that had enacted sodomy laws. Employment benefits are not universally accorded to partners of homosexual individuals in the United States. Homosexuals are officially barred from military service despite the new "don't ask, don't tell" policy, denied basic civil rights that are extended to other groups, and unwelcome in most churches and religious groups. If they are parents, homosexuals may be denied parental rights and custody of their children. Many states prohibit gays and lesbians from adopting a child, and only the biological parent in a gay relationship has parental rights in most states.

Some progress has been made, however, toward changing negative attitudes about homosexuality. For example, homosexuality is no longer considered to be a mental illness. In 1969, the American Psychiatric Association and the American Psychological Association declared that it was no longer considered a diagnostic classification. The conclusion still drawn by many gays and lesbians, however, is that they are not full members of society with the same constitutional rights and privileges that others have, despite the fact that they are taxed equally with heterosexuals.

Researchers have been unable to establish clearly the origins and causes of sexual orientation. The literature has a long history of holding various environmental influences as the determining factors in homosexual orientation, but that theory is considered questionable today (Dode, 2004). One psychoanalytical-based approach points to family influences in particular. It proposes that male homosexual orientation occurs because an individual has an extremely dominant mother and a relatively nondominant, emotionally distant father (Bieber, 1962). Other approaches propose that sexual orientation is a learned phenomenon among males and females, which suggests that individuals can willfully change their sexual orientation. No convincing evidence resolutely proves this as fact (Harry, 1989; Milic & Crowne, 1986; Whitam & Zent, 1984). Another hypothesis is that high levels of stress during pregnancy influ-

ence the likelihood of homosexual orientation of a woman's child because the stress acts to produce particular hormones that affect brain formation leading to the development of this orientation (Money, 1987). More current thinking is that a variety of markers point to a biological basis of sexual orientation (Brookey, 2000; McKnight, 2000).

Considerable popular support persists for the view that environmental factors are the cause of homosexual orientation. For example, many heterosexuals believe that gay people willfully choose their sexual orientation. There is no conclusive scientific support for such an opinion. In fact, evidence continues to grow supporting the position that people are born with a particular sexual orientation that is manifested after reaching puberty (McKnight, 2000; Patterson, 1995; Strickland, 1995).

Although some people have long believed that genetics and biological factors play an important role in determining sexual orientation, little convincing evidence has been found until recently. Studies comparing the sexual orientation of identical twins suggest a strong familial and genetic basis for homosexuality. Research points to a biological basis for male sexual orientation due to differences in certain brain structures found in homosexual and heterosexual individuals (Oldham & Kasser, 1999). These structures are associated with areas of the brain that govern sexual orientation and behavior. According to this view, individuals cannot choose their sexual orientation, although it is unclear how environmental factors may interact with these biological predispositions to influence sexual orientation. Other research provides data linking genetic and prenatal influences to the development of sexual orientation. For example, one study reports that women who experienced prenatal exposure to estrogens were more likely to be lesbian or bisexual in orientation (Meyer-Bahlburg et al., 1995).

Another investigation studied a group of preschool-aged girls and boys who had a condition known as congenital androgen hyperplasia (Berenbaum & Snyder, 1995). This exposure to high levels of androgen (a male sex hormone) during prenatal and early postnatal periods leads to the development of masculine characteristics. While the boys were not affected deleteriously by their condition, the researchers noted the girls preferred boys' toys and play activities over those usually associated with girls, which was believed to be a reliable predictor of homosexual orientation upon attaining puberty for these girls. Furthermore, research suggests that gay males have a greater than average number of older brothers and can be expected to be of later birth orders among their sibling constellations (Blanchard et al., 1995; Bogaert, 2003).

Various theories have tried to explain why this phenomenon is observed among gay males. The most plausible explanation may be that mothers of later-born gay men who have more brothers than average experienced something similar to an allergic reaction to the testosterone being produced by their male fetuses during pregnancy. In a manner similar to that found among pregnant women having a problem with the Rh blood factor, the degree of incomplete androgenization of the fetal brain increased with each pregnancy, culminating in a greater probability of the later children developing a homosexual orientation after puberty.

A large number of family systems in the United States today include a homosexual member. Studies estimate that individuals with exclusively homosexual orientation comprise from 7 to 12 percent of the male population and 5 to 7 percent of the female population (Bagley & Tremblay, 1998; Kinsey, Pomeroy, & Martin, 1948; Kinsey et al., 1953; Strong, 2004). According to recent Bureau of the Census figures, this estimate translates to about 23 million men and about 12 million women (U.S. Bureau of the Census, 2003). Assuming that these individuals come from an average-sized family of about four people, the potential number of people with a homosexual relative is more than 100 million, or nearly half the population of the United States. In addition, about 25 percent of the gay and lesbian population of the United States are biological parents of children from heterosexual relationships. There may be about 10 million children in the United States who have a gay or lesbian parent (Patterson, 1992).

There is no clear estimate about the number of families who know they have a homosexual member because not all homosexuals have disclosed their orientation to family members. This secrecy occurs for several reasons, many of which may relate to fear of rejection or a desire to avoid the unpleasant homophobic reactions of family members. Disclosing sexual orientation to parents and other family members is a critical experience for most gays and lesbians because of the risks involved. Nonetheless, those who make their orientation known affect change in the identity of their family of origin as family members adapt to the news.

## Family Systems with Gay or Lesbian Children

It is common for parents to develop and acquire a variety of expectations about themselves and their children. These expectations guide and shape parenting behavior and may serve as self-fulfilling prophesies for those involved in this family subsystem. Generally, these expectations are positive and reflect wishes, desires, hopes, and dreams for parents as well as children.

One of the most difficult but health-promoting acts performed by a homosexual person is disclosing this information and identity to others, especially family members. This process is known as **coming out.** Many heterosexuals do not understand the importance of this act and do not welcome the news because they have already learned negative attitudes and concepts about homosexuals and homosexuality. For homosexuals, the significance of disclosure lies in presenting themselves to others as whole, authentic people unashamed of who they are. Homosexuals share this act of intimacy in the hope that the disclosure will not result in rejection but eventually lead to honest acceptance and unconditional love (Eichberg, 1990).

● ● ● ● ● ● ● ● ● ● ● ● ● ● ● ● ● ● ● ● ● ● ● ● ● ● ● ● ● ● ● ●

### Parenting Reflection 13–1

What would you do and say if your best friend shared the news with you that one of his or her children is gay or lesbian?

● ● ● ● ● ● ● ● ● ● ● ● ● ● ● ● ● ● ● ● ● ● ● ● ● ● ● ● ● ● ● ●

Family systems theory predicts that when one family member changes in some manner, all other members of the system are also affected to some degree. A child's disclosure of his or her homosexual orientation is unlikely to be part of the vision that most parents hold for their child or for themselves as parents. The disclosure of homosexual orientation disrupts a family system largely because of the significantly negative social stigma that people commonly associate with homosexuality (Singer, 2001). Family disruption initially relates to members' difficulties in reconciling these negative attitudes, beliefs, and myths about homosexuality with what they know about the particular family member. These beliefs and stereotypes usually govern the initial reactions of family members after the gay or lesbian child discloses his or her orientation, and they may override what the family members already believe they know about the child as an individual and as a family member.

**Disclosure as a Family Crisis.** A child's disclosure of his or her homosexual orientation acts as a stressor event for the family system, which most likely produces a crisis reaction. The child's revelation challenges the family's perceptions of him or her, and a conflict develops as members attempt to reconcile negative stereotypes and beliefs about homosexuality with what they know about the child as a person (Rust, 2003).

Family systems react in predictable ways to any significant change or crisis event that may be external to the system or internal among members (Savin-Williams, 2001; Savin-Williams & Dube, 1998). According to Hansen and Hill's (1964) ABC-X model of family crisis management, family systems demonstrate common modes of reaction when their functioning is challenged by a significant stressor event. To briefly review, this model proposes that when A (a stressor event) interacts with B (the family's use of resources and abilities to cope, with the stressor) and with C (the family's definition of the stressor event), then X (a family crisis) will occur (see Figure 13–1). The family system's reaction to the stressor event is a response or process based on these complex interactions.

Family coping strategies (the B factor) differ in reaction to stressor events. These strategies include withdrawing from interactions with people outside the system, discussing the situation only among the adults, denying that there is a problem, using anger and other negative emotions, and seeking assistance from others outside the system. These coping strategies, however, may or may not

be immediately set into motion after a homosexual child's disclosure. Factors that collectively represent the system's and its members' interpretations (the C factor) may temporarily override other means that the family eventually employs to resolve the crisis of disclosure.

According to the ABC-X model, a family system's interpretation of the stressor event influences the system's reactions. The model predicts that when members perceive they are the cause of the problem, the family system as a whole suffers. The group is hampered in its ability to function in healthy, effective ways.

Some families interpret the revelation of a child's homosexuality in terms that are far more serious than those of other families. For example, many parents typically assume personal guilt for their child's homosexuality, believing they have done something wrong in their child rearing. They mistakenly believe that they have somehow performed poorly as parents and are failures (Fairchild & Hayward, 1989). Parents also report feeling sad, fearful for their child, shocked, depressed, and hurt following their homosexual child's disclosure (LaSala, 2000a; Mosher, 2001). It is more typical of siblings, however, to react with anger and confusion rather than guilt. They often experience feelings of alienation toward the homosexual sibling, who now seems to be a stranger rather than someone well known (Merighi & Grimes, 2000). Interestingly, a homosexual child often comes out to family members incrementally, reflecting the degree of emotional closeness he or she feels toward specific family members. For example, the child may tell the mother first, then the siblings, and finally the father.

Observers also note other efforts as the system attempts to interpret the disclosure (Merighi & Grimes, 2000; Waldner & Magruder, 1999). These may occur in

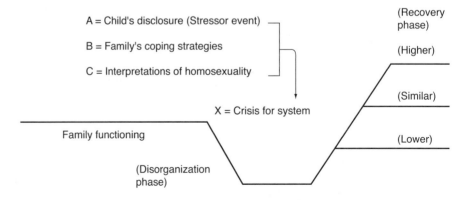

**FIGURE 13–1.** Patterns of family reactions to stress and crisis. This figure represents the process of the ABC-X model of family crisis management relating to a child's disclosure of homosexual orientation.

*Source:* Adapted from Hansen, D. A., & Hill, R. (1964). Families under stress. In H. Christensen (Ed.), *Handbook of marriage and the family*. Chicago: Rand-McNally.

two particular patterns. First, heterosexual family members frequently attempt to understand the homosexual child in relation to the family values concerning homosexuality. In reacting to the child's disclosure, parents and other family members have been exposed to, and very possibly believe, the negative stereotypes and myths about homosexuals. Most individuals know few openly gay or lesbian people to provide evidence that disputes or challenges negative stigmas and stereotypes.

In addition, sexual orientation is a private part of a person's identity, and a homosexual identity or acknowledgment is achieved late in the developmental sequence, usually in adolescence and early adulthood. Family members have had many opportunities to come to know the person without the benefit of this private knowledge about homosexual orientation, which the person may choose to disclose or family members may discover accidentally. Even if parents have suspicions about a child's homosexual orientation, the revelation of homosexuality constitutes a crisis for most parents and family systems: They may have previously assumed that the person is heterosexual like themselves. Cognitive dissonance may become evident as heterosexual family members try to reconcile negative family values about homosexuality with positive family values about the family member. Generally, the more negative the family values about homosexuality, the more negative the interpretations of and reactions to the homosexual child. These reactions may range from physical, emotional, and verbal abuse and attack to abandoning the child.

A second pattern relates to the interpretation and definition a family system makes and ascribes to the homosexual child after disclosure. The members frequently negate the child's family role as brother, son, daughter, sister, or cousin (Strommen, 1989a, 1989b). The gestalt or integrated patterns are revised to state, "There is a stranger in our midst now." Essentially, the family recognizes that it does not seem to know this person after all. What was secret and hidden (the homosexual identity and orientation) is now public to the family. This recognition raises questions about intimacy and what else the family may not know about the child.

Several factors predict the nature and strength of a family's determination of a child's disclosure as a crisis, which relate to the values that the system holds about homosexuality (Strommen, 1989a, 1989b). First, the more a family system subscribes to traditional, conservative religious teachings about homosexuality, the more

negative the reactions to, and interpretations of, a child's disclosure. Second, if family members promote traditional, rigid conservative beliefs about gender roles, then these individuals generally react negatively to any homosexual, whether or not the person is external or internal to the family system (Savin-Williams, 2001). Third, rules that govern the functioning of a family system can influence the likelihood of negative reactions to disclosure (Green, 2002). For example, some family rules relate to maintaining an image or reputation in the community ("We maintain family respectability at all costs," "As a family we solve our own problems," or "We must be as our religion teaches us"). Fourth, age and gender of family members can influence reactions in positive or negative ways. Generally, the younger children and much older adults in a family system may be more accepting and react more favorably to the disclosure than others. However, members of the same sex as the homosexual child can be expected to react more negatively than members of the opposite sex. This is especially the case for males in the family system, although fathers, brothers, uncles, and grandfathers may be expected to react unfavorably regardless of the sex of the homosexual child.

In keeping with the prediction made by the ABC-X model, the degree to which a family system interprets a stressor as disruptive becomes a self-fulfilling prophecy. After taking stock of family values relating to homosexuality and combining them with interpretations and meanings given to the homosexual child's disclosure, the system often concludes that the family is experiencing a crisis (the X result in the ABC-X model) caused by the revelation. If people perceive a child's revelation as extremely severe, their adjustments to new perceptions of the child are much more difficult. This reaction is in accord with the devastating nature people ascribe to the news.

When a family system determines that the disclosure constitutes a family crisis, the system moves into a phase of disorganization in family functioning. Families typically resist the changes that accompany the stressor event they interpret as a crisis because the ultimate goal of the system is to maintain established *homeostasis*, or balance. A child's disclosure of homosexuality temporarily disrupts the patterns of interaction and communication and the roles of all family members. They often do not know how to act toward the homosexual child after the disclosure. They may pressure the child to change his or her sexual orientation, place the child and the family into therapy, and keep the disclosure a secret from others outside the immediate or extended family. Essentially, reactions of family members disrupt the stability of the family system and tend to enhance or minimize **entropy,** disorder or chaos in effective functioning that results from lack of input from outside a family system.

The disorganization phase begins to be resolved as a family system moves into a recovery phase. Members make efforts to reach solutions that are appropriate to their particular style of functioning. Depending on the particular family system, as members attempt to reestablish homeostasis, the resolutions reached in adjusting to a homosexual member may be healthy or unhealthy. A healthy family system may initiate processes that involve **negative entropy** (attempts of the system to move away from disorder and chaos by accepting and using information from external sources) and **morphogenesis** (responses by the family system to implement changes in its rules, interactions, communications, and roles). In this way, the family moves toward positive **adaptation** in response to the homosexual child's disclosure. This tends to promote and enhance effective functioning of the family system (Figure 13–1). Such a family often seeks assistance, information, and educa-tion from outside sources that result in growth, change, innovation, and adaptation in structure and patterns.

Family systems that seek to find healthy solutions to this particular crisis may come to recognize that family secrets are unhealthy and disruptive to the effective operation of the system. Members may realize that an individual's sexual orientation is not a matter of personal choice and that no one can willfully choose to be heterosexual or homosexual. They may accept that a person's only choice is to be honest and to act authentically about his or her sexual orientation. Many family members, in seeking to understand a gay or lesbian child, acquire accurate information by educating themselves about homosexuality in appropriate ways and from reliable sources (Green, 2002; Savin-Williams, 2001). For example, they may seek out the services of psychotherapists and counselors who have expertise in homosexuality and read a variety of books on the topic. They may attend support groups devoted to helping families understand homosexual members, such as Parents and Friends of Lesbians and Gays (Parents FLAG) (Figure 13–2). These efforts facilitate a family system's ability to change its negative values about homosexuality and to create a climate of acceptance and tolerance for the homosexual child. The system's health is promoted by its understanding that differences are appropriate among members.

**FIGURE 13–2.** Support groups for family members of gays and lesbians, such as Parents FLAG, provide education and understanding for those seeking greater insight about homosexuality and the ways family systems are affected by having a homosexual member.

Some family systems do not have healthy patterns for coping with crisis, or they may be heavily influenced by the negative factors previously discussed. These families may be expected to react in ways that promote the continued dysfunctionality of the system, which may lead to serious impairments. From the perspective of family systems theory, these systems move toward higher levels of entropy and try to maintain *morphostasis* (attempts to maintain previously established family system organization, structure, and patterns) as a means of reestablishing homeostasis.

Such attempts promote even greater disorganization in the system, which prevents effective functioning. For example, members may shun and reject the gay or lesbian child; refuse to discuss anything relating to the child's homosexuality, relationships, or lifestyle; or shame the child and act in ways that express intolerance, such as disinheriting or banishing the child from the family system. When parents and other family members choose rejection as a means of resolving this crisis, the choice reflects their need to respect social conventions about homosexuality rather than express unconditional love for the homosexual family member and respect for individual differences among members. Members may blame the child for causing the disruption to the family system and resent the child for his or her actions.

The alienation heterosexual members feel when they discover they do not really know the homosexual child highlights the ineffective coping solutions they often enact. These solutions frequently include scapegoating the homosexual child, denying the child's news or refusing to discuss it, developing alliances with other heterosexual family members, or not including the child in family activities. These family systems often fail to move further toward resolving the crisis in ways that are healthy and promote effective family functioning. Instead, a hostile, ambivalent family atmosphere, especially as it relates to the homosexual child, becomes the normative family style to restore homeostasis to the system (LaSala, 2000b).

In keeping with the ABC-X model predictions regarding outcomes (see Figure 13–1), those systems that react to and resolve the crisis of a child's homosexual disclosure in unhealthy ways may reach levels of functioning similar to, or lower than, those before the crisis. In many instances, a homosexual child may withdraw his or her participation from the family system due to the negative, unaccepting reactions of members. This tends to weaken and alter the family's ability to function adequately and may be similar to losing a family member through death. In more extreme situations, a family system's unhealthy resolution may contribute to the homosexual child's likelihood of developing serious emotional depression. This depression can lead to suicide, which may account for the high suicide rate among adolescents who have difficulty accepting their homosexual orientation (Sullivan & Wodarski, 2002; van Wormer & McKinney, 2003).

Those systems that resolve the crisis in healthy ways may reach levels in recovery that are similar to, or greater than, what existed before the crisis. In these families, the pain that members initially experience after the child's disclosure becomes transformed into deeper degrees of personal growth and appreciation. Family members consider themselves to have become better people who are more open and less judgmental of others (Lewallen, 1992). Essentially, these families turn the crisis into learning experiences that can result in a better quality of life for everyone.

In reality, this description of a family system's experiences in reacting to a homosexual child's disclosure does not fully convey the deeply emotional aspects, the difficulties in reaching resolution, or the length of time each family takes to work through this process (Williamson, 1998). Parents in their role as caregivers must often struggle to resolve conflicts between their need to give unconditional love, nurturance, and visible support to a gay or lesbian child and their perceived responsibility to respect social norms that promote prejudicial and discriminatory views about homosexuality (Weinberg, 1972). If families are to respond to this crisis in healthy ways, they need to find a solution that allows their expression of unconditional love to take precedence over their need to respect socially conventional beliefs. However, to find this solution, parents most likely need to express their grief about the losses that relate to a child's homosexual orientation. These losses may include, for example, no longer being potential grandparents, no longer having a child who is conventionally similar to other children in the family, no longer anticipating marriages and relationships that are sanctioned and recognized by the community, and no longer being like other parents of heterosexual children. Parents must allow the grief and mourning process to proceed in order to heal these and many other losses. (One study, however, questions the existence of a sequential process that families experience upon receiving disclosure from a child about his or her sexual identity [Savin-Williams & Dube, 1998]). By doing so, they facilitate the healing of their family system and the reconstruction of a role definition for their homosexual child as an accepted family member. They also confront homophobic and heterosexist feelings and notions that prevent expressions of love and intimacy toward their child.

## Gay and Lesbian Families

One common belief holds that gays and lesbians do not participate in family life and that the very nature of their lifestyle is antifamily and singles-oriented (Bigner, 2000). This belief is a stereotype based on homophobic and heterosexist attitudes about gays and lesbians in American society. In reality, gays and lesbians participate in family forms that are not easily distinguished from others found in our society. It is not widely known in society at large, but a common denominator in homosexual culture is the lack of constraints that define the rigid following of norms, roles, and behaviors. As applied to family life, gays and lesbians have reinvented notions of what it means to be a family, how this family functions, and who participates in the membership (Benkov, 1994; Weston, 1997). These families are referred to as **families of choice.** Membership, roles, and rules governing this type of family structure are custom-designed according to mutually agreed conditions. As such, families of choice are formed by conscious decisions about who constitutes the family, how it is defined, and what it means to each participant. Many gays and lesbians do not feel the need to conform to family structure based on consanguinity or legally sanctioned marriage, as is the norm in heterosexual culture. They focus instead on providing a social support network based on compatibility, love, intimacy, emotional warmth, interest, and a sense of community. According to societal norms, these elements compose the essence of family life. The primary reason why gays and lesbians approach family life in this manner can be traced to the negative societal stigmas attached to homosexuality. These stigmas deny homosexuals the right to marry and bring about estrangement with families of origin in many instances. When children are involved, it is difficult to distinguish gay and lesbian families from heterosexual stepfamilies, except in the same-sex composition of adults who act as parents.

The beginning of gay and lesbian kinship formation takes place when an individual initiates what is known as the coming-out process. This multifaceted process occurs in stages and perhaps is never completed (Green, 2002). Gay and lesbian individuals develop a personal identity based on their sexual orientation, similar to that experienced by heterosexual individuals. Part of this identity is the desire to become emotionally close to another person just as heterosexuals do (Gottman et al., 2003). Gays and lesbians participate in loving, committed relationships that often endure for long periods of time and resemble those found among heterosexuals (Kurdek, 1995). Distinct differences are found, however, in gay and lesbian committed relationships. Primarily, their committed relationships strongly emphasize egalitarian functions since they are not forced to adopt and maintain traditional gender-role models, typically found among heterosexuals, that emphasize differences in social power in the relationship (Gottman et al., 2003; Kurdek, 2003).

Like other families, those formed by gays and lesbians bring strengths as well as challenges to family members. While providing individuals with a sense of togetherness and support, the families of gays and lesbians experience the trials of prejudice and discrimination and lack wide acceptance within their larger communities. The omnipresence of AIDS and its multifaceted effects can permeate all aspects of family life. These families must develop healthy ways of coping with continual stresses while maintaining the tasks of day-to-day living. By expanding the very idea of family that transcends traditional limitations, gay and lesbian families demonstrate how to deal with societal adversity in healthy ways.

**Gay and Lesbian Parents.**  Many people are probably surprised that homosexual men and women form families that include children. This situation occurs more frequently than most people believe because such families often appear to be identical to those composed of heterosexuals.

Because our culture harbors beliefs and attitudes that are antagonistic toward homosexuality, many people have a difficult time reconciling the notion that it is appropriate for gay and lesbian adults to be parents (Clarke, 2002; Tasker, 2002). It is doubtful that parenthood among gays and lesbians is a new phenomenon, but it may be more highly visible in today's society. The following discussion examines the issues relating to those gays and lesbians who have become parents and how their sexual orientation affects their children.

***Gay Fathers.***   The gay father is a newly emergent figure in homosexual culture, and researchers have relatively little information or knowledge about these individuals as compared with heterosexual fathers. Homosexual males who are fathers have a unique and more complex social-psychological environment than those of most homosexual or heterosexual men. Their challenges of adjustment relate to identity issues, acceptance of self, acceptance by other gay men, and matters relating more specifically to parenting and child custody issues (Bigner, 1996). Other concerns relate to the development of a long-term, committed relationship with another gay man who accepts and copes with children as a central issue of the relationship.

The man who is both a homosexual and a father is an enigma in our society. The term **gay father** even seems contradictory, although this contradiction is mostly a matter of semantics. *Gay* is associated with homosexuality, while *father* implies heterosexuality. The problem lies in determining how both terms may be applied simultaneously to a person with same-sex orientation who is also a parent. What complicates our understanding of this individual is that the idea of a gay father contradicts the stereotypical image of gay men, which emphasizes that gays have an antifamily lifestyle that values being single (Hain, 1999).

Researchers estimate that about 20 to 25 percent of self-identified gay men are also fathers (Bigner, 1999). This group clearly constitutes a minority within a minority in our culture. It is impossible to estimate accurately the number of gay men who are parents because many are married to women or remain *closeted*, undisclosed about their sexual orientation, for other reasons.

According to several researchers, the dilemma of the man who is both gay and a father involves the fact that he is a victim of divided personal identity (Bigner, 1996). More precisely, these men are described as socially marginal, challenged by having ties to the cultural worlds of both gays and nongays.

The process of identity development for a gay father requires a reconciliation of two polar extremes. Because each identity, homosexual and heterosexual, is essentially unaccepted by the other culture, the task for these men is to integrate both identities into a cognitive concept called *gay father*. This process is referred to as *integrative sanctioning* (Bozett, 1981a, 1981b, 1985, 1987; Bozett & Sussman, 1989). It involves the man's disclosure of his gay orientation and identity to nongays and his father identity to gays, thus forming close liaisons with people who tolerate and accept both identities simultaneously. It also involves distancing himself from others who are not tolerant and accepting. At the same time, he enhances his identity development by participating in the gay subculture.

***Why Do Gay Men Become Fathers?***   The reasons explaining why a gay man becomes a parent are not fully known because little factual information is available on gay fathers in general (Bigner, 1996; Patterson, 2000). We can speculate on one reason: A man might not be able to accept his homosexual orientation; therefore, he marries a woman and fathers children as a means of denying his true sexual orientation. Later, however, he divorces to pursue his identity as a gay man. Also, an openly gay man may willfully choose to become a father as part of a liaison established between himself and a lesbian woman because they both desire to become parents. Under these arrangements, a pregnancy is usually initiated via artificial insemination. Some gay men enter into a marriage with heterosexual women, with both partners knowing in advance the man's sexual orientation. Other marriages involve bisexual men, and many of these marriages continue intact for years. Some gay men have a genuine desire to parent children or simply want to reproduce for the same reasons often given by heterosexuals.

Gay fathers' reasons for having children are generally similar to those of nongay fathers; however, some significant differences may exist between these groups (Bigner & Jacobsen, 1989b). Nongay fathers appear to want children for traditional reasons, such as continuing a family name or providing security for parents in their old age. Gay fathers appear to place greater emphasis on the fact that parenthood conveys adult status to people in the community. This reason may be important to men who marry women in an attempt to avoid the negative social stigmas associated with homosexuality. Some of these men may use their heterosexual marriages and parental status to camouflage their homosexual orientation, most likely because they have internalized the homophobic attitudes and perceptions of society. They find it impossible to admit and reconcile their homosexual orientation and live an openly gay lifestyle. Men with such backgrounds are thought to constitute the large majority of gay fathers.

Many of these men eventually seem to come to terms with their homosexual orientation and find it impossible to live a masqueraded heterosexual lifestyle that is inauthentic, unfulfilling, and dishonest (Peterson, Butts, & Deville, 2000). These men frequently gain the courage to disclose their homosexual orientation to their wives, perhaps in conjunction with the midlife transition that ordinarily prompts much personal self-evaluation and reorientation of life goals (Sullivan & Reynolds, 2003). Their wives usually experience upsetting, disruptive reactions to the disclosure (Buxton, 1994, 2004). Few of these marriages remain intact following the man's disclosure. The men usually want to pursue the development of their homosexual identity, and the women do not wish to continue an involvement with a man who is not heterosexual and who they feel has deceived them. Some marriages survive this crisis because one or both partners feel a strong commitment to children, or because a divorce would lower the standard of living for the individual and/or the family.

The adjustment of men who divorce and pursue a homosexual lifestyle is difficult and problematic as the man acquires the new identity of gay father (Bigner, 1996). These men enter the gay subculture at some disadvantage because they come out at later ages than other gay men. They usually seek to replicate the kind of relationships they experienced or desired in their heterosexual marriages. Because they are not like most other gay men, gay fathers often experience discrimination and rejection from other gays who are not fathers. Many gay fathers are successful in forging a partnership with another gay man that is based on long-term commitment, emotional and sexual exclusivity, and economic cooperation.

Little is known about the nature of these relationships or about the gay stepfamily system that may emerge from its formation (Lynch, 2000). However, it appears that satisfaction of all people involved in a gay stepfamily is improved when efforts are made to include the gay stepfather. This is similar to what is found in heterosexual stepfamilies as a means of improving the overall success of the family system (see Chapter 12).

***Children of Gay Fathers.*** Several issues are unique to the parenting arrangements of gay fathers and their children (Patterson & Redding, 1995). These issues are summarized in Focus On 13–1.

There is no hard empirical evidence proving that the homosexual orientation of fathers or other caregivers is detrimental to children's welfare (Bigner, 1996, 1999; Patterson & Redding, 1995; Stacey & Biblarz, 2001). In fact, gay fathers are as effective as nongay fathers in their ability to parent children and provide for their care. Gay fathers are more nurturant with children and less traditional in perceiving the provider role as a prime aspect of their parenting role. They have positive relationships with children and try hard to create stable home lives for them.

These findings may be explained in the following ways. First, gay fathers may feel additional pressure to be proficient in their parenting roles because: (1) they may feel guilty about the difficulties that divorce and disclosure create for their children, and (2) they are sensitive to the fact that their parenting behavior is being scrutinized by ex-wives and others, and they may fear that custody or visitation rights will be challenged because of their sexual orientation. Second, gay fathers may be more androgynous than nongay fathers in their approach to parenting children. Their child rearing styles may incorporate a greater degree of expressiveness and more nurturant behaviors than the child rearing styles of nongay fathers do (Bigner, 1996; Bigner & Jacobsen, 1989a, 1989b). Heterosexual fathers may incorporate more elements of traditional male sex-role behavior, which is rigid and less nurturant, into their parenting behaviors.

A common fear and concern expressed in court proceedings by the judicial system, which determines the custody of children with a gay father, is that the children will also develop homosexual orientation. It should be noted that this fear masks a deeply homophobic and hostile reaction about homosexual parents rather than reflecting true concern for the best interests of children. The consensus of research is that the causes of sexual orientation are not known, but most researchers agree that sexual orientation does not seem to be transmitted from parents with a particular orientation to the children they raise (Strong, 2004). The parents of most homosexuals are heterosexual. If the sexual orientation of parents were transmissible to children, then heterosexual parents would only produce heterosexual children. In reality, this is not the case. In addition, the pattern found in the general population of the incidence of homosexual orientation appears to be replicated among sons of gay fathers (Bailey et al., 1991). More than 90 percent of

| Focus On 13–1 | **Issues Relating to Children of Gay Fathers** |
|---|---|

**The Father's Disclosure of Homosexual Orientation**

- Gay fathers have a more difficult time acknowledging and disclosing their homosexual ori... children than lesbian mothers do. This difficulty may be especially pronounced among black m...
- Gay fathers describe their children's reactions to disclosure as "none" or "tolerant and accepting."
- The age of children at the time of disclosure may affect their reaction. Those who have not experienced puberty may be more accepting than those who have.
- Children may have some difficulty relating to peers who are aware of the father's homosexual orientation, but the children apparently cope successfully with these problems, showing little harm to their self-esteem.

**Parenting Skills and Effectiveness**

- No empirical or descriptive evidence proves that having, being raised by, or living with a gay father is detrimental or harmful to the development of children.
- Most gay fathers have positive relationships with their children. Gay fathers make more serious attempts to create stable home lives and positive relationships with their children than are usually expected from traditional heterosexual parents.
- Gay fathers are similar to nongay fathers in their reasons for having children and do not differ from nongay fathers in their degree of involvement of intimacy with children.
- Gay fathers tend to be stricter, more nontraditional, and more responsive to children's needs and provide more explanations for rules than nongay fathers do.
- Sexual orientation is not a factor in determining the quality of parenting behavior and relationships.

*Sources:* Adapted from: Bigner, J. J. (2000). Gay and lesbian families. In W. C. Nichols, M. A. Pace-Nichols, D. S. Becvar, & Y. A. Napier (Eds.), *Handbook of family development and intervention* (pp. 279–298). New York, NY: Wiley; Committee on Psychosocial Aspects of Child and Family Health. (2002). Coparent or second-parent adoption by same-sex parents. *Pediatrics, 109,* 339–340; Patterson, C. J. (2000). Family relationships of lesbians and gay men. *Journal of Marriage & the Family, 62,* 1052–1069.

adult sons of gay fathers are reported to have heterosexual orientation. Apparently, these data strongly suggest that sons of gay fathers do not adopt their homosexual orientation by modeling that of their fathers, nor does living with a gay father appear to contribute in a substantial way to the sexual orientation developed by sons.

Perhaps one of the advantages that gay fathers offer to children of both sexes is the modeling of an androgynous sex role (Bigner, 1996, 1999). Psychologists have identified androgyny as the ideal gender role (Bem, 1975). Individuals who have this gender role identity and behavior manifest characteristics associated with both sexes regardless of their biological sex. Researchers have identified many advantages to having such a gender role and identity. Androgens are liked better than persons with a traditional masculine or feminine orien-

tation (Hunter & Forden, 2002). Adult males who are androgens are described as having highly developed egos, showing greater flexibility in considering options to solving problems, and having a greater and deeper respect for individual differences in others. These individuals are also described as having an accepting attitude about sexual behavior, sexual relationships, and interpersonal relationships in general with others. In addition, androgens are reported to have higher self-esteem and feelings of self-worth.

Gay fathers can generally be expected to incorporate greater degrees of androgynous behavior and identification than heterosexual fathers (Bigner, 1996, 1999; Bigner & Jacobsen, 1989a, 1989b). This may be due to gay fathers feeling less of a need to depend upon traditional male sex role behaviors and identity as heterosexual

ers appear to do. This does not imply that gay fathers
are less masculine or that they are more feminine or
effeminate as compared with heterosexual fathers, as
depicted in the traditional cultural stereotype of gay
men. Because gay fathers can combine both emotional
expressiveness and goal instrumental behaviors in their
behavioral repertoire, children can learn to adopt these
androgynous behaviors as well. It is irrational to prevent
a gay father from raising children based solely on his homosexual orientation, especially when the data strongly
indicate that sexual orientation of children, and that of
sons in particular, is not transmitted in this manner.

The benefits offered by gay fathers to their children
relate to their ability to expand their interpretations of
what it means to be a father beyond the limited traditional meanings of this family role (Bigner, 1999, 2000).
The benefits to children are likely to become even more
apparent upon reaching adulthood when their relationships with others can be expected to be based on equality rather than who holds the most social and physical
power. Researchers have found that couples in which
one person or both are androgens: (1) have higher levels
of relationship satisfaction (Wharton, 2004), (2) divide
decision making equally, (3) deemphasize the use of
power by either partner in the relationship, and (4) have
greater long-term life satisfaction that extends far into
the years of late adulthood than couples with a traditional or undifferentiated gender role orientation. This
information provides even greater credibility to the consistent research findings that children experience no
harmful influence on their developmental progress by
being raised by, or living with, a gay father.

**Lesbian Mothers.**   The parenting experiences and
situations of lesbian mothers are generally similar to
those of gay fathers; however, researchers observe differences in family dynamics (Golombok, 1999; Mooney-
Somers & Golombok, 2000; Tasker, 1999). Lesbian
women differ from gay men in the ways in which they
become involved as parents. For example, although
many women acknowledge their homosexual orientation after being married to a man and having children,
many other lesbians use artificial insemination as a
means of achieving parenthood (Stevens et al., 2003;
Vanfraussen, Ponjaet-Kristoffersen, & Brewaeys, 2003).
Adoption may also occur more frequently among lesbian
women and couples than among gay men and couples
(McClellan, 2001).

Lesbian couples face legal and social challenges
when they form a committed relationship and use artificial insemination to conceive children (McClellan,
2001). From a legal standpoint, the use of artificial insemination has a number of uncertainties, particularly if
a couple performs the process themselves instead of
consulting a physician. The laws of most states commonly recognize the biological mother's legal custody of
the child, which leaves the nonbiological or social
mother with no legal parental rights unless she legally
adopts the child conceived by insemination. However,
many states do not permit the names of two women to
appear on a child's birth certificate nor allow adoption by
a nonbiological mother. Furthermore, custody rights of
fathers are relatively unclear in these situations as well,
even if the identity of the father who has donated sperm
is known. There continues to be legal testing of these
rights in various court cases that will set precedents for
the future in this matter. Generally speaking, if the father is known to the lesbian-led family, it is possible to
have legal documents written that spell out legal rights
and responsibilities of fathers regarding custody and
visitation, for example.

For many lesbian couples, parenthood via insemination is a well-planned, deliberate, major life decision often
involving complex issues such as who will be the biological
mother and how to choose a donor (known or anonymous),
for example (Chabot & Ames, 2004). As such, children are
greatly valued, wanted, and desired; such motivation for
parenthood may bode well in both short- and long-term
consequences for both mothers and children.

**Lesbian Family Dynamics.**   Families formed by gay
men or lesbian women share qualities in common with
heterosexually formed stepfamilies (Erera & Fredriksen,
1999; Lynch, 2000). This is particularly the case with lesbian mothers, who more frequently have custody of
children produced in a former heterosexual marriage
(Hall & Kitson, 2000; Lorah, 2002). Other similarities
may involve relationship issues in the new stepfamily.
The partner of the lesbian biological mother (the children's stepparent or social parent) is rejected by the
stepchildren, the stepchildren and stepparent compete
for the attention and affection of the biological mother,
and conflicts erupt over territoriality in the home.

Distinct differences within lesbian family systems
distinguish them from other family forms, although it is
important to remember that the families of gay men and

lesbian women are not pathological (Tasker, 2002). Rather, these families experience challenges that other family systems do not face because of the larger society's negative attitudes and stereotypes about homosexuality. Four unique characteristics describe lesbian family systems due to the more active parental roles found in their structure as compared with those of gay men (Bennett, 2003; Ciano-Boyce & Shelley-Sireci, 2002; Dundas & Kaufman, 2000; Johnson & O'Connor, 2001; Nelson, 1999; Thompson, 2002). First, they experience a lack of legitimacy because they are not recognized as a family unit by their community; this lack of legitimacy presents unique problems, such as in family dealings with school systems. Second, these families must address issues unique to their status, such as more frequent confrontation with the stigmas associated with homosexuality. Gay fathers without full-time child custody do not usually experience these challenges. Parents often instruct children to keep the adults' sexual orientation a secret from others outside the family. Researchers observe a lack of community support for two lesbian women who are raising children as a family. For example, these individuals are sometimes evicted from rented residences or terminated from employment when their sexual orientation becomes public knowledge. As a result, lesbian parents may isolate themselves and their children from other families. The pressure of maintaining family secrets is unhealthy to the effective functioning of that family in relation to others and to the functioning of individuals within the system. These mothers may fear losing custody of children more intensely than gay fathers do, which makes this possibility a continual threat to the well-being of the lesbian family (Siegenthaler & Bigner, 2000). Children may not be allowed to invite friends home to play because the parents fear exposure, and the children may be shunned by others because they are seen as different.

Third, these families usually experience strained relationships with ex-spouses and other relatives. The negative feelings of ex-spouses may be compounded during postdivorce interactions due to the lesbian mothers' fears of losing custody of children. But despite all these problems, children of lesbian mothers are well adjusted, and families typically find creative and healthy ways for responding to the crises they experience.

Fourth, division of labor and parental roles take on unique assignments and situations. Each family must decide what each mother will be called, for example.

Each family will need to determine if one mother or the other will be designated as the primary caregiver.

Both lesbians and gay men base the structure of their committed relationship on the androgynous principle of equality of partners (Gottman et al., 2003). This differs considerably from the structure typically found among heterosexual couples that uses gender to determine who does what in the relationship. Lesbian families with children typically report sharing household responsibilities, but the biological mothers can be expected to be more involved in child care while the nonbiological mothers report working longer hours in their employment. Children are found to be more well adjusted, however, when both mothers divide the child-care responsibilities equally (Bennett, 2003; Ciano-Boyce & Shelley-Sireci, 2002).

***Children of Lesbian Mothers.*** The issues relating to children of lesbian mothers do not differ significantly from those relating to children of gay fathers. The main differences are that children of lesbians live in a different type of family system and have a different kind of parenting experience. However, no differences in general adjustment, gender role identity, or cognitive or behavioral functioning are consistently reported in studies comparing children of lesbian and nonlesbian mothers (Golombok et al., 2003; Tasker, 2002; Vanfraussen, Ponjaert-Kristoffersen, & Brewaeys, 2003).

Four principal issues are relevant to children of lesbian mothers (Chrisp, 2001; Johnson & O'Connor, 2001; Kershaw, 2000; McClellan, 2001; Paechter, 2000; Stevens et al., 2003; Vanfraussen, Ponjaert-Kristoffersen, & Brewaeys, 2002, 2003): (1) dealing with the mother's disclosure of her sexual orientation, (2) dealing with the uniqueness of having a lesbian mother and its effect on the parent-child relationship, (3) coping with custody concerns, and (4) dealing with the homophobic and heterosexist reactions of others.

First, like the children of gay fathers, those growing up in lesbian family systems confront the dual challenge of coping both with their parents' divorce and with the fact that their mother is different from other mothers. While this difficulty is similar to what children of gay fathers experience, the differences are compounded by the fact that these children live with their mother. Most gay fathers are largely absent from the daily lives of their children. In this respect, children of lesbian mothers share similarities with children of heterosexual mothers who become single parents after divorce.

Boys are more accepting of their mother's disclosure of homosexuality than girls. However, researchers generally find that the more accepting and relaxed the mother is about her sexuality, the more accepting the child is about having a lesbian mother. Another unique situation occurring in lesbian families is the matter of whether and how to inform children who are conceived by artificial insemination by donor (AID). Many children of lesbian mothers become aware of the uniqueness of their particular families in early childhood and begin to ask questions about their father. Typically, most children react positively to this news and are not harmed significantly if teased by peers in later years of childhood about their families and parentage.

Second, the context of the parent-child relationship changes after the mother discloses her sexual orientation. Girls develop more concerns about becoming homosexual than boys, perhaps due to their sex-role identification with the mother, although research does not bear out this fear becoming a reality (Stacey & Biblarz, 2001). Girls also tend to compete with their mother's partner for the mother's attention more than boys do. However, after the mother's disclosure, the family system appears to relax rigid definitions of family roles and allows greater flexibility in the parent-child relationship. The self-esteem of children of divorced lesbian mothers is no different from that of children of divorced heterosexual mothers. Children of both mothers experience problems that relate more directly to the effects of parental divorce than to the mother's sexual orientation.

Third, child custody can be a highly charged issue in lesbian families. It is a central concern of most lesbian mothers, particularly those who live in constant fear of losing their parental rights because of their sexual orientation. Most children of lesbian mothers wish to remain in their care and establish stable, significant relationships with a mother's female partner. Lesbian mothers, like gay fathers, are subject to a suspicious, homophobic legal system that assumes that children living in homosexual families will be sexually molested, become homosexuals themselves, and experience peer ostracism if the parents' sexual orientation becomes public knowledge. These issues directly relate to custody and parental rights that can threaten the continuation of a meaningful parent-child relationship in these family systems.

Finally, because these family systems exist in a hostile social environment that provides little support for their existence, many lesbian mothers turn to their children for implicit approval of their sexual orientation. At the same time, conflict may develop because mothers do not want their children to feel significantly different from other children. This is an especially troublesome problem for adolescents of lesbian mothers. When working through this concern in a therapeutic manner, children and lesbian parents learn that the child should not necessarily be expected to accept the parent's sexual orientation completely. However, it is important that the child come to respect the parents' lifestyle and the ways in which it is expressed. Some children also need assistance in working through the confusion between the love-hate feelings they have for their mother and the guilt that accompanies those feelings, which may relate to the mother's sexual orientation (Johnson & O'Connor, 2001).

● ● ● ● ● ● ● ● ● ● ● ● ● ● ● ● ● ● ● ● ● ● ● ● ● ● ● ●

## Parenting Reflection 13–2

Suppose you are a lawyer representing a gay or lesbian parent in a custody hearing. What evidence would you present and what would you say to demonstrate to a judge that sexual orientation of a parent is irrelevant in determining the ability to parent children effectively and in healthy ways?

● ● ● ● ● ● ● ● ● ● ● ● ● ● ● ● ● ● ● ● ● ● ● ● ● ● ● ●

● ● ● ● ● ● ● ● ● ● ● ● ● ● ● ● ● ● ● ● ● ● ● ● ● ● ● ●

***Focus Point.***   Some family systems include a homosexual member. A child's disclosure of his or her homosexual orientation frequently acts as a stressor event that disrupts family system functioning. Many parents and family members are influenced by the negative social stigma and images associated with homosexuality. The ABC-X model facilitates an understanding of a family system's reaction to the news of a child's homosexuality.

Family members frequently try first to understand the homosexual child in terms of these negative beliefs. They also may negate the child's family role as the system attempts to reconstruct a new role definition for the child that includes the notion of the child's sexual orientation. Healthy families resolve their conflicts about a child's homosexuality, for example, by educating themselves, participating in therapy, and participating in special support groups. By acting in these ways, family functioning resumes at the level prior to the child's disclosure or becomes even more efficient as a result. Unhealthy families fail to resolve these conflicts, which perpetuates the disruption in the family system for all members.

Not all parents are heterosexual; some are gay or lesbian. Their families, however, are not significantly different from other family systems, although unique challenges and problems are particular to their situations. Experiences of gay fathers are similar to those of lesbian mothers, but each type of family system faces unique challenges. Homosexuality per se does not prevent or hinder someone from being an effective parent. Research fails to support common assertions that these families create an unhealthy environment that harms children.

........................................................

## POINTS TO CONSIDER

■ Some family systems in the United States include a homosexual member. A child's disclosure of homosexuality to parents and family members frequently serves as a stressor event to the family system. The ABC-X model facilitates an understanding of family members' reactions to this crisis event. Most parents and family members are strongly influenced by negative images and beliefs about homosexuality and homosexuals that color their initial reactions to a child's disclosure. The sources that a family uses to cope with the disclosure may also be negatively biased.

■ Family systems may interpret the disclosure by reacting in ways that are healthy or unhealthy. At first, the system may seek to understand the homosexual child by applying learned negative beliefs and images to the child. Family values usually conflict with family members' positive knowledge of the child. The system may negate the homosexual child's role when dealing with this conflict. Healthy families resolve their conflicts about having a homosexual child by educating themselves about what competent, respectable researchers know about homosexuals and homosexuality. They may seek therapy for themselves, the child, and/or the family system to learn how to adjust to the crisis. And they may participate in support groups for relatives of gays and lesbians. In this way, families change their negative beliefs about homosexuals and learn to extend unconditional love and acceptance as a new family role is created for the homosexual child.

■ Gay men and lesbian women become parents for a variety of reasons. Research generally finds that these individuals act effectively as parents and that children are not harmed by living with, and being raised by, a homosexual parent. Many gay and lesbian families experience problems and circumstances that are similar to those encountered by heterosexual single-parent family and stepfamily systems.

# CHAPTER 14

# Adolescent Parents

## Focus Questions
■ ■ ■ ■ ■ ■ ■ ■ ■ ■

1. What are the principal reasons contributing to adolescent parenthood? How prevalent is this problem?
2. What are the implications for the adolescent girl and boy who initiate a pregnancy?
3. Are there short- and/or long-term consequences?
4. What kinds of community support are available for teenagers who become parents?
5. What is being done to prevent or decrease teen pregnancies?

■ ■ ■ ■ ■ ■ ■ ■ ■ ■

Pregnancy among adolescents is not a new phenomenon in the United States. However, it has always been described as a problem that has both short- and long-term consequences for the adolescent parents, their child, and their families of origin.

The rate of adolescent pregnancies has been declining over the past 15 years and reached a point in 2002 not seen since the 1950s (see Figures 14–1 and 14–2). This decline has been observed in every ethnic group surveyed in the United States while continuing to occur more frequently among minority ethnic groups except Asian/Pacific Islanders (Martin et al., 2003). While the number of teenage marriages in the United States has declined in recent years, the overwhelming majority of adolescents who become pregnant carry the pregnancy to term and retain custody of the child.

Two groups of females are considered at risk when pregnant: those *under* age 15 and those *over* age 35 (U.S. Bureau of the Census, 2003). In relation to teenage pregnancy, the term **risk** refers to the dangers to health and well-being that a teenage girl and her baby may encounter when the girl experiences pregnancy during a period of her life that is developmentally off-time.

A teenage girl and the father of her baby experience a variety of short- and long-term negative consequences. These consequences and the associated complications of teenage parenthood are discussed in this section. The majority of research presented here focuses on the issues relating to teenage girls who become pregnant. Although an increasing number of investigations examine the effects of fatherhood for teenage boys,

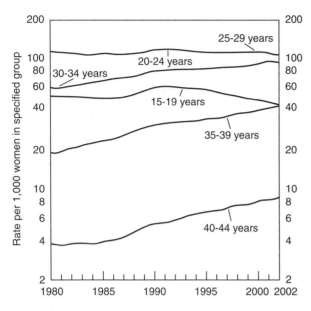

**FIGURE 14–1.** Birth rates by age of mother between 1980 and 2002 in the United States.

*Source:* Martin, J. A., Hamilton, B. E., Sutton, P. D., Ventura, S. J., Menacker, F., & Munson, M. L. (2003). Births: Final data for 2002. *National Vital Statistics Reports, 52*(10). Hyattsville, MD: National Center for Health Statistics.

researchers continue to focus on teenage girls who conceive and experience pregnancy.

## INCIDENCE, CAUSES, AND OUTCOMES OF TEENAGE PREGNANCY

### Primary Factors

Less than 800,000 adolescent girls became pregnant in 2002, continuing a decline in the birth rate among this age group that began about 10 years previously (Martin et al., 2003). This figure equates to about 1 in 8 girls between ages 13 and 19. Of those who become pregnant, about 10 percent experience miscarriage or have stillbirths; about 29 percent experience induced abortion, and about 61 percent carry the pregnancy to term and give birth. Less than half of these girls marry before giving birth; most are classified as unwed mothers. About 90 percent of the unwed girls who give birth choose to retain custody of their baby (Federal Interagency Forum on Child and Family Statistics, 2003). The vast ma-

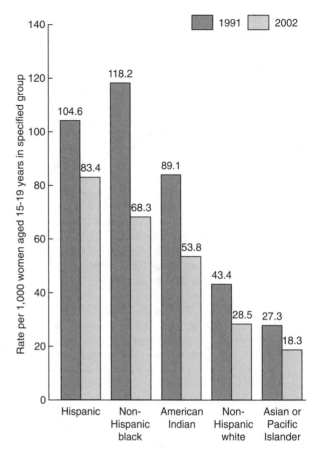

**FIGURE 14–2.** Birth rates for teenagers by race and/or Hispanic Origin for 1991 and 2002.

*Source:* Martin, J. A., Hamilton, B. E., Sutton, P. D., Ventura, S. J., Menacker, F., & Munson, M. L. (2003). Births: Final data for 2002. *National Vital Statistics Reports, 52*(10). Hyattsville, MD: National Center for Health Statistics.

jority of adolescents who give birth belong to black and Hispanic groups rather than whites.

Most adolescent girls do not become pregnant voluntarily (Wakschlag & Hans, 2000). The majority become pregnant because birth control methods obviously are not used during sexual intercourse. For some, pregnancy occurs because of rape. The basic reasons that explain why teenagers become pregnant (see Focus On 14–1), however, are traced to the following four factors:

1. Increased frequency of sexual intercourse taking place at earlier ages than in the past
2. Social influences that de-emphasize the negative stigma once associated with teen pregnancy

**Focus On 14–1**

## Contributing Causes of Teenage Pregnancy

- Serious emotional problems, such as lack of adequate social adjustment, extreme feelings of isolation, loneliness, or a low level of self-esteem
- Extreme embarrassment about sexual matters causing gross lack of correct information about conception and contraception
- Negative feelings about intercourse among girls, which can lead to rejecting the time and effort necessary to ensure safer sexual practices and experiences
- Religious beliefs that may control or inhibit sexual activity but also compound guilt feelings that interfere with a sexually active teen's effective use of contraceptives and other safe sex practices
- Eagerness and impulsiveness to participate in sexual activity without taking the time and effort to ensure safe experiences
- Desire to punish a parent toward whom angry feelings or resentments may be harbored
- Guilty or negative self-image or self-esteem that prevents the teenager from feeling that he or she deserves to be protected from the consequences of sexual intercourse
- A desire to prove and substantiate one's masculinity or femininity
- A desire to be recognized as a person with adult social status
- An attempt to create a captive love or trap a mate
- A desire to receive unconditional love from another person (perceiving a baby as a substitute for parental or marital love)
- A syndrome of behavior problems, including conduct disorders, involvement in criminal activity, or participation in delinquent behaviors such as substance abuse
- Certain family background markers, such as a single-parent versus a first-marriage family of origin, a parent who was sexually active as a teenager, older siblings who are sexually active, experiencing a particular type of parental supervision in adolescence, and racial or ethnic background

*Sources:* Breedlove, G. K., Schorfheide, A. M., & Wieczorek, R. R. (2000). *Adolescent pregnancy.* White Plains, NY: March of Dimes Birth Defects Foundation; Kirby, D. (1999). *Looking for reasons why: The antecedents of adolescent sexual risk-taking, pregnancy, and childbearing.* Washington, DC: National Campaign to Prevent Teen Pregnancy; Kirby, D. (2001). *Emerging answers: Research findings on programs to reduce teen pregnancy: Full report.* Washington, DC: National Campaign to Prevent Teen Pregnancy.

3. Lack of adequate contraceptive knowledge and use by sexually active teenage males and females

4. Personal attitudes about sexuality, pregnancy, and parenthood

Some believe that adolescent childbearing is an adaptive strategy for disadvantaged individuals because it occurs frequently among poverty-level and ethnic minorities (Kirby, 1999). From this standpoint, adolescent parenthood may be considered beneficial because there can be economic benefits to adolescent parents by becoming qualified for public assistance, for example. Others assert that adolescent parenthood is actually a cause for disadvantaged status. From this view, teen childbearing is thought to contribute heavily to keeping individuals in a position where they fail to complete

their education, which in turn keeps them from obtaining jobs that pay well or which maintain their condition of receiving public assistance (Collins, 2000). The overwhelming evidence from research suggests that parenthood is largely undesirable among adolescents, regardless of the outcomes for the young parents or their children (Breedlove, Schorfheide, & Wieczorek, 2000).

***More Teens Are Sexually Active.*** Researchers believe that there has been a continued increase in the incidence of sexual intercourse among teenagers that was first observed almost 35 years ago (Alan Guttmacher Institute, 1999). Some researchers estimate that about one-fourth of all teenage girls have participated in sexual intercourse by age 15 and that four out of five have had intercourse by age 19. This estimate contrasts with the figures for teenage boys. About a third have had sexual intercourse by age 15, an estimate that increases to about 85 percent by age 19. Apparently, young adolescents rarely participate in sexual intercourse, but it becomes increasingly common as age increases during this period of life.

Research suggests that many teenagers are sexually active at younger ages than most adults imagine (Alan Guttmacher Institute, 1999; Kellogg, Hoffman, & Taylor, 1999). For the most part, sexual activity among teenagers is believed to occur frequently and with a variety of partners. Instead of being promiscuous, however, adolescents often become intensely involved with one person over a period of time that involves sexual intimacy. Sexual activity increases the risks of negative consequences, including exposure to sexually transmitted diseases (e.g., AIDS), pregnancy, and a variety of deleterious psychosocial effects (Kirby, 2001; Weinstock, Berman, & Cates, 2004). Researchers are particularly concerned about the spread of the AIDS-causing HIV virus among teenagers, who have a high level of sexual activity that is largely unsafe and unprotected (Tinsley, Lees, & Sumartojo, 2004). Because the virus can also pass through the placenta during pregnancy and infect the developing fetus, many adolescent mothers and their children may experience this devastating disease in the coming years.

Several antecedent conditions contribute to the age at which teens become sexually active and to the number of different partners (Alan Guttmacher Institute, 1999; Baumer & South, 2001; Franke-Clark, 2003; Phillips, 2003; Raffaelli & Crockett, 2003; Susman, Dorn, & Schiefelbein, 2003):

■ The level of sex hormones associated with puberty may increase at earlier ages in children than in the past. These hormones establish the interest in and motivation for sexual activity.

■ Adolescents' cognitive and emotional development usually lags behind physical development; therefore, teenagers may not be completely aware of the risks involved in early, unprotected sexual activity. For example, cognitive distortions may give rise to their belief that others, not themselves, are vulnerable to these risks.

■ Factors derived from the family of origin can influence the sexual activity of teenagers. For example, teens may be influenced by the past sexual history of the mother during her adolescence, older siblings who are sexually active, living in a single-parent

rather than a first-marriage family system, unhealthy levels of family cohesion and adaptability, highly involved mother-daughter and negative father-daughter relationships, and the quality of the parent-child relationship. All these factors may affect the degree to which a child subscribes to family values regarding sexual behavior. In addition, the degree of adolescent girls' permissiveness about sexual activity may be related to a large number of sexually active girlfriends, or having sisters who are sexually active, especially if an adolescent sister has become a mother herself.

■ Peer influences may affect a teen's sexual involvement. Many feel a great deal of social pressure to become sexually active—especially girls, who may be particularly susceptible to coercion from a male to participate in sexual intercourse.

■ Sociocultural factors, such as religious participation, ethnic background, or the family of origin's socioeconomic status, may influence the probability of a teen's participation in sexual activity.

Changes have occurred in social attitudes about teenage sexual activity and those who become pregnant. In the past, pregnancy was a degrading, humiliating status that destroyed an adolescent girl's reputation and ability to fully participate in adolescent social development. Boys were taught that it was wrong to impregnate a girl outside of marriage. In the past, an adolescent girl who became pregnant had limited alternatives in dealing with her situation. She could try to arrange an illegal, dangerous abortion, or she could leave her community to bear her child in a facility for unwed mothers. These institutions were often managed and sponsored by charitable agencies or religious groups.

Today, such attitudes no longer influence the course and outcomes of teenage pregnancies. Abortion on demand is legal in the United States, although teenagers' access to such procedures is regulated to some degree. Fewer social stigmas are associated with teenage pregnancy, and families are more supportive of pregnant teenagers by providing various forms of emotional, financial, and physical assistance. A variety of community programs also assist both expectant teenagers and those who have become parents. For example, some programs offer teens the opportunity to continue their education with as few disruptions as possible. Most teenage girls who choose to continue their pregnancy retain custody of their babies. Many of these young mothers receive the assistance of family members, especially their own mothers, in caring for the babies and raising them to maturity as fully integrated family members.

Most pregnancies among teenagers occur because of their failure to use contraception and safer sex practices. Few teenagers are reported to desire pregnancy when they participate in sexual activity, but it happens for a number of reasons (Alan Guttmacher Institute, 1999). Many adults are puzzled about why sexually active teenagers fail to use protective measures that will prevent the possibility of pregnancy. The explanation relates to the meanings adolescents attach to contraceptive use. For example, to use contraception is an obvious admission of sexual activity (Kosunen et al., 2003). Teenagers' use of contraception reflects their understanding that consequences, such as pregnancy and disease, can result from such activity and that they are negative outcomes. Seeking and obtaining contraceptive devices have certain social, economic, and psychological costs that teenagers must weigh against the risks and costs of pregnancy. It also must be negotiated with a sexual partner, which many teens find embarrassing and feel inept at discussing. Contraceptives must be used regularly because many birth control methods must be performed daily or with each sexual act.

## Parenting Reflection 14–1

What are the pros and cons about health clinics located in junior and senior high schools dispensing contraceptives to any student who requests these?

The personal attitudes of adolescents play an important role in influencing their use or nonuse of contraceptives (Strong, 2004). The total life situation of adolescents from low-income family systems tends to promote feelings of fatalism, emotional depression, and apathy. These attitudes work against the effective use of contraception among those who are sexually active. Teenagers may be influenced in their sexual activity and use of contraception by a variety of cognitive distortions and beliefs about their ability to become pregnant. These distortions relate among some teenagers to a flaw in cognitive processing at this life stage called the *personal fable*. They may not use contraception because of the erroneous, irrational belief that other people become pregnant but not them.

### What Influences Teenagers to Use Contraception?

American adolescents, in comparison with those of other countries studied, use contraception less consistently and effectively (Hyde & DeLamater, 2000). As a result, we observe the high rates of adolescent pregnancy and parenthood here as compared with significantly lesser rates in other developed countries, such as England, Sweden, and Japan (Blum, 2001).

When preventative methods are used, however, researchers find that certain antecedent conditions are associated with the use of contraception and safer sex practices among teenagers (Kershaw et al., 2003; Longmore et al., 2003; Topolak, Williams, & Wilson, 2001). Psychosocial factors, such as perceiving oneself as being sexually active, are crucial. Apparently, having the cognitive and psychological maturity to perceive oneself in this way without guilt is vital in influencing a teen's use of birth control. In addition, if teens are able to delay becoming sexually active until late adolescence, the chances improve for their use of contraception because they have developed the abilities that promote effective sexual decision-making skills.

As teenagers become more sexually experienced, they tend to use contraception more regularly and correctly and bypass feelings of embarrassment that prevent younger adolescents from obtaining and using contraception. Furthermore, if teenagers from disadvantaged backgrounds can be assisted in continuing their educational experiences, then their chances improve for using contraception accordingly.

Families can influence contraceptive use in providing or failing to provide information to teenagers about birth control. Parents who disapprove of and do not tolerate adolescent sexuality and sexual activity are more likely to have teens who become pregnant. Researchers generally find that, contrary to popular opinion, the parents' openness to communicate and support tends to increase adolescents' use of contraceptives.

When parents are not involved in communications with adolescents about sexual activity and pregnancy, peers become an important source of influence and information for teenagers (Zabin & Cardona, 2002). When peers approve of contraceptive use, teenagers whose parents do not approve or do not discuss it appear to be influenced in positive ways to also use contraception. On the other hand, if the peer group is not using contraceptives, then the teenager will most likely follow suit.

When teenagers who are sexually active have access to family planning services either in their schools or communities, there is a greater likelihood of preventing pregnancies (Topolak, Williams, & Wilson, 2001). School sex-education programs do not appear to have a significant effect on promoting teen sexual behavior or on increasing the likelihood of adolescent pregnancy in one way or another (Conner & Dewey, 2003).

***Marriage as a Solution.***    Teenagers typically do not choose marriage as a consequence of becoming pregnant (U.S. Bureau of the Census, 2003). Most frequently, the decision not to marry but to continue the pregnancy is influenced by a teenage girl's mother and the baby's father (Haveman, Wolfe, & Pence, 2001). Regardless of whether teens become married or not, however, the poorest socioeconomic outcomes occur when adolescents become parents, and marriage does not significantly improve their situation. Such marriages at this time and under these circumstances are also considered to be high risk and prone to early divorce.

Another factor contributing to the decision about teen marriage relates to welfare benefits (Boonstra, 2000). Teenagers who are unmarried are more likely to receive welfare than are teens who are married. Racial background is also a contributing factor. Black adolescents who become pregnant are less likely to become married than white adolescents (Zabin & Cardona, 2002). This may be partly due to fewer numbers of employable, marriageable black males. The greater tendency among blacks to remain unmarried may also reflect differences in family system values; the families may be more tolerant of unmarried parenthood in general. The decision not to marry and to carry a pregnancy to term implies that teenagers must rely on their families of origin for support and assistance. In reality, unmarried teens receive less assistance from their families than do those who are married. In this manner, then, public assistance is a necessary and essential resource for many adolescent mothers.

***Adoption as an Alternative.***    Adoption has been chosen less frequently as an option in adolescent pregnancy as more teenage girls choose to continue their pregnancies and retain custody of their babies (Miller & Coyl, 2000). This is especially the case among African American and Latino teens and among those from lower socioeconomic backgrounds. The adoption alternative is believed by some to be a better one for teen mothers, since it enables the girl to continue her education, attend to otherwise normal adolescent developmental tasks, and help her to avoid experiencing a disadvan-

taged state of life. Others argue, however, that the decision to place a baby for adoption produces negative feelings of guilt, grief, and loss that can have long-term effects. These feelings can harm a girl's psychological well-being and adversely affect her future sexual and intimate relationships. These negative results of placement may be a long-term consequence rather than something that is observed in the time shortly following a child's adoption.

Placing a baby for adoption is a difficult decision for a teen mother to make and carry out. Although there is little research on how this process is experienced, it appears that those who choose to relinquish their baby have less influence from the child's father and more education. They often come from families with higher incomes, have high education and career aspirations, and are still in high school. Many adolescent girls who relinquish their babies for adoption may rationalize this decision by noting that they feel unready or unable to be a parent and to provide an adequate environment for their child.

Although most teenagers choose not to terminate their pregnancy by abortion or to place their baby for adoption, significant consequences result from the decision to retain custody of the child and to assume a parenthood role. As might be expected, teen mothers who choose to relinquish their child are reported to have more positive attitudes about adoption than those who choose to retain custody and assume parenthood status. The next section discusses these consequences for the adolescent mother and father, as well as for their child, when they decide to assume parenthood status.

• • • • • • • • • • • • • • • • • • • • • • • • • • • • • • • • • • • •

***Focus Point.***    A variety of factors explain or contribute to teenage pregnancy. The most obvious relate to the failure to use contraceptives among those who are sexually active. The majority of teens carry a pregnancy to term although a substantial proportion choose to have an abortion. Most of the girls who give birth choose to retain custody of their baby, and most do not marry either during or following their pregnancy. Adoption has increasingly declined as a means for resolving teen pregnancy.

• • • • • • • • • • • • • • • • • • • • • • • • • • • • • • • • • • • •

## Adolescent Mothers

There are several short- and long-term consequences of parenthood for teenagers (Moore & Brooks-Gunn, 2002): (1) educational implications, (2) effects on marriage and family relations, (3) health considerations, (4) actual and potential labor-force participation, and (5) effects on the parent-child relationship. These consequences generally relate to the teenage mother rather than the father because research literature has focused almost exclusively on how pregnancy and parenthood affect adolescent girls.

**Educational Implications.** Pregnancy appears to be the most common reason for why an adolescent girl drops out of school and fails to complete her high school education (Alan Guttmacher Institute, 1999; Moore & Brooks-Gunn, 2002). This is especially the case if the girl is African American. The younger the girl at the time of her conception, the less likely she is to return to school following the birth of her baby. It is possible, however, that teenage pregnancy rates might be higher when adolescent girls leave school early before finishing rather than vice versa (Fergusson & Woodward, 2000).

The most obvious, and perhaps most long-term, effect of a girl's educational disruption relates to economic consequences (Fergusson & Woodward, 2000). The lack of a high school diploma severely restricts the types of jobs available and the level of income earned. Typically, one can expect to have less prestigious jobs, less job satisfaction, and a less-satisfactory quality of life.

Some school systems today are aware that these dire consequences can affect adolescent girls for their lifetime. Special programs promote their continuation in school, teach parenting and family life skills, and assist in vocational development. These programs are discussed in greater detail later in this chapter.

**Marriage and Family Relations.** Adolescent pregnancy is likely to hasten early marriage, but this option is not necessarily an appropriate solution. Teenage marriages are likely to be high risk, highly unstable, and prone to end shortly by divorce (Moore & Brooks-Gunn, 2002). About 60 percent of adolescents who marry divorce within 5 years, as compared with 20 percent of those who marry in their early adulthood years (Lichter & Graefe, 2001).

The classic study of adolescent marriage and parenthood (deLissovoy, 1973a, 1973b) points to the unhappy nature of teenage marriages. DeLissovoy studied the relationships of working-class, rural adolescents who were 17 years old and under. The adolescent husbands were generally more dissatisfied than the adolescent wives. For example, these young men felt that their wives did not participate enough in sexual activities, while the

young women felt that husbands wanted too much sex. This dissatisfaction increased even more after 30 months of marriage. The young husbands were much more dissatisfied with the frequency of sexual activity, the degree of social activity, and opportunities to interact with mutual friends. For example, they wished to continue their buddy relationships and to participate in sports after school. The young wives felt left out and lonely because many had been dropped by former friends.

Most research suggests that the correlates of early childbearing and marriage produce much of the unhappiness rather than the pregnancy or the age of the couple (Barber, 2001; Haveman, Wolfe, & Pence, 2001). The correlates include educational disruption, restricted job opportunities, and limited earning potential.

**Health Implications.** Early studies of adolescent pregnancy reported many adverse physical complications for the young mother, including elevated death rates, increased prevalence of maternal toxemia, precipitate or prolonged delivery, anemia, postpartum infections, and hemorrhage (Children's Defense Fund, 1996, 2003). Other research, however, suggests that attributing these physical complications solely to the mother's age is questionable since other factors, such as quality of life conditions induced by poverty, can cloud this issue (Haveman, Wolfe, & Pence, 2001). The health risks associated with adolescent pregnancy may be minimized if adolescent girls receive adequate and timely prenatal care and supervised nutrition (Borja & Adair, 2003). Obtaining adequate prenatal care, however, is more likely the exception rather than common practice among most adolescent girls who become pregnant. Inadequate nutrition also presents significant problems because teenagers are generally reputed to have deficient diets. Poor nutrition exacerbates problems associated with teen pregnancy by interfering with the normal growth patterns of the young mother. It also increases the likelihood that the baby will have a low birth weight, which jeopardizes survival and increases the chances of other birth complications (Stevens-Simon, Nelligan, & Kelly, 2001).

Mental health is also negatively affected by early childbearing (Turner, Sorensen, & Turner, 2000). Teen mothers have less social support and personal resources in coping with stress. In addition, the accumulation of major, potentially traumatic events they may experience as a single parent tend to greater mental health risks.

**Labor Force Participation and Economic Consequences.**   When teenage girls drop out of school because of pregnancy, their future is jeopardized because of the broad impact on their ability to provide adequate incomes for themselves and their children (Haveman, Wolfe, & Pence, 2001). Most girls who fail to complete their high school education lack the entry-level skills that allow them to compete successfully in the job market. The income of adolescent mothers is about one-half that of mothers who have their first child in early adulthood (U.S. Bureau of the Census, 2003).

Because of the combined effects of the loss of educational opportunities, the lack of sufficient support networks, the unavailability of adequate child care, extensive medical expenses, and other related factors, teenage parents face major economic consequences during this time of their lives (Bissell, 2000). Both short- and long-term effects are evident when teenagers become parents. Their economic resources are often severely limited, and their parents are frequently unable to provide the type and level of financial support that will help to ensure adequate prenatal care, equipment, and living conditions. Teen mothers usually lack the adequate resources to become effective parents, have fewer perceived alternatives to parenthood (such as completing their educations), and fail to see parenthood as being personally or socially restrictive (Jaffee, 2002).

Economic instability in the months following a marriage between teen parents who have both dropped out of school often causes separation within at least 2 years. In the long run, teenage parents can expect to hold low-paying, low-level jobs in which little satisfaction and economic gain are evident. Another economic consequence is that children born to teenage parents ultimately are more costly to a parent than those born to women who have their first birth in their 20s (Alan Guttmacher Institute, 1999; Children's Defense Fund, 2003). This relates to the loss of potential income created by dropping out of school, the average national annual income and hourly wage among women according to their level of educational attainment, and the direct costs of having additional children. The lack of adequate job skills and educational qualifications also causes adolescent mothers to seek financial assistance from public welfare programs (Collins, 2000).

**Parent-Child Relations.**   Adolescents who become parents can expect to be a single parent and to have large families, as compared to individuals who wait until their early adulthood years to have children (Wakschlag & Hans, 2000). Some investigations report that adolescent mothers are as competent as older mothers and that their interactions with infants and children are usually appropriate. However, other studies report that teenage parents have troublesome relationships with their children that may be abusive (Stevens-Simon, Nelligan, & Kelley, 2001).

While significant data point to problematic parent-child relationships among adolescents who are mothers, it does appear that there can be positive outcomes for children under certain circumstances (Luster et al., 2000). Children of adolescent mothers have been found to score high on certain measures that examine intellectual functioning when the mothers have more years of education, are employed, have fewer children on average than others in their position, live in more desirable neighborhoods, and are living with a male partner.

Several studies point to the risks of poor teen parenting, which are highlighted by the following characteristics (deLissovoy, 1973a, 1973b; Jaffee, 2002; Moore & Brooks-Gunn, 2002; Stevens-Simon, Nelligan, & Kelly, 2001):

■ Lack of knowledge about children's developmental needs
■ Less sensitivity to behavior cues from infants
■ Lack of interest in playing with children
■ Less interaction time with children that is accentuated by ambivalent feelings about parenthood and a greater tendency to use physical punishment

The work by deLissovoy (1973a, 1973b) is particularly illuminating in this regard. Both adolescent mothers and fathers were questioned shortly after the birth of their baby regarding their knowledge of the developmental norms and events of infant growth and development. Teenagers are grossly ignorant about when to expect certain developmental events during infancy, which has broad implications regarding the ability of these young parents to provide quality, nurturant caregiving for infants and children. For example, teenage parents indicate that toilet training should begin at 24 weeks (6 months) of age and that beginning to teach infants about obedience to parental direction should begin at either 26 weeks or 36 weeks. How would parents and child react if this training actually did begin when the parents believed the infant's appropriate chronological age had been reached?

Adolescent parents typically demonstrate a range of nurturant caregiving behaviors toward children that include immature, egotistical styles as well as those in which attempts are made to recognize and meet the needs of both the parent and child (Moore & Brooks-Gunn, 2002). Other work suggests that rather than being at immediate risk of abuse and neglect due to parental ignorance, children of teenage parents may experience a delayed effect in this regard (Jaffee et al., 2001). Adolescent mothers tend to have more births, lower incomes, fewer sources of social support, interrupted educational experiences, and lower quality of life that serve as sources of stress in mediating long-term child abuse and neglect (Borkowski et al., 2002).

When adolescent mothers are compared with older mothers, however, the teen mothers are found to have competent parenting skills in a number of aspects (Brophy-Herb & Honig, 1999; Hess, Pappas, & Black, 2002). Other factors rather than age alone may mediate the negative effects that children of teenage parents experience by virtue of their parenting. Social class background, for example, may produce differences in children's development manifested via maternal knowledge, attitudes, and behaviors that determine the quality of parenting experiences for children. These studies are unclear in their findings about the greater probability of abusiveness among teenage parents.

One researcher has described a "culture" of teen parenting (Higginson, 1998). This culture is depicted as emphasizing competition to be the best parent regardless of the area in question, such as in the ability to provide material possessions for children, the physical and cognitive development of children, and knowledge of parenting skills and abilities. This competition is observed between teen mothers and with older mothers. The competitiveness is believed, in part, to be driven by the teen mothers' overwhelming motivation to prove that they do not match, in any respect, the negative stigmas and stereotypes associated with adolescent parenthood. The consuming desire is to behave in ways as a parent that persuade and convince others that they are not abusive, welfare-dependent, or incompetent.

Despite their general ignorance about child development and caretaking, adolescent girls who are either pregnant or parents are found to be more realistic than their nonpregnant cohorts in their expectations about child development milestones (Stern & Alvarez, 1992). This level of knowledge might be attributed to the participation of pregnant and parental adolescents in spe-

cial education programs that prepare them for parenthood. This finding, however, is diminished by the fact that pregnant adolescents showed significantly fewer positive attitudes about caretaking than those who were not pregnant. This information has important implications for later parenting behavior. It is not clear if adequate knowledge about children's developmental milestones can offset such negative attitudes about caring for them by their adolescent mothers.

Adolescent mothers are reported to be more likely to feel emotionally depressed, nervous, tense, fretful, and ambivalent about their parenthood status (Schweingruber & Kalil, 2000). They are also less likely to feel positive about their child and about parenthood than older mothers are (Stevens-Simon, Nelligan, & Kelly, 2001). The less positive outlook is reflected in adolescent mothers' perceptions of infants as being more difficult in comparison with the view held by older mothers. The importance of this kind of perception among teen parents relates to the child's later development.

**Focus Point.** Adolescent mothers generally have a difficult time acting in their parental capacity. A variety of short- and long-term consequences occur when adolescents assume this family role. Generally, adolescent parenthood is developmentally off-time in contemporary American society.

## Adolescent Fathers

Adolescent fathers have not received the same degree of attention from researchers as young mothers (Figure 14–3); therefore, information about these young men continues to be scant in comparison (Gielen & Roopnarine, 2004). The dearth of research may be due to the attitude held by many in society that it is more important for adolescent fathers to be identified so that they may assume their legal responsibilities for their out-of-wedlock child. Those studies that have been performed examine personality characteristics, a father's involvement during a girl's pregnancy and after the child's birth, his role in pregnancy resolution decisions, his problems, and social outcomes associated with becoming an adolescent father (Thornberry, Smith, & Howard, 1997).

Because most adolescent girls who become mothers choose to retain custody of their baby and do not marry, an equal number of adolescent boys and young men are absent or nonresidential fathers. Although adolescent

**FIGURE 14–3.**   Research about adolescent parenthood has focused almost exclusively on the teenage girls who become pregnant. Comparatively little is known about adolescent males who father children.

mothers do not seem to be labeled today by stereotypes, a stereotype of adolescent fathers depicts them as uncaring, uninvolved, and immature (Stainer-Person, 1998). This may be partly true for some adolescent fathers—those who do not acknowledge their role in impregnating an adolescent girl—but it is not true for all. Researchers describe these young fathers as frightened, withdrawn, confused, and guilty about what has happened (Heaven, 2001). Many feel overwhelmed by the girl's pregnancy and may use denial as a defense mechanism to avoid the anxiety associated with their responsibility.

In many respects, adolescent fathers resemble those teenagers who are not fathers. However, a number of distinctive characteristics describe their particular situation (Fagot et al., 1998; Madden-Derdich, Herzog, & Leonard 2002; Saunders, 2002; Xie, Cairns, & Cairns, 2001). For example, more teen fathers are members of minority groups. Teen fathers typically have lower high school GPAs than nonfathers. Their relationship with the mother of their child is long term and stable. Most

are nonresidential fathers but are involved with their child and the mother. They do not view teen parenthood as a negative life event because this is supported in their communities and families, and they feel that contraception is the responsibility of their female partner.

Adolescent fathers' lack of involvement in pregnancy resolution decisions may partly relate to the lack of clarity in their role as fathers. This confusion tends to shape their behavior as parents (Madden-Derdich, Herzog, & Leonard 2002; Xie, Cairns, & Cairns, 2001). For example, some adolescent mothers rely on the men in their extended families and social networks to act as fathers for their children. Different men may enact the role at various times in a child's life: for example, the mother's current husband, the biological father, or the mother's biological father or stepfather. Once children are born, however, the majority of young fathers have contact with their child and the mother. In addition, the extent, nature, and context of the teen father's involvement with his child may be highly dependent on the mother's support and expectations.

Many fathers of children born to adolescent girls are in their 20s, and the girls perceive them to be authority figures (Alan Guttmacher Institute, 1999). Investigators commonly report that adolescent fathers have been involved in an intimate relationship with their child's mother for a long time and frequently continue to maintain this relationship after the child's birth. Although many young men state that they love the mother, the relationship is often characterized by a lack of commitment and little promise for continuation into the future. One study, however, notes that economic issues affect almost all of these young fathers (Rozie-Battle, 2003). For these young men, who are usually out of work, joblessness accounts for a diminished role as a father. In addition, it is possible to presume that a grandfather's presence could preclude the involvement of a teen father with his child, but this does not appear to be the case. The grandfather's support may increase the likelihood of a young teen father's involvement with his child (Madden-Derdich, Herzog, & Leonard 2002).

The problems that these young men experience by virtue of their socioeconomic status and their educational and lifestyle experiences are poignant. They are essentially no different from the difficulties of many adolescent mothers. For example, both teen mothers and fathers typically have problems with the adolescent girl's parents, experience situations that are developmentally off-time, and find that they are ill prepared to be parents (Schweingruber & Kalil, 2000).

The fact that less research attention has been given to the adolescent father perhaps reflects both legal and social attitudes about these young men. It is difficult to prove the legal paternity of a child. Although sophisticated laboratory tests are available using DNA fingerprinting techniques, these methods are controversial and expensive. The laws governing the custody and legal rights of out-of-wedlock children traditionally have recognized the rights of the biological mother over those of the father. These laws, which have origins in old English common law, were adapted in the formative years of the United States. They have not been questioned until recently when fathers became interested in establishing their rights and access to out-of-wedlock children. Recently, lawsuits argued in front of the Supreme Court have reversed the biological mothers' traditional rights, clearly outlining the legal rights of anyone who fathers a child out-of-wedlock. These rights range from custody and visitation to the child's rights to inheritance and support. They also guarantee a father's access to professional services when exercising his parental rights.

What factors would one assume to place teenage males at risk for becoming fathers? Researchers have identified these as not related or contributing to the likelihood of teen fatherhood (Anda et al., 2001; Thornberry, Smith, & Howard, 1997):

■ Coming from a home without a biological father or a home that offers less supervision
■ Parental emotional depression
■ Presence of family violence
■ Commitment to school performance

However, these factors appear to predispose someone to become an adolescent father:

■ Being a teen of color
■ Being educationally disadvantaged
■ Having parents who assumed this role early in life
■ Having parents with little formal education
■ Involvement with delinquent or deviant behavior (e.g., drug use, early sexual activity)
■ Experiencing adverse childhood conditions (e.g., household members who were substance abusers, mentally ill, or criminals)

More significantly, the cumulative, interactive effect of several of these domains place a young man at

high risk for fatherhood during adolescence. While not all teen males experiencing these kinds of circumstances become fathers, the mechanisms that prevent this in some but not others is not clear at this time.

A variety of social and educational programs have been developed to help teenagers address the change in their lives when they become parents. These programs are discussed in the next section.

## Parenting Reflection 14–2

Can parents of teenage expectant parents be held responsible in any way for this situation?

*Focus Point.* Researchers have studied adolescent mothers more than adolescent fathers. The adolescent father's parental role is less well defined than the adolescent mother's, although both parents share some of the same outcomes of pregnancy. Adolescent fathers have certain legal rights as parents. Most continue to maintain a relationship with the child's mother after the baby's birth.

## SUPPORTS FOR ADOLESCENT PARENTS

A teenager who becomes a parent receives more support from the community today than in the past. Until about 20 years ago, the only type of assistance available was a residential service program where adolescents could live while awaiting their baby's birth. Today, this type of service may continue to be helpful to some pregnant adolescents, especially those who have left their family or have dropped out of school. Services also target teens who are experiencing serious substance abuse, are abused by their family or boyfriend, or have run away from home. In many places, however, community services have been expanded to include a number of other social and human service programs that address the needs of pregnant teens and those who become parents. Some of these programs also assist in preventing repeat teen pregnancy and parenthood (Akinbami, Cheng, & Kornfeld, 2001).

The programs generally fall into one or more classifications, depending on whether they address educational needs, interpersonal skills, parenting skill development, or a combination. Regardless of the type of program, researchers identify those that are successful in their goals as: (1) programs that provide individual attention to the participants, and (2) multicomponent, multiagency, community-wide programs involving, for example, parents, schools, and religious groups to reach those teens most in need of services (Nitz, 1999; Stevens-Simon, 2000; Urban Institute, 1999). Programs that attempt to facilitate change in the lives of families with teenage mothers are also effective in minimizing the deleterious effects of adolescent pregnancy on the quality of life. Essentially, these programs offer long-term benefits to their adolescent participants (Honig & Morin, 2001).

The federal government has provided funding in the Adolescent Family Life Act for programs that address adolescent sexual activity, which often leads to pregnancy. Most programs advocate abstinence or delayed sexual activity as a means of preventing pregnancy rather than focusing on contraceptive uses (Perrin & DeJoy, 2003). Teens who are sexually abstinent report they have not had sex because they fear pregnancy or contracting diseases (Blinn-Pike, 1999). These programs are controversial and little evaluative data substantiates the effectiveness of programs that promote delaying sexual activity or abstinence in lowering pregnancy rates. Programs that provide counseling, peer education, or services to increase contraceptive use seem to be more effective in preventing adolescent pregnancy than these other approaches (Key, Barbosa, & Owens, 2001; Philliber, 1999). Furthermore, those programs that inform teenagers that there is a high risk of contracting sexually transmitted diseases and that pregnancy can ruin their lives appear to be more effective (Alan Guttmacher Institute, 1999).

## Educational Programming

Many different types of programs have been developed to mainstream pregnant adolescents into public schools or to maintain the public school educational programs of those who are already parents (Hoyt & Broom, 2002). Some programs support the continuation of a teenager's education while providing child development and parenting information that promotes competent caregiving skills. A main function of these programs is to lower the high drop-out rate observed among teenage girls who become pregnant. Disruption of schooling has long-

range, largely negative effects on teen parents and their children. Other programs offer child-care services as a means of promoting school attendance while providing other students with opportunities to observe infant and child behavior as part of child development and parenting courses (Akinbami, Cheng, & Kornfeld, 2001).

Pregnant or married adolescents were formerly expelled from school or not allowed to participate in regular school programming or extracurricular activities. Recent government and judicial rulings have determined that school districts discriminate against these teenagers by establishing and enforcing policies that restrict their access to educational experiences. Many school districts in larger metropolitan areas have established special support programs especially for pregnant teenagers or those who are already parents. These programs address the impending birth and provide special instruction in parenting skills, maternal and child nutrition and health care, and prenatal care. They also teach required academic subjects.

Day-care services can provide practical experiences with infants and young children. One experimental program pairs adolescent mothers with older women who serve as mentors, role models, and friends (Waller, Brown, & Whittle, 1999). This apparently helps the young mothers learn parenting skills and acquire child development knowledge, motivates their participation in educational experiences, and results in fewer behavior problems. Other programs feature peer education approaches and basing programmatic features on what teens themselves believe are the best ways to prevent pregnancies, such as via more access to contraceptive information (Hacker et al., 2000; Philliber, 1999).

When teenagers participate in such programs, they enhance their rate of returning to or staying in school programs that lead to a high school diploma. Research reports that subsequent births among teen mothers are diminished when they remain in school, live at home with their parents, and are engaged in educational or work activities (Key, Barbosa, & Owens, 2001; Manlove, Mariner, & Papillo, 2000; Stevens-Simon, 2000).

## Promoting Parenting Skills and Preventing Future Pregnancies

Participation in special programs can help teenagers who are pregnant or who already have children improve their parenting skills and prevent future unplanned, unwanted pregnancies (Ammen, 2000; Key, Barbosa, & Owens, 2001). When teenagers have education and information about sexuality, child development, contraception, and parenting, that knowledge may result in certain outcomes: (1) increase in the number of teens using birth control, (2) reduction of repeat pregnancies, and (3) reduction of child-abuse cases. These programs are as effective with teen fathers as they are with teen mothers (Brown, Saunders, & Dick, 1999). However, more programs are aimed at meeting the needs of adolescent mothers.

One way to assess the effectiveness of teen parenting programs is to measure child outcomes following parents' participation (Jaffee et al., 2001). If a program is truly successful, it will help teen parents to do a competent job of parenting children that will be evident in a child's cognitive, emotional, intellectual, and physical development. This assessment does not exclude the importance of the maternal or paternal outcomes.

Many programs include information about child development norms and appropriate expectations for infant and child behavior. This information improves parenting skills and attempts to prevent abuse from teen parents with inappropriate expectations (Stevens-Simon, Nelligan, & Kelly, 2001). Programs give teen parents and expectant teens opportunities to observe infants and young children. They offer lectures about child development and use special learning tools to promote appropriate parental attitudes and expectations.

Some programs are developed specifically to prevent adolescent pregnancy, but the variety of approaches seems to have limited results in achieving this goal. For example, peer education involves students who train other students about the hazards and negative consequences of teen pregnancy (Akinbami, Cheng, & Kornfeld, 2001; Philliber, 1999). Small adolescent support groups discuss sexuality and sexual issues to promote responsible sexual decision making. Some programs work specifically with minority groups that are especially at risk for adolescent pregnancy and for other behavior problems that interfere with attaining a high quality of life.

Some contend that the dilemma of adolescent parenthood can be most effectively addressed by implementing programs directed at the root of the issue: adequate sex education for teenagers that results in effective contraceptive practices (Urban Institute, 1999). This is a controversial problem. It is commonly as-

serted in many communities that sex education programs only stimulate teens' interest in having early sexual experiences that lead to pregnancies. Research has not been able to provide a clear answer to the credibility of this assertion (Alan Guttmacher Institute, 1999). However, despite methodological problems in investigating this issue, some evidence suggests that contraceptive use and the ability to engage adolescents to effectively use contraception are associated with their participation in sex education programs. Youths who participate in sex education programs have been found to delay participating in sexual intercourse rather than initiating this early or experiencing increases in sexual activity.

● ● ● ● ● ● ● ● ● ● ● ● ● ● ● ● ● ● ● ● ● ● ● ● ● ● ● ● ● ● ●

## Parenting Reflection 14–3

Why don't sex education programs in junior and senior high schools have a greater effect on reducing the number of teenage girls who become pregnant each year? Why don't programs that stress abstinence or delayed sexual activity have a greater impact?

● ● ● ● ● ● ● ● ● ● ● ● ● ● ● ● ● ● ● ● ● ● ● ● ● ● ● ● ● ● ●

The federal government has been interested in developing programs that help prevent teen pregnancy. The Adolescent Family Life Act of 1981 was passed as an effort to achieve this goal but with the stipulation that demonstration programs it funded would advocate abstinence as the most effective means of eliminating teen pregnancy and that certain topics, such as abortion and contraceptive practices, would not be included in the curriculum. The effectiveness of such programs in preventing pregnancies by discouraging adolescent participation in intercourse is not clear (Perrin & DeJoy, 2003).

One of the latest and perhaps most realistic strategies for helping teens avoid pregnancy makes use of a teaching device that looks, feels, and sounds like a real baby (Martin, 1996) (see Figure 14–4). Manufactured and developed by Realityworks, Inc., the highly realistic tool is effective in helping young adolescent girls and boys have experiences that parents of a newborn often encounter. Despite its cost, it is used in teen pregnancy prevention programs offered by many middle and senior high schools in the United States.

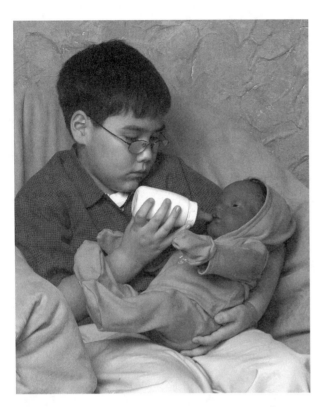

**FIGURE 14–4.**   Teaching devices, like RealCare®
Baby II, may help teens avoid early parenthood.
*Source:* Courtesy of Realityworks, Inc., 2709 Mondovi Road,
Eau Claire, WI 54701, (715) 830–2040, (800) 830–1416,
http://www.realityworks.com.

The baby is equipped with computer chips and a
small speaker that allow it to replicate realistically the
different kinds of cries made by a real baby when it is
hungry, wet, or sleepy. The chips can be programmed to
record how long the doll cries before being picked up
and the preferred position in which the baby is to be
held without crying. The teaching device can also
record if the doll has been shaken violently or hit, for example. Other models of the doll replicate the cries of an
infant born addicted to some substance via its mother's
addiction.

In a typical teen pregnancy prevention program using RealCare Baby II, each student (male and female)
typically is assigned the baby's care for 48 hours. During
this time, students experience the demands that a newborn makes on its caregiver because the baby can be programmed to cry to be fed every 4 hours around the clock,
cry and soil its diaper at irregular intervals, and so on.

Many adolescent girls entering these programs often plan
on having a baby soon after graduation or at some time
before completing their education. But after two sleep-
less nights and dealing with the hassles and demands of
caring for a simulated baby by themselves as well as attending to school responsibilities, most conclude that
they'll wait until they are much older before becoming a
parent. Interestingly, in one class, all of the instances
where the simulators were ignored or physically abused
occurred when they were being cared for by boys.

There is limited research on the effectiveness of the
simulation in reducing or preventing teen pregnancies
in the communities where programs use it as a teaching
aid. However, it is likely that such experiences are more
effective than other approaches in building empathy
with what it must be like to be a teen mother or father
(Mallery, 2002).

••••••••••••••••••••••••••••••••••••••••••••••••••••••

***Focus Point.***   Programs that address the needs of adolescent parents are available in many communities in the
United States. These programs offer a number of social
and human services that assist adolescent parents and
help to prevent future pregnancies. Public school systems provide special programs that help teen parents
pursue their educational goals. They also offer psychological support and training in parenting skills.
••••••••••••••••••••••••••••••••••••••••••••••••••••••

## POINTS TO CONSIDER

- Teenagers continue to become parents today although there has been a decline in recent years in the
  numbers who carry a pregnancy to term. Four basic
  factors influence teen pregnancy: (1) increased incidence of sexual activity among adolescents; (2) lack of
  adequate contraceptive knowledge and use; (3) social
  influences; and (4) personal, family, and community
  attitudes about teen pregnancy.
- The majority of pregnant adolescents elect to keep
  their baby following birth. A minority place their infants for adoption. Some choose to get married; however, married adolescents are at high risk for divorce
  within a relatively short period of time.
- Teen pregnancy has consequences for adolescent
  mothers and fathers, their child, their families of origin, and society. Most of these consequences are long
  term in nature and scope. Adolescent mothers may

expect interruptions or disruptions in their education; less-than-positive implications regarding the health of the mother and child; the probability of lower economic status caused by low-paying, unsatisfying jobs; large families; and the likelihood of a troubled relationship with the child due to poor parenting skills.

■ Relatively little is known about adolescent fathers as compared with adolescent mothers because these young men usually play a less well-defined role in adolescent parenthood. A variety of characteristics distinguish these young men from those within their age range who are not fathers.

■ A variety of support programs and services may be available in many communities to assist adolescent parents. These are designed to help adolescent parents complete their education and learn adequate parenting skills. The programs also work to prevent pregnancies among adolescents and repeat pregnancies among those who are parents.

## CHAPTER 15

# Abusive Parents and Foster Care

### Focus Questions
■ ■ ■ ■ ■ ■ ■ ■ ■ ■

#### Abusive Parents

1. What are the major issues relating to parental abuse and neglect of children?

2. How are abusive parents and their children characterized? What are the major consequences of abuse for children?

3. What intervention strategies help parents to control their abusiveness and provide treatment for children?

#### Foster Care

1. What is foster care?

2. Why are children placed in foster care?

3. What are some characteristics of foster children?

4. What are foster parents like, and why does someone become a foster parent?

5. What are some of the particular challenges facing foster parents?

6. What are some outcomes of foster children?

7. What can be done to improve the foster care system?

■ ■ ■ ■ ■ ■ ■ ■ ■ ■

Many families in the United States experience problems and situations that can affect their ability to function in healthy ways. Effective parenting in these families is difficult to achieve due to several factors that operate against this optimal goal. Families can be considered at high risk due to economic, health, psychological, or social factors that challenge effective functioning. Many families find they can successfully cope with such challenges by seeking help from professionals, social networks, relatives, and other sources. They learn to use healthy means for dealing with difficult circumstances. Other families, who perhaps are not especially healthy in general, often fail to respond to such challenges in healthy ways, and their status becomes even more endangered as a result. While every family can expect to experience crises at some time and frequently for a long period of time, each reacts in different ways to address and resolve crises.

This chapter discusses situations that have not yet been addressed in the text. These challenges are significant and represent issues that are specific to some families in the United States today. No family system is perfect or without problems that can threaten its ability to function effectively and in healthy ways. However, this chapter describes drastic situations. First, those families in which one or both parents abuse their children physically, sexually, and/or emotionally are examined. Abusive parents present a clear risk to their children, and the effects of such treatment can have lasting detrimental, even life-threatening, effects for children. When abuse occurs in families, such behavior of one or both parents creates an unhealthy family environment that damages all members. It frequently leads to dissolution of a family via divorce, and parental rights may be terminated. Second, most children in foster care are placed because of parental abuse, and parental rights frequently are terminated either temporarily or permanently. We examine the nature of this system in the

United States and in the process are exposed to a current debate about how it functions imperfectly and why.

## ABUSIVE PARENTS

The media and other sources of cultural conditioning have led us to believe that most families are happy groups of people committed to nurturing, sustaining, and supporting each other. This is a highly romanticized notion of family life that ignores important and unpleasant realities of daily family interaction. Only within the intimacy of family systems do some people feel permitted to harm one another in physical, sexual, or emotional ways. For some, the family system is a battleground where atrocities to others occur with all-too-frequent regularity (Brandt, 2002; Gelles, Loseke, & Cavanaugh, 2004) (see Focus On 15–1).

Early explanations of family functioning recognized conflict as inevitable in human relations. This was thought to occur because both individuals and social

| **Focus On 15–1** | **Facts About Child Abuse and Neglect** |

- An estimated 896,000 children were victims of child abuse or neglect in 2002.
- More than 60 percent of child victims experienced neglect. Almost 20 percent were physically abused; 10 percent were sexually abused; and 7 percent were emotionally maltreated.
- Children ages birth to 3 years had the highest rates of victimization at 16.0 per 1,000 children. Girls were slightly more likely to be victims than boys.
- American Indian or Alaska Native and African American children had the highest rates of victimization when compared to their national population.
- Child fatalities are the most tragic consequence of maltreatment. In 2002, an estimated 1,400 children died due to abuse or neglect.
- Three-quarters (76 percent) of children who were killed were younger than 4 years old; 12 percent were 4 to 7 years old; 6 percent were 8 to 11 years old; and 6 percent were 12 to 17 years old.
- Infant boys (younger than 1 year old) had the highest rate of fatalities.
- One-third of child fatalities were attributed to neglect. Physical abuse and sexual abuse also were major contributors to fatalities.
- More than 80 percent of perpetrators were parents. Female perpetrators, who were mostly mothers, were typically younger than male perpetrators, who were mostly fathers.
- Women comprised a larger percentage of all perpetrators than men, 58 percent compared to 42 percent.
- Of all parents who were perpetrators, less than 3 percent were associated with sexual abuse. Of all perpetrators of sexual abuse, nearly 29 percent were other relatives, and nearly one-quarter were not relatives or child-care providers.

*Source:* National Clearinghouse on Child Abuse and Neglect. (2003). *Child maltreatment 2002: Summary of key findings.* Washington, DC: Author.

agencies tended to promote personal interests and needs over the welfare of the group. One of the primary tenets of the Freudian theory of personality development stresses the dual nature of human relations in which opposite emotions, such as love and hate, can be held simultaneously in relation to a love object. Recent research on family violence illustrates a returning interest in learning more about this unpleasant aspect of family life (Wallace, 2004; Winkler, 2004).

## Definitions and Prevalence of Family Violence

Family researchers have only recently begun to study the issue of violence in families. Since the late 1960s and early 1970s, several cultural and social factors have promoted this interest (Gelles, Loseke, & Cavanaugh, 2004). First, there has been increased public sensitivity to the violence connected with the military hostilities in many regions of the world, such as the Middle East, Ireland, and the former USSR; the assassinations of public officials and celebrities; large-scale demonstrations of civil disobedience; widespread acts of terrorism; and the high homicide rates in large cities. Second, the women's movement has played a major role in focusing public attention on the issue of violence toward women and children, especially wife battering, marital rape, and incest. Third, researchers have been able to demonstrate that valid research can be conducted on this sensitive issue, although it poses many methodological problems (Miller-Perrin, Perrin, & Barnett, 2004).

There continues to be some confusion among researchers and the general public over what constitutes abuse, violence, and neglect within a family system. **Abuse** and **neglect** are sometimes interchangeable terms; they often refer to acts of physical aggression that result in injury and to nonphysical acts of maltreatment that are thought to cause harm to a person (Gelles, Loseke, & Cavanaugh, 2004). In some instances, abuse includes problems resulting from physical assault that have medical diagnoses and symptoms, and neglect refers to acts of parental negligence, such as failing to supervise children or properly provide for their nutritional needs. While this is a basic notion of abuse, **maltreatment** of children and adolescents is the term increasingly used. This term includes those acts that define abuse and neglect as well as radical parental acts, such as excessive punishment, child abandonment, infanticide, murder of chil-

dren, and abandonment of a child's corpse. **Violence** is a rather broad concept that includes what many consider to be legitimate acts of force against family members, which often fall under the guise of discipline and parental control of children. The term also relates to illegitimate acts of violence, including those occurring as part of family conflict. Hitting is acceptable behavior in many families because many parents consider spanking a child to be necessary and normal parental behavior.

A generally accepted definition of family violence is described as "an act carried out with the intention or perceived intention of causing physical pain or injury to another person" (Gelles & Cornell, 1997). Examples of such acts range from spanking, shoving, hitting, slapping, pinching, shooting, cutting, or pulling to those acts that cause psychological harm or injury.

Violence in families can be directed at both children and adults and perpetrated by one against the other. Child abuse and neglect have received a great deal of attention from both researchers and the media. Even though there is a wide variety of types of abuse (see Figure 15–1) and researchers may differ in their definitions and understandings of the types of violence in families, a general categorization of physical and psychological abuse has emerged. This is especially the case for those acts that constitute child abuse and maltreatment (see Focus On 15–2).

## Models of Family Violence

Seven basic models or theoretical explanations focus on why parents and children act violently against one another (Brandt, 2002; Garbarino et al., 2004; Gelles &

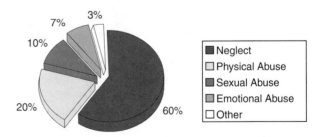

**FIGURE 15–1.** Percentage of children experiencing different types of abuse and neglect in the United States, 2002.

*Source:* National Clearinghouse on Child Abuse and Neglect. (2003). *Child maltreatment 2002: Summary of key findings.* Washington, DC: Author.

---

**Focus On 15–2**    **Classifications of Child Abuse and Neglect**

- *Physical abuse:* Infliction of any type of injury on a child, such as burns, bites, cuts, and welts
- *Sexual abuse:* Forcing, tricking, or coercing sexual behavior between a young person and an older person, with an age difference of at least 5 years between the perpetrator and the victim; includes fondling body parts, penetration of the child's body by nonsexual objects or the offender's sexual organs, and noncontact behaviors, such as voyeurism or pornography
- *Physical neglect:* Failure to provide a child with an adequate and nurturing home environment that provides the basic necessities of food, clothing, shelter, and supervision
- *Medical neglect:* Failure to provide a child with medical treatment when physical conditions necessitate such care (except in instances prohibited by religious beliefs)
- *Emotional abuse:* Speech, actions, and interactions that tend to destroy emotional well-being and a sense of self-worth and those that hamper healthy personal and social development
- *Emotional neglect:* Failure to show concern for a child and his or her activities
- *Abandonment:* Failure to make provisions for the continual supervision of a child
- *Multiple maltreatment:* A combination of several types of abuse or neglect

*Sources:* Gelles, R. J., & Cornell, C. P. (1997). *Intimate violence in families* (3rd ed.). Thousand Oaks, CA: Sage Publications; Gelles, R. J., Loseke, D. R., & Cavanaugh, M. M. (2004). *Current controversies on family violence.* Thousand Oaks, CA: Sage Publications; Wallace, W. (2004). *Family violence: Legal, medical and social perspective* (4th ed.). Boston: Allyn & Bacon.

---

Cornell, 1997; Gelles, Loseke, & Cavanaugh, 2004; Myuwiler, 2004; Wallace, 2004):

1. The **psychiatric model** assumes that abusive individuals in a family system are deviant or mentally and/or emotionally ill. This model isolates the personality characteristics of the offender as the primary cause of the abusive behavior. It attempts to link personality patterns or traits with the tendency to perform abusive acts and with other behavior patterns, such as borderline personality organization, alcoholism, substance abuse, and mental illness.

2. The **ecological model** examines the child and the family from a systems theory perspective. It explores the child's development within the family system and the functioning of the family system within its community. For example, when the community supports parental use of physical force against children but does not provide support for families in stress, the likelihood of family violence increases. From this viewpoint, abusiveness is a family problem that affects everyone, and the entire family must receive treatment to become healthy.

3. The **sociological model** stresses that social values and attitudes about violence shape violent behavior in family systems. From a cultural point of view, the use of physical force, particularly against children, is a sanctioned aspect of parenting behavior. Violence is a means of settling disputes and conflicts with others. The model also emphasizes that adults' violent behavior toward children is a reaction to stress and frustration. The strengths of these stimuli are closely related to the social status of the family system. People from lower social classes are thought to experience greater environmental stress and to express their reactions through violent behavior that is often directed at children and other family members. Another tenet of this approach emphasizes that family structure and organization lend their influence to violent behavior. Crowded living conditions, high levels of unemployment, strained financial resources, and social isolation from other families place additional stress on the parent-child microenvironment, which can result in abusive behavior. Additionally, being an adolescent parent or living in a stepfamily situation may also increase the possibility of this behavior due to stressful living conditions.

4. The **social psychological model** covers a variety of approaches that explain violence among family members. Interaction patterns, the transmission of violent behavior from one generation to the next, and environmental stress are cited as prime motivators of violent behavior in families. According to this model, violence is learned by modeling and serves as a coping mechanism in response to stress. In addition, child abuse is considered a product of inconsistent punishment used by many parents. Violence may also be learned within the sibling microenvironment as a means of solving problems.

5. The **patriarchy model** emphasizes that violence occurs in families due to the traditional social dominance of adult males, which places women in a subordinate position and condones the use of violence to support male dominance.

6. The **exchange/social control model** suggests that violence occurs in families when the costs of being violent do not outweigh its rewards. For example, the rewards of violent behavior might be getting one's own way, assuming superiority over others, gaining revenge, or expressing anger and frustration. The costs might include receiving violent behavior in retaliation, being arrested and jailed, or becoming divorced. These costs also act as social controls to prevent and limit the possibility of violent behavior, but three factors tend to limit the strength of such costs in controlling violence: (1) inequality of the sexes, (2) the privacy of the family, and (3) subscription to cultural beliefs in machismo, or ultramasculinity that is expressed in aggressive, hostile, and violent ways.

7. The **information processing approach** proposes that neglectful parents fail to process information appropriately about children's need for care because of four possibilities: (1) they do not perceive behavioral cues given by children, (2) they interpret such signals from children as not requiring a parental caregiving response, (3) they are aware that a parental response is required but fail to have one available, or (4) they choose a response that is either inappropriate or never implemented.

## Factors Associated with Family Violence

Researchers describe several social-psychological variables related to the incidence and variety of violent be-

haviors expressed in families (Gallimore, 2002; Garbarino, 2001; Garabarino et al., 2004; Gelles & Cornell, 1997). First, a **cycle of violence** appears to be manifested in two basic ways:

1. Individuals who had violent and abusive childhoods tend to become abusers of their own children.

2. A three-phase sequence in the expression of violent behavior begins with increasing tension, a loss of control manifested by violent behavior, and a reconciliation period characterized by the offender's contriteness and the victim's forgiveness.

Second, *socioeconomic status* of a family system is associated with expressions of violence, particularly in families from lower socioeconomic groups where the quality of life, environmental stresses, and cultural conditioning or standards may be felt more keenly and intensely than they are in other social groups.

Third, *stress* is closely related to domestic violence. Acts of violence or abuse form part of a person's coping mechanisms for stress. Sources of stress may include poverty, unemployment or part-time employment, financial problems, pregnancy and childbirth, or single parenthood.

Fourth, *social isolation* from other families increases the risk of abusive behavior directed toward children or a spouse. This may be a contributing factor to the likelihood of abuse occurring in single-parent families. The social networks provided by interactions with other families tend to act as a control mechanism to reduce the risk of such behavior.

In addition to these four variables, several other conditions can be linked to family violence. There is an association between **substance abuse** by parents and physical abuse and neglect of children. Substance abuse or chemical dependency, especially involving alcohol, may play a role in 50 to 90 percent of cases of physical abuse of children by parents. Intoxication and chemical dependency impair judgment, increase irritability, and enhance emotionally depressive reactions, thus increasing the likelihood of mistreating children.

Another factor associated with child abuse and neglect is *family form*. A majority of reported cases of child abuse occur in single-parent families. Rather than being a function primarily of single-parent household status, abuse of children may be more likely to occur in these homes because of the diverse effects of poverty on single-parent family functioning. Additionally, family form plays a role in that stepfathers appear to be more likely to abuse children rather than biological fathers.

• • • • • • • • • • • • • • • • • • • • • • • • • • • • • • • • •

## Parenting Reflection 15–1

You are grocery shopping and have just witnessed a parent viciously slapping and shaking her preschool-age boy. The child is screaming and crying loudly and the parent is continuing to yell at the child, calling him names and shaming him for what he has done. What do you do?

• • • • • • • • • • • • • • • • • • • • • • • • • • • • • • • • •

## Characteristics of Abusive Parents

Because it is unlike other family problems, parental abuse of children requires different approaches in understanding the causes and motivations of such behaviors (Kotch, Muller, & Blakely, 1999). In these instances the parent generally has an extremely difficult time dealing with a child's behavior and handling a problem of which he or she may or may not be consciously aware. No one characteristic is common to all abusive parents, although statistics point to the mother rather than father as being more likely to be the abusive parent (National Clearinghouse on Child Abuse and Neglect, 2003). Researchers observe several attributes in various combinations in those adults who are prone to be abusive to their children. These characteristics are outlined in Focus On 15–3.

The child-rearing patterns of these individuals typically reflect a rigid, harsh authoritarian approach. For example, abusive mothers characteristically express inconsistency, hostility, and protectiveness (paradoxically) toward their children, often almost simultaneously. They seek to gain control over their children's behavior through methods based on producing a child's anxiety and guilt as well as through physical punishment (Timmer, Borrego, & Urquiza, 2002).

Although these characteristics of abusive and neglectful parents are general and broad in nature, it is important to distinguish between the characteristics of parents who behave in different ways that result in child

---

**Focus On 15–3**

## Characteristics of an Abusive Parent

■ Had an unhappy childhood
■ Was mistreated or abused as a child by parent(s)
■ Had parents who failed to provide an adequate model of good parenting
■ Is socially isolated from family, friends, or neighbors; has few outside contacts of an intimate nature
■ Has low self-esteem; perceives self as inadequate, unlovable, incompetent, or worthless
■ Is emotionally immature; may be considered an adult child emotionally; has a dependent personality
■ Sees little joy or pleasure in life; may be clinically depressed
■ Holds distorted perceptions and unrealistic expectations of children
■ Is adverse to the idea of spoiling his or her child; strongly believes in physical punishment as a means of teaching children and helping them learn family patterns; practices an authoritarian child-rearing style; displays minimal nurturing behaviors to child; displays frequent outbursts of temper
■ Has severely limited ability to empathize with others, particularly with his or her children; displays a general insensitivity to the needs of others

*Sources:* Feindler, E. L., Rathus, J. H., & Silver, L. B. (2003). *Assessment of family violence: A handbook for researchers and practitioners.* Washington, DC: American Psychological Association; Flowers, R. B. (2000). *Domestic crimes, family violence, and child abuse: A study of contemporary American society.* Jefferson, NC: McFarland & Company; Heyman, R. E., & Slep, A. M. S. (2002). Do child abuse and interparental violence lead to adulthood family violence? *Journal of Marriage and the Family, 64,* 864–870; Institute of Medicine Staff Board. (2002). *Confronting chronic neglect: The education and training of health professionals on family violence.* Washington, DC: National Academy Press; Malley-Morrison, K., & Hines, D. (2003). *Family violence in a cultural perspective: Defining, understanding, and combating abuse.* Thousand Oaks, CA: Sage Publications; National Clearinghouse on Child Abuse and Neglect. (2003). *Child maltreatment 2002: Summary of key findings.* Washington, DC: Author; Stark, E. (2000). *Everything you need to know about family violence.* New York: Rosen Publishing Group.

---

**Parenting FAQs 15–1**

**My husband has become physically violent with me and our two children. I'm increasingly afraid of being here with him, especially when he's drinking heavily, but I'm also afraid of leaving. What can I do?**

**A:**   I can understand your dilemma, but you must understand that you are the only parent who's capable of providing your children with the protection they need and deserve, and you deserve to take care of yourself as well. You can do a few things before your husband begins to react violently. (1) Learn what seems to trigger his tendency to be physically abusive and when he is likely to become abusive so that you can begin to assess the level of danger to you and your children. (2) Make plans about how to leave, where to go that is safe, and what to take with you. (3) Inform one of your neighbors about the situation and give permission to call the police if the neighbor suspects something wrong is happening at your house. (4) Teach your oldest or most responsible child how to dial 911 if your husband begins to act violently toward you or your children.

When a violent attack is happening, you can take several steps to protect you and your children. (1) Leave immediately or lock yourself and the children into a place of safety. (2) Call 911 or have a child do this. (3) Scream so loudly that neighbors will hear you. (4) If someone is injured, leave immediately for the hospital emergency room.

If you leave your home, you will need to plan a safe escape. Put enough money in a safe place to pay for a motel room, food, gas, and telephone calls for at least a weekend. Have clothing packed for a weekend for yourself and your children. Keep nearby necessary documents, including copies of his and your driver's licenses, social security numbers, birth certificates, bank accounts, insurance policies, and/or income tax records.

Most communities have safe shelters for women and their children. Find out where these may be in your community and what you must do in case you need to go to a shelter for assistance. Community mental health agencies are also places to go for help in emergencies and for professional assistance. Some church organizations also provide assistance in situations like yours.

---

maltreatment. These different types of abusive and neglectful parents are briefly outlined here.

**Parents Who Physically Neglect Children.**   Physical neglect of children constitutes the most frequently reported type of maltreatment of children by parents. This accounts for an estimated 60 percent of all reported child abuse in the United States (National Clearinghouse on Child Abuse and Neglect, 2003) (Parenting FAQs 15–1). Parents who neglect their children physically fail to provide for basic needs, such as sufficient food for nutritional requirements, supervision, or medical care. Such inadequate care for children results in fatalities with about the same frequency as that occurring with physical abuse.

Parents who are reported for child neglect the first time are found to have recently experienced a family crisis due to illness or other health problem, divorce, or desertion (Institute of Medicine Staff Board, 2002). As might be expected, parents who chronically are physically neglectful of their children typically have poor parenting skills and abilities.

Such parents often live in poverty and experience high levels of stress that are accompanied by emotional depression and anxiety due to unemployment, inadequate nutrition, high levels of substance abuse, and low incomes. These are multiproblem families with a chaotic home environment and low personal functioning. The families are socially isolated and maintain closed boundaries that do not allow access to support systems in their community. The closed nature of these families also makes them resistant to assistance and therapy to help them overcome or cope with their problems. Parental neglect of children can be damaging to children. Our society must take this problem seriously. Although this type of child maltreatment may be overshadowed by the more dramatic aspects of physical and sexual abuse of children, it is not simply a by-product of poverty that can be dismissed as inevitable.

**Parents Who Physically Abuse Children.** Many parents who physically abuse children are not aware that what they do is wrong and harmful (Flowers, 2000; Stark, 2000). They perceive their parental responsibilities to be in authority over children. This approach is manifested in strong beliefs about the necessity of using physical punishment in teaching children how to behave, but even more significantly as a means of achieving control over children's misbehavior. They generally have low tolerance levels for children's behavior, being impatient and quick to anger. They may be described as having poor empathic abilities and as being insensitive to children's needs and natures. Some are belligerent, even paranoid, and as a result experience many negative interactions with other people both within and outside of the family. Physical abuse of children usually occurs when these parents are responsible for young children in situations that they find highly stressful and are without sufficient support and resources to cope (Stark, 2000).

Other factors coincide to culminate in abusive actions of these parents toward their children. These adults are vulnerable to stress and typically cope poorly. They have been found to experience significantly more stressful and stress-producing events in their lives than parents who do not abuse their children physically (Runyon et al., 2004).

Being abused as a child is an important predictor of whether someone will abuse their children physically as a parent. Substance abuse also plays a significant role in the behavior of abusive parents toward their children (Shultz, 2001). Alcohol abuse is especially associated with placing children at risk for physical abuse. The abusive behavior often occurs when parents are intoxicated and in even less control than usual of their actions. It is also likely that when substance abuse plays a role in the incidence of child abuse, the perpetrator grew up in a family where at least one parent was a substance abuser.

**Parents Who Emotionally Abuse Children.** Researchers have conducted fewer studies of emotionally abusive parents than other abusive types (Wark, Kruczek, & Boley, 2003). This may be due to the diffi-

culty in identifying parental behaviors that fall into this category. It is also difficult to prove that emotional abuse has occurred between parents and children because the evidence is not as obvious when compared with other types of abuse. It also may be possible that emotional abuse of children is more widespread as acceptable parental behavior (Straus & Field, 2003).

Parents who emotionally abuse children most likely experience low levels of self-esteem (Miller-Perrin, Perrin, & Barnett, 2004). They are found to have poor coping skills and child management techniques. This deficiency may give rise to situations in which parents express their anger and impatience with children in ways that damage the children's self-esteem as well. As difficult as it may seem to understand, the attainment of adulthood does not automatically confer emotional maturity upon an individual. Some parents experienced difficult childhood and adolescent developmental paths that have impaired their ability to grow in healthy ways emotionally. Some are the products of homes in which their parents suffered addictions to drugs, work, gambling, or other substances. Such life experiences tend to result in creating a distorted emotional makeup known as an **adult child** (Ramey, 2004). Until adults who are disadvantaged by stagnated emotional development can receive help in moving forward toward developmentally healthy emotional progress, it is highly likely their children will experience emotional abuse as well.

When parents become emotionally abusive, they express their impatience, frustration, rage, personal hurt, and disappointment with their children in various ways that damage the children's sense of trust and emotional well-being. Discounting a child's feelings and actions through name calling, putdowns, or sarcasm is considered emotional abuse. Telling children they will never amount to anything worthwhile is abusive. Other examples include shaming children when they make mistakes, handing down punishments that are humiliating, not allowing children to express feelings, or ostracizing children as punishment by not speaking to them, ignoring their presence, or destroying their favorite toys. When children are abused in these ways, it increases the likelihood they will become emotionally depressed (Doyle, 2001). This difficult mental state is observed to be four times as prevalent in children who have been abused than among children who have not been mistreated by parents. Because emotional depression is associated with suicidal ideation, these children are also at greater risk of suicide than others.

**Parents Who Sexually Abuse Children.**   It is difficult for most people to imagine that adults are interested in engaging in sexual activity with children, especially if those involved are members of the same family (Focus On 15–4). There is a strong taboo against incest in almost all human societies. **Incest** is sexual activity between members of the same family and is considered to be an aspect of sexual abuse involving children. Children cannot give consent to such activity. Especially in families where children are taught to obey their parents and other elders, children are incapable of declining and may not understand what they are consenting to do with an adult perpetrator (Witters-Green, 2003). Sexual abuse by parents is rare, occurring in an estimated 3 percent of families (National Clearinghouse on Child Abuse and Neglect, 2003). The majority of adults who sexually molest children are other relatives and nonrelatives with whom the child is familiar.

Until about 40 years ago, researchers thought that little sexual abuse or incestuous activity took place in American families. But when child abuse legislation was instituted at this time, requiring such cases to be reported, researchers discovered that sexual abuse of children was more widespread than they had imagined. People have become more open in publicly disclosing their sexual abuse in childhood. Celebrities such as TV star Roseanne and former Miss America Marilyn Van Debur have publicly acknowledged that they were sexually abused as children by family members. This has stimulated many people who experienced similar abuse as children to seek treatment and to help others acknowledge these experiences as part of their healing process. Although it may be impossible to gather exact figures showing the extent of sexual abuse of children, one national estimate is that almost 1 million children experienced abuse of some nature in 2002 (McDonald and Associates, 2004). Of this number, an estimated 10 percent were sexually abused.

Sexual harassment is strongly similar to sexual abuse and involves inappropriate sexual touching and insinuations between parents and children. Children are abused sexually when parents engage in genital fondling, anal or vaginal intercourse, or oral-genital contact, for example. There are many risks involved with such activities for all concerned, but especially for the child.

Families in which sexual abuse of children has occurred are characterized as having poor boundary controls among members, especially between parents and children, poor quality of the adult marriage relationship, less harmony and stability in the family system as a whole, and a father who was probably physically abused as a child and acted violently within the family as an adult (Engel, 2000; Ferrara, 2001). Families in which sexual abuse of children has occurred are observed to have significantly greater difficulties in regulating anger and greater degrees of chaos or difficulties in managing roles (Howes et al., 2000). Some insights have emerged about the attitudes of men who have perpetrated sexual abuse that may serve to motivate such behavior. When compared to other men who have physically abused children, male incest offenders hold deviant attitudes that endorse male sexual entitlement in general and perceive children to be sexually attractive and sexually motivated. They minimize the harm caused to children by sexual activity with adults, especially family members. In addition, interviews with perpetrators reveal that these individuals, regardless of their gender, see their incestuous actions as fair and loving and a statement of their professed care for their child victims (Eldridge, 1997). Such views serve to minimize and discount any possible harm that they perceive children could experience from their behavior.

## Treatment and Intervention for Abusive Parents

**Programs for Abusive Parents.**   A wide variety of assistance is available to abusive parents (Feindler, Rathus, & Silver, 2003; Harway, 2000; Malley-Morrison & Hines, 2003). Usually, this assistance focuses on the individual adult but addresses the needs of the entire family. Services may include medical care, counseling, psychotherapy, marriage and family therapy, mediation, support groups, telephone crisis information, day care, parenting education, and temporary foster care for children. Some programs emphasize skill development that enhances parental prosocial attitudes and interpersonal relationships. Others address family support needs as a means for prevention and early intervention (Winkler, 2004). In instances that include legal involvement, courts may order the family to participate in therapeutic programs using parent education and psychotherapy (Wallace, 2004). In other instances, parents may seek out these services voluntarily.

**Focus On
15–4**

## Myths About Sexual Abuse of Children

Perpetrators who molest and sexually abuse children often harbor misconceptions about their actions and the effects of their behavior on children. Likewise, many people may not fully understand the ramification of children's sexual abuse. Listed here are some of the major myths about sexual abuse of children and the facts that destroy their credibility.

- *Myth:* The typical perpetrator is an old man who entices children with offers of candy.
  *Fact:* There is no typical perpetrator; children may be abused by anyone, including adult women or men, older children or adolescents, relatives or nonrelatives. However, abuse is more likely to happen by adult males than females, and the perpetrator is likely to be someone with whom the child is familiar.

- *Myth:* Children are more likely to be abused by an adult gay male.
  *Fact:* Children are more likely to be abused by a heterosexual male who is a family member such as a stepfather. In addition, a pedophile is sexually attracted to children regardless of their biological sex.

- *Myth:* Children will forget what happened if they are sexually abused.
  *Fact:* Sexual abuse has long-term consequences that can affect victims into their adult years, manifesting in sexual difficulties, depression, and post-traumatic stress reactions, for example. Short-term effects also manifest in the form of school and peer problems, sleep disorders, regressive behaviors, and other changes in behavior.

- *Myth:* Children can make up stories about being sexually abused.
  *Fact:* Children rarely lie about being sexually abused; they lack the knowledge of explicit sexual behavior if they have not been abused.

- *Myth:* If children are sexually abused, they acted in such a way to entice the adult into such acts.
  *Fact:* Sexual abuse of children happens because an adult or older child allows this to occur. The perpetrator is always responsible for the offense.

- *Myth:* If a child reacts sexually to the perpetrator or does not object, then he or she has consented to the sexual actions.
  *Fact:* Children are incapable of making such decisions about sexual activity because they lack the ability to make sexual decisions.

- *Myth:* If a child is sexually abused by someone of the same sex, then he or she will grow up to become homosexual.
  *Fact:* Sexual orientation is not determined in this manner.

- *Myth:* Children who are sexually abused grow up to become pedophiles.
  *Fact:* There are no statistics or research findings to support this assertion.

- *Myth:* Only girls are sexually abused.
  *Fact:* Boys are often victims of sexual abuse although girls outnumber them as victims.

- *Myth:* The damage that occurs from sexual abuse as a child cannot be healed.
  *Fact:* Children need to be supported by family members when sexual abuse has occurred. Treatment can take place in childhood as well as in adulthood and healing can be achieved.

*Sources:* Adapted from American Academy of Child and Adolescent Psychiatry. (1998). *Child sexual abuse*. Washington, DC: Author; American Academy of Pediatrics. (2000). *Sexual abuse*. Washington, DC: Author; American College of Obstetricians and Gynecologists. (2000). *Adult manifestations of child sexual abuse*. Washington, DC: Author; McDonald, et al. (2004). *Child maltreatment 2002*. Washington, DC: National Clearinghouse on Child Abuse and Neglect.

It is unclear if these programs are completely effective in preventing future child abuse and neglect by parents (Garbarino et al., 2004). Using certain criteria to measure effectiveness, some critics observe that most treatment programs are not always successful for participants. Programs that emphasize parent education and early intervention with those prone to abuse may be more effective than others, especially in producing short-term effects for the parents (Dore & Lee, 1999). Programs may be most beneficial if abusive parents participate in support groups, such as Parents Anonymous or Parents in Distress, in addition to the parenting programs. These support groups are composed of self-referred individuals who are disturbed by their abusive behavior and fearful of the effects of continued abuse on their children and families. The groups are modeled after Alcoholics Anonymous. Group members meet weekly to discuss their problems and provide mutual support during and between meetings. Members are instructed to call another member when they feel most likely to commit an abusive act against someone in their family. Many communities also have safe houses that provide temporary shelter and initial assistance to women and their children who have been in abusive family situations (Correia & Rubin, 2002).

Family therapy using a systems theory approach may provide the most promise of effectiveness in helping both parents and children (Gelles, Loseke, & Cavanaugh, 2004). When families are treated by a competent therapist, all the elements related to the abuse are involved: the perpetrator, the victim, and the relationship.

*Focus Point.*   Violence in families is an unpleasant reality. Child abuse and neglect have received a great deal of attention in recent years. Seven basic theoretical approaches explain why abuse and neglect occur. Several psychological and social factors are associated with a variety of violent behaviors directed toward children and other family members. Parents who abuse and neglect children have particular characteristics. The types of abusiveness range from physical neglect and abuse to emotional and sexual abuse of children. Intervention and treatment programs have been developed, but results are generally unclear.

# FOSTER CARE

Some parents are separated from their children and may be denied visitation or even parental rights because of their abusive and neglectful behavior. Accompanying a dramatic increase in the number of families who experience poverty and related challenges is an equally dramatic increase in the number of children experiencing out-of-home placements. When a community or state agency has determined that children are not safe in their parents' home or that it is not in their best interest to be exposed to an unhealthy parent-child environment, children can be legally removed from their homes.

The most common placement is into **foster care** or **family foster care.** In this setting, children are cared for by trained and licensed adults who provide substitute parental care. Some of these homes are especially intended for children with special needs. Another kind of foster care is provided by a child's relatives. In each of these settings, the foster parents are compensated for the service they provide, although costs often exceed the amount that is provided by the supervising agency.

## Demographic Data on Foster Care in the United States

The federal government collects information relating to foster care and publishes this information annually (Children's Bureau, 2003). The most current data from 2000 to 2001 are summarized here.

- The number of children in foster care was 542,000, up 40 percent from 1990. The average age was 10.1 years. The largest numbers were between 11 and 15 years old followed by those between 6 and 10 years of age.
- The majority of children experienced foster care for at least 2 years but less than 5. The average length for all children was 2 years, 9 months.
- About 81 percent of all children in foster care are white or African American. Black children are overrepresented in the foster care population, however, as compared to those in the general population.
- The large majority of foster children are cared for by a nonrelative.
- Most children in foster care wish to be reunited with their parents or to be adopted. These goals are most often attained when foster care is terminated.

Parental abuse and neglect account for the most common reasons for placement into foster care. As many as 80 percent of all families involved in child protective services are affected by alcohol or drug problems (Children's Defense Fund, 2003).

---

### Parenting Reflection 15–2

Suppose you are a case worker for a child protective service. How would you explain what was happening and why to a child who is being placed into foster care because their parents had been charged with running a methamphetamine operation in the family home? How would you respond to this child's assertion that this was happening because her parents didn't love her?

---

## Foster Parents

Foster parents may be married or single, heterosexual or homosexual. They come from all social backgrounds and may or may not be fully employed outside their home (Lindon, 2004). Every state has its own criteria for accepting individuals as foster parents. Some commonalities in these criteria are that individuals must: (1) be 21 years of age minimum; (2) lack a criminal record or history of child abuse or neglect; (3) have a regular source of income; (4) successfully complete training in foster care; (4) be Red Cross certified in first aid; and (5) be approved with an inspection of their home.

Adults who become foster parents often are motivated by their own childhood experiences in foster care or by altruistic interests in meeting the needs of children who come from difficult family circumstances (Barber & Delfabbro, 2004). Many of the children arrive with emotional and behavioral problems and may have been placed repeatedly since being removed from their parents' care (Cox, Orme, & Rhoades, 2003).

Foster parents are uniquely challenged by dealing with a variety of issues not experienced typically by other adults who care for children (Orme & Buehler, 2001). These issues include: (1) connecting with and supervising a child who often has been abused, may be rejected or unloved by his or her parents, and thus has innumerable trust issues; (2) being paid little for demanding work; (3) dealing with a variety of agencies,

bureaucracies, social workers, and even angry, defensive biological parents; (4) having little community support or respect for being a foster parent. These issues frequently account for the high rate of burnout observed among many foster parents (The Pew Charitable Trust, 2004a, 2004b).

---

### Parenting Reflection 15–3

You are in charge of developing a training program for potential foster parents. What would be the major topics you would include in the 16 hours of training taking place in two-hour sessions for two months? What outside speakers would you invite to address the trainees?

---

Despite the odds, many foster parents and the children they care for have good outcomes (Bueler et al., 2000; Golding, 2003; Kufeldt, Simard, & Vachon, 2003). Certainly, those foster parents who have the greatest degrees of support from their child welfare system are the most likely to have good outcomes: children successfully completing their education, having satisfying relationships with peers and in intimate relationships, and avoiding conflicts with law enforcement. Such support frequently is the form of therapeutic participation, appropriate supervision and involvement from social work agencies, and adequate economic support from the child welfare system. Many foster children come to prefer living with their foster parents than with biological parents. Many hope for and gain adoption by foster parents, who may have pursued this course as a means of testing out a situation with a child prior to adoption.

On the other hand, the outcome of foster care can be disappointing for both adults and children when children remain too long in this type of care, have histories of traumatic maltreatment by biological parents and other adults, and have had many different placements, for example (Holland & Gorey, 2004; Lee, 2004). Some 40 percent of adult welfare recipients or prisoners were in foster care as children (Dumaret, Coppel-Batsch, & Couraud, 1997). Other research findings report that adult outcomes of placement in foster care as a child can range from higher incidence of emotional depression to greater likelihood of marital unhappiness and social isolation.

One study of the foster care system identifies several ways that involvement in this system exacts certain costs for both foster children and parents (The Pew Charitable Trust, 2004a):

1. The difficulties for foster children to overcome feelings of insecurity and to develop and maintain important relationships with adults

2. The price of frustration, exasperation, and confusion exacted from poor communications between social agencies and judicial systems and the foster children and parents they supervise

3. The failure of the foster care system to respond sensitively to the individual needs and differences of participants

4. The cost that results from not receiving timely help for all parties, foster children, foster parents, and biological parents

5. Burnout by foster parents and those who provide supervision, caused by shortcomings in the system (e.g., inadequate training, lack of adequate staffing, etc.)

6. The stigma associated with the concept of foster care and associated involvement with this system as a child or as a parent

Numerous governmental, charitable, and social agencies have studied a variety of options to improve the foster care system in the United States. A central goal is to move children out of this system and into adopted homes as quickly as possible. Since its inception, foster care has had the goal of providing only temporary, short-term care for children when parental rights have been terminated or questioned. Currently, many children may remain in foster care longer than is healthy. The obvious solution is to shorten their stay and attempt to provide adoption as an exit from foster care as quickly as possible (The Pew Charitable Trust, 2004b). Two options that have been studied as viable solutions include: (1) improving federal financing mechanisms that will facilitate faster exit of children from foster care and into adoption with the eventual goal of eliminating the need for foster care, and (2) improving the ability of the judicial system to make better decisions more quickly that are in the child's best interest for personal safety and welfare.

*Focus Point.*   When children are removed from their parents' care, they are placed into foster care or family foster care. This frequently occurs due to parental abuse and neglect and is intended as a temporary solution in providing care for children. Data collected by the federal government indicates that the length of stay in the foster care system is far from temporary for most children. In addition, certain demographic variables are characteristic of children in foster care.

Foster parents usually are not related to foster children, although some children are cared for by relatives. Foster parents resemble other adults in most communities and must meet criteria established by state social agencies to be licensed. In addition, they must complete approved training to be a foster parent. These parents face challenges unique to their situation of caring for unwanted or neglected children. The majority of children placed in foster care grow to achieve acceptable outcomes as adults. Some of the greatest problems arising within the foster care system may be alleviated by shortening the time children spend in this system and moving them into adoptive homes.

## POINTS TO CONSIDER

### Abusive Parents

■ Violence in families occurs in a variety of ways and is frequently directed at children. Although it is difficult to obtain accurate information regarding the extent of such violence, child abuse appears to be the most prominent type of maltreatment among family members.

■ Seven basic models explain why violence takes place in families.

■ A number of social-psychological factors are associated with abusiveness, including a cycle of violence, a family's socioeconomic status, influence of stress, social isolation from other families, and family form.

■ Parents who abuse their children share a variety of characteristics that often reflect a poor parenting experience in their own childhoods. Children are not only neglected but abused physically, sexually, and emotionally.

■ A variety of approaches is available to assist and treat abusive parents.

### Foster Care

■ Children are separated from parents and parental rights terminated when children are abused or live in an unsafe home environment. When this occurs, they are usually placed into the foster care system to be cared for, most frequently by a nonrelative.

■ Most of the children in the foster care system are white or African American. The average length of stay in the system is slightly over 2½ years. Most children wish to remain with their foster families or to be adopted.

■ Adults who become foster parents must meet criteria established by the state in which they reside and become certified by attending a training course. They assume this role for a variety of reasons, often because they wish to have a trial period of observing a potentially adoptive child.

■ Foster parenting is a challenge often because children have been abused, are suspicious of adults, and have emotional or behavior problems. Foster parents must deal with different agencies and officials. The pay they receive for housing and caring for a child is quite low, and most payments are intended to cover the cost of caring for a foster child. A high degree of burnout is observed among many foster parents.

■ Outcomes for foster children can be devastating or positive. The majority fare well as adults.

■ Many observers note that the foster care system in the United States is in serious difficulty in that certain costs are observed among foster children, foster parents, and the foster care system that provides supervision. The best recommendation for improving the system is to speed up the time to move children from the system into adoptive homes.

# References

Adams, J. (2004). *When our grown kids disappoint us: Letting go of their problems, loving them anyway, and getting on with our lives*. New York: Simon & Schuster.

Adams, K., & Fey, J. (2003). *Helping your child recover from sexual abuse*. Seattle: University of Washington Press.

Adesman, A., & Adesmec, C. A. (2004). *Parenting your adopted child: A positive approach to building a strong family*. New York: McGraw-Hill.

Aggarwal, S., & Verma, T. (1987). Aggressiveness among children: A function of differential training by mothers. *Indian Psychological Review, 32*, 15–19.

Ahrons, C. R., & Tanner, J. L. (2003). Adult children and their fathers: Relationship changes 20 years after parental divorce. *Family Relations, 52*, 340–351.

Ainsworth, M. (1973). The development of infant-mother attachment. In B. Caldwell & H. Riciuti (Eds.), *Review of child development research* (Vol. 3). Chicago: University of Chicago Press.

Ainsworth, M. (1977). Attachment theory and its utility in cross-cultural research. In P. Leiderman, S. Tulkin, & A. Rosenfield (Eds.), *Cultural and infancy: Variations in the human experience*. New York: Academic Press.

Akinbami, L. J., Cheng, T. L., & Kornfeld, D. (2002). A review of teen-tot programs: Comprehensive clinical care for young parents and their children. *Adolescence, 36*, 381–393.

Alan Guttmacher Institute. (1999). *Teen sex and pregnancy*. New York: Author.

Aldous, J. (1978). *Family careers: Developmental change in families*. New York: Wiley.

Allen, M., & Burrell, N. A. (2002). Sexual orientation of the parent: The impact on the child. In M. Allen & R. Preiss (Eds.), *Interpersonal communication research: Advances through meta-analysis* (pp. 125–143). Mahwah, NJ: Lawrence Erlbaum Associates.

Allgeier, E. R., & Allgeier, R. A. (2000). *Sexual interactions* (5th ed.). Boston: Houghton-Mifflin.

Amato, P. R. (2003). Reconciling divergent perspectives: Judith Wallerstein, quantitative family research, and children of divorce. *Family Relations, 52*, 332–339.

Amato, P. R., & Gilbreth, J. G. (1999). Nonresident fathers and children's well-being: A meta analysis. *Journal of Marriage and the Family, 61*, 557–573.

Ambert, A. M. (1992). *The effect of children on parents*. New York: Haworth Press.

Ambert, A. M. (1994). An international perspective on parenting: Social change and social constructs. *Journal of Marriage and the Family, 56*, 529–543.

American Academy of Pediatrics. (1999). *Guide to your child's nutrition: Making peace at the table and building healthy eating habits for life*. Washington, DC: Author.

American Academy of Pediatrics Committee on Drugs. (1994). The transfer of drugs and other chemicals into human milk. *Pediatrics, 93*, 137–150.

American Academy of Pediatrics Committee on Substance Abuse. (1993). Fetal alcohol syndrome and fetal alcohol effects. *Pediatrics, 91*, 1004–1006.

American Academy of Pediatrics Committee on Substance Abuse. (2001). *Substance abuse: A guide for professionals* (2nd ed.). Washington, DC: Author.

American Bar Association. (1996). *The ABA guide to family law*. New York: Times Books/Random House.

American Bar Association. (2001). *A judge's guide: Making child-centered decisions in custody cases*. Chicago: Author.

American Psychiatric Association. (2000). *Diagnostic and statistical manual of mental disorders: Text revision*. Washington, DC: Author.

Ammen, S. A. (2000). A play-based parenting program to facilitate parent-child attachment. In H. G. Kaduson & C. E. Schaefer (Eds.), *Short-term play therapy for children* (pp. 345–369). New York: Guilford Press.

Anand, K. J. (2003). Early exposure to marijuana and risk of later drug use. *Journal of the American Medical Association, 290*, 330–332.

Anda, R. F., Chapman, D. P., Felitti, V. J., Edwards, V., Williamson, D. F., Croft, J. B., & Giles, W. H. (2002). Adverse childhood experiences and risk of paternity in teen pregnancy. *Obstetrics and Gynecology, 100*, 37–45.

Anderson, A. S. (2003). Nutrition and pregnancy—motivations and interests. *Journal of Human Nutrition & Dietetics, 16*, 64–66.

Anderson, E. R., Greene, S. M., Hetherington, E. M., & Clingempeel, W. G. (1999). The dynamics of parental remarriage: Adolescent, parent, and sibling influences. In E. M. Hetherington (Ed.), *Coping with divorce, single parenting, and remarriage: A risk and resiliency perspective* (pp. 295–319). Mahwah, NJ: Lawrence Erlbaum.

Arditti, J. A. (1999). Rethinking relationships between divorced mothers and their children: Capitalizing on family strengths. *Family Relations, 48*, 109–119.

Aries, P. (Ed.). (1992). *A history of private life, Vol. 1: From pagan Rome to Byzantium*. Cambridge, MA: Harvard University Press.

Arnett, J. J. (2003). *Adolescence and emerging adulthood: A cultural approach*. Upper Saddle River, NJ: Prentice Hall.

Arnold, F., Culatao, R., Buripakdi, C., Chung, F., Fawcett, J., Iritani, T., Lee, W., & Wu, T. (1975). *The value of children* (Vol. 1). Honolulu: University of Hawaii Press.

Astington, J. W. (1993). *The child's discovery of the mind*. Cambridge, MA: Harvard University Press.

Azar, B. (1997). It may cause anxiety, but day care can benefit kids. *APA Monitor, 28*, 13.

Bagley, C., & Tremblay, P. (1998). On the prevalence of homosexuality and bisexuality, in a random community survey of 750 men aged 18 to 27. *Journal of Homosexuality, 36*, 1–18.

Bailey, J. M., Willerman, L., & Parks, C. (1991). A test of the maternal stress theory of human male sexuality. *Archives of Sexual Behavior, 20*, 277–286.

Baldwin, D. A., & Moses, I. J. (1996). The ontogeny of social information gathering. *Child Development, 67*, 1915–1939.

Balkcom, C. T. (2002). African American parental involvement in education. A phenomenological study of the role of self-efficacy. *Dissertation Abstracts International, 63*, 495.

Bandura, A. (1977). *Social learning theory*. Englewood Cliffs, NJ: Prentice Hall.

Barber, J. G., & Delfabbro, P. H. (2004). *Children in foster care*. New York: Routledge.

Barber, M. D., Lambers, A., Visco, A. G., & Bump, R. C. (2000). Effect of patient position on clinical evaluation of pelvic organ prolapse. *Obstetrics & Gynecology, 96*, 18–22.

Barber, N. (2001). On the relationship between marital opportunity and teen pregnancy: The sex ratio question. *Journal of Cross-Cultural Psychology, 32*, 259–267.

Barth, R. P., Webster, D. II, & Lee, S. (2002). Adoption of American Indian children: Implications for implementing the Indian Child Welfare and Adoption and Safe Families Acts. *Children and Youth Services Review, 24*, 139–158.

Baumer, E. P., & South, S. J. (2001). Community effects on youth sexual activity. *Journal of Marriage & the Family, 63*, 540–554.

Becerra, R. M. (1998). The Mexican-American family. In C. H. Mindel, R. W. Haberstein, & R. Wright, Jr. (Eds.), *Ethnic families in America: Patterns and variations* (pp. 153–171). Upper Saddle River, NJ: Prentice Hall.

Becvar, D. S., & Becvar, R. J. (1998). *Systems theory and family therapy: A primer* (2nd ed.). New York: University Press of America.

Beeghly, M., Frank, D. A., Rose-Jacobs, R., Cabral H., & Tronick, E. (2003). Level of prenatal cocaine exposure and infant-caregiver attachment behavior. *Neurotoxicology & Teratology, 25*, 23–38.

Bellows, B. B. (2004). *Sex education: Index and analysis of new information for parents, schools, churches, and counselors.* Washington, DC: ABBE Publishers Association.

Belsky, J. (1988). The "effects" of infant day care reconsidered. *Early Childhood Research Quarterly, 3*, 235–273.

Belsky, J. (1990). Child care and children's socioemotional development. *Journal of Marriage and the Family, 52*, 885–903.

Belsky, J., & Rovine, M. J. (1988). Nonmaternal care in the first year of life and the security of infant-parent attachment. *Child Development, 59*, 157–168.

Belsky, J., & Rovine, M. J. (1990). Patterns of marital change across the transition to parenthood: Pregnancy to three years postpartum. *Journal of Marriage and the Family, 52*, 5–19.

Bem, S. (1975). Sex-role adaptability: One consequence of psychological androgyny. *Journal of Personality and Social Psychology, 31*, 634–643.

Bem, S. (1989). Genital knowledge and gender constancy in preschool children. *Child Development, 60*, 649–662.

Benedek, E. P., & Brown, C. F. (2004). *How to help your child overcome your divorce: A support guide for families.* New York: Newmarket Press.

Benkov, L. (1994). *Reinventing the family: The emerging story of lesbian and gay parents.* New York: Crown Publishers.

Bennett, S. (2003). Is there a primary mom? Parental perceptions of attachment bond hierarchies within lesbian adoptive families. *Child & Adolescent Social Work Journal, 20*, 159–173.

Benokraitis, N. V. (2004). *Marriages and families: Changes, choices, and constraints* (5th ed.). Upper Saddle River, NJ: Prentice Hall.

Berenbaum, S. A., & Snyder, E. (1995). Early hormonal influences on childhood sex-typed activity and playmate preference: Implications for the development of sexual orientation. *Developmental Psychology, 31*, 31–42.

Berger, R. (2000). Remarried families of 2000: Definitions, description, and interventions. In W. C. Nichols, M. A. Pace-Nichols, D. S. Becvar, & A. Y. Napier (Eds.), *Handbook of family development* (pp. 371–390). New York: Wiley.

Berk, L. E., & Landau, S. (1993). Private speech of learning disabled and normally achieving children in classroom academic and laboratory contexts. *Child Development, 64*, 556–571.

Bernstein, N. (2004, March 7). Behind fall in pregnancy, a new teenage culture of restraint [Electronic version]. *New York Times.*

Bianchi, S. M., Milkie, M., Sayer, L., & Robinson, J. (2000). Is anyone doing the housework? *Social Forces, 79*, 191–228.

Bickart, T. S., & Jablon, J. (2004). *What every parent needs to know about 1st, 2nd, and 3rd grades: An essential guide to your child's education.* Naperville, IL: Sourcebooks.

Bieber, I. (1962). *Homosexuality.* New York: Basic Books.

Bigner, J. J. (1972). Parent education in popular literature: 1950–1970. *Family Coordinator, 21*, 313–319.

Bigner, J. J. (1996). Working with gay fathers: Developmental, post-divorce, and therapeutic issues. In R-J. Green & J. S. Laird (Eds.), *Lesbian and gay couple and family relationships: Therapeutic perspectives* (pp. 370–403). San Francisco: Jossey-Bass.

Bigner, J. J. (1999). Raising our sons: Gay men as fathers. *Journal of Gay and Lesbian Social Services, 10*, 61–77.

Bigner, J. J. (2000). Gay and lesbian families. In W. C. Nichols, M. A. Pace-Nichols, D. S. Becvar, & A. Y. Napier (Eds.), *Handbook of family development and intervention* (pp. 279–298). New York: Wiley.

Bigner, J. J., & Jacobsen, R. B. (1989a). Parenting behaviors of homosexual and heterosexual fathers. *Journal of Homosexuality, 18*, 173–186.

Bigner, J. J., & Jacobsen, R. B. (1989b). The value of children for gay and heterosexual fathers. *Journal of Homosexuality, 18*, 163–172.

Bigner, J. J., Jacobsen, R. B., Miller, J. A., & Turner, J. G. (1982). The value of children for farm families. *Psychological Reports, 50*, 793–794.

Bigner, J. J., Jacobsen, R. B., & Phelan, G. K. (1981). Cultural correlates of parent-nonparent stereotypes: A multivariate analysis. *Home Economics Research Journal, 9*, 184–192.

Bigner, J. J., & Yang, R. K. (1996). Parent education in popular literature: 1972–1990. *Family and Consumer Sciences Research Journal, 25*, 3–27.

Bird, C. E. (1997). Gender differences in the social and economic burdens of parenting and psychological distress. *Journal of Marriage and the Family, 59*, 809–823.

Bissell, M. (2000). Socio-economic outcomes of teen pregnancy and parenthood: A review of the literature. *Canadian Journal of Human Sexuality, 9*, 191–204.

Bitler, M., & Zavodny, M. (2002). Did abortion legalization reduce the number of unwanted children? Evidence from adoptions. *Perspectives on Sexual and Reproductive Health, 34*, 25–33.

Blanchard, R., Zuckey, K. J., Bradley, S. J., & Hume, C. S. (1995). Birth order and sibling sex ratio in homosexual male adolescents and probably prehomosexual feminine boys. *Developmental Psychology, 31*, 22–30.

Blasco, T. M. A., & Verney, T. R. (2003). Assisted reproductive technology: Psychological effects on offspring. *Journal of Prenatal & Perinatal Psychology & Health, 17*, 225–233.

Blinn-Pike, L. (1999). Why abstinent adolescents report they have not had sex: Understanding sexually resilient youth. *Family Relations, 48*, 295–301.

Bloch, J. S. (2003). The ultimate discipline guide. *Child, 18*, 88–89.

Bloomfield, H. H. (2004). *Making peace in your stepfamily: Surviving and thriving as parents and stepparents.* San Diego, CA: Peace Publishing.

Bluestone, C., & Tamis-LeMonda, C. S. (1999). Correlates of prenting styles in predominantly working- and middle-class

African American mothers. *Journal of Marriage and the Family, 61,* 881–893.

Blum, R. W. (2001). Trends in adolescent health: Perspectives from the United States. *International Journal of Adolescent Medicine & Health, 13,* 287–295.

Bogaert, A. F. (2003). The interaction of fraternal birth order and body size in male sexual orientation. *Behavioral Neuroscience, 117,* 381–384.

Bongar, B., & Beutler, L. E. (Eds.). (1995). *Comprehensive textbook of psychotherapy: Theory and practice.* New York: Oxford University Press.

Boonstra, H. (2000). Welfare law and the drive to reduce "illegitimacy." *The Guttmacher Report on Public Policy, 3,* 7–10.

Borders, L. D., Black, L. K., & Pasley, B. K. (1998). Are adopted children and their parents at greater risk for negative outcomes? *Family Relations, 47,* 237–241.

Borja, J. B., & Adair, L. S. (2003). Assessing the net effect of young maternal age on birth weight. *American Journal of Human Biology, 15,* 733–740.

Borkowski, J. G., Bisconti, T., Weed, K., Willard, C., Keogh, D. A., & Whitman, T. L. (2002). The adolescent as parent: Influences on children's intellectual, academic, and socioemotional development. In J. G. Borkowski & S. L. Ramey (Eds.), *Parenting and the child's world: Influences on academic, intellectual, and social-emotional development* (pp. 161–184). Mahwah, NJ: Lawrence Erlbaum.

Bormann, C., & Stockdale, D. (1979). Values of children: Relationships between mothers and daughters. *Home Economics Research Journal, 8,* 58–65.

Bornstein, R. F., & Masling, J. M. (Eds.). (2002). *The psychodynamics of gender and gender role.* Washington, DC: American Psychological Association.

Boss, P. (1988). *Family stress management.* Beverly Hills, CA: Sage Publications.

Bourgeois, F. J. (2004). *Obstetrics and gynecology.* Philadelphia: Lippincott, Williams, & Wilkins.

Bowen, M. (1978). *Family therapy in clinical practice.* New York: Aronson.

Bowie, F. (2004). *Cross-cultural approaches to adoption.* New York: Routledge.

Bozett, F. W. (1981a). Gay father: Evolution of the gay father identity. *American Journal of Orthopsychiatry, 51,* 552–559.

Bozett, F. W. (1981b). Gay fathers: Identity conflict resolution through integrative sanctioning. *Alternative Lifestyles, 4,* 90–107.

Bozett, F. W. (1985). Gay men as fathers. In S. Hanson & F. W. Bozett (Eds.), *Gay and lesbian parents* (pp. 35–70). New York: Sage Publications.

Bozett, F. W. (1987). Gay fathers. In F. W. Bozett (Ed.), *Gay and lesbian parents* (pp. 3–22). New York: Praeger.

Bozett, F. W., & Sussman, M. B. (1989). Homosexuality and family relations: Views and research issues. In F. W. Bozett & M. B. Sussman (Eds.), *Homosexuality and family relations* (pp. 15–28). New York: Harrington Park Press.

Bradbury, T. N., Fincham, F. D., & Beach, S. R. H. (2000). Research on the nature and determinants of marital satisfaction: A decade review. *Journal of Marriage and the Family, 62,* 964–980.

Bramlett, M. D., & Mosher, W. D. (2002). Cohabitation, marriage, divorce, and remarriage in the United States. *Vital Health Statistics, 23(22).* Hyattsville, MD: National Center for Health Statistics.

Brandt, D. (2002). *Homes of fear: The curse of family violence.* Monrovia, CA: World Vision International.

Breedlove, G. K., Schorfheide, A. M., & Wieczorek, R. R. (2000). *Adolescent pregnancy.* White Plains, NY: March of Dimes Birth Defects Foundation.

Broderick, C. B. (1993). *Understanding family process: The basics of family systems theory.* Thousand Oaks, CA: Sage Publications.

Brodzinsky, D. M., & Pinderhughes, E. (2002). Parenting and child development in adoptive families. In M. H. Bornstein (Ed.), *Handbook of parenting: Children and parenting, Vol. 1* (2nd ed., pp. 279–311). Mahwah, NJ: Lawrence Erlbaum.

Bronfenbrenner, U. (1979). *The ecology of human development.* Cambridge, MA: Harvard University Press.

Bronfenbrenner, U. (1985). The parent-child relationship and our changing society. In L. E. Arnold (Ed.), *Parents, children, and change.* Lexington, MA: Lexington Books.

Bronfenbrenner, U. (1986). Ecology of the family as a context for human development: Research perspectives. *Developmental Psychology, 22,* 723–742.

Bronfenbrenner, U. (1993). Ecological systems theory. In R. H. Wozniak (Ed.), *Development in context* (pp. 44–78). Hillsdale, NJ: Erlbaum.

Brookey, R. A. (2000). Saints or sinners: Sociobiological theories of male homosexuality. *International Journal of Sexuality & Gender Studies, 5,* 37–58.

Brophy-Herb, H. E., & Honig, A. S. (1999). Quality of adolescent mother-infant interactions and clinical determinations of risk status. *Early Child Development & Care, 152,* 17–26.

Brown, H. N., Saunders, R. B., & Dick, M. J. (1999). Preventing secondary pregnancy in adolescents: A model program. *Health Care for Women International, 20,* 5–15.

Bryson, K., & Casper, L. M. (1999). Coresident grandparents and grandchildren. *Current Population Reports, P-23-198.* Washington, DC: U.S. Government Printing Office.

Bubolz, M. M., & Sontag, S. (1993). Human ecology theory. In P. Boss, W. J. Doherty, R. LaRossa, W. R. Schumm, & S. K. Steinmetz (Eds.), *Sourcebook of family theories and methods: A contextual approach* (pp. 419–448). New York: Plenum Press.

Bueler, C., Orme, J. G., Post, J., & Patterson, D. A. (2000). The long-term correlates of family foster care. *Children & Youth Services Review, 22,* 595–625.

Bulterys, M. (2001). What's new in perinatal research? U.S. and international update. Retrieved from http://www.cdc.gov/mmwr/PDF/rr/rr4702.pdf

Burgess, E. (1926). The family as a unity of interacting personalities. *Family, 7,* 3–9.

Buriel, R., Mercado, R., Rodriguez, J., & Chavez, J. M. (1991). Mexican-American disciplinary practices and attitudes toward child maltreatment: A comparison of foreign- and native-born mothers. *Hispanic Journal of Behavioral Sciences, 13,* 78–94.

Burns, D. (1999). *Feeling good: The new mood therapy.* New York: Morrow/Avon.

Buxton, A. P. (1994). *The other side of the closet: The coming-out crisis for straight spouses and families.* New York: Wiley.

Buxton, A. P. (1999). The best interest of children of gay and lesbian parents. In R. M Galatzer-Levy & L. Kraus (Eds.), *The scientific basis of child custody decisions* (pp. 319–356). Chicago: University of Chicago Press.

Buxton, A. P. (2004). Paths and pitfalls: How heterosexual spouses cope when their husbands or wives come out. *Journal of Couple and Relationship Therapy, 3(2/3),* 95–110.

Cabrera, N. J. (2003). In their own voices: How men become fathers. *Human Development, 46,* 250–258.

Caldwell, M. (2004). *Adoption: Using technology and time-tested techniques to expedite a safe, successful adoption: Your step-by-step guide.* Nevada City, CA: American Carriage House Publishing.

Callan, V. J., & Gallois, C. (1983). Perceptions about having children: Are daughters different from their mothers? *Journal of Marriage and the Family, 45*, 607–612.

Cancian, F. M., & Oliker, S. J. (2000). *Caring and gender*. Walnut Creek, CA: Alta/Mira.

Capps, R., Fix, M., & Reardon-Anderson, J. (2003). *Children of immigrants show slight reductions in poverty, hardship*. Washington, DC: The Urban Institute.

Caputo, R. K. (2001). The intergenerational transmission of grandmother-grandchild co-residency. *Journal of Sociology and Social Welfare, 28*, 79–86.

Carlson, B. E. (1986). Children's beliefs about punishment. *American Journal of Orthopsychiatry, 56*, 308–312.

CDC-NCBDDD. (2002). FAS and other prenatal alcohol-related conditions. Retrieved from http://www.cdc.gov/ncbddd/fas/faqs.htm

Centers for Disease Control and Prevention. (2002). *Overweight children and adolescents 6–19 years of age, according to sex, age, race, and Hispanic origin: United States, selected years 1963–65 through 1999–2000*. Hyattsville, MD: U.S. Department of Health and Human Services.

Centers for Disease Control and Prevention. (2003, December 31). *Adolescent and school health, sexual behaviors*. Retrieved from http://www.cdc.gov/nccdphp/dash/sexualbehaviors/index.htm#data

Chabot, J. M., & Ames, B. D. (2004). "It wasn't let's get pregnant and go do it'": Decision making in lesbian couples planning motherhood via donor insemination. *Family Relations, 53*, 348–356.

Chakraborty, R. (2002). Better late than never. *Femina, 43*, 94–96.

Chamberlain, P., & Patterson, G. R. (1995). Discipline and child compliance in parenting. In M. H. Bornstein (Ed.), *Handbook of parenting, Vol. 4: Applied and practical parenting* (pp. 205–225). Hillsdale, NJ: Lawrence Erlbaum.

Cherlin, A. J., & Furstenberg, F. F. (1986). *The new American grandparent*. New York: Basic Books.

Chiang, Y.-Y., & Finley, G. E. (2001). Is adoptee status a risk or protective factor for the experience of adoptive parental divorce? Paper presented at the 63rd Annual Conference of the National Council on Family Relations, Rochester, NY.

Children's Bureau. (2003). The adoption and foster care analysis and reporting system (AFCARS) report: Preliminary FY 2001 estimates as of March 2003. Washington,

DC: U.S. Department of Health and Human Services, Administration for Children and Families, Administration on Children, Youth and Families. Retrieved from www.acf.hhs.gov/programs/cb

Children's Defense Fund. (1996). *The state of America's children yearbook, 1996*. Washington, DC: Author.

Children's Defense Fund. (2003). *The state of children in America's union 2002*. Washington, DC: Author.

Chinnaiya, A., Venkat, A., Dawn, C., Chee, W. Y., Choo, K. B., Gole, L. A., Meng, C. T. (1998). Intrahepatic vein fetal blood sampling: Current role in prenatal diagnosis. *Journal of Obstetrics & Gynaecology Research, 24*, 239–246.

Chrisp, J. (2001). That four letter word—sons: Lesbian mothers and adolescent sons. *Journal of Lesbian Studies, 5*, 195–209.

Christensen, F. B., & Smith, T. A. (2002). What is happening to satisfaction and quality of relationships between step/grandparents and step/grandchildren? *Journal of Divorce & Remarriage, 37*, 117–133.

Chugani, H. T., Behen, M. E., Muzik, O., Juhasz, C., Nagy, F., & Chugani, D. C. (2001). Local brain function activity following early deprivation: A study of postinstitutionalized Romanian orphans. *NeuroImage, 14*, 1290–1301.

Ciano-Boyce, C., & Shelley-Sireci, L. (2002). Who is mommy tonight? Lesbian parenting issues. *Journal of Homosexuality, 43*, 1–13.

Cicero, S., Curcio, P. Papageorghiou, A., Sonek, J., & Nicholaides, K. (2001). Absence of nasal bone in fetuses with trisomy 21 at 11–14 weeks of gestation: An observational study. *Lancet, 358*, 1665–1667.

Cicirelli, V. G. (2000). An examination of the trajectory of the adult child's caregiving for an elderly parent. *Family Relations, 49*, 169–175.

Clarke, J. I., & Dawson, C. (1998). *Growing up again: Parenting ourselves, parenting our children* (2nd ed.). Center City, MN: Hazelden Information and Educational Services.

Clarke, V. (2002). Resistance and normalization in the construction of lesbian and gay families: A discursive analysis. In A. Coyle & C. Kitzinger (Eds.), *Lesbian and gay psychology: New perspectives* (pp. 98–116). Malden, MA: Blackwell Publishers.

Coley, R. L. (2001). (In) visible men: Emerging research on low-income, unmarried, and minority fathers. *American Psychologist, 56*, 743–753.

Coll, B. (1991). Consider the children: Is parenthood being devalued? *Psychological Record, 41*, 303–314.

Collins, M. E. (2000). Impact of welfare reform on teenage parent recipients: An analysis of two cohorts. *American Journal of Orthopsychiatry, 70*, 135–140.

Collins, W. A., Maccoby, E. E., Steinberg, L., Hetherington, E. M., & Bornstein, M. H. (2000). Contemporary research in parenting: The case for nature and nurture. *American Psychologist, 55*, 218–232.

Coltrane, S. (1990). Birth timing and the division of labor in dual-earner families: Exploratory findings and suggestions for further research. *Journal of Family Issues, 11*, 157–181.

Committee on Obstetric Practice. (2002). ACOG committee opinion: Exercise during pregnancy and the postpartum period. *International Journal of Gynaecology & Obstetrics, 77*, 79–81.

Conner, J. M., & Dewey, J. E. (2003). Reproductive health. In M. H. Bornstein & L. Davidson (Eds.), *Well-being: Positive development across the life course: Crosscurrents in contemporary psychology* (pp. 99–107). Mahwah, NJ: Lawrence Erlbaum.

Connolly, C. M. (2005). A process of change: The intersection of the GLBT individual and their family of origin. *Journal of GLBT Family Studies, 1*, 5–20.

Connor, K. A. (2000). *Continuing to care: Older Americans and their families*. New York, NY: Falmer.

Consumer Product Safety Commission. (2004). Think toy safety. Retrieved from http://www.cpsc.gov/cpscpub/pubs/281.pdf

Conway, M. B., Christensen, T. M., & Herlihy, B. (2003). Adult children of divorce and intimate relationships: Implications for counseling. *Family Journal: Counseling & Therapy for Couples & Families, 11*, 364–373.

Cook, A. S., & Oltjenbruns, K. A. (1998). *Dying and grieving: Lifespan and family perspectives*. New York: Harcourt Trade Publishers.

Coontz, S. (1992). *The way we never were: American families and the nostalgia trap*. New York: Basic Books.

Coontz, S. (1998). *The way we really are: Coming to terms with America's changing families*. New York: Basic Books.

Correia, A., & Rubin, J. (2002). *Housing and battered women*. Washington, DC: Department of Justice, Office of Violence Against Women.

Cowan, C. P., & Cowan, P. A. (1992). *When partners become parents: The big life change for couples*. New York: Basic Books.

Cox, F. D. (2001). *Human intimacy: Marriage, the family, and its meaning.* Belmont, CA: Brooks/Cole.

Cox, M. E., Orme, J. G., & Rhoades, K. W. (2003). Willingness to foster children with emotional or behavioral problems. *Journal of Social Service Research, 29,* 23–51.

Cox, M. J., Paley, B., Burchinal, M., & Payne, C. C. (1999). Marital perceptions and interactions across the transition to parenthood. *Journal of Marriage and the Family, 61,* 611–625.

Cox, S. M., Werner, C. L., Gilstrap, L. C., & Cunningham, G. F. (2001). *Williams obstetrics* (21st ed.). New York: McGraw-Hill.

Crimmins, E. M. (2001). Americans living longer, not necessarily healthier lives. *Population Today,* February/March, *1,* 8.

Daly, D. (2003). Trust me—I'm a midwife. *Practising Midwife, 6,* 32–33.

Damewood, M. D. (2001). Ethical implications of a new application of preimplantation diagnosis. *Journal of the American Medical Association, 285,* 3143–3144.

Day, R. D., Peterson, G. W., & McCracken, C. (1998). Predicting spanking of younger and older children by mothers and fathers. *Journal of Marriage and the Family, 60,* 79–94.

DeBlander, T., & DeBlander, D. (2004). *Parents by choice: An insightful guide exploring adoption to build your family.* Lincoln, NE: iUniverse.

Delahunt, W. A. (2002). On the first anniversary of the enactment of the Child Citizenship Act of 2001. *Congressional Record–Extensions, 148*(18).

Delfos, M. F. (2003). *Anxiety, ADHD, depression, and aggression in childhood.* London: Jessica Kingsley Publishers.

deLissovoy, V. (1973a). Child care by adolescent parents. *Children Today, 2,* 22–25.

deLissovoy, V. (1973b). High school marriages: A longitudinal study. *Journal of Marriage and the Family, 35,* 245–255.

Dembo, M. H., Switzer, M., & Lauritzen, P. (1985). An evaluation of group parent education: Behavioral, PET, and Adlerian programs. *Review of Educational Research, 55,* 155–200.

DeNavas-Walt, C., Cleveland, R., & Webster, B. H., Jr. (2003). Income in the United States: 2002. *Current Population Reports, 60–221.* Washington, DC: U.S. Bureau of the Census.

Detzner, D. F., & Xiong, B. (1999). Southeast Asian families straddle two worlds. *NCFR Report,* June, 14–15.

DiClemente, Carlo C. (2003). *Addiction and change: How addictions develop and addicted people recover.* New York: Guilford.

Dinkmeyer, D. (1979). A comprehensive and systematic approach to parent education. *Journal of Family Therapy, 7,* 46–50.

Dinkmeyer, D., & Driekurs, R. (2000). *Encouraging children to learn.* New York: Brunner/Mazel.

Dinkmeyer, D., & McKay, G. D. (1981). *Parents' handbook: Systematic training for effective parenting.* Circle Pines, MN: American Guidance Service.

Dipietro, J. A., Millet, S., Costigan, K. A., Gurewitsch, E., & Caulfield, L. E. (2003). Psychosocial influences on weight gain attitudes and behaviors during pregnancy. *Journal of the American Dietetic Association, 103,* 1314–1319.

Dode, L. (2004). *A history of homosexuality.* Victoria, BC, Canada: Trafford.

Doherty, W. J., Kouneski, E. F., & Erickson, M. F. (1998). Responsible fathering: An overview and conceptual framework. *Journal of Marriage and the Family, 60,* 277–292.

Doherty, W. J., Kouneski, E. F., & Erickson, M. F. (2000). We are all responsible for responsible fathering: A response to Walker and McGraw. *Journal of Marriage and the Family, 62,* 570–574.

Donnelly, A. C. (Ed.). (2000). *Classic papers in child abuse.* Thousand Oaks, CA: Sage.

Dore, M. M., & Lee, J. M. (1999). The role of parent training with abusive and neglectful parents. *Family Relations, 48,* 313–325.

Doyle, C. (2001). Surviving and coping with emotional abuse in childhood. *Clinical Child Psychology & Psychiatry, 6,* 387–402.

Dresner, B. H. (2000). Sex-role stereotyping: Changes in attitude of 3-, 4-, and 5-year-old children. *Dissertation Abstracts International, 61* (6-A), 2177.

Driekurs, R. (1950). *The challenge of parenthood* (Rev. ed.). New York: Duell, Sloan, & Pearce.

Dumaret, A.-C., Coppel-Batsch, M., & Couraud, S. (1997). Adult outcome of children reared for long-term periods in foster families. *Child Abuse & Neglect, 21,* 911–927.

Dundas, S., & Kaufman, M. (2000). The Toronto lesbian family study. *Journal of Homosexuality, 40,* 65–79.

Duvall, E. M. (1988). Family development's first forty years. *Family Relations, 37,* 127–134.

Duvall, E. M., & Miller, B. C. (1985). *Marriage and family development* (6th ed.). New York: Harper & Row.

Dyer, E. (1963). Parenthood as crisis: A restudy. *Journal of Marriage and the Family, 25,* 196–201.

Edgar, T. (1985). The little house out back: Key to encouragement. *Individual Psychology, 41,* 483–488.

Eichberg, R. (1990). *Coming out: An act of love.* New York: Plume.

Eisenberg, A. (2002). *What to expect pregnancy planner.* New York: Workman.

Eldridge, H. (1997). *Therapist guide for maintaining change: Relapse prevention for adult male perpetrators of child sexual abuse.* Thousand Oaks, CA: Sage.

Elkin, F., & Handel, G. (1989). *The child and society: The process of socialization* (5th ed.). New York: Random House.

Engel, B. (2000). *Families in recovery: Healing the damage of childhood sexual abuse.* New York: McGraw-Hill.

Erel, O., Oberman, Y., & Yirmiya, N. (2000). Maternal versus nonmaternal care and seven domains of children's development. *Psychological Bulletin, 126,* 727–747.

Erera, P. I., & Fredriksen, K. (1999). Lesbian stepfamilies: A unique family structure. *Families in Society, 80,* 263–270.

Erikson, E. (1950). *Childhood and society.* New York: Norton.

Erikson, E. (1964). *Insight and responsibility.* New York: Norton.

Erikson, E. (1982). *The life cycle completed.* New York: Norton.

Erikson, E., Erikson, J., & Kivnick, H. (1986). *Vital involvement in old age.* New York: Norton.

Eshleman, L. (2004). *Becoming a family: Promoting healthy attachments with your adopted child.* Lanham, MD: Taylor.

Everett, C. A., & Everett, S. V. (2000). Single-parent families: Dynamics and treatment issues. In W. C. Nichols, M. A. Pace-Nichols, D. S. Becvar, & A. Y. Napier (Eds.), *Handbook of family development and intervention* (pp. 323–340). New York: Wiley.

Eyer, D. (1992). *Maternal-infant bondings: A scientific fiction.* New Haven, CT: Yale University Press.

Fagot, B. I., Pears, K. C., Capaldi, D. M., Crosby, L., & Leve, C. S. (1998). Becoming an adolescent father: Precursors and parenting. *Developmental Psychology, 34,* 1209–1219.

Fairchild, B., & Hayward, N. (1989). *Now that you know: What every parent should know about homosexuality* (Updated ed.). New York: Harcourt Brace Javonovich.

Federal Interagency Forum on Child and Family Statistics. (2003). *America's children:*

*Key national indicators of well-being: 2003*. Washington, DC: U.S. Government Printing Office.

Feindler, E. L., Rathus, J. H., & Silver, L. B. (2003). *Assessment of family violence: A handbook for researchers and practitioners*. Washington, DC: American Psychological Association.

Fenwick, J., Gamble, J., & Mawson, J. (2003). Women's experiences of Caesarean section and vaginal birth after Caesarian: A birth rites initiative. *International Journal of Nursing Practice, 9*, 10–17.

Fergusson, D. M., & Woodward, L. J. (2000). Teenage pregnancy and female educational underachievement: A prospective study of a New Zealand birth cohort. *Journal of Marriage and the Family, 62*, 147–161.

Ferrara, F. F. (2001). *Childhood sexual abuse: Developmental effects across the lifespan*. Belmont, CA: Wadsworth.

Fields, J. (2001). Living arrangements of children: 1996. *Current Population Reports, P70–74*. Washington, DC: U.S. Bureau of the Census.

Fields, J. (2003). Children's living arrangements and characteristics: March 2002. *Current Population Reports, P20–547*. Washington, DC: U.S. Bureau of the Census.

Fields, J., & Casper, L. M. (2001). America's families and living arrangements: March 2000. *Current Population Reports, P20–537*. Washington, DC: U.S. Bureau of the Census.

Fields, J., & Lynne, M. C. (2001). America's families and living arrangements: March 2000. *Current Population Reports, P20–537*. Washington, DC: U.S. Bureau of the Census.

First, J. A., & Way, W. L. (1995). Parent education outcomes: Insights into transformational learning. *Family Relations, 44*, 104–109.

Fix, M., Zimmerman, W., & Passel, J. S. (2001). *The integration of immigrant families in the United States*. Washington, DC: The Urban Institute.

Flavell, J. H., Miller, P. H., & Miller, S. A. (2001). *Cognitive development* (4th ed.). Englewood Cliffs, NJ: Prentice Hall.

Fleming, A. S., Ruble, D. N., Flett, G. L., & Shaul, D. L. (1988). Postpartum adjustment of first-time mothers: Relations between mood, maternal attitudes, and mother-infant interactions. *Developmental Psychology, 24*, 71–81.

Flowers, R. B. (2000). *Domestic crimes, family violence, and child abuse: A study of contemporary American society*. Jefferson, NC: McFarland.

Floyd, N. M. (1985). "Pick on somebody your own size": Controlling victimization. *Printer, 29*, 9–17.

Fox, G. L., Bruce, C., & Combs-Orme, T. (2000). Parenting expectations and concerns of fathers and mothers of newborn infants. *Family Relations, 49*, 123–131.

Framo, J. L., Weber, T. T., & Levine, F. B. (2003). *Coming home again: A family-of-origin consultation*. Philadelphia: Brunner-Routledge.

Francis-Connolly, E. (2003). Constructing parenthood: Portrayals of motherhood and fatherhood in popular American magazines. *Journal of the Association for Research on Mothering, 5*, 179–185.

Frank, D. A., Augustyn, M., Knight, W. G., Pell, T., & Zuckerman, B. (2001). Growth, development, and behavior in early childhood following prenatal cocaine exposure. *Journal of the American Medical Association, 285*, 1613–1625.

Franke-Clark, M. J. (2003). The father-daughter relationship and its effect on early sexual activity. *Dissertation Abstracts International: Section B: The Sciences & Engineering, 63* (8-B), 3957. Ann Arbor, MI: University Microfilms International.

French, V. (1995). History of parenting. In M. H. Bornstein (Ed.), *Handbook of parenting*. (Vol. 2, pp. 263–285). Mahwah, NJ: Lawrence Erlbaum.

Funderberg, F. F. (1994). *Black, white, and other*. New York: Morrow.

Gabbe, S. G., Niebyl, J. R., & Simpson, J. L. (2003). *Obstetrics: Normal and problem pregnancies* (4th ed.). Philadelphia: Elsevier.

Galinsky, E. (1987). *The six stages of parenthood*. Reading, MA: Addison-Wesley.

Galinski, J. H., & Kopp, C. B. (1993). Everyday rules for behavior: Mothers' requests to young children. *Developmental Psychology, 29*, 573–584.

Gallimore, T. (2002). Unresolved trauma: Fuel of the cycle of violence and terrorism. In C. E. Stout (Ed), *The psychology of terrorism: Clinical aspects and responses* (Vol. II, pp. 143–164). Westport, CT: Praeger/Greenwood.

Ganong, L., & Coleman, M. (2000). Remarried families. In C. Hendrick & S. Hendrick (Eds.), *Close relationships: A sourcebook* (pp. 155–168). Thousand Oaks, CA: Sage.

Ganske, M. G. (2003). Beyond "no." *Parenting, 17*, 134–136, 138.

Garbarino, J. (1980). Changing hospital childbirth practices. A developmental perspective on prevention of child maltreatment. *American Journal of Orthopsychiatry, 50*, 588–597.

Garbarino, J. (2001). An ecological perspective on the effects of violence on children. *Journal of Community Psychology, 29*, 361–378.

Garbarino, J., Hammond, W. R., Mercy, J., & Yung, B. R. (2004). Community violence and children: Preventing exposure and reducing harm. In K. I. Maton & C. J. Schellenbach (Eds.), *Investing in children, youth, families, and communities: Strengths-based research and policy* (pp. 303–320). Washington, DC: American Psychological Association.

Gelles, R. J., & Cornell, C. P. (1997). *Intimate violence in families* (3rd ed.). Thousand Oaks, CA: Sage.

Gelles, R. J., Loseke, D. R., & Cavanaugh, M. M. (2004). *Current controversies on family violence*. Thousand Oaks, CA: Sage.

Gerlach, P. (2003). *Build a co-parenting team: After divorce or remarriage*. Philadelphia: Xlibris.

Gerson, K. (1993). *No man's land: Men's changing commitments to family and work*. New York: Basic.

Gerson, M. J., Berman, L. S., & Morris, A. M. (1991). The value of having children as an aspect of adult development. *Journal of Genetic Psychology, 152*, 327–339.

Gibbs, J. T. (2003). Biracial and bicultural children and adolescents. In J. T. Gibbs & L. N. Huang (Eds.), *Children of color: Psychological interventions with culturally diverse youth* (pp. 145–182). San Francisco: Jossey-Bass.

Gielen, U. P., & Roopnarine, J. L. (2004). *Childhood and adolescence*. Westport, CT: Praeger.

Ginott, H. (1965). *Between parent and child*. New York: Macmillan.

Glenn, H. S., Erwin, C., & Nelen, J. (2000). *Positive discipline for your stepfamily: Nurturing harmony, respect, unity, and joy in your new family*. New York: Crown Publishing Group.

Glenn, N. D. (1990). Quantitative research on marital quality in the 1980s: A critical review. *Journal of Marriage and the Family, 52*, 818–831.

Gnaulati, E., & Heine, B. J. (2001). Separation-individuation in late adolescence: An investigation of gender and ethnic differences. *Journal of Psychology, 135*, 59–70.

Golding, K. (2003). Helping foster careers, helping children: Using attachment theory to guide practice. *Adoption and Fostering, 27,* 64–73.

Goldschneider, F. K., & Goldschneider, C. (1998). The effects of childhood family structure on leaving and returning home. *Journal of Marriage and the Family, 60,* 745–756.

Golombok, S. (1999). New family forms: Children raised in solo mother families, lesbian mother families, and in families created by assisted reproduction. In L. Balter & C. S. Tamis-LeMonda (Eds.), *Child psychology: A handbook of contemporary issues* (pp. 429–446). Philadelphia: Psychology Press/Taylor & Francis.

Golombok, S., Cook, R., Bish, A., & Murray, C. (1995). Families created by the new reproductive technologies: Quality of parenting and emotional development of children. *Child Development, 66,* 285–296.

Golombok, S., & MacCallum, F. (2003). Practitioner review: Outcomes for parents and children following non-traditional conception: What do clinicians need to know? *Journal of Child Psychology & Psychiatry & Allied Disciplines, 44,* 303–315.

Golombok, S., Murray, C., Brinsden, P., & Abdalla, H. (2003). Social versus biological parenting: Family functioning and the socioemotional development of children conceived by egg or sperm donation. In M. E. Hertzig & E. A. Farber (Eds.), *Annual progress in child psychiatry and child development: 2000–2001* (pp. 155–175). New York: Brunner-Routledge.

Goode, W. J. (1993). *A theory of role strain.* New York: Irvington.

Goodrich, S. M. (1990). *Boundaries: Development of self within a family system.* Dissertation Abstracts International, *50,* 4218.

Gordon, S. (2000). Pregnancy and birth: Mother's helper. *Parents, 75,* 157.

Gordon, S. (2004). *When living hurts: For teenagers, young adults, their parents, leaders, and counselors.* New York: U A H C Press.

Gordon, T. (1975/2000). *Parent effectiveness training: The tested way to raise responsible children.* New York: Wyden.

Gormly, A. V., Gormly, J. B., & Weiss, H. (1987). Motivations for parenthood among young adult college students. *Sex Roles, 16,* 31–39.

Gottman, J. M., Levenson, R. W., Gross, J., Frederickson, B. L., McCoy, K., Rosenthal, L., Ruef, A., & Yoshimoto, D. (2003). Correlates of gay and lesbian couples' relationship satisfaction and relationship dissolution. *Journal of Homosexuality, 45,* 23–43.

Grace, D. M. (2003). Should adopted children be granted access to the identity of their birth parents? A psychological perspective. *Australian Journal of Psychology, 55,* 44–45.

Grall, T. S. (2003). Custodial mothers and fathers and their child support: 2001. *Current Population Reports, Series P60–225.* Washington, DC: U.S. Bureau of the Census.

Gray, M. R., & Steinberg, L. (1999). Unpacking authoritative parenting: Reassessing a multidimensional construct. *Journal of Marriage and the Family, 61,* 574–587.

Graziano, A. M., & Namaste, K. A. (1990). Parental use of physical force in child discipline: A survey of 679 college students. *Journal of Interpersonal Violence, 5,* 449–463.

Green, R.-J. (2002). Coming out to family . . . in context. In E. Davis-Russell (Ed.), *The California School of Professional Psychology handbook of multicultural education, research, intervention, and training* (pp. 277–284). San Francisco: Jossey-Bass.

Greenfield, P. M., & Suzuki, L. K. (2001). Culture and parenthood. In J. C. Westman (Ed.), *Parenthood in America* (pp. 20–33). Madison: University of Wisconsin Press.

Grieco, E. M., & Cassidy, R. C. (2001). Overview of race and Hispanic origin. *Census 2000 Brief.* Washington, DC: U.S. Bureau of the Census.

Groleger, U., Tomori, M., & Kocmur, M. (2003). Suicidal ideation in adolescence— An indicator of actual risk? *Israel Journal of Psychiatry & Related Sciences, 40,* 202–208.

Haberstroh, C., Hayslip, Bert, Jr., & Wohl, E. (2001). Perceptions of grandparents and stepgrandparents by young adults. *The Gerontologist, 41,* 35.

Hacker, K. A., Amare, Y., Strunk, N., & Horst, L. (2000). Listening to youth: Teen perspectives on pregnancy prevention. *Journal of Adolescent Health, 26,* 279–288.

Haig, D. (1995). Prenatal power plays. *Natural History, 104,* 9.

Hain, D. (1999). *Stopping stereotypes: Gays, lesbians, and alcoholism.* Tempe, AZ: Do It Now Foundation.

Hall, K. J., & Kitson, G. C. (2000). Lesbian stepfamilies: An even more "incomplete institution." *Journal of Lesbian Studies, 4,* 31–47.

Hallahan, D. P., & Kauffman, J. M. (2004). *Introduction to learning disabilities.* Boston: Allyn & Bacon.

Hansen, D. A., & Hill, R. (1964). Families under stress. In H. Christensen (Ed.), *Handbook of marriage and the family* (pp. 355–375). Chicago: Rand-McNally.

Harry, J. (1989). Parental physical abuse and sexual orientation in males. *Archives of Sexual Behavior, 18,* 251–261.

Harway, M. (2000). Families experiencing violence. In W. C. Nichols, M. A. Pace-Nichols, D. S. Becvar, & A. Y. Napier (Eds.), *Handbook of family development and intervention* (pp. 391–414). New York: Wiley.

Hatheway, J. (2003). *Gilded age roots of American homophobia.* New York: Palgrave Macmillan.

Haveman, R., Wolfe, B., & Pence, K. (2001). Intergenerational effects of nonmarital and early childbearing. In L. L. Wu & B. Wolfe (Eds.), *Out of wedlock: Causes and consequences of nonmarital fertility* (pp. 287–316). New York: Russell Sage Foundation.

Hawkins, D. B. (2003). *When you're living in a stepfamily.* Colorado Springs, CO: Cook Communications Ministries.

Hayslip, B., Jr. (2003). The impact of a psychosocial intervention on parental efficacy, grandchild relationship quality, and well-being among grandparents raising grandchildren. In B. Hayslip, Jr., & J. H. Patrick (Eds.), *Working with custodial grandparents* (pp. 163–176). New York: Springer.

Hayslip, B., & Goldberg-Glen, R. (Eds.). (2000). *Grandparents raising grandchildren: Theoretical, empirical and clinical perspectives.* New York: Springer.

Heaven, P. C. L. (2001). *The social psychology of adolescence.* Basingstoke, England: Palgrave.

Herek, G. M. (1984). Beyond homophobia: A social psychological perspective on attitudes toward lesbians and gay men. *Journal of Homosexuality, 10,* 1–21.

Herek, G. M. (1993). The context of antigay violence: Notes on cultural and psychological heterosexism. In L. D. Garnets & D. C. Kimmel (Eds.), *Psychological perspectives on lesbian and gay male experiences* (pp. 89–107). New York: Columbia University Press.

Hess, C. R., Papas, M. A., & Black, M. M. (2002). Resilience among African American adolescent mothers: Predictors of positive parenting in early infancy. *Journal of Pediatric Psychology, 27,* 619–629.

Hewlett, B. S., Lamb, M. E., Shannon, D., Leyendecker, B., & Scholmerich, A. (1998). Culture and early infancy among central African foragers and farmers. *Developmental Psychology, 34,* 653–661.

Higginson, J. G. (1998). Competitive parenting: The culture of teen mothers. *Journal of Marriage and the Family, 60,* 135–149.

Hildebrand, V., Phenice, L. A., Gray, M. M., & Hines, R. P. (2000). *Knowing and serving diverse families* (2nd ed.). Upper Saddle River, NJ: Merrill/Prentice Hall.

Himes, C. L. (2001). Social demography of contemporary families and aging. In A. J. Walker, M. Manoogian-O'Dell, L. A. Mc-Graw, & D. L. G. White (Eds.), *Families in later life: Connections and transitions* (pp. 47–50). Thousand Oaks, CA: Pine Forge.

Hobbs, D. (1965). Parenthood as crisis: A third study. *Journal of Marriage and the Family, 27,* 367–372.

Hobbs, D., & Wimbish, J. (1977). Transition to parenthood by black couples. *Journal of Marriage and the Family, 39,* 677–689.

Hobbs, F., & Stoops, N. (2002). *Demographic trends in the 20th century.* Census 2000 Special Reports, Series CENSR-4. Washington, DC: U.S. Government Printing Office.

Hofferth, S. L., Reid, L., & Mott, F. L. (2001). The effects of early childbearing on schooling over time. *Family Planning Perspectives, 33,* 259–267.

Hoffman, L. (1973). Deviation-amplifying process in natural groups. In J. Haley (Ed.), *Changing families* (pp. 135–168). New York: Grune & Stratton.

Hoffman, W., & Manis, J. (1979). The value of children in the United States: A new approach to the study of fertility. *Journal of Marriage and the Family, 41,* 583–596.

Hoffnung, M. (1992). *What's a mother to do? Conversations on work and family.* Pasadena, CA: Trilogy Books.

Holland, P., & Gorey, K. M. (2004). Historical, developmental, and behavioral factors associated with foster care challenges. *Child & Adolescent Social Work Journal, 21,* 117–135.

Holmes, T. H., & Rahe, R. H. (1967). The social readjustment scale. *Journal of Psychosomatic Research, 11,* 213–218.

Holyfield, L. (2003). *Moving up and out: Poverty, education, and the single parent family.* Philadelphia: Temple University Press.

Honein, M. A., Paulozzi, L. J., Mathews, T. J., Erikson, J. D., & Wong, L.-Y. C. (2001). Impact of folic acid fortification of the U.S. food supply on the occurrence of neural tube defects. *Journal of the American Medical Association, 285,* 2981–2986.

Honig, A. S., & Morin, C. (2001). When should programs for teen parents and babies begin? Longitudinal evaluation of a teen parents and babies program. *Journal of Primary Prevention, 21,* 447–454.

Houseknect, S. K. (1987). Voluntary childlessness. In M. B. Sussman & S. K. Steinmetz (Eds.), *Handbook of marriage and the family* (pp. 369–418). New York: Plenum.

Howes, P. W., Cicchetti, D., Toth, S. L., & Rogosch, F. A. (2000). Affective, organizations, and relational characteristics of maltreating families: A system's perspective. *Journal of Family Psychology, 14,* 95–110.

Hoyt, H. H., & Broom, B. L. (2002). School-based teen pregnancy prevention programs: A review of the literature. *Journal of School Nursing, 18,* 11–17.

Hughes, D. (2003). Correlates of African American and Latino parents' messages to children about ethnicity and race: A comparative study of racial socialization. *American Journal of Community Psychology, 31,* 15–33.

Hui, P. W., Lam, Y. H., Tang, M. H., Ng, E. H., Yeung, W. S., & Ho, P. C. (2003). Amniotic fluid, human chorionic gonadotrophin, and alpha-fetoprotein levels in pregnancies conceived after assisted reproduction. *Prenatal Diagnosis, 23,* 484–487.

Hunter, A. E., & Forden, C. (Eds.). (2002). *Readings in the psychology of gender: Exploring our differences and commonalities.* Needham Heights, MA: Allyn & Bacon.

Hyde, J. S., & DeLamater, J. D. (2000). *Understanding human sexuality* (7th ed.). New York: McGraw-Hill.

Ifejika, S. (2003). *Growing pains: A how to manual for parents and young adults.* Frederick, MD: PublishAmerican.

Ihinger-Tallman, M., & Pasley, K. (1997). Stepfamilies in 1984 and today—A scholarly perspective. In I. Levin & M. B. Sussman (Eds.), *Stepfamilies: History, research, and policy* (pp. 19–40). New York: Haworth Press.

Ingersoll-Dayton, B., Neal, M. B., & Hammer, L. B. (2001). Aging parents helping adult children: The experience of the sandwiched generation. *Family Relations, 50,* 262–271.

Institute of Medicine Staff Board. (2002). *Confronting chronic neglect: The education and training of health professionals on family violence.* Washington, DC: National Academy Press.

Itzkoff, S. W. (2003). Intervening with mother nature: The ethics of human cloning. *Mankind Quarterly, 44,* 29–42.

Jacobsen, R. B., Bigner, J. J., & Hood, S. (1991). Black versus white single parents and the value of children. *Journal of Black Studies, 21,* 302–312.

Jaffee, S. R. (2002). Pathways to adversity in young adulthood among early childbearers. *Journal of Family Psychology, 16,* 38–49.

Jaffee, S., Caspi, A., Moffitt, T. E., Belsky, J., & Silva, P. (2001). Why are children born to teen mothers at risk for adverse outcomes in young adulthood? Results from a 20-year longitudinal study. *Development & Psychopathology, 13,* 377–397.

Jarrett, R. L. (1995). Growing up poor: The family experiences of socially mobile youth in low-income African American neighborhoods. *Journal of Adolescent Research, 10,* 111–135.

John, R. (1998). Native American families. In C. H. Mindel, R. W. Haberstein, & R. Wright, Jr. (Eds.), *Ethnic families in America: Patterns and variations* (pp. 382–421). Upper Saddle River, NJ: Prentice Hall.

Johnson, D. C., Harrison, B. C., Burnett, M. F., & Emerson, P. (2003). Deterrents to participation in parenting education. *Family & Consumer Sciences Research Journal, 31,* 403–424.

Johnson, S. M., & O'Connor, E. (2001). *For lesbian parents: Your guide to helping your family grow up happy, healthy, and proud.* New York: Guilford Publications.

Jones, D. J., Forehand, R., Brody, G. H., & Armistead, L. (2002). Positive parenting and child psychosocial adjustment in inner-city single-parent African American families: the role of maternal optimism. *Behavior Modification, 26,* 464–481.

Jones, R. H. (Ed.). (2004). *The last mile home: An anthology of addiction and recovery.* New York: Welcome Rain Publishers.

Jordan, D-L. (2003). *How to succeed as a single parent.* London: Hodder & Stoughton.

Joselevich, E. (1988). Family transitions, cumulative stress, and crises. In C. J. Falicov (Ed.), *Family transitions: Continuity and change over the life cycle.* New York: Bruner/Mazel.

Judges of the 29th Judicial District of Kansas. (1985). *An informational program for separating/divorcing parents with minor children.* Whandotte, KS: Wyandotte County Bar Association.

Julian, T. W., McHenry, P. C., & McKelvey, M. W. (1994). Cultural variations in parenting: Perceptions of Caucasian, African-American, Latino, and Asian-American parents. *Family Relations, 43*, 30–37.

Kalish, S. (1995). Multiracial births increase as U.S. ponders racial definitions. *Population Today, 23*, 1–2.

Kaslow, F. W. (2000). Families experiencing divorce. In W. C. Nichols, M. A. Pace-Nichols, D. S. Becvar, & Y. A. Napier (Eds.), *Handbook of family development and intervention* (pp. 341–368). New York: Wiley.

Kazdin, A. E., & Benjet, C. (2003). Spanking children: Evidence and issues. *Current Directions in Psychological Science, 12*, 99–103.

Keck, G. C., & Kupecky, R. M. (2004). *Parenting the hurt child: Helping adoptive families heal and grow*. Colorado Springs, CO: Pinon Press.

Kelder, L. R., McNamara, J. R., Carlson, B., & Lynn, S. J. (1991). Perceptions of physical punishment: The relation to childhood and adolescent experiences. *Journal of Interpersonal Violence, 6*, 432–445.

Kelley, M. L., Grace, N., & Elliott, S. N. (1990). Acceptability of positive and punitive discipline methods: Comparisons among abusive, potentially abusive, and nonabusive parents. *Child Abuse and Neglect, 14*, 219–226.

Kellogg, N. D., Hoffman, T. J., & Taylor, E. R. (1999). Early sexual experiences among pregnant and parenting adolescents. *Adolescence, 34*, 293–303.

Kendall-Tackett, K. A. (2001). *The hidden feelings of motherhood: Coping with stress, depression, and burnout*. Oakland, CA: New Harbinger Publications.

Kennedy, R. (2004). *Interracial intimacies: Sex, marriage, identity, and adoption*. New York: Knopf.

Kershaw, S. (2000). Living in a lesbian household: The effects on children. *Child & Family Social Work, 5*, 365–371.

Kershaw, T. S., Niccolai, L. M., Ethier, K. A., Lewis, J. B., & Ickovics, J. R. (2003). Perceived susceptibility to pregnancy and sexually transmitted disease among pregnant and nonpregnant adolescents. *Journal of Community Psychology, 31*, 419–434.

Key, J., Barbosa, G. A., & Owens, V. J. (2001). The Second Chance Club: Repeat adolescent pregnancy prevention with a school-based intervention. *Journal of Adolescent Health, 28*, 167–169.

Kim, H. H. (2004). *Learning disabilities*. Farmington Hills, MI: Greenhaven Press.

Kinsey, A. C., Pomeroy, W. B., & Martin, C. E. (1948). *Sexual behavior in the human male*. Philadelphia: Saunders.

Kinsey, A. C., Pomeroy, W. B., Martin, C. E., & Gebhard, P. H. (1953). *Sexual behavior in the human female*. Philadelphia: Saunders.

Kirby, D. (1999). *Looking for reasons why: The antecedents of adolescent sexual risk-taking, pregnancy, and childbearing*. Washington, DC: National Campaign to Prevent Teen Pregnancy.

Kirby, D. (2001). *Emerging answers: Research findings on programs to reduce teen pregnancy: Full report*. Washington, DC: National Campaign to Prevent Teen Pregnancy.

Knowles, C. (1997). *Family boundaries: The invention of normality and dangerousness*. Peterborough, ON, CA: Broadview Press.

Knox, D., & Leggett, K. (2000). *Divorced dad's survival book: How to stay connected with your kids*. Cambridge, MA: Perseus.

Koerner, S. S., Jacobs, S. L., & Raymond, M. (2000). When mothers turn to their adolescent daughters: Predicting daughters' vulnerability to negative adjustment outcomes. *Family Relations, 49*, 301–309.

Kopera-Frye, K., Wiscott, R. C., & Begovic, A. (2003). Lessons learned from custodial grandparents involved in a community support group. In B. Hayslip, Jr., & J. H. Patrick (Eds.), *Working with custodial grandparents* (pp. 243–256). New York: Springer.

Kornhaber, A. (2002). *The grandparent guide: The definitive guide to coping with the challenges of modern grandparenting*. New York: McGraw-Hill.

Kosunen, E., Kaltiala-Heino, R., Rimpela, M., & Laippala, P. (2003). Risk-taking sexual behavior and self-reported depression in middle adolescence—a school-based survey. *Child: Care, Health & Development, 29*, 337–344.

Kotch, J. B., Muller, G. O., & Blakely, C. H. (1999). Understanding the origins and incidence of child maltreatment. In T. P. Gullotta & S. J. McElhaney (Eds.), *Violence in homes and communities: Prevention, intervention, and treatment* (pp. 1–38). Thousand Oaks, CA: Sage.

Kourtis, A., Bulterys, M., Nesheim, S., & Lee, F. (2001). Understanding the timing of HIV transmission from mother to infant. *Journal of the American Medical Association, 285*, 709–712.

Krauss, M. W. (2000). Family assessment within early intervention programs. In J. P. Shonkoff & S. J. Meisels (Eds.), *Handbook of early childhood intervention* (2nd ed.,

pp. 290–308). New York: Cambridge University Press.

Kravetz, J. D., & Federman, D. G. (2002). Cat associated zoonoses. *Archives of Internal Medicine, 162*, 1945–1952.

Krebs, L. L. (1986). Current research on theoretically based parenting programs. *Individual Psychology, 42*, 375–387.

Kropf, N. P., & Burnette, D. (2003). Grandparents as family caregivers: Lessons for intergenerational education. *Educational Gerontology, 29*, 361–372.

Kuczynski, L., & Kochanska, G. (1995). Function and content of maternal demands: Developmental significance of early demands for competent action. *Child Development, 66*, 616–628.

Kufeldt, K., Simard, M., & Vachon, J. (2003). Improving outcomes for children in care: Giving youth a voice. *Adoption and Fostering, 27*, 8–19.

Kurdek, L. A. (1995). Lesbian and gay couples. In A. R. D'Augelli & C. J. Patterson (Eds.), *Lesbian, gay, and bisexual identities over the lifespan: Psychological perspectives* (pp. 243–261). New York: Oxford University Press.

Kurdek, L. A. (2003). Differences between gay and lesbian cohabitating couples. *Journal of Social and Personal Relationships, 20*, 411–436.

Kurjak, A., Kupesic, S., Matijevic, R., Kos, M., & Marton, U. (1999). First trimester malformation screening. *European Journal of Obstetrics, Gynecology, and Reproductive Biology, 85*, 93–96.

Kyman, W. (1991). Maternal satisfaction with the birth experience. *Journal of Social Behavior and Personality, 6*, 57–70.

Kyriacou, C. (2002). A humanistic view of discipline. In B. Rogers (Ed.), *Teacher leadership and behavior management* (pp. 40–52). London: Paul Chapman Publishing.

Laird, J. (2003). Lesbian and gay families. In F. Walsh (Ed.), *Normal family processes: Growing diversity and complexity* (3rd ed., pp. 176–209). New York: Guilford.

Lal, S. (2002). Orphaned, adopted, and abducted: Parents and children in twentieth-century America. *Radical History Review, 84*, 174–184.

Lamanna, M. A., & Reidman, A. (2003). *Marriages and families: Making choices in a diverse society* (8th ed.). Belmont, CA: Wadsworth/Thomson Learning.

Lamaze, F. (1958). *Painless childbirth: Psychoprophalactic method*. New York: Harper & Row.

LaRossa, R. (1986). *Becoming a parent*. Thousand Oaks, CA: Sage.

Larzelere, R. E., Klein, M., Schumm, W. R., & Alibrando, S. A. (1989). Relations of spanking and other parenting characteristics to self-esteem and perceived fairness of parental discipline. *Psychological Reports, 64*, 1140–1142.

LaSala, M. C. (2000a). Gay male couples: The importance of coming out and being out to parents. *Journal of Homosexuality, 39*, 47–71.

LaSala, M. C. (2000b). Lesbians, gay men, and their parents: Family therapy for the coming-out crisis. *Family Process, 39*, 67–81.

Laszloffy, T. A. (2002). Rethinking family development theory: Teaching with the systemic family development (SFD) model. *Family Relations, 51*, 206–214.

Lawrence, F. R., & Blair, C. (2003). Factorial invariance in preventive intervention: Modeling the development of intelligence in low birth weight, preterm infants. *Prevention Science, 4*, 249–261.

Layne, S. L. (2004). *Over land and sea: The story of international adoption*. Gretna, LA: Pelican Publishing.

Leboyer, F. (1976). *Birth without violence*. New York: Knopf.

Lee, C. D. (2004). A guidebook for raising foster children. *Child & Adolescent Social Work Journal, 21*, 191–194.

LeMasters, E. E. (1957). Parenthood as crisis. *Marriage and Family Living, 19*, 352–355.

LeMasters, E. E. (1977). *Parents in modern America* (Rev. ed.). Homewood, IL: Dorsey.

Lester, T. P. (Ed.). (2003). *Gender nonconformity, race, and sexuality: Charting the connections*. Madison: University of Wisconsin Press.

Levine, J. A., & Pitt, E. W. (1998). *New expectations: Community strategies for responsible fatherhood*. New York: Families and Work Institute.

Levinson, D., et al. (1978). *Seasons of a man's life*. New York: Knopf.

Leviton, A., & Cowan, L. (2002). A review of the literature relating caffeine consumption by women to their risk of reproductive hazards. *Food & Chemical Toxicology, 40*, 1271–1310.

Levy-Shiff, R. (1994). Individual and contextual correlates of marital change across the transition to parenthood. *Developmental Psychology, 30*, 591–601.

Lewallen, E. (1992, October 30). Early pain transforms into deep appreciation. *Rocky Mountain United Methodist Reporter, 139*, 13.

Leyden, S. (2002). *Supporting the child of exceptional ability: At home and school*. London: David Fulton.

Lichter, D. T., & Graefe, D. R. (2001). Finding a mate? The marital and cohabitation histories of unwed mothers. In L. L. Wu & B. Wolfe (Eds.), *Out of wedlock: Causes and consequences of nonmarital fertility* (pp. 317–343). New York: Russell Sage Foundation.

Lindon, J. (2004). *Working with children and young people in residential and foster care*. Boston: International Thomson Business Press.

Lino, M. (2003). *Expenditures on children by families, 2002*. U.S. Department of Agriculture, Center for Nutrition Policy and Promotion. Miscellaneous Publication No. 1528–2002. Washington, DC: U.S. Government Printing Office.

Longmore, M. A., Manning, W. D., Giordano, P. C., & Rudolph, J. L. (2003). Contraceptive self-efficacy: Does it influence adolescents' contraceptive use? *Journal of Health & Social Behavior, 44*, 45–60.

Lorah, M. A. (2002). Lesbian stepmothers: A grounded theory study of women who cohabit with biological, custodial mothers of children from previous heterosexual relationships. *Dissertation Abstracts International, 62*, 4074.

Lowenstein, L. F. (2002). Joint custody and shared parenting: Are courts listening? *Family Therapy, 29*, 101–108.

Luster, T., Bates, L., Fitzgerald, H., Vanderbelt, M., & Key, J. P. (2000). Factors related to successful outcomes among preschool children born to low-income adolescent mothers. *Journal of Marriage and the Family, 62*, 113–146.

Lynch, J. M. (2000). Considerations of family structure and gender composition: The lesbian and gay stepfamily. *Journal of Homosexuality, 40*, 81–95.

Lytton, H., & Romney, D. M. (1991). Parents' differential socialization of boys and girls: A meta-analysis. *Psychological Bulletin, 109*, 267–296.

Maccoby, E. (1984). Middle childhood in the context of the family. In W. Collins (Ed.), *Development during middle childhood: The years from six to twelve*. Washington, DC: National Academy of Sciences.

Maccoby, E., & Jacklin, C. (1974). *The psychology of sex differences*. Stanford, CA: Stanford University Press.

Macmillan, C., Madder, L. S., Brooders, P., Chase, C., Hotelman, J., Laky, T., Male, K.,

Mullins, C. A., & Velez-Boras, J. (2001). Head growth and neurodevelopment of infants born to HIV-1-infected drug-using women. *Neurology, 57*, 1402–1411.

Madden-Derdich, D. A., Herzog, M. J., & Leonard, S. A. (2002). The coparental involvement of teen-aged fathers: The mediating role of mothers' desire to have fathers involved. Paper presented at the 64th Annual Conference of the National Council on Family Relations, Houston, Texas.

Magen, Z., Levin, T., & Yeshurun, D. (1991). Parent counseling as a means of change: A study of an Adlerian approach. *International Journal for the Advancement of Counseling, 14*, 27–39.

Mallery, J. G. (2002). Practicing parenting? Effects of computerized infant simulators on teenage attitudes toward early parenthood. *The Journal of Early Education and Family Review, 9*, 18–28.

Malley-Morrison, K., & Hines, D. (2003). *Family violence in a cultural perspective: Defining, understanding, and combating abuse*. Thousand Oaks, CA: Sage.

Mallon, G. P. (2004). *Gay men choosing parenthood*. New York: Columbia University Press.

Manlove, J., Mariner, C., & Papillo, A. R. (2000). Subsequent fertility among teen mothers: Longitudinal analyses of recent national data. *Journal of Marriage and the Family, 62*, 430–448.

Manning, W. D., & Smock, P. J. (2000). "Swapping" families: Serial parenting and economic support for children. *Journal of Marriage and the Family, 62*, 111–122.

Mannis, V. S. (1999). Single mothers by choice. *Family Relations, 48*, 121–128.

March of Dimes Foundation. (2002). *Toxoplasmosis* (fact sheet). Wilkes Bare, PA: Author.

Marieb, E. N. (2003). *Human anatomy and physiology* (6th ed.). Redwood City, CA: Benjamin/Cummings.

Marsiglio, W. (2004). When stepfathers claim stepchildren: A conceptual analysis. *Journal of Marriage and the Family, 66*, 22–39.

Marsiglio, W., Hutchinson, S., & Cohan, M. (2000). Envisioning fatherhood: A social psychological perspective on young men with kids. *Family Relations, 49*, 133–142.

Martin, C. (1996). Baby Think It Over: Doll vocal about teen pregnancy. *The Denver Post*, 1G–2G.

Martin, J. A., Hamilton, B. E., Sutton, P. D., Ventura, S. J., Menacker, F., & Munson, M. L. (2003). Births: Final data for 2002. *National Vital Statistics Reports, 52*(10). Hyattsville, MD: National Center for Health Statistics.

Martin, J. A., Hamilton, B. E., Ventura, S. J., Menacker, F., & Park, M. M. (2002). Births: Final data for 2000. *National Vital Statistics Reports, 50*(5). Hyattsville, MD: National Center for Health Statistics.

Martin, P., & Midgely, E. (1999). *Immigration in the United States. Population Bulletin 54*(2). Washington, DC: Population Reference Bureau.

Mattessich, P., & Hill, R. (1987). Life cycle and family development. In M. Sussman & S. Steinmetz (Eds.), *Handbook of marriage and the family*. New York: Plenum Press.

May, E. T. (1997). *Barren in the promised land: Childless Americans and the pursuit of happiness*. Cambridge, MA: Harvard University Press.

McBride-Chang, C., & Chang, L. (1998). Adolescent-parent relations in Hong-Kong: Parenting styles, emotional autonomy, and school achievement. *Journal of Genetic Psychology, 159*, 421–435.

McClellan, D. L. (2001). The "other mother" and second parent adoption. *Journal of Gay & Lesbian Social Services, 13*, 1–21.

McCranie, E. W., & Simpson, M. E. (1986). Parental childrearing antecedents of Type A behavior. *Personality and Social Psychology Bulletin, 12*, 493–501.

McDonald, Walter R. and Associates. (2004). *Child maltreatment 2002*. Washington, DC: National Clearinghouse on Child Abuse and Neglect.

McElderry, D. H., & Omar, H. A. (2003). Sex education in the schools: What role does it play? *International Journal of Adolescent Medicine & Health, 15*, 3–9.

McGuinness, T., & Pallansch, L. (2000). Competence of children adopted from the former Soviet Union. *Family Relations, 49*, 457–464.

McKay, A., Fisher, W., Maticka-Tyndale, E., & Barrett, M. (2001). Adolescent sexual health education: Does it work? Can it work better? An analysis of recent research and media reports. *Canadian Journal of Human Sexuality, 10*, 127–135.

McKnight, J. (2000). Editorial: The origins of male homosexuality. *Psychology, Evolution & Gender, 2*, 223–228.

McLoyd, V. C., Cauce, A. M., Takeuchi, D., & Wilson, L. (2000). Marital processes and parental socialization in families of color: A decade review of research. *Journal of Marriage and the Family, 62*, 1070–1093.

Mereu, G., Fa, M., Ferraro, L., Cagiano, R., Antonelli, T., Tattoli, M., Ghiglieri, V., Tanganelli, S., Gessa, G. L., & Cuomo, V. (2003). Prenatal exposure to a cannabinoid agonist produces memory deficits linked to dysfunction in hippocampal long-term potentiation and glutamate release. *Proceedings of the National Academy of Sciences, 100*, 4915–4920.

Merighi, J. R., & Grimes, M. D. (2000). Coming out to families in a multicultural context. *Families in Society, 81*, 32–41.

Meyer, D. J. (2003). *Living with a brother or sister with special needs: A book for sibs*. Seattle: University of Washington Press.

Meyer-Bahlburg, H. F. L., Ehrdardt, A. A., Rosen, L. R., Gruen, R. S., Veridiano, N. P., Vann, F. H., & Newhalder, H. F. (1995). Prenatal estrogens and the development of homosexual orientation. *Developmental Psychology, 31*, 12–21.

Mikesell, R. H., Lusterman, D.-D., & McDaniel, S. H. (Eds.). (1995). *Integrating family therapy: Handbook of family psychology and systems theory*. Washington, DC: American Psychological Association.

Milic, J. H., & Crowne, D. P. (1986). Recalled parent-child relations and need for approval of homosexual and heterosexual men. *Archives of Sexual Behavior, 15*, 239–246.

Miller, B. C., & Coyl, D. D. (2000). Adolescent pregnancy and childbearing in relation to infant adoption in the United States. *Adoption Quarterly, 4*, 3–25.

Miller, L. G., & Albrecht, K. M. (2004). *The infant and toddler child development guide*. Beltsville, MD: Gryphon House.

Miller, M. W., Astley, S. J., & Clarren, S. K. (1999). Number of axons in the corpus callosum of the mature macaca nemestrina: Increases caused by prenatal exposure to ethanol. *Journal of Comparative Neurology, 412*, 123–131.

Miller-Perrin, C. L., Perrin, R. D., & Barnett, O. W. (2004). *Family violence across the lifespan: An introduction* (2nd ed.). Thousand Oaks, CA: Sage.

Minuchin, S. (1974). *Families and family therapy*. Cambridge, MA: Harvard University Press.

Mitchell, B. (1998). Too close for comfort? Parental assessments of "Boomerang Kid" living arrangements. *Canadian Journal of Sociology, 23*, 21–46.

Mitchell, B. A., & Gee, E. M. (1996). "Boomerang kids" and midlife parental marital satisfaction. *Family Relations, 45*, 442–448.

Molter, N. C. (2003). Creating a healing environment for critical care. *Critical Care Nursing Clinics of North America, 15*, 295–304.

Money, J. (1987). Sin, sickness, or status? Homosexual gender identity and psychoneuroendocrinology. *American Psychologist, 42*, 384–399.

Monk, C., Fifer, W. P., Meyers, M. M., Sloan, R. P., Trien, L., & Hurtado, A. (2000). Maternal stress responses and anxiety during pregnancy: Effects on fetal heart rate. *Developmental Psychology, 36*, 67–77.

Mooney-Somers, J., & Golombok, S. (2000). Children of lesbian mothers: From the 1970s to the new millennium. *Sexual & Relationship Therapy, 15*, 121–126.

Moore, M. R., & Brooks-Gunn, J. (2002). Adolescent parenthood. In M. H. Bornstein (Ed.), *Handbook of parenting, Vol. 3: Being and becoming a parent* (2nd ed., pp. 173–214). Mahwah, NJ: Erlbaum.

Morgan, S. P., Botev, N., Chen, R., & Huang, J. (1999). White and nonwhite trends in first birth timing: Comparisons using vital registration and Current Population Surveys. *Population Research and Policy Review, 18*, 339–356.

Morris, D. (1986). *The illustrated naked ape*: A zoologist's study of the human animal. New York: Crown.

Morris, D. (1996). *The human zoo: A zoologist's classic study of the urban animal*. New York: Kodansha International.

Morse, A. (2003). *SCHIP and access for children in immigrant families*. Washington, DC: National Conference of State Legislatures.

Mosher, C. M. (2001). The social implications of sexual identity formation and the coming-out process: A review of the theoretical and empirical literature. *Family Journal: Counseling & Therapy for Couples & Families, 9*, 164–173.

Mueller, M. M., & Elder, G. H. (2003). Family contingencies across the generations: Grandparent-grandchild relationships in holistic perspective. *Journal of Marriage & the Family, 65*, 404–417.

Murdock, G. P. (1949). *Social structure*. New York: Macmillan.

Murphy, A. (2003). Daddy boot camp: How an increasingly popular program prepares rookie fathers to hit the ground crawling. *Child, 18*, 85–86, 88, 90.

Murphy, M.-K., & Knoll, J. (2003). *International adoption: Sensitive advice for prospective parents*. Chicago: Chicago Review Press.

Myuwiler, J. (2004). *Family violence*. Farmington Hills, MI: Gale Group.

National Clearinghouse on Child Abuse and Neglect. (2003). *Child maltreatment 2002: Summary of key findings*. Washington, DC: Author.

National Institute for Child Health and Human Development. (1999, January 26). NICHD child care study investigators to report on child care quality: Higher quality care related to less problem behavior (news release). Retrieved from http://www.nichd.gov/new/release/daycar99

National Institute for Child Health and Human Development. (2003, July 16). Child care linked to assertive, noncompliant, and aggressive behaviors: Vast majority of children within normal range (news release). Retrieved from http://www.nichd.gov/new/releases/child care.cfm

Neil, E. (2002). Contact after adoption: The role of agencies in making and supporting plans. *Adoption and Fostering, 26,* 25–38.

Nelsen, J., & Delzer, C. (1999). *Positive discipline for single parents: Nurturing cooperation, respect, and joy in your single-parent family.* New York: Crown.

Nelson, D. B., Grisso, J. A., Joffe, M. M., Brensinger, C., Shaw, L., & Datner, E. (2003). Does stress influence early pregnancy loss? *Annals of Epidemiology, 13,* 223–229.

Nelson, F. (1999). Lesbian families: Achieving motherhood. *Journal of Gay & Lesbian Social Services, 10,* 27–46.

Newburn-Cook, C. V., White, D., Svenson, L. W., Emianczuk, N. N., Bott, N., & Edwards, J. (2002). Where and to what extent is prevention of low birth weight possible? *Western Journal of Nursing Research, 24,* 887–904.

NICHD Early Child Care Research Network. (1999). Child outcomes when child care center classes meet recommended standards for quality. *American Journal of Public Health, 89,* 1072–1077.

NICHD Early Child Care Research Network. (2000a). Characteristics and quality of child care for toddlers and preschoolers. *Applied Developmental Science, 4,* 116–135.

NICHD Early Child Care Research Network. (2000b). The relation of child care to cognitive and language development. *Child Development, 71,* 960–980.

Nitz, K. (1999). Adolescent pregnancy prevention: A review of interventions and programs. *Clinical Psychology Review, 19,* 457–471.

Noy-Sharav, D. (2002). Good enough adoptive parenting—the adopted child and self-object relations. *Clinical Social Work Journal, 30,* 57–76.

Oldham, J. D., & Kasser, T. (1999). Attitude change in response to information that male homosexuality has a biological basis. *Journal of Sex & Marital Therapy, 25,* 121–124.

O'Rand, A. M., & Krecker, M. L. (1990). Concepts of the life cycle: Their history, meanings, and use in the social sciences. *Annual Review of Sociology, 16,* 241–262.

Orme, J. G., & Buehler, C. (2001). Foster family characteristics and behavioral and emotional problems of foster children: A narrative review. *Family Relations, 50,* 3–15.

Orthner, D. K., Bowen, G. L., & Beare, V. G. (1990). The organization family: A question of work and family boundaries. *Marriage and Family Review, 15,* 15–36.

Osborn, S. T. (2004). *A special kind of love: For those who love children with special needs.* Nashville, TN: Broadman & Holman.

Ostrea, C. (2003). *Family bound: One couple's journey through infertility and adoption.* Lincoln, NE: iUniverse.

Paechter, C. (2000). Growing up with a lesbian mother: A theoretically-based analysis of personal experience. *Sexualities, 3,* 395–408.

Papernow, P. L. (1984). The stepfamily cycle: An experimental model of stepfamily development. *Family Relations, 33,* 355–363.

Papernow, P. L. (1993). *Becoming a stepfamily.* San Francisco: Jossey-Bass.

Parens, H. (1995). *The development of aggression in early childhood.* Northvale, NJ: Jason Aronson.

Paris, E. (2000). Conscious parenting. *Journal of Prenatal & Perinatal Psychology & Health, 14,* 346–347.

Pasley, K., & Ihinger-Tallman, M. (1987). *Remarriage.* Beverly Hills, CA: Sage.

Patterson, C. J. (1992). Children of lesbian and gay parents. *Child Development, 63,* 1025–1042.

Patterson, C. J. (1995). Sexual orientation and human development: An overview. *Developmental Psychology, 31,* 3–11.

Patterson, C. J. (2000). Family relationships of lesbians and gay men. *Journal of Marriage & the Family, 62,* 1052–1069.

Patterson, C. J., Fulcher, M., & Wainright, J. (2002). Children of lesbian and gay parents: Research, law, and policy. In B. L. Bottoms & M. Bull Kovera (Eds.), *Children, social science, and the law* (pp. 176–199). New York: Cambridge University Press.

Patterson, C. J., & Redding, R. E. (1995). Lesbian and gay families with children: Implications of social science research for policy. *Journal of Social Issues, 52,* 29–50.

Paul, H. A. (2000). *Is my child OK? When behavior is a problem, when it's not, and when to seek help.* New York: Dell.

Pavao, J. M. (2004). *The family of adoption: Completely revised and updated.* Boston: Beacon Press.

Perez, A., O'Neil, K., & Gesiriech, S. (2004). *Demographics of children in foster care.* Washington, DC: Pew Commission on Children in Foster Care.

Perrin, K. K., & DeJoy, S. B. (2003). Abstinence-only education: How we got here and where we're going. *Journal of Public Health Policy, 24,* 445–459.

Perry, J. L. (2004). *Right to be wanted, right to be loved: Telling children about adoption.* Philadelphia: Xlibris Corp.

Peterson, J., Song, X., & Jones-DeWeever, A. (2003). *Life after welfare reform: Low-income single parent families, pre- and post-TANF.* Washington, DC: Institute for Women's Policy Research.

Peterson, L. M., Butts, J., & Deville, D. M. (2000). Parenting experiences of three self-identified gay fathers. *Smith College Studies in Social Work, 70,* 513–521.

Pew Charitable Trust, The. (2004a). *Voices from the inside.* Washington, DC: Author.

Pew Charitable Trust, The. (2004b). *Fostering the future: Safety, permanence, and well-being for children in foster care.* Washington, DC: Author.

Philliber, S. (1999). Peer programs to prevent teen pregnancy: what have we learned? *PPFY Network, 2,* 4–5.

Phillips, S. (2003). Adolescent health. In A. M. Nezu & C. M. Nezu (Eds.), *Handbook of psychology: Health psychology* (Vol. 9, pp. 465–485). New York: Wiley.

Piaget, J. (1967). *Six psychological studies.* New York: Random House.

Piaget, J., & Inhelder, B. (1969). *The psychology of the child.* New York: Basic Books.

Piper, B., & Balswick, J. C. (1997). *Then they leave home: Parenting after the kids grow up.* Downers Grove, IL.: InterVarsity Press.

Pittman, F. S. (1987). *Turning points: Treating families in transition and crisis.* New York: W. W. Norton.

Plotkin, S. A. (2001). Rubella eradication. *Vaccine, 19,* 3311–3319.

Population Reference Bureau. (2003a). Diversity, poverty characterize female-headed households. Retrieved from http://www.prb.org/Template.cfm?Section=PRB&template=/ContentManagement/ContentDisplay.cfm&ContentID=8277

Population Reference Bureau. (2003b). *Traditional families account for only 7 percent of U.S. households.* Retrieved from http://www.ameristat.org

Power, T. G., & Chapieski, M. L. (1986). Child rearing and impulse control in toddlers: A naturalistic investigation. *Developmental Psychology, 22,* 271–275.

Price, E. (2004). *Divorce and teens: When a family splits apart.* Berkeley Heights, NJ: Enslow Publishers.

Proctor, B. D., & Dalaker, J. (2003). Poverty in the United States: 2002. *Current Population Reports, P60–222.* Washington, DC: U.S. Bureau of the Census.

Pryor, J., & Rodgers, B. (2001). *Children in changing families: Life after parental separation.* Malden, MA: Blackwell.

Radke-Yarrow, M., Zahn-Waxler, C., & Chapman, M. (1983). Children's prosocial dispositions and behavior. In M. E. Hetherington (Ed.), *Handbook of child psychology* (Vol. 4, pp. 138–156). New York: Wiley.

Raffaelli, M., & Crockett, L. J. (2003). Sexual risk taking in adolescence: The role of self-regulation and attraction to risk. *Developmental Psychology, 39,* 1036–1046.

Ramey, M. (2004). *Adult children, adult choices: Outgrowing codependency.* Chicago: Sheed & Ward.

Reeves, C. R. (2003). *Childhood: It should not hurt!* Huntersville, NC: LTI Publishers.

Reichman, N. E., & Teitler, J. O. (2003). Effects of psychosocial risk factors and prenatal interventions on birth weight: Evidence from New Jersey's HealthStart program. *Perspectives on Sexual & Reproductive Health, 35,* 130–137.

Reynolds, G. P., Wright, J. V., & Beale, B. (2003). The roles of grandparents in educating today's children. *Journal of Instructional Psychology, 30,* 316–325.

Rholes, W. S., Simpson, J. A, Campbell, L., & Grich, J. (2001). Adult attachment and the transition to parenthood. *Journal of Personality & Social Psychology, 81,* 421–435.

Richardson, R. W. (1999). *Family ties that bind: A self-help guide to change through family of origin therapy.* Vancouver, British Colombia, Canada: Self-Counsel Press.

Rigazio-DiGilio, S. A., & Cramer-Benjamin, D. (2000). Families with learning disabilities, physical disabilities, and other childhood challenges. In W. C. Nichols, M. A. Pace-Nichols, D. S. Becvar, & A. Y. Napier (Eds.), *Handbook of family development and intervention* (pp. 415–438). New York: Wiley.

Riley, L. A., & Glass, J. L. (2002). You can't always get what you want—Infant care preferences and use among employed mothers. *Journal of Marriage and the Family, 64,* 2–15.

Ring, S. (2001). Use of role playing in parent training: A methodological component

analysis of systematic training for effective parenting. *Dissertation Abstracts International: Section B: the Sciences & Engineering, 61* (11-B), 6121.

Ripley, R. J. (2003). *My child has special needs: A journey from grief to joy.* Enumclaw, WA: Pleasant Word.

Rock, E. A. (2002). Empathy in the easily aroused child. *Dissertation Abstracts International: Section B: the Sciences & Engineering, 63* (4-B), 2101.

Rogoff, B. (1990). *Apprenticeship in thinking: Cognitive development in social context.* New York: Oxford University Press.

Rolls, B. J., Engell, D., & Birch, L. L. (2000). Serving portion size influences 5-year-old but not 3-year-old children's food intake. *Journal of the American Dietetic Association, 100,* 232–234.

Roopnarine, J. L., Hooper, F. H., Ahmeduzzaman, M., & Pollack, B. (1993). Gentle play partners: Mother-child and father-child play in New Delhi, India. In K. MacDonald (Ed.), *Parent-child play* (pp. 287–304). Albany: State University of New York Press.

Rose-Jacobs, R., Cabral, H., Posner, M. A., Epstein, J., & Frank, D. A. (2002). Do "we just know"? Masked assessors' ability to accurately identify children with prenatal cocaine exposure. *Journal of Developmental & Behavioral Pediatrics, 23,* 340–346.

Rossi, A. (1968). Transition to parenthood. *Journal of Marriage and the Family, 30,* 26–39.

Rossi, A. (1977). A biosocial perspective on parenting. *Daedalus, 106,* 1–31.

Roxburgh, S., Stephens, R. C., Toltzis, P., & Atkins, I. (2001). The value of children, parenting strains, and depression among urban African American mothers. *Sociological Forum, 16,* 55–72.

Rozie-Battle, J. (2003). Economic support and the dilemma of teen fathers. *Journal of Health & Social Policy, 17,* 73–86.

Runyon, M. K., Deblinger, E., Ryan, E. E., & Thakkar-Kolar, R. (2004). An overview of child physical abuse: Developing an integrated parent-child cognitive-behavioral treatment approach. *Trauma, Violence & Abuse, 5,* 65–85.

Rushton, A. (2003). Support for adoptive families: A review of current evidence on problems, needs and effectiveness. *Adoption and Fostering, 27,* 41–50.

Russell, C. S. (1974). Transition to parenthood: Problems and gratifications. *Journal of Marriage and the Family, 36,* 294–301.

Rust, P. C. (2003). Finding a sexual identity and community: Therapeutic implications and cultural assumptions in scientific models of coming out. In L. D. Garnets, & D. C. Kimmel (Eds.), *Psychological perspectives on lesbian, gay, and bisexual experiences* (2nd ed., pp. 227–269). New York: Columbia University Press.

Rys, G. S., & Bear, G. G. (1997). Relationship aggression and peer relations: Gender and developmental issues. *Merrill-Palmer Quarterly, 43,* 87–106.

Sanders, M. R., Cann, W., & Markie-Dadds, C. (2003). The triple P-positive parenting programme: A universal population-level approach to the prevention of child abuse. *Child Abuse Review, 12,* 155–171.

Santrock, J. W. (2004). *Adolescence* (10th ed.). New York: McGraw-Hill.

Satir, V. (1972a). Family systems and approaches to family therapy. In G. D. Erikson & T. P. Hogan (Eds.), *Family therapy: An introduction to theory and technique.* Monterey, CA: Brooks/Cole.

Satir, V. (1972b). *Peoplemaking.* Palo Alto, CA: Science and Behavior Books.

Satyen, L. (2003). Rethinking ADHD: Integrated approaches to helping children at home and at school. *Journal of Family Studies, 9,* 276–277.

Saunders, J. A. (2002). African American teen parents and their non-parenting peers: Differences in high school and young adulthood. *DAI-A, 62,* 4335.

Savin-Williams, R., & Dube, E. M. (1998). Parental reactions and self-esteem among gay and lesbian youths. *Journal of Homosexuality, 18,* 1–36.

Savin-Williams, R., & Ream, G. L. (2003). Suicide attempts among sexual-minority male youth. *Journal of Clinical Child & Adolescent Psychology, 32,* 509–522.

Savin-Williams, R. C. (2001). *Mom, Dad. I'm gay. How families negotiate coming out.* Washington, DC: American Psychological Association.

Scher, M. S., Richardson, G. A., & Day, N. L. (2000). Effects of prenatal crack/cocaine and other drug exposure on electroencephalographic sleep studies at birth and one year. *Pediatrics, 105,* 39–48.

Schmitz, C. L., & Tebb, S. S. (2003). *Diversity in single-parent families: Working from strength.* Chicago: Lyceum Books.

Schneider, M. L., Roughton, E. C., Koehler, A. J., & Lubach, G. R. (1999). Growth and development following prenatal stress exposure in primates: An examination of ontogenetic vulnerability. *Child Development, 70*, 253–274.

Schutter, L. S., & Brinker, R. P. (1992). Conjuring a new category of disability from prenatal cocaine exposure: Are the infants unique biological or caretaking casualties? *Topics in Early Childhood Special Education, 11*, 84–111.

Schwartz, L. L. (2000). Families by choice: Adoptive and foster families. In W. C. Nichols, M. A. Pace-Nichols, D. S. Becvar, & A. Y. Napier (Eds.), *Handbook of family development* (pp. 255–278). New York: Wiley.

Schwarzchild, M. (2000). *Helping your difficult child behave*. Lincoln, NE: iUniverse.

Schwebel, D. C., & Plumert, J. M. (1999). Longitudinal and concurrent relations among temperament, ability estimation, and injury proneness. *Child Development, 70*, 700–712.

Schweingruber, H. A., & Kalil, A. (2000). Decision making and depressive symptoms in black and white multigenerational teen-parent families. *Journal of Family Psychology, 14*, 556–569.

Secunda, V. (2004). *Losing your parents, finding your self: The defining turning point of adult life*. Collingdale, PA: DIANE Publishing.

Shapiro, J. P., Schrof, J. M., Tharp, M., & Friedman, D. (1995, February 27). Honor thy children. *U.S. News and World Report*, 39–49.

Shultz, S. K. (2001). Child physical abuse: Relationship of parental substance use to severity of abuse and risk for future abuse. *Dissertation Abstracts International: Section B: the Sciences & Engineering, 62*(1-B), 605. Ann Arbor, MI: University Microfilms International.

Siegenthaler, A., & Bigner, J. J. (2000). The value of children to lesbian and nonlesbian mothers. *Journal of Homosexuality, 39*, 73–92.

Silverstein, L. B., & Auerbach, C. F. (2002). Deconstructing the essential father. In A. E. Hunter & C. Forden (Eds.), *Readings in the psychology of gender: Exploring our differences and commonalities* (pp. 245–262). Needham Heights, MA: Allyn & Bacon.

Simons, R. L., Whitbeck, L. B., Conger, R. D., & Wu, C. (1991). Intergenerational transmission of harsh parenting. *Developmental Psychology, 27*, 159–171.

Sinclair, J. C. (2003). Weighing risks and benefits in treating the individual patient. *Clinics in Perinatology, 30*, 251–268.

Singer, A. (2001). Coming out of the shadows: Supporting the development of our gay, lesbian, and bisexual adolescents. In M. McConville & G. Wheeler (Eds.), *The heart of development* (Vol. 11, pp. 172–192). Cambridge, MA: GestaltPress Book.

Skinner, B. F. (1938). *The behavior of organisms*. New York: Appleton-Century-Crofts.

Skinner, J. H. (2001). Acculturation: Measures of ethnic accommodation to the dominant American culture. *Journal of Mental Health and Aging, 7*, 41–52.

Skinner, K. B., Bahr, S. J., Crane, D. R., & Call, V. R. A. (2002). Cohabitation, marriage, and remarriage: A comparison of relationship quality over time. *Journal of Family Issues, 23*, 74–90.

Skolnick, A., & Skolnick, J. (1971). *Family in transition: Rethinking marriage, childrearing, and family organization*. Boston: Little, Brown.

Smith, C., Perou, R., & Lesesne, C. (2002). Parent education. In M. H. Bornstein (Ed.), *Handbook of parenting* (Vol. 4, 2nd ed., pp. 389–410). Mahwah, NJ: Erlbaum.

Smith, D. (2003). The older population in the United States: March 2002. *Current Population Reports*, P20–546. Washington, DC: U.S. Bureau of the Census.

Smith, P. K., Smees, R., Pellegrini, A. D., & Menesini, E. (2002). Comparing pupil and teacher perceptions for playful fighting, serious fighting, and positive peer interaction. In J. L. Roopnarine (Ed.), *Conceptual, social-cognitive, and contextual issues in the fields of play: Play & culture studies* (Vol. 4, pp. 235–245). Westport, CT: Ablex Publishing.

Smith, R. L. (2002). Using solution-focused techniques with reconstructed family systems. In R. E. Watts & J. Carlson (Eds.), *Techniques in marriage and family counseling* (Vol. 2, pp. 63–68). Alexandria, VA: American Counseling Association.

Sobol, M. P., Daly, K. J., & Kelloway, E. K. (2000). Paths to the facilitation of open adoption. *Family Relations, 49*, 419–424.

Sokol, R. J., Jr., Delaney-Black, V., & Nordstrom, B. (2003). Fetal alcohol spectrum disorder. *Journal of the American Medical Association, 290*, 2996–2999.

Somers, M. D. (1993). A comparison of voluntarily childfree adults and parents. *Journal of Marriage and the Family, 55*, 643–650.

Sood, B., Delaney-Black, V., Covington, C., Nordstrom-Klee, B., Ager, J., Templin, T., Janisse, J., Martier, S., & Sokol, R. J. (2001). Prenatal alcohol exposure and childhood behavior at age 6 to 7 years: I. Dose-response effect. *Pediatrics, 108*, 461–462.

South, S. J. (1999). Historical changes and life course variation in the determinants of premarital childbearing. *Journal of Marriage and the Family, 61*, 752–763.

Spock, B. (2004). *Dr. Spock's baby and child care* (8th ed.). New York: Simon & Schuster.

Stacey, J. (1996). *In the name of the family: Rethinking family values in the post-modern age*. Boston: Beacon Press.

Stacey, J., & Biblarz, T. J. (2001). (How) does the sexual orientation of parents matter? *American Sociological Review, 66*, 159–183.

Stainer-Person, K. E. (1998). Individual, familial, and parental factors associated with teenage pregnancy. *Dissertation Abstracts-International: Section B: the Sciences & Engineering, 59*(3-B). Ann Arbor, MI: University Microfilms International.

Staples, R. (1999). Interracial relationships: A convergence of desire and opportunity. In R. Staples (Ed.), *The black family: Essays and studies* (pp. 129–136). Belmont, CA: Wadsworth.

Staples, R., & Mirande, A. (1980). Racial and cultural variations among American families: A decennial review of the literature on minority families. *Journal of Marriage and the Family, 42*, 887–903.

Stark, E. (2000). *Everything you need to know about family violence*. New York: Rosen Publishing Group.

Steinberg, L., & Silk, J. S. (2002). Parenting adolescents. In M. H. Bornstein (Ed.), *Handbook of parenting* (Vol. 1, 2nd ed., pp. 103–133). Mahwah, NJ: Erlbaum.

Steinberg, L. D. (2004). *Adolescence*. New York: McGraw-Hill.

Steinmetz, S., Clavan, S., & Stein, K. F. (1990). *Marriage and family realities: Historical and contemporary perspectives*. New York: Harper & Row.

Stern, M., & Alvarez, A. (1992). Knowledge of child development and caretaking attitudes: A comparison of pregnant, parenting, and nonpregnant adolescents. *Family Relations, 41*, 297–302.

Stevens, M., Perry, B., Burston, A., Golombok, S., & Golding, J. (2003). Openness in lesbian-mother families regarding mother's sexual orientation and child's conception by donor insemination. *Journal of Reproductive & Infant Psychology, 21*, 347–362.

Stevens-Simon, C. (2000). Participation in a program that helps families with one teen pregnancy prevent others. *Journal of Pediatric and Adolescent Gynecology, 13*, 167–169.

Stevens-Simon, C., Nelligan, D., & Kelly, L. (2001). Adolescents at risk for mistreating their children. Part I: Prenatal identification. *Child Abuse & Neglect, 25*, 737–751.

Stifter, C. A., Coulehan, C. M., & Fish, M. (1993). Linking employment to attachment: The mediating effects of maternal separation anxiety and interactive behavior. *Child Development, 64*, 1451–1460.

Strassberg, Z., Dodge, K. A., Pettit, G. S., & Bates, J. E. (1994). Spanking in the home and children's subsequent aggression toward kindergarten peers. *Development and Psychopathology, 6*, 445–462.

Straus, M. A. (1991a). Discipline and violence: Physical punishment of children and violence and other crime in adulthood. *Social Problems, 38*, 133–154.

Straus, M. A. (1991b). New theory and old canards about family violence research. *Social Problems, 38*, 180–197.

Straus, M. A. (1994). *Beating the devil out of them: Corporal punishment in American families.* New York: Lexington.

Straus, M. A., & Field, C. J. (2003). Psychological aggression by American parents: National data on prevalence, chronicity, and severity. *Journal of Marriage and the Family, 65*, 795–808.

Straus, M. A., & Stewart, J. H. (1999). Corporal punishment by American parents: National data on prevalence, chronicity, severity, and duration in relation to child and family characteristics. *Clinical Child and Family Psychology Review, 2*, 55–70.

Straus, M. A., & Yodanis, C. L. (1996). Corporal punishment in adolescence and physical assaults on spouses in later life: What accounts for the link? *Journal of Marriage and the Family, 58*, 825–841.

Strickland, B. R. (1995). Research on sexual orientation and human development: A commentary. *Developmental Psychology, 31*, 137–140.

Strommen, E. F. (1989a). Hidden branches and growing pains: Homosexuality and the family tree. *Marriage and Family Review, 14*, 9–34.

Strommen, E. F. (1989b). "You're a what?": Family member reactions to the disclosure of homosexuality. *Journal of Homosexuality, 18*, 37–58.

Strong, B. (2004). *Human sexuality: Diversity in contemporary America.* New York: McGraw-Hill.

Studd, J. W. (2004). *Progress in obstetrics and gynecology.* Philadelphia: Elsevier.

Sullivan, G., & Reynolds, R. (2003). Homosexuality in midlife: Narrative and identity. *Journal of Gay & Lesbian Social Services, 15*, 153–170.

Sullivan, M., & Wodarski, J. S. (2002). Social alienation in gay youth. *Journal of Human Behavior in the Social Environment, 5*, 1–17.

Sullivan–Bolyai, J., Hull, H. F., Wilson, C., & Corey, L. (1983). Neonatal herpes simplex virus infection in King County, Washington: Increasing incidence and epidemiologic correlates. *Journal of the American Medical Association, 250*, 3059–3062.

Susman, E. J., Dorn, L. D., & Schiefelbein, V. L. (2003). Puberty, sexuality, and health. In R. M. Lerner & M. A. Easterbrooks (Eds.), *Handbook of psychology: Developmental psychology* (Vol. 6., pp. 295–324). New York: Wiley.

Swinford, S. P., DeMaris, A., Cernkovich, S. A., & Giordano, P. C. (2000). Harsh physical discipline in childhood and violence in later romantic involvements: The mediating role of problem behaviors. *Journal of Marriage and the Family, 62*, 508–519.

Swize, J. (2002). Transracial adoption and the unblinkable difference: Racial dissimilarity serving the interests of adopted children. *Virginia Law Review, 88*, 1079–1118.

Talmadge, L. D., & Talmadge, W. C. (2003). Dealing with the unhappy marriage. In S. B. Levine & C. B. Risen (Eds.), *Handbook of clinical sexuality for mental health professionals* (pp. 75–92). New York: Brunner- Routledge.

Tanner, J. M. (1990). Foetus into man (2nd ed.). Cambridge, MA: Harvard University Press.

Tasker, F. (1999). Children in lesbian-led families: A review. *Clinical Child Psychology & Psychiatry, 4*, 153–166.

Tasker, F. (2002). Lesbian and gay parenting. In A. Coyle & C. Kitzinger (Eds.), *Lesbian and gay psychology: New perspectives* (pp. 81–97). Malden, MA: Blackwell.

Taylor, M. K. (2001). *Grandparent visitation rights: A legal research guide.* Buffalo, NY: William S. Hein.

Therrien, M. & Ramirez, R. R. (2000). The Hispanic population in the United States: March 2000. *Current Population Reports, P20–535.* Washington, DC: U.S. Census Bureau.

Thompson, G. L. (2003). *What African American parents want educators to know.* New York: Praeger.

Thompson, J. M. (2002). *Mommy queerest: Contemporary rhetorics of lesbian maternal identity.* Amherst, MA: University of Massachusetts Press.

Thornberry, T. P., Smith, C. A., & Howard, G. J. (1997). Risk factors for teenage fatherhood. *Journal of Marriage and Family, 59*, 505–522.

Thornton, A., & Young-DeMarco, L. (2001). Four decades of trends in attitudes toward family issues in the United States: The 1960s through the 1990s. *Journal of Marriage and the Family, 63*, 1009–1037.

Timmer, S. G., Borrego, J., Jr., & Urquiza, A. J. (2002). Antecedents of coercive interactions in physically abusive mother-child dyads. *Journal of Interpersonal Violence, 17*, 836–853.

Tinsley, B. J., Lees, N. B., & Sumartojo, E. (2004). Child and adolescent HIV risk: Familial and cultural perspectives. *Journal of Family Psychology, 18*, 208–224.

Tobin, C. (2002). *The parent's problem solver: Smart solutions for everyday discipline dilemmas and behavior problems.* New York: Crown.

Topolak, R., Williams, V., & Wilson, J. (2001). Preventing teenage pregnancy: A multifaceted review. *Journal of Psychological Practice, 7*, 33–46.

Townsend, L. (2003). Open adoption: A review of the literature with recommendations to adoption practitioners. *Journal of Child and Adolescent Mental Health, 15*, 1–11.

Treffers, P. E., Hanselaar, A. G., Helmerhorst, T. J., Koster, M. E., & van Leeuwen, F. F. (2001). Consequences of diethylstilbestrol during pregnancy: 50 years later still a significant problem. *Ned Tijdscjr Geneeskd, 145*, 675–680.

Trosper, T. B. (2002). Parenting strategies in the middle class African-American family. *Dissertation Abstracts International, 63*, 864.

Tubman, J. G., Wagner, E. F., & Langer, L. M. (2003). Patterns of depressive symptoms, drinking motives, and sexual behavior among substance abusing adolescents: Implications for health risk. *Journal of Child & Adolescent Substance Abuse, 13*, 37–57.

Tully, L. A., Moffitt, T. E., & Caspi, A. (2003). Maternal adjustment, parenting and child behaviour in families of school-aged twins conceived after IVF and ovulation induction. *Journal of Child Psychology & Psychiatry & Allied Disciplines, 44*, 316–325.

Turnbull, R., & Cilley, M. (1999). *Explanations and implications of the 1997 amendments to the IDEA.* Upper Saddle River, NJ: Prentice Hall.

Turner, R. J., Sorenson, A. M., & Turner, J. B. (2000). Social contingencies in mental health: A seven-year follow-up study of teenage mothers. *Journal of Marriage and the Family, 62*, 777–791.

Urban Institute. (1999). *Get organized: A guide to preventing teen pregnancy.* Washington, DC: Author.

U.S. Bureau of the Census. (2002). *Statistical abstract of the United States.* Washington, DC: U.S. Government Printing Office.

U.S. Bureau of the Census. (2003). *Statistical abstract of the United States.* Washington, DC: U.S. Government Printing Office.

Vanfraussen, K., Ponjaert-Kristoffersen, I., & Brewaeys, A. (2002). What does it mean for youngsters to grow up in a lesbian family created by means of donor insemination? *Journal of Reproductive & Infant Psychology, 20,* 237–252.

Vanfraussen, K., Ponjaert-Kristoffersen, I., & Brewaeys, A. (2003). Family functioning in lesbian families created by donor insemination. *American Journal of Orthopsychiatry, 73,* 78–90.

Van Houten, R., & Hall, R. V. (2001). *The measurement of behavior: Behavior modification* (3rd ed.). Austin, TX: PRO-ED.

VanLaningham, J., Johnson, D. R., & Amato, P. (2001). Marital happiness, marital duration, and the U-shaped curve: Evidence from a five-wave panel study. *Social Forces, 78,* 1313–1341.

van Poppel, F. W. A., Oris, M., & Lee, J. Z. (2004). *The road to independence: Leaving home in western and eastern societies, 16th to 20th centuries.* New York: Peter Lang.

van Spronsen, F. J., Molendijk, H., Erwich, J. J., & Smit, G. P. (2003). Inherited metabolic diseases and pregnancy: Consequences for mother and child. *Nederlands Tijdschrift voor Geneeskunde, 147,* 235–240.

van Wormer, K., & McKinney, R. (2003). What schools can do to help gay/lesbian/bisexual youth: A harm reduction approach. *Adolescence, 38,* 409–420.

Varon, L. (2003). *Adopting on your own: The complete guide to adoption for single parents.* Collingdale, PA: DIANE Publishing.

Veevers, J. E. (1973). The social meanings of parenthood. *Psychiatry, 36,* 291–310.

Veevers, J. E., & Mitchell, B. A. (1998). Intergenerational exchanges and perceptions of support within "boomerang kid" family environments. *International Journal of Aging & Human Development, 46,* 91–108.

Visher, E. B., & Visher, J. S. (1996). *Therapy with stepfamilies.* New York: Brunner/Mazel.

von Bertalanffy, L. (1968). General systems theory and psychiatry. In S. Arieti (Ed.), *American handbook of psychiatry* (Vol. 1, pp. 247–300). New York: Basic Books.

von Bertalanffy, L. (1974). *General systems theory.* New York: Braziller.

Vontver, L. A. (2003). *Appleton and Lange's review of obstetrics and gynecology.* New York: McGraw-Hill.

Vygotsky, L. S. (1962). *Thought and language.* Cambridge, MA: MIT Press.

Vygotsky, L. S. (1987). Thinking and speech. In R. W. Reiber & A. S. Carton (Eds.), *The collected works of L. S. Vygotsky: Problems of general psychology* (Vol. 1, pp. 37–285). New York: Plenum.

Wajda-Johnston, V. A. (2003). Children of addiction: Research, health, and public policy issues. *Addictive Disorders & Their Treatment, 2,* 105.

Wakschlag, L. S., & Hans, S. L. (2000). Early parenthood in context: Implications for development and intervention. In C. H. Zeanah, Jr. (Ed.), *Handbook of infant mental health* (2nd ed., pp. 129–144). New York: Guilford Press.

Waldenstroem, U. (1999a). Experience of labor and birth in 1111 women. *Journal of Psychosomatic Research, 47,* 471–482.

Waldenstroem, U. (1999b). Effects of birth centre care on fathers' satisfaction with care, experience of the birth and adaptation to fatherhood. *Journal of Reproductive & Infant Psychology, 17,* 357–368.

Waldner, L. K., & Magruder, B. (1999). Coming out to parents: Perceptions of family relations, perceived resources and identity expression as predictors of identity disclosure for gay and lesbian adolescents. *Journal of Homosexuality, 37,* 83–100.

Walker, A. J., & McGraw, L. A. (2000). Who is responsible for responsible fathering? *Journal of Marriage & the Family, 62,* 563–569.

Wallace, W. (2004). *Family violence: Legal, medical and social perspective* (4th ed.). Boston: Allyn & Bacon.

Waller, M. A., Brown, B., & Whittle, B. (1999). Mentoring as a bridge to positive outcomes for teen mothers and their children. *Child and Adolescent Social Work Journal, 16,* 467–480.

Wallerstein, J. S., & Blakeslee, S. (2003). *What about the kids? Raising your children before, during and after divorce.* New York: Hyperion Press.

Wallerstein, J. S., Lewis, J. M., & Blakeslee, S. (2001). *The unexpected legacy of divorce: A twenty-five year landmark study.* New York: Hyperion Press.

Walsh, W. (2002). Spankers and nonspankers: Where they get their information on spanking. *Family Relations, 51,* 81–88.

Wark, M. J., Kruczek, T., & Boley, A. (2003). Emotional neglect and family structure: Impact on student functioning. *Child Abuse & Neglect, 27,* 1033–1043.

Watson, J. B. (1928). *Psychological care of infant and child.* New York: Norton.

Wegar, K. (2000). Adoption, family ideology, and social stigma: Bias in community attitudes, adoption research, and practice. *Family Relations, 49,* 363–370.

Weight, C. E. (2004). *Divorce in America: A reference handbook.* Santa Barbara, CA: A B C-Clio.

Weinberg, G. (1972). *Society and the healthy homosexual.* New York: St. Martin's Press.

Weinraub, M., Horvath, D. L., & Gringlas, M. B. (2002). Single parenthood. In M. H. Bornstein (Ed.), *Handbook of parenting: Vol. 3. Being and becoming a parent* (2nd ed., pp. 109–140). Mahwah, NJ: Erlbaum.

Weinstock, H., Berman, S., & Cates, W., Jr. (2004). Sexually transmitted diseases among American youth: Incidence and prevalence estimates, 2000. *Perspectives on Sexual and Reproductive Health, 36,* 6–10.

Weis, R. (2002). Parenting dimensionality and typology in a disadvantaged, African American sample: a cultural variance perspective. *Journal of Black Psychology, 28,* 142–173.

Westheimer, R. K., & Lopater, S. (2004). *Human sexuality: A psychosocial perspective.* New York: Lippincott, Williams, & Wilkins.

Weston, K. (1997). *Families we choose: Lesbians, gays, kinship.* New York: Columbia University Press.

Wharton, A. S. (2004). *The sociology of gender: An introduction to theory and research.* Malden, MA: Blackwell.

Whipple, E. E., & Ritchey, C. A. (1997). Crossing the line from physical discipline to child abuse: How much is too much? *Child Abuse and Neglect, 21,* 431–444.

Whitam, F. L., & Zent, M. (1984). A cross-cultural assessment of early cross-gender behavior and familial factors in male homosexuality. *Archives of Sexual Behavior, 13,* 427–439.

Wiehe, V. R. (1990). Religious influence on parental attitudes toward the use of corporal punishment. *Journal of Family Violence, 5,* 173–186.

Wilcoxon, S. A. (2002). Permission to speak freely: Consent and intervention with the noncustodial parent and children. In R. E. Watts & J. Carlson (Eds.), *Techniques in marriage and family counseling* (Vol. 2, pp. 109–116). Alexandria, VA: American Counseling Association.

Wiley, A. R., Warren, H. B., & Montanelli, D. S. (2002). Shelter in a time of storm: Parenting in poor, rural African-American communities. *Family Relations, 51,* 265–273.

Williams, S. S., Norris, A. E., & Bedor, M. M. (2003). Sexual relationships, condom use, and concerns about pregnancy, HIV/AIDS, and other sexually transmitted diseases. *Clinical Nurse Specialist, 17,* 89–94.

Williamson, D. S. (1998). Disclosure is a family event. *Family Relations, 47,* 23–25.

Winkler, R. (2004). *The family—Where violence begins, recognizing and stopping it.* Lincoln, NE: iUniverse.

Witters-Green, R. (2003). Parental expression of physical intimacy with young children: Influences on subjective norms about what is appropriate. *Dissertation Abstracts International: Section B: the Sciences & Engineering, 64 (3-B), 1556.* Ann Arbor, MI: University Microfilms International.

Wood, B., & Talmon, M. (1983). Family boundaries in transition: A search for alternatives. *Family Process, 22,* 347–357.

Wood, C., & Davidson, J. (2003). Helping families cope: A fresh look at parent effectiveness training. *Family Matters, 65,* 28–33.

Woodhill, B. M., & Samuels, C. A. (2003). Positive and negative androgyny and their relationship with psychological health and well-being. *Sex Roles, 48,* 555–565.

Xie, H., Cairns, B. D., & Cairns, R. B. (2001). Predicting teen motherhood and teen fatherhood: Individual characteristics and peer affiliations. *Social Development, 10,* 488–509.

Yellowbird, M., & Snipp, C. (1998). American Indian families. In R. Taylor (Ed.), *Minority families in the United States* (pp. 234–248). Upper Saddle River, NJ: Prentice Hall.

Zabin, L. S., & Cardona, K. M. (2002). Adolescent pregnancy. In G. M. Wingood & R. J. DiClemente (Eds.), *Handbook of women's sexual and reproductive health: Issues in women health* (pp. 231–253). New York: Kluwer Academic/Plenum Publishers.

Ziegahn, S. J. (2002). *The stepparent's survival guide: A workbook for creating a happy blended family.* Oakland, CA: New Harbinger Publications.

# Index

Closed adoption, 110
Closeted, 263
Cocaine use during pregnancy, 121
Cognitive development in preschoolers, 162
Cognitive theory, 62
Cohan, M., 16
Coleman, M., 25
Coley, R.L., 147
Coll, B., 99
Collins, M.E., 272, 277
Collins, W.A., 197
Colonial America, 9–10, *10*
Coltrane, S., 106
Combs-Orme, T., 147
Coming out, 257
Communication styles in family systems
        theory, 42–43
Community services for special needs
        children, 188–189
Computer usage in school-age children, 182
Conditional love, 74, 75
Confucian training doctrine, 34
Conner, J.M., 275
Connolly, C.M., 255
Connor, K.A., 212, 213
Contextual communication in family systems
        theory, 42
Contraception, 274–275
Conway, M.B., 224
Cook, A.S., 162
Coontz, S., 7, 8, 14, 15, 21, 147
Coppel-Batsch, M., 297
Coregulation, 176
Cornell, C.P., 287, 288, 289
Correia, A., 295
Coulehan, C.M., 142
Couraud, S., 297
Cowan, C.P., 103, 113, 114
Cowan, L., 121
Cowan, P.A., 103, 113, 114
Cox, F.D., 106
Cox, M.E., 296
Cox, M.J., 102
Cox, S.M., 126, 127, 128, 129
Coyl, D.D., 275
Cramer-Benjamin, D., 186, 187, 189
Crimmins, E.M., 212
Criticism and parenting styles, 71, 72
Crockett, L.J., 273
Crowne, D.P., 256
Cultural influences, 13, 14–15. *See also*
        Ethnic diversity in contemporary
        families
Cycle of violence, 289

Dalaker, J., 26
Daly, K.J., 110
Daly, R.D., 130

Damewood, M.D., 126
Dating, 201
Davidson, J., 83, 86
Dawson, C., 15, 16, 42, 70, 73, 76, 139, 157,
        177, 209
Day, N.L., 121
Day, R.D., 69
Day care, 167–169
DeBlander, D., 109
DeBlander, T., 109
DeJoy, S.B., 281, 282
Delahunt, W.A., 111
DeLamater, J.D., 274
Delaney-Black, V., 119
Delfabbro, P.H., 296
Delfos, M.F., 160
DeLissovoy, V., 146, 276, 277
Delzer, C., 230
Dembo, M.H., 79
Democratic child training, 79–82
DeNavas-Walt, C., 25
Departure stage of parenthood, 13
Detzner, D.F., 37
Developmental concept of infancy, 134
Developmental role of parenthood, 11–13
Developmental time, 13, 15
Deville, D.M., 264
Dewey, J.E., 275
Dick, M.J., 282
DiClemente, C.C., 4
Dimensions of parenting, 19
    attitudes about parenting, 13, 18
    characteristics of parenthood and parent-
        child relations, 6–7
    child influences, 13, 16–17
    concepts of parenthood, 4–6
    configuring the parenthood role, 13–18
    cultural influences, 13, 14–15
    developmental role of parenthood, 11–13
    developmental time, 13, 15
    disciplinary approach, 13, 17
    educational needs, 3–4
    "family," 6
    family ecological factors, 13, 17–18
    family of origin influences, 13, 16
    Galinsky's stages of parenthood, 12–13
    historical changes in parent-child
        relations, 7–11
    parenthood as a developmental role, 6–7
    parenthood as a social construct, 7
    primary parenting functions, 13, 15–16
    synchrony of parental style and child
        development, 15
Dinkmeyer, D., 79
Dipietro, J.A., 118
Direct-entry midwife, 130
Discipline, 65–67
    abandonment, 71, 72

abuse, 74, 75
abusive corporal punishment, 67–68
approach to parenthood, 13, 17
assertive care, 73, 74, 75
clear understandings, 70–73
conditional love, 74, 75
criticism, 71, 72
equifinality's applicability, 67
feelings and motivations of children, 68
individual differences, 70
indulgence, 75, 76
ineffective methods, 86–87
marshmallowing, 70, 71, 72
negative nurturance, 74–76
negative structure, 71–73
neglect, 75, 76
negotiable rules, 71, 72
nonnegotiable rules, 71, 72
nurturance, 73–76
opportunities to reason and make
        choices, 68–70
positive nurturance, 74–76
positive structure, 71–73
rigidity, 71, 72
spanking, 69
supportive care, 73, 75, 76
Diversity of contemporary families, 20, 27,
        38. *See also* Ethnic diversity in
        contemporary families
birth rates, 23–24
blended families, 29
boomerang kids, 29
coresident grandparents and
        grandchildren, 30–31
divorce, 24
ethnic diversity, 31–37
family characteristics and concepts,
        21–22
family functions, 22
family income, 25
features of contemporary families, 22–26
gay families, 29–30
homelessness, 25–26
lesbian families, 29–30
marriage, 22–23
poverty, 25–26
remarriage, 24–25
renested families, 29
single-parent families, 24, 27–28
stepfamilies, 29
working mothers, 25
Divorce, 24, 218–220
adult reactions, 220–222
child custody, 225–229
children's reactions, 222–225
Dode, L., 256
Doherty, W.J., 99, 146, 147
Donnelly, A.C., 4